W9-BKQ-419

Programming in Assembly Language: MACRO-11

Edward F. Sowell
California State University, Fullerton

▲▼

Addison-Wesley Publishing Company
Reading, Massachusetts
Menlo Park, California
London • Amsterdam
Don Mills, Ontario • Sydney

Sponsoring Editor: James T. DeWolf
Production Manager: Karen M. Guardino
Production Editor: William J. Yskamp
Text Designer: Marie E. McAdam
Illustrator: Robert Gallison
Cover Designer and Illustrator: Harold Pattek
Art Coordinator: Loretta M. Bailey
Manufacturing Supervisor: Hugh J. Crawford

This book is in the Addison-Wesley Series in Computer Science

Consulting Editor
Michael A. Harrison

Library of Congress Cataloging in Publication Data

Sowell, Edward F.
  Programming in assembly language, MACRO-11.

  Includes index.
  1. MACRO-11 (Computer program language) I. Title.
QA76.73.M23S68   1984   001.64′24   83-3774
ISBN 0-201-07788-4

Reprinted with corrections, May 1984

EFGHIJ-MA-89876

In memory of
Pleamon Jackson Sowell

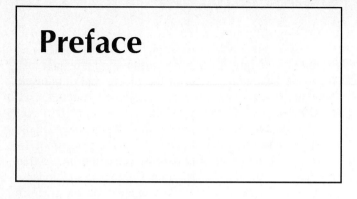

Preface

Background

The study of assembly language remains an essential element of the computer science curriculum in spite of the increasing use of high-level languages. The justifications for this study are twofold. First, there are still programming tasks that are best done in assembly for reasons of efficiency and access to machine capabilities not available in high-level languages. The versatile computer scientist or programmer must therefore be able to code in assembly language when the need arises. The second reason is more fundamental: Assembly is really just a way of expressing the actual native language of the computer; namely, machine code. The study of assembly is therefore, in a sense, a study of the machine. Important issues that come up naturally in this study include fundamental instructions that a computer is capable of carrying out; the concept of the hardware word as the basic unit of memory; the way that the machine stores and accesses data and instructions; the instruction execution cycle that constitutes the most fundamental characteristic of a digital computer; the fundamental aspects of computer input and output; and important data structures such as stacks, queues, lists, and pointers. Thus the study of assembly language can serve as a bridge between the skills learned in an introductory programming course and many advanced topics that the student will study in greater depth in later courses.

The Aim of This Book

This book is written for students who have had only one prior course in introductory programming (in any high-level language), and no prior exposure to assembly language, number theory, logic, or computer architecture. The dependence on the programming course is actually minimal. For example, it is not assumed that the student is thoroughly familiar with any particular programming language. All concepts are developed from the beginning. Some of the things that should aid the student in using this book are the frequent examples explained in detail, end-of-chapter summaries, and answers to selected problems.

This book is also written for the instructor. In particular, it will be appreciated by instructors who are teaching assembly of MACRO-11 for the first time. To this end, the book organization is in the order of classroom presentation, so that a course outline for the core material will closely follow the Contents. Additionally, sufficient exercises are presented so that different assignments can be given in alternate semesters. Because of the inclusion of material on operating system interaction, and on the use of editors and debugging tools, it should not be necessary to develop supplementary handouts for most installations. The appendixes provide complete details of these matters in RSTS/E, RSX-11M, RT-11, and the UNIX system environments.†

Because of the detailed explanations and examples, the book will also be useful for self-study. Those already familiar with an assembly language may find the discussion too detailed and the pace too slow, especially in early chapters. Nonetheless, such readers will appreciate that nearly every PDP-11 instruction is discussed and most are presented with examples.

Approach

The pedagogic approach taken in this text reflects its principal aim, namely, guiding first- and second- year students in the study of assembly and machine language programming. To this end, the order of presentation is designed to keep the motivation level high, and the new-concept load low. Rather than presenting all related instructions at once, as would be done in a manual, a small group of instructions and a single addressing mode are presented first, followed by examples using only this subset of the language. These instructions were selected to provide a repertoire sufficient to work a small class of programming problems. Assembler directives (pseudo-ops) are introduced in the same manner. This knowledge of MACRO-11 is then gradually expanded, enlarging the class of workable problems and programming competence in a metered way. Machine code translation and execution on the machine are emphasized throughout this process.

As a rule, young computer science students like to use the computer more than they like to deal with abstract information. Capitalizing on this, the book moves into programming as quickly as possible. In Chapter 1, examples and exercises get the student onto the machine. Number theory is initially covered only in sufficient depth to provide necessary positive-integer skills in binary,

---

† VAX, VMS, PDP, DEC, RSX, RMS, UNIBUS, LSI-11 and MASSBUS are trademarks of Digital Equipment Corporation. UNIX is a trademark of Bell Laboratories.

octal, and hex. By deferring the remainder of number theory to a later chapter, motivation is kept high. Naturally, the initial subset of the language has been carefully selected to require only positive integers.

Input and output (I/O) can be major stumbling blocks in learning (and teaching!) assembly. The primary approach taken in this book is to sidestep the issue until the student's level of programming skill is high enough to properly handle I/O. In the meanwhile, we use the On-line Debugging Technique (ODT) to load input directly into registers or memory, and to examine contents after program execution. This approach has an important side benefit. It requires the student to think in terms of data and instructions as they actually exist in memory, rather than allowing the assembly mnemonics to be viewed as the end product of the exercise. Also there is no better way to develop skills in the octal base than to examine memory using a debugging tool. Recognizing that some instructors will want to use terminal I/O rather than the ODT approach, preprogrammed octal I/O routines are presented in Appendix E. Programmed I/O using the device registers with polling, and interrupt-driven I/O are covered in later chapters.

Another central idea in the pedagogical approach of this book is that most students learn best in going from the specific to the general, rather than the reverse. It is for this reason that instructions are demonstrated by simple examples as well as being given in the general form. This theory of learning also supports the basic approach of using a specific assembly language and computer instead of working in terms of an idealized, imaginary computer and contrived assembly language. With the approach taken here, students "learn by doing" in a real computing environment. It is well known that although machine and assembly code is highly machine-specific the basic *concepts* remain the same for practically any modern computer. This means that students who learn MACRO-11 on the PDP-11 will be able to transfer much of this knowledge to learning another machine and assembly language on their own.

The Computing Environment

The PDP-11 family of computers and the MACRO-11 assembler are the vehicles for the presentation. Maximum benefit will be derived if students have access to such equipment and software, either through a central facility (e.g., PDP-11/70 with a multiuser operating system) or stand-alone machines such as LSI-11/03 or PDP-11/23. However, in situations in which this is not possible, there are sufficient examples of actual machine interaction so that much could be learned without a machine.

The decision to include actual machine interaction examples in the text required the selection of a particular operating system for the body of the book. The widely used Digital Equipment Corporation (DEC) timesharing operating system called RSTS/E was selected for this purpose. Sections and figures in the text that are affected by the operating system are marked "[OS]," alerting the non-RSTS/E user to check Appendix D for equivalent information on RT-11,

RSX-11M, and the UNIX system. Although the details are not given here, the RSX-11M information is generally applicable also to VAX computers operating in compatibility mode.

Uniform input and output, regardless of which operating system is used, is provided by three macros modeled after the RT-11 macros .TTYIN, .TTYOUT, and .PRINT. Versions of these suitable for RSTS/E, RSX-11M, and the UNIX system are provided in Appendix D. *The instructor should have these macros installed before instruction begins if they are not presently on the system to be used.* Once these are installed, all examples in the text will operate essentially as shown without modification.

How to Use This Book

Programming in Assembly Language: MACRO-11 is intended for a one-semester (three hours per week) or one-quarter (four hours per week) course in assembly language and machine organization. Such a course will fulfill the CS-3 requirement, *Introduction to Computer Systems,* in Curriculum 78 recommended by the Association for Computing Machinery, and typically enrolls students with one prior programming course. Chapters 1 through 9 will provide the core material for this course, with supplemental topics selected from Chapters 10 through 15. A longer course can cover Chapters 10 through 15 more thoroughly.

Two course formats were tried while the book was being tested at California State University, Fullerton. In both cases, 27 one-hour lectures (two per week) were allocated for covering core and supplemental advanced topics. In one test format, the third hour each week was used for classroom discussion, in-class machine interaction, use of editors, working examples, and so on. In the second test format, the two hours of lecture was supplemented by a two-hour laboratory meeting in which the students worked at terminals with an instructor present. Both formats work well, although the latter is preferable if resources are available.

Chapters 1, 2, and 3 provide an introduction to the course. Chapter 1 shows by example what is meant by machine and assembly programming, and explains the process of creating a program with an editor, as well as assembling, linking, and running it on the machine. Chapter 2 is intended to give the student essential skills in base conversion and nondecimal arithmetic with positive integers. The organization of the PDP-11 in terms of memory, registers, data paths, and block structure is discussed in Chapter 3. The instruction execution cycle is also covered in Chapter 3. These chapters can be covered easily in the first four lectures, with the majority of that time devoted to Chapter 2.

Chapter 4 begins the process of introducing instructions, addressing modes, and directives. The subset introduced here will allow only "straight-line" programs, manipulating positive integers in registers. Manual translation, assembler listing, and the use of the On-line Debugging Technique (ODT) are also introduced here. Two or three lectures will be required to cover this chapter.

The purpose of Chapter 5 is to enlarge the student's repertoire sufficiently to allow programming with branches and loops, and to use data organized in arrays. (The full treatment of data structures is deferred until Chapter 11.) Unsigned branching instructions are described without specific reference to condition codes. The student is given several standard "templates" for programming decision structures and loops. Immediate, relative, register deferred, and autoincrement and autodecrement addressing modes are introduced. Three to four lectures should be allocated for this chapter.

Chapter 6, "Computer Arithmetic," returns to number theory, covering the two's complement system and arithmetic involving negative integers. It also introduces the condition codes, and then the signed branch instructions. Other arithmetic concepts discussed here include shift and rotate operations, double-precision arithmetic, and the multiply and divide operations, both in hardware and software forms. Four lectures will be adequate for this chapter, although an extra lecture will be required for thorough coverage of the software multiply and divide algorithms.

The purpose of Chapter 7 is to introduce the character (byte) data handling capability of the machine. This includes coverage of the ASCII code, byte instructions, and byte directives. Logical bit instructions are also discussed here. Three lectures will be required to cover this material.

Input and output are finally discussed in Chapter 8. By this point the student has a sufficient grasp of the language to deal with the intricate steps involved in I/O. Character I/O using system-supplied macros (as shown in Appendix D) is discussed first, followed by programmed I/O through the device registers using polling. This is followed by a detailed explanation of octal and decimal I/O routines. At least three lectures will be required for this chapter.

Chapter 9 presents the concepts of subroutines and stacks. Basic ideas of subroutines, including elementary usage in MACRO-11, are presented first, followed by a thorough introduction of stacks. This leads into a discussion of linkage and argument transmission. Four lectures will suffice for this chapter if the instructor is selective in classroom coverage of the several argument transmission methods presented in the chapter. Chapter 9 concludes the normal core material for the course.

The remaining lectures to supplement the core material can be selected from Chapters 10 through 15. Chapter 10 covers the macro definition facility of MACRO-11, as well as assembly expressions, symbols and direct assignment, repeat directives, and conditional assembly. The assembly process is also outlined in Chapter 10. Chapter 11 contains a complete discussion of the PDP-11 addressing modes, filling gaps and unifying the addressing mode picture developed in earlier chapters. This prepares the student for the main topic of Chapter 11—data structures. Chapter 12 presents the fundamental ideas of recursion, then shows its implementation with MACRO-11 subroutines. Floating-point operations, using both the FIS option and the FP11 coprocessor, are covered in Chapter 13. Traps and interrupts are the principal topics of Chapter 14, with interrupt-driven I/O being the major example. Software interrupts are also covered. Chapter 15 is devoted to programming considerations that are not often covered in an introductory course, but that are important in larger projects. These include modular programming, programming style and standards, linkage and memory maps, position-independent code, and the creation and use of libraries.

Acknowledgments

This book is a result of the combined efforts of many people. I especially wish to acknowledge the contributions of Vaclav Rajlich (University of Michigan, Ann Arbor) who provided some of the original organizational ideas, and Raymond Bagley (California State University, Fullerton) who provided assistance and insights throughout the project. My constant assistant from beginning to end has been Phyllis Mercer, who not only typed the manuscript, but also acted as general editor and counselor while the book was undergoing development and classroom testing at CSUF. Also, Gene Rose and Mahadeva Venkatesan (CSUF) were immensely helpful in their thorough proofreading, checking of examples, and editorial suggestions. The reviewers of the manuscript, including James Bueg and Joseph Grimes (California Polytechnic State University, San Luis Obispo), Thomas W. Lynch (Northwestern University), Dennis Volper (University of California, Irvine), William Franks (San Diego, California), and Harold Stone (University of Massachusetts, Amherst), are also acknowledged for their helpful criticisms and suggestions, many of which are incorporated into this text. I am also grateful for the help provided by James Bueg, Michael Herrera (CSUF), Richard Nelson (CSUF), and Gary Valencia (CSUF) in developing Appendix D. In addition to expressing my gratitude to the several hundred students who provided feedback during the testing period, I wish to also acknowledge the proofreading and programming done by Tzu-Ming Hong, Eduardo Malamut, and Craig Verbeck. Whatever shortcomings this book may have should be attributed to myself. There would have been more without the able assistance of these people.

Fullerton, California   E.F.S.
January 1984

Contents

Preliminaries

Binary, Octal, and Decimal Number Systems

PDP-11 Hardware Organization and Characteristics

Introduction to Assembly Language Programming

5 Programs with Branches and Simple Data Structures

6 Computer Arithmetic

7 Character Data

Macros, Conditional Assembly and Other MACRO-11 Features

Traps and Interrupts

Programming Considerations

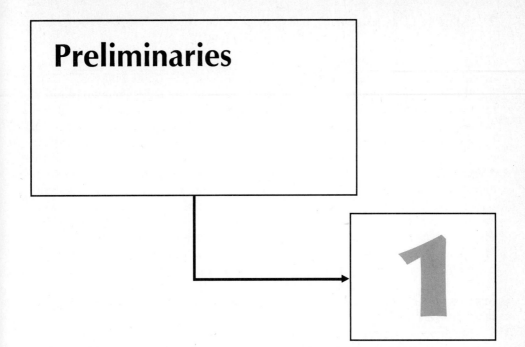

1.1 Programming Concepts

A digital computer is a machine that is capable of accepting a prepared sequence of instructions and carrying them out. The PDP-11 series of computers discussed in this book, for example, has over 100 different instructions, called its *instruction set*, and can be configured with sufficient memory space to retain a sequence of many thousands of these instructions. Preparation of a sequence of these instructions to accomplish some desired purpose is called **programming** of the computer. The sequence of instructions, or some set of statements from which they can be derived, is called a **program.**

There are many different ways in which a program can be expressed. We begin our discussion by considering the most fundamental way in which a program can be expressed; that is, when it is expressed in terms of numerical instruction codes, called **machine code,** recognizable directly by the machine. An example of this is

```
0   001   000   001   000   100
0   110   000   010   000   100
0   110   000   011   000   100
0   000   000   000   000   000
```

Although difficult to recognize, this is a segment of a program in the "machine language" of the PDP-11 computer; it causes the PDP-11 to add three numbers. It may be observed here that the instructions in this native language of the PDP-11, like those for other digital computers, are strings of 1's and 0's called bit

1

(*b*inary dig*it*) strings. Each particular pattern has a very precise meaning to the machine; these meanings were imparted to the machine by its builders.

It is possible, although not always practical, to program the computer entirely in terms of such bit patterns. The machine itself has a set of 16 or more switches across the front (see Fig. 1.1) so that an operator can set a particular switch up to represent a 1 and down to represent a 0. Depressing another momentary-contact switch "deposits" the instruction code set on the switches into memory. The process can be repeated until an entire program has been entered. After entry, the program can be executed. It is easy to see that the process is tedious and time-consuming. Therefore programming is not often done in this way. Another disadvantage is that programs expressed in this way are very difficult for *human beings* to read. This is important because most programs sooner or later have to be modified to meet a new need, requiring the programmer (or perhaps another programmer) to review them long after they were originally written. The most distinguishing quality of machine code is that it is the easiest form of a program for the machine to understand; at the same time, it is the most difficult for human beings to understand.

Machine code programs are often expressed in a slightly different form that makes them easier (although still not easy!) for human beings to read. If we begin at the right in each instruction in the program above and replace each group of three binary digits according to the rule

```
000 = 0
001 = 1
010 = 2
011 = 3
100 = 4
101 = 5
110 = 6
111 = 7
```

we arrive at

```
010104
060204
060304
000000
```

This is said to be "octal" (base 8) representation, whereas the original version is expressed in binary (base 2). This is merely a convenience for human beings because the machine actually works in terms of binary instructions. When it becomes necessary for a programmer to write out a machine language instruction, he or she most often will do so in octal. It is not often necessary to write programs in machine language.

The inconvenience of machine language programming is overcome to a large extent by the use of **assembly language programming.** The fundamental idea of

Figure 1.1   Front panel of PDP-11 computer. (Photograph by Charles B. Blanton, CSUF Media Center.)

assembly language is that each machine language instruction has a short, meaningful symbol that is more easily recognized by human programmers than are the binary or octal representations. Such symbols are called **mnemonics** because they are intended to have the quality of being easily remembered. For example, ADD is the mnemonic for the addition instruction.

Rewriting the program segment above in terms of the PDP-11 assembly language (called MACRO-11) produces

```
MOV   R1,R4
ADD   R2,R4
ADD   R3,R4
HALT
```

It is much easier to see how this program works. The program assumes that there are three numbers, each stored in one of the **registers** R1, R2, and R3, which may be viewed as "number boxes." In the first instruction, the contents† of R1 is moved into a fourth box R4 (destroying whatever was there before). Next, the contents of R2 is added to the contents of R4, producing a partial sum of the contents of R1 and R2, with the result being placed back in R4. The contents of R3 is likewise added to R4, producing the final result of R1 + R2 + R3, leaving it in R4. The last instruction, HALT, stops the computer.

---

† In this text, the word "contents" will be construed to be a singular noun meaning "the number contained in a location."

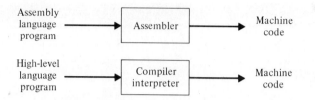

Figure 1.2 Translation of assembly or high-level language to machine code.

This example demonstrates the correspondence between machine and assembly language programming. It should be understood, however, that ultimately every program, however expressed originally, must be reduced to machine code prior to execution because the computer "understands" only its own native language. Thus when one writes a program in assembly language, it is with the expectation that it will be *translated* into machine code. Now, very little would be gained from programming in assembly language if this translation had to be done by the programmer, i.e., by hand. Fortunately, this problem has a solution—namely *another* program (written earlier by someone else!) that can read the assembly language and can generate automatically the patterns of 1's and 0's representing the corresponding machine code. Such a program is called an **assembler,** and most likely already exists on the computer system that you will be using. The process is shown in Fig. 1.2. The programmer creates the program in assembly language and passes it through the assembler, producing machine code.

Programming in assembly language is easier than programming in machine code, but not quite as easy as using a "high-level" language such as BASIC or Pascal. Contrast, for example, the single BASIC statement

        LET W = X + Y + Z

with the assembly language program above that accomplishes essentially the same thing, i.e., it adds three numbers together. It is seen that a single BASIC statement expresses what it took three **instructions** to express in MACRO-11. Moreover, the meaning, at least to those familiar with conventional notation of algebra, is much clearer. This is true in general: A high-level language program is easier for human beings to read and is more compact in its original (source) form than are assembly language programs. We must not forget, however, that, as with assembly language programs, high-level language programs have to be translated to machine code prior to execution. The preexisting program that does this job for high-level languages is called a **compiler** or, in some cases, an **interpreter.** This process is also shown in Fig. 1.2.

1.2 Why Assembly Language?

Because it is usually easier to program in high-level languages, one might ask, "Why use assembly language?" The answer to this question depends heavily on the particular problem being addressed. One thing that usually indicates the desirability of assembly language is the requirement for extremely fast execution of the final program. As a rule, compilers and interpreters generate machine code that uses more machine instructions than a well-designed assembly language program uses: Fewer instructions often mean faster execution. The actual size of the machine language program is sometimes critical as well. Computers aboard spacecraft, for example, may have limited memory, so that the shorter programs created by talented assembly language programmers may be an important advantage or even a necessity. Another reason may be that a compiler or interpreter is *not available* for the host computer, or those available may be limited in some way, precluding the use of some useful feature of the machine. This happens very frequently in the task known as "systems programming" and, as a result, most computer installations will have at least one programmer who works with assembly language.

Programmers must examine their tasks in view of these factors in making the decision. If the problem does not need extremely efficient, compact code and if a suitable high-level language translator is available, one most likely should not use assembly language. We also point out that a study of assembly language develops a deeper understanding of the computer itself that will improve one's programming skills in any language. This in itself is enough cause for one to learn assembly language.

1.3 Support Programs [OS]†

Solving a problem on a computer always involves more than just the program, regardless of the language selected. For example, one must somehow "enter" the program into the computer before it can be executed. As already observed, if it is not in the native language of the machine, it must be assembled, compiled, or interpreted, and, as we shall later see, "linked" to other preexisting programs that it needs to execute. Finally, one must instruct the computer to run the program, and enter any necessary input data. In most cases, the programmer is assisted in these tasks by the **operating system,** and a number of supporting **system programs** available on the computer being used. Here we briefly introduce these concepts, using the RSTS/E operating system as an example. A more complete treatment of the use of these support systems is presented in Appendixes B, C, and D.

The creation of an assembly language program is aided by a system program called an **editor.** Several are usually available on PDP-11 computers. The one selected for use here is EDT (called the DEC Editor in Digital Equipment Corporation literature). This or any other editor allows the programmer to create and save programs as files on the mass storage device serving the computer. Commands to the editor also allow the correction of typographical errors, or later modification of the program. One task facing the beginning assembly language

---

† We shall mark sections that depend on the operating system in this way. [OS] means to consult Appendix D if you are not using RSTS/E.

programmer is the mastery of EDT or some other available editor program so
that programs can be easily created and modified.

An example will demonstrate the procedure. After signing on to the computer,
enter

```
EDT   MYPROG.MAC
```

The system responds with an asterisk (we show responses by the machine with
an underline), that should be answered with I, standing for input.

```
*I
```

The program can now be entered. A simple one that can actually be executed
is

```
          .TITLE    FIRST TRY
          .MCALL    . PRINT, .EXIT
START:    .PRINT    #MSG1
          .EXIT
MSG1:     .ASCIZ    / HI THERE!/
          .END      START
```

Note: This will work only if .PRINT and .EXIT have been installed on your
computer. See Appendix D or consult your instructor or computer center staff.

Simultaneously pushing the "control" and "Z" keys (called control-Z and
written ^Z) will cause the system to respond with another asterisk, to which the
user responds with EX, standing for EXIT from the EDT program. This also
saves the results. The complete sequence, which should be tried, is

```
EDT MYPROG.MAC
*I
          .TITLE    FIRST TRY
          .MCALL    . PRINT,.EXIT
START:    .PRINT    #MSG1
          .EXIT
MSG1:     .ASCIZ    /HI THERE!/
          .END      START
^Z
*EX
```

This creates a "file" or permanent copy of these entered lines on your disk
space. If typing errors are made, they can be corrected using other features of
EDT as explained in Section B.2.

To assemble this program, the MACRO-11 assembler must be invoked. Although slight variations may also work at your facility, the following sequence
will nearly always work.

```
RUN   $MACRO
*MYPROG.OBJ,MYPROG.LST=MYPROG.MAC
 ERRORS DETECTED = 0
*^Z
```

The assembler responds with an error count, which should be 0. After printing the error count, the assembler provides another * prompt, to which you should respond with ˆZ to leave the assembler.

Before it can be executed, your assembled program must be "linked" with existing, system-supplied programs to help it work. This process is called linking, and is done by a system program called LINK. To execute LINK, enter

```
RUN   $LINK
*MYPROG.SAV,MYPROG.MAP=MYPROG.OBJ
*ˆZ
```

The executable program is now in the MYPROG.SAV file. To execute your program, then enter

```
RUN   MYPROG.SAV
```

whereupon it will print

```
HI THERE!
```

Note: (If it doesn't, see Section D.3.1.)

The process described above is shown diagrammatically in Fig. 1.3. Each of the four steps—editing, assembling, linking, and execution—requires the use of a system program, invoked by entering their names. Each system program receives your program in one form and creates from it a different version. For example, EDT receives keyboard entries of MACRO-11 statements and creates a source file, conventionally identified as **name.MAC**, where name is selected by the programmer. The file is automatically saved on mass storage. The assembler, MACRO-11, accepts name.MAC as input, and produces two files as output—name.OBJ and name.LST. Both are also saved. The LST file is a "listing" that can be printed or displayed on your terminal; it gives the assembled program (as octal addresses and instructions) as well as the assembly language itself. Any errors encountered by the assembler will also be included in LST. To see the LST file, enter

```
PIP   MYPROG.LST
```

We make use of a system-provided program that is called the Peripheral Interchange Processor or PIP. Another system program, TYPE, will work equally well. The interpretation of the LST file is given in Section 4.7. The OBJ file, on the other hand, is "machine code," sometimes called the *object* version of your program and cannot be listed at your terminal. It is in the binary form needed by the LINK program.

The OBJ version becomes input to the LINK program, which also creates two files. The first of these, name.MAP, can be printed or displayed and has information useful to an experienced programmer. The second, name.SAV is, like name.OBJ, in binary and therefore cannot be printed. However, it is the complete, ready-to-execute program along with all necessary system routines. The complete terminal activity for this example is shown in Fig. 1.4. Note that

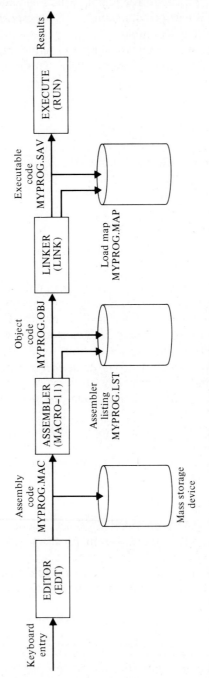

Figure 1.3 Procedure for creating and running a MACRO-11 program.

8

```
EDT MYPROG.MAC
*I
            .TITLE FIRST TRY
            .MCALL .PRINT, .EXIT
START:      .PRINT #MSG1
            .EXIT
MSG1:       .ASCIZ \HI THERE!\
            .END START
^Z
[EOB]
*EX
MYPROG.MAC 6 lines

Ready

RUN $MACRO
*MYPROG.OBJ,MYPROG.LST=MYPROG.MAC
ERRORS DETECTED:  0
*^Z

Ready

RUN $LINK
*MYPROG.SAV,MYPROG.MAP=MYPROG.OBJ
*^Z

Ready

RUN MYPROG.SAV
HI THERE!

Ready
```

Figure 1.4 Complete terminal activity for a simple MACRO-11 exercise. [OS]

the system responses are underlined. The response <u>Ready</u> indicates that the computer is ready for the next command.

1.4 Summary

We have seen that a computer program, in its most fundamental form, is a set of *instructions* represented as bit patterns in successive locations in the computer's memory. These bit patterns are recognizable *by the hardware of the machine itself* and are therefore referred to as *machine code*. These bit patterns can also be represented in octal. Assembly language is a way of expressing such a program in "human readable" form and there is a system-provided program (called an *assembler*) that converts assembly language to machine code.

Briefly mentioned was the relation between assembly language and still more convenient higher-level languages, which raised the question, "Why use assembly language?" The answer to this may be greater execution speed, more compact programs, or the mere absence of high-level language translators for the target machine.

We have also covered, at least briefly, how to actually create, assemble, link, and execute a simple MACRO-11 program. If a machine is available, the reader should repeat the given examples and work the provided exercises because there is no substitute for practice.

1.5 Exercises

1.1 Go to your computer center and determine which text editor you should use. If your editor is different from EDT, then find out how to do the examples in this text with your editor.

1.2 Create the program given in Sec. 1.3 using your system text editor. Assemble, link, and run this program.

1.3 Using Appendix D, the reference manuals available in the computer center, or materials from your instructor, determine how to do the following things on your computer system.

a) Obtain a directory listing of your permanent files.

b) Erase a file.

c) Rename a file.

d) Merge two files.

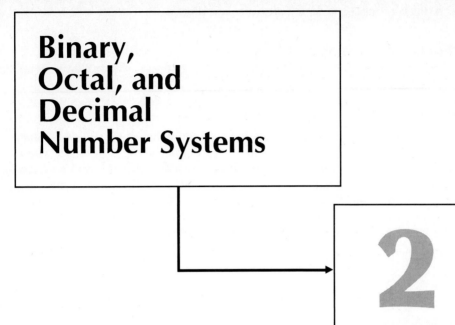

Binary, Octal, and Decimal Number Systems

2.1 Numbers for Machines and People

As we have already noted, digital computers work internally in terms of binary codes. This is almost universally true because it is easy to devise electronic hardware that can represent two different states, e.g., on and off, and binary codes require only two different symbols, 0 and 1. Thus there is a natural match between electronic machines and binary codes. On the other hand, human beings are adapted to working principally with the decimal representation of numbers using the arabic digit symbols 0, 1, 2, ..., 9. In order to bridge this gap, we therefore digress from our discussion of programming to review the fundamental notions of number representation, conversion of bases and arithmetic operations in the machine-preferred systems. We focus on binary, octal (shorthand binary!), and the familiar decimal system.

The term "representation" is used in this discussion to distinguish the manner in which we choose to *write or store* a number from the number itself. For example, 16 people or 16 pounds of corn can be represented with arabic numerals in decimal as we have here, roman numerals, tally marks, or any one of many other numeric representation systems. Regardless of the method of representation, however, the abstract concept of the number is the same. This is an important distinction to keep in mind as we proceed.

2.2 Positional Notation and Bases

As we are taught in elementary school, a number such as 428 in the arabic decimal system can be viewed as a sum of products.

$$4 \times 10^2 + 2 \times 10^1 + 8 \times 10^0 = 428.$$

Here we are acknowledging that each digit position has a certain **place value,** i.e., from right-to-left 1, 10, 100, 1000, etc., that multiplies the digit value. These are obviously the successive powers of 10, i.e., 10^0, 10^1, 10^2, 10^3, and so forth, so that the place value of a decimal digit is 10 raised to the power of its position, counting from 0 at the least significant digit. Here 10 is said to be the "base" of the decimal number system. Where there is any possibility for ambiguity, we note the base of the representation used by a subscript, e.g., 428_{10}.

In general, a positional notation number in any base can be expressed as

$$N = \sum_{i=0}^{m-1} D_i b^i \tag{2.1}$$

where the D_i are the m individual digits and b is the base.

Binary (base 2) and octal (base 8) numbers employ the same kind of positional notation. For example, the binary number 101_2 can be viewed as

$$1 \times 2^2 + 0 \times 2^1 + 1 \times 2^0.$$

If we express the place values, e.g., 2^2, 2^1 and 2^0, as *decimal* numbers, we achieve the decimal equivalent of this number.

$$1 \times 4 + 0 \times 2 + 1 \times 1 = 5_{10}.$$

Similarly, the binary number 11111 is

$$1 \times 2^4 + 1 \times 2^3 + 1 \times 2^2 + 1 \times 2^1 + 1 \times 2^0 = 31_{10}.$$

This last example demonstrates that the largest possible value of a number composed of a specified number of digits occurs when each digit has the largest value allowed by the base. In general, if the base is b and there are m allowed digits, the decimal representation of the largest allowed number is

$$b^m - 1.$$

In the example above, this is $2^5 - 1 = 31_{10}$. The importance of this observation is that in a fixed word length machine, the largest number that can be represented in binary positional representation is determined by the word length.

As we have already seen in Chapter 1, octal numbers are used primarily as a more convenient way for human beings to write binary codes. (See Section 1.1.) However, it is also true that the octal numbers are the positional representation in base 8, so that we can also view them as sums of place value times digit products. For example, applying Eq. (2.1), 165_8 is

$$1 \times 8^2 + 6 \times 8^1 + 5 \times 8^0 = 117_{10}.$$

We have seen that the significance of the base of a number system is that it determines the *place values* in a positional notation. In going from right to left, each successive place value is the base times the previous place value. It is also important to note that the base determines the number of unique symbols required in a positional number system. For example, in the binary system, base 2, we need two symbols (0 and 1), while in the decimal system we need ten symbols (0, 1, 2, ..., 9). As should be evident, the octal system, base 8, requires eight symbols (0, 1, 2, ..., 7). The reason for this is simply that there must be enough symbols to "span" the distance between place values. Consider the simple process of numbering mileposts along a highway using the decimal system and beginning at 0. The post at the end of the ninth mile is marked 9, and the next post must mark the end of the tenth mile. We observe that because we have chosen the decimal system, the second digit place value is 10, and therefore we have no need for another symbol; we can mark the post with two of the already used symbols, i.e., a 1 and a 0. Indeed, if there *had* been an eleventh symbol, it would have been possible to mark the post two different ways that would be a redundant system and confusing. On the other hand, had there been only nine symbols, 0 through 8, we would not have had any symbol to mark the post at the end of the ninth mile! Thus the selection of base in a positional notation determines the required number of symbols. Table 2.1 shows the symbols commonly used for the widely used bases.

The hexadecimal system, base 16, is another system that allows an easy shorthand for binary numbers. Although not used in programming the PDP-11, it is widely used in connection with other computers. It is also a positional notation system so that we can interpret the number 169_{16} as

$$1 \times 16^2 + 6 \times 16^1 + 9 \times 16^0 = 361_{10}.$$

Observe now, however, that we need 16 symbols to span the range between place values of successive digits, and that the customary ten arabic digits are insufficient. This problem is solved by using the *alphabetic* characters A, B, C, D, E, and F to augment the digits 0, 1, 2, ..., 9 as shown in Table 2.1. Thus the number E4A, for example, is

$$14 \times 16^2 + 4 \times 16^1 + 10 \times 16^0 = 3658_{10}$$

TABLE 2.1
Digit Symbols for Various Bases

Base	Name	Digit Symbols
2	Binary	0 1
8	Octal	0 1 2 3 4 5 6 7
10	Decimal	0 1 2 3 4 5 6 7 8 9
16	Hexadecimal	0 1 2 3 4 5 6 7 8 9 A B C D E F

where we have made use of Eq.(2.1) and the facts that E has the decimal value of 14 and A has the decimal value of 10.

2.3 Arithmetic Operations in Binary and Octal

From time to time it will be necessary for the assembly language programmer to perform simple addition and subtraction in binary and octal. The rules learned in elementary school for performing these operations in decimal have to be modified slightly to account for the different bases. We will show these operations by example, and encourage the reader to practice using the exercises provided at the end of the chapter.

2.3.1 Addition

Addition is performed one digit at a time, working from the right. When the sum of digits exceeds the value of the highest symbol available in the base, one must "carry" the excess into the next position. In binary the highest symbol value is 1, so 1 plus 1 generates a 0 and a carry as shown in the following simple examples.

$$
\begin{array}{cccc}
1 & 1 & 11 & 101 \\
+1 & +0 & +01 & +100 \\
\hline
10 & 1 & 100 & 1001
\end{array}
$$

A slightly more difficult case occurs when more than two digits have to be added. Consider, for example, the following.

$$
\begin{array}{r}
1 \\
1 \\
+1 \\
\hline
11
\end{array}
$$

In performing this we added the first two 1's getting a carry to the second-digit position. The 0 added to the remaining 1 yields 1 in the first digit. Because there are no second-place 1's in the summands, the final result is just the carry generated by the first addition. A more interesting case occurs when adding four 1's.

$$
\begin{array}{r}
1 \\
1 \\
1 \\
+1 \\
\hline
100
\end{array}
$$

Adding the first two 1's yield 0 with a 1 carried to position two. Adding the third summand to the first-position 0 yields 1. Adding this first-position 1 to the fourth summand yields 0 and *another* carry to the second position. We must then *add the two carries,* yielding a 0 as the final second-position value, and a carry into the third position.

As a final example of binary addition, consider

```
  111
+ 111
 1110
```

We note here that we added a number to itself, so that the result should be twice the number. Our answer of 1110 is indeed twice 111, and demonstrates an important principle: Multiplying a binary number by 2 shifts the bit pattern left by one bit, with a 0 filling in the first position. Said another way, multiplying by 2 adds a 0 at the right. This operation is commonly called an **arithmetic shift left.** The reader will recognize that this is similar to the effect that multiplying by 10 has on a decimal number. Indeed, when any number is multiplied by its base, a 0 digit is added to the right.

Addition of octal numbers follows similar rules. In this case, however, the highest available digit has the value 7, so that any partial sum greater than 7 necessitates a carry. Some examples will demonstrate the octal technique.

a)	1	b)	3	c)	4	d)	5	e)	7	f)	7	g)	77
	+4		+4		+4		+4		+4		+7		+1
	5		7		10		11		13		16		100

Examples (a) and (b) yield sums that are 7 or less and therefore involve no carries. In (c), 4 added to 4 yields a *value* of 8, but there is no *single symbol* for 8 in octal. Rather than writing 8, we therefore write the amount by which the sum *exceeds* 8, in this case 0, and carry a 1. In example (d), the sum of 4 and 5 exceeds 8 by 1, so we write a 1 and carry a 1 to the next digit. The reader can confirm that this technique leads to the answers given for examples (e), (f), and (g) also. Example (g) demonstrates that 77 is the largest value that can be represented by a two-digit octal number; adding 1 causes a carry into the third position.

When there are more than two octal summands, there may be more than one carry to be added into the adjacent position. For example, consider

```
  7
  7
+ 7
 25
```

Addition of the first two 7's yields 6 with a carry of 1 to the second-position digit. The first-position 6 added to the third 7 yields a 5 with *another* carry to the second-position digit. Finally, the two carries are added to yield 2 in the second position. The reader may wish to test his or her skills by verifying the following examples of octal addition.

a)	576	b)	777	c)	123
	472		777		456
	677		111		712
	2167		2107		1513

2.3.2 Subtraction

Subtraction is only slightly more difficult than addition. Rather than carrying, we may have the need to "borrow" from the digit to the left, in a manner completely analogous to decimal subtraction. We will demonstrate first with binary, then octal. We defer the consideration of negative numbers until Chapter 6. Therefore we do not consider in this chapter problems that would lead to negative results.

When no borrowing is required, the subtraction process is completely straightforward.

$$\begin{array}{ccc} 1 & 11 & 111 \\ -1 & -10 & -101 \\ \hline 0 & 01 & 010 \end{array}$$

Now consider the case when there is a 1 to be subtracted from a 0, e.g.,

$$\begin{array}{r} 10 \\ -1 \\ \hline 1 \end{array}$$

Here it is necessary to borrow from the second position before subtracting the 1. The following scratch-work shows the process and compares it to the analogous situation in decimal subtraction.

Note that borrowing a 1 from the next binary digit reduces that digit by 1, and converts the 0 to a 2. The 1 can then be subtracted from this 2, yielding the answer. If the position to be borrowed from is itself a 0, it is necessary to borrow also from the *next higher* digit. Note the following example.

Here we borrowed from the third position giving the second position a value of 2. This allowed borrowing from the second position, leaving it as a 1 and making the first-position value 2. The subtrahend can now be subtracted from the first-position 2, giving a 1. Finally, the second-position value is brought down giving the correct answer.

Note in the examples above that in the borrowing process we chose to express the sum of the borrow and the minuend digit in *decimal* form rather than in binary form. That is, observe that we could either write (and think!) in binary as in the following

$$\overset{10}{\cancel{1}\,\cancel{0}}$$
$$\underline{-1}$$
$$1$$

or in decimal

$$\overset{2}{\cancel{1}\,\cancel{0}}$$
$$\underline{-1}$$
$$1$$

We choose the latter because then we can use the subtraction facts we learned for decimal arithmetic, rather than learning their counterparts in binary, octal, or whatever base we happen to need.

   The following examples further demonstrate the process of binary subtraction, and should be verified by the reader.

a)	1110	b)	1000	c)	1010
	-1101		-111		-0101
	0001		0001		0101

   Subtraction of octal numbers parallels the process in decimal or binary. That is, we proceed digit by digit from right to left subtracting the subtrahend from the minuend. For example,

$$774$$
$$\underline{-153}$$
$$621$$

In this case it is impossible to discern that octal subtraction is being done because every digit of the subtrahend is smaller than the corresponding digit in the *minuend*. When this is not the case, one must borrow from the digit to the left. This is the same as in decimal, except in octal the borrow gives 8_{10} rather than 10_{10}. Observe this in the following example, where we again choose to "borrow in decimal."

13			11			9			11		
$\cancel{1}$ 14			3 $\cancel{3}$ 12			5 $\cancel{1}$ 9			$\cancel{3}$ 11		
$\cancel{1}\,\cancel{6}\,\cancel{6}$			$\cancel{4}\,\cancel{4}\,\cancel{4}$			$\cancel{6}\,\cancel{2}\,\cancel{1}$			$\cancel{1}\,\cancel{4}\,\cancel{3}$		
$-\quad 7\;7$			$-1\;5\;6$			$-4\;3\;2$			$-\quad 4\;6$		
6 7			2 6 6			1 6 7			7 5		

Octal subtraction is an especially important skill when working with addresses of memory locations.

2.4 Conversion of Bases

We have already observed that the same number can be represented in many different bases. The conversion from one base to another is something that every assembly language programmer has to do regularly. Therefore, some proficiency in this skill is necessary. Here we will show selected conversion techniques for

binary to octal
octal to binary
octal to decimal
binary to decimal
decimal to octal
decimal to binary

2.4.1 Binary to Octal

The conversions from binary to octal and octal to binary are particularly easy, as we have already seen. One must memorize the short table

Octal	Binary
0	000
1	001
2	010
3	011
4	100
5	101
6	110
7	111

Then a binary number is simply partitioned into groups of 3 bits, starting at the right, and the corresponding octal digit is substituted for each group. Examples follow.

Binary: 011 001 110   111 101 110 000 001
Octal: 3   1   6   7   5   6   0   1

If the binary number has a length that is not divisible by 3, simply add 0's at the left as required. Conversion from octal to binary is simply the reverse of the above. For example,

Octal: 7   5   2   1
Binary: 111 101 010 001

2.4.2 Binary and Octal to Decimal

We have also already seen conversion from binary and octal to decimal. This can be done by using the formula Eq. (2.1) repeated here

$$N = \sum_{i=0}^{m-1} D_i b^i$$

where

D_i = value of the ith digit *represented in decimal,* and

b^i = base raised to the ith power and *represented in decimal.*

Several examples of this are given in Section 2.1.

There are other methods for conversion to base 10. One binary-to-decimal conversion that can be done without the aid of powers-of-two tables is called the **double dabble** method. The steps are

1. Double the MSB.
2. Add the next bit. (This is the "dabble.")
3. Double the result.
4. Repeat from step 2 until there are no more bits.

MSB means "Most Significant Bit," that is, the leftmost bit of the number. Although this method can, with practice, be done without writing anything down, we show a step-by-step example below for clarity.

Example 2.1 Convert 1011101 to decimal using double dabble.

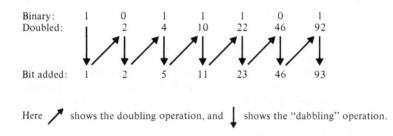

Here ⟋ shows the doubling operation, and ⟱ shows the "dabbling" operation.

See also Exercise 2.8.

2.4.3 Decimal to Binary
Conversion from decimal to octal or binary is significantly more difficult than the reverse. Theoretically, the formula given previously could be used, but this is not a practical method for hand calculations. To see why, consider conversion of 42_{10} to binary by Eq. (2.1).

$$4 \times 10^1 + 2 \times 10^0.$$

In order for *conversion* to take place, each of these numbers must be expressed in the target base, binary, and the arithmetic must be carried out in binary. Let's do this just once.

$$100 \times 1010 + 10 \times 1 = 101010.$$

The reader can prove this to be correct by converting back to decimal. Note, however, that to do it this way we had to know the binary representation of 4, 2, 10, and 1, and had to know how to perform multiplication in binary. These are not particularly difficult concepts, but on the other hand most of us have far better skills in *decimal* arithmetic. Most programmers therefore apply different methods for the reverse conversions. Decimal to binary can be done quite easily with a subtractive method because the coefficients on the place values are always 0 or 1. The method goes rapidly with a calculator and a powers-of-two table such as shown inside the back cover of this book. One simply attempts to subtract the largest possible power of 2, and records a 1 for the corresponding bit when successful or a 0 otherwise. The following example demonstrates this method.

Example 2.2 (Subtractive method)

Convert 42_{10} to binary.

$$42 - 32 = 10 \quad D_5 = 1$$
$$D_4 = 0$$
$$10 - 8 = 2 \quad D_3 = 1$$
$$D_2 = 0$$
$$2 - 2 = 0 \quad D_1 = 1$$
$$D_0 = 0$$

Therefore $42_{10} = 101010$.

Example 2.3 (Remainder Method) An alternative approach is known as the division or *remainder* method. With this method, the number is divided by the base and the quotient and remainder are written separately. The quotient is then divided by the base, again writing the resulting quotient and remainder. This process is repeated until the quotient is zero. The succession of remainders is the number in the new base. The following example demonstrates this method. Convert 93_{10} to binary.

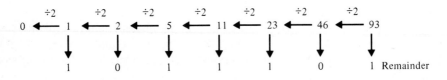

Therefore $93_{10} = 1011101_2$. Note that this method is the inverse of the double dabble method. This is evidenced by the similarity in intermediate results. (See Example 2.1.)

2.4.4 Decimal to Octal

Decimal to octal conversion can be done in several different ways. Some prefer to convert first to binary using the subtractive or remainder method, then perform the easy binary-to-octal conversion. Direct decimal-to-octal conversion by the subtractive method is complicated by the fact that the octal digits act as multipliers on the place value. One must first determine the largest power of 8 that can be subtracted. The first octal digit is then the number of times that this power can be subtracted. Repetition of the process gives the rest of the digits, as shown in the following example.

Example 2.4 (Subtractive Method) Convert 656_{10} to octal.

$$
\begin{array}{rl}
656 & \\
-512 & \quad (8^3 = 512) \qquad \text{(Subtracted once; } D_3 = 1.) \\
\hline
144 & \\
-64 & \quad (8^2 = 64) \qquad \text{(Subtracted twice; } D_2 = 2.) \\
\hline
80 & \\
-64 & \\
\hline
16 & \\
-8 & \quad (8^1 = 8) \qquad \text{(Subtracted twice; } D_1 = 2.) \\
\hline
8 & \\
-8 & \\
\hline
0 & \quad (8^0 = 1) \qquad \text{(Subtracted zero times; } D_0 = 0.)
\end{array}
$$

Therefore $656_{10} = 1220_8$.

An alternate method for decimal-to-octal conversion is called the division or remainder method. Here one divides the number by 8 repeatedly; on each division the next digit of the result is given by the *remainder*.

Example 2.5 (Remainder Method) Convert 656_{10} to octal.

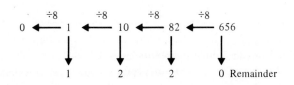

Therefore $656_{10} = 1220_8$. It is observed that the procedure is the same as used in decimal to binary conversion by the remainder method; only the base is different.

2.5 Summary

Assembly-language programming is complicated by the fact that the machine works with binary numbers, while people are more familiar with decimal numbers. Some effort is necessary to bridge this gap.

We first distinguished between the abstract concept of a number and the way we choose to represent it; 13_{10} is a *representation* of a baker's dozen, but so is 1101_2. It was seen that *positional notation* is used in binary and octal (base 8) number systems as well as the familiar decimal system. The *place values* and the number of required *digit symbols* are determined by the base of a positional number system. The place values are found by raising the base to the position index, counting from 0 at the rightmost digit.

The number of symbols required is equal to the base. The value of a positional number is the sum of the products of place values and the occupying digits. If the digits and place values are expressed in a *different base,* the number is *converted* to that base. We have also discussed the mechanics of simple arithmetic in the binary and octal systems. Addition was seen to be much the same as decimal addition. However, it was found necessary to recognize the impact of the base on the *carry* operation. For example, in octal we saw that $7 + 1 = 10$ because there is no symbol for 8 in octal, and 8 is the place value of the second digit. Similarly, in subtraction the borrow operation provides an additional 8 in octal or 2 in binary, analogous to 10 in decimal. We found, however, that we could make use of our decimal addition and subtraction "facts" learned in elementary school by representing borrows in decimal.

The chapter concludes with discussion of a number of algorithms for converting from one base to another. We found that binary to octal, or the reverse, was a simple substitution process. This ease of conversion is in fact the only justification for the use of octal; it is a "shorthand" for binary. Slightly more difficult are the conversions from binary or octal to decimal. The positional notation, sum-of-products formula is the most straightforward method for converting to decimal from either binary or octal. The alternate "double dabble" method is applicable for binary to decimal conversion. The more difficult conversions are *from decimal* to binary or octal. The sum-of-products formula would work, but not many of us have sufficient facility in base 8 or base 2 arithmetic to make this attractive. Instead, we demonstrated the use of the subtraction-of-powers method and the remainder method for conversion to either binary or octal. Most will find one or the other of these most suitable to their needs. Do not overlook the fact that you can convert first to binary, if you find that easy, and then convert the binary to octal by substitution.

2.6 Exercises

2.1 Convert the following binary numbers to decimal using either the direct sum-of-powers definition or the double dabble technique.

a) 11110111	**b)** 10000001	**c)** 1100100
d) 1010011100101110	**e)** 1010	**f)** 10101001
g) 10000000	**h)** 1111101000	**i)** 10011100010000
j) 10101101	**k)** 11111111	**l)** 11000011010100000

2.2 Perform the indicated binary arithmetic.

   a) $101010 + 10101 =$

   b) $10000000 - 1 =$

   c) $1111 + 111 =$

   d) $1111 - 111 =$

   e) $10000000 - 1010101 =$

f) 1100100 − 101111 =

g) 110110110 + 111111111 =

h) 100110011001 + 110000111001 =

i) 1 + 11 + 111 + 1111 =

j) 11 + 1001 + 11011 + 1010001 =

k) 1 + 111 − 110 + 111110100 − 11100001 =

l) 1111101000 − 1100100 − 1010 − 1 =

2.3 Convert the following binary numbers to octal and decimal.

a) 1010	**b)** 10101101	**c)** 10000001
d) 1111101000	**e)** 10111111	**f)** 1010011100101110

2.4 Convert the following decimal numbers to octal and binary.

a) 15	**b)** 384	**c)** 169
d) 1000	**e)** 255	**f)** 65535

Try both the subtraction of powers and remainder methods.

2.5 Convert the following octal numbers to decimal and binary.

a) 314	**b)** 164735	**c)** 177777
d) 147	**e)** 377	**f)** 123456

2.6 Perform the indicated arithmetic. All values are in octal.

a)	432 +371	**b)**	063257 +025653	**c)**	063254 −025667
d)	375 −177	**e)**	145 654 +717	**f)**	563 351 +666

2.7 Perform the indicated arithmetic. All values are in hexadecimal.

a)	E12A +0E5B	**b)**	1 2EF + ABCD	**c)**	FF92 −EA89
d)	AC79 −79AC	**e)**	1234 +9876	**f)**	FF − 19

2.8 In this chapter we saw a method to convert binary numbers to decimal using the double dabble technique. This technique can be generalized readily to create a fast method for converting octal numbers to decimal. In fact double dabble (and its generalization) is simply an efficient way to evaluate the positional polynomial representation of the number to be converted. Can you generalize double dabble for octal to decimal conversion? Explain why your generalization works. (*Hint:* Convert octal 1672 to decimal.

$$((1 \times 8 + 6) \times 8 + 7) \times 8 + 2 = 954.$$

What was done?) Try your generalization with the following octal numbers.

a) 1762   **b)** 1750   **c)** 255   **d)** 123456

PDP-11 Hardware Organization and Characteristics

3

3.1 Overview

A clear understanding of assembly and machine language programming cannot be developed without some understanding of the basic characteristics of the machine itself. In this chapter we discuss the characteristics of the PDP-11 architecture that are essential to successful MACRO-11 assembly programming. This includes the structure of the fundamental units of memory (i.e., words and bytes), the organization of all of the words comprising the memory unit, the general registers, and the processing unit. The fundamental instruction cycle is also discussed.

3.2 Words and Bytes

A digital computer must have the capability to store information (instructions and data) in the form of binary numbers or "bit patterns." This capability is provided by the central memory unit composed of a large number of individual memory units called "words." Each word of memory, also called a memory location, has the capability of accepting and retaining 16 bits of information. While this is accomplished in various electronic ways, the programmer is concerned only with the fact that "bit patterns" can be stored in each word. Diagrammatically

Figure 3.1 The 16-bit word.

this can be shown as in Fig. 3.1. Each "box" can hold either a 1 or a 0. In such a word, we can store any information that can be represented by a binary code. For example, it is possible to represent a decimal number as a binary number. As a specific case, let's work with the decimal number 76 that is 01001100 in binary. The binary representation of this number can be stored in the rightmost 7 bits of a 16-bit word, as shown in Fig. 3.2. Note that leading 0's do not change the value of a binary number any more than they would in the decimal representation.

The information to be stored need not, however, be binary representation of numbers. Observe, for example, that the program shown in Section 1.1, when represented as *binary* machine code, can be stored in four such words. Further, we shall later see that by assigning binary codes to alphabetic or other characters, e.g., "A," "B," "#," and "?," they too can be stored in these 16-bit words. Indeed, *any* information can be represented by some kind of binary code and therefore can be stored in a word. Conversely, a bit pattern in a word can have many different meanings; the particular meaning depends on *how it is used*.

For convenience of discussion, it is sometimes necessary to refer to particular bits within the word. For this purpose it is conventional (at least on the PDP-11) to assign position numbers beginning with 0 at the right, so that the leftmost bit is numbered 15. Additionally, one sometimes refers to the rightmost bit as the least significant bit (LSB), and that at the left end as the most significant bit (MSB). This terminology refers to the numeric interpretation of the word contents. As we saw in Chapter 1, the MSB contributes 2^{15} to the value of the contained number, while the LSB contributes only 2^0.

It is sometimes more convenient to view the 16-bit word as composed of two 8-bit halves called "bytes." In this case the rightmost half is called the **low byte** and the leftmost, the **high byte.** The term "byte" here refers to half of a word. A byte is often a more convenient unit of information capacity than a bit or a word is because much data processing is concerned with nonnumeric data, and 8 bits are sufficient to represent a *character* (e.g., A, B, and #) using a suitable code. Moreover, a significant feature of the PDP-11 computer is that there are many instructions that perform operations on bytes rather than on words.

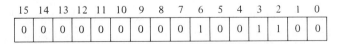

Figure 3.2 Binary representation of decimal 76 stored in a 16-bit word.

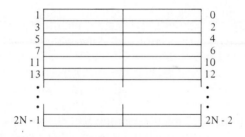

Figure 3.3 Memory unit comprising N words.

3.3 The Central Memory Unit

The computer has a large number (several thousand) of words as described above, together comprising the **central memory** unit (CM). This is often shown diagrammatically as in Fig. 3.3.

As noted previously, each word in the CM is divided into two bytes. By virtue of the hardware design, each byte in the memory unit has a unique "address," indicated in Fig. 3.3 by the numbers down the side. Note that the low bytes are numbered 0, 2, 4, 6, 10, 12, . . . , i.e., *even* numbers, while the high bytes have the odd addresses. By convention, the *word address* is the same as the address of its lower byte. Thus we have word addresses as: 0, 2, 4, 6, 10, 12, ...

The size of the memory unit, usually given in bytes, can be from 4096 (4K) to 65536 (64K) or more depending on the particular installation. Often the machine has a much larger memory partitioned into a number of smaller regions. This allows many simultaneous users.

3.4 The General Registers

The PDP-11 also has a number of memory elements other than the CM called **general registers.** General registers are similar to the words in the CM, but are physically and functionally different. The general registers, often called simply **registers,** are 16 bits in length as are the words. However, data can be moved in and out of the registers much faster than they can in the case of the CM, a factor that is one of the registers' principal virtues. There are only eight registers, however, and they are usually designated R0, R1, . . . , R7 as in Fig. 3.4.

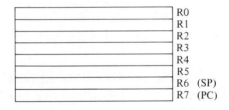

Figure 3.4 The general registers.

As we become familiar with MACRO-11, it will be seen that registers have a variety of uses in programming. Most often, data that must be accessed many times will first be moved to a register to take advantage of the greater speed of access. Results needed much later or infrequently are moved back to the CM, freeing the limited number of registers for other uses. It will also be noted later that MACRO-11 relies heavily on the registers for holding addresses of locations in the CM.

Registers R0 through R5 may be employed for any purpose, but R6 and R7 have very special functions that preclude most other uses. Register R7 is called the program counter (PC) meaning that it always contains the central memory address of the next instruction to be fetched for execution. This is discussed more fully in connection with the Instruction Execution Cycle below. Register R6 is called the stack pointer (SP). Its use will not be explained until more advanced programming techniques are discussed in Chapter 7. For the present, the reader is simply cautioned not to use R6.

3.5 Instruction Execution Cycle

One of the most fundamental characteristics of a digital computer is its ability to execute automatically, one after another, a series of stored instructions. The procedure whereby this is carried out is referred to as the **Instruction Execution Cycle.** Another physical component of the machine, the **Arithmetic Logic Unit** (ALU), must be explained in connection with the execution cycle. The ALU is the device that actually "understands" the bit patterns that represent machine code. It is designed to automatically fetch the contents of the memory location whose address is in the program counter, PC, then decode and execute it. In order that the *next* instruction will be accessible to the ALU, it must, after fetching the instruction but before executing it, increment the PC. Because instructions are stored in consecutive *words* whose addresses are those of the low bytes, this incrementation is by 2. Moreover, because the PC must be incremented before execution, the pending instruction must be temporarily stored within the ALU. The Instruction Execution Cycle can be described by the following algorithm.

1. Set PC to the address of the first instruction of the program.
2. Fetch the contents of the CM location whose address is found in PC. Save this instruction within the ALU.
3. Increment PC by 2.
4. Decode the instruction and, if indicated by the instruction, fetch the operands.
5. Execute the instruction and, if necessary, store the results. If HALT, stop.
6. Repeat from step 2.

It must be recognized that the Instruction Execution Cycle is built into the machine itself. It is repeated continuously after being initiated and until a HALT instruction is encountered.

As an example, consider the short program

Address	Octal Machine Code	Assembly Code
000000	010104	MOV R1,R4
000002	060204	ADD R2,R4
000004	000000	HALT

As explained earlier, this program must be assembled, linked, and run. The RUN command, in effect, sets the PC to the address 000000 and initiates the instruction execution cycle. The contents of 000000, namely, 010104, is first fetched into the ALU. PC is then incremented to 000002. Then the 010104 is decoded, and found to say, "Move the contents of register 1 to register 4." The ALU obtains the contents of R1 and places it into R4. Having completed this instruction, the ALU is ready to begin again and obtains the contents of 000002, namely, 060204. PC is incremented to 000004. The 060204 is then decoded to say, "Add contents of R2 to R4." The ALU therefore obtains the contents of R2 and R4, adds these values, and returns the results to R4, completing the instruction. Once again the ALU fetches the contents of the memory location "pointed at" by the contents of PC. This time it is found to be 000000. Before execution, PC is incremented to 000006. Upon decoding, the instruction is found to be the HALT command, and therefore the instruction cycle is stopped. Observe that the contents of 000006 was *not* fetched because of the HALT.

The execution cycle bears close study because it is closely tied to proper understanding of the PDP-11 instructions and methods of addressing. In particular, observe that PC is incremented *before* the decoding of the instruction. This will be of great importance when we later observe that the contents of PC may be used to help locate operands for the instruction. The reader will also observe that at the beginning of each cycle the ALU, rather blindly, accepts whatever it finds in the memory location pointed at by the PC and attempts to interpret it as an instruction. If the programmer inadvertently places a *data* item before the HALT instruction, the ALU will treat it as an instruction. This often will result in the error message

M-TRAP TO 10 AT USER PC n

which means illegal instruction, but if the data item by chance has a valid interpretation as an instruction, the results are unpredictable but most likely wrong.

It would appear from the above that PC is incremented exactly by 2 each cycle. It should be noted, however, that some addressing methods, to be discussed later, require operands or addresses of operands to be placed in the word or words immediately following the instruction. In these cases, this method of addressing is detected in the process of decoding the instruction, and PC is automatically incremented accordingly to skip this operand data and get to the next valid instruction. Instructions using these addressing methods are referred to as two- or three-word instructions and will be further discussed later.

3.6 PDP-11 Architecture

The term ''architecture'' as used in connection with computers refers to the way that the components of the machine are designed and interact with each other. The architecture of a particular computer can be described with various levels of detail. Here, we shall look at the PDP-11 architecture only in sufficient detail to improve our programming perspective.

As we have seen above, the principal components are the central memory (CM) unit and the central processing unit (CPU). All computers have these elements in common. Additionally, all computers have what are called *peripheral devices,* which may include printers, terminals, magnetic tape and disk storage units, clocks, and other devices that send/receive data to/from the computer itself. On the PDP-11, these components interact with each other as shown in Fig. 3.5, which can be called the overall architecture or ''block structure'' of the PDP-11 machine. The Arithmetic Logic Unit (ALU), Processor Status Word (PSW), and General Registers (GRs) are shown as subelements of the CPU in this diagram. The lines in the diagram represent data flow paths between the components. It is seen that the data can go directly between the PSW and GRs and the ALU. They are said to have dedicated links with one another. On the other hand, transfers to and from memory or peripheral devices must go through a shared communication link called a **bus.** On PDP-11 computers this is called UNIBUS™, which is a trademark used by DEC for their particular implementation of the bus concept. Basically, a bus is just a group of wires that carries data and control information as electrical signals. All devices are connected to it in parallel, and there is circuitry that coordinates access by each device. At any one time, only two devices can be communicating with one another over the bus. Once granted access to the bus, a device can use it for one cycle, which lasts approximately one-millionth of a second. During this time the data transfer takes place and the bus can be relinquished to another device.

Because of this sharing, a relatively complex control process is needed to coordinate usage of the bus. That is, devices must request usage, await permission, await acknowledgment of the receiver, transfer data and/or addresses, and finally relinquish control of the bus to another device. This means that data transfer between memory and the CPU is relatively slow compared with the speed of the data transfer between the GRs and the CPU. Therefore, in programs for which execution speed is critical, it is important to minimize the number of data items transferred to and from memory.

One measure of program efficiency is the number of memory accesses (**fetches**) and stores that is required. The term **fetch** refers to the CPU obtaining the contents of one word from CM, and **store** is when the CPU transfers the contents of one word to CM. For each instruction execution cycle, there will be, as a minimum, the fetch of the instruction itself. As we shall see in a later chapter, some instructions occupy as many as three words, so up to three fetches may be required to get the instruction. Depending on the addressing method used to find the operands, as many as three additional fetches and a store may have to

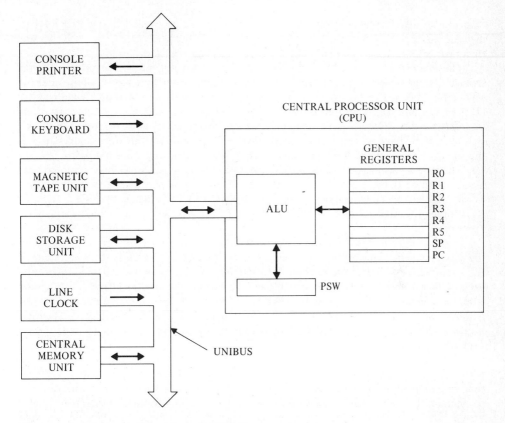

Figure 3.5   Block structure of small PDP-11 computers.

be performed in order to obtain and store data. For each of these fetches and stores, the bus must be accessed as discussed above. These factors provide strong arguments for carefully choosing the addressing method from those presented in subsequent chapters. Note that when an instruction uses the GRs only, the only fetch is to get the instruction itself. This means that whenever possible intermediate results should be kept in registers.

3.7 Summary

An essential feature of the digital computer is the ability to store information. We have seen that the basic unit of information storage capacity is the *word* (also called a location). The word is of a definite size or *length*, established by the designers of the machine, measured in *bits;* the PDP-11 has a word length of 16 bits. Any kind of information that can be represented by a 16-bit binary code can be stored in such a word; this includes machine-code instructions as well as data.

It is sometimes more convenient to view each word as composed of two *bytes* of 8 bits each. This convenience derives from the fact that certain kinds of data, particularly character codes (alphabetic data), can be stored in 8 bits, and that the PDP-11 has instructions that can operate on individual bytes. Within each word, we refer to the rightmost 8 bits as the *low byte,* and the other 8 as the *high byte.*

The *central memory* (CM) unit is a collection of several thousand words, allowing storage of large programs and extensive amounts of data. Each byte has a definite *address* that can be referred to by instructions, allowing necessary data to be found when needed by the program. We noted that the address numbers of bytes are conventionally written in *octal* (base 8). Since some things, for example instructions, must be stored in *words only,* we often have to refer to *word addresses.* By definition, the word addresses are the same as those of the low byte, and consist of a sequence of *even numbers.*

The PDP-11 also has a special, smaller memory called the *general registers* or *registers.* These also hold 16 bits but are faster than central memory and play a key role in addressing as we shall see in later chapters. The registers are usually designated as R0, R1, . . . , R7, although R6 and R7 have aliases of SP and PC, respectively, indicating their special purposes.

Another topic in this chapter was the *Instruction Execution Cycle.* This term describes the process carried out by the *Arithmetic Logic Unit* (ALU), which is the subsystem of the computer responsible for fetching instructions from memory and carrying them out. We saw that the ALU repeatedly goes through the execution cycle, fetching the instructions from the memory location whose address is held in the PC (program counter). The ALU automatically advances the PC (by 2) after fetching the instruction, but before executing it, thereby causing a sequence of instructions in successive words in memory to be executed.

Yet another topic discussed in this chapter was the *PDP-11 architecture.* This term refers to the organization of the various components and the data flow paths. We saw that communication between the ALU and the GRs is via *dedicated link,* whereas that for memory is over a *shared link* called a *bus.* One of the implications of this is the longer time that it takes to access data from memory, which argues in favor of keeping intermediate results in the GRs. The efficiency of an instruction was explained in terms of the number of *fetches* and *stores* from and to the CM that are required.

3.8 Exercises

3.1 For each of the following decimal numbers, show its internal representation as it would exist in a PDP-11 CM location. Give the binary, octal, and hexadecimal representations, first for the entire word, then for the high and low bytes.

a) 29652   **b)** 43957   **c)** 465

d) 19754   **e)** 05693   **f)** 65535

3.2 Assume that a word of CM on the PDP-11 has the hexadecimal number ABB5 stored in it. Give the binary, hexadecimal, and octal contents of the high and low bytes.

3.3 If a word of CM on the PDP-11 with address 014632 contains the octal number 164321, what is the octal contents of the byte with address 014633? What is the octal contents of the byte with address 014632?

3.4 In Sec. 3.5 we saw that CM addresses are temporarily placed in R7. From this fact, determine the largest address that an instruction can be stored in on the PDP-11.

3.5 Assume that we have in CM the program segment given below.

Address	Contents
.	.
.	.
.	.
001056	010301
001060	060105
001062	010103
001064	060305
001066	010102
001070	000000
001072	000500

   a) What is the contents of PC immediately after 060105 has been fetched and before this instruction has been executed?

   b) What is the contents of PC when execution stops?

3.6 Discuss the implications of the instruction MOV R1,PC. What effect might this have? Does it appear to be good programming practice?

3.7 How many unique bit patterns can be represented with the PDP-11 word? with the byte?

3.8 List five valid *word* addresses in binary and in octal.

3.9 Discuss the meanings of the terms "fetch" and "store." How many fetches and stores are required by the instructions

```
MOV   R1,R2
MOV   R3,R2
MOV   R2,R1
```

Introduction to Assembly Language Programming

4

4.1 Overview

In Chapter 1 we saw that assembly language programs consist of a sequence of simple instructions each of which causes a certain action to be taken by the computer. The PDP-11 has a large set of these instructions, some of which cause operations to be carried out on data (operand instructions) and others that affect the execution sequence in the program (control instructions). In this chapter we discuss five of these instructions—MOV, ADD, CLR, INC, and HALT. The first four of these are operand instructions that exemplify single- and double-operand formats. The last, HALT, is a simple control instruction.

These five instructions allow us to develop the fundamental concept of assembly language programming with simple programs and without unnecessary complications. These instructions will also serve as models for more advanced instructions introduced in later chapters. Because branching instructions are not covered, the programs that can be considered in this chapter are restricted to those with straightline logic, i.e., strictly sequential execution of the instructions.

The five instructions of this chapter also provide us with a basis for initial discussion of **addressing.** This term refers to the manner in which the data to be operated on by the instruction, i.e., the **operands,** are identified. We restrict our discussion to a single addressing mode (register addressing), postponing exploration of the full PDP-11 addressing capabilities until later chapters. In this way we allow the concept of addressing to be firmly established in the context of simple, straightline programs. This restriction does limit the programs we can write to those operating only on the registers. Data that are stored in memory will remain out of our reach temporarily.

The restricted set of instructions and addressing modes also allows us to begin development of skill in **translation** to machine code. Translation is important because the best understanding of assembly language programming comes by trying to visualize the resulting maching code instead of thinking solely in terms of the assembly language mnemonics. The idea here is simply that every assembly language instruction translates into 16-bit binary patterns in one or more sequential words. For convenience, however, we will write these as their octal equivalents.

This chapter also introduces the idea of **assembler directives.** These are lines embedded in an assembly language program that are *not* PDP-11 instructions, but rather they are instructions to the assembler. Directives are sometimes called pseudo-ops because they look like other mnemonic codes recognized by the assembler, but do not result in machine instructions. In keeping with the theme of this chapter, we again restrict our discussion to a small initial subset of the available directives, in particular, .TITLE and .END.

The chapter also includes two sections dealing with program execution and debugging. The first, Section 4.7, deals with how to read a MACRO-11 listing. It will be recalled that the listing is produced by the assembler and shows the results of the translation in human-readable form. Section 4.8 is an introduction to the PDP-11 On-line Debugging Technique, ODT. This is a system program that allows the programmer to interact with and examine the results of the program as it executes. This provides an extremely powerful learning mechanism, as well as affording a means for finding programming errors.

4.2 Five Instructions—MOV, ADD, CLR, INC, and HALT

4.2.1 MOV

When you are programming in assembly language, you will often find it necessary to move a piece of data from one place to another. For example, a value may be stored in memory and the program may require it in a register, or you may wish to transfer the result of an operation from one register to another or to memory. In fact, in large programs this is often one of the most frequent operations. To facilitate this, MACRO-11 has the MOV instruction. For example,

    MOV   R1,R2

causes the contents of register R1 to be moved into register R2. More precisely, the bit pattern in register R1 is *copied* into R2, leaving R1 unchanged. For example, if R1 and R2 initially contain

    R1:   0 001 010 000 011 111
    R2:   1 101 000 000 100 001

then after MOV R1,R2 is executed they will contain

R1:   0 001 010 000 011 111
R2:   0 001 010 000 011 111

Note that the previous contents of R2 has been lost or overwritten in the process.

4.2.2 ADD

Another widely used instruction is ADD. As might be expected, the purpose of this instruction is to add one number to another. For example, if we have

R1:   0 000 000 000 000 010
R2:   0 000 000 001 001 010

and the instruction

ADD   R1,R2

is executed, the registers will then contain

R1:   0 000 000 000 000 010
R2:   0 000 000 001 001 100

Note that the contents of R1 remains unchanged, while the sum is placed in R2. Also observe that the original contents of R2 is overwritten with the result of the addition.

The MOV and ADD instructions are what we call double-operand instructions. That is, it is necessary to indicate the *source* and *destination* registers for the MOV operation or, in the case of ADD, the registers containing the two numbers to be added. There is a convention in MACRO-11 that the first operand is called the source and the second operand is called the destination in most double-operand instructions. That is

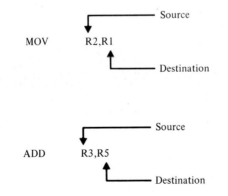

or

Actually, the second operand of the ADD instruction is at once the source of the second summand and the destination for the sum. Nonetheless, we refer to it as the destination operand, emphasizing that results always go to the second operand.

4.2.3 CLR

Very often a procedure within a program will begin by initializing registers or memory locations to 0. This is called clearing, and the MACRO-11 instruction to do it is the CLR instruction. Unlike the MOV and ADD instructions, there is only a *single operand* for CLR, namely, the register to be cleared. For example, if we have in register R4

        R4:   0 001 111 000 010 011

and the instruction

        CLR   R4

is executed, R4 will then be

        R4:   0 000 000 000 000 000

In later chapters we will see how CLR can also be used to clear words and bytes in memory in addition to registers.

4.2.4 INC

The need to add unity to a quantity occurs frequently in programming. MACRO-11 provides a single-operand instruction, INC, specifically for this purpose. To demonstrate its use, assume that R2 initially contains

        $25_{10} = 0\ 000\ 000\ 000\ 011\ 001_2$.

Then if

        INC   R2

is executed, we will have

        R2:   0 000 000 000 011 010

that the reader will recognize as 26_{10}.

The INC instruction can be used in conjunction with the CLR instruction to initialize a register to 1. That is

        CLR   R2
        INC   R2

will result in R2 being set to unity.

4.2.5 HALT

The MOV, ADD, CLR, and INC instructions are similar to one another in that they operate on data, i.e., they each have one or two operands. The next instruction we will examine, HALT, has no operands. Its role is simply to stop the instruction execution cycle. (See Section 3.5.) It is placed at the *logical end* of the program, i.e., after the last instruction to be executed. Often this will be different from the *physical end* of the program because nonexecutable lines, e.g., data storage, are sometimes placed after the last executable instruction. In Section 4.5 we will see how to mark the physical end of the program.

If you are using MACRO-11 with an operating system such as RSTS, the HALT instruction causes an error report saying that your program was halted. This is purely informative and can be ignored. If desired, the system "macro instruction" .EXIT can be used instead of HALT, as shown in the example in Section 1.3. This will require that you also include the .MCALL .EXIT line at the beginning of the program. The use of .EXIT will, however, introduce machine code that cannot be explained in terms of the material covered thus far; it is for this reason that HALT is used in our examples.

4.3 Register Addressing Mode

It should be apparent that if the machine uses an item of data, it is necessary to identify where the data item is stored. Specifying the locations of data items to be used in an operation is referred to as *addressing*. The PDP-11 has a variety of different ways of doing this, called *addressing modes*. However, in this chapter only the direct *register addressing mode* is considered.

As discussed in Section 3.4, the PDP-11 has eight general registers. For the MACRO-11 assembly language, these registers are identified by the special symbols

    %0   %1   %2   %3   %4   %5   %6   %7

In most installations, however, one can use Rn in place of %n for n = 0,1,...,5. For example, the instruction

    MOV   %2,%5

can be equivalently written as

    MOV   R2,R5

The latter form is the preferred and usual notation. In Chapter 10, it will be shown that the programmer can "equate" Rn to %n if it is not done automatically at his or her installation.

Registers %6 and %7 have special significance. For this reason these registers are usually known by the special system definitions

    SP = %6   Stack pointer
    PC = %7   Program counter

Normally the SP and PC registers are not to be used for general data storage. The meaning and significance of these special registers will be discussed in later chapters. Note that the assembler does not recognize the symbols R6 and R7; SP and PC, or %6 and %7, must be used to refer to these registers.

System-supplied functions (such as .PRINT) often use R0 for their own purposes and therefore will destroy its previous contents. One should be careful about depending on a value in R0 after the use of such a function. The problem of saving and restoring registers is discussed in Chapter 9.

4.4 Translation to Machine Code

In Chapter 1 we saw that every assembler instruction can be translated into an equivalent machine language instruction. We shall now see how this is done for the instructions that use the direct register addressing mode.

4.4.1 Double-operand Instructions

Every instruction is represented by a unique binary code called an operation code or **opcode.** In the case of double-operand instructions, such as ADD and MOV, the opcodes are four bits in length. Specifically, we have

Instruction	Opcode	
	Binary	Octal
MOV	0001	01
ADD	0110	06

(Note that for convenience we will most often use the octal representation.)

Addressing modes are also represented by binary or octal codes. For register mode addressing, the octal code is 0n. Here the 0 implies register mode addressing, and the octal digit n indicates the register involved.

The translation of an entire instruction is composed of the translation of the opcode together with translation of the operand addressing codes. An example will clarify this. Given the assembly language instruction

        MOV   R4,R2

we have

        MOV $\Rightarrow$ 01 (Opcode)
        R4 $\Rightarrow$ 04 (Addressing code)
        R2 $\Rightarrow$ 02 (Addressing code)

where $\Rightarrow$ is read as "implies." Thus the translation of the instruction is

        010402 (Octal)

and the binary equivalent is

        0 001 000 100 000 010 (Binary)

Similarly,

        ADD   R1,R5

translates to

060105 (Octal)

or

0 110 000 001 000 101 (Binary)

In general, all double-operand MACRO-11 instructions have the format indicated below

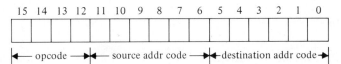

From a hardware point of view, this means that the ALU looks at the four leftmost bits to see what operation to perform. By examining the address fields, bits 0 through 5 and 6 through 11, the ALU can tell where to obtain the operands.

The operand address fields of double-operand instructions are each 6 bits in length. Each is further divided into two subfields as shown below.

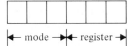

We have already seen that for register mode addressing the mode is binary 000. The 3-bit register field is just sufficient to allow for binary representations of registers 0 through 7. This is not a coincidence, but instead is the result of thoughtful work by the designers of the PDP-11. The reader may also surmise that the PDP-11 could have as many as eight different addressing modes because the mode subfield is also 3 bits in length. This is indeed so; direct register mode addressing is just the first to be considered, with others to be introduced as the need arises. A complete treatment of this topic is presented in Chapter 11.

4.4.2 Single-operand Instructions

Single-operand instructions, e.g., CLR and INC, have a different format in the word from that used for double-operand instructions. Specifically, the need for a single-operand address field allows more bits to be used for the opcode. For the two single-operand instructions discussed so far, we have the following opcodes.

Instruction	Opcode	
	Binary	Octal
CLR	0 000 101 000	0050
INC	0 000 101 010	0052

The address code consisting of two octal digits (6 bits) is placed at the right, completing the instruction. The register addressing mode address code is the same as for double-operand instructions. Thus we have the following translation examples.

Instruction	Translation
	(Octal)
CLR R1	005001
INC R4	005204
CLR R0	005000
INC R5	005205

As in the case of double-operand instructions, the single-operand instructions must be stored in 16-bit words. The format is indicated below.

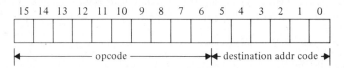

From this it can be seen that the opcodes for single-operand instructions are 10 bits in length. The single-operand field is referred to as the destination, implying that the action is taken on the contents of the given address. This address code field is subdivided and used exactly as it is in the double-operand format.

4.4.3 No-operand Instructions
Translation of the HALT instruction is quite simple because it has no operands. The opcode for HALT is

000000 (Octal)
0 000 000 000 000 000 (Binary)

Thus the execution cycle continues until the ALU finds a memory location with all bits set to 0.

4.5 Assembly Language Directives, Labels, and Comments

An assembly directive is an instruction to the assembler that tells it something about *how* the program is to be assembled. We shall restrict the discussion here to two directives that are necessary or helpful in simple programs. These are

.TITLE   name
.END   label

The directive **.TITLE name** simply assigns a programmer-selected name to the program. It is used as the first line of the program. The effect of this will be that the operating system will print out this name whenever the program is executed or listed. It is merely a convenience and is not required. Nonetheless, its use is encouraged.

A label is an identifier attached to a line in your program. Although you can attach a label to any line, customarily labels are attached only to those lines that need to be referred to elsewhere in the program. Labels can be any combination of characters beginning with a letter. They can be of any length, but only the first six characters are recognized. For example the labels L23456, L234567, and L23456Y are all equivalent because they all start with the same first six characters. When a label is encountered during an assembly, it is assigned the value that represents the next location to be used to assemble an instruction or data. The program can use this label in any place in which the corresponding value could be used. When defining a label, it is the leftmost item in the assembly line and must be suffixed with a colon. The following is an example of a label definition.

```
START:    MOV    R4,R5                ; Move R4 to R5
```

During assembly, START will be defined to have the value of the address of the MOV instruction. Every label must be unique in the first six characters. If the same (or equivalent) label is defined more than once in a program, an error will be reported.

An example of a label reference is

```
.END    START
```

The **.END label** directive is required and does two things. First, it represents the physical end of the program. That is, the assembler will process line after line until it reaches an .END directive. Thus any lines after the .END will not be assembled. The second function of the .END directive is to indicate the entry point of the program. That is, if one writes

```
.END    A
```

where A is a label in the program, the program counter will be initialized to the address assigned to A before execution begins. In many examples in this text, we use

```
.END    START
```

because we customarily use START as a meaningful label for the first executable instruction in the program.

In MACRO-11, text following ";" is treated as commentary. This is demonstrated in the MOV instruction above.

4.6 Example Programs

With the instructions and the addressing mode discussed thus far, a limited range of simple programs can be written. The examples below are designed to exercise these tools on problems of minimal complexity.

Example 4.1 Let us consider first a program to compute the sum of the contents of R1, R2, and R3, and place the result in R0. The contents of R1, R2, and R3 are not to be changed in the process. The algorithm we shall use is as follows.

1. Copy contents of R1 into R0.
2. Add contents of R2 to R0.
3. Add contents of R3 to R0.
4. Stop.

The corresponding MACRO-11 program is shown in Fig. 4.1, and the translation into machine code is shown in Fig. 4.2. In the translation it is seen that there are four instructions, each occupying one word. We have assumed that the program was loaded into memory beginning at location 000000. Observe that .TITLE and .END START do not result in any machine code because they are assembly directives. Also the assembler treats anything to the right of a semicolon as comment, so that the lines 2, 3, and 4 in the assembly code result in no machine code. In this example we also demonstrate some elements of programming style. In particular, note that

1. The program has a title block indicating what it does and what registers are used. This is placed immediately after the .TITLE directive.
2. Labels begin in Column 1.
3. Instructions and directives begin in Column 9.
4. Operands begin in Column 17.
5. Comments begin in Column 33.

While these rules of style are not mandatory, they tend to make programs more readable and therefore we encourage adherence to them. Also observe that the example program accepts no input data and generates no output. Those familiar with programming in high-level languages will find this curious, and may ask, "Why not read in R1, R2, and R3, and print out R0?" The answer is that input and output (I/O) are considerably more difficult in assembly language, and we choose therefore to postpone considering them until more programming skills

```
        .TITLE ADDITION
;
;  ADDS R1, R2 AND R3 INTO R0
;
START:
        MOV    R1,R0      ;ADD THREE
        ADD    R2,R0      ; NUMBERS
        ADD    R3,R0      ;  INTO R0
        HALT
        .END   START
```

Figure 4.1 MACRO-11 program to add R1, R2, and R3 into R0.

Address	Contents
(Octal)	(Octal)
000000	010100
000002	060200
000004	060300
000006	000000

Figure 4.2 Translation of program ADDITION.

have been developed. In order to circumvent this problem, we will learn in Section 4.8 how to set and examine memory locations and registers using the On-line Debugging Technique (ODT).

Example 4.2 Suppose that it is necessary to *interchange* the contents of two registers. For example, suppose we have

R4:   000002
R5:   000004

and we wish to have

R4:   000004
R5:   000002

One way of accomplishing this is with the algorithm

1. Copy contents of R4 into R0.
2. Copy contents of R5 into R4.
3. Copy contents of R0 into R5.
4. Stop.

The program and translation are shown in Figs. 4.3 and 4.4. You should be able to easily confirm that the program works and that the translation is correct.

```
        .TITLE SWITCH
;
;   INTERCHANGE R4 AND R5
;
START:
        MOV     R4,R0
        MOV     R5,R4
        MOV     R0,R5
        HALT
        .END    START
```

Figure 4.3 MACRO-11 program to interchange R4 and R5.

Address	Contents
(Octal)	(Octal)
000000	010400
000002	010504
000004	010005
000006	000000

Figure 4.4 Translation of interchange program.

Example 4.3 Consider the calculation of the sixth Fibonacci number. Fibonacci numbers are the sequence of integers that obey the rule that each number in the sequence is the sum of the previous two. That is

$$F(n) = F(n - 1) + F(n - 2)$$

starting with

$$F(1) = F(2) = 1.$$

Here is a list of the first six Fibonacci numbers.

n	F(n)
1	1
2	1
3	2
4	3
5	5
6	8

An algorithm to calculate F(6) is as follows.

0. Initialize R1 and R2 to 1.

1. Copy R2 in R0.

2. Add R1 to R2.

3. Copy R0 into R1.

4. Repeat steps 1, 2, and 3 three more times.

The strategy behind this algorithm is that R1 and R2 always contain the previous and current Fibonacci numbers, respectively. The next Fibonacci number is therefore the sum of R1 and R2, as indicated by step 2. However, because the

Address	Contents
000000	005001
000002	005002
000004	005201
000006	005202
000010	010200
000012	060102
000014	010001
000016	010200
000020	060102
000022	010001
000024	010200
000026	060102
000030	010001
000032	010200
000034	060102
000036	010001
000040	000000

```
        .TITLE FIBONACCI
;
;   CALCULATES 6TH FIBONACCI NUMBER AND
;       PLACES IT IN R2
;
START:
        CLR     R1          ;INITIALIZE
        CLR     R2          ; R1 AND R2
        INC     R1          ;   TO 1
        IN      R2          ;
        MOV     R2,R0       ;CALCULATE
        ADD     R1,R2       ;  F(3)
        MOV     R0,R1       ;
        MOV     R2,R0       ;CALCULATE
        ADD     R1,R2       ;  F(4)
        MOV     R0,R1       ;
        MOV     R2,R0       ;CALCULATE
        ADD     R1,R2       ;  F(5)
        MOV     R0,R1       ;
        MOV     R2,R0       ;CALCULATE
        ADD     R1,R2       ;  F(6)
        MOV     R0,R1       ;
        HALT
        .END    START
```

Figure 4.5 MACRO-11 program to calculate sixth Fibonacci number.

Figure 4.6 Translation of FIBONACCI.

sum is to be placed in R2, a copy of the current value (which is the current Fibonacci number) must be set aside for safekeeping; this is the justification for step 1. After execution of step 2, R2 has the new current Fibonacci number, R0 has the previous one, and R1 has the no longer needed value from the still earlier stage. Step 3 therefore moves R0 into R1 reestablishing the pattern. After steps 1, 2, and 3 are done the first time, R2 will have F(3). After steps 1, 2, and 3 are completed for the fourth time, R2 will have the desired result, F(6).

The MACRO-11 implementation of the Fibonacci algorithm is shown in Fig. 4.5 with the corresponding translation to machine code in Fig. 4.6. It is seen that after initialization, the MOV, ADD, MOV instruction sequence is simply inserted four times. (The last MOV R0,R1 is unnecessary, but is included to retain the similarity in each stage.)

You will probably observe in this problem the opportunity to save programming effort and program size by looping back to reuse the same code rather than repeating it. In the next chapter we will develop this capability and will revisit this problem at that time.

4.7 Interpretation of Assembly Listings

When a MACRO-11 program file is submitted to the assembler (see Section 1.3), two output files are generated—the object file and the listing. The object file is intended only for machine interpretation, but the listing file is for the programmer to read. It contains much useful information including errors uncovered by the assembler. Examination of the listing is especially helpful when one is just beginning to understand the translation process performed by the assembler because it shows the machine code and the mnemonics side by side. It is also a source of enlightenment if the program is not working as anticipated. Errors are often caused by a misunderstanding of the meaning of the mnemonic codes, and it is therefore very helpful to see exactly how the assembler translates them.

In this section we use the assembler listing for Example 4.3 to explain its contents and format. Figure 4.7 shows this listing. The top line of the listing shows the name of the program as given in the .TITLE directive, along with the date and time of the assembly. The version of the assembler, which changes from time to time as DEC modifies it, is also shown on this line. The program is then printed. Each line appearing in the source program is assigned a number. We see that lines 1 through 4 have nothing but the source statements, which appear at the right. Beginning with line 5, however, there are two 6-digit octal numbers preceding the source statements. The first is the relative memory location address assigned to the translated instruction. We say relative address here because it is relative to the first instruction in the program. Later we will see that the entire program may be loaded for execution in an entirely different position in memory, but this need not concern us for the moment. The second 6-digit octal number is the machine code translation of the MACRO-11 source on the same line. These numbers will be found to correspond to the translation

```
FIBONACCI        MACRO V04.00  19-FEB-83 15:21:00 PAGE 1

       1                                       .TITLE FIBONACCI
       2                               ;
       3                               ;  CALCULATES 6TH FIBONACCI NUMBER AND
       4                               ;     PLACES IT IN R2
       5                               ;
       6 000000                        START:
       7 000000    005001                      CLR    R1          ;INITIALIZE
       8 000002    005002                      CLR    R2          ;  R1 AND R2
       9 000004    005201                      INC    R1          ;   TO 1
      10 000006    005202                      INC    R2          ;
      11 000010    010200                      MOV    R2,R0       ;CALCULATE
      12 000012    060102                      ADD    R1,R2       ;  F(3)
      13 000014    010001                      MOV    R0,R1       ;
      14 000016    010200                      MOV    R2,R0       ;CALCULATE
      15 000020    060102                      ADD    R1,R2       ;  F(4)
      16 000022    010001                      MOV    R0,R1       ;
      17 000024    010200                      MOV    R2,R0       ;CALCULATE
      18 000026    060102                      ADD    R1,R2       ;  F(5)
      19 000030    010001                      MOV    R0,R1       ;
      20 000032    010200                      MOV    R2,R0       ;CALCULATE
      21 000034    060102                      ADD    R1,R2       ;  F(6)
      22 000036    010001                      MOV    R0,R1       ;
      23 000040    000000                      HALT
      24           000000'                      .END   START


SYMBOL TABLE

START    000000R

. ABS.   000000      000
         000042      001
ERRORS DETECTED:   0
```

Figure 4.7   Assembler listing for FIBONACCI.

we developed in Fig. 4.6. Observe that the addresses of successive memory locations are incremented by 2 because they are *word* addresses. Also, because they are octal numbers, the count goes from 00006 to 000010, from 000016 to 000020, and so on.

Earlier we pointed out that assembly directives are not MACRO-11 instructions. In the listing, this is quite clear because .TITLE and .END do not have corresponding machine code instructions. The 00000' associated with .END START will be used by the operating system to tell where to begin execution. It is *not* an instruction.

Following the program listing, the listing file has the **symbol table.** This is discussed in detail in Chapter 15. Here we will simply note that in this table the programmer can see a list of all symbols that were used in the program and the values assigned to them by the assembler. In our example, the only one is START, which is a label. The assembler has assigned to it a value 000000, which is the address of the instruction for which START is a label. The R implies that this is *relative* to the beginning of the program.

Our example has a message **ERRORS DETECTED = 0.** Had there been any errors detectable by the assembler, they would have been marked on the line where they occurred and the total printed at the bottom of the listing. Table G.1 presents a list of assembler error messages and their most likely causes.

The last three lines of the listing file indicate conditions under which the assembly took place. This information is useful when one must carefully allocate memory resources. This could be the case when very large programs are assembled and linked. The last line is an echo of the command that caused the assembly to take place.

Figure 4.7 represents a relatively uncomplicated listing. As our programs increase in complexity, we will examine the corresponding listings to see the effects.

4.8 Use of the On-line Debugging Technique (ODT) [OS]

This section shows how to use the On-line Debugging Technique, ODT, which may be helpful in debugging MACRO-11 programs. Here we develop the concept of such a tool and show simple examples of its use. More details for using ODT with RSTS/E are provided in Section C.2. Other sections of Appendix C show these operations using other operating systems.

MACRO-11 programs that are not working properly are sometimes difficult to debug because errors are often caused by misunderstanding of the opcodes and/or addressing modes. A powerful method of debugging such a program is a software tool that allows execution of the program to some preselected stopping point, called a breakpoint, then allows the examination of the contents of each register and memory location. ODT is such a software tool. Many commands are provided by ODT, including setting breakpoints, running the program, examining locations, modifying locations and single-step execution.

To use ODT, you link it to your MACRO-11 program with LINK. Then when you issue a RUN command for your program, ODT takes over. From that point you issue ODT commands, such as setting breakpoints, running the program, and examining contents. To use ODT effectively, you will need to look at your MACRO-11 listing as described in the previous section. Note that we continue the practice of showing the machine response with an underline.

It is assumed that you have a MACRO-11 output object file such as PROG1.OBJ. (See Section 1.3.) Enter the sequence

```
RUN $LINK
*PROG1.SAV,PROG1.MAP = PROG1.OBJ,ODT/T
```

The system then responds

Transfer Symbol?

to which you respond

```
O.ODT
*^Z
```

At this point you have an executable file named PROG1.SAV that consists of your program linked with ODT. To execute, enter

```
RUN    PROG1.SAV
```

The response will be

```
ODT    R01-04
*
-
```

It now awaits your ODT commands. Normally, you would next want to set **breakpoints** at the addresses of instructions where you want it to stop. ODT will stop *prior* to execution of the breakpoint instruction. The usual sequence of commands is then

1. Set breakpoints at locations where you want the program to stop. See your MACRO-11 listing to decide where to place them.
2. Run the program using the G command.
3. Examine register and memory locations.

The most important commands are

Setting a breakpoint:	*address;B example: *1124;B
Removing a breakpoint:	*;0B
Examine a memory location:	*address/contents (ODT prints the contents)
Modify a memory location:	*address/contents new-contents
Look at contents of R1:	*$1/contents
Modify contents of R2:	*$2/contents new-contents
Examine Proc. Status Word:	*$S/contents
Start program execution:	*address;G (example: *1100;G)
Continue execution after HALTing at a breakpoint:	*;P
Enable single instruction mode:	*;1S
Run program for next n instructions:	*n;P
Disable single instruction mode:	*;S
Stop (return to RSTS):	*^C

Note: Execution continues until a HALT, breakpoint, system error, or completion occurs.

Because LINK normally assigns addresses to your program beginning with 1000 (octal), this number must be added to the addresses shown in your assembler listing in order to arrive at the addresses for ODT commands. For example, to look at address 20 in your assembler listing, enter 1020 as the ODT address.

A complete terminal session using ODT to check the workings of the Example 4.3 program is shown in Fig. 4.8. Here we have previously assembled the program as shown in Fig. 4.7, and the object program exists as EXP4P3.OBJ. We LINK to this the system supplied ODT object program as shown in the first four lines of Fig. 4.8. Issuing the RUN command causes the message ODT R01-04 followed

```
RUN $LINK
*EXP4P3.SAV,EXP4P3.MAP=EXP4P3.OBJ,ODT/T
Transfer symbol? O.ODT
*^Z

Ready

RUN EXP4P3

ODT  R01-04
*1040;B
*1000;G
B0;001040
*1000/005001
 001002 /005002
 001004 /005201
 001006 /005202
 001010 /010200
 001012 /060102
 001014 /010001
 001016 /010200
 001020 /060102
 001022 /010001
 001024 /010200
 001026 /060102
 001030 /010001
 001032 /010200
 001034 /060102
 001036 /010001
 001040 /000000
*$1/000005
*$2/000010
*^C
```

Figure 4.8 ODT execution of FIBONACCI.

by * on a fresh line. At the *, ODT has control and awaits our command. After looking at the listing, Fig. 4.7, we choose to set a breakpoint at location (relative) 40, which contains the HALT instruction. Noting that the program is loaded (by LINK) beginning at location 1000, we realize that 40 is really at 1040, so we give ODT the command

   *1040;B

It accepts this command and responds with another *. We now wish to execute the program beginning at location 1000, so we respond

   *1000;G

It then executes the program through location 1036, stops, and reports the location which *would* have been executed next.

   B0;001040

After this, it gives us another * allowing further commands. We choose to examine the entire program in memory, so we issue the command

   *1000/

to which it responds with the contents of location 001000. We then depress the **linefeed** key, which automatically displays the next location and its contents. Repeated depressing of the linefeed key will eventually result in the display of the entire program. Observe that this corresponds to listing the machine code, differing only in that the location addresses have all been offset by 1000. After seeing the contents of 1040, we depress carriage return, which generates a command prompt.

After examining the program as it resides in memory, we choose to examine the register contents. This is done by entering, in response to the *, a $n, where n is the desired register number. Thus we examine R1 and R2 and see 000005_8 and 000010_8, which we recognize as the fifth and sixth Fibonacci numbers. We exit from ODT by using ^C that returns control to the operating system.

Another important command available in ODT is the setting of registers or memory locations. To demonstrate this, let us execute the program of Example 4.2 under control of ODT. Figure 4.9 shows the listing, and the sample terminal session with ODT is shown in Fig. 4.10. In Fig. 4.10, the first two ODT commands set registers 4 and 5 to 31_8 and 100_8. (Their original values of 000000 and 010062 are left over from previous uses of these registers and are of no concern to this example.) In the third and fourth commands we assure ourselves that R4 and R5 have the assigned values. We then set the breakpoint to 1006 (the HALT) and execute the program from 1000. When it reaches the breakpoint, we reexamine R4 and R5. It is evident that the program does work as planned. As a final exercise, we examine the entire program, confirming that the translation developed in Fig. 4.4 was correct.

The preceding two examples show how we enter data into our programs and read the results until we develop the necessary skills for true I/O. While this method is not suitable for practical programs, it is quite adequate for our immediate needs. Moreover, it is very instructive to see exactly the form that our programs take in the memory of the machine.

```
SWITCH   MACRO V04.00   19-FEB-83 15:40:09 PAGE 1

        1                                        .TITLE SWITCH
        2                                   ;
        3                                   ;   INTERCHANGE R4 AND R5
        4                                   ;
        5 000000                            START:
        6 000000   010400                       MOV   R4,R0
        7 000002   010504                       MOV   R5,R4
        8 000004   010005                       MOV   R0,R5
        9 000006   000000                       HALT
       10 000010                                .BLKW  20
       11           000000'                      .END   START


        SYMBOL TABLE

        START     000000R

        . ABS.    000000      000
                  000050      001
        ERRORS DETECTED:   0
```

Figure 4.9 Assembler listing for SWITCH.

```
RUN $LINK
*SWITCH.SAV,SWITCH.MAP=SWITCH.OBJ,ODT/T
Transfer symbol? O.ODT
*^Z

Ready

RUN SWITCH

ODT  R01-04
*$4/000000 31
*$5/010062 100
*$4/000031
*$5/000100
*1006;B
*1000;G
B0;001006
*$4/000100
*$5/000031
*1000/010400
001002 /010504
001004 /010005
001006 /000000
*^C
```

Figure 4.10   ODT execution of SWITCH.

4.9 Simplified Input and Output (Optional) [OS]

Normally, a computer program is written to allow its user easily to change the values that it operates on. For example, the program in Example 4.1 would be much more useful if a user who did not necessarily understand MACRO-11 programming could cause it to add *any* three numbers. That is, we would like to allow the user to **input** the three summands, perhaps from a terminal keyboard. Additionally, for a user unfamiliar with machine code and ODT, we should have a means of displaying the results. This would be called **output.**

Input and output (I/O) are surprisingly complicated tasks when considered at their most fundamental levels. These complexities arise for several reasons, including differences between the representation of data internal to and external from the computer. Also, external devices such as keyboards and printers tend to be much slower than the CPU, and the program must compensate for this difference in speed. Finally, the facilities for input and output available to the programmer vary considerably from one computer installation to another. This complexity of I/O presents a dilemma for those just beginning the study of assembly language programming (and for those who teach it!). We would naturally like to be able to allow program input conveniently and to display program results *early* in our studies, but the programming skills necessary to handle the complexities of I/O cannot be developed until we are well into the subject. One approach to this dilemma is to sidestep it through the use of ODT. We showed this approach in the preceding example, where we wrote programs without I/O, and used ODT to set input data registers and examine the contents of registers in which results were placed. The disadvantages of this approach are obvious. Another approach is to use **preprogrammed subroutines** that perform the required operations for input or output. This approach is described below. The principal disadvantage is that it introduces into the program concepts that cannot be fully understood by the beginning programmer. Many will be willing to accept this disadvantage in order to be able to do I/O earlier in the study of assembly language programming.

The preprogrammed I/O subroutines to be used here are called GETOCT and PUTOCT. GETOCT gets an octal integer from the keyboard and leaves it in R0. PUTOCT prints the number found in R0 on the user's console. These subroutines can be made available in your MACRO-11 program in any one of several ways as described in Appendix E. In the examples below, we assume that they have been assembled and exist in the file called GPOCT.OBJ in the RSTS/E account of the user.

Usage of GETOCT and PUTOCT is not difficult. The instruction

```
JSR    PC,GETOCT
```

anywhere in the program causes an asterisk (*) to be printed or displayed on the screen, and a pause to allow input of an *octal* number (000000 to 177777). The value typed in will be stored as a binary number in R0. Similarly, the instruction

```
JSR    PC,PUTOCT
```

will result in the binary number stored in R0 being printed or displayed on the screen in *octal*. We shall defer explanation of the full meaning of the JSR instruction until Chapter 9. For now, it is sufficient to say that JSR PC,*name* will cause a jump to subroutine name with return to the instruction following the JSR instruction. The translation of JSR PC,name is

```
004767
relative address of name
```

where the relative address word is the address of the subroutine name relative to the current PC.

As an example of the use of GETOCT and PUTOCT, we revise Example 4.1 to allow input of the three numbers to be added and the printing of their sum. The necessary revisions are shown in the listing in Fig. 4.11. Observe that for input of each number we use a JSR PC,GETOCT followed by a MOV R0,Ri where Ri is the register into which the input value is to be placed. To print the result, we simply use JSR PC,PUTOCT because the result already resides in R0; otherwise it would have been necessary to move the result to R0 before the JSR PC,PUTOCT.

Note that another line has been added to the program in Fig. 4.11, immediately after the .TITLE line.

```
.GLOBL GETOCT,PUTOCT
```

This line tells the assembler that the two labels GETOCT and PUTOCT are not

```
        .TITLE GET/PUTOCT DEMONSTRATION
        .GLOBL GETOCT, PUTOCT
;
;    READS AND ADDS THREE NUMBERS FROM THE KEYBOARD
;
START:
        JSR   PC,GETOCT    ;INPUT 1ST NUMBER TO R0
        MOV   R0,R1        ;SAVE 1ST NUMBER IN R1
        JSR   PC,GETOCT    ;INPUT 2ND NUMBER TO R0
        MOV   R0,R2        ;SAVE 2ND NUMBER IN R2
        JSR   PC,GETOCT    ;INPUT 3RD NUMBER TO R0
        ADD   R1,R0        ;ADD 1ST NUMBER TO SUM
        ADD   R2,R0        ;ADD 2ND NUMBER TO SUM
        JSR   PC,PUTOCT    ;PRINT THE SUM
        HALT
        .END START
```

Figure 4.11 Using GETOCT and PUTOCT to add three numbers.

defined in this program, but rather are **global** symbols (symbols that are defined in another program that is assembled external to this one). This allows their address to go undetermined until the linkage step.

Figure 4.12 shows a complete terminal session using the GETOCT and PUTOCT subroutines. Assembly is exactly as before. However, the LINK step is revised to access the GETOCT and PUTOCT subroutines. As explained previously, these subroutines are assumed to exist as machine code (i.e., preassambled) in a file called GPOCT.OBJ saved under your account number. If this is not the case, see Appendix E. Execution is as before, except now the program prints * and awaits keyboard entry; it does this three times. After the third number has been entered, the program prints the results (in octal) on the user's console device.

```
RUN $MACRO
*EX4P11.OBJ,EX4P11.LST=EX4P11.MAC
ERRORS DETECTED:  0
*^Z

Ready

RUN $LINK
*EX4P11.SAV,EX4P11.MAP=EX4P11.OBJ,GPOCT.OBJ
*^Z

Ready

RUN EX4P11
*11111
*22222
*33333
066666
?M-Halt at user PC 001032
Ready

RUN EX4P11
*34
*38
SOME CHARACTER WAS NOT OCTAL. START OVER.
*37
*33
000126
?M-Halt at user PC 001032
Ready
```

Figure 4.12 Terminal session using GETOCT and PUTOCT.

4.10 Summary

This chapter has introduced five fundamental instructions and one addressing mode. The instructions are

```
MOV    Rn,Rn      ; double operand.
ADD    Rn,Rn      ; double operand.
CLR    Rn         ; single operand.
INC    Rn         ; single operand.
HALT              ; no operand.
```

The addressing mode introduced here was the direct *register mode,* which enables us to work only with data in the general registers. Use of memory for our data must await introduction of other addressing modes in later chapters. By considering this single addressing mode and small set of instructions, we were able to focus better on the underlying concepts of assembly language programming.

The process of *translation* from assembly language mnemonics to machine code was examined in detail for each of these instructions and register addressing. We saw that for each instruction there is a unique *opcode* in the form of a binary number (but most often *represented* in octal). Additionally, there is a binary code for the operand address, called the *address code,* also represented most often in octal. The opcode together with the operand address codes comprise the machine code translation of the assembly language instruction. You should be able to carry out such translations with ease once the ideas are firmly understood.

This chapter also introduced the idea of *assembly directives* using .TITLE and .END as examples. Directives are instructions *to the assembler* telling it *how* to assemble the program. They do not result in any machine code in the actual assembled program. More directives will be introduced in later chapters as the need arises.

This chapter included several examples that demonstrated the instructions and addressing modes introduced. From these examples you can see the elements and structure of a MACRO-11 program. The examples also provided us with practice in translation from assembly to machine code.

Also presented were two important aids for the assembly language programmer—the *listing file* generated by the MACRO-11 assembler, and the *On-line Debugging Technique* (ODT). The listing shows us exactly how the assembler translated our program and where it stored each instruction relative to the program beginning. ODT is a system-provided program that allows us to interact with our own program during execution. We demonstrated the use of ODT as a mechanism for entering data into our program and examining results produced by the program. ODT will serve as our principal I/O mechanism until we develop I/O facilities in later chapters. However, those who wish to use interactive I/O earlier can use the subroutines GETOCT and PUTOCT introduced in Section 4.9.

4.11 Exercises

4.1 Translate the following MACRO-11 instructions into octal machine code.

a) MOV R5,R3   b) ADD R0,R0   c) CLR R4

d) INC R1   e) ADD %1,%6   f) HALT

g) ADD SP,%4   h) MOV PC,R3

4.2 Translate the following PDP-11 octal machine code to MACRO-11. This is called "disassembly."

a) 010402   b) 000000   c) 060102

d) 005204   e) 010101   f) 005003

4.3 The following questions can be answered by considering the instruction formats for PDP-11 code.

a) How many single-operand instructions can the PDP-11 have?

b) How many double-operand instructions can the PDP-11 have?

c) Suppose the PDP-11 designers had wanted 16 registers instead of 8. How must the format for double-operand instructions be modified in order to allow use of all 16 registers? Give the limitations of this format.

4.4 The following is a PDP-11 program given in octal. What is the contents of the affected registers when it halts?

```
005000
005200
010001
005200
060100
000000
```

4.5 Discuss the differences between instructions and directives.

4.6 Assemble the following MACRO-11 program putting the first instruction into location 000000.

```
            .TITLE EXAMPLE
START:
            CLR R0
            INC R0
            ADD R0,R0
            ADD R0,R0
            ADD R0,R0
A:          HALT
            .END START
```

a) What value will the label A have?

b) What value will the label START have?

c) What is the contents of the memory location that A labels?

d) What is the contents of the memory location that START labels?

4.7 Compare the assembler listing in Fig. 4.7 with the ODT listing given in Fig. 4.8. Why are the addresses different?

4.8 Write a MACRO-11 program to reverse the order of the contents of R1, R2, R3, and R4. Run the program, using ODT to load 10_8, 20_8, 30_8, and 40_8 into R1, R2, R3, and R4, and to show that they have been reversed after execution. Submit the listing and execution results.

4.9 Repeat Exercise 4.8 but use the input/output subroutines discussed in Sec. 4.9 to establish the initial contents of the registers and to print out the final contents. Ask your instructor how to access GETOCT and PUTOCT, or see Appendix E.

Programs with Branches and Simple Data Structures

5

5.1 Overview

The previous chapter introduced a limited set of instructions and a single addressing mode that allowed us to undertake simple programming problems in assembly language. This restricted MACRO-11 subset allowed us to maintain a focus on the concepts of instructions, addressing, and translation. It is not a practical subset, however, because it does not allow repetitive calculations or even the use of central memory. In this chapter we will expand our programming capability by introducing several new instructions and addressing modes. In particular, we introduce **branching** instructions and their supporting comparison instructions. With the branches introduced, it will be possible to build **loops** for **repetitive** calculations. The discussion is limited, however, to those branches and comparisons that deal with **signless** integers, i.e., the MACRO-11 unsigned branches. Signed branches are deferred until after the discussion of a system allowing negative numbers in Chapter 6.

In order to allow use of central memory for our data, we introduce in this chapter several new addressing modes, some of which are useful in working with linear data structures such as arrays. These include the **immediate, relative, autoincrement** and **autodecrement** modes.

In this chapter it will become evident that when addressing modes that refer to memory are used, the program must set aside storage space for the data in the central memory. New assembler directives (.BLKW and .WORD) will be introduced for this purpose.

It is shown that memory reference addressing modes can generate instructions that require two or three memory words. The translation technique in these cases is discussed, as well as the effects on the appearance of the listing file.

5.2 MACRO-11 Branching

It will be recalled that machine language instructions are stored sequentially in the central memory, and that the execution cycle normally fetches them sequentially for execution. The need often arises to alter the sequence of instructions depending on conditions that arise in the calculations. One example would be when one or more instructions are to be performed or skipped depending on the outcome of a previous calculation. Another is when a sequence of instructions is to be repeated a number of times. Any alteration of the normal fetching of instructions from sequential memory locations is called a *branch*.

There are several PDP-11 instructions that can be used to cause branching. They work by *resetting* the PC to the destination address, whereupon the normal sequential fetching and execution resumes. The branching instructions include an unconditional branch and several groups of related conditional branches. We shall first discuss the **unsigned conditional branches,** followed by the unconditional branch instruction.

The conditional branches require a two-step process—the setting of a "condition" followed by a branch that depends on the condition. For the present, we may think of the condition as simply the outcome of a comparison or subtraction. To set the condition, we may use either the compare instruction, CMP, or the subtract instruction, SUB. This is then followed by the appropriate branch instruction. An example of this is

```
CMP     R1,R2
BHI     PLACE
```

Here the contents of R1 will be compared with that of R2. The following BHI instruction will then cause a branch to a label PLACE if the contents of R1 is greater than that of R2. If, on the other hand, R1 is less than or the same as R2, the branch will not take place. Instead, the instruction immediately following the BHI instruction will be executed.

There are other branch instructions that can be used in the same way. Those considered in this chapter include

BHI	Branch if HIgher
BLO	Branch if LOwer
BEQ	Branch if EQual
BHIS	Branch if HIgher or Same
BLOS	Branch if LOwer or Same
BNE	Branch if Not Equal

The workings of these instructions are shown in the following examples.

Example 5.1   R1 is set to 100_8 and R2 to 50_8.

```
CMP     R1,R2
BHI     A
```

Control will be transferred to A.

Example 5.2   R1 is set to 100_8 and R2 to 50_8.

```
CMP     R1,R2
BLO     A
```

Control will *fall through* the BLO instruction to the code that follows in sequence.

Example 5.3   R1 is set to 25_8, R2 to 50_8.

```
CMP     R1,R2
BLO     A
```

Control will be transferred to A.

Example 5.4   R1 is set to 25_8, R2 to 25_8.

```
CMP     R1,R2
BLO     A
BHI     B
```

Control will fall through both branches.

Example 5.5   R1 is set to 25_8, R2 to 25_8.

```
CMP     R1,R2
BHIS    A
```

Control will be transferred to A.

Example 5.6   R1 is set to 50_8, R2 to 25_8.

```
CMP     R1,R2
BHIS    A
```

Control will be transferred to A.

Example 5.7   R1 is set to 50_8, R2 to 50_8.

```
CMP     R1,R2
BLOS    A
```

Control will be transferred to A.

Example 5.8   R1 is set to 50_8, R2 to 100_8.

```
CMP     R1,R2
BLOS    A
```

Control will be transferred to A.

Example 5.9   R1 is set to 100_8, R2 to 50_8.

```
CMP     R1,R2
BEQ     A
BNE     B
```

Control will be transferred to B. Note that any unlabeled instruction following this BNE B cannot be reached.

In these examples, we have used only the CMP instruction to set the condition in each case. This instruction, in effect, performs a subtraction, forming the result of the first argument minus the second argument (in the examples, R1 minus R2) in the ALU. It is important to note, however, that CMP *has no effect on either operand*. It merely establishes a condition to determine if subsequent branching should be done.

There are other instructions that can be used to set branching conditions. For example, the SUB instruction performs subtraction, placing the result of the *second operand minus the first into the second operand*. At the same time, conditions are set for subsequent branch instructions. Note that the roles of the operands are *reversed* from those of the CMP instruction. An example will clarify this.

Example 5.10   R1 is set to 50_8 and R2 to 100_8.

```
SUB     R1,R2
BHI     A
```

Now the first operand is subtracted from the second and the result (30_8) is positive. Because branches, in effect, examine the previous result relative to *zero,* the branch to A will take place.

The choice between CMP and SUB as a means of setting a branch condition depends on whether the difference will be needed later. The SUB instruction makes this difference available, whereas the CMP does not.

There is often a need to branch depending on the *existing* state of a register or memory location, i.e., without comparing or subtracting. This can be done using the TST instruction. The two instructions

```
TST     R1
BHI     A
```

will cause a branch to A if the contents of R1 is positive. The contents of R1 remains unchanged.

It should also be recognized that *many* other instructions will act to set branching conditions. If there is any doubt that the conditions are properly set, a TST or CMP should be done immediately preceding the branch. This is discussed further when we take up condition codes in Chapter 6.

The simplest of all branching statements has been left until last. This is the **unconditional branch,** BR. It has a single operand, namely the label to which control is to be transferred. For example,

    BR   A

will branch to A regardless of what precedes or follows it. The usefulness of this instruction will become apparent in later examples. An instruction without a label following immediately after an unconditional branch indicates a good possibility of error. This is because in normal circumstances an instruction after an unconditional branch can be reached only by another branch instruction. Therefore one would label this instruction to be used as a branch target.

5.3 Translation of Branches

The translation process for branching instructions is quite different from other instructions. Each branch instruction has a **base code** that can be represented as a 6-digit octal number. For example, the base code for BHI is 101000_8. Table 5.1 shows the base codes for the branches discussed so far. The machine code translation of a branch instruction is the *sum* of the base code plus the offset. By offset we mean the number of *words* that the PC will have to advance to reach the destination label. Consider the following example.

Example 5.11   Show the translation of the following program segment.

Address		Instruction	Translation
000100		CMP R1,R2	020102
000102		BHI A	101003
000104		MOV R2,R3	010203
000106		MOV R1,R2	010102
000110		MOV R3,R1	010301
000112	A:	HALT	

Note that the label A is three words beyond where the PC is *after the BHI instruction has been fetched.* To get to A, PC must therefore advance three words. Therefore the translation is

    101000 + 3 = 101003.

Several points need to be stressed here. First, the offset is measured in *words,* not bytes. Also, it is expressed in octal, as is the base code, and the addition is octal, naturally. We have already pointed out that the offset is relative

TABLE 5.1
Unsigned Branches

Instruction	Base Code
BHI	101000
BLO	103400
BLOS	101400
BHIS	103000
BEQ	001400
BNE	001000
BR	000400

to the address *following* the branch because the PC has already been advanced by the Instruction Execution Cycle. For larger offsets, counting is awkward, and it may be easier to calculate the offset by subtraction of addresses. In the example above, we have

$$
\begin{array}{r}
000112 \\
-\,000104 \\
\hline
000006 \text{ bytes } = 3 \text{ words.}
\end{array}
$$

The offsets are limited to 177_8 because the PDP-11 design allows only eight bits for this information. If it is necessary to branch to more distant places in the program, the JMP instruction (Section 6.10) must be employed.

When we consider loop control structures we will see the need for branching *backwards* in the program. The same formula applies for translation, but in this case the offset is negative. Because we have elected to defer discussion of negative numbers until the next chapter, we will also defer rigorous treatment of backward branches. We can, however, show a method of translation without elaboration. Consider the following program that assumes that R0 is initialized prior to its execution.

Address		Instruction	Offset from B	Offset from C	Translation
000100		CLR R1			005001
000102		CLR R2			005002
000104	A:	CMP R1,R0		373	020100
000106	B:	BEQ OUT		374	001403
000110		ADD R1,R2	0	375	060102
000112		INC R1	1	376	005201
000114	C:	BR A	2	377	000773
000116	OUT:	HALT	3	0	000000

The offset columns are aids in manual translation. To generate the column for the forward branch, i.e., B to OUT, we place a 0 at the statement *after* the branch statement. Then we count words, in octal by 1's, in the forward direction to the destination label, OUT. This shows that OUT is offset by 3, so the translation for the forward branch is

   001400 + 3 = 001403.

To generate the offset column for the backward branch, C to A, count *downward* from 377 beginning *at the branch instruction.* Thus we get 373 as the offset for the *backward branch,* and the translation is

   000400 + 373 = 000773.

We see then that offsets for forward or backward branches can be found by following these simple counting procedures. Note, however, that the count forward or backward is in *octal* so that, for example, if the backward branch was further back we would continue 372, 371, 370, *367,* 366, ... Later we will see that in the special system used for signed numbers in the PDP-11, 377 is −1, 376 is −2, and so on. Thus when we add 373 to 000400, we are actually *subtracting* 5. This is discussed in detail in Chapter 6.

When the branch destination label is far removed from the branch instruction the method above becomes awkward. Instead, you can use the following rules to find the offset. If we represent the branch instruction address as α and the destination address as β, we have for the offset

if $\beta > \alpha$ (forward branch), $\text{offset} = \dfrac{\beta - \alpha - 2}{2}.$

if $\beta < \alpha$ (backward branch), $\text{offset} = 377 - \dfrac{\alpha - \beta}{2}.$

The arithmetic required in these formulas must be done in octal. For example,

$$\text{offset} = \frac{116 - 106 - 2}{2} = \frac{6}{2} = 3,$$

and

$$\text{offset} = 377 - \frac{114 - 104}{2} = 377 - \frac{10}{2} = 377 - 4 = 373.$$

The field allowed for the operand of a branch instruction is 8 bits in length. This limits the branching distance to 177_8 words forward and 200_8 words backward, as measured from the address following the branch instruction.

It should not be inferred from this discussion that the assembly language programmer normally goes through this tedious, manual offset calculation and translation process. Rather, the *assembler* does this automatically. Nonetheless, the programmer should fully understand the process so that machine code can be recognized as correct (or incorrect!) as the occasion may demand.

5.4 Implementing Decision and Loop Structures

Certain cases of conditional branching arise frequently in programming. It is worthwhile to develop standard implementations for these cases. Three of the most common cases are the **single-alternative decision** structure, the **double-alternative decision** structure, and a **loop** structure. Collectively, these are called **control** structures. Logical flowcharts for these control structures are shown in Fig. 5.1. Those familiar with modern high-level languages will recognize these as the IF-THEN, IF-THEN-ELSE, and WHILE structures.

While there are many different ways that these structures could be implemented in MACRO-11, there is some value to adopting a standard implementation for each. Doing this will speed up the programming effort by reducing the number of choices facing the programmer, and will also make the program easier for others to understand. To this end, we present a single implementation for each

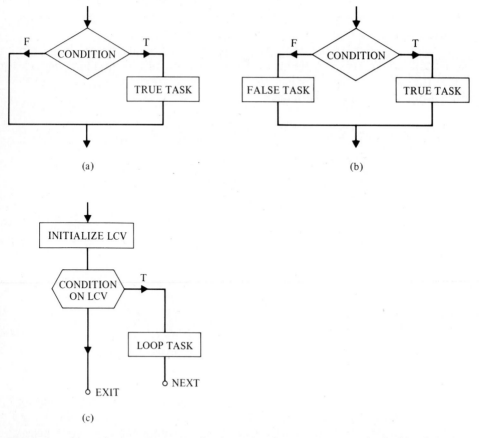

Figure 5.1 Control structures: (a) single-alternative decision structure; (b) double-alternative decision structure; (c) loop structure (leading decisions).

structure in Fig. 5.1. Later in the chapter we will offer other more efficient implementations for some of these.

5.4.1 Single-alternative Decision Structures
The suggested MACRO-11 implementation of the single-alternative decision structure is

Set condition
Branch to END on *complement* of condition

```
_____

_____      (True task)

_____
```

END:
           (Program continues.)

Note that the appropriate branch instruction must be selected to skip the true task if the *complement* (i.e., the logical inverse) of the condition is true. This is a necessity because control falls through a branch if branching does not take place. An example will clarify this.

Example 5.12   Suppose we wish to increment R0 only if R1 is *greater than or equal to* R2. We then write

```
          CMP      R1,R2           ;  CONDITION IS SET
          BLO      END             ;  BR OUT IF NOT TRUE
          INC      R0              ;  TRUE TASK
END:
```
           (Program continues.)

Note that the BLO (branch if R1 is *less* than R2) is the complement of the condition for which R0 is to be incremented.

5.4.2 Double-alternative Decision Structures
For the double-alternative decision structure, we suggest the following implementation.

```
          Set condition
          Branch to ELSE on complement of condition
THEN:          _____

               _____      (True task)

               _____

          BR   END
ELSE:          _____

               _____      (False task)

               _____

               _____

END:
```
           (Program continues.)

Observe that we again branch around the true task if the condition *complement* is true. In this structure, however, the branch is to the false task, commonly labeled ELSE. Attention is also called to the BR END instruction, which is necessary to prevent execution of the false task after completion of the true task.

Let us now consider the following example of the double-alternative decision structure.

Example 5.13   Suppose R1 is to be incremented by 1 if it is less than R0, or by 2 if it is greater than or equal to R0. The instructions to accomplish this using the standard structure are

```
            CMP     R1,R0        ; CONDITION IS SET
            BHIS    ELSE1        ; BRANCH TO ELSE1 IF R1 >= R0
THEN1:      INC     R1           ; TRUE TASK
            BR      END1
ELSE1:      INC     R1           ; FALSE
            INC     R1           ;    TASK
END1:
```

                        (Program continues.)

As a matter of programming style, it is possible to indent the instructions in the true and false tasks. This helps to improve program readability. This, however, is not customarily done in assembly language programming. Note that use of the labels THEN1, ELSE1, and END1 is optional and strictly a matter of style. In particular, the THEN1 label is unnecessary because control will automatically fall through the BHIS if R1 is smaller than R0. Many programmers choose to omit THEN labels because each added symbol in the program adds to the amount of memory required in the assembly process. On very large programs, this can be a problem. On the other hand, these labels do improve readability, especially for those who are not thoroughly familiar with the MACRO-11 instructions. Note that because each label in a program must occur only once, we append an integer (1 in this case), to the labels. If other structures occur in the same program, we would use THEN2, ELSE2, END2, etc.

5.4.3 Loop Structures
Loop structures are often helpful and may be essential whenever the same set of instructions needs to be executed repeatedly. An example of this is in Fig. 4.5 where we saw that the instructions

```
    MOV     R2,R0
    ADD     R1,R2
    MOV     R0,R1
```

occur four times. If a loop structure had been used, this program would be significantly shorter. Moreover, if the instructions have to be done many times, it will be impractical to write the program any other way.

There are many different ways to implement loop structures in assembly language. Here we will show a versatile implementation of a WHILE loop, which is not greatly different from the WHILE loops familiar to high-level language programmers. The general structure is

```
          Initialize LCV
WHILE:    Set condition using LCV
          Branch to END on complement of condition

          ____
          ____  (Loop task)
          ____

          Update   LCV
          BR    WHILE
END:
          (Program continues.)
```

Here LCV stands for loop control variable, which is the quantity examined when the loop condition is set. It must be initialized prior to the first execution of the instruction that sets the condition, and updated prior to looping back after each execution of the loop task.

The looping will continue while the tested condition remains true, and control will branch to the loop end the first time this condition is false. The following example shows how to multiply two integers using this structure.

Example 5.14 Suppose that the two numbers to be multiplied are in R1 and R2, and that their product is less than 32767. We will perform the multiplication by adding R2 to R0 exactly R1 times. Register 3 will serve as our LCV. The necessary instructions are

```
          CLR      R0
          MOV      R1,R3              ; INITIALIZE LCV AND CONDITION
WHILE1:   TST      R3                 ; SET CONDITION
          BLOS     END1               ; CHECK COMPLEMENT
          ADD      R2,R0              ; LOOP TASK
          DEC      R3                 ; UPDATE LCV
          BR       WHILE1
END1:
          (Program continues.)
```

Let us now go through this program segment line by line and understand how it works. R0 is cleared because it will be the destination register for holding the running sum. The LCV, R3, is initialized by moving the first multiplicand, R1, into it. The TST instruction compares R3 with 0, setting the condition for the subsequent BLOS instruction. Note that BLOS is the complement condition in the sense that we wish to execute the loop task only if R3 is *greater than 0,* whereas BLOS will branch if R3 is *less than or the same as 0.* The loop task is a single instruction in this example, and adds the second multiplicand, R2, to

R0. This is followed by *decrementing* the LCV, R3, and an unconditional branch back to the instruction at WHILE1.

The decrement instruction, DEC, subtracts unity from the single operand. It is a single-operand instruction with a translation format exactly the same as the INC instruction discussed in Section 4.4.2. Its operation code is 0053.

The reader will find it helpful to select small integers for R1 and R2 and follow through the entire sequence, verifying that the algorithm works. Also, check to see that it performs correctly for either operand being 1 or 0.

We caution that the preceding example is not an efficient way to multiply. In fact, the PDP-11 has a multiply instruction that is preferable. On machines that do not support the multiply instruction, there are much more efficient algorithms. (See Section 6.14.)

The loop implementation developed above is quite versatile. Note that it can be used as an indexed loop similar to the BASIC FOR loop or the FORTRAN DO loop. In this case, the LCV is an index that is incremented beginning with an assigned initial value and until the assigned limit value is reached. This is coded in the following way if we identify R3 as the LCV, R2 as the initial value, R4 as the limit value, and R5 as the step or increment value.

```
          MOV      R2,R3          ; INITIALIZE INDEX
WHILE1:   CMP      R3,R4          ; SET CONDITION
          BHI      END1           ; CHECK COMPLEMENT
          _____                ; LOOP TASK
          _____
          _____
          _____

          ADD      R5,R3          ; INCREMENT INDEX
          BR       WHILE1
END1:
```

(Program continues.)

Note that the loop will be done only when the index is less than or equal to the limit value, R4. In particular, it will not be done at all if the initial value exceeds the limit value. This is similar to the way the DO loop is implemented in some (but not all) FORTRAN compilers. In the following section we consider other loop implementations that offer certain efficiencies.

5.5 Efficient Loop Structures

The loop control structure described in Section 5.4 has the advantage of looking like the WHILE structure in modern high-level languages. There are penalties for this appearance, however, namely, program length and execution time. Very often programs are written in assembly language specifically for compactness and speed advantages over high-level languages. One, therefore, looks for the most efficient assembly language structures.

As an alternative, more efficient loop structure, consider the following.

```
           Initialize LCV

REPEAT:

           _____
           _____   (Loop task)
           _____

           Update LCV
           Set condition for loop
           Branch to REPEAT if condition is true
```

We note that in this structure there is a single branch, whereas in the structure given in Section 5.4 two were required. Thus there is a saving in program length. More importantly, one execution cycle time interval is saved on each pass through the loop. In programs with many loops to be repeated thousands of times, the savings can be substantial.

This loop structure has another important difference when compared with the earlier one. Note that the loop task is performed *at least once,* even if the loop condition is not met. This is because it uses the **method of trailing decisions,** instead of leading decisions. With this structure it is therefore necessary to use greater care in initializing the loop control variable, and to branch around the entire structure under conditions for which the task is not to be done at all. With leading decisions, i.e., the WHILE structure, the loop exit without task execution when the conditions are not met upon entry is a built-in feature.

It is possible to construct a loop in MACRO-11 that is efficient as well as possessing the advantages of leading decisions. The structure having both features is

```
           Initialize LCV
           BR WHILE

LOOP:      _____
           _____   (Loop task)
           _____

           Update LCV
WHILE:     Set condition for loop
           Branch to LOOP if condition is true
```

Observe that although the loop task appears before the decision physically, it occurs after the decision logically. This is, therefore, the logical equivalent of the WHILE structure presented in Section 5.4. It is more efficient, however, because the unconditional branch to WHILE is executed only once. Its only disadvantage is that the physical location of the loop task before the condition test will appear "out of place" to those more familiar with structured languages.

The frequently encountered need to loop a specified number of times has an even more efficient implementation. This is with the use of the SOB instruction

(Subtract One and Branch on nonzero). This instruction performs an automatic decrement of the specified register *and* branches if the result is not zero. Suppose that the number of times that the loop is to be executed is stored in R1. The following implementation will accomplish this

```
LOOP:     _____

          _____

          _____     (Loop task)

          _____

          SOB     R1,LOOP
```

This is similar to

```
LOOP:     _____

          _____

          _____

          DEC     R1
          BNE     LOOP
```

Thus the use of the SOB instruction results in saving one instruction execution cycle per loop pass. This will be a preferred structure for highly efficient code when the loop is to be performed a known number of times upon entry to the loop. Another advantage of the SOB instruction is that it does not alter the condition codes. It loses its advantages if exit from the loop is dependent on more complicated conditions.

The method of leading decisions can also be used with the SOB instruction. This is done by placing a branch instruction just above LOOP, which transfers control directly to the SOB instruction at the end of the loop. The loop control register must be initialized with exactly the number of times that the loop is to be executed.

The SOB instruction translates as a single word machine instruction of the following format: 077nff. Here n is the number of the register specified in the assembly instruction, and ff is the branch offset. The offset is determined by the assembler and is the number of words from the location *following* the SOB instruction to the label. For example, the instructions

```
A:  CLR     (R1)+
    SOB     R2,A
```

translate to

```
005021
077202
```

Here ff is seen to be 2 because A is two words before the word that follows the SOB. Note, however, that only *backward* offsets are allowed because SOB is intended specifically for loops. Also, because ff is allocated only six bits in the instruction word, the maximum offset is 63_{10}, which results in a maximum backwards branch of 62 words measured from the SOB words. Note that SOB is an optional instruction not available on all PDP-11 computers.

5.6 Immediate and Relative Addressing

Up to this point we have dealt with only one addressing mode, register addressing. This limits our programming capability considerably because it does not allow access to data in the central memory. We now wish to introduce two addressing methods that allow the use of CM for program data, namely, *immediate* and *relative* addressing. An important advantage of these methods is that they give us other ways to initialize program variables.

We avoid calling the immediate and relative addressing methods *addressing modes*. These methods are actually just special cases of more general PDP-11 addressing modes. More will be said on addressing modes in Chapter 11.

5.6.1 Immediate Addressing
Immediate addressing is exemplified by

    MOV   #25,R4

and

    MOV   #A,R5

The presence of the # (called "sharp") indicates immediate addressing. The meaning of the operand #25 is the *number 25*. Therefore in the first example above, we are moving 25_8 into R4. This is a frequent use of immediate addressing, i.e., putting a numerical value into a register or memory location.

The meaning of the operand #A requires careful thought and we call attention to the fact that it is often misunderstood. To develop the correct understanding of this operand, note that the assembler *assigns a value* to every *symbol* that it finds in the program. Most often, the symbol will be a *label* in the program. In this case the assembler assigns to the label A the value of the memory location address where it placed the translated code for the attached instruction. In Example 5.11, A is a label on the HALT instruction, and the assembler has placed this instruction into location 000112. Thus it has assigned to A the value 000112. Therefore if the instruction MOV #A,R5 occurred anywhere in that program, it would, *upon execution,* place the address of the HALT instruction into register five. (The octal value placed in R0 will be 000112 plus the loading point address determined when the program is LINKed. See Section 15.4 for detailed discussion of execution-time addresses.) Note that #A does *not* mean the contents of A, although it is often mistakenly thought to mean that.

The discussion above relates to the assembly language syntax for immediate addressing, and how it is used. We now discuss its translation into machine code, which will reveal why it is called *immediate* addressing. Whenever the assembler encounters the form "#symbol" (e.g. #A or #25) in the program, it determines the numerical value of "symbol" and stores it in the memory location immediately following that in which the instruction itself is placed. It also assigns the code 27 to the operand field of the instruction format. For example, the instruction

MOV   #25,R3

translates to

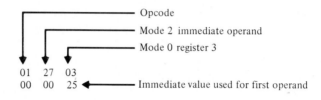

We observe here that one line of assembly language generates *two* words of machine code. The instruction MOV #25,R3 is therefore called a *two-word instruction*. The reason for calling this immediate addressing is now apparent; the value to be used is immediately after the instruction.

The fact that this is a two-word instruction raises the question of proper positioning of the program counter for the next instruction. That is, our previous understanding of the instruction execution cycle indicated that PC is incremented by 2 prior to execution of the fetched instruction, in this case 012703. Will it therefore attempt to *execute* the data item 000025? The answer is *no* for the following reason: Whenever the ALU decodes the instruction and finds an address code of 27, it automatically increments the PC by 2. The PC is therefore pointing at the word *following* the 000025 where, presumably, the next instruction will reside.

Before leaving immediate addressing, let us briefly discuss a possible usage error. This is when the programmer writes

MOV   #A,R4

thinking that this moves the *contents* of a memory location labeled A into R4. Actually it moves the *address* of A into R4. The same erroneous thinking could lead a programmer to the statement

MOV   R4,#A

but the result is different. Here, we are instructing the *assembler* to place the address of A into the memory location following the MOV instruction. When it is executed, the contents of R4 is moved into the same location, overwriting what was there before. This leads us to say that if there is an immediate mode indication for the *destination address* for any instruction that *changes* the destination, this is probably an error. Note, however, that the instruction

CMP   R5,#15

is correct and is often used. There is nothing wrong here because the CMP instruction does not affect the destination address.

5.6.2 Relative Addressing

Relative addressing allows us to store, retrieve, and otherwise operate on data *anywhere* in CM, rather than just immediately after the instruction. Relative addressing is indicated to the assembler by a symbol or expression *without prefix* in an operand field. For example, in the instruction

MOV   A,R4

the first operand is in the relative mode. This says, in effect, to take the *contents* of a memory location labeled A and move it into register 4. Here the symbol A plays a role identical to variables in high-level languages. The instruction

MOV   A,X

is equivalent to the FORTRAN statement

X = A

in that they both say, "Copy the contents of A into the location identified by X." Note that here, for the first time, we are doing operations directly on memory.

The assembly language programmer must take specific steps to allocate memory locations for symbols to be used in relative addressing. This is done by use of assembler directives such as **.BLKW** and **.WORD.** To demonstrate their use, consider the problem of interchanging the contents of two registers using a memory location for intermediate storage. The program segment to do this might be

```
          . . .
          . . .
          . . .
          MOV      R1,SAVE
          MOV      R2,R1
          MOV      SAVE,R2
          . . .
          . . .
          . . .
          HALT
SAVE:     .BLKW    1
          . . .
          . . .
          . . .
```

Here we assume that meaningful values have been placed into the registers R1 and R2. The .BLKW 1 is a directive that causes the assembler to reserve one word immediately after the HALT instruction. In this example, the address of this word would be assigned to the symbol SAVE. The first MOV instruction then copies the contents of R1 into this location, and the third one copies it into R2.

The .WORD directive allows the assignment of an initial value into a reserved memory location. To demonstrate this, consider the following program segment that adds 1, 10, and 100 (all octal), leaving the result in R0.

```
        MOV    A,R0
        ADD    B,R0
        ADD    C,R0
        HALT
A:   .WORD 1
B:   .WORD 10
C:   .WORD 100
```

Here one word each has been allocated for A, B, and C, and they have been initialized *by the assembler* to be 1, 10, and 100, respectively. We emphasize that this takes place at assembly time rather than at execution time because the distinction is important. In particular, note that instructions can alter the contents of a memory location initialized by .WORD. Consider the example below.

```
             . . .
             . . .
             . . .
X:           .WORD   4
START:  CLR      X
             . . .
             . . .
             . . .
```

This sequence is clearly not useful code because the CLR instruction cancels the effect of the .WORD directive. A more likely error would be

```
        . . .
        . . .
        . . .
        CLR      X
        . . .
        . . .
        . . .
X:   .WORD   4
        . . .
        . . .
        . . .
```

where the programmer perhaps thinks that the .WORD directive will cause X to be reset to 4 during execution. It will not. Moreover, there is another trap in this example, and that is the implication that .WORD 4 generates an instruction, whereas it does not. In fact, the appearance of .WORD or .BLKW anywhere after the first instruction should be preceded by a HALT or an unconditional branch. Otherwise, the current contents will be interpreted as an instruction, even though the programmer probably intended it as data.

Let us now consider the machine code translation of relative addressing. It will then become apparent why it is so named. As with immediate addressing, relative addressing employs the word immediately following the instruction. In this case, however, the information stored there, automatically, by the assembler, *helps to find the operand,* rather than actually *being* the operand as it is for immediate addressing. We use a simple example to demonstrate how this works. The occurrence of the sequence

```
     MOV     X,R2
     . . .
     . . .
     . . .
     HALT
X:   .WORD   45
```

translates to

Address	Machine Code
000100	016702
000102	000676
	.
	.
	.
001000	000000
001002	000045

In this translation we assumed that the MOV instruction was stored in location 000100, and that location 001002 is reserved for X. The address code for relative addressing is 67; the assembler assigns this to the address field of the first operand upon finding a *symbol* or expression† there. Into the following word, it places the *address* of the first operand *relative* to the *current* value of the PC. In this case the relative address is 000676. To see why this is the correct number and how the assembler determines it, we must examine the way the machine responds to the 016702 instruction. Upon fetching this instruction, the normal execution cycle causes PC to be incremented by 2, yielding 000102. When the ALU finds 67 in the first operand field, it fetches the contents of the memory location pointed at by PC, i.e., the word after the instruction, and *again* increments PC by 2. Because the address code is 67, it *adds* the contents of PC to the value

---

† Expressions are not discussed until Chapter 10.

it found in the preceding address, and uses the result as the absolute address of the operand. In this case it gets the operand from

$$
\begin{array}{r}
000104 \\
+\,000676 \\
\hline
001002
\end{array}
$$

that we see to be the proper address for X. Note that PC is left pointing at the word following the relative address location.

Let us now consider the case when two operands employ relative addressing. For example, suppose we wish to translate the following program segment.

```
        SUB     ARG1,ARG2
        MOV     R1,ARG1
        HALT
ARG1:   .WORD   4
ARG2:   .WORD   2
```

It is seen that both operands of the SUB instruction employ relative addressing. This affects the translation in that SUB becomes a *three*-word instruction; that is, we need a word for the instruction itself, a word for the relative address of the first operand, and a word for the relative address of the second operand. The translation follows.

Address	Machine Code (before Execution)
000100	166767
000102	000010
000104	000010
000106	010167
000110	000002
000112	000000
000114	000004
000116	000002

The translation of the SUB instruction itself is

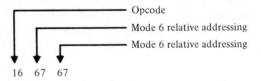

The relative address of the first operand is

$$
\begin{array}{r}
000114 \\
-\,000104 \\
\hline
000010
\end{array}
\quad
\begin{array}{l}
\text{True address of ARG1} \\
\text{PC after relative address is fetched}
\end{array}
$$

This follows because the true address is 000114 and PC will be 000104 after the relative address is fetched. The relative address of the second operand is found similarly.

$$\begin{array}{rl} 000116 & \text{True address of ARG2} \\ -\underline{000106} & \text{PC after relative address is fetched} \\ 000010 \end{array}$$

Note that PC is left at 000106 after the fetch of the second argument's relative address. The rest of the translation proceeds as before.

It is also possible for a double-operand instruction to use immediate addressing for the first operand and relative addressing for the second. A very common example is of the form

ADD   #15,B

that translates as a three-word instruction. Let us assume that this instruction is assembled beginning at address 000106, and that a word has been assigned for B at location 000222. The translation is then

Address	Machine
000106	062767
000110	000015
000112	000106

The verification of the relative address of B is left as an exercise.

From the examples above we can derive formulas for the relative address. If we designate the address of the first word of the instruction by α, and the address of its *first relatively addressed* operand by β, the relative address of that operand is

$$\text{Relative address} = \beta - \alpha - 4. \tag{5.1}$$

This equation would apply whenever the relative address will reside in the second word of a two- or three-word instruction. These cases include MOV A,R1; MOV R1,A; MOV A,B; CMP A,#12. The first two are two-word instructions, with the second word containing the relative address of A, determined by Eq. (5.1). The second two instructions are three-word instructions, but because A is the first relatively addressed operand, its relative address is also given by Eq. (5.1). If two operands are relatively addressed, e.g., ADD X,Y the relative address of the *second* operand is given by

$$\text{Relative address} = \beta - \alpha - 6. \tag{5.2}$$

where α and β have the same meanings as above. The same equation applies for the relative address of A in instructions such as

ADD   #25,A

Summarizing, Eq. (5.1) applies where the relative address will reside in the *second* word, and Eq. (5.2) applies whenever it will reside in the *third* word of a multiword instruction.

5.7 Deferred, Autoincrement, and Autodecrement Addressing

In the preceding section we found that data in central memory could be individually referenced by the use of relative addressing. It will be observed, however, that with relative addressing a separate symbol is needed to label each individual data item used. For example, if three values are to be added, it is necessary to write

```
    MOV    A,R1
    ADD    B,R1
    ADD    C,R1
    . . .
    . . .
    . . .
    HALT
A:  .WORD 5
B:  .WORD 3
C:  .WORD 12
```

Clearly, this method of addressing is practical only for a few data items to be referenced. If the task is to add or otherwise manipulate a large collection of data, i.e., an **array,** a more convenient addressing method is required. Because of the frequent need to work with arrays of data usually stored in sequential central memory locations, MACRO-11 provides several addressing modes especially designed for this purpose. In this section we describe the autoincrement and autodecrement modes, both of which are useful in dealing with arrays. Both are based on the concept of indirect or **deferred** addressing that we shall therefore take up first.

5.7.1 Register Deferred (Indirect) Addressing
When we write

```
    MOV    R1,R2
```

we tell the processor to move the value found in register 1 into register 2. Thus the register addressing mode gives the processor the necessary information to find the values to be operated on (the operands) in a very *direct* way. We shall now contrast this with an alternate way of finding the operands, called *indirect* or *deferred* addressing.

Using what is called **register deferred** addressing we might write the MACRO-11 instruction

```
    MOV    (R1),R2
```

Here we are telling the processor that the central memory *address* of the operand is to be found in R1. This is often called deferred or indirect addressing because the processor first gets the address of the operand, then uses that address to find the operand itself.

An analogy may be helpful in understanding deferred addressing. Books in a library are organized on the shelves according to topic. If you know the *author* of a particular book, however, the librarian will be likely to direct you to the card catalog. In the card catalog, you will find the *location* (address) of the book, but not the book itself. Thus the librarian who refers you to the card catalog is telling you the book's address *indirectly*. This is the same concept as a register having in it the *address* of an operand, rather than the operand itself.

Register deferred addressing is indicated in either of two mnemonic forms in MACRO-11. The first, which we shall use most frequently as a matter of style, is a register symbol enclosed in parentheses. For example, in the instruction

```
SUB     (R4),A
```

we are employing register deferred addressing for the first operand. This will cause the value found in the memory location whose address is contained in R4 to be subtracted from the current value in the location whose address is A. The alternate method uses the "commercial at" character (@). For example,

```
SUB     @R4,A
```

will be interpreted exactly as the previous example.

Because indirect addressing requires an address to be in a register, an instruction using this mode is usually preceded by an instruction placing an address into the register. A typical sequence is therefore

```
MOV     #X,R5
ADD     B,(R5)
```

While it is not necessary that the address be placed in a register *immediately* before its use in register deferred addressing, it is necessary to do so somewhere prior to its use. Programs are more easily understood if this is done close to where it is used.

It will be observed that the instruction

```
ADD     B,X
```

has the same effect as the preceding example. Both add the contents of B to the contents of X. Nonetheless there is an important advantage to the deferred addressing method in that with it the operand address can be easily *changed* by subsequent operations on the register. For example, if we write

```
MOV     #X,R5
ADD     B,(R5)
ADD     #2,R5
ADD     B,(R5)
```

we are adding B to X, and to the *succeeding* memory word as well, without the need for another label. This advantage becomes very important when working with arrays of memory locations, as demonstrated in the following example.

Example 5.15   Suppose we wish to clear 100_8 successive memory words beginning at location RESULT. Using the loop structure suggested earlier, we can write the following program.

```
            MOV      #RESULT,R2      ; INITIALIZE RESULT ADDR
            MOV      #100,R3         ; INITIALIZE LCV
  WHILE:    TST      R3
            BLOS     END
            CLR      (R2)            ; CLEAR RESULT ARRAY
            ADD      #2,R2           ; UPDATE POINTER TO NEXT
                                       ARRAY ELEMENT

            DEC      R3
            BR       WHILE
  END:
            HALT
  RESULT:   .BLKW    100
            .END
```

The first instruction places the *address* of the first word in the block of 100_8 words reserved for RESULT into R2. The loop control variable, R3, is then initialized to 100_8. Because the loop structure works exactly as described earlier (see Section 5.4.3), we will not repeat the details, but go directly to the loop task. On the first pass the instruction CLR (R2) clears the first word of the array stored at the address RESULT. Then R2 is incremented by 2, so that now R2 contains the address of the *second* word in the block of 100_8 words. The next time through the loop, the CLR (R2) will, therefore, clear the second word, and the ADD instruction will increment R2 to the third word. This continues until all 100_8 locations are cleared. Note that this could not have been done easily using relative addressing.

We shall revisit this example and improve the program somewhat when we take up autoincrement addressing.

When using register deferred addressing to reference successive elements in an array of data, the register can be viewed as a *pointer* into the array. That is, the register always contains the address of the next element, and is said to point at it. This allows discussion of deferred addressing in more concise terms. For example, we can simply say "R2 points at" rather than saying that "R2 contains the address of."

Register deferred addressing has the address code $1n$ where n is the register number employed. Thus the instruction

```
  SUB    (R3),(R1)
```

translates as

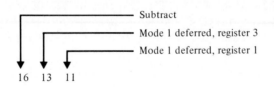

5.7.2 Autoincrement and Autodecrement Addressing

The need to increment the pointer register by 2 as in the preceding example occurs so often that it is provided automatically in the autoincrement addressing mode. To show how this works, we replace the two instructions (CLR and ADD) in the loop task in the preceding example by

    CLR   (R2)+

that accomplishes exactly the same result. The " + " sign *following* the closing parenthesis indicates to the assembler that we are using *autoincrement* addressing. As with register deferred addressing, the operand is found in the memory location whose address is contained in R2. Now, however, the *register contents is incremented by 2 after the operand is fetched.* Thus the ADD #2,R2 instruction is not needed. This has the advantage of greater execution speed and also reduces the number of instructions required.

Autodecrement addressing is a companion to autoincrement addressing. It has the effect of *decrementing* the employed register by 2, and it does this *before* the operand is fetched. An example is

    MOV   −(R5),R1

that first decrements R5 by 2, then uses the result as an address. Whatever it finds at that address it copies into R1. If R5 was originally 001034, for example, this instruction would move the contents of memory location 001032 into R1, and would leave R5 set at 001032. In contrast, the instruction

    MOV   (R5)+,R1

moves the contents of 001032 into R1, leaving R5 set at 001034. Note that the assembly mnemonic has the " + " *following* the operand symbol (autoincrement) while the " − " *precedes* the operand symbol (autodecrement). This is suggestive of the way in which the instructions work.

If both operands in a double-operand instruction use autoincrement and/or autodecrement addressing, careful thought must be given to the addresses actually referenced. The rule is that the operands are fetched and the registers are incremented or decremented *one at a time* beginning with the first operand. Consider the instruction

    ADD   (R1)+,(R1)+

where R1 initially contains 000100. The first operand is fetched from 000100, and R1 is incremented to 000102. The contents of 000100 is therefore added to the contents of location 000102 and R1 is *subsequently* incremented to 000104.

Let us now consider two frequent errors in autoincrement/decrement addressing. The instruction

      CMP   (R1)+,−(R1)

may not have the expected result because R1 is both incremented and decremented after fetching the first operand. This means that the first operand and the second operand are precisely the same memory word! This instruction leaves R1 unchanged. The only effect is that the conditions have been set so that a branch on equal (BEQ) instruction will branch. As another example of this type of situation, consider the instruction

      CMP   (R3),(R3)+

Both operands are addressed before R3 is incremented. Therefore we again have the case in which both operands are the same memory word, but in this case there is a difference. After the instruction is finished, R3 has been incremented by 2. This instruction has the effect that we have set up the conditions so that a branch on equal (BEQ) instruction will branch and that R3 gets incremented. This is an unusual, but sometimes useful, operation. A more normal instruction is

      CMP   (R3)+,(R3)

The value to which R3 initially points is compared with the value in the next sequential memory word. In the process, R3 gets incremented so that the instruction finishes with R3 pointing at the second word.

The autoincrement and autodecrement addressing modes are frequently used with the TST instruction purely as a means of incrementing or decrementing a register by 2. For example,

      TST   (R1)+

will increment R1 by 2, while

      TST   −(R5)

will decrement R5 by 2. This requires fewer instruction words and executes faster than two INC (DEC) instructions or an ADD #2,R1 (SUB #2,R1) instruction, which accounts for the frequent usage. Usually, whenever TST (Rn)+ or TST −(Rn) appears without being followed immediately by a branch, this usage is indicated.

The address codes for the autoincrement and autodecrement modes are

      2*n* (Autoincrement)
      4*n* (Autodecrement)

where n is the number of the register employed. For example, the translation of

ADD $-(R3),(R2)+$

is

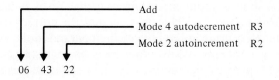

06   43   22

5.8 Examples [OS]

Example 5.16   The decimal integers from 1 to 10 are to be placed in a block of ten words. The program is to add the tenth to the first, leaving the result in the first word, add the ninth to the second leaving the result in the second word, and so on for the rest of the block. Thus, upon halting, the first five words of the block should contain 11_{10}.

The listing file for an assembled MACRO-11 program to do this is shown in Fig. 5.2. In this program R2 is used as a pointer that is initialized to the top of the array beginning at A; this is done by the MOV #A,R2 instruction. Similarly, R3 is a pointer initialized at one word beyond the end of the array, which is labeled EOA (end of A). A loop then begins, with the single instruction task of

```
EXAMPLE 5.16    MACRO V04.00   19-FEB-83 15:49:07 PAGE 1

      1                                        .TITLE EXAMPLE 5.16
      2 000000  012702  000022'        START:  MOV   #A,R2
      3 000004  012703  000046'                MOV   #EOA,R3
      4 000010  020302                 WHILE:  CMP   R3,R2
      5 000012  101402                         BLOS  END
      6 000014  064322                         ADD   -(R3),(R2)+
      7 000016  000774                         BR    WHILE
      8 000020  000000                 END:    HALT
      9 000022  000001  000002  000003 A:      .WORD 1,2,3,4,5,6,7,10,11,12
        000030  000004  000005  000006
        000036  000007  000010  000011
        000044  000012
     10 000046                         EOA:    .BLKW 1
     11          000000'                        .END  START



      SYMBOL TABLE

      A 000022R     END 000020R     EOA 000046R      WHILE 000010R

      START 000000R
      . ABS.  000000     000
              000050     001
      ERRORS DETECTED:   0
```

Figure 5.2   Listing for Example 5.16.

adding the value pointed at by R3 to that pointed at by R2. Autoincrement addressing is used on R2 and autodecrement is used on R3, so that each time through the loop a new sum is generated. Registers R2 and R3 are also used as loop control variables; so long as R3 is greater than R2 (after each has been incremented or decremented) the loop will continue. When the two pointers meet in the middle, the loop is terminated. Observe that R3 is initialized to address one word *beyond* the end of A. This ensures that the correct word is addressed when it is decremented *prior* to fetching of the operand in the ADD instruction.

Figure 5.2 also shows how multiword instructions are displayed in the MACRO-11 listing file. The two MOV instructions use immediate addressing for their first operands. The addresses of these operands are shown on the same lines as the translated instructions. For example, the address of A is shown as 000022', which can be confirmed by looking at the symbol table, or in the address column where storage is allocated for A. Because this address is actually only *relative* to the beginning of this program, the assembler marks it with a single quote character ('), indicating that when the program is linked and loaded, this number will be changed. Note that because the first instruction occupies two words, the addresses go from 000000 to 000004 in the address column of the listing.

In line 9 of the listing, we see the beginning of the block of words reserved for the A array. The values given in the .WORD directive are displayed three words per line. Thus on the first line the assembler shows us that 000001, 000002, and 000003 are stored in words 000022, 000024, and 000026. The next line begins with the address 000030 followed by three more word contents. This continues until all words are displayed. The single word reserved with the label EOA by the .BLKW directive is stored at 000046. Note that the assembler does *not* give this word a value, so that line 10 has only the address.

Figure 5.3 shows how the assembled program is linked with ODT and executed. In Fig. 5.3(a) the preexecution contents of memory are displayed using ODT. Note that the LINK process has added 1000_8 to all addresses given in the listing file. The program therefore resides between 001000 and 001020, with the block for the A array beginning at 001022. The ten integers are shown in their octal representations in locations 001022 through 001044. In Fig. 5.3(b), we see execution of the program with a breakpoint set at the HALT instruction. Following execution, the contents of memory holding the A array are again displayed. We see that the first half of the array now contains octal 000013, which is of course decimal 11 as desired.

Example 5.17 An array of data comprised of N values is to be stored beginning at a CM location labeled DATA. The program is to sort the data into ascending order.

We choose to perform the task using a straightforward bubble sort technique. In this method, N passes are made through an array of N values. On each pass,

```
RUN $LINK
*EX5P16,EX5P16=EX5P16,ODT/T
Transfer symbol? O.ODT
*^Z

Ready

RUN EX5P16

ODT  R01-04
*1000/012702
001002 /001022
001004 /012703
001006 /001046
001010 /020302
001012 /101402
001014 /064322
001016 /000774
001020 /000000
001022 /000001
001024 /000002
001026 /000003
001030 /000004
001032 /000005
001034 /000006
001036 /000007
001040 /000010
001042 /000011
001044 /000012
001046 /000000
001050 /000000
```

```
*1020;B
*1000;G
B0;001020
*001024/000013
001026 /000013
001030 /000013
001032 /000013
001034 /000006
001036 /000007
001040 /000010
001042 /000011
001044 /000012
001046 /000000
001050 /000000
*^C

Ready
```

(a)   (b)

Figure 5.3   ODT execution of Example 5.16: (a) memory contents before execution; (b) execution and resulting effects on memory.

each successive value is compared with its successor, and if it is found to be larger than the successor the two are interchanged. We forgo easy improvements to this algorithm in the interest of simplicity. The MACRO-11 listing is shown in Fig. 5.4. In this program R1 is the loop control variable for the outer loop, and R2 for the inner loop. Register 3 serves as a pointer into the DATA array, and as such is initialized to the first address in the DATA block before each entry to the inner loop. The inner loop performs a pass through the array, comparing adjacent values and doing an interchange on any pair that is out of order. Note that a single pass requires advancing the pointer $N - 1$ times where N is the length of the array. It is known that N such passes will ensure a completely ordered array.

To further explain the operation of this algorithm, we shall use the term "current" to represent the memory location pointed at by R3, or its contents, when the CMP instruction is encountered. The term "next" is used to represent the next higher location or its contents. Note that in the compare instruction, the first operand employs autoincrement addressing and represents the current array element, while the second operand represents the next array element by register deferred addressing. The exchange process is then *skipped* if the current value is less than or the same as the next value. The exchange process employs

```
EXAMPLE 5.17    MACRO V03.01 14-JAN-83 10:27:37 PAGE 1

    1                                                      .TITLE  EXAMPLE 5.17
    2 000000  016767  000064  000064   START:     MOV     N,NM1
    3 000006  162767  000001  000056              SUB     #1,NM1
    4 000014  016701  000050              MOV     N,R1
    5 000020  005701           WHILE1:    TST     R1
    6 000022  101421                      BLOS    END1
    7 000024  012703  000074'             MOV     #DATA,R3
    8 000030  016702  000036              MOV     NM1,R2
    9 000034                   WHILE2:
   10 000034  005702                      TST     R2
   11 000036  101411                      BLOS    END2
   12 00C040  022313                      CMP     (R3)+,(R3)
   13 000042  101405                      BLOS    END3
   14 000044  014304                      MOV     -(R3),R4
   15 000046  005723                      TST     (R3)+
   16 000050  011343                      MOV     (R3),-(R3)
   17 000052  005723                      TST     (R3)+
   18 000054  010413                      MOV     R4,(R3)
   19 000056                   END3:
   20 000056  005302                      DEC     R2
   21 000060  000765                      BR      WHILE2
   22 000062                   END2:
   23 000062  005301                      DEC     R1
   24 000064  000755                      BR      WHILE1
   25 000066                   END1:
   26 000066  000000                      HALT
   27 000070  000004           N:         .WORD   4
   28 000072                   NM1:       .BLKW   1
   29 000074  000004  000003  000002   DATA:      .WORD   4,3,2,1
      000102  000001
   30                                              .BLKW   10
   31                                              .BLKW   20
   32          000000'                             .END    START


        SYMBOL TABLE

        DATA 000074R    END1 000066R    N 000070R    START 000000R
        WHILE2 000034R
        END3 000056R    END2 000062R    NM1 000072R   WHILE1 000020R

        . ABS.  000000    000
                000164    001
        ERRORS DETECTED:  0
```

Figure 5.4 Listing of program for Example 5.17.

autoincrement, autodecrement, and register deferred addressing. The strategy employed is

1. Place the current value into R4 for safekeeping.
2. Place the next value into the current location.
3. Retrieve the current value and place it into the next location.

The exchange begins by autodecrementing the pointer in the first MOV so that the current value is copied into R4. The following TST then advances the pointer so that the second MOV picks up the next value as its first operand. Autodecrement of the destination operand of this instruction causes the next value to be copied into the current location, leaving the pointer at this location.

The second TST again advances the pointer to the next location so that it is properly positioned for the destination operand of the third MOV. Observe that there is an equal number of increments and decrements, so that R3 is left pointing at the next location, as it was when the interchange began.

It is worthwhile noting that there are other ways to accomplish the interchange that could be more efficient. However, addressing modes and/or instructions not yet discussed would be required. The method we have shown provides an interesting exercise in the use of autoincrement, autodecrement, and register deferred addressing. The reader who follows this example carefully will have no further difficulty with these modes.

Figure 5.5 shows the execution of Example 5.17 with ODT. Figure 5.5(a) shows the memory contents before execution. Figure 5.5(b) shows that the contents of locations 001074 through 001102 have indeed been sorted after execution.

```
RUN $LINK
*EX5P17,EX5P17=EX5P17,ODT/T
Transfer symbol? O.ODT
*^Z

Ready

RUN EX5P17
ODT  R01-04
*1000/016767
001002 /000064
001004 /000064
001006 /162767
001010 /000001
001012 /000056
001014 /016701
001016 /000050
001020 /005701
001022 /101421
001024 /012703
001026 /001074
001030 /016702
001032 /000036
001034 /005702
001036 /101411
001040 /022313
001042 /101405
001044 /014304
001046 /005723
001050 /011343
001052 /005723
001054 /010413
001056 /005302
001060 /000765
001062 /005301
001064 /000755           *1066;B
001066 /000000           *1000;G
001070 /000004           B0:001066
001072 /000000           *1074/000001
001074 /000004           001076 /000002
001076 /000003           001100 /000003
001100 /000002           001102 /000004
001102 /000001           001104 /000000
001104 /000000           *
001106 /000000           Ready

      (a)                      (b)
```

Figure 5.5   Execution of Example 5.17 with ODT.

Example 5.18 Assume the following initializations of the registers and memory locations prior to execution of each of the sample instructions given.

Register	Contents	Location	Contents
R0	000512	000500	000001
R1	000504	000502	000002
R2	000506	000504	000003
R3	000502	000506	000004
		000510	000005
		000512	000006

Instruction	Affected Address of Register	New Contents
a) CLR (R0)	000512	000000
b) CLR (R0)+	000512	000000
	R0	000514
c) CLR −(R1)	000502	000000
	R1	000502
d) MOV (R2),−(R2)	000504	000004
	R2	000504
e) MOV #512,R0	R0	000512
ADD (R0),−(R3)	000500	000007
	R3	000500
f) SUB (R1),(R1)+	000504	000000
	R1	000506
g) SUB (R1)+,(R1)	000506	000001
	R1	000506
h) MOV (R0)+,−(R0)	no effect	

5.9 Successive Refinements of Loops (Optional)

There are many important points to remember in the process of efficient loop construction. A very important point is to remain flexible in thinking. Rigid structures make templates to guide one's development of first cut programs, but the next step is refinement. To illustrate this point, consider the following simple program.

```
        MOV    #ADR1,R1   ; POINT TO 1ST ARRAY.
        MOV    #ADR2,R2   ; POINT TO 2ND ARRAY.
        MOV    COUNT,R3   ; NUMBER OF ARRAY WORDS.
WHILE:  TST    R3         ; TEST THE LOOP COUNTER.
        BEQ    END        ; HAVE COMPLETED THE LOOP TASK.
        ADD    (R1)+,(R2)+ ; ADD WORD FROM 1ST ARRAY TO 2ND.
        DEC    R3         ; DECREMENT THE LOOP COUNTER.
        BR     WHILE      ; GO AROUND THE LOOP AGAIN.
    END:
```

This program adds the words of the array at ADR1 to the corresponding words of the array at ADR2. COUNT is the number of additions to be done. As a simple refinement we observe that both the MOV COUNT,R3 and the DEC R3 instructions test R3. This means that the TST instruction is redundant.

```
                MOV     #ADR1,R1      ; POINT TO 1ST ARRAY.
                MOV     #ADR2,R2      ; POINT TO 2ND ARRAY.
                MOV     COUNT,R3      ; NUMBER OF ARRAY WORDS.
     WHILE:     BEQ     END           ; HAVE COMPLETED THE LOOP TASK.
                ADD     (R1)+,(R2)+   ; ADD WORD FROM 1ST ARRAY TO 2ND.
                DEC     R3            ; DECREMENT THE LOOP COUNTER.
                BR      WHILE         ; GO AROUND THE LOOP AGAIN.
     END:
```

This refinement may not seem significant. The point to remember is that one good refinement may open paths to allow other refinements. The BR WHILE instruction can be replaced by a BNE instruction so that we have a speed gain for large values of COUNT without sacrificing any loss of efficiency (even in the zero loop case).

```
                MOV     #ADR1,R1      ; POINT TO 1ST ARRAY.
                MOV     #ADR2,R2      ; POINT TO 2ND ARRAY.
                MOV     COUNT,R3      ; NUMBER OF ARRAY WORDS.
                BEQ     END           ; HAVE COMPLETED THE LOOP TASK.
     WHILE:     ADD     (R1)+,(R2)+   ; ADD WORD FROM 1ST ARRAY TO 2ND.
                DEC     R3            ; DECREMENT THE LOOP COUNTER.
                BNE     WHILE         ; GO AROUND THE LOOP AGAIN.
     END:
```

Now it is clear that the DEC R3, BNE WHILE set can be replaced by a simple SOB R3,WHILE instruction.

```
                MOV     #ADR1,R1      ; POINT TO 1ST ARRAY.
                MOV     #ADR2,R2      ; POINT TO 2ND ARRAY.
                MOV     COUNT,R3      ; NUMBER OF ARRAY WORDS.
                BEQ     END           ; HAVE COMPLETED THE LOOP TASK.
     WHILE:     ADD     (R1)+,(R2)+   ; ADD WORD FROM 1ST ARRAY TO 2ND.
                SOB     R3,WHILE      ; DECREMENT AND LOOP IF NOT ZERO.
     END:
```

We have created a program that is at once simple to understand and more efficient both in memory space and execution time. Something else was gained that was so subtle that you may not have even noticed. That is, this program is also globally more flexible than the original one. The SOB instruction does its operation without altering the conditions set by any previous test. This allows for more testing conditions to occur and to be used easily while going around the loop. This is a subtle point that may eventually become clear as you gain more experience with larger programs.

5.10 Summary

This chapter has introduced several new instructions and addressing methods that greatly enlarge our programming capability in MACRO-11 assembly language. Three new instructions used to establish branching conditions are *CMP, SUB,* and *TST*. Seven branching instructions—*BHI, BLO, BEQ, BNE, BHIS, BLOS,* and *BR*—were introduced. Recall that both CMP and SUB do a subtraction. However, SUB subtracts the first operand from the second and places the result in the second, while CMP subtracts the second from the first and does not permanently place the result. Thus CMP only establishes branching conditions. TST is also used to set branching conditions, but examines only a single operand comparing it with zero. All conditional branching instructions decide whether or not to branch based on conditions set by preceding instructions such as SUB, CMP, or TST. The conditional branches discussed in this chapter are intended for use with *unsigned numbers*. Conditional branching involving negative numbers is discussed in Chapter 6.

It was seen that branch instructions have a translation process different from the other instructions. The operand field of a branch instruction is an 8-bit relative address (or *offset*). The actual address is automatically generated (when needed) by adding the current PC value to the relative address. It was seen that the branch instructions can be used to build three important classes of control structures—*single-alternative decision structures, double-alternative decision structures,* and *loops*. Standard implementations of these were presented and demonstrated in examples. Rigid adherence to the use of these standard forms is not necessary. However, the forms can be used to simplify the programming task and make programs more readable.

New addressing methods introduced include immediate, relative, register deferred, autoincrement, and autodecrement. All of these methods allow us to reference data in the CM. *Immediate* is indicated by a "*#symbol*" where symbol can be any numeric value or label. The numerical value is stored *immediately* after the instruction word. *Relative addressing* is indicated by a symbol appearing alone as an operand. The symbol is assumed to be a label, and the assembler determines its address *relative* to the PC and stores this address in the word after the instruction word. In later chapters we will see that the symbols for both of these modes can be replaced by expressions or can be defined other than as labels.

The *autoincrement* and *autodecrement* methods of addressing allow reference to contiguous blocks of CM using a single register. This makes them suitable for working with arrays. Both of these methods use the concept of deferred or indirect addressing, which is also exemplified in the *register deferred* method. In deferred addressing, the *address* of the operand is in the register, rather than the operand value itself. This is convenient because registers can be incremented or decremented, causing the same instruction to reference sequential memory locations as it is encountered repeatedly in a loop. Register deferred operands are indicated by registers enclosed in parentheses, e.g., (R5). Here we say that R5 points to the operand in memory. Such usage must of course be preceded by an instruction that places a valid address into the register employed, e.g., MOV #A,R5. Autoincrement addressing is indicated by a (+) sign *following* a register enclosed in parentheses, e.g., (R2)+. As suggested by this notation, R2 is incremented *after* the operand is fetched from the CM location pointed at by R2. In autodecrement, the operand is written —(R4) which causes the register to be *decremented before* the operand value is fetched.

We found that use of CM to store data obligates the programmer to allocate room. This is done by the use of the assembler directives *.BLKW n* that sets aside *n* words, or .WORD $n_1, n_2, \ldots, n_k$ that sets aside k words and initializes them to the given values $n_1, n_2, \ldots, n_k$.

5.11 Exercises

5.1 On a separate sheet, set up a table with BHI, BLO, BLOS, BHIS, BEQ, BNE, and BR across the top, and a, b, . . . , h down the left side. Indicate by X which branches will occur after CMP R1,R2 with the following values of R1 and R2.

R1	R2		R1	R2
a) 017552	017552	**b)** 000705	000613
c) 104311	004311	**d)** 000000	000000
e) 177602	000176	**f)** 000001	104631
g) 001016	054272	**h)** 177777	017777

5.2 Translate the following branch instructions, assuming that the branch operand label A is at the given address.

Addr of Branch Instruction	Branch Instruction		A
a) 001002	BHI	A	001012
b) 001010	BLO	A	001024
c) 000444	BLOS	A	000464
d) 010246	BHIS	A	010240
e) 010642	BEQ	A	010636
f) 021364	BNE	A	021264
g) 022434	BR	A	022422

5.3 We want to set R2 to 3 if R0 is greater than R1, or to set R2 to 4 if R0 is less than or equal to R1. Implement this in MACRO-11 using first the standard control structure, then, in the most compact and efficient way you can devise, using the instructions introduced so far. How many memory words and execution cycles did you save with the more efficient method?

5.4 Write a MACRO-11 program to sort the contents of R1 through R4 into ascending order. Use the decision structures and loop implementations presented in this chapter. Translate manually, then assemble and run using ODT or GETOCT/PUTOCT for I/O.

5.5 Revise the FIBONACCI program in Fig. 4.5 to compute F(n) where n is a value stored in R5. Demonstrate this program using ODT or GETOCT/PUTOCT. How large can n be while still producing a valid result?

5.6 Translate the following into machine code.

```
ADD     #62, R4
MOV     #100,R1
```

5.7 Translate the following into assembly.

012700

000073

005700

5.8 Translate the following into machine code.

```
L1:
        DEC       A
        BEQ       L1
        BR        L2
        .BLKW     5
L2:     MOV       #A,R1
        MOV       A,R2
        HALT
  A:    .WORD     10
```

a) Assuming that this segment of code is loaded beginning at 1000_8, what value does the assembler assign to A?

b) To what value does the assembler initialize the *contents* of A?

c) What value is stored in A at HALT?

d) What is the value in R2 at HALT?

e) What is the value in R1 at HALT?

5.9 Identify the branch instruction and offsets implied by the following machine code branches. Also, state how many *words* forward or backward they will branch, *measured from the branch instruction*.

a) 000577   **b)** 000770   **c)** 001405

d) 103376   **e)** 001774   **f)** 103401

g) 001766   **h)** 101375

5.10 Before *each* instruction below, assume that memory and registers are set as follows.

Memory		Registers	
120:	000000	R0:	000000
122:	000701	R3:	000124
124:	000456		
304:	000537		
456:	000174		
524:	000304		
700:	000663		

Indicate the effects of each instruction on the register and memory.

a) CLR   R3   **b)** CLR   (R3)

c) CLR   (R3)+   **d)** CLR   −(R3)

e) MOV   R3, R0   **f)** MOV   (R3),R0

g) MOV   (R3)+,R0   **h)** MOV   −(R3),R0

i) MOV   −(R3),−(R3)   **j)** MOV   −(PC),−(PC)

5.11 Translate the following program into machine code. Also, indicate the final contents of all registers and memory locations affected by the program as they would be after execution.

```
START:    MOV      N,R1
          MOV      #A,R2
          MOV      #B,R3
LOOP:     TST      R1
          BEQ      OUT
          CMP      (R2)+,(R3)+
          BHI      L1
          CLR      −(R2)
          TST      (R2)+
L1:       DEC      R1
          BR       LOOP
OUT:      HALT
N:        .WORD    4
A:        .WORD    1,2,3,4
B:        .WORD    4,3,2,1
          .END     START
```

5.12 Write a program that reverses the contents of an array of length N beginning at A. That is, if A is initially 1,2,3,4, it should be 4,3,2,1 after execution. Your program should work with arrays of any size up to 1000 octal without changing any instructions. Use either ODT or GETOCT/PUTOCT to initialize N and A and demonstrate your program.

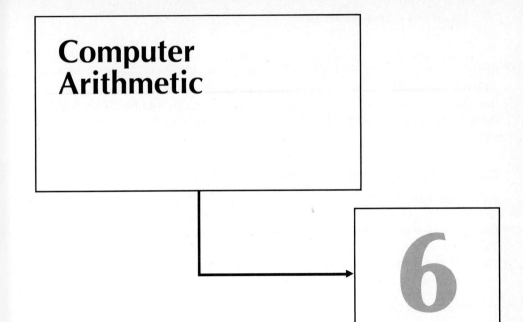

Computer Arithmetic

6

6.1 Overview

Up to this point our focus has been on elements of programming. In order to maintain this focus, we have discussed numbers and arithmetic operations in a somewhat superficial way. In this chapter we change this focus to numbers and calculations with numbers, which we call **computer arithmetic.**

Arithmetic operations impose certain requirements on the computer and language not dealt with up to this point. In particular, a complete arithmetic capability requires the concept of negative numbers, whereas we have up to this point dealt only with positive integers. In this chapter we introduce a number system used in the PDP-11 computer, called the **two's complement system,** that allows negative numbers. We shall then see that such numbers make use of a special class of PDP-11 instructions. This includes, in particular, the **signed branch** instructions.

Understanding of signed numbers and these new instructions requires that we consider another element of the computer hardware, namely the **Processor Status Word** (PSW). This special register monitors developments during calculations and allows us to guard against erroneous results.

Other new instructions introduced in this chapter because of their particular importance in arithmetic operations include the shift and rotate instructions that allow us to deal with word contents on a bit-by-bit basis. We also take up the multiply and divide instructions available on most PDP-11 computers.

When dealing with arithmetic it is possible to encounter numbers too large to be stored in a single word in the positional binary representation. To deal with this we introduce the concept of **multiple-precision** representation of integers that allows us to use two or more words to store a single number. This requires the introduction of new PDP-11 instructions for **add–carry** and **subtract–carry** operations.

6.2 The Two's Complement Number System

6.2.1 Concepts

In Chapter 1 it was shown that the number of bits available, i.e., the word length, limits the size of numbers that can be stored using binary positional notation. There we saw, for example, that a 3-bit binary number can represent only eight different numerical values. We used these combinations to represent the eight octal digits 0, 1, 2, 3, 4, 5, 6, and 7. That is

Binary	Octal
000	0
001	1
010	2
011	3
100	4
101	5
110	6
111	7

Similarly, with 16-bit words such as we have in the PDP-11, there are $2^{16} = 65536_{10}$ different bit patterns that can be used to represent zero and the positive integers up to 65535_{10}. We now note that if we used *all* of these available bit patterns for *positive* numbers, we have none to represent negative numbers. If the programmer wishes to use negative numbers, it will be necessary to assign some of the bit patterns for their representation.

There are many ways that this could be done. For example, using a 3-bit word length for convenience of demonstration, we could make the following assignments.

111	-3
110	-2
101	-1
100	-0
000	$+0$
001	$+1$
010	$+2$
011	$+3$

This would give us a way to represent the integers from -3 to $+3$, and as a bonus we would have a -0 as well as a $+0$ (for whatever value that might be!). This system could be used, but poses some slight inconveniences. For example, one might expect that $2 + (-1)$ should come out $+1$. In this system, however, we have

$$
\begin{array}{rl}
010 & (\ 2) \\
+\,101 & (-1) \\
\hline
111 & (-3)
\end{array}
$$

which is -3 instead. This difficulty could of course be overcome by devising new rules for subtraction. Indeed, some computers do use such a system. However, there is another system that was viewed as a better one by the designers of the PDP-11 computers. This is called the *two's complement* system, and is used on many other digital computers as well as the PDP-11.

The two's complement system offers an attractive way to divide the available bit patterns of a fixed word length into positive and negative integers. To demonstrate this system we will again use a 3-bit word for convenience. The positive integers are represented by the positional binary numbers

Decimal System	Two's Complement System (3-bit)
0	000
1	001
2	010
3	011

The negative numbers are represented by defining 111 to be -1 and then counting *downward* as the numbers become more negative as shown below.

Decimal System	Two's Complement System (3-bit)
0	000
-1	111
-2	110
-3	101
-4	100

With this system we observe that the integers between -4 and $+3$ can be represented, including a single 0. However, if we attempt to go beyond $+3$, we get 100 that is the same as the pattern assigned to -4. Similarly attempting to achieve a value more negative than -4 yields 011 that is really a $+3$. It is therefore very important to recognize the range limits with this (or any other) digital representation of numbers.

The two's complement property of generating the most negative number by exceeding the positive range by 1 and vice versa invites a circular representation of the real line as shown in Fig. 6.1. You may also observe the similarity between this system and an automotive odometer that goes back to 0 after reading 99999.

The two's complement system has many interesting and convenient properties. For example, subtraction obeys familiar rules.

$$
\begin{array}{rr}
010 & (\ 2) \\
+\,111 & (-1) \\
\hline
1 \leftarrow \quad 001 & (+1)
\end{array}
$$

Here we have shown that $(+2) + (-1)$ produces $+1$, using the conventional rules for binary addition and ignoring the carry from the MSB. Also, the negative of a number is produced by subtracting it from 0 (assuming a borrow into the MSB).

$$
\begin{array}{rr}
1 \rightarrow \quad 000 & (\ 0) \\
-\,011 & -(+3) \\
\hline
101 & (-3)
\end{array}
$$

This property in fact gives the two's complement system its name. The term "complement" in mathematics means the amount that will make a value "complete." The complement of an acute angle is the value one must add to obtain 90 degrees. The two's complement of an n-bit binary number is the value that must be added to yield 2^n which, in a sense, is complete. Thus we can determine

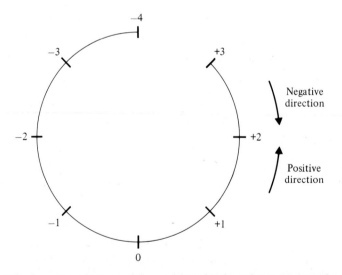

Figure 6.1 Circular representation of the real line for the 3-bit two's complement system.

the two's complement of an n-bit binary number by subtracting it from 2^n. This is what we did, in effect, when we subtracted 011 from 000 with a carry into the MSB in the preceding example.

Many find it easier to determine the two's complement of a number by taking the one's complement and adding 1. This can be shown to be mathematically equivalent to subtracting it from 2^n. It is easy because the one's complement is found simply by "flipping the bits," i.e., change 1's to 0's and 0's to 1's. Addition of the 1 usually requires only a few carries, and the entire process is often quicker than the subtraction process implied in the definition. The following examples show both methods.

Example 6.1

a) Find the two's complement of 01010111. By the definition,

```
  100000000    (2ⁿ)
−  01010111    (Minus original number)
   10101001    (Two's complement)
```

By one's complement plus 1,

```
  10101000    (One's complement of original number)
+        1    (Plus 1)
  10101001    (Two's complement)
```

b) Find the two's complement of 111. By the definition,

```
  1000
−  111
   001
```

By one's complement plus 1,

```
  000
+   1
  001
```

c) Find the two's complement of 0100111011000101. By the definition,

```
  10000000000000000
−  0100111011000101
   1011000100111011
```

By one's complement plus 1,

```
  1011000100111010
+                1
  1011000100111011
```

d) Show that the two's complement *of the two's complement* of a number, say

0110, yields the original number. By one's complement plus 1

1001	(One's complement)
+ 1	
1010	(Two's complement)

0101	(One's complement)
+ 1	
0110	(Original number)

The last example demonstrates the important property $-(-N) = N$ in the two's complement system.

There is the possibility of confusion stemming from several usages of the term "two's complement." This term is used as the name of the number system, as an adjective describing a number in this system, and as an arithmetic operation. When we say, "Find the two's complement of" or "Take the two's complement of," we refer to an arithmetic operation otherwise known as negation. When we say, "A two's complement number," i.e., using the term as an adjective, we are identifying the representation system employed. Note in particular that "two's complement" used as an adjective is not synonymous with *negative*. Indeed, in the examples above we found that by two's complementing 111 (a negative number) we achieved 001 (a positive number). *Both* 111 and 001 can be viewed as two's complement numbers. We have already noted that either could also be viewed simply as positive integers in a 3-bit positional binary system. Saying that they are two's complement numbers is a necessary clarification, and says nothing about their sign.

6.2.2 The 16-bit and 8-bit Two's Complement Systems

The PDP-11 computer has a 16-bit word length and therefore allows 2^{16} different bit patterns. As already noted, these can be used exclusively to represent positive integers, in which case the allowable range is 0 to 65535. By use of the 16-bit two's complement system, however, this same word can be used to represent the range -32768_{10} to $+32767_{10}$. The scheme of representation is shown in Table 6.1. Note that as with the 3-bit two's complement system, the largest positive value is a 0 in the MSB with the rest set to 1, and the largest negative value is a 1 in the MSB with the rest set to 0. Noting that *all* negative numbers have MSB equal to 1, we see why the MSB is often called the **sign bit**. Table 6.1 also lists the **octal translation** of the bit patterns, which we call 16-bit two's complement octal. In Fig. 6.2(a) we show the 16-bit two's complement system on a circular "real" line to emphasize that exceeding the allowed range, positive or negative, produces an erroneous result.

It is sometimes convenient or necessary to work in terms of 8-bit two's complement numbers rather than those of 16. Table 6.2 shows this system, with the circular diagram appearing in Fig. 6.2(b). The similarities to the 8-bit and

TABLE 6.1
16-bit Two's Complement System

Decimal	Two's Complement (Binary)	Two's Complement (Octal)
−32768	1 000 000 000 000 000	100000
−32767	1 000 000 000 000 001	100001
−32766	1 000 000 000 000 010	100002
.	.	.
.	.	.
.	.	.
−2	1 111 111 111 111 110	177776
−1	1 111 111 111 111 111	177777
0	0 000 000 000 000 000	000000
1	0 000 000 000 000 001	000001
2	0 000 000 000 000 010	000002
.	.	.
.	.	.
.	.	.
32765	0 111 111 111 111 101	077775
32766	0 111 111 111 111 110	077776
32767	0 111 111 111 111 111	077777

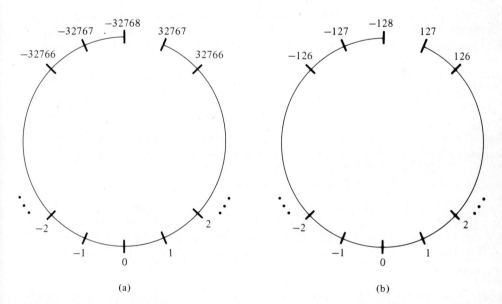

(a) (b)

Figure 6.2 Circular representation of the real line for (a) 16-bit and (b) 8-bit two's complement systems. (Numbers shown in base 10.)

16-bit systems are quite apparent in the binary representation. Attention is called to the octal representation, however, where differences are apparent. The most significant octal digit in the 8-bit system has a maximum value of 3, compared to 1 in the 16-bit system. This is because when 8-bit numbers are grouped by threes from right to left, *two bits* remain to represent the most significant octal digit. For the 16-bit system, there is only *one bit* for the most significant octal digit.

Tables 6.1 and 6.2 should be studied until negative and positive numbers can be readily recognized in both systems, whether written in octal or binary. For the 16-bit two's complement system, an octal number with a leading 1 is negative. A leading 0 or 1 in the 8-bit system indicates a positive number, while a leading 2 or 3 indicates negative. In the binary form, a 1 in the MSB indicates negative in either system. Comparison of the negative 8-bit numbers in binary representation with the negative 16-bit numbers similarly represented reveals an important fact: The representations are the same except for eight more leading 1's in the 16-bit representation. Similarly, the 8-bit and 16-bit positive numbers differ only by eight more leading 0's. Thus one could convert from 8-bit to 16-bit representation by *extending the sign bit to the left*. This is an important property called **sign extension,** used when we take up bit and byte manipulations later.

6.2.3 Two's Complement Arithmetic

Facility in two's complement arithmetic is important to the assembly language programmer. Here we demonstrate the most common operations—addition, subtraction, and negation. In this discussion, the MSB is called the fifteenth bit, and the adjacent one, the fourteenth.

Addition of two positive two's complement numbers is no different from adding positional binary numbers, provided that the allowable range is not exceeded. When it is exceeded, the result is not valid. For example, adding 3 to 32766_{10} produces

$$
\begin{array}{r}
0\ 111\ 111\ 111\ 111\ 110 \\
+\underline{0\ 000\ 000\ 000\ 000\ 011} \\
1\ 000\ 000\ 000\ 000\ 001 \quad \text{(Overflow)}
\end{array}
$$

that is -32767_{10}. Here an *overflow* is said to have occurred. Note that this condition is marked by a carry from the fourteenth to the fifteenth bit. Because the fifteenth bit is reserved for the sign, the carry invalidates the result.

However, if there is *also* a carry out of the MSB, there is no overflow. This is demonstrated by the following example.

$$
\begin{array}{r}
1\ 100\ 000\ 000\ 000\ 000 \\
+\underline{0\ 100\ 000\ 000\ 000\ 000} \\
1 \leftarrow 0\ 000\ 000\ 000\ 000\ 000 \quad \text{(Correct result)}
\end{array}
$$

TABLE 6.2
8-bit Two's Complement System

Decimal	Two's Complement (Binary)	Two's Complement (Octal)
−128	10 000 000	200
−127	10 000 001	201
−126	10 000 010	202
.	.	.
.	.	.
.	.	.
−2	11 111 110	376
−1	11 111 111	377
0	00 000 000	000
1	00 000 001	001
2	00 000 010	002
.	.	.
.	.	.
.	.	.
125	01 111 101	175
126	01 111 110	176
127	01 111 111	177

Subtraction can be carried out either by following the normal rules of binary subtraction, or by negating the subtrahend and adding. If the minuend is larger than the subtrahend and both are positive, normal subtraction is no different from that discussed in Chapter 2. Let us consider then the more interesting case of subtracting a larger positive number from a smaller one, for example, 2 − 3. We use the 3-bit two's complement system for convenience.

$$
\begin{array}{ll}
1 \rightarrow 010 & (2) \quad \text{(Minuend)} \\
\underline{-011} & \underline{-(3)} \quad \text{(Subtrahend)} \\
111 & (-1)
\end{array}
$$

Note that by simply borrowing from an imaginary bit to the left of the MSB we arrived at the correct result. This same result can be obtained by forming the two's complement of the subtrahend (i.e., negating it) and adding.

$$
\begin{array}{ll}
010 & (\ 2) \\
\underline{+101} & \underline{+(-3)} \\
111 & (-1)
\end{array}
$$

Some will find this a more convenient method because addition may be easier than subtraction.

The operations above can also be carried out entirely in the *octal* representation of two's complement numbers. In fact, most assembly language programmers learn to think and work entirely in octal (or hexadecimal depending on the computer). We have already considered octal addition in Chapter 2; this remains unchanged for the two's complement system if the sum is within the allowed range. Even if one or both of the addends are negative, the rules do not change. For example, the 16-bit two's complement octal numbers below are both negative.

$$
\begin{array}{rr}
100002 & (-32766_{10}) \\
+\,177776 & +(\qquad -2_{10}) \\
\hline
1 \leftarrow \quad 100000 & (-32768_{10})
\end{array}
$$

In determining the most significant digit, it is necessary to remember that its maximum value is 1. Therefore, in this example the leftmost 1's, together with the carry from the adjacent position, generate a 1, and a final carry, which is ignored.

The negation operation, i.e., two's complementing, can also be carried out entirely in octal. It is only necessary to observe the *maximum value* that each digit can take on as you follow the rules previously established. Let us consider the negation of the 8-bit two's complement octal number 142. First find its one's complement by subtracting each digit from its maximum possible value.

$$
\begin{array}{ll}
\quad 377 & \text{(Maximum value of each digit)} \\
-\,142 & \\
\hline
\quad 235 & \text{(One's complement of 142)} \\
+\quad 1 & \\
\hline
\quad 236 & \text{(Two's complement of 142)}
\end{array}
$$

Observe that this is a negative number by virtue of the leading 2. (See Table 6.2.)

The problem sometimes arises that a negative two's complement octal number is given and we need to know its decimal equivalent. The easy way to do this is to *negate* the number, i.e., form its two's complement, then convert the result to decimal and append the customary minus sign. For example, suppose we are given 346 and told that it is in an 8-bit two's complement octal representation (we could *not* tell this just by looking at it!). Because its leading digit is 3, it is negative. Its two's complement is

$$
\begin{array}{l}
\quad 377 \\
-\,346 \\
\hline
\quad 031 \\
+\quad 1 \\
\hline
\quad 032_8 = 26_{10}
\end{array}
$$

Therefore two's complement $346_8 = -26_{10}$.

Two's complement octal subtraction is facilitated by negation. That is, rather than performing subtraction, we can take the two's complement of the subtrahend and add. In the following example we find the difference 177573 − 000163 in which both operands are 16-bit two's complement octal representations. Observe that we are subtracting a positive number from a negative number, so we expect a negative result.

$$
\begin{array}{rl}
177777 & \text{(Maximum digit values)} \\
-\,000163 & \text{(Subtrahend)} \\
\hline
177614 & \text{(One's complement)} \\
+\qquad 1 & \\
\hline
177615 & \text{(Two's complement)} \\
+\,177573 & \text{(Minuend)} \\
\hline
177410 & \\
\end{array}
$$

It is left as an exercise for the reader to show that this is correct by converting the original numbers to decimal and carrying out the subtraction. The result is -248_{10}.

6.3 Two's Complement Numbers and the PDP-11

The PDP-11 computer is designed to make use of the two's complement system. We do not wish to imply, however, that *all* numbers *must* be so represented on this machine. In fact, the computer stores *bit patterns,* on which the programmer can place whatever interpretations he or she wishes. Sometimes it is most convenient to place in a word, or view its contents as, a 16-bit, positive positional notation binary number. Other times we wish to use the same words to store 16-bit two's complement numbers (positive or negative). Although seldom done on the PDP-11, it would also be possible to devise some other system of representing both positive and negative numbers with the same 16-bit words.

The reason that one might say that the PDP-11 "uses" the two's complement system is that all instructions that are affected by algebraic sign or require negative numbers *assume* the two's complement representation. For example, as we saw in Chapter 5, a backwards branch of four words has an offset of 374, which is the 8-bit two's complement representation of −4. Also, any negative result will be automatically represented in the two's complement system. For example, when the instructions

```
CLR     R1
DEC     R1
```

are executed, we would expect to find in R1 the octal number 177777, which is −1. There are many other examples of this. Consider the immediate addressing example below.

```
MOV     # − 14,R3
```

After execution of this we would find 177764 in R3, which is -14_8 in 16-bit two's complement representation.

The PDP-11 has a special instruction for creating the two's complement for a number. Naturally, this instruction has the mnemonic NEG. For example,

```
MOV     #14,R1
NEG     R1
```

will place 177764 in R1. This is a single-operand instruction with the operation code 0054DD, where DD is the operand address code. The operand can of course use any of the addressing modes, e.g., register or relative.

When we take up the subject of signed branch instructions in a later section of this chapter, we will see another important implication of the two's complement system on the PDP-11. That is, a set of branching instructions is included especially for two's complement numbers.

6.4 Condition Codes and the Processor Status Word

In our earlier discussion of branching instructions, we used the loosely defined concept of "setting a condition" for a branch. (See Section 5.2.) We shall now refine this understanding by examining the mechanism whereby the machine establishes and retains these conditions.

The outcome of an instruction execution can be described in terms of four "condition codes," designated N, Z, V, and C. These codes are stored in four bits in a special register called the **Processor Status Word.** The approximate meanings of these codes, clarified in the discussion to follow, are

N: Negative condition code, which is set to 1 if the previous result was less than 0.

Z: Zero condition code, which is set to 1 if the previous result was 0.

V: OVerflow condition code, which is set to 1 if the previous result exceeded the valid range of 16-bit two's complement numbers.

C: Carry condition code, which indicates whether or not the previous operation caused a carry out of or a borrow into the MSB. Set to 1 if a previous operation *caused* a carry or a borrow.

It is important to remember that *many* instructions cause the condition codes to be set or cleared. We will develop the more important situations below. Table A.1 can be consulted to see exactly how any particular instruction will affect these codes.

The importance of the condition codes is that they allow the programmer to take appropriate action when a particular condition arises. We have already seen this with the unsigned conditional branch instructions, which are affected by the outcome of previous instructions, e.g., SUB or CMP. Here we merely point out that information about the outcome of previous operations is represented in terms of the four condition codes. We shall see that the condition codes have many other important uses, including guarding against invalid results.

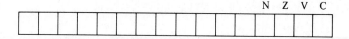

Figure 6.3   Processor status word.

Because the condition codes are *set* or *cleared* during execution of one instruction and must be *examined* in execution of a subsequent instruction, their values must be temporarily stored. This is done in the PSW. The PSW is a 16-bit register, but we are concerned here only with the four least significant bits that contain the current values of N, Z, V, and C. This is shown in Fig. 6.3.

The sections that follow show several important usages of the information represented by the condition codes in the PSW.

6.5 Using the C Condition Code to Detect Unsigned Overflow

Earlier discussion pointed out that if we use the entire 16-bit word length to represent only positive (i.e., unsigned) numbers, the maximum possible value is $2^{16} - 1 = 65535_{10}$. It was also mentioned that it is entirely possible to perform an arithmetic operation that would produce a larger result, in which case the machine-produced result is in error. Unless the program is written to detect this error and to take appropriate action, however, the computer will simply proceed, using the incorrect value. The C condition code provides a means of detecting this error.

To see how the carry condition code (sometimes called the carry bit) can help us, consider the following four examples, each of which operates on 16-bit *positive integers*.

Addition

```
    1 111 111 111 111 111              (65535)
  + 0 000 000 000 000 001            + (   +1)
  1 ← 0 000 000 000 000 000   (Error)   (    0)
```

Subtraction (by two's complement and add)

```
    0 000 000 000 000 010              (    2)
    1 111 111 111 111 100            + (   -4)
    1 111 111 111 111 110   (Error)   (65534)
```

Addition

```
    1 111 111 111 111 110              (65534)
  +                     1            + (   +1)
    1 111 111 111 111 111   (Correct)  (65535)
```

Subtraction (by two's complement and add)

$$
\begin{array}{ll}
\quad 0\ 000\ 000\ 000\ 000\ 100 & \qquad (\quad 4) \\
\quad \underline{1\ 111\ 111\ 111\ 111\ 110} & \qquad \underline{+(-2)} \\
1 \leftarrow 0\ 000\ 000\ 000\ 000\ 010 \quad \text{(Correct)} & \qquad (\quad 2)
\end{array}
$$

A study of these examples reveals that erroneous results are produced whenever the maximum values would be exceeded. In the addition problems, we see that an error is accompanied by a carry out of the MSB, while a correct result does not generate such a carry. In subtraction, on the other hand, a *correct result* of a two's complement addition generates a carry from the MSB, and an error does not generate such a carry.

The PDP-11 is designed to take advantage of these properties; it does so by the way the C condition code is set by addition and subtraction operations. Specifically, we have

After ADD instructions
$\quad$ C = 0 $\quad$ if there was not a carry from MSB.
$\quad$ C = 1 $\quad$ if there was a carry from MSB.

After SUB, or CMP instructions
$\quad$ C = 1 $\quad$ if there *was not* a carry from MSB.
$\quad$ C = 0 $\quad$ if there *was* a carry from MSB.

Thus we see that for 16-bit *unsigned* numbers C = 0 indicates a valid result while C = 1 indicates an invalid result. (Later we shall see, however, that this conclusion is not warranted for two's complement numbers.)

The programmer can use this property and the **Branch on Carry Set (BCS)** instruction to take corrective action as shown below.

```
ADD     X,Y
BCS     ERROR
```

Here ERROR is the label of an instruction that initiates the appropriate corrective action. For example, one may wish to simply halt execution at ERROR. The BCS instruction examines the C condition code and branches if it is *set*, i.e., if it is 1. The same instruction would detect an unsigned overflow error after any instruction that affects the C condition code.

Again we caution that the C condition code, used as shown here, is a valid test only for unsigned numbers. Error checking for signed numbers is discussed below.

6.6 Using the V Condition Code to Detect Signed Overflow

If the results of arithmetic operations are to be viewed as two's complement numbers, the C condition code is not a valid test for an overflow. This is because bit 15 (i.e., the MSB) is, in a sense, reserved for the sign in the two's complement system, and any carries that change it create errors. The C condition code would not reflect this. The V condition code is therefore provided to allow checking for this kind of overflow.

The V condition code is based on the fact that a carry from bit 14 to bit 15 (without a compensating carry out of bit 15) produces a result with an obviously incorrect sign bit. For example, addition of two positive numbers should yield a positive result. Yet, if we add 1 to the largest allowable positive 16-bit *two's complement number* we get

$$
\begin{array}{ll}
0\ 111\ 111\ 111\ 111\ 111 & (32767\ ) \\
\underline{+0\ 000\ 000\ 000\ 000\ 001} & \underline{+(+1\ )} \\
1\ 000\ 000\ 000\ 000\ 000\ \text{(Error)} & (-32768_{10})
\end{array}
$$

Because both operands were positive, the sign bit of 1 is a clear indication of an erroneous result due to overflow. Similarly, adding two negative numbers should give a negative result. However, when we add -1 to -32768_{10} we get

$$
\begin{array}{ll}
1\ 000\ 000\ 000\ 000\ 000 & (-32768\ ) \\
\underline{+1\ 111\ 111\ 111\ 111\ 111} & \underline{|\ (-1\ )} \\
1\leftarrow0\ 111\ 111\ 111\ 111\ 111\ \text{(Error)} & (32767_{10})
\end{array}
$$

The positive result is obviously in error. Moreover, if there is a carry out of the MSB without a compensating carry into it, the result is in error.

In addition to the observations above, it should also be apparent that if the operands are of opposite signs, no overflow error can occur as a result of *addition*. You should be able to demonstrate this to yourself.

Because the V condition code is designed to reflect two's complement overflow, it is set or cleared after **addition** according to the following rule.

V = 1   if both operands are of the same sign and the result is of the opposite sign.

V = 0   otherwise, i.e., operands of opposite signs, or both have the same sign as result.

Thus we see that the V = 1 is a reliable indicator of two's complement overflow in addition.

The rules whereby the PDP-11 determines if two's complement overflow has occurred in *subtraction* are slightly more complex. Once again, these rules are based on what sign the result has in relation to the operands. To explain these rules, we shall use the notation S to represent the subtrahend and M to represent the minuend. Note that with the SUB instruction, the first operand is S and the second M, while with CMP the two are reversed.

There are only four possibilities for the signs of the operands.

1. Subtrahend and minuend positive, designated here (S^+, M^+).
2. Subtrahend and minuend negative (S^-, M^-).
3. Subtrahend negative and minuend positive (S^-, M^+).
4. Subtrahend positive and minuend negative (S^+, M^-).

In cases 1 and 2, no error is possible because a result smaller than either operand *must* result. In case 3, the result should be positive; if the result is negative (i.e., has same sign as S), it is in error. In case 4, the result should be negative; if the result is positive (i.e., has same sign as S), it is in error. Observe from the preceding analysis that an error is indicated whenever S and M are of *opposite* signs and the result is the *same sign as* S. In all other situations, the result is correct. Thus we have the following rules which the PDP-11 applies in determining V when SUB or CMP is executed.

V = 1   if subtrahend and minuend are of opposite sign *and* the result is of the same sign as the subtrahend.

V = 0   otherwise.

It will be observed that, as with addition, V = 1 is therefore an indication of a two's complement overflow during subtraction.

    When the addition and subtraction effects on V are compared, it is found that for *either* operation V = 1 is a reliable indicator of overflow in two's complement arithmetic. Thus the instruction

    BVS   ERROR

will "trap" a two's complement overflow after any instruction. Here ERROR is the label for the first statement in an error-handling sequence of instructions. The instruction BVS means **B**ranch on **OV**erflow **S**et. Thus it branches to ERROR only if V is 1.

6.7 Using N and Z Condition Codes to Detect Negative and Zero

Of the four condition codes, N and Z are the easiest to understand and use. The N condition code is set by any operation that produces a negative result. The machine simply examines the MSB of the result and sets N to 1 if it is 1. It will be observed from Table 6.1 that a zero result will not cause N to be set to 1.

    The Z condition code is set to 1 by any operation that produces a zero result and cleared by any nonzero result. The machine will examine all 16 bits of the result and, if they are all zero, it sets Z to 1.

    There are four branch instructions that use only the N or Z condition codes. These are

    BEQ   Branches if Z = 1.
    BNE   Branches if Z = 0.
    BMI   Branches if N = 1.
    BPL   Branches if N = 0.

Usage of BEQ and BNE is straightforward and unaffected by the representation of the data. This is because zero is the same bit pattern regardless of whether the data are represented as positive integers or as two's complement numbers.

Typical usage would be

```
TST    (R1)
BEQ    L1
```

where a branch to label L1 will take place if the location pointed at by the address in R1 contains zero.

The instructions BPL and BMI should be used with great caution. First observe that they have no recommended usage when working with 16-bit positive integers. This is because any result greater than 32767_{10} will have a 1 in the MSB, causing the N condition code to be set and BMI to branch. Usage with two's complement numbers is also hazardous. For example the instructions

```
CMP    M,S
BPL    L2
```

where M and S are two's complement numbers will *not* branch if

$$M = 077777_8 \quad (32767_{10})$$

and

$$S = 177776_8 \quad (-2_{10}).$$

This is because the subtraction causes an overflow from bit 14 to the MSB, producing an (erroneous) negative result. This could be handled by checking for overflow (using BVC or BVS) before the BPL. In Section 6.9, however, we will see that the *signed branch instructions* deal with overflow properly. The BPL and BMI instructions will be found to have utility in certain advanced programming situations. (See, for example, Section 8.8.2.)

6.8 Signed Conditional Branch Instructions

With the preceding understandings of the two's complement number system, and the condition codes, we are in a position to deal with the signed branch instructions. These are BGE, BLT, BGT, and BLE. Simply stated, these branch instructions are intended to be used only with two's complement numbers, whereas the previously discussed (Chapter 5) unsigned branch instructions BHIS, BLO, BHI, and BLOS should be used only with 16-bit positive integers.

The need for different branch instructions for two's complement numbers can best be seen in terms of diagrams of the real line. Figure 6.4(a) shows the real line for the positive integers that can be represented with 16-bit, positional binary notation, and Fig. 6.4(b) shows the real line for the 16-bit two's complement system. Let us choose the two numbers,

$$M = 177776_8$$

and

$$S = 077777_8,$$

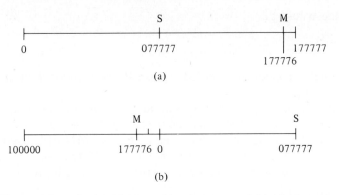

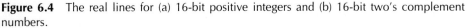

(b)

Figure 6.4 The real lines for (a) 16-bit positive integers and (b) 16-bit two's complement numbers.

and show them on both of these diagrams. It is seen that, when viewed as positive integers, M is greater than S, whereas the opposite is true if they are viewed as two's complement numbers.

If the programmer wishes to view the values of M and S as positive integers, the instructions

```
CMP     M,S
BHI     OUT
```

can be relied upon to branch to OUT if and only if M lies to the right of S in Fig. 6.4(a). However, if M and S are to be viewed as two's complement numbers, these instructions *do not* guarantee a branch to OUT when M is algebraically greater than S. Indeed, the example in Fig. 6.4(b) clearly shows that M = 177776 is *less* than S = 077777, yet the instructions above will cause the branch to occur. If M and S are to be two's complement numbers and we wish a branch to OUT if and only if M > S, we should write instead

```
CMP     M,S
BGT     OUT
```

The CMP instruction performs exactly the same operation, regardless of the programmer's view of the representation of the operands. However, the BGT instruction will properly assess the two's complement comparison and branch to OUT if M is *algebraically* larger than S. We shall see below that BGT and the other signed branch instructions do this by examining the N, V, and Z condition codes in the PSW. From a programming perspective, it is often sufficient to note that the preceding branch occurs whenever M lies to the right of S in Fig. 6.4(b).

To see how the signed branch instructions use the information in the PSW, let us begin with the BLT instruction. We have already seen that subtraction (CMP or SUB) sets the V code whenever overflow occurs in a two's complement sense. This condition code can therefore be used to decide when to branch. This may be seen in Fig. 6.5, where we show the ten possible relationships between two nonzero operands of a subtraction-type instruction (CMP or SUB). From study of the figure from a purely algebraic point of view, it is seen that cases (c), (d), (g), and (h) should branch upon execution of

```
CMP      M,S
BLT      L1
```

That is, M is to the left of (algebraically less than) S in each of these cases, and one would hope that the computer would be able to recognize this. Indeed it can, and it does so by examination of the N and V condition codes. The condition codes that would result from subtraction of S from M in each case of Fig. 6.5 are shown in Table 6.3. (The determination of these condition codes using rules established in Sections 6.5, 6.6, and 6.7 is left as an exercise.) It will be observed

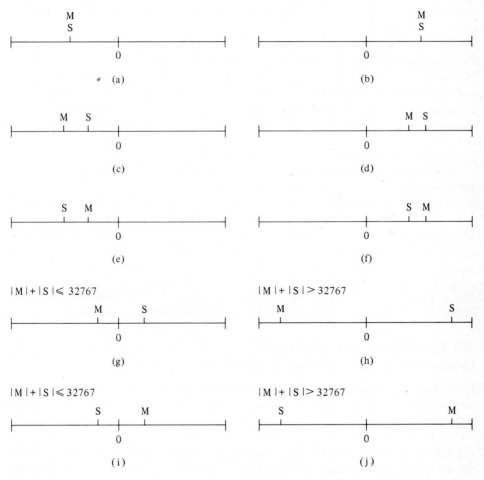

Figure 6.5   Ten cases of subtraction of two's complement numbers. (M = minuend, S = subtrahend.)

TABLE 6.3
Evaluation of Signed Branch Instructions in
Terms of Condition Codes (Cases defined in Fig. 6.5)

Case	Condition Codes		
	NZVC	N∀V	Z∨(N∀V)
(a)	0 1 0 0	0	1
(b)	0 1 0 0	0	1
(c)	1 0 0 1	1	1
(d)	1 0 0 1	1	1
(e)	0 0 0 0	0	0
(f)	0 0 0 0	0	0
(g)	1 0 0 0	1	1
(h)	0 0 1 0	1	1
(i)	0 0 0 1	0	0
(j)	1 0 1 1	0	0

that the four cases in which M < S are unique in having the "exclusive or" of N and V, i.e., N∀V, equal to 1. ("Exclusive or" means that one or the other is 1 but not both.) Thus N∀V = 1 is a reliable indication of whether or not M is indeed less than S. It is therefore the quantity that the PDP-11 has been designed to check upon execution of BLT. Conversely, examination of Table 6.3 reveals that N alone is not sufficient; it would branch incorrectly for case (j), and would not branch for case (h) as it should.

Because BGE is the logical complement of BLT, N∀V also provides a basis for its decision. That is, BGE branches if N∀V = 0.

The BLE conditional branch instruction is analogous to BLT, except that it must also branch if the result of the subtraction is 0. Thus the condition to be checked is Z∨(N∀V) that will be true (i.e., 1) if N∀V is 1 or Z is 1. Examination of Fig. 6.4 and Table 6.3 reveals that BLE will branch for cases (a) and (b) as well as for all those cases for which BLT will branch. The logical complement of BLE is BGT. Therefore BGT will branch only under those conditions for which BLE will not branch, that is, BGT branches when Z∨(N∀V) = 0.

6.9 Condition Codes and the Unsigned Conditional Branch Instructions

In Section 5.2 we discussed a number of branching instructions intended for use with unsigned integers. There we described their operation from a strictly algebraic point of view. We now wish to show that these branch instructions in fact depend on the condition codes Z and C for their operation.

Let us examine first the BLO instruction that is supposed to branch when the minuend is less than the subtrahend with both treated as 16-bit positive integers. Figure 6.6 shows all possible relationships between two positive integers.

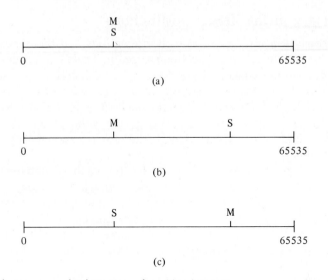

Figure 6.6   Three cases of subtraction of positive integers.

It is apparent from the figure that only in case (b) should BLO branch after CMP M,S. Table 6.4 shows the corresponding Z and C condition codes, where it will be observed that case (b) is the only case where C = 1. It is for this reason that C = 1 is the condition the PDP-11 checks for the BLO instruction. In fact, the machine code translation for the BLO instruction is exactly the same as for the BCS instruction.

Because M ≥ S is the logical complement of M < S, the BHIS instruction also examines C and branches if C = 0. It has the same machine code as BCC.

The instruction BLOS will branch if the minuend is less than or equal to the subtrahend. Thus the check is based on C∨Z = 1. As may be seen in Table 6.4, this occurs for cases (a) and (b). Note that BLOS is the unsigned equivalent of BLE.

The instruction BHI is the logical complement of BLOS. Therefore this instruction causes a branch if C∨Z = 0.

TABLE 6.4
Evaluation of Unsigned Branch
Instructions in Terms of Condition Codes

Case	Z	C	C∨Z
(a)	1	0	1
(b)	0	1	1
(c)	0	0	0

6.10 Summary of the Branch Instructions

We have discussed a number of branch instructions and their intended usage. All of these branch instructions are summarized in Table 6.5, grouped according to their most common usage. Those listed under General Usage can be safely used for any kind of data, i.e., positive integers or two's complement integers. All other branch instructions have recommended usage for either positive integers (unsigned) or two's complement integers (signed). Although an experienced programmer may find other valid usages, the novice should adhere to these recommendations.

Table 6.5 also provides the base codes for each branch instruction. As explained in Section 5.3, the translation of any branch is obtained by adding the base code to the PC offset (measured in words, not bytes) necessary to reach the target label. We take this opportunity to remind you that this offset is limited to 177_8 forward or 200_8 backward. Branches to more distant points can be achieved by inverting the logic and branching over a JMP instruction. For example, to

TABLE 6.5
Branch Instructions

Instruction and Usage	Assembly Mnemonic		Base Code	Branch Condition
General Usage				
Unconditional **BR**anch	BR	L	000400	Unconditional
Branch if **EQ**ual	BEQ	L	001400	$Z = 1$
Branch **N**ot **E**qual	BNE	L	001000	$Z = 0$
Unsigned Branch Instructions				
Branch if **HI**gher	BHI	L	101000	$C \vee Z = 0$
Branch if **LO**wer	BLO	L	103400	$C = 1$
Branch if **HI**gher or **S**ame	BHIS	L	103000	$C = 0$
Branch if **LO**wer or **S**ame	BLOS	L	101400	$C \vee Z = 1$
Unsigned Overflow Checking				
Branch on **C**arry **S**et	BCS	L	103400	$C = 1$
Branch on **C**arry **C**lear	BCC	L	103000	$C = 0$
Signed Branch Instructions				
Branch if **G**reater **T**han	BGT	- L	003000	$Z \vee (N \forall V) = 0$
Branch if **L**ess **T**han	BLT	L	002400	$N \forall V = 1$
Branch if **G**reater than or **E**qual to	BGE	L	002000	$N \forall V = 0$
Branch if **L**ess than or **E**qual to	BLE	L	003400	$Z \vee (N \forall V) = 1$
Signed Overflow Checking				
Branch if **O**verflow **S**et	BVS	L	102400	$V = 1$
Branch if **O**verflow **C**lear	BVC	L	102000	$V = 0$
Sign Checking				
Branch if **PL**us	BPL	L	100000	$N = 0$
Branch if **MI**nus	BMI	L	100400	$N = 1$

jump to a distant label A when R0 is higher than R1, we could code

```
        CMP  R0,R1
        BLOS SKIP
        JMP  A
SKIP:
```

The translation of a JMP is

000167
rel addr

where rel addr is the PC-relative address of the destination label.

6.11 Setting the Condition Codes

In the examples presented thus far, we have always placed an instruction specifically intended to set the condition codes immediately before the conditional branch. This practice leads the beginning programmer quickly to correct programs, but sometimes is unnecessary. In fact, practically all instructions will affect the condition codes, and it may well be that an instruction needed for some other reason will set the condition codes properly for the branch. For example, suppose we wish to move the contents of A into R2 and branch to L2 if the transferred number was negative. We can write

```
MOV      A,R2
BLT      L2
```

without doing a specific TST R2. This is because MOV will clear V and set or clear N according to whether the number moved was negative or positive, and these condition codes are the only ones needed by BLT. A programmer who is concerned by program speed and size will examine the code with this in mind and remove unnecessary CMPs and TSTs. Consult Table A.1 to see exactly how every PDP-11 instruction affects, and is affected by, the condition codes.

Occasionally you will want to set or clear one or more condition codes *unconditionally*. You can do this by using one of the no-operand instructions given in Table 6.6. In the interest of efficiency, however, you should be sure that such an instruction is really required. Most often the conditions established by other instructions are adequate.

6.12 Shift and Rotate Instructions

An important property of positional binary representation is that a number is multiplied by 2 simply by shifting the bit pattern to the left and adding a 0 at the right. For example, 3_{10} is written in binary as

0 000 000 000 000 011

TABLE 6.6
Condition Code Set/Clear Instructions

Assembly Mnemonic	Operation Code	Effects on PSW†			
		N	Z	V	C
CLC	000241	–	–	–	0
CLV	000242	–	–	0	–
CLZ	000244	–	0	–	–
CLN	000250	0	–	–	–
CCC	000257	0	0	0	0
SEC	000261	–	–	–	1
SEV	000262	–	–	1	–
SEZ	000264	–	1	–	–
SEN	000270	1	–	–	–
SCC	000177	1	1	1	1

† In this table, – means unaffected.

If we shift the pattern to the left by one bit we get

0 000 000 000 000 110

which is 6_{10}. It should also be apparent that shifting one bit to the right will divide by 2.

These facts form the basis for many arithmetic algorithms on a binary machine. For this and other reasons to be developed later, most computers have shift instructions that accomplish the operation above. In MACRO-11 we have

ASL   D

for Arithmetic Shift Left, and

ASR   D

for Arithmetic Shift Right. These instructions can be used to multiply or divide by 2. Their operation is shown diagrammatically in Fig. 6.7. Observe that the carry bit in the PSW "catches" the bit that is displaced out of the word.

These instructions are called *arithmetic* shifts because of the way that they treat the leftmost and rightmost bits. Shifting with ASL automatically "zero fills" at the right, accomplishing the desired effect of multiplying by 2. The right shift, ASR, will automatically replicate the leftmost bit, thereby retaining the correct sign. For example, if the number is

1 101 101 111 110 000

an ASR will produce

1 110 110 111 111 000

This yields the correct result; we have divided a negative number by 2 and have obtained a negative result. If the leftmost bit was a 0, i.e., a positive number, ASR would add 0's at the left to produce a positive number half as large. We call attention to the fact that shifting too far to the left produces an overflow, as should be expected. For example, suppose we have the positive number

0 100 000 000 000 000

that is 16384_{10}. ASL would produce

1 000 000 000 000 000

that is -32768_{10}. This erroneous result developed because

$$2 \times 16384_{10} = 32768_{10}$$

that is 1 larger than the maximum allowable 16-bit two's complement number. In this event the V condition code would be set, indicating an overflow. Similarly, if we have the large negative number in R1

1 000 000 000 000 001

and ASL R1 is executed, we get the erroneous result

0 000 000 000 000 010

Again, this operation would cause V to be set.

Although the ASL and ASR instructions are designed to work with 16-bit two's complement numbers, ASL also works well with 16-bit unsigned integers. When this is the case, the C bit can be used to detect an overflow, as can be seen in Fig. 6.7(a). Using ASR with unsigned integers is not recommended

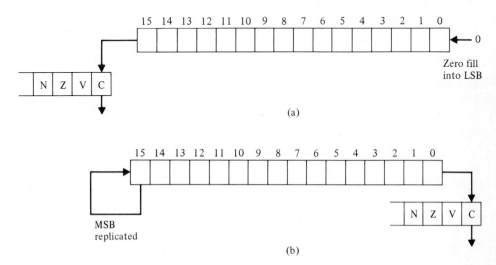

Figure 6.7   Operation of the (a) ASL and (b) ASR instructions.

because any such number greater than 32767_{10} will result in an error in the shifted result. This is caused by the replication of the MSB.

When an odd number is divided by 2, a fractional part results. In a system that does not retain fractional parts, i.e., two's complement or positive integers, we must examine what happens. Consider first the positive 16-bit two's complement number

0 000 000 000 000 011

that is 3_{10}. An ASR will produce

0 000 000 000 000 001

that is 1_{10}. Now consider -3_{10}, that is

1 111 111 111 111 101

An ASR produces

1 111 111 111 111 110

that is -2_{10}. These results can best be explained in terms of the real line. As shown below, the result is truncated to the integer *at its left*.

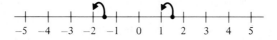

Thus we see that the ASR produces the largest integer that is less than or equal to the original number divided by 2. In mathematics this would be called the "floor function." Many readers will recognize this as being similar to the INT function in BASIC or FORTRAN.

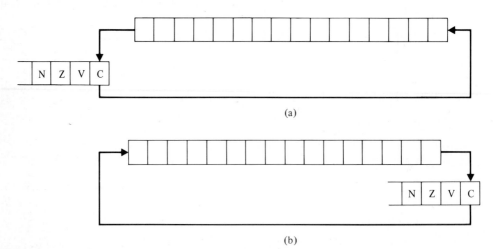

(a)

(b)

Figure 6.8 Operation of the (a) ROL and (b) ROR instructions.

MACRO-11 has two other instructions that can be used to shift bit patterns. These are ROL (*RO*tate *L*eft) and ROR (*RO*tate *R*ight). The difference between these and the ASL and ASR instructions can be seen by comparing Figs. 6.7 and 6.8. The ROL and ROR instructions rotate the C-bit back into the word instead of discarding it. Note that 17_{10} successive RORs *or* 17_{10} successive ROLs leave the operand unchanged. These instructions find use in multiple-precision arithmetic as discussed below.

6.13 Double-precision Representation

There are many problems in which the magnitude of the numbers involved exceeds the capacity of a single 16-bit word. One way to overcome this limitation is to simply use more than one word to store the values. For example, if we wish to store 15632457613_8, we can use two successive words

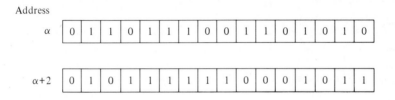

Here we have placed the binary codes for the least significant octal digits beginning in the second word $\alpha + 2$ and continuing into the preceding word. With this arrangement we can store 32-bit two's complement integers, allowing a "dynamic range" of

20000000000_8 (-2147483648_{10})

to

17777777777_8 $(+2147483647_{10})$.

This is called *double precision*. Although this concept can be extended to use more than two words (multiple precision), we will focus on double precision in this discussion. In practice, use of still larger numbers would probably be through the use of the *floating-point* representation to be discussed in Chapter 13.

Because the PDP-11 arithmetic instructions work on 16-bit numbers, special programming is required to perform 32-bit operations. This is accomplished by performing the operations on the high and low words separately, accounting for carries or borrows across the word boundary. We will demonstrate this by showing how to add two double-precision numbers. For convenience, we will use 3-bit words because the concept is the same regardless of the word length.

Consider the addition for A = 13_{10} to B = 14_{10} with each stored in two 3-bit words. We can represent this diagrammatically as follows.

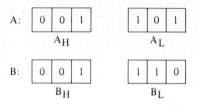

Here we use A_H and B_H to represent the words used to store the high-order bits of each number, and A_L and B_L for the words in which their low-order bits are stored. Now observe that the addition of A_L to B_L yields a 3-bit result and a carry.

B_L: 110
A_L: $+\underline{101}$
B_L: $1 \leftarrow 011$

Clearly the carry bit must be added to B_H:

B_H: 001
Carry: $+\underline{001}$
B_H: 010

To complete the operation, we add A_H to B_H.

B_H: 010
A_H: $+\underline{001}$
B_H: 011

The final result is

that, when viewed as a 6-bit number, is 27_{10}.

These operations can be implemented in MACRO-11 by use of the C condition code and the **AD**d Carry (ADC) instruction.

It will be recalled that C is set after addition if there was a carry out of the 16th bit. Otherwise it is cleared. The carry bit can be *added* to an operand by use of ADC. The operations above are then implemented as

```
ADD    AL,BL      ; ADD LOW WORDS
ADC    BH         ; ADD CARRY TO HIGH WORD
ADD    AH,BH      ; ADD HIGH WORDS
```

This, of course, assumes that the high and low 16-bit segments of A and B were previously stored in locations labeled AH, AL, BH, and BL.

Double-precision subtraction can be done similarly. To subtract B from A, we first subtract B_L from A_L. If a borrow was required from the A_H word, a

1 must be *subtracted* from A$_H$ to reflect this fact. The C condition code will be set if such a borrow occurred, so this can be accomplished by use of the SuBtract Carry instruction, SBC. The double-precision subtraction is then accomplished by

```
SUB  BL,AL
SBC  AH
SUB  BH,AH
```

The result is then found in the two successive words, AH and AL. The double-precision subtraction algorithm depends on the fact that the C condition code (the carry bit) is set if there was a borrow *into* the MSB. In Section 6.7 it was explained that C was set if there was *not* a carry *out of* the MSB. We now point out that these are merely two different ways of saying the same thing. That is, subtraction can be viewed either as negating the subtrahend and adding, or as actual binary subtraction. From the first point of view, subtracting a larger number from a smaller one generates a *carry out of* the MSB. From the second point of view a *borrow into* the MSB is required. This is seen in the following example, using a 3-bit word for convenience.

Negate and add

```
101    (Subtrahend)
011    (Two's complement of subtrahend)
100    (Minuend)
111    (Difference)
```

(No carry generated out of 3rd bit, so C = 1.)

Binary subtraction

$$1 \rightarrow \quad 100 \quad \text{(Minuend)}$$
$$- \underline{101} \quad \text{(Subtrahend)}$$
$$111$$

(A borrow was required into the 3rd bit, so C = 1.)

This observation leads some to call C the "borrow" bit in subtraction. However, we choose to call it the carry bit or the C condition code in any context. Regardless of terminology or points of view, the C bit is properly set in addition or subtraction so that the instructions above for double-precision addition and subtraction work.

Double-precision negation can best be explained as complementing A$_H$, negating A$_L$, and somehow allowing the possible carry out of the A$_L$ negation to propagate into A$_H$. This suggests the sequence

```
COM      AH
NEG      AL
add 1 to AH if negation caused carry
```

The problem, however, is that the C condition code is *cleared* rather than set because of a carry that is caused by a NEG operation, as in subtraction. Therefore, to accomplish the desired effect, we *add 1* to A$_H$ beforehand, and then *subtract* the C condition code. This suggests the following instructions.

```
COM     AH
INC     AH
NEG     AL
SBC     AH
```

However, noting that complementing and incrementing is simply negation, we finally arrive at

```
NEG     AH
NEG     AL
SBC     AH
```

for double-precision negation. Note that the *order* of these instructions is very important. Carrying out these operations by hand with a few double-precision numbers will show more clearly how they work.

6.14 Multiplication and Division

Multiplication and division are significantly different from addition and subtraction. Indeed, many small computers, including some smaller PDP-11 machines, do not have instructions for these operations. If this is the case, the programmer must carry out multiplication and division by use of the more primitive addition and subtraction instructions. This is called "software" multiply and divide. If your PDP-11 is a larger machine, it is probably equipped with the Extended Instruction Set (EIS), in which case it will support the multiply and divide (MUL and DIV) instructions. These are called "hardware" multiply and divide because these extra instructions are provided through the use of special additional circuits.

In the paragraphs below, we will discuss both software and hardware multiply and divide. The former is instructive even if MUL and DIV are available on your machine. However, if the hardware instructions are available, they are usually preferable.

6.14.1 Multiplication

Software multiplication can best be explained in terms of a simple example. Suppose we wish to multiply 3_{10} by 5_{10}. In binary, "longhand" multiplication takes the following form.

```
      0 1 1
  ×   1 0 1
      0 1 1
    0 0 0
  0 1 1
  0 1 1 1 1
```

Observe that each partial product is just the first multiplicand shifted to the left. Also note that whenever a zero-bit occurs in the second multiplicand, the partial product is zero and *need not* be added. This suggests the following algorithm.

1. Clear the result register.
2. Shift the *second* multiplicand to the right.
3. If the bit shifted out at the right was a 1, add the first multiplicand to the result.
4. Shift the first multiplicand to the left.
5. If the second multiplicand is not 0, repeat from step 2.

This algorithm is expressed as a MACRO-11 program in Fig. 6.9. Observe that the algorithm works only for 16-bit positive integers. We should add instructions to branch to an appropriate error action if overflow occurs in the multiplication process. This program could be placed in a larger program where multiplication is required. In a later chapter we will see that it could also be written as a subroutine for more convenient usage.

If your machine has the Extended Instruction Set it will allow use of the multiply instruction MUL. This instruction has two operands, the first of which can use any addressing mode. The second operand, however, *must be a register*. For example,

    MUL   S,R3

will multiply the contents of the memory location reserved for S by the contents of R3, placing the result into R3. The only complexity involved in using MUL is caused by the fact that the result may exceed 16 bits; we saw this above when we obtained a 5-bit product by multiplying two 3-bit numbers. It is for this reason that MUL is designed to produce optionally a 32-bit result. When the 32-bit result is desired, the programmer must use an even register (R0, R2, R4) for the destination operand. The result will then be placed in the indicated register *and the next one*. The high-order bits are placed in the even register, and the low-order bits are placed in the following odd register. If only a 16-bit result is needed, an odd register (R1, R3, R5) must be used.

```
            .TITLE MULTIPLY
        ;
        ;   MULTIPLICATION USING SHIFTING
        ;   INPUT:
        ;           R1 =FIRST MULTIPLICAND
        ;           R2 =SECOND MULTIPLICAND
        ;   OUTPUT:
        ;           R0 =PRODUCT
        ;
START:  CLR     R0              ;CLEAR RESULT REG & CARRY BIT
LOOP:   ROR     R2              ;SHIFT RIGHT AND CHECK
        BCC     L1              ;    SHIFT OUT BIT.
        ADD     R1,R0           ;ADD  R1 IF LSB=1
L1:     ASL     R1              ;SHIFT R1
        TST     R2              ;CLEAR CARRY AND REPEAT IF
        BNE     LOOP            ;    ANY MORE R2 BITS.
        HALT
        .BLKW   20
        .END START
```

Figure 6.9 Software multiplication using shifting.

An example will clarify this. Suppose we wish to multiply 16_8 by 2_8. Because the result is clearly small enough to fit in 16-bits, we use an odd register.

```
MOV    #16,R3
MUL    #2,R3
```

The result in R3 is

0 000 000 000 011 100

On the other hand, if we wish to multiply 077775_8 by 4_8, which will produce a result with more than 16 bits, we must use an even register.

```
MOV    #77775,R2
MUL    #4,R2
```

to get the result

```
R2:    0 000 000 000 000 001    (High-order word)
R3:    1 111 111 111 110 100    (Low-order word)
```

The reader should carry out this multiplication to see that the binary result is the concatenation of these two words. Of course, special programming must be done to use this 32-bit result. This was discussed above. (See Section 6.13.)

The translation of the MUL instruction is

070RSS

where 070 is the opcode, R is the *register* of the destination operand (i.e., 0, 1, . . . , 5) and SS is the address code of the source operand. The latter can be any mode, i.e., register, register deferred, or immediate. Thus the translation of the first example above is

```
012703    MOV #16,R3
000016
070327    MUL #2,R3
000002
```

Attention is called to the fact that the register comes *before* the source operand in the machine code, which is the opposite of the assembly language mnemonics.

Note that the V bit is always cleared by the MUL instruction. This is because a two-word result cannot overflow. The C bit is set if the result is less than -2^{15} or greater than or equal to 2^{15}. Therefore the C bit can be used to check if the result is too large for a 15-bit result.

6.14.2 Division

Like multiplication, division can be done either with hardware (if the Extended Instruction Set is available) or by means of an algorithm using more fundamental instructions. We will first examine division algorithms and second, the DIV instruction provided by the EIS.

Division algorithms vary in complexity and efficiency. The simplest algorithm, namely, repeated subtraction of the divisor from the dividend, is also the least efficient. Because of its simplicity, we will look at it first. To see how it works, consider the division of 27_{10} by 5_{10}. The quotient can be viewed as the number of times that 5_{10} can be subtracted from 27_{10} *without* a negative result. Performing the operations in binary, we have

Number of times subtracted

```
                    11011
                 -   101      1
                    10110
                 -   101      2
                    10001
                 -   101      3
                    01100
                 -   101      4
                    00111
                 -   101      5 = quotient
Remainder           00010
                 -   101      6
Negative result     11001
```

By this process we get the answer as 5_{10} with a remainder of 2_{10}. A MACRO-11 program employing this method is shown in Fig. 6.10. We have simplified the program by assuming that the dividend and divisors are positive integers. This limitation can be removed by checking R1 and R2 prior to the division. A more fundamental shortcoming of the successive subtraction method is its inefficiency for large dividend and small divisor. In this case, the number of subtractions can be quite large. Consider, for example, division of 65535_{10} by 1_{10} using this algorithm.

```
            .TITLE DIVISION ONE
        ;
        ;
        ;       DIVISION BY SUCCESSIVE SUBTRACTION
        ;
        ;           DIVIDEND  = R1   (POSITIVE)
        ;           DIVISOR   = R2   (POSITIVE)
        ;           QUOTIENT  = R0
        ;           REMAINDER = R1
        ;
START:      CLR     R0               ;INITIALIZE QUOTIENT
            BR      WHILE            ;USE LEADING DECISIONS
LOOP:       SUB     R2,R1            ;SUBTRACT DIVISOR
            INC     R0               ;AND INCREMENT QUOTIENT
WHILE:      TST     R1               ;LOOP WHILE REMAINDER
            BGE     LOOP             ;   IS POSITIVE
            ADD     R2,R1            ;CORRECT FOR
            DEC     R0               ;   OVERSUBTRACTION
            HALT
            .END    START
```

Figure 6.10   Division of positive integers using successive subtraction.

A much more efficient division algorithm can be developed using the shift instructions. One frequently used algorithm is similar to "longhand" division used in decimal arithmetic. To see how this works, consider division of 27_{10} by 5_{10}, carried out in binary in a manner similar to the familiar decimal division technique.

$$\begin{array}{r} 00101 \\ 101\overline{)11011} \\ \underline{101} \\ 00111 \\ \underline{00101} \\ \end{array}$$

Remainder $\qquad 00010$

Study of this technique shows that we determine if the divisor can be subtracted from the MSB. If it cannot be subtracted, we place a 0 in the quotient at the corresponding bit position, and then consider the *two* most significant bits. In the example, this continues until the divisor is compared to the three most significant bits of the dividend. Because 101 *can* be subtracted from 110, we place a 1 in the quotient and carry out the subtraction. The process then repeats until there are no further bits in the divisor. The remainder is the outcome of the last subtraction.

This can be implemented in MACRO-11 using shifting operations. The strategy is to use two words to hold the dividend. We choose R0 and R1, with the highest-order bits stored in R0. Thus R0 contains those bits from which we wish to subtract the divisor at each step.

After each subtraction or attempted subtraction, we execute a double-precision arithmetic shift, bringing the next MSB into R0.

The following example will clarify this method. We use a 6-bit word length for convenience, and the same dividend and divisor as before. The result is developed in R5. The results of successive left shifts and subtractions are shown below.

	R0	R1	R5
Initial:	000000	011011	000000
Shift:	000000	110110	000000
Shift:	000001	101100	000000
Shift:	000011	011000	000000
Shift:	000110	110000	000000
Subtract:	000001	110000	000001
Shift:	000011	100000	000010
Shift:	000111	000000	000100
Subtract:	000010	000000	000101

In this table, shift means that a double-precision shift is done on (R0,R1), *and* that R5 is shifted. After four shifts, we see that R0 is larger than the divisor R2, so we subtract R2 from R0 and increment R5. After two more shifts, R0 is again greater than R2 and we subtract R2 again, and again increment R5. The process stops after six shifts because this guarantees that all bits in the dividend have gone into R0. Note that shifting R5 each time (R0,R1) is shifted ensures that each new quotient bit, either 0 or 1, gets put in the correct position. It is evident from this example that the quotient (5_{10}) is left in R5, and the remainder resides in R1.

The procedure above is implemented in MACRO-11 in Fig. 6.11. We have added a preliminary check that will determine if the division would result in a value larger than could be represented as a 16-bit positive integer. If this occurs, the C condition code is set before halting; otherwise, it is cleared.

The program in Fig. 6.11 is restricted to positive integers whose quotient is less than or equal to $2^{16} - 1$. It can be modified to work on positive or negative two's complement numbers by performing a preliminary check on the signs of the inputs. One method would be to set an auxiliary register to 1 if either but not both of the operands are negative, then negate those operands that are negative. The division would then be carried out as positive integers, and the result negated if the auxiliary register is set. The overflow check should also be modified to reflect the smaller range of two's complement numbers, and a different overflow flag value selected. Normally, the V condition code is used for this purpose.

Before leaving this algorithm, let us consider an improvement that would not require use of R5. Observe from the earlier example that the low-order bits in R1 are 0 because of the shifting. In effect, the low-order positions in R1 are therefore unused as the solution progresses. This observation suggests that the quotient could be allowed to develop in R1. That is, we could increment R1

```
              .TITLE DIVISION TWO
        ;
        ;       INPUT:
        ;           (R0,R1)= HIGH AND LOW WORDS OF DIVIDEND (POSITIVE)
        ;           R2      = DIVISOR (POSITIVE)
        ;       INTERMEDIATE USAGE:
        ;           R0      = REMAINDER
        ;           R5      = QUOTIENT
        ;       OUTPUT:
        ;           R0      = QUOTIENT
        ;           R1      = REMAINDER
        ;
        START:  CMP     R2,R0           ;CHECK FOR POTENTIAL
                BLOS    OVERFL          ;   OVERFLOW OF RESULT
                MOV     #20,R3          ;INITIALIZE LCV (DEC 16)
        LOOP:   ASL     R5              ;SHIFT RESULT
                ASL     R1              ;DOUBLE PRECISION SHIFT
                ROL     R0              ;   OF DIVIDEND
                CMP     R0,R2           ;SEE IF DIVISOR CAN
                BLO     ENDLP           ;   BE SUBTRACTED
                SUB     R2,R0           ;SUBTRACT DIVISOR
                INC     R5              ;PUT 1-BIT IN QUOTIENT
        ENDLP:  SOB     R3,LOOP         ;LOOP IF MORE BITS
                MOV     R0,R1           ;PUT RESULTS IN
                MOV     R5,R0           ;   DESIGNATED REGISTERS
                CLC                     ;NORMAL EXIT
                HALT
        OVERFL: SEC                     ;C SET IF RESULT TOO BIG
                HALT
                .BLKW 20
                .END    START
```

Figure 6.11   Efficient software division using shifting.

instead of R5, and delete the ASL R5, saving one instruction and one register. In some instances, seemingly small improvements like this one may be important.

If the Extended Instruction Set is available, software division is not necessary. The hardware division instruction provided in this extension has the assembly language mnemonic of

DIV   S,Rn

where S is the divisor, and can be addressed in any mode. The second operand, Rn, *must be an even-numbered register*. The dividend is assumed to be in the indicated even register and *in the adjacent odd register*. For example if we write

DIV   R3,R0

it is assumed that the 32-bit dividend is in R0 and R1.

After the division, the 16-bit quotient is placed in R0, with the remainder in R1. Both operands can be two's complement representations; the sign of the quotient will be determined from the operands in the expected way. The remainder is given the sign of the quotient.

The format of the machine code for DIV is the same as for MUL. The 7-bit opcode is 071, with 3 bits for the register number and 6 bits for the source operand address code. As with MUL, the register field comes first, which is opposite of the mnemonic order. For example,

DIV   #4,R2

translates to

071227
000004

It is possible to have values of the dividend and divisor such that the quotient would exceed the range of 16-bit two's complement number. If this occurs, the V bit is set. The C bit is set if the divisor is 0. The N and Z bits are set according to whether the result is negative or 0 in the usual manner.

6.15 Summary

This chapter has dealt with numbers and operations on numbers in MACRO-11. First, we developed the concept of the *two's complement system* as a means of representing both positive and negative numbers. Although other systems are possible, the two's complement system is heavily favored by the PDP-11 instruction set. We saw that the two's complement system has several interesting properties, such as allowing a subtraction mechanism of taking the two's complement of (i.e., *negating*) the subtrahend and adding. It was shown that the real line in a two's complement system is "circular" in the sense that exceeding the allowed range of positive numbers produces negative values, and vice versa. Because one bit is used for the sign, the allowable range for two's complement numbers is less than for positive integers in the same word length.

Condition codes were introduced and related to arithmetic operations. These codes, N, Z, V, and C, are represented by the four least significant bits in the processor status word (PSW). We saw that each of these has its special uses in checking the outcome of instructions. In general, N is set when a negative result is produced, and Z is set if a zero result is produced. C and V serve several functions, but in general indicate unsigned overflow or signed overflow, respectively. A group of branching instructions, BVC, BVS, BCC, and BCS, is available for checking the C and V bits so that appropriate action can be taken if overflow occurs. We found that the condition codes provide a means for evaluating signed and unsigned branching conditions. We saw that the difference between two 16-bit numbers will have two different interpretations, depending on whether the numbers are viewed to be positive integers or two's complement integers. The PDP-11 therefore has a set of conditional branch instructions for unsigned comparisons (BHI, BLO, BHIS, and BLOS), and a different set for signed comparisons (BGT, BLT, BGE, and BLE). These instructions use one or more of the condition codes to determine whether or not to branch. It was also observed that condition codes are set or cleared by many instructions; a conditional branch will react according to the condition codes' current state, regardless of which instruction was responsible for establishing the state. In passing, we noted that the branch instructions have a limited transfer range, but they can be used in conjunction with the JMP instruction to transfer to more distant addresses.

In order to expand our arithmetic capability, we introduced several other new instructions. These include NEG, ROL, ASL, ROR, ASR, MUL, and DIV. NEG performs a two's complement operation on its operand, producing a value of equal magnitude but opposite sign. The shift instructions ROL (Rotate Left), ROR (Rotate Right) "circulate" the bits in a word (one position) to the left or right. It is important to remember that the C-bit (C condition code) is involved in this circulation. For example, in ROR the least significant bit moves into C and the contents of C rotates into the MSB of the word. Arithmetic shift left (ASL) and arithmetic shift right (ASR) also shift the bit pattern, but in such a way as to provide useful arithmetic operations. ASL adds 0 at the right, providing a convenient multiplication by 2. ASR replicates the MSB, providing a division by 2 while preserving the original algebraic sign. The shift instructions provide a means for efficient multiplication and division. The multiplication and division algorithms presented provide examples of these newly introduced instructions. However, many PDP-11 computers have "hardware multiply and divide" represented by the MUL and DIV instructions. These are more efficient and convenient if available.

The chapter also introduced the concept of double-precision representation. Here, two words are used, providing 32 bits to represent a single integer. This allows much larger values in a MACRO-11 program. We noted that special steps are required to perform addition, subtraction, and negation of double-precision numbers. This required treating the high and low words separately and accounting for carries or borrows across the word boundary with the add carry (ADC) or subtract carry (SBC) instructions.

6.16 Exercises ────────────────────────────────

6.1 Convert the following decimal numbers to 16-bit two's complement octal representation.

a) 14	**b)** -14	**c)** 6954
d) 30000	**e)** -28481	**f)** -195

6.2 Convert the following 16-bit two's complement octal numbers to decimal.

   a) 066666   **b)** 166666   **c)** 100432

   d) 000101   **e)** 177774   **f)** 077770

6.3 Perform the following arithmetic. All numbers are 16-bit two's complement, expressed in octal. Indicate if overflow has occurred, and whether result is positive or negative.

a)	133177	**b)**	177777	**c)**	177776	**d)**	000643
	+017774		+177777		−000002		−144401
e)	100101	**f)**	076432	**g)**	000001	**h)**	177777
	−077774		+023467		−177777		+000002

6.4 On a separate sheet of paper, create a table with the branch instructions BPL, BEQ, BHIS, BMI, BLT, BLO, BGT, BHI, BLE, and BLOS across the top and the letters a, b, c, . . . , j down the side. In each position of this table, indicate with an X if the branch will occur after a CMP A,B instruction for each pair of A and B given below. All values are octal.

	A	B
a)	017522	017522
b)	104311	104311
c)	177602	000176
d)	054272	001016
e)	177705	177613
f)	004640	017227
g)	105352	176051
h)	151547	031246
i)	177642	077640
j)	077640	100642

6.5 Determine the N, Z, V, and C condition codes after CMP A,B is performed for each of the pairs of A and B given in Exercise 6.4.

6.6 What is the contents of R0 after the following instructions?

```
MOV      # − 1,R0
ASR      R0
ASR      R0
ASR      R0
ROL      R0
```

6.7 Write a program to count the number of 1-bits (i.e., the number of bits that contain the digit 1) in a 16-bit number that is stored in R1. For example, the number 0101111001101011 has ten 1-bits. Execute the program using ODT and demonstrate that it works.

6.8 Revise the division algorithm given in Fig. 6.11 to work with positive or negative two's complement numbers for dividend and divisor. Execute the program using ODT, and verify that it works; show cases that cause overflow also.

6.9 Write a program that will sort an array of positive and negative two's complement numbers into ascending order. Demonstrate its operation using ODT.

6.10 Devise a program that adds two 48-bit two's complement numbers. Demonstrate your program using ODT. Try it with the octal numbers

0000037777777777

and

0000077777600001.

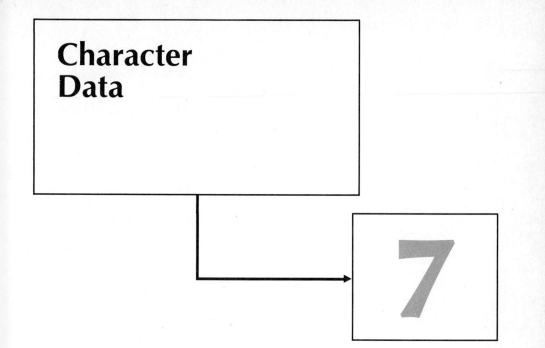

Character Data

7

7.1 Overview

A great deal of the information processed by computers is composed of strings of alphabetic, numeric, and other character data. Examples of this include lists of mailing addresses, parts lists for inventory control, and the like. Even information that is essentially numeric in nature (i.e., produced by or used in arithmetic operations) must be converted to equivalent character representations in order to be communicated to or from devices, such as printers or terminals, that are external to the computer. The importance of processing character data causes us to now turn our attention to the facilities of the PDP-11 and MACRO-11 for handling information in this form.

In this chapter we begin by describing how character data are represented digitally, namely, the American Standard Code for Information Interchange, usually called ASCII (pronounced "ask'-ee"). With this standard, each symbol used in representing printed information, as well as certain nonprinting "control characters," is assigned a 7-bit code. We then introduce several new MACRO-11 directives used to store (or reserve space for) bytes of character in the central memory.

The 7-bit ASCII character codes fit conveniently into the 8-bit bytes on the PDP-11. A part of the chapter is devoted to describing MACRO-11 instructions that operate on bytes. We will see that most of the instructions previously introduced for operations on words have versions that perform the same functions on bytes. These instructions are essential for efficient programming when the data are character in nature. Finally, this chapter introduces a number of instructions that enable the programmer to examine or manipulate individual bits in words and registers.

All of the topics above are important when we take up input and output in Chapter 8.

7.2 Character Codes

Digital computers, as we have seen earlier, are designed to store and manipulate binary information, i.e., patterns of 1's and 0's. If we wish to use such a machine to process character information, it is therefore necessary to use binary representations or "codes" for the characters to be processed. For example, the alphabet can be represented as follows.

Character	Binary Code
A	1000001
B	1000010
C	1000011
.	.
.	.
.	.

Then when we wish to store an A (uppercase), we could put into the low or high byte of a PDP-11 word

15	14	13	12	11	10	9	8	7	6	5	4	3	2	1	0
								0	1	0	0	0	0	0	1

Conversely, when this bit pattern is *found* in a byte, we could interpret it as an uppercase A. Note that there is nothing inherent in this bit pattern *compelling* us to interpret it in this way; it could equally well be interpreted as a representation of the positive integer 65_{10}. It is the *context*, i.e., how the data are used, that determines what this bit pattern means.

7.3 The American Standard Code for Information Interchange (ASCII)

Many possible codes could be used to represent characters. The only true requirement is that there be enough bit patterns to represent each character needed. The system shown above is called ASCII, standing for the American Standard Code for Information Interchange. ASCII has been defined as a 7-bit code, so that there are $2^7 = 128_{10}$ unique bit patterns or codes, and 128_{10} characters can therefore be represented. These codes have been assigned to the alphabetic, numeric, and other characters as shown in Table 7.1. In this table we follow the customary practice of giving the octal representations of the binary codes. Internally, they are of course represented in binary.

In Table 7.1 there are 95 characters that appear in printed media. These are the so-called printing characters that include 26 uppercase letters, 26 lowercase letters, 32 punctuation characters (e.g., ".", " + ", ")", etc.), 10 numeric characters,

TABLE 7.1
The ASCII Codes

Octal Code	Char	Octal Code	Char	Octal Code	Char	Octal Code	Char
000	NUL	040	SP	100	@	140	
001	SOH	041	!	101	A	141	a
002	STX	042	"	102	B	142	b
003	ETX	043	#	103	C	143	c
004	EOT	044	$	104	D	144	d
005	ENQ	045	%	105	E	145	e
006	ACK	046	&	106	F	146	f
007	BEL	047	'	107	G	147	g
010	BS	050	(	110	H	150	h
011	HT	051	)	111	I	151	i
012	LF	052	*	112	J	152	j
013	VT	053	+	113	K	153	k
014	FF	054	,	114	L	154	l
015	CR	055	−	115	M	155	m
016	SO	056	.	116	N	156	n
017	SI	057	/	117	O	157	o
020	DLE	060	0	120	P	160	p
021	DC1	061	1	121	Q	161	q
022	DC2	062	2	122	R	162	r
023	DC3	063	3	123	S	163	s
024	DC4	064	4	124	T	164	t
025	NAK	065	5	125	U	165	u
026	SYN	066	6	126	V	166	v
027	ETB	067	7	127	W	167	w
030	CAN	070	8	130	X	170	x
031	EM	071	9	131	Y	171	y
032	SUB	072	:	132	Z	172	z
033	ESC	073	;	133	[	173	{
034	FS	074	⟨	134	\	174	|
035	GS	075	=	135	]	175	}
036	RS	076	⟩	136	^	176	~
037	US	077	?	137	_	177	DEL (RUB)

and the blank character. The remaining 33 codes have no printed equivalent but have special significance to the equipment that transmits, receives, prints, or generates data. These are called the "control characters" and are represented in the table by their standard designations. An example of a control character is LF that stands for linefeed and has an octal code of 012_8.

The ASCII codes have several properties that make them convenient for manipulation in the computer. First, observe that the codes for the numeric characters 0, 1, 2, . . ., 9 are sequential octal (or binary) numbers—060, 061, 062, . . ., 071. The importance of this lies in the fact that the *character code* for a digit can be obtained by adding octal 060 to the digit. For example, if we have the number 4

0 000 000 000 000 100

and we add octal 060, then we get

0 000 000 000 110 100

that is 000064 in octal. By ignoring the high byte, this is octal 064, which from Table 7.1 is the ASCII code for the numeric character 4. Because of this property of the code, 060_8 is called the "ASCII base." When we discuss output of octal and decimal numbers in Chapter 8, we will see that this is done by computing the *numeric value* of each digit and adding the ASCII base. Below we will see that the ASCII codes are then sent to the printer that responds by printing the appropriate character.

Another useful property is that the lowercase character codes are obtainable by adding 40_8 to the uppercase codes. A still more useful property is that each successive alpha code is one greater than the last. This means that sorting into alphabetic order can be done using arithmetic comparisons. We see that all characters as shown in Table 7.1 are in a "natural" order with regard to their ASCII codes. This is called the "collating sequence" for the character set.

7.4 Storage of ASCII

Because ASCII is a 7-bit code, we can store one code in each byte. That is we can "pack" two ASCII characters per word. For example, we could store the message HI in a word as follows.

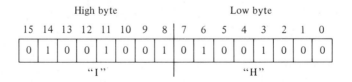

Note that the 7-bit code leaves an unused bit at the left in each byte. Sometimes this bit is used as a means of detecting an error. (See Section 8.7.)

In this discussion, however, it is assumed to be unused and to be always 0. Another observation is that we chose to store the first character of the message on the right and the second on the left. This may seem backwards but, in fact, is a very logical order. Because the right byte has the lowest address, we are storing the first character in the first address, the second character in the second address, and so on. If we wished to store a longer message, such as HI THERE!!, we would continue in the same manner, using as many bytes as necessary. Below, for example, we arbitrarily start this message at address 500.

High byte address																		Low byte address
000501	0	1	0	0	1	0	0	1	0	1	0	0	1	0	0	0	000500
000503	0	1	0	1	0	1	0	0	0	0	1	0	0	0	0	0	000502
000505	0	1	0	0	0	1	0	1	0	1	0	0	1	0	0	0	000504
000507	0	1	0	0	0	1	0	1	0	1	0	1	0	0	1	0	000506
000511	0	0	1	0	0	0	0	1	0	0	1	0	0	0	0	1	000510

By converting the bit patterns in each byte to character form, it will be seen that we have stored the message as follows.

Word Address	Contents Interpreted as ASCII
000500	"IH"
000502	"T "
000504	"EH"
000506	"ER"
000510	"!!"

The instructions and directives available in MACRO-11, which are discussed below, make such storage of ASCII messages easy to do.

Often it is necessary to examine the contents of a memory location, i.e., a word, and to interpret its contents as ASCII character codes; this was done in the example above. To do this it is necessary to view the word as *two separate bytes,* and convert each byte into octal. Then the corresponding characters can be identified with the ASCII codes in Table 7.1. For example, the word contents

044510

is converted to binary as

0 100 100 101 001 000

Viewed as two bytes we have

01 001 001   01 001 000

that readily decodes to

    111   110

or

    "I"   "H"

Observe that the correct translation is *not* obtained by simply "splitting" the six octal digits that represent the *word* contents (e.g., 044 510 does not represent IH). This difficulty arises because an 8-bit byte is not evenly divisible by three (the number of binary digits needed to represent an octal digit). It should be apparent that if hexadecimal representation were used instead of octal, this problem would not arise. It is for this reason that hexadecimal is rapidly superseding octal as the favored shorthand representation for binary numbers in the computer industry. Because octal is built into MACRO-11 and other PDP-11 software, however, it will probably always be used with these machines.

7.5 ASCII and Peripheral Devices

Let us now examine the use of ASCII external to the computer, i.e., in the peripheral devices. The peripheral devices, such as terminals and printers, have character codes *incorporated into their designs*. For example, an ASCII printer is designed to print the symbol A when it receives the bit pattern 1000001, a B when it receives 1000010, and so on. Conversely, an ASCII keyboard will generate a bit pattern 1000001 when an uppercase A is typed using the shift and A keys.

On a "full" ASCII keyboard, each of the 128_{10} different codes can be generated by some combination of one or more keys. Some of the control characters, such as linefeed (LF) and carriage return (CR), have single keys that generate them. Any control character, however, can be generated by depressing the CTRL key and the key indicated in the sixth column of Table 7.1. For example, the character called BS (010_8) can be generated with the CTRL and H keys. For this reason control characters without assigned keys are often represented in the form CTRL-H or ^H. While the key or keys required to generate a particular code may vary from one keyboard to another, the meanings and usages of the codes are standardized to a large extent. For example, a 007_8 code (0000111_2) will ring the bell on the device, provided that one has been installed.

Here we qualify the device as ASCII because, as noted above, other code systems are possible. One other widely used code is EBCDIC(ebb-see-dick), meaning Extended Binary Coded Decimal Interchange Code. Many terminals, particularly those manufactured by IBM, use these codes. When such a terminal is used in conjunction with an ASCII-oriented computer such as the PDP-11, the character codes must be translated as they go to and from the computer. Modern timesharing operating systems incorporate software that automatically detects the character codes generated by the terminal and performs the translation without the knowledge of the user.

We also point out that some computers use special, nonstandard codes to represent character data *internally*. That is, the data may be received from an external device as ASCII or EBCDIC, and translated to a different code for internal representation. Many Control Data Corporation computers are in this category.

7.6 Character (Byte) Oriented Directives

It will be recalled that we used assembler directives to reserve space for, or to initialize words of memory with, numbers. There are corresponding directives to initialize bytes of memory with character codes.

Two frequently used directives are .ASCII and its companion, .ASCIZ. These are used to initialize successive bytes in memory to the ASCII codes for character strings. For example,

.ASCII /Computer 67/

will initialize 11 bytes of memory to the ASCII codes for the characters in the string "Computer 67". The first character code is stored in the *next available byte,* after the assembler has translated the preceding instruction or directive. For example, the sequence

```
          HALT
MSG1:     .ASCII /Computer 67/
```

will generate

Word Contents	Byte Contents	
000000	000	000
067503	157	103
070155	160	155
072165	164	165
071145	162	145
033040	066	040
????67	???	067

Note that because the number of characters was odd, and we started in a low byte (this was necessary because HALT is an *instruction* and hence must be loaded into a *word*), the high byte of the last word is undefined in this example. The ASCII codes for the characters are as shown in Table 7.1.

To emphasize that .ASCII loads character codes beginning in the next available *byte,* let us consider the sequence

```
HALT
.ASCII /PDP/
.ASCII /-11/
```

This generates

Word Contents	Byte Contents	
000000	000	000
042120	104	120
026520	055	120
030461	061	061

Here we see that the "—" (055) is stored in the high byte left over after storing the second "P" in the first string. This example also shows that long messages can be built up using successive .ASCII directives.

The .ASCIZ directive works exactly like .ASCII except that the *null* character, 000, is added after the last character in the given string. For example,

```
HALT
.ASCIZ /+*#/
```

will generate

Word Contents	Byte Contents	
000000	000	000
025053	052	053
000043	000	043

The importance of .ASCIZ is that the null character 000 can be used to mark or flag the end of a message. Indeed, it is so used by a system-supplied method for printing strings of ASCII characters. This is discussed further in Chapter 8.

In these examples we have arbitrarily used the slash (/) to mark the beginning and end of the string, i.e., to *delimit* the string. If the / character is to be *part* of the string to be stored, then it cannot be used as the delimiter. In such a case, use any character that is not otherwise used in the string as a delimiter, e.g., *, ., ", etc. As an example, consider

```
.ASCII *4/3*
```

where we use * as the delimiter because the string "4/3" contains a "/."

It is often desired to store the character codes for the nonprinting characters, for example, linefeed, carriage return, or bell. There are several ways of doing this. One way is with the use of the .ASCII or .ASCIZ directives, in which case the *octal codes* are enclosed in ⟨. . .⟩ symbols. For example, to store linefeed, carriage return, and bell followed by a null, we would write

```
.ASCIZ ⟨12⟩⟨15⟩⟨7⟩
```

that (assuming that we began at an even address) results in

Word Contents	Byte Contents	
006412	015	012
000007	000	007

This can be combined with a string enclosed in delimiters.

    .ASCIZ /RING BELL/⟨7⟩

Note that when this is done, we put the ⟨7⟩ *outside* of the string delimiters; otherwise the ⟨7⟩ would be considered as a string of three characters rather than the desired control character.

When we were working with numeric data, we sometimes found it necessary to set aside *n* words of memory using the .BLKW n directive. The corresponding directive to reserve one or more bytes is .BLKB n. For example, to set aside 10_8 bytes, we use

    .BLKB 10

When the assembler encounters this directive, it skips the next 10_8 bytes before assigning an address to the succeeding instruction or directive. Note that this directive *does not* store specified values in these bytes, but merely reserves them for future use. Typically, one would use .BLKB expecting the *program* to generate results to be stored in the reserved bytes, perhaps using the byte-oriented instructions discussed later in this chapter.

In passing, observe that the directives

    .BLKB 20

or

    .BLKW 10

do exactly the same thing, provided that they start with an even address. They are identical in effect because a block of 10_8 sequential words is equivalent to 20_8 sequential bytes. Nonetheless, it is good practice to use .BLKB to reserve space eventually to be used for byte-sized data (characters) while .BLKW should be used for allocating space for word-sized data (numeric values).

There is also a directive called .BYTE that corresponds to the .WORD directive. This can be used to initialize bytes to *numeric* values. For example, if

    .BYTE   4,2,177,15

begins at an even address, it would store

Word Contents	Byte Contents	
001004	002	004
006577	015	177

Observe that exactly the same contents (bytes and words) would be obtained as a result of

    .WORD   1004,6577

However, it is better programming practice to use the directives that match the data type.

We close this section with another directive, .EVEN, that is important when working with byte data. The use of .EVEN causes the assembler to place the *next* instruction or directive beginning in the next *even* address, i.e., word address. To see situations in which this would be necessary, consider the sequence

```
L:          .ASCII /X1 = /
            .EVEN
START:      CLR   R0
            INC   R0
              .
              .
              .
```

Here the programmer wishes to initialize a string of three bytes immediately before the first instruction. Because three is odd, if the .EVEN were not used, the assembler would attempt to assemble the CLR R0 instruction into an odd address, which is illegal. In order to avoid this problem, it is good practice to use .EVEN between all byte-oriented storage or initialization directives and the following instruction or word-oriented directive.

7.7 Byte-oriented Instructions

Several of the PDP-11 instructions that we have discussed in the context of word-length data also have forms that operate on byte-length data. The assembly mnemonics for the byte-oriented instructions are simply the word-oriented instructions with B added at the right. For example,

```
MOVB     A,B
```

will move the contents of the byte whose address is A to the byte whose address is B. Other byte-oriented instructions include CLRB, INCB, DECB, NEGB, TSTB, and CMPB as well as the shift, rotate, add–carry, and subtract–carry instructions. The arithmetic ADD and SUB instructions, however, have no byte-oriented form. (Table A.1 shows all instructions and indicates which have byte forms.)

The byte instructions perform the same operations as their word-oriented counterparts. The major differences, in addition to operating on 8-bit data rather than on 16-bit data, have to do with addressing. First, the CM address of the operands of byte-oriented instructions (except SWAB—see below) can be even or odd, i.e., either low or high bytes can be addressed. This means that character codes can be "packed" two per word, and either byte can be individually manipulated. Another consequence of this is that the autoincrement and the autodecrement addressing modes increment or decrement by 1 rather than 2 if the instruction is byte-oriented.

Let us now examine some cases of byte-oriented instructions and their effects. In Example 7.1 we show 10 byte-oriented instructions.

Example 7.1 It is assumed for this example that the registers and memory are set as indicated below before *each* of these instructions is executed.

Register	Contents	Word Address	Byte Contents	
R0	000512	000500	102	101
R1	000503	000502	104	103
R2	000506	000504	106	105
R3	000502	000506	110	107
R4	000515	000510	112	111
		000512	114	113
		000514	300	100

The instructions for each case are given in the first column below. The second column shows the word addresses or the registers that are affected by the instructions. The last two columns give the contents of the affected words and/or registers after the instructions have been executed. Both word (16-bit) and byte (8-bit) forms are shown in octal.

Instruction		Affected Word	Resulting Contents (Octal)	
		Address or Register	Word Form	Byte Form
a) CLRB	R0	R0	000400	001 000
b) MOVB	(R4),R1	R1	177700	377 300
c) MOVB	−(R4),R1	R1	000100	000 100
d) CLRB	(R0)	000512	046000	114 000
e) CLRB	(R1)+	000502	000103	000 103
		R1	000504	001 104
f) MOVB	−(R3),(R2)+	000506	044102	110 102
		R3	000501	001 101
		R2	000507	001 107
g) ASLB	(R1)	000502	104103	210 103
h) SEC				
ROLB	−(R4)	R4	000514	001 114
		000514	140201	300 201
		C bit	Cleared	
i) NEGB	−(R2)	R2	000505	001 105
		000504	135105	272 105
j) SWAB	R3	R3	041001	102 001
k) SWAB	(R3)	000502	041504	103 104

In case (a), we see that the CLRB instruction operating on a register clears only the *low* byte, leaving the high byte unchanged. (To see this, you must convert R0 contents to binary, clear the low byte, and then interpret the bit pattern as two 8-bit bytes). In general, byte operations on registers affect only the low byte. The exception to this is the MOVB instruction with a register as *destination* operand will perform *sign-extension* (see Section 6.2.2) based on the MSB of the source byte. This is shown in cases (b) and (c). This provides a means for generating a 16-bit representation of an 8-bit two's complement number.

Cases (b) and (c) also show the usage of deferred and autodecrement addressing with byte-oriented instructions. Note that in case (b) the source operand is the contents of byte 000515, which is pointed at by R4; it is the high byte of the word with address 000514. The contents, 300, (a negative number) gets put into the low byte of R1, and the *negative* sign bit gets extended into the high byte (i.e., the 8-bit two's complement number 300_8 is equivalent to the 16-bit two's complement number 177700_8). In case (c), R4 is decremented to yield 000514. Then the contents of byte 000514 is placed in the low byte of R1. In this case the sign bit is a 0, so sign extension clears the high byte of R1.

Other examples of deferred and autoincrement addressing in byte instructions are shown in cases (d), (e), and (f). The reader should verify the results of these instructions. The shift and rotate byte instructions behave as they would for words except that only eight bits are involved. This is demonstrated in cases (g) and (h). In case (g), the high byte of word 000502 is shifted left with zero fill *at the right of the high byte,* i.e., into the eighth bit. Note that in case (h) the C condition code rolls into the LSB of the low byte, and C receives the MSB of the same byte. Thus these instructions work exactly like their word-oriented counterparts as shown in Figs. 6.7 and 6.8.

The NEGB instruction replaces the operand byte by its two's complement value. This is demonstrated in case (i). The other byte in the same word is unaffected.

This example covers one additional byte-oriented instruction, SWAB. This instruction interchanges (swaps) the two bytes in the operand word. Observe that the operand of SWAB must be a register or a word address, i.e., even.

In translation of byte instructions, observe that their opcodes are the same as corresponding word instructions except that the MSB is set to 1. For example,

```
MOVB    (R1),(R2)
```

translates to

```
111112
```

Condition codes for the byte-oriented instructions are set or cleared according to the same rules used for the corresponding word-oriented instructions. However, allowance is made for the shorter length of the byte. That is, the C condition code is set if the result would exceed $2^8 - 1$ interpreted as a positive integer. Also, the V bit is set if the result would be outside of the range -128_{10} to 127_{10}. (We caution, however, that INCB and DECB do not affect the C condition code, just as INC and DEC do not).

7.8 Character Constants

It is often necessary to use an ASCII character in byte-oriented instructions. For example, it may be desired to compare the contents of a memory location (byte) with the ASCII code for S. One could use the octal code, 123_8

```
CMPB    #123,C
```

However, this makes it difficult for another programmer to see what is being done. A better way is to use the facility of MACRO-11 for representing character constants. This is a single quote followed by a single character. The example above then becomes

CMPB   #'S,C

This causes the *assembler* to look up the ASCII code for S and place it in the low byte of the word following the instruction (i.e., immediate addressing due to #). A double quote will cause the assembler to translate the following *two* characters into a 16-bit operand.

7.9 Logical Bit Instructions

The PDP-11 has several instructions that perform logical operations, e.g., "and," "or," "complement," and "exclusive or" on a bit-by-bit basis. These instructions find usage in certain programming problems, and in particular in the input of characters as discussed in Chapter 8. Although we base our discussion here on the word form of these instructions, each (except "exclusive or") has a byte equivalent.

Let us first review the logical operators "and," "or," "complement," and "exclusive or" for single bits. Table 7.2 is the "truth table" for these operators that defines the outcome for each possible combination of single-bit operands. This shows, for example, that "and," symbolized by $\wedge$, is true (i.e., 1) if and only if both operands are 1. The "or" operator, symbolized by $\vee$, is true if *either* operand is true. The "exclusive or," symbolized by $\veebar$, is true if one *but not both* of the operands are true. Complement, symbolized by $\sim$, is true if the single operand is false, and false if the operand is true.

The last column in Table 7.2, labeled BIC, is not as familiar as the other logical operations, but is an available PDP-11 instruction and plays an important role in programming. In effect, it says "If a_1 is true, then the result is false regardless of a_2. However, if a_1 is false, then the result is the same as a_2". In other words, it *clears* bits in a_2 whenever there is a 1 bit in a_1.

The PDP-11 has an instruction for each of these logical operators. The MACRO-11 mnemonics are as follows.

TABLE 7.2
Truth Table for Logical Operators

Operands		Operators				
a_1	a_2	BIT (AND) $a_1 \wedge a_2$	BIS (OR) $a_1 \vee a_2$	XOR $a_1 \veebar a_2$	COM $\sim a_1$	BIC $(\sim a_1) \wedge a_2$
0	0	0	0	0	1	0
0	1	0	1	1	1	1
1	0	0	1	1	0	0
1	1	1	1	0	0	0

```
BIT    M,D    ; Bit test (AND) (does not change D)
BIS    M,D    ; Bit set (OR)
XOR    Rn,D   ; Exclusive OR
COM    D      ; Bit complement
BIC    M,D    ; Bit clear
```

These instructions examine the operands on a bit-by-bit basis and, except for BIT, establish the destination bit patterns according to the rules in Table 7.2.

In the most common usage of these instructions, the first operand is often called a "mask" because it can be viewed as a bit pattern that "masks out" the unwanted portion of the second operand. For example, if we wished to clear all bits in a word A except the rightmost three, we could use

```
BIC    #177770,A
```

The BIC instruction follows the rules established in the last column in Table 7.2, i.e., the first operand (the mask) is *complemented*, then ANDed with the second. To see this more clearly, suppose that A was 164325_8. Then we have

```
1 111 111 111 111 000 (Mask)
0 000 000 000 000 111 (~mask)
1 110 100 011 010 101 (A)
0 000 000 000 000 101 (Final A)
```

We see that the three LSBs have been left undisturbed while all others have been cleared or "masked out." Thus one can clear bits in the destination by placing a 1 in the corresponding mask bit.

The BIS instruction will cause the destination operand bits to be *set* whenever there is a 1 in the mask. For example, using the byte-oriented equivalent BISB

```
MOVB    #143,A
BISB    #360,A
```

sets 1's in the leftmost four bits of A while leaving the rightmost four bits unchanged. This produces 363_8 in A as shown below.

```
  11110000    (360)
  01100011    (143)
  11110011    (363)
```

The "exclusive or," XOR, *complements* the destination bits selectively wherever there is a 1 bit in the mask. For example,

```
MOV    #077777,R1
MOV    #170707,A
XOR    R1,A
```

causes A to be set as shown below.

```
0 111 111 111 111 111    (077777)   (Mask)
1 111 000 111 000 111    (170707)   (Original A)
1 000 111 000 111 000    (107070)   (Final A)
```

Note that XOR is a single-word instruction with a machine code format similar to MUL and DIV. That is, the translation is 074RDD where R is a register and DD is the destination referenced by any addressing mode. The assembly mnemonics therefore require that the *first* operand be a *register*. The XOR does *not* have a byte equivalent.

An interesting usage of the XOR is in exchanging the contents of two registers. That is,

```
XOR      R1,R2
XOR      R2,R1
XOR      R1,R2
```

will transfer the contents of R1 to R2, and R2 to R1 without using any other registers. The reader can demonstrate that this works with any convenient bit patterns in R1 and R2.

The BIT instruction differs from the others in that it does not change either operand. It is similar in this respect to the CMP instruction, and it is used in much the same way. That is, it is an efficient test before a branch instruction. Logically, it performs a bit-by-bit AND as shown in Table 7.2. A typical usage occurs when it is desired to execute a branch if a particular bit pattern exists in one of the operands. Consider, for example, the need to branch to OUT only if bit four is set, disregarding all other bits. A mask with this bit set is 000020_8. We therefore write the instructions

```
BIT      #20,R1
BNE      OUT
```

Because all but the fourth bit in 20_8 is 0, the BIT (AND) operation will yield a 0 in all bits other than the fourth, regardless of R1. A 1 in the fourth bit of R1 will produce a 1 in the result (formed only in the ALU); since this is not 0, BNE will branch. A 0 in the fourth bit of R1 will produce a 0 result, so the BNE will not branch. Masks can be selected to cause a variety of branching conditions using BIT. Note that the 0 result occurs when the second operand *does not* equal the mask; it is for this reason that the branch instruction must reflect the *complement* of the desired branching condition.

As the last bit-oriented instruction we consider COM, meaning complement. It has a single operand, and each bit in this operand is complemented. Thus

```
MOV    #707,A
COM    A
```

modifies A as indicated below.

```
0 000 000 111 000 111      (000707)   (A)
1 111 111 000 111 000      (177070)   (~A)
```

As we noted in Chapter 6, this would be called the "one's complement" of A.

7.10 A Programming Example

As an example of the character manipulation capabilities of MACRO-11, let us consider the following problem.

Example 7.2   Assume that a sentence is stored in a block of successive bytes beginning at the label S. Write a MACRO-11 program that will compute the number of words in the sentence and the length of each word. The number of words is to be placed in a memory location labeled N and the lengths are to be placed in N successive *bytes* (as 8-bit positive integers) beginning at L. Assume that each word is separated from the next by exactly one blank, and that the sentence ends with a period.

Figure 7.1(a) shows the level-1 flowchart for a solution to this problem. We use register R2 as a word counter, R1 to point at the location in L where the length of the current word is developed, and R0 to point at the current character in the sentence. The two pointers are initialized to the beginnings of their arrays prior to entering a WHILE loop. Each pass through the body of this loop counts the characters in the next word, placing the count into the next byte in the length array L. Upon completion of a pass, the sentence character pointer is left pointing at the first character of the next word, or if a period is present, at the period. The word length array pointer is incremented so that it points to the next byte in the L array for the next pass through the loop. The word counter R2 is also incremented in the body of the loop.

Because the character pointer R0 is left at the period, it can act as a loop control variable. That is, if the contents of the byte pointed at by R0 is a ".", the last word has been found. Upon exit from this loop, as a last step we move the word count into location N as required by the problem statement.

The refinement of the major loop body is shown in Fig. 7.1(b). It begins by initializing the word length (to be stored in the byte pointed at by R1) to 0, then enters a WHILE loop that is repeated so long as the character pointed at by R0 is not a delimiter. Note that R0 is incremented as part of the condition check, but only if a "." is not found. The body of this loop increments the length of the current word.

The assembly program for the flowchart in Fig. 7.1 is shown in Fig. 7.2. For the most part, because the instructions correspond quite closely to the flowchart blocks described above, we shall omit a detailed description of the program operation and focus on the usage of the byte directives and instructions. First, observe that we use byte comparisons (CMPB) when comparing characters. This is especially important in an instruction such as in line 11 because the pointer R0 can take on *odd* values. The word form would not allow an odd (high-byte) address for the operand in deferred addressing. Even if this were not a problem, it would be illogical to compare a full 16 bits when it is only 8 bits that need to be compared to establish equality of two characters.

Note that the pointer R0 is incremented using autoincrement addressing in line 16. This advances R0 to the first character of the next word if one is present.

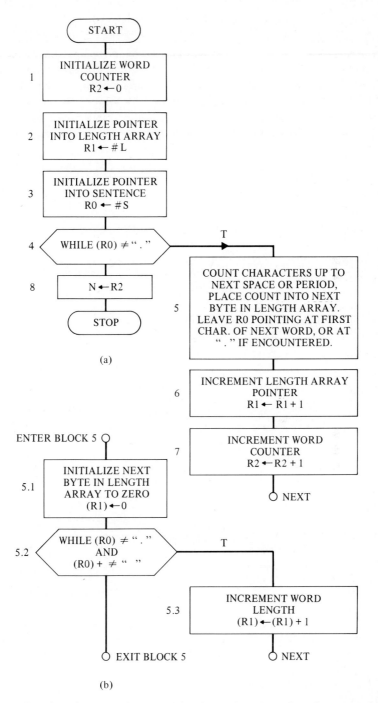

Figure 7.1 Flowchart for Example 7.2: (a) level-one flowchart; (b) refinement of block 5.

However, if the delimiter is a period, R0 is *not* incremented. The body of the innermost loop then has a single instruction (line 18) incrementing the word length counter. Note that we use the byte form of the increment instruction because the problem statement required that the length counts be stored in bytes rather than words. This is efficient usage of memory because word lengths will always be well within the range accommodated by 8-bit, positive integers.

We purposely have left some inefficiencies in this program to allow discussion of the refinement process that most programmers go through in arriving at a final

```
EXP7P2   MACRO V03.01  17-JAN-83 12:32:26  PAGE 1


    1                                          .TITLE   EXP7P2
    2                                  ;
    3                                  ;    PROGRAM TO DETERMINE NUMBER OF WORDS AND LENGTHS
    4                                  ;              IN A SENTENCE.
    5                                  ;
    6 000000                          START:
    7 000000   005002                          CLR     R2              ;INITIALIZE WORD COUNTER
    8 000002   012701   000131'                MOV     #L,R1           ;INITIALIZE LENGTH ARRAY POINTER
    9 000006   012700   000056'                MOV     #S,R0           ;INITIALIZE CHARACTER POINTER
   10 000012                          WHILE1:
   11 000012   121027   000056                 CMPB    (R0),#'.        ;GET WORD IF NO PERIOD
   12 000016   001414                          BEQ     OUT1
   13 000020   105011                          CLRB    (R1)            ;INITIALIZE CURRENT WORD LENGTH
   14 000022   121027   000056        WHILE2:  CMPB    (R0),#'.        ;PERIOD ENDS WORD & SENTENCE
   15 000026   001405                          BEQ     OUT2
   16 000030   122027   000040                 CMPB    (R0)+,#'        ;SPACE ENDS WORD
   17 000034   001402                          BEQ     OUT2
   18 000036   105211                          INCB    (R1)            ;INCREMENT CURRENT WORD LENGTH
   19 000040   000770                          BR      WHILE2          ;CHECK NEXT CHARACTER
   20 000042   005201                 OUT2:    INC     R1              ;INC. LENGTH ARRAY POINTER
   21 000044   005202                          INC     R2              ;INC. WORD COUNTER
   22 000046   000761                          BR      WHILE1          ;GET NEXT WORD
   23 000050                          OUT1:
   24 000050   010267   000156                 MOV     R2,N            ;PLACE WORD COUNT INTO N
   25 000054   000000                          HALT
   26 000056      124      110    111 S:       .ASCII/THIS IS A SAMPLE/
      000061      123      040    111
      000064      123      040    101
      000067      040      123    101
      000072      115      120    114
      000075      105
   27 000076      040      123    105          .ASCII/ SENTENCE WITH EIGHT WORDS./
      000101      116      124    105
      000104      116      103    105
      000107      040      127    111
      000112      124      110    040
      000115      105      111    107
      000120      110      124    040
      000123      127      117    122
      000126      104      123    056
   28 000131                          L:       .BLKB    100
   29                                          .EVEN
   30 000232                          N:       .BLKW    1
   31                                          .BLKW    20
   32           000000'                        .END     START


SYMBOL TABLE

L 000131R    OUT1 000050R    S 000056R    WHILE1 000012R    WHILE2  000022R
N 000232R    OUT2 000042R    START 000000R

.  ABS.   000000    000
          000274    001
ERRORS DETECTED:   0
```

Figure 7.2 MACRO-11 listing for Example 7.2.

program. Note that we increment R1 in the instruction in line 20. This could be done alternatively by changing line 13 to autoincrement addressing. However, this would leave R1 pointing one byte beyond where it should be when line 18 is reached. This would have to be fixed by decrementing R1 immediately after setting it at the address of L at line 8. Whereas this may seem to have gained nothing—trading one instruction for another—it is in fact an improvement: We have eliminated an instruction inside the *inner* loop, at the cost of adding one outside of both loops. This saves a number of execution cycles equal to the number of characters in the sentence minus one. If this algorithm was to be incorporated into a larger program, and had to be executed thousands of times, such improvements may be quite important.

Let us make some other observations before leaving Fig. 7.2. The CMPB instruction at line 11 is seen to be translated as 121027; the one in the MSB indicates the byte form of the instruction. The addressing mode of the second operand is 27 (immediate), so the operand itself is placed in the following word. Examination of Table 7.1 shows that 056 is the ASCII code for the period. Thus the mnemonic operand #'*character* tells the assembler to place the ASCII code for *character* into the next location. Note that it is placed in the *low byte,* with the high byte filled with 0's. (We could alternately say that the high byte is assigned the "null character.")

Note how the assembler listing displays the translation of the .ASCII directive. At line 26, for example, we see the octal ASCII codes for the characters in the string, printed three per line. Obviously the assembler has provided us with the *byte* contents rather than the word contents. Also, the addresses given relate to bytes rather than words. That is, the character codes 124, 110, and 111 are stored in addresses 000056, 000057, and 000060. The end of the first .ASCII string is stored in byte 000075, and the beginning of the second is stored in 000076. Line 28 shows the allocations of 100_8 bytes for the byte array L. Note that it begins at byte 000131 and would therefore end at byte 000230. However the *word* allocated for N is at address 000282 rather than 000231 because of the .EVEN directive. This is important because the value assigned to N by the assembler is used as an address for the word instruction MOV R2,N at line 24.

Figure 7.3 shows execution of the program under ODT. We first set a breakpoint at the HALT, location 1054. After execution to the breakpoint, we examine the memory locations where the sentence is stored. By using the back-slash key, \, we cause ODT to display the contents of each byte, interpreted as octal, *and* as an ASCII character. This is shown in Fig. 7.3(a). In Fig. 7.3(b) we examine the bytes where the word lengths have been stored. The octal interpretation of these bytes gives the length of each word in the sentence. The ASCII interpretations of these bytes are seen to be certain control characters, which are not of concern in this example. However, you may wish to compare the byte contents with Table 7.1 to verify that they are indeed the control characters. For example, ^E is printed for the code 005 that Table 7.1 shows to be the control character called ENQ. By examining the registers we see that R0, the sentence character pointer, is left pointing at location 001130 that is seen to be the period. (See Fig. 7.3a.)

```
RUN EX7P2

ODT  R01-04
*1054;B
*1000;G
B0;001054
*1056\124 =T
001057 \110 =H
001060 \111 =I
001061 \123 =S
001062 \040 =
001063 \111 =I
001064 \123 =S
001065 \040 =
001066 \101 =A
001067 \040 =
001070 \123 =S
001071 \101 =A
001072 \115 =M
001073 \120 =P
001074 \114 =L
001075 \105 =E
001076 \040 =
001077 \123 =S
001100 \105 =E
001101 \116 =N
001102 \124 =T
001103 \105 =E
001104 \116 =N
001105 \103 =C
001106 \105 =E
001107 \040 =
001110 \127 =W
001111 \111 =I
001112 \124 =T
001113 \110 =H
001114 \040 =
001115 \105 =E
001116 \111 =I
001117 \107 =G
001120 \110 =H
001121 \124 =T
001122 \040 =
001123 \127 =W
001124 \117 =O
001125 \122 =R
001126 \104 =D
001127 \123 =S
001130 \056 =.
```

```
001131 \004 =^D
001132 \002 =^B
001133 \001 =^A
001134 \006 =^F
001135 \010 =
001136 \004 =^D
001137 \005 =^E
001140 \005 =^E
001141 \000 =
*$0/001130
*$1/001141
*$2/000010
*;P
?M-Halt at user PC 001056
Ready
```

(a)   (b)

Figure 7.3 Execution of Example 7.2 program under ODT. [OS]

Similarly, R1 is left pointing at the byte where the *next* word length would have been placed had the sentence been longer. The number of words in the sentence, $10_8 = 8_{10}$, is seen to be in register R2 and in the location assigned to N, namely, 001232.

7.11 Summary

Chapter 7 has covered a range of topics related to the manipulation of nonnumeric, i.e., character data, with the PDP-11. We began by observing that some binary code is necessary for representing character data on a binary digital computer. The ASCII code was presented in detail because most peripheral devices communicate with the PDP-11 using this system, and MACRO-11 has features that make it a convenient choice. It is a 7-bit code, so that a single character fits neatly into an 8-bit byte. We saw that most often character strings are "packed" into successive bytes in memory.

There are two byte-oriented directives in MACRO-11 that allow initialization of blocks of successive bytes to ASCII codes. The directive .ASCII /string/ places the codes for each character in string into the next available memory bytes; .ASCIZ /string/ does the same, but adds a null character at the end. Other byte-oriented directives include .BLKB n which reserves n bytes without initialization, and .BYTE $v_1, v_2, \ldots, v_n$ which initializes the next n bytes to the values $v_1, v_2, \ldots, v_n$.

Because character manipulation is a frequent need, and the character codes reside in bytes, the PDP-11 has byte-oriented forms of many instructions. These include CLRB, COMB, INCB, DECB, NEGB, TSTB, MOVB, CMPB, ADCB, SBCB, and the rotate and shift instructions. These operate essentially the same as the previously introduced word instructions having the same mnemonics but without the B. The byte-oriented instructions allow us to move byte-sized data to and from individual bytes in memory. We saw that certain differences therefore arise in addressing the operands. For example, in INCB (R1), R1 can contain any address, whereas INC (R1) requires that R1 be a word address (i.e., an even address). More importantly, the autoincrement and autodecrement modes increment the register by 1 when used in a byte-oriented instruction. This is convenient when the objective is to manipulate successive bytes because adjacent byte addresses differ by 1. For example, CLRB (R1)+ in the body of a loop will clear successive bytes beginning at the byte address in R1 upon entry to the loop.

It was observed that operations *between* bytes and words can also be done. In particular, MOVB A,R1 will move the 8 bits found in (byte) address A into the low byte of register R1 and *sign extend* into the high byte of R1. This is in effect a *conversion* of an 8-bit two's complement number to its 16-bit equivalent. On the other hand, MOVB R1,A will move the low byte of R1 into the byte reserved for A. Except for MOVB with a register as the second operand, the byte-oriented instructions with register operands refer to the low byte in the register. Because the high byte of the registers cannot be addressed, the SWAB instruction is provided that interchanges the high and low bytes of the single operand.

Frequently it is necessary to have a "character constant" as an operand. This can be done using the single (or double) quote in MACRO-11. That is, CMPB A,#'B will compare the byte stored in A with the ASCII code for B, while CMP R0, #"AB will compare the 16 bits in R0 with those implied by the character string "AB."

The chapter also dealt with bit manipulation instructions, including BIT, BIC, BIS, and their byte-oriented equivalents BITB, BICB, and BISB. These perform logical operations on a bit-by-bit basis for two operands. Most often the first or source operand is viewed as a "mask" that "selects" or identifies the bits of concern in the second operand. For example, BIT #4,R1 will produce a nonzero result if and only if bit two of R1 is set; all other bits in R1 are of no consequence because the corresponding bits in the mask are zero. Similarly, BIS (logical OR) will set bits in the second operand wherever a 1 occurs in the mask, and BIC clears bits in the second operand wherever a 1 occurs in the mask. Note, however, that BIC and BIS *change the second operand* while BIT acts only to set or clear the N and Z condition codes. We also described the operation of the "exclusive or," XOR that will set a bit in the destination operand if there is a 1 in the corresponding position in *either* the first operand or the second, but not in both. This has the effect of complementing the destination bits in the positions selected by 1's in the mask. The XOR does not have a byte equivalent, and must have a *register* as the first operand. It is available only if the machine has the Extended Instruction Set (EIS) that is standard on larger PDP-11s and available (as an option) on the PDP-11/03 and LSI-11 processors.

The chapter ended with an example that showed the use of byte directives and instructions in character manipulation.

7.12 Exercises

7.1 Determine the ASCII characters represented by the following 8-bit octal codes.

a) 155	**b)** 033	**c)** 123	**d)** 015
e) 012	**f)** 007	**g)** 054	**h)** 040
i) 066	**j)** 177		

7.2 Show the byte contents in octal and binary for the ASCII representation of the following characters.

a) /	**b)** r	**c)** R	**d)** .
e) NUL	**f)** 0	**g)** 8	**h)** ˆB
i) |	**j)** ⟨		

7.3 Indicate the characters represented in each byte of the following 16-bit words whose contents are given in octal below. Be sure to give your answer in the correct order, remembering that the low byte holds the first character.

a) 027056	**b)** 047557	**c)** 042500	**d)** 035127
e) 070555	**f)** 040502	**g)** 006412	**h)** 020101
i) 024051	**j)** 030061		

7.4 Determine the contents of each byte as a result of the following directives.

```
.ASCII     /YOU CAN LEARN ONLY/
.ASCIZ     / BY PRACTICE!!/
```

7.5 What do the directives .ASCII /AB/, .BYTE 101,102, and .WORD 41101 have in common? Which is preferred and why?

7.6 Show the contents of each byte as a result of

```
.ASCIZ     /HI THERE!/⟨15⟩⟨12⟩⟨7⟩
```

7.7 Explain why you cannot use terminal keys themselves to generate the nonprinting characters in the .ASCIZ directive in Exercise 7.6, but must use the ASCII codes, e.g., 15, 12, and 7, for generating carriage return, linefeed, and bell.

7.8 The following program "decodes" a coded message stored in CODE and puts the decoded message into CLEAR. Explain how it works, and what the message says. What is stored in the last byte of CLEAR at completion?

```
1                  .TITLE DECODE
2      START:   MOV     #CODE,R1
3               MOV     #CLEAR,R2
4      LOOP:    MOVB    (R1),R3
5               ADD     #10,R3
```

```
6                      MOVB   R3,(R2)+
7                      CMPB   (R1)+,#370
8                      BNE    LOOP
9                      HALT
10     CODE:           .BYTE  105,131,133,152,147,45,51,51,370
11     CLEAR:          .BLKB  11
12                     .END   START
```

7.9   For each of the cases below, show the outcome of BIT R1,R2; BIC R1,R2; BIS R1,R2; and XOR R1,R2. Present your results in a table with a row for each case and a column for each instruction. (For BIT, show the N, Z, and V condition codes only. For the others, show the contents of R2 in octal.)

	R1	R2
a)	170707	141311
b)	177600	147757
c)	177770	177777
d)	000777	177777
e)	004000	177777

7.10   Modify Example 7.2 so that words can be delimited by any number of commas or spaces. Run your program with ODT to verify its correctness.

7.11   Write a program that examines a sentence and determines the number of times that each ASCII alphabetical character appears. Place the counts for each character in an array of bytes beginning at C. (*Hint:* The ASCII code minus 101_8 plus the address of C can be used as a pointer into C. Run your program with ODT to verify its correctness.)

7.12   Assume that a block of bytes beginning at M has somehow been filled with ASCII characters. The MSB in each of these bytes has supposedly been set to "even parity," meaning set to 0 or 1 as required to give an even number of 1 bits. However, errors may have occurred such that a byte may no longer be in true parity. Write a program sequence that will examine each byte and move each character that doesn't have a parity error (i.e., that has an even number of bits) to a new array beginning at D. The MSBs in D should all be cleared. Errors in M should appear as DEL (177_8) in D.

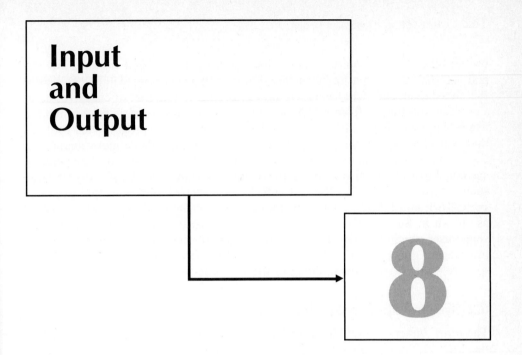

8.1 Overview

Most programs require certain items of data in order to begin, called the input data, and generate results that must be communicated to the user, called the output data. For example, a program that is to determine the sum of two numbers requires these numbers as input data, and the sum must be output data. In Section 4.8 we were able to sidestep these matters by using ODT to load the input directly into memory locations or registers, and to examine the results in the locations or registers where they were generated. As an alternative procedure, we showed the use of preprogrammed routines for octal input/output (I/O) in Section 4.9. These methods allowed the complications of I/O to be temporarily set aside, but neither is very practical for real programs. In this chapter we therefore take up the matter of I/O, with the objective of learning how to write programs that accept general data entry from the terminal keyboard and print or display data back to the terminal.

We will be concerned in this chapter with I/O of two kinds of data—data that have numerical meaning (i.e., representations of numbers), and data that do not (i.e., character data). We will take up character data first because the internal representation of the data is the same as the external representation, namely, ASCII character codes. Thus no translation or conversion is necessary prior to sending character data to the display, and character data received from the keyboard are already properly coded for use in the program. Numerical data, on the other hand, require a translation upon input or output because internal and external representation forms are different. However, we will find that after this translation, the I/O of numbers proceeds exactly like that of character data.

Input and output from a MACRO-11 program can be simplified through the use of what we shall call *I/O macros*. These are in fact preprogrammed routines that deal with much of the detail of inputting or outputting one or more characters. These routines may be available as part of the support programs of the operating system. Most of the discussion in this chapter assumes the availability of three such macros, called .TTYIN, .TTYOUT, and .PRINT that are often available on RSTS/E and RT-11 systems. (If they are not available, they must be installed as shown in Section D.5). For those who are learning MACRO-11 on a small single-user machine, we provide a discussion of the more detailed I/O steps involved in that case. This discussion may also be of interest to those wishing to develop a better understanding of the I/O process.

8.2 System-supplied Macros

The term "macro," in addition to its use as the name of the assembler used on the PDP-11, has a general meaning in computer science. A macro name is a single mnemonic used to invoke the assembly of a predefined *group* of assembly lines. In the following discussions when we say "macro," we mean a mnemonic that is not formally part of the MACRO-11 language, but will be recognized by the assembler and cause a group of machine language instructions to be inserted into the machine language version of the program. Macros usually perform a particular task that is required at many places in the program. In Chapter 10 we will learn how to write macro definitions. Here, however, we wish simply to become familiar with the term so that it can be used in connection with input and output of character data.

Many PDP-11 installations operate under one of the Digital Equipment Corporation operating systems, such as RSTS/E, RT-11, RSX-11, or under UNIX™ operating systems developed by Bell Laboratories. Such systems can be provided with a library of macros that simplify MACRO-11 I/O programming. (See Section D.5.) One of these, called .TTYOUT, is designed to send a single ASCII character to the user's output device, normally the terminal printer or screen. A variation of this is the macro called .PRINT that prints a *string* of characters. Another, called .TTYIN, is designed to accept character data from the user's input device, normally the terminal keyboard. The MACRO-11 programmer can include and use these macros in his or her program to facilitate input and output of program data.

Any program that uses system supplied macros must list these macros in an assembler directive statement called .MCALL, at the beginning of the program. For example, if we wish to use .PRINT, .TTYIN, and .TTYOUT, we must include the directive

```
.MCALL .PRINT,.TTYIN,.TTYOUT
```

This should be placed immediately after the .TITLE directive. This directive tells the assembler to recognize .PRINT, .TTYIN, and .TTYOUT as names of macros to be found in the system macro library. If these mnemonics are then used later in the program, the corresponding machine code instructions are automatically inserted in the assembled program.

The .TTYIN, .PRINT, and .TTYOUT macros are usually installed as part of the RT-11 operating system library. If you are using RSTS/E, RSX-11M, or the UNIX system, you may have to install them as discussed in Section D.5. If the examples shown in this chapter do not work, discuss this matter with your instructor or computer center staff.

In the discussion in following sections it will be seen that .TTYIN, .PRINT, and .TTYOUT use R0. It is therefore necessary to save the contents of R0 elsewhere *before* each use of any of these macros if such contents are going to be needed later. Failure to observe this rule is a frequent source of error.

8.3 The .TTYOUT Macro

The .TTYOUT macro is the easiest to use of the three I/O macros discussed here. Suppose it is desired to print the character whose ASCII code resides in the low byte of R1. This is accomplished by the macro reference

```
.TTYOUT    R1
```

For example,

```
MOVB       #'X,R1
.TTYOUT    R1
```

will print an "X". In this example we used register addressing for the operand of .TTYOUT. Other addressing modes can be used as well. For example, using immediate addressing

```
.TTYOUT    #102
```

will print a "B" (because octal 102 is the ASCII code for B). Finally, using relative addressing

```
        .TTYOUT L1
          .
          .
          .
L1:     .ASCII /Q/
```

will cause a "Q" to be printed.

The .TTYOUT macro sends a *single* character to be printed on the display device, and therefore does not provide the familiar carriage return and linefeed after printing. This causes the *next* printed item to be placed adjacent to the last on the same line. If this is not desired, the carriage return and linefeed codes can be sent by separate .TTYOUTs. For example,

```
.TTYOUT #102    ;  Display B.
.TTYOUT #15     ;  Send Carriage Return.
.TTYOUT #12     ;  Send Linefeed.
```

Alternatively, one could use the .PRINT macro described below that automatically sends a carriage return and linefeed after printing.

Although it is not evident in the MACRO-11 code, the .TTYOUT macro uses R0. A frequent error is to overlook this fact, expecting R0 to be unchanged after using .TTYOUT. The following example shows this error.

```
          MOV       #5,R0
          MOV       #L1,R1
LOOP:     .TTYOUT   (R1)+          ;(Incorrect)
          SOB       R0,LOOP
          HALT
L1:       .ASCII    /HELLO/
```

The programmer may hope that this would print out the word HELLO as the loop is executed in this program. However, the loop control variable, R0, is being changed by .TTYOUT, so that results are unpredictable. A different register should be used for the loop control variable.

8.4 The .PRINT Macro

The .PRINT macro is also quite useful and easy to use. It should be used when an entire line, including a carriage return and linefeed, is to be printed. Typical usage is to print a message

```
.PRINT #MSG
```

where MSG is a label for the first location in a block of memory locations containing a string of characters to be printed. The character codes stored in MSG and each successive byte thereafter will be sent to the terminal display. This will continue until a null byte (000) is encountered, and then a carriage return and linefeed are sent. We have already seen this used in Chapter 1 to print a message. This is a very common usage.

The message to be printed is stored using the .ASCIZ directive that automatically ends the message string with a null byte. The message is stored at any convenient point in the program, and the .PRINT is placed at the point where the printing is to be done during program execution.

In addition to fixed messages initialized by .ASCIZ, the .PRINT macro can be used to print strings of ASCII character codes *calculated* by the program. To demonstrate this, consider the following example.

Example 8.1   Print the entire set of printable ASCII characters, that is, those with codes beginning with octal 040 and ending with 176.

Because these codes are sequential, they can be generated by initializing a register, say R1, to 040 and incrementing it in a loop. Each successive value

```
                .TITLE   ASCII
        ;
        ;               DISPLAY THE ASCII PRINTING CHARACTERS
        ;                    USING THE .PRINT MACRO
        ;
                .MCALL   .PRINT        ;FIND .PRINT IN LIBRARY
        START:  MOV      #40,R0        ;INITIALIZE TO SPACE CHAR
                MOV      #CHAR,R1      ;INITIALIZE ARRAY POINTER
        WHILE:  CMPB     R0,#177       ;CHECK FOR DEL CHAR
                BHI      OUT           ;  AND STOP IF REACHED.
                MOVB     R0,(R1)+      ;STORE CHAR & INC. POINTER
                INC      R0            ;CREATE NEXT CHARACTER
                BR       WHILE
        OUT:
                CLRB     (R1)          ;STORE NULL BYTE
                .PRINT   #MSG          ;PRINT OUTPUT LABEL
                                       ;  AND OUTPUT ARRAY.
                HALT
        MSG:    .ASCII/ASCII PRINTING CHARACTERS:/<15><12><7>
        CHAR:   .BLKB    140           ;RESERVE BYTE ARRAY
                .END     START
```

Figure 8.1   Program to print the ASCII printable characters (Example 8.1).

```
RUN EXP8P1.SAV
ASCII PRINTING CHARACTERS:
 !"#$%&'()*+,-./0123456789:;<=>?@ABCDEFGHIJKLMNOPQRSTUVWXYZ[\]^_`abcdefghijklmno
pqrstuvwxyz{|}~
?M-Halt at user PC 001036
Ready
```

Figure 8.2   Execution of the program for Example 8.1.

can be stored in the next location in a byte array beginning at the label CHAR. After this array has been filled in this manner, the .PRINT macro can be used to print it. Remember that a null byte must be placed after the last valid character code to "turn off" the .PRINT process.

The listing for the MACRO-11 program is shown in Fig. 8.1. As described above, the program first fills the array CHAR with the ASCII codes, followed by the null byte. The subsequent .PRINT #MSG causes the message created by the .ASCII directive to be printed. The ⟨15⟩ ⟨12⟩ ⟨7⟩ cause carriage return, linefeed, and bell character codes to be sent to the display after the message. This positions the next printing at the beginning of the next line, and rings the bell. Note that because we used .ASCII rather than .ASCIZ, the .PRINT macro continues after printing the MSG string rather than stopping. In this way we cause MSG and the results to be printed by a single use of .PRINT. Results of executing this program are shown in Fig. 8.2. Note that as with .TTYOUT, the .PRINT macro disturbs R0.

8.5 The .TTYIN Macro

The role of the .TTYIN macro is to allow keyboard entry of a single ASCII character into your program. By using it repeatedly, any number of characters can be entered.

Usage of .TTYIN is slightly more complicated than the usage of .TTYOUT and .PRINT. In order to explain the .TTYIN, we must first introduce the concept of a **buffer.**

A buffer is group of memory locations that acts as temporary storage for data that are being transferred from one place to another. Data are first placed in the buffer, then withdrawn, and moved to a final destination. Buffers are often required or desirable when there is a large difference in the rate of inflow and outflow of data. In the case of inputting data from a keyboard, for example, the data can be placed in the buffer by the operator at a relatively slow rate while the CPU is doing other tasks. When the buffer is full, or when the user has finished a line of input, the CPU is allowed to read the data from the buffer.

The .TTYIN macro uses the buffer concept and the programmer must take this into account when using it. Characters are accepted into the buffer from the keyboard until the carriage return key is pressed. After the ASCII code for the carriage return (015_8) is placed in the buffer, a linefeed code (012_8) is *automatically placed in the buffer.* This linefeed code is supplied by the operating system, much the same as a typewriter will automatically linefeed when the carriage is returned.

In addition to filling the buffer, the .TTYIN execution causes the first character of the line to be removed from the buffer and to be placed into R0. On the other hand, if .TTYIN is executed and the buffer has something in it, the next character is removed and placed into R0, without further keyboard entry. A new line is not accepted into the buffer until it has been emptied. An example will clarify the process.

Suppose it is desired to accept two characters from the keyboard and to store them in two successive bytes beginning at label A. To accomplish this, we include these instructions at the appropriate place in our program.

```
MOV     #A,R1       ;  INITIALIZE R1 TO ADDRESS OF A
.TTYIN              ;  FILLS BUFFER AND GETS
                    ;  FIRST CHARACTER INTO R0
MOVB    R0,(R1)+    ;  SAVE FIRST CHAR. IN A
.TTYIN              ;  GETS SECOND CHAR. INTO R0
MOVB    R0,(R1)     ;  SAVE SECOND CHAR. IN A+1
.TTYIN              ;  CLEAR CR IN BUFFER
.TTYIN              ;  CLEAR LF IN BUFFER
```

When this program executes, it will pause at the first .TTYIN and wait for keyboard entry. Suppose the user inputs

QB⟨CR⟩

After completion of this input, indicated by the carriage return ⟨CR⟩, the contents of R0 and the .TTYIN buffer are

Low byte of R0:	Q

.TTYIN buffer:	B	C_R	L_F			

Note that the second character entered is in the first position in the buffer. The first MOVB instruction places the Q into the byte in memory labeled A, and advances R1 to address A + 1. After execution of the second .TTYIN, the contents of R0 and the buffer is

Low byte of R0:   B

.TTYIN buffer:

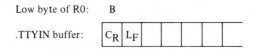

Note that the execution of .TTYIN caused the next character in the buffer to be moved into R0, and removed from the buffer; it *did not* cause the buffer to accept further keyboard entry because it was not empty.

After moving the second character into the location pointed at by R1, we placed two additional .TTYIN macro references. The purpose of these is to *empty the buffer* so that it is ready for reuse the next time we want to get a line of characters from the keyboard. The first of these two .TTYINs leaves R0 and the buffer as follows.

Low byte of R0:   〈CR〉

.TTYIN buffer:

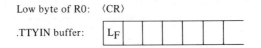

After the next, we have

Low byte of R0:   〈LF〉

.TTYIN buffer:

It is very important to note here that our purpose was to place the first two input characters into A and A + 1. This we have done. We also emptied the buffer so that it could be used later; this was also an important step. The fact that we have left a linefeed character in R0 is not important; it will be overwritten the next time R0 is used.

To see why it is important to leave the .TTYIN buffer empty, consider the following example. Suppose a programmer wishes to accept a *single* character from each of two separate lines of keyboard entry and check to see if they are equal. To meet this need, the following (incorrect) program segment is written.

```
.TTYIN
MOVB      R0,A
.TTYIN
MOV       R0,B
CMPB      A,B
BEQ       L1
    .
    .
```

One might think that two entry lines of the same character, e.g.,

Q⟨CR⟩
Q⟨CR⟩

would result in a branch to L1. However, it does *not* because the first .TTYIN leaves the buffer and R0 to be

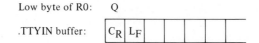

Low byte of R0: Q

.TTYIN buffer: C_R | L_F

Thus the Q gets put into the byte of address A. The second .TTYIN gives

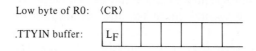

Low byte of R0: ⟨CR⟩

.TTYIN buffer: L_F

Thus ⟨CR⟩ gets put into the byte of address B, and we see that Q (ASCII 121) gets compared with ⟨CR⟩ (ASCII 015). Incidentally, the second line of keyboard input, Q⟨CR⟩, will be ignored by the program, and will cause an error response from the operating system at the conclusion of the program.

The examples above assumed that the entry lines from the keyboard had only the number of characters anticipated by the programmer. This permitted us to empty the buffer by inserting two .TTYINs after the last expected character was read to clear out the ⟨CR⟩ and ⟨LF⟩. One cannot always anticipate, however, the length of the line that the user will actually put in. Suppose, for example, that the program asks for a yes or no response, and then checks only the first character to see if it is a Y or N. Perhaps the user will actually type "YES⟨CR⟩", or even "YES, THANK YOU⟨CR⟩". What is needed to solve this problem is a set of instructions that will take the single character from the .TTYIN buffer, save it, and then clear all remaining characters. Because the end of the line will be marked with a ⟨LF⟩, the following instructions will do this.

```
G1:     .TTYIN           ;  GET BUFFER & FIRST CHAR.
        MOVB   R0,S      ;  SAVE FIRST CHAR.
L1:     .TTYIN           ;  CLEAR
        CMPB   R0,#12    ;     REST OF
        BNE    L1        ;        BUFFER
                   .
                   .
                   .
        HALT
S:      .BLKB   1
```

8.6 Examples Using .PRINT, .TTYIN, and .TTYOUT

Now that we have seen how the .TTYOUT, .PRINT, and .TTYIN macro instructions work, let's consider examples that employ them.

Example 8.2   Prepare a MACRO-11 program that accepts a line of keyboard entry consisting of uppercase alpha characters. After the line is entered, it should then be printed as the corresponding lower case characters.

The MACRO-11 program for this problem is shown in Fig. 8.3. The first section of the program prints a prompt message, rings the bell, and then awaits a line of keyboard input.

The entire line is accepted by the .TTYIN buffer the *first time* the .TTYIN macro is executed. On this execution, the character entered first is also placed in R0. The BIC instruction clears bits 8 through 15. This is done as a precaution because bit 8 may be set as a parity bit (see Section 8.7), and if so will cause subsequent comparisons with the 7-bit ASCII codes to fail.

The ADD instruction creates a lowercase character from an uppercase one. This addition is bypassed for ⟨CR⟩, ⟨LF⟩, and space characters. The character created by the addition is stored in the next byte in B and the pointer R1 is incremented. The criterion for looping back for more characters from the buffer is whether or not a linefeed character has been encountered.

After completion of the loop, it will be noted that we have stored the carriage return and linefeed as well as the lower case characters in B. This causes ⟨CR⟩ and ⟨LF⟩ codes to be sent to the output display, resulting in a carriage return and linefeed action to take place. Because .PRINT *automatically* sends ⟨CR⟩ ⟨LF⟩, we could have omitted these characters from the array. As is shown in Fig. 8.4, the way we have programmed it gives a blank line after the output.

```
        .TITLE  UPPER TO LOWER
        .MCALL  .PRINT,.TTYIN
;
;       LINE OF UPPERCASE
;       ECHOED AS LOWERCASE
;
START:
; GET LINE OF INPUT & PUT INTO B ARRAY
;
        MOV     #B,R1   ;INITIALIZE B ARRAY POINTER
        .PRINT  #PROMT
LOOP:   .TTYIN          ;GET CHAR.&/OR FILL BUFFER
        BIC     #177600,R0;CLEAR PARITY BIT
        CMPB    R0,#15  ;SKIP IF CR
        BEQ     L1
        CMPB    R0,#12  ;    OR LF
        BEQ     L1
        CMPB    R0,#40  ;    OR SPACE.
        BEQ     L1
        ADD     #40,R0  ;MAKE LOWERCASE
L1:     MOVB    R0,(R1)+ ;SAVE IN B ARRAY
        CMPB    R0,#12  ;REPEAT TIL LF
        BNE     LOOP
        CLRB    (R1)    ;NULL BYTE TO TURN OFF .PRINT
;
;       PRINT   THE B ARRAY
;
        .PRINT  #B
        HALT
PROMT:  .ASCIZ/ENTER LINE OF UPPERCASE ALPHA CHARACTERS:/<7>
        .EVEN
B:      .BLKW   120     ;80. CHARACTER ARRAY
        .END    START
```

Figure 8.3   Program for Example 8.2.

```
RUN EXP8P2
ENTER LINE OF UPPERCASE ALPHA CHARACTERS:
ALL IS QUIET ON THE WESTERN FRONT
all is quiet on the western front

?M-Halt at user PC 001072
Ready
```

Figure 8.4   Execution of the program for Example 8.2.

Example 8.3   Write a MACRO-11 program that accepts a single octal digit from the keyboard, then asks the user to enter a line with at least the number of characters indicated by the octal digit. Regardless of the entered line length, print out only the number of characters indicated by the octal digit.

The MACRO-11 program is shown in Fig. 8.5. The first .PRINT prompts the user for the octal digit. When read in, this digit is saved in R1 so that subsequent usages of .TTYIN will not destroy it. Assuming that the user enters only one digit and no other characters, the next two .TTYINs will clear the buffer. We then print MSG2 that acknowledges the digit and asks for a line. Note that the .TTYOUT will print the digit on a fresh line because the preceding .PRINT issued carriage return and linefeed characters. The next .PRINT, for MSG3, will appear on the same line as the digit, however, because .TTYOUT *does not* issue carriage return and linefeed.

The digit entered will actually be the *ASCII Code* for the octal digit, so we have to convert it to binary in order to use it as a loop control variable. This

```
        .TITLE DEMO OF I/O MACROS
        .MCALL  .TTYIN,.TTYOUT,.PRINT
;
;       THIS PROGRAM ACCEPTS A SINGLE OCTAL
;       DIGIT,PRINTS IT OUT,THEN ACCEPTS THAT
;       NUMBER OF OTHER ASCII CHARACTERS AND
;       PRINTS THEM OUT.  ITS PURPOSE IS TO
;       DEMONSTRATE .TTYIN,.TTYOUT AND .PRINT.
;
START:
        .PRINT  #MSG1
        .TTYIN                  ;ACCEPT OCTAL DIGIT
        MOV     R0,R1           ;SAVE IN R1
        .TTYIN                  ;CLEAR THE CR IN .TTYIN BUFFER
        .TTYIN                  ;CLEAR THE LF IN .TTYIN BUFFER
        .PRINT  #MSG2
        .TTYOUT R1              ;PRINT IT OUT
        .PRINT  #MSG3
        MOV     #LINE,R2        ;INITIALIZE POINTER FOR LINE
        SUB     #60,R1          ;CONVERT TO BINARY (LCV)
L1:     .TTYIN                  ;LOOP TO ACCEPT
        MOVB    R0,(R2)+        ;   CHARACTERS
        SOB     R1,L1           ;      INTO LINE.
L2:     .TTYIN                  ;CLEAR OUT
        CMPB    R0,#12          ;   .TTYIN BUFFER
        BNE     L2              ;      TO LF
        CLRB    (R2)            ;STORE NULL BYTE AT END OF LINE
        .PRINT  #LINE           ;PRINT IT
        HALT
MSG1:   .ASCIZ  /ENTER AN OCTAL DIGIT/
MSG2:   .ASCIZ  /THANK YOU! NOW ENTER AT LEAST/
MSG3:   .ASCIZ  / CHARACTERS IN A LINE./
LINE:   .BLKB   100
        .END START
```

Figure 8.5   Program for Example 8.3.

```
RUN EXP8P3
ENTER AN OCTAL DIGIT
7
THANK YOU! NOW ENTER AT LEAST
7 CHARACTERS IN A LINE.
ABCDEFGHIJKL
ABCDEFG
?M-Halt at user PC 001112
Ready
```

Figure 8.6 Execution of the program for Example 8.3.

is done by subtracting the so-called ASCII base, 60_8. (See Chapter 7.) The subsequent loop accepts the entered line and stores the number of characters indicated by the converted value; these characters are stored in a byte array beginning at LINE. The second loop clears the .TTYIN buffer.

After storing the specified number of entered characters in LINE, we clear the next byte, creating the "null character," 000. The subsequent .PRINT #LINE will print all characters in LINE up to this null character. The operation of this program is shown in Fig. 8.6.

We call attention to the fact that this program fails if the user does not follow directions precisely. We leave as an exercise the determination of what happens if more than one character is entered when the digit is asked for, or if *fewer* than the specified number of characters is entered for the line. Fixing these "bugs" is also an interesting exercise.

8.7 Error Checking Using Parity (Optional)

Data being transmitted to or from a computer are sometimes distorted by malfunctioning of the transmission system. The term "line noise" is often used to describe this problem. This is most likely to occur when the data are being transmitted over long distances—on telephone lines, for example. However, line noise can occur even between a terminal and nearby computer if the components are faulty or not properly adjusted. Some types of errors can actually develop within the computer itself. Because of these realities, computer programs are sometimes written to check for errors and, if any errors are found, to report their occurrence so that appropriate action can be taken. If you are working on a large, well-maintained system, this checking is probably not necessary because it is done by hardware and system programs. In some situations, however, checking for errors is the programmer's responsibility.

One frequently encountered error is the loss of a bit. For example, an ASCII "A" character code may be transmitted as

1000001

and arrive at its destination as

0000001

Here it is seen that the MSB has been changed to a 0. The opposite can also occur, i.e., the data might be received as

1100001

where bit five has been changed from a 0 to a 1. In either case the receiver has gotten a character code that is different from the one sent and an error is said to have occurred.

Errors of the type described above can be discovered if the transmitter and the receiver employ what is called a *parity system*. We shall first describe the *even* parity system. In this system the transmitter sends 8 bits rather than 7. The new bit, appended at the left, is set to a 1 or a 0 depending on whether the 7-bit code has an odd or even number of 1 bits. For example, instead of sending the normal ASCII "A" code, it would send

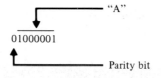

Note that the parity bit is set at 0 here because this will give the 8-bit code an *even* number of 1 bits. On the other hand, if a "C" was to be sent, the transmitter sends

Again, note that the parity is set so as to give an even number of 1 bits in the transmitted code.

If the receiver is told that the transmitter is transmitting *even parity* as described above, the incoming character codes can easily be checked for accuracy. That is, the program can count the number of 1 bits in each character as it is received. If it is not an even number, an error should be reported. The development of a program to do this was left as an exercise in Chapter 7. It is also possible to provide this checking with the operating system software, or by hardware means. In large timesharing systems this is most often the case, so that the MACRO-11 programmer often does not need to be concerned with parity.

It should be apparent that an *odd* parity system will work equally as well as an even parity system. In this system, the sender appends a parity bit to make the number of 1 bits odd, and the receiver checks for an odd number.

Either the even or odd parity suffers from an obvious deficiency. If *two* bits are flipped during transmission, the receiver will not be able to detect the error. It is usually felt, however, that if the equipment is well designed and maintained, this type of error is unlikely. Moreover, any serious malfunction will most likely be revealed in other ways, such as obviously incorrect results of the computations. Error checking algorithms that are more elaborate are sometimes used.

We saw above that the parity system is dependent on the receiver knowing whether even or odd parity is being used by the sender. External transmitting devices such as terminal keyboards usually can be set, by means of switches or special wiring, to generate either even or odd parity. The receiver must then be set accordingly either through proper programming or by settings on the hardware that provides this function.

Note that if a parity system is in use, it is necessary to remove or ignore the parity bit in the program. To see the need for this, suppose we wish to see if an incoming character is an ASCII "C." If the character is received into R0, we might perform the following check.

    CMPB   R0,#'C

The assembler will translate the second operand as an ASCII "C" plus 0 bits appended at the left. The translated machine code is therefore

Binary	Octal
1010000000010111	120027
0000000001000011	000103

However, if a "C" *plus even parity* is received into R0, it will contain (assuming that sign extension took place as in MOVB A,R0)

    R0:   1111111111000011   177703

Obviously these are not the same, so that a subsequent BEQ would not branch, even though the received character was a "C."

The solution to this problem is **masking,** using the BIC instruction. (See Section 7.8.) Recalling that BIC clears the destination operand wherever a 1 bit occurs in the mask (the first operand), we need a mask of

Binary	Octal
1111111110000000	177760

Therefore we change our program as follows.

    BIC   #177600,R0
    CMPB   R0,#'C

This will ensure that the MSBs of both operands of the CMPB instruction are zero, and therefore that only the 7-bit ASCII code has an effect on the comparison.

In the example above we masked out all bits to the left of the 7-bit ASCII code. This is the customary practice because when a single byte is read into a register one cannot always predict what will be in the high byte. For example, the input software such as .TTYIN (often beyond the programmer's awareness) may leave the high byte at its previous value, clear it, or set it following the rules of sign extension from the low byte. Rather than worry about its possible contents, most programmers prefer to simply clear it along with the MSB of the low byte using the mask above.

8.8 I/O without an Operating System (Optional)

The preceding sections dealt with input/output when the program is to execute on a machine with an operating system, e.g., RSTS/E. The macros from the system macro library, .TTYIN, .TTYOUT, and .PRINT, provided us with access to the I/O routines within the operating system, allowing relatively straightforward input and output of character codes. However, when the computer being used *does not* have an operating system (for example, a rudimentary PDP-11/03), it will be necessary to program the more detailed steps involved in I/O.

It is also important to note that the discussion in this section applies *specifically* to situations in which the user program has access to the so-called *device registers* (see below). This is usually the case on a single-user machine, such as most configurations of the PDP-11/03. Multiuser systems, such as RSTS/E, *do not* allow programs other than the operating system itself to access these registers, and the procedures described here are not applicable. Thus if you are using a RSTS/E or other multiuser system, you should use .TTYIN, .TTYOUT, and .PRINT, or their equivalents for I/O as described above. See Section D.5 on the operating system used on your computer for details on this matter.

The methods described here are known as "programmed I/O" using "polling." Other I/O methods are discussed in Chapter 14.

8.8.1 Device Registers

External devices such as terminals communicate with the CPU through special addresses collectively called *device registers*. Although these registers are not actually part of CM, they have addresses exactly like CM locations. There are several of these on a typical configuration, allowing it to communicate with the operator's console, disk storage units, tape storage units and the like. Here we are concerned only with those for the operator's console. Such a console may be a cathode ray tube (CRT) terminal, or a printing terminal. Either device is composed of two parts, a keyboard and a display. Each has two associated device registers as we describe below.

The two registers associated with the keyboard are called the *keyboard status register* (KSR) and the *keyboard data register* (KDR). These registers are shown in Fig. 8.7. Note that each has a specific address that is assigned at the time that the computer is assembled. (Although it is possible to have other addresses by special order, the addresses shown are standard.)

The KSR and the KDR work together to make keyboard-generated character codes available to the CPU. The character code from the keyboard is accepted

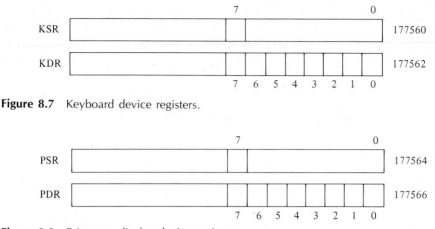

Figure 8.7   Keyboard device registers.

Figure 8.8   Printer or display device registers.

into bits 0 through 7 of the KDR. The KSR indicates by the state of bit 7 whether or not the KDR is ready to be read by the CPU. That is, when a key is pressed, the corresponding ASCII code is sent to the KDR. However, because the keyboard and intermediate circuitry require some amount of time to act, this code cannot be assumed to be immediately available to the CPU. As soon as it is ready, however, bit 7 of the KSR is set to 1. The CPU can therefore check the KSR in order to see if the code can be read from the KDR. When the CPU *does* access the KDR, e.g., by a MOV instruction, KDR is *cleared*.

The KSR and KDR can be thought of as 16-bit registers. However, only bit 7 of KSR has any significance. Similarly, the high byte of KDR is never used.

Another important point to note with regard to KSR and KDR is that they cannot be changed by the program. That is, it is possible to use these registers as *source* operands, but not destination operands.

The printer or display unit also has a status and a data register, which we shall call the Printer Data Register (PDR) and Printer Status Register (PSR). These are shown in Fig. 8.8. The PDR and PSR work in conjunction with one another similarly to KSR and KDR. In this case, however, the printer reads the character code from PDR and begins to print it. While this printing is going on, bit 7 of the PSR is set at 0. When the printing process is complete, bit 7 of PSR is set to 1. This indicates to the program that PDR is empty and ready to accept another character code.

We note that PSR can be used as a destination address only. Although it makes little sense to do so, if used as a source address, it would produce a 0 operand value.

8.8.2   Printing a Character
With the understanding above of the printer device registers we are prepared to write a program to print a character. The strategy to be employed is as follows.

```
LOOP:   TSTB   177564        ;TEST PRINTER STATUS
        BPL    LOOP          ;     REGISTER
        MOVB   R0,177566     ;PRINT R0
```

Figure 8.9 MACRO-11 procedure for printing a character.

```
LOOP:   TSTB   177560        ;TEST KEYBOARD STATUS
        BPL    LOOP          ;     REGISTER
        MOVB   177562,R0     ;GET CHARACTER INTO R0
        BIC    #177600,R0    ;CLEAR BITS 7-15
```

Figure 8.10 MACRO-11 procedure for reading a character.

1. Test bit 7 of the PSR
2. If bit 7 of PSR is clear, repeat from step 1.
3. When bit 7 of PSR is set to 1, move the character code to be printed to PDR.

Steps 1 and 2 constitute an "idle loop," the only purpose of which is to "kill time" until the printer is ready. This is called "polling." As soon as bit 7 of PSR becomes 1, i.e., the printer is ready, we go to step 3 which moves the code of the character to be printed into the PDR. The printer handles the process from this point.

MACRO-11 code to accomplish the printing strategy above is shown in Fig. 8.9. Note that we examine bit 7 of PSR (address 177564) by doing a TSTB followed by BPL. This works because BPL examines *only* the N condition code of the program status word, and N is set by TSTB only if the MSB of the *byte* is 1. We assume that the character code to be printed is stored in the low byte of R0 prior to entering this procedure.

8.8.3 Reading a Character

Reading a character code from the keyboard follows a strategy similar to printing as described above. That is, we repeatedly examine the "ready" bit in the KSR. When it is set, we know that the keyboard has completed the placing of the character code into KDR, and it can therefore be read by the CPU. This is shown in the procedure in Fig. 8.10, which places the result in register R0. Note that after the KDR is placed in R0, we clear bits 7 through 15. This ensures that register R0 will have only the 7-bit ASCII code in bits 0–7 of the low byte with 0's elsewhere, as explained in Section 8.7.

8.9 Input and Output of Octal and Decimal Numbers

In earlier chapters we have specified the starting-point data for our numerical example problems by using ODT, immediate addressing, e.g., MOV #2,R0, or the initialization directives .WORD and .BYTE. These methods are not desirable for actual programs because they require the user of the program to be very familiar with MACRO-11. Moreover, if the data are established by instructions or directives, rerunning the program for new data requires reassembling and relinking on every use.

We now therefore take up the matter of accepting an item of numerical data from the keyboard and converting it to the binary internal representation. Conversion is necessary because the keyboard generates a sequence of ASCII codes for the numeric *characters*, whereas internally we want the *binary* number. For example, keyboard entry of the octal number 776 sends the three 8-bit codes (assuming no parity has been added).

00110111	(ASCII "7")
00110111	(ASCII "7")
00110110	(ASCII "6")

However, the true binary value of 776_8 is

0 000 000 111 111 110 (776_8)

Thus we somehow have to convert from the sequence of input ASCII codes to the binary representation of the *value* implied by that sequence.

The conversion process will depend on the input representation. That is, the baker's dozen could be entered in the decimal system as "13," or in the octal system as "15;" yet the internal representation is

0 000 000 000 001 101

in either case. We shall begin our discussion with the conversion of multidigit *octal* numbers, entered from the keyboard, to their binary internal forms. This is called octal input.

8.9.1 Octal Input

We shall develop an algorithm for this conversion based on three essential facts.

1. Keyboard entry of a number begins with the most significant digit and proceeds to the least significant digit. That is, when "176" is entered, the computer receives the "1" first.

2. The entered digits, assumed to be 0, 1, . . . , 7, are received by the computer as ASCII codes.

3. For a single octal digit, the binary value is obtained by subtracting 060_8 from the ASCII code. That is,

00110111	(ASCII "7")
− 00110000	(060_8)
00000111	(7_8)

These observations suggest the following algorithm.

1. Clear the result register, R1.

2. Accept a valid ASCII character between "0" and "7" into R0.

3. Subtract 60_8 from R0, giving the binary representation of the value of the digit.

4. Multiply the result register R1 by 10_8 (octal "shift" left). This step is required for digits after the first, and does no harm for the first.

5. Add the binary representation of the new digit value to the result register.

6. Repeat from step 2 until there are no more digits.

To see how this works, consider a simple example. Suppose the entered octal digits are "24." The contents of R0 and R1 *after* each step are shown below (octal is used for convenience; clearly, *binary* is stored):

Step	R0	R1	Notes
1	?	000000	Clear R1.
2	000062	000000	Accept "2."
3	000002	000000	Subtract 60_8.
4	000002	000000	Octal shift R1.
5	000002	000002	Add new digit.
2	000064	000002	Accept "4."
3	000004	000002	Subtract 60_8.
4	000004	000020	Octal shift R1.
5	000004	000024	Add new digit.

Observe that the key to the success of this algorithm is that we shift the previous result to the left one octal digit, then add the new digit. This is, in effect, just like writing each new digit at the right of those received previously.

Figure 8.11 shows a MACRO-11 program that employs the algorithm above. It has been enhanced by prompting for input by *, and checking for invalid characters.

After prompting for input, the input line is read, and the first character is placed in R0 by .TTYIN. If the character is a carriage return, it loops back to get the expected linefeed, and branches out. Otherwise, the character is checked to see that it lies within the range of valid octal digits ($060–067_8$). Note that for the first check, we subtract the ASCII code for a 0 from R0. If the code is less than 60_8, we know that it is not a valid numerical character and branch to the error-handling section of the program at L2. (Recall that the carry bit is set after a subtract that required a borrow into the MSB). If it passes the first test, we check to see if it is perhaps too large to be an ASCII code for a valid octal digit. Now, however, we have the *binary value* in R0 because 60_8 has already been subtracted. Thus if R0 is greater than or equal to octal 10 (decimal 8), we know that a bad digit was entered, and branch to L2. After such an error, a message is printed and the process is restarted from the top, clearing the result register and issuing another prompt.

The octal conversion code is composed of the two instructions—MUL and ADD. The MUL #10,R1 is an octal shift as described earlier. (If MUL is not available, three ASL R1 instructions will suffice.) The ADD instruction adds the binary value of the new digit. The BR L1 after ADD ensures that we loop back

```
        .TITLE OCTAL INPUT
        .MCALL  .TTYIN, .TTYOUT, .PRINT
;
;    ACCEPT KEYBOARD OCTAL (0-177777) TO
;    BINARY NUMBER IN R0
;
START:  CLR     R1              ;CLEAR RESULT REGISTER
        .TTYOUT #'*
L1:     .TTYIN                  ;GET DIGIT
        CMPB    R0,#15          ;IF CR
        BEQ     L1              ;LOOK FOR LF
        CMPB    R0,#12          ;IF LF
        BEQ     OUT             ;NUMBER IS COMPLETE
        SUB     #60,R0          ;CONVERT DIGIT TO BINARY
        BLO     L2              ;INVALID DIGIT
        CMPB    R0,#10
        BHIS    L2              ;INVALID DIGIT
        MUL     #10,R1          ;MULT. CURRENT RESULT BY 10 OCT
        ADD     R0,R1           ;ADD NEW DIGIT
        BR      L1              ;GET NEXT DIGIT
L2:     .TTYIN                  ;BAD CHAR. HANDLING
        CMPB    R0,#12          ;CLEAR TTYIN
        BNE     L2              ;   BUFFER
        .PRINT  #MSG
        BR      START           ;AND START OVER
OUT:    MOV     R1,R0           ;PUT RESULT IN R0
        HALT
MSG:    .ASCIZ  /BAD NUMBER, START OVER/
        .END    START
```

Figure 8.11 MACRO-11 program for octal input.

until all digits have been read and converted. The exit from the loop occurs upon obtaining the linefeed character that follows all keyboard entry through .TTYIN. The final step in the program is to place the result into R0 because this is the customary register in which to leave the result of an input operation.

It should be observed that while the program in Fig. 8.11 accepts octal numbers in the range of 0 to 177777, the interpretation of these numbers by the program is arbitrary. That is, number 177776 could be entered, and interpreted as a positive integer (65534_{10}), or as a two's complement number (-2_{10}). Thus in a sense it allows entry of negative numbers, even though a minus sign will not be accepted.

8.9.2 Decimal Input

The algorithm and program described above for octal input can, with only minor modifications, be used for decimal input. Indeed, the steps are the same except that the digits 8 and 9 must be accepted, and the current value must be multiplied by *decimal* 10 before adding the new digit. The program in Fig. 8.11 could be modified to accept decimal by the following two changes.

1. Change the invalid digit test to decimal 10 rather than to octal 10. This accepts the digits through "9."

2. Change MUL #10,R1 to MUL #10.,R1. This does a decimal shift rather than an octal shift.

8.9.3 Output of Octal Numbers

A numerical value is usually represented as either a two's complement or positive binary integer in a 16-bit memory location or register on the PDP-11. As such, it cannot be printed directly. For example, a common error by a beginning programmer is as follows (incorrect example).

```
        MOV     #52,A
        .PRINT  #A
        HALT
A:      .BLKW   1
```

Here the programmer may think that "52" will be printed. The reason that this will not work is that the .PRINT #A expects to find *ASCII codes* at address A, whereas instead there is the binary equivalent of 52_8, i.e.,

A: 0 000 000 000 101 010 (52_8)

Interpreted as ASCII, this is the "*" character followed by a null character.

If we wish to print a number, we must first convert it from its internal binary representation to a series of ASCII codes. This can be done by the subtractive method discussed in Section 2.4.3 in connection with "Decimal to Octal" conversion. This process works equally well for converting from binary to octal.

To apply the subtractive method with octal, one works with a powers-of-8 table.

n	8^n (in octal)
0	1
1	10
2	100
3	1000
4	10000
5	100000

The n in this table can be viewed as the digit position index in a multidigit octal number, and the power can be viewed as the "place value." For example, in the octal number 142365, the digit 5 is in position 0; because the place value of this position is 1, this digit contributes 5×1 to the value.

The conversion strategy is to start with the highest place value and subtract it as many times as possible from the number being converted. The number of times it can be subtracted is obviously the digit value for that place. Then the next highest place value is repeatedly subtracted to find the next digit, and so on. Note that this strategy determines the digits from left to right. This is important because this is the order in which they must be printed.

As an example, consider determination of the octal digits for the binary number

0 001 110 000 011 010 (016032_8)

By the subtraction method we determine the octal digits one at a time as shown in the table below (we show the work in octal, for convenience, but the computer will carry it out in binary).

Place Value	Can Be Subtracted	Remainder	Digit
100000	0 times	016032	$D_5 = 0$
10000	1 time	006032	$D_4 = 1$
1000	6 times	000032	$D_3 = 6$
100	0 times	000032	$D_2 = 0$
10	3 times	000002	$D_1 = 3$
1	2 times	000000	$D_0 = 2$

Observe that because the 16-bit PDP-11 word will allow an octal number of no more than six digits, we do not need powers of 8 greater than 8^5.

A MACRO-11 program using this strategy is shown in Fig. 8.12. The values placed in R0 by earlier parts of the program will be printed. The program uses two arrays—PV and A. The PV array holds the place values, while A is a byte array that will store the ASCII codes of the octal digits as they are determined.

The two pointers into these arrays, R1 and R3, are initialized prior to entry into the major loop of the program. The major loop, beginning at NEXT and extending to the SOB instruction, is executed six times; each time through this loop a new digit is determined and stored in A as its ASCII code.

Inside the major loop is another loop, beginning at COUNT and extending to BHIS. The body of this inner loop increments the current digit value and subtracts the current place value from the number in R0. Exit from the loop occurs when the subtraction results in a borrow into the MSB, which means

```
        .TITLE  OCTAL OUTPUT
        .MCALL      .PRINT
;
;       THIS PROGRAM WILL PRINT THE NUMBER FOUND
;       IN R0 AS A 6-DIGIT OCTAL NUMBER
;
START:  MOV     #01632,R0       ;EXAMPLE VALUE TO BE PRINTED
        MOV     #PV,R1          ;INITIALIZE PLACE VALUE POINTER
        MOV     #6,R2           ;INITIALIZE LCV (6 DIGITS)
        MOV     #A,R3           ;INITIALIZE RESULT DIGIT POINTER
NEXT:   MOV     #-1,R4          ;INITIALIZE DIGIT VALUE
COUNT:  INC     R4              ;UPDATE DIGIT VALUE
        SUB     (R1),R0         ;SUBTRACT PLACE VALUE
        BHIS    COUNT           ;   UNTIL OVERSUBTRACTED
        ADD     (R1)+,R0        ;CORRECT OVERSUBTRACT
        ADD     #60,R4          ;CONVERT DIGIT TO ASCII
        MOVB    R4,(R3)+        ;STORE CHAR. IN PRINT ARRAY
        SOB     R2,NEXT         ;REPEAT FOR NEXT DIGIT
        .PRINT  #A              ;PRINT RESULT
        HALT
PV:     .WORD   100000,10000,1000,100,10,1  ;PLACE VALUES
A:      .BLKB   6               ;RESULT ARRAY
        .BYTE   0               ;NULL BYTE FOR .PRINT
        .EVEN
        .END    START
```

Figure 8.12   MACRO-11 program to print an octal number.

that we have "oversubtracted." Therefore, upon exit from the loop, we correct for the oversubtraction by adding the current place value back into R0. This process *counts* the number of times the place value can be subtracted. At this point we have the *binary value* of the digit in R4; the ASCII equivalent is found by adding the ASCII base, 60_8, to R4. This result is then saved in the next byte of A, and the A array pointer is incremented automatically.

After exit from the major loop, all digits have been determined and their ASCII codes are in A. The .PRINT #A macro then sends these ASCII codes to the printer or display, completing the program.

8.9.4 Output of Decimal Numbers

With minor modification, the algorithm presented in the previous section also works for printing decimal numbers. First, observe that in decimal the place values are different, i.e., the second digit in a decimal number is worth 10 *decimal* rather than 10 *octal*. Second, the largest decimal number that can be represented in a 16-bit word can be expressed in five decimal digits (i.e., 65535) rather than the six required octal digits (i.e., 177777). These observations lead us to the following modifications to the program in Fig. 8.12 in order to make it convert binary numbers to decimal.

1. Initialize the LCV to 5 rather than 6. That is: MOV #5,R2.
2. Change the place values to decimal. That is,

   PV: .WORD 10000., 1000., 100., 10., 1.

   (*Note:* The assembler interprets numbers followed by "." as decimal.)
3. Change the storage array to five digits; that is

   A: .BLKB 5

With these minor modifications, the program will convert the 16-bit binary number in R0 to decimal output.

It must be recognized that the program modified as suggested treats the contents of R0 as a positive integer. That is, if R0 is

1 111 111 111 111 110

it will print 65534, not −2. If it is desired to treat R0 as a two's complement number (that might be negative), the program would have to be modified. This modification is left as an exercise.

8.10 Summary _____

The topic of this chapter has been input and output (I/O). We first examined the input and output of ASCII characters using the "macros" (meaning large instructions) often supplied in the operating system library. These macros included .TTYOUT that prints a single character, .TTYIN that reads a single character, and .PRINT that prints an array of characters. It was pointed out that these macros or their equivalents will have to be installed on your system before they can be used if they are not already in place in the library. It was also noted that some type of system macros are *necessary* if you are working on a multiuser, timesharing computer system. This is because such a system must necessarily control access to the so-called device registers (also called I/O ports). However, small "stand-alone" computers do not require and may not have these macros. In this case, the input process involves moving the input character from the keyboard data register, but only *after* looping until the keyboard *status* register indicates that the character is ready, a process called *polling*. Similarly, output requires moving a character to the printer data register after its status register indicates that it is ready.

A section in this chapter dealt with the idea of *parity* as a means of error checking. The central concept here is setting bit 7 (otherwise unused for a 7-bit ASCII character code) so as to give an *even* number of 1 bits (even parity), or an *odd* number of 1 bits (odd parity). Then when the code is transmitted and one of the bits gets reversed (flipped from 1 to 0 or 0 to 1), the receiver can detect the error by counting the bits. If such a system is employed, the program can check for parity transmission errors. Even if no errors are detected, it will be necessary to ignore the MSB in any comparison with 7-bit ASCII codes in the program. This is facilitated with "masking" using the BIC instruction introduced in Chapter 7.

The last sections of the chapter dealt with input and output of numerical data. We observed that input required that the incoming ASCII codes representing octal (or decimal) digits had to be converted to binary and added into the developing internal value. The algorithm that we examined for doing this took advantage of the fact that keyboard entry produces the most significant digit first. Therefore, to ensure that each digit was added in at its correct place value required only that we *shift* the previous sum one digit to the left. This shift was achieved by multiplying by 10_8 for octal input, or by 10_{10} for decimal input. Indeed, we found that the algorithm could be converted to decimal input merely by changing the multiplier from 10_8 to 10_{10}, and extending the range of allowable digits. Numerical output required that we convert the internal binary representation to the series of ASCII codes required for octal (or decimal) representation. We found that an algorithm using repeated subtraction worked well for this purpose. In this algorithm, we found each digit, beginning at the left, by determining how many times the place value could be subtracted. An array of place values, selected by a pointer, made this process straightforward and efficient.

After determination of each digit *value* by this process, we converted it to an ASCII code and stored it for later printing. Again, we found that decimal output could be achieved by very minor modifications to the octal routine.

8.11 Exercises

8.1 Indicate what will happen upon execution of the following instructions:

    a) .TTYOUT #53   **b)** MOV #7,B   **c)** A: .ASCIZ /X + Y/
                                 .TTYOUT B   S: .PRINT #A

    d) .TTYIN   **e)** .TTYIN
         MOVB   R0,B   .TTYIN
         .PRINT   #B   .TTYOUT R0

8.2 Write a program segment that will prompt the user with a ")", then accept a single character *on the same line as the prompt,* then echo this character on the next line, and position the printer at the beginning of the next line.

8.3 Modify the program in Example 7.2 to accept the sentence from the keyboard, store it, then determine and print out the number of words and the length of each word. You may use .PUTOCT (see Sec. 4.9) or the program shown in Fig. 7.2. Label the results.

8.4 Write a program that accepts a sentence as all uppercase alpha characters, then prints it out with only the first character uppercase and the rest lowercase.

8.5 Write a program that accepts two characters from the keyboard, stores them in a memory location, then prints out the resulting bit pattern. (*Hint:* Use shift instructions to allow examination of each bit, and print out the ASCII character for either 0 or 1 as the case may be.)

8.6 Write a program that accepts two characters from the keyboard, stores them in a memory location, then prints out the word contents as four hexadecimal digits. (*Hint:* Use shifts and BIC with the appropriate mask to examine the bits in groups of four. Use these four bits to determine the appropriate ASCII code to print.)

8.7 Write a program that will accept up to 20 octal numbers in the range 0–177777 from the keyboard and sort them into descending order, treating them as positive integers. Print out the sorted list of numbers.

8.8 Work Exercise 8.7 but treat the numbers as two's complement numbers.

8.9 Write a program that behaves like a four-function, Reverse Polish calculator. That is, it should accept two octal numbers, then an operator, either " + ", " − ", "*", or "/". It should then print out the result. For example 20, 2, * should produce 40.

8.10 Modify the octal input and output programs given in this chapter to work in decimal, but with the numbers restricted to positive integers.

8.11 Modify the octal input and output programs given in this chapter to work with positive or negative integers.

8.12 Write a program segment that would work like .PRINT on a machine that allows access to the device registers.

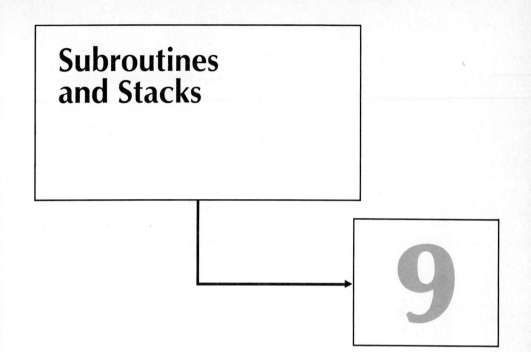

Subroutines and Stacks

9.1 The Need for Subroutines

Programs that we have examined up to this point have been small and relatively simple in terms of purpose. However, it will be found that programs addressing more significant problems become large and unwieldy if one relies solely on the methods presented so far. That is, complex programs that incorporate all of the detailed steps in a single, large set of instructions are difficult to develop, and confusing to those who wish to understand how they work. What we need then is some mechanism for dividing a large, complex programming task into a group of small, simple tasks. By far the most important of the programming concepts that allow efficient, straightforward construction of sophisticated programs is the **subroutine.**

This chapter shows how subroutines are written and used in MACRO-11. We will first develop the essential concepts, and show their application through simple examples. Full understanding of the MACRO-11 subroutine call requires that we then introduce the concept of a data structure called a **stack.** This is an important concept in its own right, but plays a key role in MACRO-11 subroutine calls. Other related matters are also discussed in this chapter, such as how to "pass" information to and from the subroutine, and how to avoid disturbing the contents of the general registers during subroutine execution. Finally, we shall examine how subroutines can be developed and assembled separately for later use in any other program.

This chapter also introduces four new addressing modes—**index, index deferred, autoincrement deferred,** and **autodecrement deferred**—used in connection with argument transmission.

9.2 Characteristics of Subroutines

A subroutine is a group of instructions that has a purpose *subordinate* to the main purpose of a program. These instructions are usually physically separated from the main program. This separation is made possible by two special instructions, namely JSR (*Jump to Subroutine*) and RTS (**Return** *from Subroutine*). JSR is placed in the "calling" program and causes control to be transferred to the first instruction in the subroutine. Unlike a branch instruction, however, a JSR causes the machine to "remember" where it was, so that control can be transferred back to the calling program upon completion of the subroutine. The RTS instruction performs this return transfer. It is placed in the subroutine (usually at the end) and causes control to be transferred back to the calling program, specifically to the instruction following the JSR.

Usually, subroutines have a single purpose and are small. However, any number of instructions of any type can occur in the subroutine before the RTS, and the entire module will be executed each time control is transferred to the subroutine. It is important to note that control can be transferred to the subroutine from any number of places in the main program, and even from other subroutines. This is possible because the computer remembers where it was, so that control can be transferred back to the correct place after subroutine execution.

Subroutines contribute to programming efficiency and clarity in a number of ways. First, they allow the details of subordinate computations to be removed from the main program. This helps the programmer because attention can remain focused on the principal problem being attacked, rather than becoming distracted with details of subordinate computations. Anyone who has to read the program will also benefit from this approach. This advantage is intensified in situations in which the same calculations have to be repeated at several places in the program. Rather than repeating the instructions, they can be written once as a subroutine and used, by means of JSR instructions, from anywhere in the program as often as needed. This method conserves memory space as well as programming effort.

9.3 Elementary Subroutine Usage

In its simplest form, MACRO-11 subroutine usage is by means of the instruction

```
JSR     PC,label
```

appearing in the program. This instruction will cause control to be transferred to label, which is attached to the first instruction in the subroutine. That is, PC is set to the address of label as assigned by the assembler.

The subroutine itself, occurring anywhere in the program (or even separately assembled), has the following form.

label: instruction 1
          instruction 2
          .
          .
          .
          RTS   PC

The RTS instruction causes control to be passed back to the instruction following the JSR PC,label instruction. That is, PC is set to the address of the instruction following the one containing the JSR. (Note that in JSR PC,label we are using relative addressing, so that PC is reset to two words beyond JSR.)

There are variations of the JSR and RTS instructions, but the form above represents the most straightforward, and not uncommon, usage.

An example of this is shown in Fig. 9.1. Here we have written a program that will divide the original contents of two numbers, stored in A and B, by 8, making use of a simple subroutine to perform the division. The main program is placed at the beginning, and the subroutine at the end, although this order is not important. DIV8 has been selected as a label, or name, for the subroutine.

Let us examine how this program works. The main program first moves the contents of A into R0 because DIV8 actually operates on R0. By placing A into R0, we are doing what is called "passing" or "transmitting" the argument to the subroutine; other methods of doing this are discussed later. The first JSR PC,DIV8 causes control to be passed to the first instruction in the subroutine, ASR R0, which divides by two. Two more ASR R0 instructions in the subroutine leave R0 at one-eighth of its entry value. The RTS PC instruction then causes

```
            .TITLE      EXAMPLE 9.1
        ;
        ;    DIVIDE A AND B BY 8 USING A SUBROUTINE
        ;
        START:    MOV     A,R0        ;DIVIDE A BY 8
                  JSR     PC,DIV8     ;  AND PLACE BACK
                  MOV     R0,A        ;    INTO A
                  MOV     B,R0        ;
                  JSR     PC,DIV8     ;NOW B
                  MOV     R0,B        ;
                  HALT
        A:        .WORD   16
        B:        .WORD   24
        ;    END OF MAIN PROGRAM
        ;
        DIV8:
        ;
        ;    DIVISION BY 8 SUBROUTINE

                  ASR     R0
                  ASR     R0
                  ASR     R0
                  RTS     PC
        ;    END OF SUBROUTINE
                  .END    START
```

Figure 9.1   Example of simple subroutine usage.

control to be passed back to the main program, specifically, to the MOV R0,A instruction that stores the result back into A.

The next sequence of instructions in the main program divides B by 8. This time the value stored in B is moved into R0, and control is passed to DIV8. Upon completion, RTS PC returns control to the MOV R0,B instruction. Note that each time RTS PC is reached, control passes back to the instruction immediately following the most recent JSR PC,DIV8 instruction. As noted previously, this is because it can "remember" where it came from. Below we will see exactly how the PDP-11 accomplishes this.

Subroutines are of great benefit to the programmer, but they also require consideration of factors that would not come up otherwise. These factors are

1. *Linkage:* Linkage, used here in a slightly different sense from the way we referred to the LINK step in Section 1.3, refers to the mechanism whereby control is transferred to the subroutine, and returned to the proper place after completion.

2. *Argument transmission:* Subroutines usually have certain required inputs and generate certain results. Therefore, there must be a mechanism for transmitting data to and from the subroutine. This is an especially important consideration when the subroutine is used for different input values from different points in the program, and when the subroutine is assembled separately.

3. *Side effects:* Ideally, a subroutine should perform a single task, leaving the world otherwise undisturbed. Any changes to memory or registers other than the intended changes are called "side effects," and are undesirable.

These considerations are taken up in the following paragraphs. We shall begin with a study of the data structure known as a stack because this can play a role in each of these considerations.

9.4 Stacks

A stack is a way of organizing objects such that the most recently added item is also the next one accessible for removal. The classic example is a stack of dinner plates in a cafeteria: Clean plates are placed on top of the stack, and are also removed from the top. The stack of dishes often lies on a platform supported by a spring, so that each plate added "pushes" the stack down farther, and each one removed causes the stack to "pop" up.

There is a way of organizing data that is completely analogous to the stack of cafeteria plates. Naturally, it is called a stack. It is an appropriate structure whenever the last item to be put into the set of data items is the next one needed for retrieval. Many problems in computer science require just such an organization. MACRO-11 offers convenient means of using data stacks in assembly programming.

A data stack will occupy a group of adjacent locations in the central memory. These locations are specifically set aside for the stack, either by the programmer or by LINK at the time the program is linked. In any event, we can picture the stack as shown in Fig. 9.2, where we assume that 10_8 words have been reserved for it.

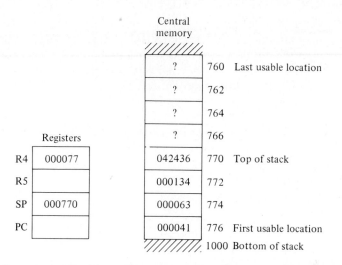

Figure 9.2 Data stack with 10_8 words.

First observe that the so-called bottom of the stack is one word higher in memory than the first actual data position. Each added piece of data goes into the next *lower* memory location. As it is shown, there are four entries in the stack, with the number 042436_8 occupying the "top" position. Words above the top will have some (probably nonzero) contents, but with respect to the stack they are regarded as empty. We show this with a question mark.

Although any register could be used for the purpose, R6 is conventionally used to hold the address of the current "top of stack." It is for this reason that SP (meaning Stack Pointer) is used instead of R6 in MACRO-11. It is sometimes called the "system" stack pointer for reasons discussed in Section 9.5.

An item of data can be placed in the stack (at the top) by use of the MOV instruction and autodecrement addressing on the destination operand. For example, suppose the stack and registers are as shown in Fig. 9.2. If the instruction

    MOV   R4,-(SP)

is executed, the result will be as shown below.

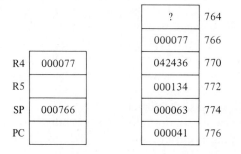

This instruction is often called a "push," in analogy to the action of pushing another plate onto the stack of cafeteria dishes. In order to remove an item from the stack, we use the MOV instruction with autoincrement addressing on the source operand. For example, if the registers and memory are as left by the previous example and the instructions

```
MOV     (SP)+,R5
MOV     (SP)+,R4
```

are executed, we have

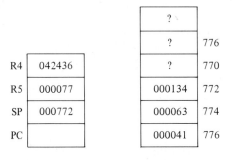

A study of this will reveal that we have removed ("popped") the top two stack entries and placed them into R5 and R4, respectively. Furthermore, this action has left the stack pointer pointing at the new top of the stack. Note that we again regard the locations above the pointer as empty, even though the previous values remain undisturbed in this example.

In general, then, stack data items are added or removed by the instructions

```
MOV     S,-(SP)     ;   Push S onto stack
MOV     (SP)+,D     ;   Pop top of stack into D
```

After either push or pop instructions, the stack pointer is left properly positioned for the next push or pop operation. The other operand in each of these instructions can use any addressing mode.

It is interesting to note that the same stack can be used for many different purposes, so long as three simple rules are followed. One rule is to always remove from the stack whatever you place there. For example, a certain value could be placed on top of the stack at the beginning of a program. The stack can be used for any number of pushes and pops throughout the program, and so long as every push was matched with a pop, the original value can be popped from the top of the stack at the end of the program. The second rule is to remove items in the reverse order of their placement in the stack. For example, if A, B, and C are pushed onto the stack, they must be popped off as C, B, and A. The third rule is not to depend on any value above the current stack pointer. The reasons for this are discussed below.

Space for the stack is usually allocated immediately preceding the program instructions. If a linking program, such as LINK in RSTS/E, is used, the programmer does not have to take special actions because the program will be loaded beginning at some offset provided by the linker, usually 1000_8. This has the effect of reserving 1000_8 words immediately before the first instruction, most of which are available for the stack (locations 0–300 may be used by the operating system). Moreover, the stack pointer will be set automatically at the offset point when the program is loaded. These two automatic actions have the effect of providing stack space immediately preceding the program, and this stack can be freely used within the program. This is often called the "system stack."

If a program is written for a PDP-11 computer without an operating system, or if a larger stack is needed, it will be necessary to allocate space and set the stack pointer within the program. A sequence of directives and instructions to do this is shown below.

```
        .TITLE    name
        .BLKW     1000     ;  RESERVE 512 WORDS FOR STACK
START:  MOV       PC,SP    ;  SET POINTER TO
        TST       -(SP)    ;      BOTTOM OF STACK

              .
              .
              .
```

The directive .BLKW 1000 causes the assembler to skip over (i.e., not place instructions in) $1000_8 = 512_{10}$ words. The first instruction is then assembled at location 1000_8, which is also the intended bottom of the stack. During *execution,* the MOV instruction is fetched and PC is advanced to 1002. This is the value that is therefore moved into SP by the MOV instruction. The next instruction decrements SP by 2, leaving it at 1000_8 which is the bottom of the stack. Subsequent pushes will store data beginning at 776_8, 774_8, 772_8, and so on.

The technique above can also be used to establish other stacks if more than one are needed in a program. If more than one stack are used, registers other than SP can be selected as pointers.

It is important to observe the size of the stack as it is being used. That is, if 1000_8 words have been reserved for it, no more than 512_{10} items can be placed in the stack. If it is attempted to push more items onto the stack, either adjacent data will be overwritten or an addressing error will occur. Attempting to pop more items from the stack than were placed there will result in the contents of locations beyond the bottom (i.e., higher addresses) being fetched. No error messages will result, although it is almost certain that the results obtained will be wrong.

The preceding discussion is based on the idea of a stack of words. It is also possible to use a stack in which the items are bytes rather than words. In this case the push and pop instructions would be

```
MOVB    SB,-(Rn)    ; PUSH  BYTE
MOVB    (Rn)+,DB    ; POP   BYTE
```

Here SB and DB are assumed to be byte-sized operands. We have used the byte form of the move instruction, so the pointer register will be incremented or decremented by one. A register other than SP (R6) must be used because SP is *always incremented by 2 even in byte instructions*. This is so because otherwise SP might be left at an odd address that would be invalid for its usage in subroutine calls as discussed below.

9.5 The System Stack

Above, it was stated that any of the general registers (other than R7) can be used as a stack pointer. Most often, however, SP (R6) is used. When SP is used, the stack is referred to as the system or hardware stack. This is because some instructions, notably JSR and interrupts, have need of a stack, and automatically use R6 as a pointer. Note that the system stack will be wherever SP is initialized as described previously. The user program having need of a data stack can freely use the same stack pointer and stack space by observing the three rules mentioned in Section 9.4.

9.6 Subroutine Linkage and the System Stack

We have previously noted that the principal difference between a normal branch and a subroutine jump (JSR) is the ability to return. We will now examine how the PDP-11 has provided for this transfer to and from subroutines. This is called linkage, and the system stack plays a major role.

The most general form of the subroutine call is

    JSR   Rn,label

This is translated by the assembler to

    004n67
    rel addr

where n is the number of the register chosen to be the linkage register, and rel addr stands for the relative address of the subroutine entry point. Normally, the entry point would be the first instruction in the subroutine, although multiple entry points are allowed. Any register except SP, the stack pointer, can be used as the linkage register. Also, the second operand can use any addressing mode although relative is the most common. The action taken upon execution of the JSR instruction may be thought of as three distinct steps that take place during a *single* execution cycle. These are

1. The contents of the linkage register is saved on the stack, i.e.,

    SP ← SP − 2
    (SP) ← Rn

2. The contents of PC is saved in the linkage register, i.e.,

    Rn ← PC

3. PC is set to its current value plus rel addr, i.e.,

PC ← PC + rel addr

The effect of this is to transfer control to label while saving the correct return point in the linkage register, Rn. The role of the stack is to provide a place to save the *previous contents* of the linkage register, so that Rn can be automatically restored after the subroutine is complete.

The general form of the subroutine return is

RTS   Rn

where Rn is the *same* linkage register used for the JSR. Its effect is the following two steps, both carried out in one execution cycle.

1. PC is reset to the contents of Rn, i.e.,

PC ← Rn

2. The saved contents of Rn is restored from the stack, i.e.,

Rn ← (SP)
SP ← SP + 2

Because the saved contents of PC is the address of the instruction *following* the JSR, this causes control to be returned to the proper place for resumption of the calling program. Upon this return, the linkage register has been properly restored to the value it had before the transfer.

We see now how the stack is used in subroutine linkage, i.e., to provide a mechanism for protecting the contents of the linkage register. At first encounter, this might seem to be convenient, but not essential. Couldn't one simply use a register for linkage that did not contain valuable data? To see the true importance of using the stack, you must consider the linkage problem in "nested" subroutines, i.e., the case in which one subroutine calls another subroutine.

An example of subroutine nesting is shown in Fig. 9.3. Here the main program

```
            .TITLE    NESTED SUBS
            .MCALL    .PRINT
START:      MOV       #77,R4
S:          JSR       R4,A

AR:         HALT

A:          JSR       R4,B
BR:         RTS       R4

B:          JSR       R4,C
CR:         RTS       R4

C:          .PRINT    #MSG
D:          RTS       R4
MSG:        .ASCIZ    /HERE I AM IN SUBROUTINE C/
            .END      START
```

Figure 9.3   Nested subroutines. (See also Fig. 9.4.)

calls subroutine A, subroutine A calls subroutine B, and subroutine B calls subroutine C. Because our intention is to examine only the linkage process, we have chosen subroutines that themselves do nothing useful.

Figure 9.4 shows the contents of the stack, PC, and the linkage register R4 as this program executes. Note that each instruction has been given a label for convenient reference. The successive states of the stack are shown *before* the instruction indicated at the bottom has been executed. Thus after the first instruction has been executed, the stack is empty and the address of the next instruction, S, is in PC. After the first JSR is executed, the return address is placed in R4, and the previous contents of R4 has been saved in the stack. Now the instruction at A is another JSR, so the return address for it must be placed in R4. First, however, the address for return from subroutine A, i.e., AR, is saved in the stack. Similarly, after executing the JSR at B we see that the return points for both of the earlier subroutine calls are in the stack. It should be apparent that subroutines can be nested to any level by this scheme, limited only by the reserved stack space. The process of always saving the previous contents of the linkage register on the stack ensures that the return address for each earlier subroutine call is saved for future use. Moreover, these addresses are available in exactly the order in which they are needed.

The right three panels in Fig. 9.4 show the stack, PC, and linkage register as control returns to the main program. Observe that the linkage register always has the proper return point regardless of which routine we are in. At the conclusion, the original contents of R4 is restored. This demonstrates how the system stack can be jointly used by subroutine calls and program data.

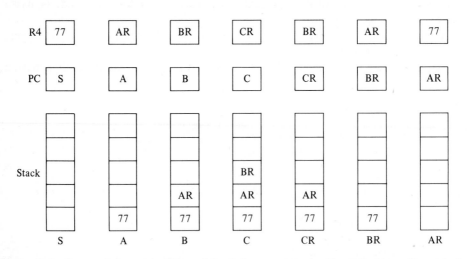

Figure 9.4 States of the stack, PC, and the linkage register for Fig. 9.3. *Note:* The state is shown *immediately before* the instruction indicated with the label at the bottom has been executed.

9.7 Using PC as Linkage Register

We noted earlier that the most common usage of the JSR and RTS instruction is with the form

    JSR   PC,label

and

    RTS   PC

It is now evident that this form of the instruction uses the PC as the linkage register, and is just a special case of the more general form.

The way in which this form works can be explained in exactly the same terms used in describing the more general case. That is, the JSR, PC,label instruction causes the following action.

1. The contents of the linkage register (i.e., the contents of PC) is saved in the stack

    SP   ←   SP − 2
    (SP) ← PC

2. The return address is stored in the linkage register. Because the PC is the linkage register, this amounts to

    PC ← PC

    This has no effect, but neither does it do any harm.

3. The PC is reset to the subroutine entry label

    PC ← label

    The effect of all of this is to leave the *return address* at the top of the stack.

When RTS PC is encountered, the following actions take place.

1. The PC is set to the contents of the linkage register. Because PC is the linkage register, we have

    PC ← PC

    that again has no effect.

2. The linkage register is reset to the previous value, which is removed from the stack.

    PC ← (SP)
    SP ← SP + 2

A careful study of these steps, and comparison with the general case, reveals only a slight difference; that is, the return is *caused by the restoration of the linkage register* when we use RTS PC; in the general case, it is caused by the restoration of PC *from* the linkage register. However, the effect is exactly the same, namely, return to the proper place in the calling program.

It will also be observed that using the PC as the linkage register does not compromise our ability to nest subroutine calls. Each successive subroutine jump simply places another return address on the stack. Afterwards, as the RTS PC is encountered in each subroutine, the proper return address is popped off the stack.

Even though both methods of subroutine transfer have the same effect, there are sometimes reasons to prefer one over the other. One advantage of using RTS Rn is that the return address is more directly available. For example, when using ODT it may be desired to determine the return address during subroutine execution. It is easier to examine a register than it is to examine the top of the stack. Also, some argument transmission methods are more easily implemented using a non-PC register for linkage. This is because arguments are sometimes stored immediately following the subroutine transfer instruction. In this case the arguments can be more easily found and used if this address is in a register rather than on the stack.

Nonetheless, the simplicity of JSR PC has some appeal if for no other reason than being easier to understand. This easier understanding can derive from omitting the unnecessary PC to PC transfer step in the explanation above. With this simpler view, we have for jump to the subroutine

1. Push return address onto stack.

   SP ← SP − 2
   (SP) ← PC

2. Set PC to transfer address.

   PC ← label

And for return,

3. Pop return address from the stack into PC.

   PC ← (SP)
   SP ← SP + 2

This explanation, although not showing precisely what takes place, adequately describes the effects and is much simpler than the detailed explanation for the more general case.

It should also be noted that by using PC for linkage, we avoid the use of a general-purpose register, leaving it for other uses. This may be critical in a program in which all registers are needed.

9.8 Translation of the Subroutine Instructions

The JSR instruction has the machine code

    004RDD

where R is the linkage register number and DD is the destination address code. The destination address can be in any mode, but is usually relatively addressed, i.e., DD = 67. As an example, consider the instruction

    JSR   PC,SUB1

where SUB1 is the entry point label for the subroutine. Let us assume that the
address of SUB1 is 100_8 words beyond the JSR instruction. Recalling that the
PC is two words beyond the JSR instruction after the JSR and its operands have
been fetched, the relative address of SUB1 is

$$2 \times 100_8 - 4 = 174_8.$$

The translation is then

    004767
    000174

If the address of the entry point label is lower than the address of the JSR, the
relative address will be a negative number, expressed as 16-bit two's complement.
For example, if SUB1 was 100_8 words before the JSR, the translation would be

    004767
    177574

It will be observed that because a full word is available for the relative address,
a JSR instruction can transfer control over a wide range. The transfer label can
be up to 16384 words after the JSR instruction, or up to 16383 words before it.
   The RTS instruction is translated as

    00020R

where R is the linkage register number, e.g., RTS PC always translates as 00207.

9.9 Register Protection

Ideally, a subroutine should carry out a specific intended purpose and do nothing
else. If nonintended changes occur as a result of calling the subroutine, it is said
to have side effects. Side effects tend to make programming more difficult and
more subject to errors.
   One step that can be taken to prevent side effects is to "protect" the registers
upon transfer to the subroutine. This is accomplished easily using the system
stack. The idea here is to push all registers used in the subroutine onto the stack
immediately upon entry into the subroutine. They are then popped off the stack,
in reverse order, immediately before the RTS instruction. For example, a subroutine
that makes use of registers R0 and R1 would be written

    SUB: (Entry point)
            MOV   R0,−(SP)
            MOV   R1,−(SP)
            (Body of subroutine)
            MOV   (SP)+,R1
            MOV   (SP)+,R0
            RTS   PC

It should be evident that this use of the stack does not interfere with its normal usage for linkage purposes. This is because we have observed the rule that all items pushed onto the stack must be popped off it.

9.10 An Example

We will now consider an example that demonstrates the definition and usage of a subroutine.

Example 9.1 Suppose we need a subroutine that performs division using the shifting method as shown in Fig. 6.11. This algorithm uses registers R0, R1, and R2 for transmission of input arguments, and returns the results in R0 and R1. The user would therefore expect R0 and R1 to change as a result of calling the subroutine. However, examination of the algorithm shows that R3 and R5 are also changed. When we write the subroutine we therefore must save R3 and R5 on the stack for restoration after the division is complete.

```
              .TITLE DIVISION TWO
DIV2:
;
;          INPUT:
;              (R0,R1)= HIGH AND LOW WORDS OF DIVIDEND (POSITIVE)
;              R2     = DIVISOR (POSITIVE)
;          INTERMEDIATE USAGE:
;              R0        = REMAINDER
;              R5        = QUOTIENT
;          OUTPUT:
;              R0        = QUOTIENT
;              R1        = REMAINDER
;
              MOV     R3,-(SP)        ;SAVE R3
              MOV     R5,-(SP)        ;   AND R5 ON STACK
              CMP     R2,R0           ;CHECK FOR POTENTIAL
              BLOS    OVERFL          ;   OVERFLOW OF RESULT
              MOV     #20,R3          ;INITIALIZE LCV (DEC 16)
LOOP:         ASL     R5              ;SHIFT RESULT
              ASL     R1              ;DOUBLE PRECISION SHIFT
              ROL     R0              ;   OF DIVIDEND
              CMP     R0,R2           ;SEE IF DIVISOR CAN
              BLO     ENDLP           ;   BE SUBTRACTED
              SUB     R2,R0           ;SUBTRACT DIVISOR
              INC     R5              ;PUT 1-BIT IN QUOTIENT
ENDLP:        SOB     R3,LOOP         ;LOOP IF MORE BITS
              MOV     R0,R1           ;PUT RESULTS IN
              MOV     R5,R0           ;   DESIGNATED REGISTERS
              CLC                     ;NORMAL EXIT
              BR      DIV2E                               \
OVERFL:       SEC                     ;C SET IF RESULT TOO BIG
DIV2E:        MOV     (SP)+,R5        ;RESTORE R5
              MOV     (SP)+,R3        ;   AND R3
;
;    RETURN TO CALLER
;
              RTS     PC
;
;    CALLING PROGRAM
;
START:
              CLR     R0              ;SET DIVIDEND HIGH WORD
              MOV     #33,R1          ;   AND LOW WORD
              MOV     #2,R2           ;SET DIVISOR
              JSR     PC,DIV2         ;DO THE DIVIDE
              HALT                    ;STOP
              .BLKW   20              ;BUFFER
              .END    START           ;THIS ESTABLISHES PROG. START POINT
```

Figure 9.5 Division with shifting using subroutine.

```
RUN DIV2

ODT  R01-04
*$3/176314 133333
*$5/010062 155555
*1072;B
*1054;G
B0;001072
*$0/000015
*$1/000001
*$2/000002
*$3/133333
*$5/155555
*;P
?M-Halt at user PC 001074
Ready
```

Figure 9.6   Execution of example in Fig. 9.5. [OS]

Figure 9.5 shows the subroutine implementation and use. Comparing this with Fig. 6.11 shows that the following changes have been made. First, we have given the procedure a name by putting label DIV2 at the beginning.

The first instructions upon entry push R3 and R5 onto the stack. At the end of the division process, we pop R5 and R3 off the stack, then return to the calling program. Note that the HALTs have been removed and replaced by the return instruction.

Following the subroutine we have placed a sample calling program with the entry label START. Because of the .END START directive, this will be the place that execution begins when the assembled version of Fig. 9.5 is executed. The first three instructions set up the dividend in R0 and R1, and the divisor in R2. The JSR PC,DIV2 then calls the subroutine, which transfers control to the label DIV2. Upon reaching the RTS PC, control is returned to the HALT instruction in the calling program.

Figure 9.6 demonstrates the program and subroutine shown in Fig. 9.5. In order to show that R3 and R5 are indeed protected, we use ODT to place arbitrary values in them before executing the program. A breakpoint is then set at the HALT instruction, and execution is initiated at the label START (location 1054). By examining registers R0 and R1 when the breakpoint is reached, we see that 33/2 is 15 with remainder 1 (observe octal arithmetic). By examining R3 and R5, we see that they have been restored to their original values.

9.11 Methods of Argument Transmission

Up to this point we have used the registers to communicate input data to a subroutine, and the results back to the calling program. This method is the most convenient and is often used if the number of arguments is small. In this section we shall discuss five other methods that can be used when there are many arguments.

9.11.1 Transferring Address of Arguments through Registers

Transferring *addresses* through registers is almost as simple as passing *values* through registers. However, there are occasions when it will be an advantage to transfer addresses. One such occasion occurs when the subroutine has arrays as either input or output. In this case, by passing the address of the array, whose space is reserved by the calling program, we avoid the execution time that would be needed to transfer all of the values. Also, this saves memory because the subroutine makes use of the same array space reserved in the calling program.

Example 9.2 As an example of this method, consider a subroutine to find the largest number in an array of 1000_8 integers. The subroutine and calling program are shown in Fig. 9.7.

In Fig. 9.7, observe that we use immediate addressing to place the necessary addresses into the argument registers first, then jump to the subroutine. After return, we use the octal output routine described in Section 4.9 to print the

```
 1                                          .TITLE BIGGEST
 2                                          .MCALL  .EXIT
 3                                          .GLOBL  PUTOCT
 4                                      ;
 5                                      ;   PROGRAM TO DEMO PASSING ADDRESSES
 6                                      ;       (FINDS LARGEST IN ARRAY)
 7                                      ;
 8 000000  012700  000032'      START:  MOV   #N,R0    ;PLACE ADDR OF ARRAY LENGTH IN R0
 9 000004  012701  000034'              MOV   #A,R1    ;PLACE ADDR OF ARRAY IN R1
10 000010  012702  000046'              MOV   #BIG,R2  ;PLACE ADDR OF RESULT IN R2
11 000014  004767  000030              JSR   PC,FINDIT ;FIND LARGEST NO. IN ARRAY
12 000020  016700  000022              MOV   BIG,R0   ;PRINT RESULT
13 000024  004767  000000G             JSR   PC,PUTOCT ;  IN OCTAL
14 000030                              .EXIT          ;EXIT USING SYSTEM EXIT ROUTINE
15 000032  000005              N:       .WORD  5
16 000034  000103  000022  000004  A:   .WORD  103,22,4,777,177777
   000042  000777  177777
17 000046                      BIG:     .BLKW  1
18                                      ;
19                                      ;   END OF MAIN PROGRAM
20                                      ;
21 000050                      FINDIT:
22                                      ;   SUBROUTINE TO FIND LARGEST NO. IN ARRAY
23                                      ;       (R0)=NO. OF ELEMENTS IN ARRAY
24                                      ;       (R1)=FIRST ELEMENT IN ARRAY
25                                      ;       (R2)=RESULT RETURNED
26                                      ;
27 000050  011112                       MOV   (R1),(R2) ;INITIALIZE BIG
28 000052  010146                       MOV   R1,-(SP)  ;PROTECT REGISTERS
29 000054  010446                       MOV   R4,-(SP)  ;
30 000056  011004                       MOV   (R0),R4   ;INITIALIZE LCV
31 000060  022112              AGAIN:   CMP   (R1)+,(R2);CMP NEXT VAL WITH BIG
32 000062  003402                       BLE   L1        ;REPLACE IF
33 000064  014112                       MOV   -(R1),(R2);  IT WAS BIGGER
34 000066  005721                       TST   (R1)+     ;READVANCE POINTER
35 000070  077405              L1:      SOB   R4,AGAIN
36 000072  012604                       MOV   (SP)+,R4  ;RESTORE REGISTERS
37 000074  012601                       MOV   (SP)+,R1
38 000076  000207                       RTS   PC
39                                      ;   END OF FINDIT
40                                      ;
41                                      .BLKW 20
42          000000'                     .END START

SYMBOL TABLE

A 000034R   BIG 000046R    L1 000070R    PUTOCT= ****** G    START 000000R
AGAIN 000060R    FINDIT 000050R    N 000032R

. ABS.   000000    000
         000140    001
```

Figure 9.7 Using addresses for argument passing.

```
LINK
*EXP9P2,EXP9P2=EXP9P2,GPOCT
*^Z
```

<u>Ready</u>

```
RUN EXP9P2
000777
```

<u>Ready</u>

Figure 9.8　Linking and executing program in Fig. 9.7. [OS] *Note:* This will not work unless GPOCT.OBJ is in your account. See Section E.1.

result. Inside the subroutine, addressing is done using the register deferred or autoincrement modes. This allows the instructions to refer to data stored in the main programs, minimizing the need for moving data.

　　Linkage and execution of this program are shown in Fig. 9.8. Note that we had to link the program and subroutine shown in Fig. 9.7 to the existing input/output routine called GPOCT. (See Section 4.9.) The program correctly selects 777 as the largest of the five numbers stored in A. The number 177777 may appear to be greater, but it is a *negative* number and we have used a signed branch, BLE, in the subroutine.

9.11.2 In-line Argument Values
The general form of the JSR instruction affords the MACRO-11 programmer another convenient means of passing subroutine arguments. This is called "in-line argument values" because the argument values are placed immediately after the JSR instruction.

Example 9.3　As an example, suppose we wish to pass two input arguments, X and Y, to a subroutine SUB1 and accept the result, say the difference between X and Y, into a third argument, Z. A subroutine and calling program using this method is shown in Fig. 9.9.

　　In this program we use the octal input routine GETOCT to accept values for X and Y from the keyboard. We then transfer to SUB1 using R5 as the linkage register. The arguments are stored immediately after the JSR instruction. This would cause a problem upon return if the PC was reset in the normal way. However, in the subroutine we use autoincrement addressing with R5 to access the arguments, and in the process R5 is advanced to the word following the last argument. This assures proper linkage for the return because JSR R5 resets PC to the final contents of R5. With this method great care must be used in matching the number of arguments in the subroutine and calling program. Otherwise, the linkage register will not contain the correct return address.

　　Let us examine in greater detail how this example works. Upon entry to the subroutine, R5 contains the address of the word following the JSR R5 instruction. Because X is in this word, the MOV (R5)+,R1 instruction gets X, advances R5 by 2, and puts X into R1. Because of the advancement, R5 now points at Y,

```
SUBTRACT           MACRO V03.01 14-JAN-83 14:45:13 PAGE 1
     1                                           .TITLE  SUBTRACT
     2                                           .MCALL  .EXIT,.PRINT
     3                                           .GLOBL  GETOCT,PUTOCT
     4                                  ;
     5                                  ;         PROGRAM TO DEMO PASSING ARGUMENTS AS
     6                                  ;         IN-LINE VALUES.
     7                                  ;
     8 000000                          START:
     9 000000                                    .PRINT  #MSG
    10 000006   004767   000000G                 JSR     PC,GETOCT   ;GET X
    11 000012   010067   000022                  MOV     R0,X
    12 000016                                    .PRINT  #MSG1
    13 000024   004767   000000G                 JSR     PC,GETOCT   ;GET Y
    14 000030   010067   000006                  MOV     R0,Y
    15 000034   004567   000070                  JSR     R5,SUB1     ;COMPUTE DIFFERENCE
    16 000040                          X:        .BLKW   1           ;ALLOCATE WORD FOR X
    17 000042                          Y:        .BLKW   1           ;ALLOCATE WORD FOR Y
    18 000044                          Z:        .BLKW   1           ;ALLOCATE WORD FOR Z
    19 000046                                    .PRINT  #MSG2
    20 000054   016700   177764                  MOV     Z,R0        ;PRINT DIFFERENCE X-Y
    21 000060   004767   000000G                 JSR     PC,PUTOCT
    22 000064                                    .EXIT               ;EXIT USING SYSTEM ROUTINE
    23 000066      111      116   120  MSG:      .ASCIZ/INPUT X:/
       000071      125      124   040
       000074      130      072   000
    24 000077      111      116   120  MSG1:     .ASCIZ/INPUT Y:/
       000102      125      124   040
       000105      131      072   000
    25 000110      104      111   106  MSG2:     .ASCIZ/DIFFERENCE IS:/
       000113      106      105   122
       000116      105      116   103
       000121      105      040   111
       000124      123      072   000
    26                                           .EVEN
    27                                  ;
    28                                  ;         END OF MAIN PROGRAM
    29                                  ;
    30 000130                          SUB1:
    31                                  ;
    32                                  ;         SUBROUTINE TO COMPUTE DIFFERENCE
    33                                  ;           (R5)=X
    34                                  ;           (R5+2)=Y
    35                                  ;           (R5+4)=X-Y
    36                                  ;
    37 000130   010146                            MOV     R1,-(SP)    ;PROTECT REGISTER R1
    38 000132   012501                            MOV     (R5)+,R1    ;GET X
    39 000134   162501                            SUB     (R5)+,R1    ;GET Y AND SUBTRACT
    40 000136   010125                            MOV     R1,(R5)+    ;PUT RESULT INTO Z
    41                                  ;           AND ADVANCE PC TO RETURN
    42                                  ;           ADDRESS.
    43 000140   012601                            MOV     (SP)+,R1
    44 000142   000205                            RTS     R5
    45                                  ;
    46                                  ;         END OF SUB1
    47                                  ;
    48                                            .BLKW   20
    49          000000'                           .END    START
```

Figure 9.9   Using in-line argument values.

so that SUB (R5)+,R1 subtracts Y from R1. R5 is incremented by two in the process of getting Y, so that the MOV R1,(R5)+ places the result into Z; the autoincrement addressing here advances R5 to one word beyond Z, which we see to be the correct return point for the subroutine.

9.11.3 In-line Argument Addresses
A variation of in-line argument values is to place the *addresses* of the arguments in line, i.e., after the JSR instruction. As with in-line values, it is necessary to use the general form of the JSR, and to advance the linkage register in the

subroutine in order to leave it properly positioned for return. However, this method of argument transmission requires a new method of operand addressing that we shall take up before discussion of other aspects.

A new method of addressing is needed because the argument *addresses* are placed following the JSR instruction, so that upon entry to the subroutine the linkage register will point to an address that *contains an address,* rather than a value. For example, we can write

```
A:    JSR        R5,SUB1
      .WORD      X
```

where X is the label for the location reserved for the argument X. The assembler translates this to

```
α      :      004567
              rel addr SUB1
α+4    :      addr
```

where addr is the address reserved for X, (i.e., the value assigned by the assembler to X) and α and α+4 represent addresses in which the instruction and addr are stored. When 004567 is fetched for execution, PC is left pointing at α+2, then PC is advanced to α+4 as the destination operand is decoded. When 004567 is executed, α+4 gets placed in R5, and PC is set to the transfer address SUB1.

Now, when we wish to access the argument in the subroutine, we can look in R5 to get the address α+4, and then look in α+4 to get addr, and finally extract the contents of addr. This is called **second-level indirect addressing,** as shown in Fig. 9.10.

The PDP-11 has a second-level indirect addressing mode in which the register is incremented automatically. It is called *autoincrement deferred,* and the assembly mnemonics are

```
@(Rn)+
```

where n can be any register. To show how this works, assume that we have the

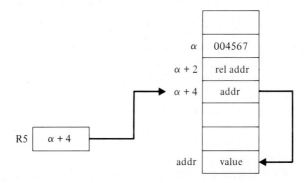

Figure 9.10   Second-level indirect addressing (autoincrement deferred).

following register and memory state.

R1:	000200
R2:	000000
000200:	000400
000400:	000111

Then when the instruction

MOV   @(R1)+,R2

is executed, we will obtain

R1:	000202
R2:	000111
000200:	000400
000400:	000111

Thus we have moved the contents of 000400 to R2, and have incremented R1 by 2.

As a companion to autoincrement deferred, the PDP-11 has autodecrement deferred. The mnemonics for this are

@−(Rn)

The only differences between this and autoincrement deferred are that Rn is decremented, and that this is done *before* fetching rather than after.

The address codes for autoincrement deferred and autodecrement deferred addressing are 3n and 5n, respectively. Thus the previous MOV example translates as

013101

Note the fact that the PDP-11 does not have second-level indirect addressing without autoincrement or autodecrement. However, the mnemonic @(Rn) is recognized by the assembler as index deferred addressing. (See Section 11.2.2.)

We can now return to the in-line address method of argument transmission.

Example 9.4   To demonstrate this method, Example 9.3 can be modified to use addresses instead of values. The listing in Fig. 9.11 shows the program with the necessary modifications. Note that we have moved the storage allocation for X, Y, and Z after the main program .EXIT. In the three words immediately following the JSR R5,SUB1 we have placed the addresses for these arguments. (Recall that the assembler determines values for the labels X, Y, and Z, and it is these values that get stored.) In the subroutine itself, we have changed the addressing mode for the arguments to autoincrement deferred. In this way we account for the fact that R5 *points to an address that contains the address* of the arguments. As each argument is referenced, the autoincrement feature advances the linkage register by two, leaving it with the correct return address. These changes make this program work exactly the same as the one in Fig. 9.9.

```
SUBTRACT          MACRO V03.01 14-JAN-83 14:49:50 PAGE 1
    1                                              .TITLE  SUBTRACT
    2                                              .MCALL  .EXIT,.PRINT
    3                                              .GLOBL  GETOCT,PUTOCT
    4                                      ;
    5                                      ;       PROGRAM TO DEMO PASSING ARGUMENTS AS
    6                                      ;       IN-LINE ADDRESSES.
    7                                      ;
    8 000000                              START:
    9 000000                                      .PRINT  #MSG
   10 000006  004767  000000G                     JSR     PC,GETOCT   ;GET X
   11 000012  010067  000050                      MOV     R0,X
   12 000016                                      .PRINT  #MSG1
   13 000024  004767  000000G                     JSR     PC,GETOCT   ;GET Y
   14 000030  010067  000034                      MOV     R0,Y
   15 000034  004567  000076                      JSR     R5,SUB1     ;COMPUTE DIFFERENCE
   16 000040  000066'                             .WORD   X           ;ADDRESS OF X
   17 000042  000070'                             .WORD   Y           ;ADDRESS OF Y
   18 000044  000072'                             .WORD   Z           ;ADDRESS OF Z
   19 000046                                      .PRINT  #MSG2
   20 000054  016700  000012                      MOV     Z,R0        ;PRINT DIFFERENCE X-Y
   21 000060  004767  000000G                     JSR     PC,PUTOCT
   22 000064                                      .EXIT               ;EXIT USING SYSTEM ROUTINE
   23 000066                              X:      .BLKW   1           ;ALLOCATE WORD FOR X
   24 000070                              Y:      .BLKW   1           ;ALLOCATE WORD FOR Y
   25 000072                              Z:      .BLKW   1           ;ALLOCATE WORD FOR Z
   26 000074     111     116     120      MSG:    .ASCIZ/INPUT X:/
      000077     125     124     040
      000102     130     072     000
   27 000105     111     116     120      MSG1:   .ASCIZ/INPUT Y:/
      000110     125     124     040
      000113     131     072     000
   28 000116     104     111     106      MSG2:   .ASCIZ/DIFFERENCE IS:/
      000121     106     105     122
      000124     105     116     103
      000127     105     040     111
      000132     123     072     000
   29                                              .EVEN
   30                                      ;
   31                                      ;       END OF MAIN PROGRAM
   32                                      ;
   33 000136                              SUB1:
   34                                      ;
   35                                      ;       SUBROUTINE TO COMPUTE DIFFERENCE
   36                                      ;       @(R5)=X
   37                                      ;       @(R5+2)=Y
   38                                      ;       @(R5+4)=X-Y
   39                                      ;
   40 000136  010146                              MOV     R1,-(SP)    ;PROTECT REGISTER R1
   41 000140  013501                              MOV     @(R5)+,R1   ;GET X
   42 000142  163501                              SUB     @(R5)+,R1   ;GET Y AND SUBTRACT
   43 000144  010135                              MOV     R1,@(R5)+   ;PUT RESULT INTO Z
   44                                      ;           AND ADVANCE PC TO RETURN
   45                                      ;           ADDRESS.
   46 000146  012601                              MOV     (SP)+,R1
   47 000150  000205                              RTS     R5
   48                                      ;
   49                                      ;       END OF SUB1
   50                                      ;
   51                                              .BLKW 20
   52         000000'                             .END START
```

Figure 9.11   Using in-line argument addresses.

9.11.4 Transmission of Address of Argument List

This method of transmitting subroutine arguments uses ideas present in several of the other methods. It is similar to the in-line address method in that it passes an address that points to a list of addresses. In this case, however, the list of argument addresses are *not* placed immediately after the JSR instruction. Therefore, the address of the list of argument addresses is passed in a register other than the linkage register.

This method is of interest for two reasons. First, it conveniently allows for a large number of arguments, without requiring that they be stored in adjacent memory locations. Second, it is the method used in the machine code generated by the FORTRAN compiler for the PDP-11 computer. Therefore, if this method is used, the resulting MACRO-11 subroutine can be called by a FORTRAN program.

We will need yet another addressing mode for this method of argument transmission. This mode is called *index mode*, and has the mnemonics

symbol(Rn)

Here, symbol can be either a numeric constant or a symbol whose value is assigned by the assembler, e.g., a label. The operation of this mode is very simple: The value of symbol is added to the contents of Rn, and the result is the address of the operand. For example, if we have

```
R1:        000200
R2:        000100
000204:    000177
```

and the instruction

```
ADD    4(R1),R2
```

is executed, there results

```
R1:        000200
R2:        000277
000204:    000177
```

Note that the contents of the location pointed at by 4 plus the contents of R1 (i.e., 000204) has been added to R2. Used in this way, this addressing mode refers to a value in a location that is *offset* by the value of the preceding constant from the base address in the register employed. This is the way in which it will be used in the argument transmission mode discussed in this section. Note that the contents of the register is an *address* when used in this manner.

In other uses of index addressing, the symbol is more conveniently viewed as the base address, and the value in the register as an offset. That is, we can write

```
MOV    X(R3),R1
```

where X is a label to which the assembler assigns an address value. During execution, the contents of R3 will be added to X to find the operand. Thus Rn is like a subscript in an array in high-level languages. Indeed, many of the array examples in earlier chapters of this book could have been worked using index addressing rather than autoincrement. Used in this manner, the symbol preceding the parenthesis is an address, and the register contains an integer that is an offset rather than an address.

The index addressing mode has the address code 6n where n is the register employed. The previous MOV instruction therefore translates as

016301
addr X

Note that the *value of the symbol* is stored after the instruction; in this case, this value is the absolute address of X.

It is also interesting to note that if R7 is used with this mode, we have what we have been calling relative addressing. Actually, relative addressing is a special case of index mode addressing when examined at the machine code level. As a convenience to assembly programmers, the special assembler mnemonics have been built into MACRO-11 for the case when the index register is R7, and this we have called relative addressing.

We can now return to transmission of the address of the argument list. With this method, the arguments themselves are stored in the calling program, and not necessarily in adjacent locations. Also, the *addresses* of these arguments are stored in an array in which the first element is the number of arguments. Let us demonstrate this with the following example.

Example 9.5   Suppose we wish to transfer the two arguments X and Y to a subroutine called SUB1, which calculates the value of $Z = X + 2Y$. We could write

| | MOV | #ARG,R5 |
| | JSR | PC,SUB1 |

```
        MOV     #ARG,R5
        JSR     PC,SUB1
          .
          .
          .
ARG:    .WORD   3,X,Y,Z
          .
          .
          .
X:      .WORD   10
          .
          .
          .
Y:      .WORD   20
          .
          .
          .
Z:      .BLKW   1
          .
          .
          .
```

Here we have used R5 to convey to the subroutine the *address* of a short array called ARG. The first element in ARG contains the number of arguments that follow. The symbols X, Y, and Z in the .WORD directive are *replaced at assembly time* by the *addresses* of locations reserved for their values, so that at execution time the ARG array contains the number of arguments and their addresses. As we have shown, the locations reserved for the arguments themselves can be anywhere, and need not be adjacent.

Let us now consider how the arguments are accessed in the subroutine. Because the address of ARG is passed in R5, any element in ARG can be found by index addressing. For example, the address of the first argument X is 2(R5), the address of Y is 4(R5), and so on. When the argument *values* are needed, they can be obtained by first using index addressing to move the address into a register, then using deferred addressing to obtain the value. For example, to compute $X + 2Y$, we could use the following instructions.

```
MOV    2(R5),R1    ;   ADDRESS OF X INTO R1
MOV    4(R5),R2    ;   ADDRESS OF Y INTO R2
MOV    (R1),R3     ;   X INTO R3
ADD    (R2),R3     ;   ADD Y
ADD    (R2),R3     ;   ADD Y AGAIN
```

This code can be shortened by using a new addressing mode called *index deferred*. Its assembly mnemonics are

@symbol(Rn)

that is just like index mode, except for the preceding @. This implies that the value found by adding the value of symbol to the contents of Rn is to be interpreted as an *address* where the operand is to be found. The addressing code for index deferred addressing is 7n. Using this mode, the code above reduces to

```
MOV    @2(R5),R3    ;   MOVE X INTO R3
ADD    @4(R5),R3    ;   ADD Y
ADD    @4(R5),R3    ;   ADD Y AGAIN
```

The complete subroutine and a demonstration calling program is shown in Fig. 9.12. In Section 9.12 we will see how this is modified for calling by a FORTRAN program.

Note that we have followed the FORTRAN convention of placing the argument count in ARG. This is done only to make the subroutine "FORTRAN-compatible." We do not use this count in this example. It could be omitted if FORTRAN compatibility is not required.

9.11.5 Transmission of Arguments Using the System Stack

Sometimes the most attractive method for argument transmission is using the system stack. This is particularly true in *recursive* subroutines, i.e., those that can "call themselves," as discussed in Chapter 12. Here we demonstrate the technique using a simple example that could be handled easily with other methods.

```
ADDRESS ARRAY   MACRO V03.01 14-JAN-83 14:58:15 PAGE 1


    1                                              .TITLE ADDRESS ARRAY
    2                                         ;
    3                                         ;   DEMONSTRATES FORTRAN-COMPATIBLE SUBROUTINE
    4                                         ;
    5                                              .MCALL   .EXIT,.PRINT
    6                                              .GLOBL   PUTOCT
    7 000000                           START:
    8 000000  012705  000030'              MOV      #ARG,R5    ;ADDRESS OF ARG ARRAY TO R5
    9 000004  004767  000050               JSR      PC,SUB1    ;COMPUTE Z =X + 2 Y
   10 000010                               .PRINT   #MSG       ;PRINT LABEL FOR OUTPUT
   11 000016  016700  000022               MOV      Z,R0       ;PRINT VALUE
   12 000022  004767  000000G              JSR      PC,PUTOCT;    OF Z
   13 000026                               .EXIT
   14 000030  000003  000040' 000042' ARG: .WORD    3,X,Y,Z    ;ARGUMENT ADDRESS ARRAY
      000036  000044'
   15 000040  000010               X:      .WORD    10         ;INITIALIZE X
   16 000042  000020               Y:      .WORD    20         ;INITIALIZE Y
   17 000044                       Z:      .BLKW    1          ;RESERVE WORD FOR Z
   18 000046     130     040    053 MSG:    .ASCIZ/X + 2 Y =/
      000051     040     062    040
      000054     131     040    075
      000057     000
   19                                              .EVEN
   20                                         ;
   21                                         ;   END OF MAIN PROGRAM
   22                                         ;
   23 000060                           SUB1:
   24                                         ;
   25                                         ;   COMPUTES Z = X + 2 Y
   26                                         ;      X=2(R5)
   27                                         ;      Y=4(R5)
   28                                         ;      Z=6(R5)
   29                                         ;
   30 000060  010346                        MOV      R3,-(SP)   ;PROTECT R3
   31 000062  017503  000002               MOV      @2(R5),R3  ;PUT X IN R3
   32 000066  067503  000004               ADD      @4(R5),R3  ;ADD Y
   33 000072  067503  000004               ADD      @4(R5),R3  ;   TWICE.
   34 000076  010375  000006               MOV      R3,@6(R5)  ;PUT RESULT INTO Z
   35 000102  012603                        MOV      (SP)+,R3   ;RESTORE R3
   36 000104  000207                        RTS      PC         ;RETURN TO CALLER
   37                                         ;
   38                                         ;   END OF SUB1
   39                                         ;
   40         000000'                        .END START
```

Figure 9.12   Using address of argument list.

Example 9.6   Suppose we need frequently to multiply by 8. Let us write a subroutine to do this, designed such that the number to be multiplied is placed on top of the stack before transfer and the result is on top of the stack upon return. The calling sequence and subroutine are then

```
          MOV       Y,-(SP)       ; Y TO TOP OF STACK

          JSR       PC,MUL8       ; MULTIPLY BY 8
A:        MOV       (SP)+,Y8      ; STORE RESULT
          HALT
Y:        .WORD     6
Y8:       .BLKW     1
MUL8:                             ; SUBROUTINE
          ASL       2(SP)         ; MULT Y  BY 2
          ASL       2(SP)         ;    AGAIN AND
```

```
ASL        2(SP)        ;          AGAIN
RTS        PC           ; RETURN
 .
 .
 .
```

This demonstrates the technique of using index addressing in the stack to reach the argument. To see this, note that the stack contents after MUL8 is reached is

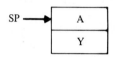

Thus the return address is pointed at by SP, and Y is in the next word, i.e., SP plus 2. Recalling that with index addressing the operand address is the sum of the preceding value and the register contents, we see that 2(SP) refers to Y. In the example the contents of this location in the stack is multiplied by 2 three times.

When the RTS PC causes the return address to be popped from the stack, the result is left at the top as desired. It is especially important when using the stack in a subroutine to remember that the return address must be at the top of the stack upon reaching RTS PC. In the example above, we are assured of this by not disturbing it at all. Alternately, it can be removed from the stack and saved in a temporary location so that arguments in the stack can be popped. It is then necessary to place the return address back on the stack immediately before return.

9.12 Separately Assembled Subroutines

The examples to this point have shown the subroutines as part of the main program that uses them. In larger programming efforts, it is most often preferred to have subroutines as completely separate "modules" that are assembled separately and saved in machine code (object) form as separate files. This has several advantages, including reduction of the size of the file that has to be continually reassembled during program development. Also, separately assembled programs can be used by many different programmers in a variety of different programs.

We have already seen an example of a separately assembled subroutine in Section 4.9. There the subroutines GETOCT and PUTOCT were assumed to exist as object modules ready to be linked with any program needing octal input and output. In this section, we shall see how such object modules can be created, and some new considerations that arise because of their separate assembly.

Example 9.7   To demonstrate separate assembly, let us modify the subroutine in Fig. 9.12 appropriately. The modified form is shown in Fig. 9.13. Comparing these two figures shows that we made the following changes.

1. Moved the subroutine instructions to a separate file called SUB1.MAC.
2. Added a .TITLE directive to the subroutine.
3. Inserted a .GLOBL SUB1 directive to the subroutine.
4. Added an .END directive in the subroutine.
5. Inserted a .GLOBL SUB1 directive in the main program.

The .GLOBL directive alerts the assembler that the listed symbols, in this case SUB1, have meaning outside of the module being assembled. In the case of the main program, the assembler will simply mark all references to this symbol as G(global) rather than flagging them as "undefined symbol" errors. In the subroutine, the assembler is alerted to the fact that some other modules, e.g., the main program, may refer to the symbol. This is indicated in the listing by SUB1 being marked G in the symbol table. When the LINK program is used as shown below, the symbol tables of all linked modules are searched for the global symbols referred to in other modules. This allows the linker to arrive at the correct addresses for subroutine transfers during execution. This process is called *resolving external references*.

In the subroutine, we have indicated that the label SUB1 is global by the directive .GLOBL SUB1. This can also be done by using a double colon following the label itself at the point at which it is defined in the subroutine. For example,

SUB1::

When this method is used, the explicit .GLOBL directive is omitted. Note that this works only for symbols *defined* in the module, so that in the main program we must use the directive .GLOBL.

Once the main program and subroutines have been placed in separate source files, they can be separately assembled, then linked and run. These steps are shown in Fig. 9.14.

Example 9.8   When the subroutine SUB1 was introduced in Example 9.5, it was pointed out that the argument passing and linkage conventions were FORTRAN-compatible. We can now demonstrate this by using the separately assembled MACRO-11 subroutine SUB1, as shown in Fig. 9.13(b), linked with a FORTRAN program. Figure 9.15(a) shows a short FORTRAN program that reads two integers, I and J, from the terminal keyboard. It then calls SUB, passing I and J as the first two arguments. The input values thus are assigned to X and Y in the MACRO-11 subroutine, and are used to compute Z, the third argument. Because the third argument in the calling program is K, K takes on the value calculated for Z.

```
 1                                                  .TITLE ADDRESS ARRAY
 2                                         ;
 3                                         ;      DEMONSTRATES SEPARATELY ASSEMBLED MAIN PROGRAM
 4                                         ;
 5                                                  .MCALL    .EXIT,.PRINT
 6                                                  .GLOBL    PUTOCT,SUB1
 7 000000                          START:
 8 000000    012705  000030'               MOV       #ARG,R5    ;ADDRESS OF ARG ARRAY TO R5
 9 000004    004767  000000G               JSR       PC,SUB1    ;COMPUTE Z =X + 2 Y
10 000010                                  .PRINT    #MSG       ;PRINT LABEL FOR OUTPUT
11 000016    016700  000022               MOV       Z,R0       ;PRINT VALUE
12 000022    004767  000000G               JSR       PC,PUTOCT;   OF Z
13 000026                                  .EXIT
14 000030    000003  000040' 000042' ARG:  .WORD     3,X,Y,Z    ;ARGUMENT ADDRESS ARRAY
   000036    000044'
15 000040    000010                  X:    .WORD     10         ;INITIALIZE X
16 000042    000020                  Y:    .WORD     20         ;INITIALIZE Y
17 000044                            Z:    .BLKW     1          ;RESERVE WORD FOR Z
18 000046       130     040     053  MSG:  .ASCIZ/X + 2 Y =/
   000051       040     062     040
   000054       131     040     075
   000057       000
19                                         ;
20                                         ;      END OF MAIN PROGRAM
21                                         ;
22            000000'                       .END START
```

SYMBOL TABLE

```
ARG   000030R   PUTOCT= ****** G   SUB1  = ****** G    Y    000042R    Z    000044R
MSG   000046R   START   000000R    X       000040R
```

```
. ABS.  000000    000
        000060    001
```

(a)

```
 1                                                  .TITLE SUB1
 2 000000                          SUB1:
 3                                                  .GLOBL    SUB1
 4                                         ;
 5                                         ;      COMPUTES Z = X + 2 Y
 6                                         ;          X=2(R5)
 7                                         ;          Y=4(R5)
 8                                         ;          Z=6(R5)
 9                                         ;
10 000000    010346                        MOV       R3,-(SP)   ;PROTECT R3
11 000002    017503  000002               MOV       @2(R5),R3  ;PUT X IN R3
12 000006    067503  000004               ADD       @4(R5),R3  ;ADD Y
13 000012    067503  000004               ADD       @4(R5),R3  ;   TWICE.
14 000016    010375  000006               MOV       R3,@6(R5)  ;PUT RESULT INTO Z
15 000022    012603                        MOV       (SP)+,R3   ;RESTORE R3
16 000024    000207                        RTS       PC         ;RETURN TO CALLER
17                                         ;
18                                         ;      END OF SUB1
19                                         ;
20            000001                        .END
```

SYMBOL TABLE

```
SUB1    000000RG

        000026     001
```

(b)

Figure 9.13 Separately assembled subroutines: (a) main program; (b) subroutine SUB1.

```
MACRO EXP9P6,EXP9P6=EXP9P6
ERRORS DETECTED:  0

Ready

MACRO SUB1,SUB1=SUB1
ERRORS DETECTED:  0

Ready

LINK EXP9P6,EXP9P6=EXP9P6,SUB1,GPOCT

Ready

RUN EXP9P6

X + 2 Y =
000050

Ready
```

Figure 9.14   Separate assembly, linkage, and execution. [OS] *Note:* This will not work unless GPOCT.OBJ is in your account. See Section E.1.

Figures 9.15(b),(c), and (d) show the compilation of the FORTRAN program, linkage, and execution. We observe that an input of 10 and 20 for I and J, respectively, produces a result of 50 as expected, thus demonstrating proper argument passing and linkage. Often FORTRAN programs can be made to execute

```
C
C          FORTRAN PROGRAM TO DEMONSTRATE
C          MACRO SUBROUTINE USAGE
C
           READ(5,*)I,J
           CALL SUB1(I,J,K)
           WRITE(7,*)I,J,K
           END

(a)


FOR
*TRY,TRY=TRY
.MAIN.
*^Z

Ready

(b)


LINK TRY,TRY=TRY,SUB1

Ready

(c)


RUN TRY
10,20
        10      20      50
STOP --

Ready

(d)
```

Figure 9.15   MACRO-11 subroutine usage with FORTRAN. [OS] (a) FORTRAN program (saved in TRY.FOR); (b) compilation; (c) linkage; (d) run.

much faster by coding key subroutines in assembly and linking as shown in this example.

9.13 Summary

This chapter has been aimed at the use of subroutines in assembly language programming. As in high-level language programming, the use of subroutines provides a mechanism for breaking a large assembly language programming task into a number of smaller ones. MACRO-11 provides a convenient means of implementing subroutines based on the use of two special instructions, JSR and RTS, and upon the so-called system stack.

The JSR instruction transfers control to the subroutine. Its most general form is

JSR   Rn,label

where Rn is any register except R6, and label is the label attached to the subroutine "entry point." The register selected is called the linkage register because the address of the instruction *after* the JSR is stored in it. This provides the information needed to transfer control back to the calling point after completion of the subroutine. Before the return address is stored in Rn, however, the then-current value in Rn is saved on the system stack, so that it can be restored after subroutine completion. This provides automatic "protection" of the linkage register. Other registers can also be protected by saving their contents on the stack, but this requires specific instructions inside the subroutine, as we saw in Example 9.1.

A simplified form of the subroutine transfer instruction is often used. This is

JSR   PC,label

In this case, the return address winds up stored on the stack. However, careful study of this form reveals it to be just a special case of the more general form. The choice depends on which method is selected for argument transmission.

The companion to the JSR is the RTS instruction. This instruction is placed in the subroutine at the place at which it is desired to return to the calling program. It reverses the effect of the JSR in the sense that the PC is reset to the proper address at which execution is to resume in the calling program, and the linkage register is restored.

In this chapter we also examined the concept of a "stack" as a general means of data organization. Its special property is that the most recently added item is the next available for removal. In MACRO-11, data are "pushed" onto the stack with MOV S,−(SP), and are "popped" off by MOV (SP)+,D.

While the stack has many other uses, it is particularly useful in subroutine transfer. We saw that the PDP-11 makes use of register R6 (alias SP) as a "system stack pointer" in the sense that the JSR instruction automatically saves the contents of the linkage register in the location pointed at by SP. Operating system software, i.e., LINK, allows a number of locations immediately preceding the user's program as a "system stack," and sets SP to its bottom when execution begins. This usually provides enough stack space to allow general usage in the program for temporary data storage, as well as subroutine linkage. We noted that one must always retrieve information from the stack in the reverse order of placing it there, and must remove all items placed there. If these rules are not followed for stack usage inside the subroutine, linkage back to the main program will be lost.

The input and output data for subroutines are called arguments, and we examined several different ways for them to be transmitted back and forth. The simplest way is to pass values through registers, but this will not suffice if there are very many arguments. We saw that an alternative is to use a register to pass an *address* where the argument can be found; this serves especially well with array arguments. Still another alternative is to reserve the storage locations for the argument values immediately after the JSR, i.e., "in line." Then, using the more general form of the JSR, the linkage register will contain the address of the first argument when the subroutine is reached. The arguments can then be accessed using autoincrement addressing with the linkage register. If all of the arguments are so referenced, the linkage register will contain the correct return address upon reaching the RTS instruction.

A variation of the in-line value transmission method is in-line addresses. Here the argument *addresses* are stored immediately after the JSR, so that upon subroutine entry the linkage register points to an address that contains the address of the first argument. Access then requires use of the autoincrement deferred addressing mode, introduced here for the first time.

Autoincrement deferred addressing is indicated by the mnemonics @(Rn)+. This addressing mode causes the quantity found in the address pointed at by Rn to be interpreted as the *address* of the operand, and afterwards the register contents to be incremented. This is called second-level indirect addressing. There is a companion autodecrement deferred mode, @−(Rn), but second-level indirect addressing is *not* available on the PDP-11 without modification of register contents.

Another very flexible argument transmission method is characterized by passing a single address through a register. This address is that of an array containing the number of arguments, followed by the addresses of the arguments. Access to the arguments is then through the use of two newly introduced addressing modes called index and index deferred addressing. The assembly mnemonics for index addressing are *symbol*(Rn), and it is understood that the operand address is the sum of *symbol* and the register contents. Index deferred is indicated by @*symbol*(Rn), where the sum of *symbol* and the register contents produce the address of the location in which the operand address can be found. The principal advantage of this method of argument transmission is the flexibility allowed in the number and storage locations of the arguments. In particular, it is used by the PDP-11 FORTRAN compiler, so that MACRO-11 subroutines using it can be called from FORTRAN programs.

As a final method of argument transmission, we considered use of the system stack. Here, arguments are simply pushed onto the stack by the calling program, and accessed internally by popping or using index addressing into the stack. Special care must be taken because of the way that the stack is used in the linkage process. This method of argument transmission plays an important role in recursive subroutines that will be discussed in Chapter 12.

The chapter concluded with consideration of separate assembly of MACRO-11 subroutines. This concept allows full achievement of the advantages of subroutines in that, after it has been tested, a subroutine can be assembled once and for all and stored in object form. Programs that use it then do not need to include its source code, but simply "link" with it before execution. This is made possible with the concept of "global" symbols in the assembly process. Use of the .GLOBL directive tells the assembler that the subroutine name is global, i.e., will be determined at linkage time; reference to it in a separately assembled calling program will not then treat it as an undefined symbol. The subroutine entry-point label must also be declared global in the subroutine itself, so that it will be placed in a list of global symbols searched by LINK.

9.14 Exercises

9.1 Enter and assemble the program shown in Fig. 9.3, and execute it using ODT. Set breakpoints at S, A, B, C, CR, BR, and AR. Examine the stack, PC and R4, at each break verifying the states shown in Fig. 9.4.

9.2 Revise the program in Fig. 9.3 so that PC is used as the linkage register and examine the stack at each state as in Exercise 9.1.

9.3 Write a MACRO-11 subroutine that accepts an octal number as ASCII characters from the keyboard and returns its binary value in R0. Include a short main program to demonstrate its use. Assemble the main program and subroutine together. Link and run using ODT to show that it works. (*Hint:* The program in Fig. 8.11 can be converted easily to a subroutine. Be sure to protect the contents of any registers used in the subroutine, other than R0.)

9.4 Write a MACRO-11 subroutine that prints the number found in R0 as a 6-digit octal number. Include a short main program to demonstrate its use. Assemble the main program and subroutine together. Link and run using ODT to show that it works. (*Hint:* The program in Fig. 8.12 can be converted easily to a subroutine. Be sure to protect the contents of all registers used in the subroutine, including R0.)

9.5 Do Exercise 9.3 for positive decimal number input.

9.6 Do Exercise 9.4 for decimal number output of a 16-bit positive integer placed in R0.

9.7 Assume the following initializations of registers and memory locations prior to execution of each of the sample instructions given. Indicate all changes in registers and memory locations as a result of each instruction.

Register	Contents	Label	Location	Contents
R0	000004	W:	000500	000001
R1	000504		000502	000002
R2	000506		000504	000506
R3	000502		000506	000500
			000510	000500
			000512	000504

a) CLR   2(R1)   b) ADD   R1,4(R2)

c) CLR   W(R0)   d) SUB   2(R1),W(R0)

e) MOV   R2,@2(R1)   f) CLR   @4(R2)

g) CLR   @(R1)+   h) DEC   @(R2)+

i) MOV   @(R1)+,@2(R1)   j) SUB   @−(R2),@(R2)+

9.8 Write a subroutine that does software multiply of 16-bit positive integers using the shifting algorithm. (See Fig. 6.9.) Also write a subroutine that computes $Z =$

$X(X + 3Y)$ where X, Y, and Z are arguments transmitted using the technique of in-line values. Write a main program that accepts values for X and Y from the keyboard and prints out Z, using the subroutine. For input/output you may use the routines developed in Exercises 9.4–9.6, or the separately assembled routines described in Sec. 4.9.

9.9 Write a subroutine that searches a character string to see if it contains a given character. Pass the address of the first character of the search string in R0 and the ASCII code of the target character in R1. Return the location of the first occurrence of the target character in the search string as a value in R0. For example, if the search string is "NOW IS THE TIME!" and the target character is "S," R0 should be set to 6. If the target is not found, R0 should be set to 0. Assume that the search string is terminated with a null character. Include a main program to demonstrate its usage with several different search strings and target characters.

9.10 Write a main program that

a) prompts the user for "Y" or "N".

b) if "Y", accepts a positive integer from the keyboard and places it on the stack.

c) when "N" is entered, calls SUB.

d) halts or exits upon return from SUB.

The subroutine SUB should print the entered values in the reverse order of entry, and then print their sum. Assemble the main program and SUB separately. Link main, SUB, and decimal or octal input/output routines together and run.

9.11 Write a subroutine that computes the inner (dot) product of two vectors, i.e., $P = X_1 Y_1 + X_2 Y_2 +, \cdots, + X_n Y_n$. Transmit arguments using in-line addresses. Separately assemble a short main program to demonstrate it. You may use either ODT or suitable decimal or octal input/output routines in this demonstration. (*Hint:* Use register deferred addressing to place addresses of X and Y *arrays* into *local* locations X0 and Y0. Then use index addressing.)

9.12 Write a subroutine that computes the sum of three numbers passing the argument values in registers. Also write a calling program to demonstrate its usage. Repeat this for the following other methods of argument transmission.

a) addresses in registers   **b)** in-line values   **c)** in-line addresses

d) addresses of argument   **e)** values in system
    list in register   stack

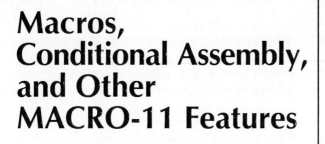

Macros, Conditional Assembly, and Other MACRO-11 Features

10.1 Overview

This chapter presents a collection of MACRO-11 features that, while not essential, greatly simplify program development. We first introduce the concept of **expressions,** and the **direct assignment** directive. The central idea of expressions is that the assembler is asked to perform elementary arithmetic prior to the translation process. The assignment directive provides a means of assigning a value that is *not* an address, at assembly time, to a symbol. One advantage of this is the ability to use mnemonic symbols in place of numeric constants in the assembly code, thus improving program clarity and allowing for easy change of a parameter. Taken together, assignment and expressions allow programs that can be more easily modified.

In the second section we take up the concept of **macro instructions,** or **macros** for short. Like subroutines, macros represent a way of coding an algorithm in one place and using it as often as necessary in other parts of the program. A macro is used simply by writing its name and operands (called arguments) much as if it were part of the MACRO-11 language. Prior to translation, the macro body is inserted in place of the reference to its name. This results in the translation being inserted "in-line" in the object code, in contrast to subroutines that require transfer of control to remotely located code.

Related to macros is the concept of the **repeat block.** This feature allows the programmer automatically to replicate a block of MACRO-11 instructions a specified number of times. MACRO-11 allows three forms of repeat blocks, each of which is discussed in this chapter.

219

Another major topic taken up in this chapter is **conditional assembly.** The idea here is that certain portions of the source code can be skipped during the translation process, depending on values assigned to certain symbols or determined from expression evaluation during assembly. This feature allows different versions of the object program to be created by making only minor changes in the source program.

The final topic of this chapter is the assembly process itself. This is presented in the form of a simplified algorithm for a two-pass assembler with some of the features found in MACRO-11.

10.2 Assembly Expressions and Assignment

10.2.1 Expressions as Operands

Up to this point we have restricted instruction operands to conform exactly to one of the given addressing modes. That is, we have allowed operands only of forms such as Rn, (Rn), A, X(Rn), etc. We now consider cases in which operands are *expressions,* such as $A+2$ or $A+\langle 2*B \rangle$ where A and B are symbols to which values are assigned during assembly. MACRO-11 allows symbolic expressions of certain limited forms, including the $+$, $-$, $*$, and $/$ operators. Note that there is no hierarchy among the operators, so that evaluation proceeds left-to-right, except for subexpressions in $\langle\ \rangle$ being evaluated first.

Using expressions as operands allows programming techniques not otherwise available. A frequent usage is to refer to a memory location that is a known number of bytes away from a location that has a label. For example,

```
MOV     A + 100,R1
```

will move the contents of the word that is 100 bytes beyond A into R1. This avoids having to assign a label to the operand byte. Note that the relative addressing mode is used here, and that the expression is evaluated during assembly. Thus if the PC-relative address of A is say 42_8, the translation of the above is

```
016701
000142
```

It is important to observe that the expression $A+100$ does *not* mean that the *value found in A* is added to 100. To remember this, keep in mind that all symbolic expressions are evaluated at *assembly* time, whereas location contents are usually determined during execution.

10.2.2 Symbols and Direct Assignment

Up to this point we have used symbols only as labels for memory locations. Actually, MACRO-11 allows a wider usage of symbols, and provides the *assignment directive* as a means of assigning values to symbols that are not labels.

Symbols have two major uses in addition to their role as labels. First, they are frequently used in place of constants in order to improve program readability.

For example, the instruction

    CMPB   R0,#CR

suggests that we are checking to see if R0 contains the carriage return control character, while

    CMPB   R0,#15

is less clear. In order for such a symbol to be used in a program, however, it must be given a value using the assignment directive.

The form of the assignment directive is

    symbol = expression

Customarily, the assignment directive begins in column one.

In the most common usage, expression is just a constant. For example, we may write

    LF = 12
            .
            .
            .
        CMPB   R0,#LF

However, the expression on the right of the equal sign could be any valid form as discussed in Section 10.2.1.

Global symbols can also be assigned values. Double equal characters indicate that the symbol is to be placed in the global symbol table for use in separately assembled modules. For example, if we write

    BEL = = 7

the symbol BEL will be defined as 7_8 in all program modules.

Symbol names follow the same rules as labels do. That is, they must begin with an alpha character and be six characters or fewer in length.

10.2.3 Advantage of Symbols and Expressions

Use of symbols and expressions can lead to more efficient programs, as well as to programs that are more easily modified. For example, let us reconsider the program in Fig. 5.4. This program makes use of the quantities N and NM1, the latter meaning $N - 1$. Note that the way we chose to program this required two words of storage for N and NM1, and required two instructions to compute NM1 at execution time. As an alternative, suppose we add the label EOD to the word beyond the end of DATA, define N and NM1 as nonlabel symbols, and make the following other changes to the program.

    N = ⟨EOD − DATA⟩/2
    NM1 = N − 1
            .
            .
            .

```
        MOV #N,R1
          .
          .
          .
        MOV #NM1,R2
          .
          .
          .
DATA:       .WORD  4,3,2,1
EOD:        (Next instruction)
```

The assembler will now assign addresses to DATA and EOD, and then compute the values of the symbols N and NM1. Note that it was necessary to change the addressing modes where N and NM1 are used because they are now values computed at assembly time rather than the contents of memory locations computed during execution. The program modified in this way is shorter by eight words and runs faster than the original program. Also, observe that it is more easily modified. If it became necessary to sort a larger array, it is necessary only to add additional values in .WORD directives between DATA and EOD. Unlike the original program, it is not even necessary to manually count the values in the array.

10.2.4 Location Counter Usage

A programming technique of occasional value is the use of the assembler **location counter** in expressions. The location counter is symbolized with a period ".''" in the assembly code, and always has a value equal to the address of the next location available for storage of translated code or data. The location counter symbol can be used where any other symbol can be used. As an example, suppose it was necessary to branch around a block of two words (4 bytes). We could write

```
        BR       .+6
A:      .WORD   74,54
        MOV     R2,R3
```

This is equivalent to

```
        BR       B
A:      .WORD   74,54
B:      MOV     R2,R3
```

However, by using the location counter we were able to accomplish the branch without introducing a destination label. As a rule, this usage is not recommended because it has less clarity than using a label, and greater care must be exercised if the program has to be modified later. More valuable usage of location counter addressing is demonstrated in Section 15.5.

When using the location counter it is important to be aware of exactly when it is advanced during the assembly cycle. The rule is that it advances *after* a line has been translated. Thus the instruction

```
A:      MOV     #.,R0
```

will place the address of the same instruction (i.e., the value of A) into R0. Note that the sequence

```
LC = .
A:        MOV     #LC,R0
```

will have the same effect because the assignment directive does not advance the location counter.

10.2.5 Pitfalls to Avoid When Using Symbolic Expressions

While use of symbolic expressions and assignments often allows savings, care must be taken to assure that the results are those intended. A common error is failing to recognize that expressions are evaluated and assignments made *at assembly time*. An example of such an error is the following (incorrect) program to clear an array beginning at A.

```
A:        .BLKW     100
START:    MOV       #100,R0
L:        CLR       A              ; (Incorrect)
          A =       A + 2
          SOB       R0,L
```

The programmer may believe that the address being cleared is incremented by 2 each time through the loop. Actually, this code has a conceptual error and, moreover, will cause assembly time error reports. Conceptually it is wrong because the expression evaluation and assignment are done only once because they are done during assembly, while the loop is repeated only during execution. Assembler errors are generated because A is first defined as a label, then its value is changed by direct assignment. On the second pass, the assembler will again encounter the label, and report it as a multiply-defined label. As a general rule, the same symbol cannot appear on the left of both an "=" and a ":" in a program.

Another common error is the attempt to increment the contents of a register using an expression. For example, the instruction

```
MOV     R1+1,B
```

may *appear* to add 1 to the contents of R1. Actually, this instruction says to move the contents of R2 to B because the addition is done *before* translation.

10.3 Macro Instructions

The concept of a subroutine, introduced in the previous chapter, provides the programmer with one method for defining a group of instructions in one place and using it elsewhere in the program. This was found to be an important advantage because it improves program clarity as well as reducing programming effort.

In this section we introduce another programming concept with similar advantages, called a **macro.** Like a subroutine, a macro is a group of instructions, defined by the programmer, that can be referred to by an assigned name. Wherever this name is referred to in the assembly source program, the entire set of defining instructions will be inserted into the source program. This results in the corresponding machine code being inserted into the object program, much the same as a normal assembler mnemonic causes a single machine code instruction to be translated. Indeed, the term "macro instruction" means literally "large instruction."

An assembler that allows the definition and use of macro instructions (macros for short) is called a macro assembler. MACRO-11 has such capability and, in fact, derives its name from this feature.

10.3.1 Definition and Use of Simple Macros

Whenever there is need to perform the same task at many different places in a program, considerable programming effort can be saved by defining a macro to do the task. This definition must precede the usage of the macro in the program.

The definition of a macro begins with the directive .MACRO and ends with the directive .ENDM. Everything between these directives is considered to be part of the macro definition. For example, a macro to interchange the contents of two registers or locations can be defined as

```
.MACRO    SWITCH,A,B,TEMP
MOV       A, TEMP
MOV       B,A
MOV       TEMP, B
.ENDM     SWITCH
```

Here we have selected SWITCH as the name of the macro, and have used three dummy *arguments,* A, B, and TEMP. Obviously, A and B represent the storage locations or registers whose contents are to be switched, and TEMP represents temporary storage. Note that while the macro name in the .ENDM directive is optional, it improves clarity when there are many macros defined.

Once a macro has been defined, it can be used as if it were part of the MACRO-11 language itself. Use of the macro above to interchange R1 and R2 using R0 as temporary storage would require only

```
SWITCH    R1,R2,R0
```

This would result in the following instructions being inserted into the source program.

```
MOV       R1,R0
MOV       R2,R1
MOV       R0,R2
```

Thus we see that the assembler substitutes the *actual* arguments for the dummy arguments, then "expands" the macro. Afterwards, the normal translation process takes place. When a macro is used, it is said to be *referenced* or *invoked*. The action of the assembler upon encountering a macro reference is called "expansion" of the macro.

The substitution process should be viewed as the replacement of the strings of characters representing the dummy arguments by the strings representing the actual arguments. With this understanding, it is easy to see the exact meaning of a particular application of a macro. For example, if we use the macro above to write

```
SWITCH    X,Y,T
```

it is evident that the resulting "expanded" code will be

```
MOV    X,T
MOV    Y,X
MOV    T,Y
```

Moreover, the same macro could be used to switch the contents of the two topmost stack locations

```
SWITCH    2(SP),(SP),T
```

that expands to

```
MOV    2(SP),T
MOV    (SP),2(SP)
MOV    T,(SP)
```

Thus it is seen that when the macro is used, its operands can be specified using any addressing mode.

Example 10.1   A complete program defining and using the macro above is shown in Figs. 10.1 and 10.2. Figure 10.1 shows the source file, in which it can be seen that the macro is used first with register addressing, then with relative addressing. Note that in the latter case it is necessary to reserve memory locations for the arguments in the main program; the macro defined in this example does not allow for any data storage.

Figure 10.2 shows how the assembler expands each reference to the SWITCH macro. Observe that the first usage results in only three words of machine code because register addressing is employed. In the second usage, relative addressing makes each MOV instruction in the expanded code translate into a three-word instruction.

Figure 10.2 also shows that the assembler *does not* generate machine code at the point at which the macro is defined. Rather, the code is generated only where the macro is used.

In the example in Figs. 10.1 and 10.2 we have included the directive

```
.LIST    ME
```

```
                    .TITLE  MACRO DEMO
                    .MCALL   .EXIT
            ;
            ;       DEMONSTRATES DEFINITION AND USE OF SIMPLE MACRO
            ;
                    .MACRO   SWITCH,A,B,TEMP
                    MOV      A,TEMP
                    MOV      B,A
                    MOV      TEMP,B
                    .ENDM
                    .LIST    ME      ; THIS CAUSES MACRO EXPANSIONS TO LIST
            ;
            ;       NOW USE THE MACRO CALLED SWITCH:
            ;
            START:
                    MOV      #3,R1
                    MOV      #4,R2
                    SWITCH   R1,R2,R0
                    MOV      #5,X
                    MOV      #6,Y
                    SWITCH   X,Y,T
                    .EXIT
            X:      .BLKW    1
            Y:      .BLKW    1
            T:      .BLKW    1
                    .BLKW    10
                    .END     START
```

Figure 10.1 Demonstration of a simple macro (source file).


```
MACRO DEMO       MACRO V03.01 13-NOV-82 17:52:25 PAGE 1

 1                                              .TITLE  MACRO DEMO
 2                                              .MCALL   .EXIT
 3                                      ;
 4                                      ;       DEMONSTRATES DEFINITION AND USE OF SIMPLE MACRO
 5                                      ;
 6                                              .MACRO   SWITCH,A,B,TEMP
 7                                              MOV      A,TEMP
 8                                              MOV      B,A
 9                                              MOV      TEMP,B
10                                              .ENDM
11                                              .LIST    ME      ; THIS CAUSES MACRO EXPANSIONS TO LIST
12                                      ;
13                                      ;       NOW USE THE MACRO CALLED SWITCH:
14                                      ;
15 000000                              START:
16 000000   012701  000003                     MOV      #3,R1
17 000004   012702  000004                     MOV      #4,R2
18 000010                                       SWITCH   R1,R2,R0
   000010   010100                             MOV      R1,R0
   000012   010201                             MOV      R2,R1
   000014   010002                             MOV      R0,R2
19 000016   012767  000005  000032             MOV      #5,X
20 000024   012767  000006  000026             MOV      #6,Y
21 000032                                       SWITCH   X,Y,T
   000032   016767  000020  000022             MOV      X,T
   000040   016767  000014  000010             MOV      Y,X
   000046   016767  000010  000004             MOV      T,Y
22 000054                                      .EXIT
   000054   104350                             EMT      ^O350
23 000056                              X:      .BLKW    1
24 000060                              Y:      .BLKW    1
25 000062                              T:      .BLKW    1
26                                              .BLKW    10
27         000000'                             .END     START


SYMBOL TABLE

START 000000R     T 000062R     X 000056R     Y 000060R

. ABS.    000000      000
          000104      001
ERRORS DETECTED:  0
```

Figure 10.2 Demonstration of a simple macro (expanded listing file).

226

This directive causes the listing file to show the expanded form of the macro, as we see in Fig. 10.2. Had this directive been omitted, such expansion would not be shown. Instead, the listing would show only the macro references as in the source file. In normal circumstances the latter is preferred because the expanded form makes the listing lengthy and cluttered. In any case, however, the assembler generates the machine code instructions for the expanded macro and inserts it into the object program at each point of reference.

10.3.2 Macros vs. Subroutines

An important distinction can be made between macros and subroutines. This is that reference to a macro inserts machine code "in-line" at each point of reference to it, whereas machine code for the subroutine exists at one place only and control is transferred to it and back each time it is used. The implications of this are important when either program size or speed is of concern. In general, the definition and use of a macro to perform a given task will result in a *larger* object program than it would have if the same task were done using a subroutine. On the other hand, transfer to and from subroutines takes longer than does sequential execution of in-line code. The magnitudes of these differences will depend on the size of the object code to do the task, and the number of times it is to be used in the program. As a general rule, small tasks should be defined as macros, and lengthy tasks should be subroutines.

10.3.3 Internal Labels

In Section 4.5, we noted that using the same label for more than one memory location could not be allowed because ambiguity would result. This is of concern when a macro has an internal label because every reference to the macro will generate a repetition of the label. For example, consider a macro to push N values stored in ARY onto the stack. This might be written as follows.

```
        .MACRO    PUSHN,ARY,N
        MOV       #ARY,R1
        MOV       N,R0
L1:     MOV       (R1)+,−(SP)
        SOB       R0,L1
        .ENDM     PUSHN
```

Then if we wished to use this to put two arrays A and B onto the stack, we would write

```
        PUSHN     A,NA
        PUSHN     B,NB
```

```
NA:     .WORD   5
A:      .WORD   1,2,3,4,5
           .
           .
           .
NB:     .WORD   7
B:      .WORD   11,12,13,14,15,16,17
```

When expanded, this would create two occurrences of the label L1, which is unacceptable. We will discuss two ways of dealing with this, namely, *argument labels* and *local labels*.

Argument labels require no new ideas. The labels internal to the macro are simply placed in the dummy argument list. At each use of the macro, a unique label is specified by the programmer as the actual argument. In the expansion process, the actual label is substituted for the dummy so that the fully expanded program has no repeated labels.

Labels as arguments are objectionable because they require careful selection of unique labels on each macro reference. Also, the requirement for specifying an actual argument that has no significance in the invoking procedure is, in general, not good programming practice. In order to overcome this, MACRO-11 provides another mechanism that uses the concept of local labels. We shall first examine local labels in general, then show how they are employed to resolve the problem of internal macro labels.

The definition of local labels depends on the idea of the MACRO-11 program being divided into a number of segments called *local symbol blocks*. This division is done automatically according to the rule that a new local symbol block begins with each *normal* label, i.e., those not constructed according to the rules for local labels as defined below. As an example, the code beginning with START: and ending with the line preceding NEXT: in Fig. 8.12 is a local symbol block, and that beginning with COUNT and ending with HALT is another. [The directive .PSECT (Section 15.4.4) and certain other directives also can be used to define local symbol blocks.]

The programmer creates a local label by making it of the form n$, where n is a decimal integer between 1 and 65535. For example, 4$, 6$, and 48$ are valid local labels. Any label so constructed will be recognized only within the local symbol block in which it is defined. This fact has two important implications.

1. Local symbols cannot be referred to from other local symbol blocks. For example, consider

```
2$:     MOV     R1,R2
           .
           .
           .
L4:
           .
           .
           .
        BR      2$
```

This will not cause a branch to the MOV instruction because L4 begins a new local symbol block. Either the BR will cause an "unrecognized symbol" error or, if there is a label 2\$ defined within the local symbol block beginning at L4, it will be the branch destination.

2. The same local label can be used in more than one local symbol block. When this is done, the assembler will treat each as a unique label.

It is the second characteristic that justifies the usage of local labels. If one uses local labels for branch destinations and loop labels, and uses normal labels for entry points for major blocks of code, there will be less chance of duplicate labels.

MACRO-11 uses the concept of local labels to eliminate effectively the possibility of duplicate labels during macro expansion. This is accomplished by putting the label in the dummy argument list with a preceding question mark "?", i.e.,

```
.MACRO      PUSHN,ARY,N,?L1
```

When this is done, the expansion process *generates* a local label n\$ with n between 64_{10} and 128_{10} to be used in place of L1. The first reference to a macro with a local label argument in any local symbol block generates 64\$, the second generates 65\$, and so on up to 127\$. The count begins at 64\$ again whenever a new local symbol block is encountered. The possibility of generating more than 64_{10} local labels in a given local symbol block is remote, but would result in illegal duplicate labels and assembler errors if it occurred. Note that automatically generated local labels represent one of the very few places that decimal numbers are used in MACRO-11.

Example 10.2   Figure 10.3 shows a listing for the PUSHN macro example with automatically generated local labels. The .LIST ME is again included to show the macro expansion. We see that the label L1 is replaced by 64\$ on the first reference, and by 65\$ on the second.

10.3.4 Nested Macros
It is possible to have a macro reference another macro. For example, suppose we wish to create a macro to save the contents of R0 through R5 on the stack. One way of doing this is

```
.MACRO      PUSH,X
MOV         X, – (SP)
.ENDM       PUSH
.MACRO      SAVREG
PUSH        R0
PUSH        R1
PUSH        R2
PUSH        R3
PUSH        R4
PUSH        R5
.ENDM       SAVREG
```

```
LOCAL SYMBOLS   MACRO V03.01 17-JAN-83 09:43:57 PAGE 1


         1                                        .TITLE LOCAL SYMBOLS
         2                                        .MCALL    .EXIT
         3                                        .MACRO    PUSHN,ARY,N,?Ll
         4                                        MOV       #ARY,R1
         5                                        MOV       N,R0
         6                               Ll:      MOV       (R1)+,-(SP)
         7                                        SOB       R0,Ll
         8                                        .ENDM     PUSHN
         9                                        .LIST ME          ;LIST MACRO EXPANSIONS
        10 000000                        START:
        11 000000                                 PUSHN     A,NA
           000000  012701  000034'                MOV       #A,R1
           000004  016700  000022                 MOV       NA,R0
           000010  012146                 64$:    MOV       (R1)+,-(SP)
           000012  077002                         SOB       R0,64$
        12 000014                                 PUSHN     B,NB
           000014  012701  000050'                MOV       #B,R1
           000020  016700  000022                 MOV       NB,R0
           000024  012146                 65$:    MOV       (R1)+,-(SP)
           000026  077002                         SOB       R0,65$
        13 000030                                 .EXIT
           000030  104350                         EMT       ^0350
        14 000032  000005                 NA:     .WORD     5
        15 000034  000001  000002  000003 A:      .WORD     1,2,3,4,5
           000042  000004  000005
        16 000046  000007                 NB:     .WORD     7
        17 000050  000011  000012  000013 B:      .WORD     11,12,13,14,15,16,17
           000056  000014  000015  000016
           000064  000017
        18                                         .BLKW     10
        19         000000'                         .END      START



SYMBOL TABLE

A 000034R      B 000050R      NA 000032R      NB 000046R      START   000000R

. ABS.  000000      000
        000106      001
ERRORS DETECTED:  0
```

Figure 10.3   Listing with expanded macro using local labels.

This technique is called *nesting* of macro *references*. The expansion of SAVREG will yield

```
MOV     R0, - (SP)
MOV     R1, - (SP)
MOV     R2, - (SP)
MOV     R3, - (SP)
MOV     R4, - (SP)
MOV     R5, - (SP)
```

It is also possible to nest macros to more than one level, i.e., to have a macro reference a macro that references another macro, and so on.

Definitions of macros can also be nested. That is, it is possible to write

```
.MACRO     ONE,X,Y
TWO        X
THREE      Y
.MACRO     TWO,W
```

```
MUL        #2,R1
MOV        R1,W
.ENDM      TWO
.MACRO     THREE,W
MUL        #3,R1
MOV        R1,W
.ENDM      THREE
.ENDM      ONE
```

Here we have defined and referenced macros named TWO and THREE internally to macro ONE. When macro ONE is referenced in a program, e.g.,

```
ONE     A,B
```

the resulting expansion is

```
MUL        #2,R1
MOV        R1,A
MUL        #3,R1
MOV        R1,B
.MACRO     TWO,W
MUL        #2,R1
MOV        R1,W
.ENDM      TWO
.MACRO     THREE,W
MUL        #3,R1
MOV        R1,W
.ENDM      THREE
```

It should be noted that the expansion yields the assembly and machine code for the references to TWO and THREE, and also the *definitions* of these two macros. Thus it would now be possible to make further references to TWO and THREE later in the program. It is not possible, however, to refer to an internally defined macro until *after* the macro in which it is defined has been referenced.

Features of MACRO-11 such as nested macro definitions have uses in advanced programming. Their importance to the beginning programmer is obviously limited.

10.3.5 More on Macro Arguments

In the preceding sections we have seen that dummy arguments in macro definitions are treated as character strings that are replaced by the corresponding actual argument strings during expansion. We will now examine some cases in which slightly different processes are used for some kinds of arguments.

One special case occurs when the dummy argument is to be replaced by an actual argument string that *contains a delimiter*. Delimiters are the characters used to separate the arguments, and include the space, comma, semicolon, and the tab key.

In this case the actual argument must be enclosed in angle brackets ⟨ ⟩, causing it to be treated as a single string during expansion. As an example, suppose we wish the capability to delay the execution of arbitrary instructions. We could define a macro instruction to do this as follows.

```
      .MACRO    DELAY,INSTR,N,?L
      MOV       R0, - (SP)     ;SAVE R0
      MOV       #N,R0          ;DELAY
  L:  SOB       R0,L           ;  N CYCLES
      MOV       (SP) + ,R0     ;RECOVER R0
      INSTR
      .ENDM
```

A typical invocation of this could be

```
  DELAY     (JSR  PC,READ),100
```

that would be expanded to give

```
          MOV     R0, - (SP)     ;SAVE R0
          MOV     #100,R0        ;DELAY
  64$:    SOB     R0,64$         ;  N CYCLES
          MOV     (SP) + ,R0     ;RECOVER R0
          JSR     PC,READ
```

Thus any time this macro is invoked, the machine will execute the SOB instruction N times before executing the indicated instruction. Without the facility provided by the angle brackets, this macro could not have been constructed because the spaces and commas used in the instruction argument, acting as delimiters, would have caused the instruction mnemonic and each of its operands to be treated as separate macro arguments.

Another special case occurs when an argument is to be treated as a number. In order to force the assembler to treat an argument as a number rather than as the corresponding character, the actual argument is preceded by a back slash "\".

Example 10.3 As an example of this consider a macro that will store the first argument in the next available location in an array beginning at A. This might be done as follows.

```
  .MACRO    NEXT,V,C
  MOV       V,A + C
  .ENDM     NEXT
  .MACRO    SAVE,V,C
  NEXT      V,\C
  C=C+2
  .ENDM     SAVE
```

To see how this works, let us examine Fig. 10.4 in which a listing with four expanded references to SAVE are shown. The symbol C is first defined to be zero, and the first reference to SAVE is at source line 12. Note that the *symbol*

C was substituted during the expansion of SAVE, yielding

```
NEXT X,\C
C=C+2
```

However, when NEXT X,\C is expanded, the \C causes the *value* of C to be substituted for the dummy argument of NEXT. This yields

```
MOV    X,A+0
```

Subsequent references to SAVE yield

```
MOV    X,A+2
MOV    Y,A+4
MOV    Z,A+6
```

and so on, due to the C=C+2 that is generated upon each expansion.

```
NESTED MACRO WITH NUMERIC ARGS. MACRO V03.01 17-JAN-83 09:51:49 PAGE 1


     1                                          .TITLE NESTED MACRO WITH NUMERIC ARGS.
     2                                          .LIST ME
     3                                          .MACRO  NEXT,V,C
     4                                          MOV     V,A+C
     5                                          .ENDM   NEXT
     6                                          .MACRO  SAVE,V,C
     7                                          NEXT    V,\C
     8                                          C=C+2
     9                                          .ENDM   SAVE
    10 000000                          START:
    11           000000                C=0
    12 000000                          SAVE    X,C
       000000                          NEXT    X,\C
       000000   016767  000026  000032 MOV     X,A+0
                 000002                 C=C+2
    13 000006                          SAVE    X,C
       000006                          NEXT    X,\C
       000006   016767  000020  000026 MOV     X,A+2
                 000004                 C=C+2
    14 000014                          SAVE    Y,C
       000014                          NEXT    Y,\C
       000014   016767  000014  000022 MOV     Y,A+4
                 000006                 C=C+2
    15 000022                          SAVE    Z,C
       000022                          NEXT    Z,\C
       000022   016767  000010  000016 MOV     Z,A+6
                 000010                 C=C+2
    16 000030   000000                 HALT
    17 000032   000010          X:      .WORD   10
    18 000034   000020          Y:      .WORD   20
    19 000036   000030          Z:      .WORD   30
    20 000040                   A:      .BLKW   100
    21           000000'                .END START



SYMBOL TABLE

A 000040R     START 000000R     X 000032R     Y 000034R
Z 000036R
C = 000010

. ABS.  000000     000
        000240     001
ERRORS DETECTED:  0
```

Figure 10.4   Nested macro call with numeric arguments.

The final case of special argument forms to be mentioned here is called **concatenation** of arguments. The way this works and a suggestion for possible usage may be seen in the following example.

```
        .MACRO     MSG,A,B
MSG'A:  .ASCII/MESSAGE 'A:/
        .ASCIZ/A'B/
        .ENDM      MSG
```

The single quote preceding (or following) a dummy argument inside the macro means that the substituted actual argument string is to be concatenated to the existing characters at that point. If we reference the above macro with

```
MSG    ONE,<:ENTER A VALUE>
```

the expansion is therefore

```
MSGONE:    .ASCII/MESSAGE ONE:/
           .ASCIZ/ONE:ENTER A VALUE/
```

This technique can be used to construct conveniently a number of messages that differ from each other only slightly. It has many other uses also, such as those shown in Section 10.4.1.

10.4 Repeat Blocks

An assembly concept with some similarity to the macro instruction is the **repeat block.** Like a macro, a repeat block causes automatic insertion of code into the assembly instructions prior to translation. However, a repeat block replicates the defining code a specified number of times at a single place in the code, rather than generating a copy at various calling points throughout the program like a macro. MACRO-11 provides three forms of repeat blocks, indicated by the directives .REPT, .IRP, and .IRPC. Each of these is discussed below.

10.4.1 Simple Repeat Blocks (.REPT)

The simple repeat block can be used when it is necessary to insert the same sequence of instructions a definite number of times at a single place in the program. The .REPT block has the form

```
.REPT     expression
(Body)
.ENDR
```

When .REPT is encountered in the assembly process, the expression is evaluated, and all instructions and directives in the body are repeated a number of times indicated by the value of the expression. As a simple case to consider, suppose it is desired to shift the contents of a memory location 4 bits to the right. Using a repeat block we could write

```
.REPT    4
ASR   X
.ENDR
```

The assembler will expand this to

```
ASR X
ASR X
ASR X
ASR X
```

The body of the repeat block can contain any instruction, macro call, or directive.

Example 10.4   To show this, let us reconsider the need for a macro to save register R0 through R5 on the stack. We will use techniques for numeric and concatenated arguments discussed in Section 10.3.5 in addition to the .REPT directive

```
.MACRO       PUSH,N
MOV          R'N, − (SP)
.ENDM        PUSH
.MACRO       SAVREG
N = 0
.REPT     6
PUSH        \N
N = N + 1
.ENDR
.ENDM        SAVREG
```

A reference to SAVREG will then generate machine code for

```
MOV     R0, − (SP)
MOV     R1, − (SP)
          .
          .
          .
MOV     R5, − (SP)
```

This expansion occurs because the sequence

```
PUSH        \N
N = N + 1
```

is printed six times after N has been initialized to 0. Because of the \ preceding N, the *value* of N is passed to the PUSH macro expansion and gets concatenated onto the R as discussed in Section 10.3.5.

10.4.2 Indefinite Repeat Blocks (.IRP)

The indefinite repeat block differs from the simple form in that symbol substitution is possible. Its general form is

```
.IRP       Symbol,⟨argument list⟩
(Body)
.ENDM      (.ENDR also acceptable)
```

This structure is placed in the program at the location where the repeated code is required. Upon expansion, the internal parameter represented by symbol is replaced by successive symbol strings in the argument list. Let us clarify this with the now-familiar need to save register contents. We could write

```
.MACRO      SAVREG
.IRP        X,(R0,R1,R2,R3,R4,R5)
MOV         X, – (SP)
.ENDM
.ENDM       SAVREG
```

Any reference of SAVREG causes the MOV X, – (SP) instruction to be repeated, with X replaced successively by R0, R1, . . . , R5. Obviously, this generates the same machine code as the other macros we defined for this purpose.

This is called an indefinite repeat block because the repetition is done for an arbitrary number of arguments. It has several similarities to the macro. Note, for example, that it has a dummy argument (symbol) and actual arguments (argument list). Also, the rules for forming arguments are the same as they are for macro arguments. Finally, the end is marked by .ENDM just as it is for a macro. However, it is not referenced by a name like a macro.

10.4.3 Indefinite Repeat with Character Argument (.IRPC)
The repeat block directive .IRPC is almost identical to .IRP. The only difference between them is that the single argument is a string of characters, each of which becomes a substitution for the dummy argument symbol. To show this as simply as possible, the code

```
.IRPC     X,(AB)
MOV       X,(R1)+
.ENDM
```

is expanded to give

```
MOV       A,(R1)+
MOV       B,(R1)+
```

It is left as an exercise to use this construction to define our SAVREG macro yet another way.

10.5 Conditional Assembly

Often a program is expected to run in several different environments. This situation can arise because of differences in the hardware, such as the possible absence of the Extended Instruction Set, or the absence of certain software, such as macros in the operating system library. The programmer can use the **conditional assembly** feature of MACRO-11 to allow for such differences within the context of a single source program.

The basic concept of conditional assembly is that assembly language instructions are included in the source program for all anticipated program variations, but certain portions are skipped in the translation process to generate a particular version of the object program. The portions included and those skipped are controlled by decision structures constructed with special assembly directives.

Let us be clear on a very important point in this discussion. That is, we are talking about decisions that are made during the *assembly* process, not during execution. These decisions must therefore be based on symbols and expressions whose values are determinable at *assembly time*. Often this is as simple as introducing a symbol to act as a flag, with an assignment directive near the beginning of the source program to give the flag a value. When it is desired to assemble a different version, the value of the flag is changed and the source program is reassembled. Later in the program, conditional assembly directives use this value to determine whether or not to assemble a particular block of instructions.

MACRO-11 provides several directives that can be used to construct conditional assembly decision structures. We will use these to describe single-alternative and double-alternative conditional assemblies.

10.5.1   Single-alternative Conditional Assembly
This is the case where there is a block of source code that is to be either assembled or skipped, as pictured in Fig. 10.5.

The implementation of Fig. 10.5 in MACRO-11 has the following general form

```
.IF        condition        argument
    (Code to be assembled if
    argument meets condition)
.ENDC
```

An alternate implementation, useful when there is only one line to be assembled or omitted, is

```
.IIF    condition    argument,    statement
```

where *statement* is any valid MACRO-11 instruction or directive.

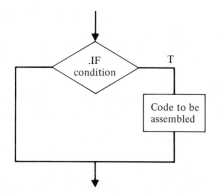

Figure 10.5   Single-alternative conditional assembly.

TABLE 10.1
Conditional Test Operators

Condition	Arguments	Assemble Block If
EQ or Z	Expression	Expression is equal to zero.
NE or NZ	Expression	Expression is not equal to zero.
GT or G	Expression	Expression is greater than zero.
LE	Expression	Expression is less than or equal to zero.
LT or L	Expression	Expression is less than zero.
GE	Expression	Expression is greater than or equal to zero.
DF	Symbol	Symbol is defined.
NDF	Symbol	Symbol is not defined.
B	⟨String⟩	Argument string is absent (blank).
NB	⟨String⟩	Argument string is not blank.
IDN	⟨String 1⟩ ⟨String 2⟩	String 1 is identical to string 2.
DIF	⟨String 1⟩ ⟨String 2⟩	String 1 is different from string 2.

Notes:

1. Expression can be any valid symbolic expression.
2. Symbol can be any valid symbol. It is found to be defined if it occurs to the left of :, =, ::, or ==.
3. String can be anything that would comprise a valid macro argument enclosed in ⟨ ⟩.

Here *condition* can be any of the several logical operators shown in Table 10.1. The first six of these assume the argument to be an expression that can be evaluated at assembly time. The value is then compared to 0 according to the condition operator, e.g., to see if it is EQual to zero, or LT (less than) zero. If the expression satisfies the condition, the code is assembled; otherwise, it is ignored. When the DF and NDF conditions are used, the argument is treated as a symbol, and a determination is made to see whether or not the symbol has been defined either as a label or by assignment. (Note that macro names, MACRO-11 instructions, and directive symbols are not recognized as defined in this sense.) The last four conditions are intended for use in macro definitions, and assume the argument to be like a macro argument. These are discussed in Section 10.5.3.

Example 10.5 As our first example of the use of conditional assembly, suppose we wish to write a program for a PDP-11/04 that does not have the "exclusive or" instruction, XOR. However, we also want the program to be converted easily to take advantage of XOR if a larger machine is later installed. To do this, let us define a flag symbol DEFXOR that is set to 0 if XOR is not available, and to a nonzero value otherwise. Then in the initial version of the source program we place the assignment directive

    DEFXOR = 0

This should be near the beginning of the program so that it can be found readily and changed later. Then we insert into the source program the conditional assembly block as follows.

```
.IF          EQ      DEFXOR
.MACRO       XOR     RN,D    ; XOR MACRO
MOV          D , -(SP)
BIC          RN, D
BIC          (SP)+,RN
BIS          RN, D
.ENDM        XOR
.ENDC
```

Because DEFXOR is zero, the macro will be expanded wherever XOR appears in the program. A study of this macro will reveal that it behaves exactly as the XOR instruction behaves, although it is longer and considerably less efficient. If DEFXOR is set to a nonzero value and the program is reassembled, the macro will not be expanded and any XOR in the program will automatically refer to the XOR *instruction*. This assembly would generate object code for a machine with the XOR instruction.

Although this example has only a macro definition in the conditional assembly block, any MACRO-11 directive or instruction can be included.

10.5.2 Double-alternative Conditional Assembly

Often there is a need to assemble one block of code if a condition is true, or a different block if the condition is false. Also, there is usually code to be assembled regardless. This is what can be called a double-alternative conditional assembly, as depicted in Fig. 10.6.

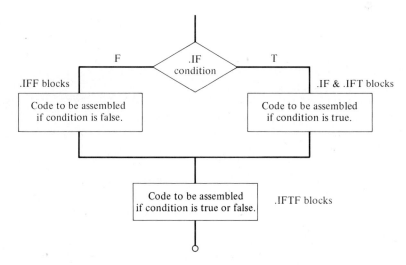

Figure 10.6 Double-alternative conditional assembly.

MACRO-11 provides for assembly control structures such as this using the conditional assembly directive described above, .IF, and three *subconditional* assembly directives .IFF (if false), .IFT (if true) and .IFTF (if true or false). The subconditional directives can appear only inside a conditional block, but can be used as often as necessary and in any order. They do not have a separate condition test; they are based on the test for the preceding .IF directive. The rule followed is that code is assembled or not assembled according to the most recent directive. That is: (1) All code following .IF or .IFT is assembled only if the condition is true, (2) all code following an .IFF is assembled only if the condition is false, (3) all code following an .IFTF is assembled regardless of whether the condition is true or false.

Example 10.6　As an example of double-alternative conditional assembly, again suppose that a PDP-11/04, which will not have the SOB instruction, is the original machine to be used, but later a larger PDP-11 with this instruction will be installed. The source code for a simple loop to clear an array that would work on either machine could be written

```
P1104 = 1    ;    PDP-11/04 VERSION
                 .IF    NE    P1104
                 .IFTF
                 MOV    #A,R2
                 MOV    #10,R1
       L1:       CLR    (R2)+
                 .IFT
                 DEC    R1
                 BNE    L1
                 .IFF
                 SOB    R1,L1
                 .ENDC
```

The results of assembling this with the P1104 flag set to 1 and 0 are

```
           P1104=1

           MOV    #A,R2
           MOV    #10,R1
     L1:   CLR    (R2)+
           DEC    R1
           BNE    L1
```

and

```
           P1104=0

           MOV    #A,R2
           MOV    #10,R2
     L1:   CLR    (R2)+
           SOB    R1,L1
```

Observe that the first three instructions are assembled in any event because they are after the .IFTF directive. Only one of the other two blocks is selected depending on whether P1104 is 0 or not 0.

10.5.3 Nonnumeric Conditional Tests

Table 10.1 shows several nonnumeric conditional tests. Among these are the DF and NDF conditions that can be used to determine if a symbol has been defined as a label or through use of the assignment directive. (Note that symbols in the permanent symbol table, i.e., the MACRO-11 instruction and directive sets, and those used as macro names *cannot* be checked with these conditional tests.)

Example 10.7 As an example of the use of NDF, consider again the need for a macro that switches the contents of two words or registers. We would like to use a word of memory for the temporary location, but do not want a different location allocated each time the macro is referenced. The following definition meets this requirement

```
        .MACRO    SWITCH,A,B
        .IF     NDF     SWTMP
        BR      .+4
SWTMP:  .WORD   1
        .ENDC
        MOV       A,SWTMP
        MOV       B,A
        MOV       SWTMP,B
        .ENDM     SWITCH
```

On the first reference to SWITCH, a memory location is reserved with the label SWTMP. The BR .+4 instruction is also inserted to branch around this word. (See Section 10.2.4.) Subsequent references to SWITCH will find SWTMP to be defined, and will simply use it rather than defining another temporary location.

The DF and NDF conditions can also be applied to logical expressions involving several symbols. The accepted logical operators are & (and) and ! (or). For example we could write

```
    .IF     DF      N!M
```

that would cause assembly of the subsequent conditional block if either N or M has been defined. If we write

```
    .IF     NDF     S&W
```

the conditional block is assembled only if S and W are both undefined, i.e., neither is defined.

The B and NB conditional tests allow the detection of omitted actual arguments when a macro is referenced.

Example 10.8 As an example, suppose a macro is needed that will move M words from array X to array Y, but if M is not specified it should assume that ten words are to be transferred. This could be written as follows.

```
        .MACRO      SAVARY,X,Y,M,?L
        .IF     B       〈M〉
        N = 10.
        .IFF
        N = M
        .ENDC
        MOV         R0, − (SP)
        CLR         R0
L:      MOV         X(R0),Y(R0)
        TST         (R0) +
        CMP         R0,#2*N
        BLO         L
        MOV         (SP) + ,R0
        .ENDM       SAVARY
```

Then if this is referenced as

```
SAVARY      X1,Y1
```

ten values are moved from X1 to Y1. On the other hand, if we write

```
SAVARY      Z,W,44
```

the code generated will move 44_8 values from Z to W.

The conditional tests IDN and DIF also enable examination of macro argument strings. In this case, two strings are involved, and they are compared to see if they are identical (IDN) or different (DIF). As an example of a possible use of these conditions, consider the SWITCH macro developed in Section 10.3.1. Suppose we wish to alert the programmer using this macro if the TEMP location is the same as one of the locations being switched because this would cause an error. To do so, modify the macro as follows.

```
.MACRO          SWITCH,A,B,TEMP
.IF     IDN     〈A〉,〈TEMP〉
.ERROR              ;TEMP SAME AS A
.ENDC
.IF     IDN     〈B〉,〈TEMP〉
.ERROR              ;TEMP SAME AS B
.ENDC
MOV     A,TEMP
MOV     B,A
MOV     TEMP,B
.ENDM   SWITCH
```

Then if in any usage of SWITCH the actual argument for either A or B is identical to that for TEMP, the .ERROR directive will be placed in the expanded source program. The .ERROR directive, used here for the first time, causes an error report in the listing. The general form of this directive is

.ERROR   symbol   ;   message

where *symbol* is any defined symbol in the program and *message* is any character string. The report in the listing will include the value of *symbol* and the message, and will be flagged with a P error code.

10.5.4 Other Conditional Assemblies in Macro
We have already noted that conditional assembly in macro definitions can be a useful programming technique. We shall now examine several other directives that enlarge this capability in MACRO-11. These include

Directive		Explanation
.MEXIT		Causes all further code in the macro to be skipped. In effect, an unconditional GO TO .ENDM in the macro expansion.
.NARG	symbol	Causes the count of actual arguments to be assigned to symbol.
.NTYPE	symbol,arg	Causes the addressing code of argument arg to be assigned to symbol.
.NCHAR	symbol,⟨string⟩	Causes the count of characters in string to be assigned to symbol.

The .MEXIT and .NARG directives are often used together.

Example 10.9   As an example, let us devise a macro that will add up to five arguments, with the sum appearing in R0. The following macro will do this.

```
.MACRO      ADDALL,A,B,C,D,E
.NARG       N
CLR         R0
.IF         EQ        N
.MEXIT
.ENDC
.IRP        X,⟨A,B,C,D,E⟩
ADD         X,R0
N=N-1
.IF         EQ        N
.MEXIT
.ENDC
.ENDR
.ENDM       ADDALL
```

Note that after clearing R0, the first conditional assembly will insert .MEXIT causing no further expansion of the macro if there are no arguments. If N is greater than 0, however, the repeat block will be expanded. On each expansion there is generated successively

```
ADD     A,R0
N = N - 1
ADD     B,R0
N = N - 1
  .
  .
  .
```

This continues until N is 0, whereupon the second conditional assembly generates an .MEXIT causing the macro expansion process to stop.

The directive .NTYPE is used for detecting the addressing mode of arguments and allowing proper action to be taken. For example, the SWITCH macro of Example 10.1 could be modified to prohibit the use of R0 as the temporary location.

```
.MACRO   SWITCH,A,B,TEMP
.NTYPE   TYPE,TEMP
.IF      EQ      TYPE
.ERROR   TYPE            ;CANNOT USE R0
.MEXIT
.ENDC
MOV      A,TEMP
MOV      B,A
MOV      TEMP,B
.ENDM    SWITCH
```

Thus if this macro is called by an uninformed user as

```
SWITCH   X,Y,R0
```

the symbol TYPE will be set to 0 (i.e., the address code for R0), causing the conditional assembly block to be expanded. This expansion generates an .ERROR directive, and exits from further macro expansion due to .MEXIT. Note that we have used the general form of the .ERROR directive; this will cause the value of the symbol TYPE to be printed in the listing along with the message

```
".ERROR   TYPE;   CANNOT   USE   R0."
```

Sometimes a macro argument will be a character string whose length is needed in the macro expansion. Consider the following example of this, which uses the .NCHAR directive.

```
.MACRO   SAVSTR,   STRING
.NCHAR   COUNT,   STRING
.EVEN
.WORD    COUNT
.ASCII   /STRING/
.EVEN
.ENDM    SAVSTR
```

When this macro is invoked, the argument string is saved, preceded by a count of its length. For example,

    SAVSTR   ⟨MACRO-11⟩

results in the expansion

    .EVEN
    .WORD   COUNT
    .ASCII   /MACRO-11/
    .EVEN

Note that the assembler *also* has assigned a *value* to COUNT, namely 8; this would be evident if we examined the translation (not given here).

10.6 The Assembly Process

Throughout this book we have referred to "the assembler" constantly, but have described it only in terms of *what* it does and not in terms of *how* it does it. A somewhat better understanding of assembly language programming can be gained by considering how the assembler works. A complete description of the MACRO-11 assembler is beyond the scope of this book, but we can gain some understanding by considering a simplified assembler with similar features.

An assembler is nothing more than a program. It can be written in any suitable programming language, including another assembly language or even in the very language that it is intended to assemble. For example, one could program a MACRO-11 assembler in MACRO-11, FORTRAN, Pascal, or BASIC. Functionally, this program may be described as a program that reads a "source program" consisting of a list of assembly instructions and directives, and produces a list of binary numbers that represent the machine language equivalent of the source program.

Most assemblers, including MACRO-11, are what we call *two-pass* assemblers. This means that the source program is processed line by line twice in coming up with the machine language program. The reason for the second pass is the possibility of a symbol occurring in an instruction or directive *before* it is defined. This is called *forward referencing*. For example, in assembling the program

    CR = 15
                CMP   A,#CR
                .
                .
                .
    A: .BLKB   100
                .
                .
                .

the symbol CR has a known value when the CMP instruction is encountered, but A does not. The value to be assigned to A cannot be determined until all intervening instructions have been assigned locations. Therefore, the CMP instruction cannot be assembled when first encountered. To resolve this problem, the first pass has as its principal purpose the building of a *symbol table*. This symbol table is a list of symbols and corresponding values, e.g.,

```
CR     15
A      000024
```

where 15 is the assigned value for CR and 24 is the address (relative to the beginning of the program) assigned by the assembler for storage at label A. The second pass through the source program then can fully translate the instructions, referring to the symbol table as required to determine immediate values, PC relative addresses, and so on.

The assembly process is facilitated by the location counter, LC, first mentioned in Section 10.2.4. Much as PC always points to the next instruction, LC always points to the next available location for assignment to an instruction or storage directive. It starts at 0 and is advanced by the number of bytes required by each instruction or directive as successive lines of source code are processed. During the first pass then, LC will always provide the value to assign to a label when one is encountered.

A simplified algorithm for a two-pass assembler is described in Fig. 10.7. In Fig. 10.7(a) we see the major steps in building the symbol table. After initializing LC to 0, we get the first source line and break it down into "tokens," i.e., symbols and punctuation. These tokens are examined to see if one of them is an .END directive that marks the end of the module. If not, the WHILE loop is entered and the tokens are examined to see if they form a MACRO-11 directive or instruction. If it is a direct assignment, the symbol and the value to the right of the " = " are placed in the symbol table. If it is a label, the symbol and the current LC are put in the symbol table. Once this has been done, the next task is to determine how much to advance LC. The "syntax" of the source line, i.e., the sequence of tokens, provides this information. For example, an instruction with two relative or immediate operands will require three words, hence LC will be advanced by six bytes, while the directive

```
.BLKB     12
```

will cause LC to be advanced by 12_8. Some directives, e.g., direct assignment, require no storage so LC is not advanced at all. After updating the LC, the next line is obtained and tokenized, and the WHILE loop is repeated. This continues until the .END token is found in some line, whereupon pass 1 concludes and pass 2 begins.

The basic structure of pass 2 is much the same as pass 1. Now, however, tokens are compared to a list of instruction mnemonics, and, if found, the corresponding opcodes are taken from a built-in table. Many instructions, such as

```
MOV     A,B
```

BEGIN PASS 1:

    INITIALIZE LC=1;
    GET THE FIRST LINE OF SOURCE CODE;
    BREAK LINE INTO TOKENS;
    WHILE LINE IS NOT .END DIRECTIVE:
        IF LINE IS ASSIGNMENT DIRECTIVE:
        THEN
            ENTER SYMBOL & VALUE INTO SYMBOL TABLE;
        IF LINE HAS LABEL:
        THEN
            ENTER LABEL & LC INTO SYMBOL TABLE;
        DETERMINE BYTES REQ'D TO ASSEMBLE LINE;
        INCREMENT LC= LC + BYTES USED;
        GET NEXT LINE OF SOURCE;
        BREAK LINE INTO TOKENS;
    NEXT;
END PASS 1;

(a)

BEGIN PASS 2:

    INITIALIZE LC = 0;
    GET FIRST LINE OF SOURCE CODE;
    BREAK LINE INTO TOKENS;
    WHILE LINE IS NOT .END DIRECTIVE:
        IF LINE IS INSTRUCTION:
        THEN
            FIND OPCODE FROM OPCODE TABLE;
            FIND SYMBOL VALUES FROM SYMBOL TABLE;
            FORM AND WRITE MACHINE CODE INSTRUCTION;
        ELSE (IT MUST BE A DIRECTIVE):
            CARRY OUT DIRECTIVE;
        WRITE LINE AND MACHINE CODE TO LISTING FILE;
        DETERMINE BYTES USED;
        INCREMENT LC = LC + BYTES USED;
        GET NEXT LINE OF SOURCE;
        BREAK LINE INTO TOKENS;
    NEXT;
END PASS 2;

(b)

Figure 10.7　Simplified algorithm for two-pass assembler: (a) pass one; (b) pass two.

will also require that symbols be looked up in the symbol table. Once the opcode and symbols are known, the machine code can be formed and stored in an output file.

If a line is not an instruction, it is examined to see if it is a directive. Some directives will require no action. For example, storage directives such as .BLKB require no action other than the normal LC advancement. Directives such as .WORD 4,5,6 will require that specific values be placed into the machine code file. The simplified algorithm shown here does not indicate actions required by more complex directives, such as .MACRO and .REPT.

The listing is also produced during pass 2. This is done by writing each assembled line, in both machine code and mnemonic forms, to the listing file. At the conclusion of pass 2, the entire symbol table is also written to this file.

When we compare the algorithm above with MACRO-11, we see that many important details have been omitted. We have already mentioned that the algorithm does not address macro expansion. Indeed, many simple assemblers do not allow macros. Other omissions include error checking, evaluation of expressions, and the details of the several steps involved. These are proper subjects for study in the general area of language processors, which also include compilers and interpreters.

10.7 Summary

This chapter has dealt with a number of MACRO-11 features that aid the programmer in developing clearly written and efficient assembly programs. We first saw that *expressions* involving symbols and constants can be used in the operand fields of instructions, and that symbols can be given values with the *assignment* directive. These features often can be used to shorten the assembled program through elimination of unnecessary execution-time arithmetic and labels. Moreover, the use of symbols makes programs more readable, and easier to maintain. The assembler *location counter,* symbolized by the period "." in the source code, can be used in expressions whenever the address of the current or next translated instruction is required. We also observed that all expressions and assignments are carried out at assembly time, a fact that must be carefully observed when using these features.

The .MACRO directive introduced in this chapter allows the programmer, in effect, to define his or her own instructions. We saw that such instructions, called *macros,* can be referred to by name after they have been defined, and any such reference causes the entire defining code to be "expanded" into the program prior to assembly, substituting actual arguments for the dummy arguments used in the definition. Macros are like subroutines in that they provide a facility for making use of a block of source code more than once. They differ in that they result in *in-line* code in the object program, rather than in jumps and returns.

Our study of macros included the problems caused by internal labels. We saw that one way of dealing with these problems is to put the internal label in the dummy argument list preceded by a question mark, e.g., ?L1. Doing this results in automatic generation of *local labels* of the form $n\$$, where n is an integer. Such labels are "known" only within the local symbol block where they are used. Local symbol blocks are program segments delimited by normal labels in the source code. Although generated automatically in macro expansion, local labels can also be introduced by the programmer, inside or outside of macros, using the n\$ naming convention. This is an effective means of avoiding multiply-defined labels.

An important extension of macro utility is achieved through *nesting*. There are two concepts here—nesting of a macro *reference* within a macro definition, and nesting of a macro *definition* within a macro definition. The latter results in the inner macro not being defined unless the outer macro is invoked.

A key feature of macros is that they are defined in terms of *dummy* arguments, for which *actual* arguments are substituted when the macros are expanded. The actual arguments are treated normally as strings that replace the dummy strings. However, by preceding an actual argument with a \, its *value* is used instead. We also saw that actual arguments that contain delimiters such as blanks or commas must be enclosed in angle brackets ⟨ ⟩.

Closely related to macros are *repeat blocks*. We saw that any one of the directives .REPT, .IRP, and .IRPC will cause all code up to the .ENDR directive to be repeated a number of times, generating in-line code. The .REPT directive repeats a fixed block of code the number of times indicated by the argument expression. Both .IRP and .IRPC perform substitutions much like a macro, and generate a number of modified blocks of code equal to the number of arguments.

With *conditional assembly directives,* it is possible to include or omit blocks of assembly code during the translation process. The basic directives are .IF and .ENDC, which set off the conditional assembly block. The .IF directive has a *condition* and an *argument.* The argument, which is often a symbol or expression, is evaluated and checked according to the specified condition. If the condition is met, the block is assembled. Otherwise, it is omitted. Subconditional assembly directives .IFT, .IFF, and .IFTF can occur within the conditional block, and allow double alternative decision structures for the conditional assembly. An important usage of conditional assembly is in making versatile macros. In this case, the conditional directives and blocks are internal to the macro definition, and the conditions are tested whenever the macros are expanded. We considered several examples of this, such as causing the macro expansion to vary depending on the number or type of actual arguments in the macro reference.

The chapter concluded with a brief look at the assembly process itself. Here we saw that the assembler is a program that makes two "passes" through the source file. On pass 1, it determines values for all symbols found, placing both the symbols and values in a symbol table. This table is then referenced as the mnemonic codes are translated to machine instructions during pass 2.

10.8 Exercises _____

10.1 Using symbols, expressions, and the assignment directive, modify the program in Fig. 8.12 so that it can be assembled for either octal output or decimal output depending only on the value assigned to a *single symbol*. That is, if B = 8., it should be assembled for octal, or if B = 10., it should be assembled for decimal.

10.2 Modify the program in Fig. 5.3 as suggested in Sec. 10.2.3. Assemble it and compare the listing to that shown in the figure. List all differences, and indicate how many words and instructions have been saved.

10.3 Translate the following instruction assuming that it will be placed in location 000500.

    MOV   #.+2,−(SP)

Explain what it does.

10.4   Write a macro that will interchange two double-precision quantities. For each argument, assume that the low word is stored in the location following the high word. Demonstrate your macro in a program.

10.5   Write a macro that will add two double-precision quantities. For each argument, assume that the low word is stored in the location following the high word. Demonstrate your macro in a program.

10.6   Show the expanded assembly code that results from the macro call

    ADDX   2,123

The definition of ADDX is as follows.

```
.MACRO      ADDX,     N,STRING
C=N
.IRPC       K,⟨STRING⟩
ADDNX        K,\C
C=C+2
.ENDR
.ENDM       ADDX
.MACRO      ADDNX, X,N
ADD         #N,A'X
.ENDM       ADDNX
```

10.7   Show the expanded assembly code that results from the macro call

    HEXSFT   A,−2

Also, describe what it does. The definition of HEXSFT is as follows.

```
.MACRO          HEXSFT,X,N
.IF         GT    N
.REPT           4*N
SEC
BIT             #1,X
BNE             .+4
CLC
ROR             X
.ENDR
.IFF
.REPT           −4*N
SEC
BMI             .+4
CLC
ROL             X
.ENDR
.ENDC
.ENDM           HEXSFT
```

10.8   Using the .IRPC directive, define a macro called SAVREG that pushes general registers R0 through R5 onto the stack.

10.9   Show how multiply-defined labels can be avoided during macro expansion by using

(a) the location counter in operand expressions, and (b) the argument concantenation operation ' in the macro definition.

10.10 Define a set of macros that simulate a Reverse Polish Notation (RPN) calculator. The following functions are required.

EN   X   ;   pushes contents of X onto stack.

EX   ;   interchanges the upper two stack entries.

PL   ;   adds the upper two stack entries and leaves sum on top of stack.

SU   ;   subtracts top of stack from second from top, leaving result on top of stack.

MU   ;   multiplies upper two stack entries and leaves product on top of stack.

DI   ;   divides top of stack into second from top, leaving result on top of stack.

NE   ;   negates top of stack.

Demonstrate these macros to evaluate the octal expression

$$\frac{((2 + 4) \times 3 + 6 - 4/2)}{6}.$$

10.11 Using conditional and subconditional assembly directives, write a macro ADDWB A1,A2,P that will generate code to add A1 to A2 regardless of whether they are byte ($P = 1$), word ($P = 2$) or double-precision ($P = 4$) quantities.

10.12 In the following problems, assume that $Z = 2$ and $W = 4$, but no other symbols are defined. Write the resulting assembly code.

a) .IF   LE   W − 3*Z
   ADD   R1 + Z,R2
   .IFF
   SUB   R1 + W,R2
   .IFTF
   MOV   Z(R1),W(R2)
   .ENDC

b) .IF   LT   W − ⟨3*Z⟩
   MOV   A,B
   .IFTF
   MOV   R1,R2
   .IFTF
   MOV   C,D
   .IFT
   ADD   A,B
   .ENDC

c) .IF   DF   Z
   .IF   NDF   W
   MUL   R4,R1
   .IFF
   ADD   R4,R1
   .ENDC
   .ENDC

d) .IF   NDF   Z
   .IF   DF   W
   MUL   R4,R1
   .IFF
   ADD   R4,R1
   .ENDC
   .ENDC

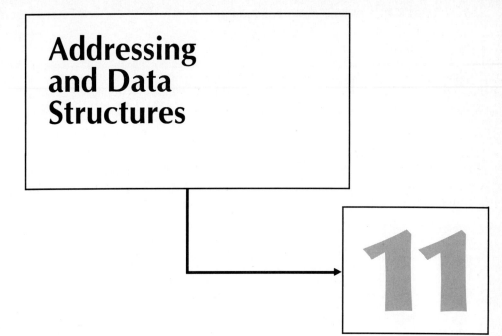

Addressing and Data Structures

11.1 Overview

Earlier chapters introduced a number of elementary assembly programming topics and the corresponding MACRO-11 instructions, addressing modes, and directives. This has given us the ability to develop modestly complex assembly programs, especially with the use of subroutines and macros. However, with the intent of maintaining a sharply focused discussion as we went along, we omitted a number of assembly programming techniques and features of MACRO-11. In particular, we introduced the various PDP-11 addressing modes on an "as-needed" basis, thus postponing the development of a unified view of this topic. Also, we have not developed an adequate understanding of how these addressing techniques can be used to implement various data structures in MACRO-11. It is the intent of this chapter to fill in these gaps. While this material is optional for an introductory course, the topics considered here are of substantial importance in many advanced assembly applications.

We begin this chapter by going back to the subject of *addressing modes*. We examine all of the addressing modes offered on the PDP-11 as a unified whole, supplementing earlier explanations where they were first introduced.

Our purpose will be to develop an understanding of the interrelationships among these modes, which is not possible when they are considered separately.

Data structure refers to the way that the data to be processed are stored in memory. There are several more or less standard organization schemes available, such as arrays, tables, stacks, queues, and linked lists. These are briefly explained, and their implementation in MACRO-11 is discussed.

11.2 The PDP-11 Addressing Modes

Address specification for instruction operands can take many different forms on the PDP-11. Although we have already seen most of these forms in the context of various examples introduced in earlier chapters, we shall now see how they fit into the overall PDP-11 addressing methodology.

11.2.1 Addressing Code Format

Let us begin this study by reexamining the address fields within the instruction word format. Recall that six bits are allocated for the address code for each operand. For example, the single-operand instructions have the format

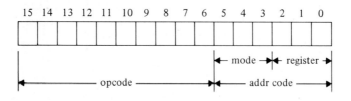

The three rightmost bits in the address code represent the *register involved* while the next three represent the *mode*.

The format above has several implications. First, observe that *all* address codes involve one of the eight registers (R0, R1, R2, ..., R5, SP, or PC). However, the *meaning* of the contents of the involved register is determined by the mode. Because the mode field is also three bits in length, there can be, and indeed there are, eight different addressing modes on the PDP-11 computer. In octal, these are 0, 1, ..., 7.

11.2.2 Mode Definitions

Each of the eight addressing modes imparts a specific meaning to the register contents, and implies a particular method of finding the operand. For example, mode 0 (register addressing) causes the contents of the register to be used as the operand, while mode 1 (register deferred) causes the contents of the register to be used as the *address* of the operand. Note that the method of finding the operand is conveyed entirely by the mode, and does not depend on which register is employed.

When learning to use any addressing mode, we are concerned with two questions. First, we need to know exactly how the operand is found. Second, we need to know what effect, if any, the addressing operation has on the employed register. These questions are answered for all addressing modes in Table 11.1. Because each of the modes has been introduced in earlier chapters, detailed explanations and examples are not repeated here. Rather, each mode is referenced to a section in which it was first introduced and in which examples can be found.

TABLE 11.1
PDP-11   Addressing Mode Explanations

Mode	Name	Assembly Mnemonics	Explanation
0	Register	Rn	Rn contains operand. Sec. 4.3
1	Register Deferred	(Rn)	Rn contains address of operand. Sec. 5.7
2	Autoincrement	(Rn)+	Rn contains address of operand. After the operand is fetched or stored, Rn is incremented (by 2 if the operation is a word operation, or by 1 if it is a byte operation, but always by 2 if R6 is used). Sec. 5.7
3	Autoincrement Deferred	@(Rn)+	Rn contains address of address of operand. After the operand is fetched or stored, Rn is incremented by 2. Sec. 9.10.3
4	Autodecrement	−(Rn)	Decrement contents of Rn by 2 if the operation is a word operation, or by 1 if it is a byte operation, but always by 2 if R6 is used. After that, Rn contains address of operand. Sec. 5.7
5	Autodecrement Deferred	@−(Rn)	Decrement contents of Rn by 2. After that, Rn contains address of address of operand. Sec. 9.10.3
6	Index	X(Rn)	Address of operand is X + contents of Rn. The value of X is stored in the word following the instruction. The PC is incremented by 2. Sec. 9.10.4
7	Index Deferred	@X(Rn)	Address of address of operand is X + contents of Rn. The value of X is stored in the word following the instruction. The PC is incremented by 2. Sec. 9.10.4

Note:

Examples of usage are shown in the indicated sections for each mode.

The modes are presented in a slightly different arrangement in Table 11.2. There we see in the left column that there are four modes that might be called "basic," namely register, autoincrement, autodecrement, and index.

Table 11.2 shows that for *each basic mode* there is a corresponding *deferred* mode (also called indirect mode). A helpful view of these modes is that the quantity determined by the basic mode is used as the operand *value,* whereas in the deferred mode the same quantity is determined, but then is used as the *address* of the operand value. For example, register mode uses the register contents as the operand value, but in register deferred mode, the contents is the *address* of the value. Taking a more complex mode, autodecrement causes the register to be decremented, then fetches the value from the memory location pointed at by the register, and uses it as the operand value. Autodecrement

TABLE 11.2
Addressing Modes (Basic vs. Deferred)

	Basic Mode		Deferred Mode	
	Mode	Mnemonics	Mode	Mnemonics
Register	0	Rn	1	@Rn or (Rn)
Autoincrement	2	(Rn)+	3	@(Rn)+
Autodecrement	4	−(Rn)	5	@−(Rn)
Index	6	X(Rn)	7	@X(Rn)

deferred, on the other hand, decrements the register, fetches the value from the memory location pointed at by the register, but then goes one step further to use that value as an *address* pointing at the actual operand. Observe that in this case because the basic mode itself uses deferred addressing, the autodecrement deferred mode is actually *second-level* deferred addressing. This is also true for modes 5 and 7.

We should make another observation in the case of modes 3, 5, and 7. Because these are second-level deferred addressing modes, we must be sure that the *first* value found in the operand determination process is a valid *word* address, i.e., an even number. This is necessary because this value will be used as an address of a location that is supposed to contain an *address*. By definition, PDP-11 addresses are 16-bit numbers and therefore cannot be stored in bytes. To see this problem more clearly, consider the index deferred mode in the following example.

```
MOV    #500,R2
MOV    @3(R2),R1    (Incorrect)
```

In trying to arrive at the first operand, the 3 is added to the contents of R2, yielding 000503. This is then used as an address of a location in which we expect to find the address of the operand. However, 000503 is the address of a high byte that cannot possibly contain a 16-bit address. Errors of this nature are not detected by the assembler, but will result in run-time errors. The way to avoid such errors is to make sure that

1. The register always contains an even numbered address in *autoincremented deferred* and *autodecrement deferred* addressing. (Observe that in keeping with this rule, these modes increment registers by 2 even with byte instructions.)

2. The sum of the register contents and the symbol in *index deferred* addressing result in an even address.

From Tables 11.1 and 11.2 it is seen that the PDP-11 does not have a second-level deferred addressing mode without indexing or register incrementing or decrementing. That is, the mode that might be symbolized as

@(Rn)

is missing from the table. In fact, however, this syntax *will* be recognized by the assembler, and translated as index deferred addressing (mode 7) with the symbol value of 0. That is

@(Rn)

is interpreted as

@0(Rn)

Thus while the *machine code* does not have simple second-level deferred addressing, the assembly language programmer can assume that it does.

11.2.3 Program Counter Addressing

You may have observed that in the preceding section there was no discussion of what we have earlier called relative addressing and immediate addressing. This is because these are not really distinct addressing modes on the PDP-11. Rather, they are special cases of modes 2 and 6 when the employed register is 7, i.e., the PC. Below we see that there are two other addressing methods that use the PC. These four methods are known collectively as **Program Counter Addressing.** Although they are only special cases of the actual PDP-11 modes, they appear to be different to the assembly language programmer because the assembler recognizes special syntax for them. They are perhaps the addressing methods most often used.

Table 11.3 shows the four program counter addressing methods recognized by the MACRO-11 assembler. Of these, immediate and relative have been discussed previously (Chapter 5), while absolute and relative deferred appear here for the first time. We shall see how these work from a practical, assembly programming point of view, as well as in relation to the fundamental modes.

We have already seen (in Chapter 5) that immediate addressing provides a method of introducing a value as an operand. Typical examples include

```
MOV     #25,R1
MOV     #ARY,R2
```

From a programming point of view, this says to move the value following the # into the second operand. Note that what follows the # is always reduced to a value at assembly time, and is therefore a constant at run time. We often use this method to introduce a constant, or to refer to an address by means of a label to which the assembler assigns a value.

To see how immediate addressing works in terms of the fundamental modes, observe from Table 11.1 that the assembler assigns an address code of 27 and stores the operand value in the word following the instruction. Because of the

TABLE 11.3
Program Counter Addressing

Address Code	Name	Assembly Mnemonics	Explanation
27	Immediate	#symbol	Operand is the value of symbol. This value is automatically stored following the instruction.
37	Absolute	@#symbol	Operand is in location whose address is the value of symbol. Symbol value is automatically stored following the instruction.
67	Relative	symbol	Operand is in location whose address is the value of symbol. The PC relative address of symbol (see Notes) is automatically stored following the instruction.
77	Relative deferred	@symbol	Address of operand is in location whose address is indicated by value of symbol. The PC-relative address of symbol (see Notes) is automatically stored following the instruction.

Notes:

1. Symbol can be a numeric constant, a label, a symbol given a value by assignment, or even an expression. In all cases, a value is first determined, then used as indicated.

2. PC-relative address is the symbol value minus the *current* PC. See Sec. 5.6.2.

Instruction Execution Cycle, register 7 (the PC) will contain the address of this location after the instruction is fetched. Now because the address code is 27 (autoincrement), according to Table 11.1, the contents of this location is fetched as the operand, *and* the register (i.e., the PC) is advanced by 2. This leaves the PC pointing at the next word that will contain another PC-addressed operand, or the next instruction.

Relative addressing has also been discussed in Chapter 5. From a programming point of view, it is a convenient way to use the contents of a memory location as an operand. For example,

ADD   B,R1

says to add the contents of the memory location whose label (i.e., address) is B to R1. Note that because the operand is the contents of a memory location, its value can change during execution; thus this mode is most naturally used when the operand is a *variable* rather than a constant.

From a machine code perspective, relative addressing is a special case of the index addressing mode. When the assembler sees a symbol as an operand, it sets the address code to 67 (i.e., mode 6, register 7) and computes the *PC-relative* address of the symbol and stores it in the next word. By PC-relative address, we mean the value assigned to the symbol (understood to be an address) *minus* the current value stored in PC. (Recall, however, that the current value means its value *after* the operand fetch. See Section 5.6.2.)

Let us now see what happens during execution with relative addressing. When the instruction is fetched, PC is advanced to the next word, where the relative address was placed by the assembler. Now, according to Table 11.1, for mode 6 the address of the operand is found by adding the contents of R7, i.e., the PC contents, to the value found after the instruction. Clearly, this "undoes" the subtraction carried out by the assembler, yielding the actual address of the operand. Note that the PC is advanced by 2 whenever mode 6 is used, so it is left pointing at the next word, containing an instruction or perhaps another PC-addressed operand.

The *absolute* and *relative deferred* addressing methods are simply deferred versions of the immediate and relative methods. That is, if we write

    TSTB   @#177564

we are testing the contents of the byte whose *address* is 177564. This translates to

    105737

    177564

When the instruction is fetched, PC will contain the address of the word containing 177564. We see from Table 11.1 that because the mode is 3 and the register is 7 the 177564 will be fetched and treated as the address of the operand, and PC will be incremented. Note that the only difference between this and immediate addressing is the way in which the "immediate" value is used. In one case it is used as the operand, and in the other, as the address of the operand.

We should also carefully compare relative and absolute addressing because they have certain similarities, but also an important difference. Note that from a programming point of view the instruction

    MOV   A,R1

has the same effect as

    MOV   @#A,R1

That is, both access the contents of the location labeled A. The difference, however, is in how they are assembled. In the first case, relative addressing is employed and it translates as

    016701
    rel addr of A

where we see that the *PC relative address* of A is stored. In the second case, we have

    013701
    addr of A

where the *absolute* address of A is seen to be stored. In many cases this will not matter because the computer will find the same operand by either method. We will examine cases in which it does make a difference when we study position-independent code in Section 15.5.

The deferred counterpart of relative addressing is exemplified by the first operand of

MOV   @ARY,R1

Here we are indicating that the address of the value to be moved to R1 is stored in the location labeled ARY. This is very similar to register deferred addressing, where the address of the operand was stored in a register.

The assembler translates the instruction above as

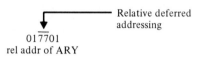

As with relative addressing, the actual address of ARY is found by adding the current PC contents to the relative address stored immediately after the instruction. However, because the mode is 7, the value found in ARY is used as the address of the actual operand.

11.2.4 Review of Index Addressing

Many of the data structures considered in this chapter rely heavily on index addressing. This mode was introduced in Section 9.10.4. Here we review it briefly so that its operation will be thoroughly understood when it is needed later in this chapter.

As shown in Table 11.1, index addressing is symbolized by

X(Rn)

Here the prefix X can be either a constant, a symbol that is a label, a symbol that is defined by direct assignment, or an expression. If it is a symbol or expression, it is replaced by its numeric value at assembly time.

Regardless of whether X is a symbol or a constant, at execution time its value is added to the contents of Rn, and the value thus determined is used as the address of the operand. For example, if R1 contains 001000, and we write

MOV   4(R1),R3

the contents of 001004 is placed in R3. The same thing is accomplished by

A=4   ;   DIRECT ASSIGNMENT OF 4 TO A
             MOV   A(R1),R4

Further, the instructions

```
A = 2
        MOV     A + 2(R1),R3
```

again do the same thing. In this case we are using the *expression* A + 2 as the prefix. At assembly time, 2 is added to the assigned value of A, so that at execution time, 4 is added to the current contents of R1.

Usage of this mode is often of the form

```
SCORE = 6
        MOV     #TABLE,R1
        MOV     SCORE(R1),R2
```

This results in the contents of the location "SCORE bytes beyond TABLE" being placed in R2. We shall see that this provides a convenient means of addressing into tables.

11.3 Arrays

11.3.1 One-dimensional Arrays

An array is a collection of similar data items, stored in a sequence of CM locations, that is identified by a single name. The simplest example is an array of integers stored in successive words beginning at some label. Storage space for arrays is usually allocated using the .BLKW or .BLKB directives, e.g.,

```
RESULT:     .BLKW 100
```

As we saw in Chapter 5, successive items in an array, called elements, can be referenced by register deferred or autoincrement/autodecrement addressing. For example, to increment all elements of RESULT by 1, we write

```
        MOV     #100,R1
        MOV     #RESULT,R2
L:      INC     (R2)+
        SOB     R1,L
```

Alternately, index addressing can be employed to address particular array elements. This method is preferred when there are parallel arrays in which corresponding elements are to be addressed. For example, the following code will add array A to array RESULT

```
        CLR     R1
L:      ADD     A(R1),RESULT(R1)
        CMP     R1,#100
        BLO     L
```

Note that accomplishing this with autoincrement or register deferred addressing would require two registers instead of the one used above.

11.3.2 Two-dimensional Arrays

The examples above use *one-dimensional* arrays. That is, an element is specifiable by a single index. For some types of data, this is a natural organization. Other types of data are more naturally viewed in a two-dimensional organization.

An example is daily time records for a group of employees, where the time worked by employee I on day J might be referred to as T(I,J). As shown in Fig. 11.1(a), this collection can be viewed as a two-dimensional array, with each row representing an employee and each column a day. Note that by convention the row index is given first, so that by T(2,1) we mean the value in the second row and first column. Also, the indexes are normally assumed to begin at 1, rather than at 0.

The CM is inherently one-dimensional, so storage of two-dimensional arrays must occur in either *column-major* or *row-major* form, as shown in Figs. 11.1(b) and (c). The choice is arbitrary unless there is a need for compatibility with other program modules that use a particular arrangement. For example, FORTRAN

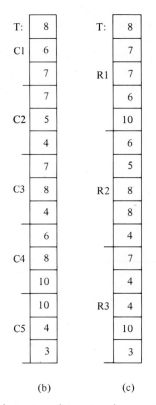

Figure 11.1 Two-dimensional array: (a) T viewed as a two-dimensional array; (b) column-major storage; (c) row-major storage.

arrays are always stored by columns. Regardless of which order is used, an assembly language program has to *compute* the proper index in the as-stored form, given the separate row-column indexes. For example, if the array has m rows and n columns and is stored by columns, the one-dimensional index of T(I,J), relative to the first element, is

$$2[(I - 1) + m(J - 1)],$$

which assumes that each element occupies two bytes. However, for better efficiency the value of this one-dimensional index is often calculated by addition rather than directly from this formula.

Example 11.1 As a simple example of programming with two-dimensional arrays, consider the need to compute the weekly total hours for each employee. A program that initializes T as shown in Fig. 11.1 and computes row-wise sums is shown in Fig. 11.2. In this program R3 holds a one-dimensional index relative to the first element in T. The sum for each row is computed by first setting R3 to a row "base index," which is the index for the first element in each row, then incrementing R3 by the number of bytes per column each time through the innermost loop. After completing a row sum, it is saved in the one-dimensional array W. The row-base index is recomputed each time through the outer loop by adding 2. This strategy should be compared with the far less efficient method of calculating R3 directly by the formula. Note that the row-base index also serves as an index for the result array W.

```
        .TITLE TWO DIM. ARRAY
START:
        MOV     M,R0     ;INIT. ROW LCV
        MOV     R0,M2    ;CALC. COL-TO-COL
        ASL     M2       ;    INDEX INCREMENT.
        MOV     N,R1     ;INIT. COL LCV
        CLR     R2       ;INIT. ROW BASE INDEX
        CLR     R3       ;INIT. 1-DIM. INDEX
        CLR     R4       ;INIT. SUM
L1:
        ADD     T(R3),R4 ;DEVELOP SUM
        ADD     M2,R3    ;INC. COL INDEX
        SOB     R1,L1    ;REPEAT FOR N COLS.
        MOV     R4,W(R2) ;STORE SUM
        CLR     R4       ;REINIT SUM
        ADD     #2,R2    ;INC.ROW BASE INDEX
        MOV     R2,R3    ;SET INDEX TO NEW ROW BASE
        MOV     N,R1     ;REINIT COL LCV
        SOB     R0,L1    ;REPEAT FOR M ROWS
        HALT
T:      .WORD   8.,6.,7. ;HOURS BY EMPLOYEE & DAY
        .WORD   7.,5.,4.
        .WORD   7.,8.,4.
        .WORD   6.,8.,10.
        .WORD   10.,4.,3.
W:      .BLKW   3        ;HOURS BY EMPLOYEE
M:      .WORD   3        ;NO. OF EMPLOYEES
N:      .WORD   5        ;NO. OF DAYS
M2:     .BLKW   1        ; 2* NO. OF DAYS
        .BLKW 20
        .END START
```

Figure 11.2 Two-dimensional array example.

11.3.3 Arrays of Records (Tables)

In the array of the preceding example, each element was a word (two bytes), containing a single entity. Sometimes it may be desired to have each array element contain several entities, in which case we would call it a record. Such an array can be called a **table.**

Example 11.2 Suppose, for example, that we wish to store a list of names and exam scores. This might be done in an array as shown in Fig. 11.3. We have defined a name *field* of ten bytes and a score field of two bytes for each record. Storage for this array could be allocated by the directive

```
TABLE:    .BLKB 108.    ;  9 RECORDS OF 12 BYTES
```

In order to place a name or score into this array, it is necessary to identify the record and the displacement of the appropriate field from the beginning of the record. Techniques for doing this are demonstrated in Fig. 11.4. This program loads the array in Fig. 11.3 from keyboard entry. R1 is used as a pointer to the first byte in each record, and R2 points to the beginning of the name field in each record. This address is moved to R0 and the subroutine GETSTR accepts keyboard characters and stores them beginning at this address. The subroutine GETOCT gets an octal number from the keyboard and places it in R0. (GETOCT and GETSTR are shown in Fig. E.1.) The subsequent MOV stores this number

Index	← 10.bytes →	← 2 bytes →
0	SMITH	77
1	JOHNSON	90
2	WELLINGTON	56
3	STUMP	65
4	DAVIDSON	72
5	GARCIA	95
6	EDWARDS	82
7	JONES	77
8	ROBERTSON	52

(a)

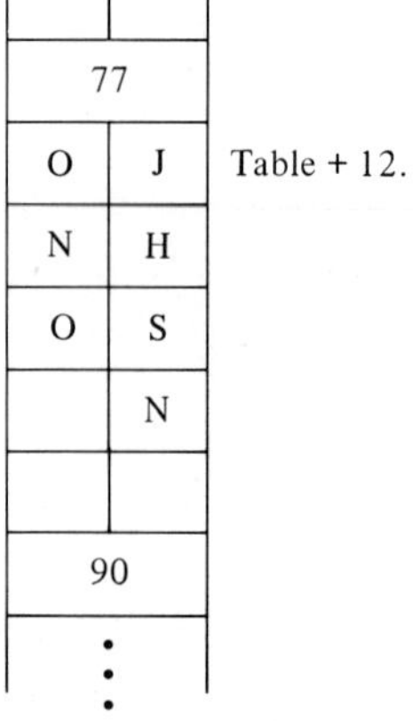

(b)

Figure 11.3 An array of records: (a) logical organization; (b) physical organization in CM.

```
                    .TITLE TABLE OF RECORDS
                    .MCALL .EXIT,.PRINT,.TTYIN
                    .GLOBL GETOCT,PUTOCT,GETSTR
        NAME=0.      ;NAME DISPLACEMENT IN RECORD
        SCORE=10.    ;SCORE DISPLACEMENT IN RECORD
        RECLEN=12. ;RECORD LENGTH
        ;
        ;
        START:
                MOV     #9.,R3          ;INIT LCV
                MOV     #TABLE,R1       ;INIT RECORD POINTER
                MOV     #TABLE+NAME,R2  ;INIT POINTER TO NAME
        L1:     MOV     R2,R0           ;GET
                JSR     PC,GETSTR       ;   NAME
                JSR     PC,GETOCT       ;GET
                MOV     R0,SCORE(R1)    ;    SCORE
                ADD     #RECLEN,R1      ;ADVANCE TO
                ADD     #RECLEN,R2      ;    NEXT RECORD
                SOB     R3,L1           ;REPEAT 9. TIMES
                .EXIT
        TABLE:  .BLKB   9.*RECLEN       ;9. RECS. OF RECLEN BYTES
                .BLKW   20              ;BUFFER
                .END START
```

Figure 11.4 Storing data in a table of records. (See Fig. 11.3.)

in the score field. Observe that we use index addressing here, so that the field displacement is added to the record pointer, yielding the CM address of the destination operand.

The two techniques for addressing into tables employed in the example above are general and should be studied carefully. When the field contains a character string, we most often need the *CM address* of the first byte, rather than the contents. This is because the PDP-11 does not have instructions that process entire strings as a single entity, making it necessary to index within the string from its starting address. Thus for strings we initialize a pointer to the NAME address in the first record. This allows autoincrement addressing within the string. Subsequently, incrementing the pointer by the record length advances it to the next record. On the other hand, when the field contains an entity that can be operated on by a single PDP-11 instruction, i.e., a byte or word, then we use index addressing to access it. Note that when we code

    MOV   R0,SCORE(R1)

the sum of SCORE and the contents of R1 provides the destination address. R1 is incremented by the record length in order to access the SCORE in the next record.

In the example above, R1 and R2 are always equal because the displacement of the name field is 0. However, this is not always the case. The way it is programmed in Fig. 11.4 ensures that the address of the NAME field is always correctly calculated even if its displacement is not 0.

11.4 Table Accessing Order

One-dimensional arrays of records, called tables, often need to be accessed in a particular order. For example, it may be desired to print out the names and scores from the array in Fig. 11.3 in an order determined by the scores, from

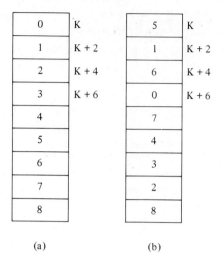

(a)   (b)

Figure 11.5 Index array for table sorting: (a) before sorting; (b) after sorting.

highest to lowest. There are several ways to accomplish this, including

1. Making repeated searches for the highest remaining score, with a system of marking each record after printing it.

2. Sorting the table prior to printing, using the score field of each record for comparison, and interchanging entire records when an out-of-order sequence is detected.

3. Doing a sort using the score field for the comparison, but rearranging only the elements of a *parallel array* of record indexes. The array of indexes is then used to select records for printing.

Method 1 might be used if the task needed to be done only once, but is wasteful if the table has to be accessed in the same order later. Methods 2 and 3 are both superior to method 1 in this respect. Method 2, however, is not ideal for large tables because it involves moving large amounts of data. Method 3, called an *index sort,* avoids this problem because only the indexes are moved while the table itself remains unchanged. We will therefore implement this method as an exercise in table access.

The index sort is based on an auxiliary array called the index array that has an element for each record in the table. The contents of each element of the index array is used to identify a particular record in the table. For example, if we have an index array K as shown in Fig. 11.5(a) and R1 contains 6, the instruction sequence

```
MOV     K(R1),R3
MUL     #12.,R3
```

will place the index for TABLE record number 3 into R3. Note that we had to multiply by 12_{10}, the record length, to get the record address from the indexes stored in K. To address the SCORE for this record, we use

```
MOV     #TABLE+SCORE(R3),R0
```

From Fig. 11.3(a), we see that this places the score 65 into R0. Obviously, if we incremented R1 by 2 and repeated this sequence, we would get the score from record 4, i.e., 72. Further, we see that if R1 is incremented as 0, 2, 4, 6, ..., this process accesses the records in whatever order is implied by the *contents* of the successive elements of K.

The aim of index sorting is then to rearrange the index array such that it contains the record indexes in the desired order. For example, we see from Fig. 11.3(a) that the maximum score is in record 5, the next highest in record 1, and so on. In Fig. 11.5(b) we see the desired sequence of indexes in K.

Example 11.3   A program that reads a table of records and performs an index sort is shown in Fig. 11.6. Reading the table is essentially the same as shown in Fig. 11.4, except that instructions have been added to create the initial index

```
        .TITLE SORT TABLE OF RECORDS
        .MCALL .TTYIN,.TTYOUT,.PRINT,.EXIT
        .GLOBL GETOCT,GETSTR,PUTOCT
NREC=9.     ;NUMBER OF RECORDS
NAME=0.     ;NAME DISPLACEMENT IN RECORD
SCORE=10.   ;SCORE DISPLACEMENT IN RECORD
RECLEN=12.  ;RECORD LENGTH
SCR=TABLE+SCORE ;
;
START:
;
;   READ TABLE
;
        CLR     R3              ;INIT. LCV/INDEX
        MOV     #TABLE,R1       ;INIT RECORD POINTER
        MOV     #TABLE+NAME,R2  ;INIT POINTER TO NAME
L1:     MOV     R2,R0           ;GET
        JSR     PC,GETSTR       ;   NAME
        JSR     PC,GETOCT       ;GET
        MOV     R0,SCORE(R1)    ;   SCORE
        MOV     R3,K(R3)        ;SET UP ARRAY OF REC INDEXES
        ASR     K(R3)           ;SO K WILL BE 0,1,2...
        ADD     #RECLEN,R1      ;ADVANCE TO
        ADD     #RECLEN,R2      ;   NEXT RECORD
        ADD     #2,R3           ;INC LCV/INDEX
        CMP     R3,#2*NREC      ;REPEAT
        BLO     L1              ;   NREC TIMES
;
;   SORT ACCORDING TO SCORES
;
L2:     MOV     #NREC-1,R0      ;INIT LCV
        CLR     R1              ;INIT K INDEX
        CLR     FLAG            ;INIT INTERCHG FLAG
L3:     MOV     K(R1),R3        ;COMPUTE
        MUL     #RECLEN,R3      ;   RECORD
        MOV     K+2(R1),R5      ;      INDEXES FROM
        MUL     #RECLEN,R5      ;      K INDEX
        CMP     SCR(R3),SCR(R5) ;OUT OF ORDER?
        BHIS    E               ;   IF YES
        MOV     K(R1),R2        ;      THEN
        MOV     K+2(R1),K(R1)   ;         INTERCHANGE
        MOV     R2,K+2(R1)      ;            INDEXES
        INC     FLAG            ;SET INTERCHG FLAG
E:      ADD     #2,R1           ;ADVANCE 1 INDEX
        SOB     R0,L3           ;CONTINUE THE PASS
        TST     FLAG            ;ANOTHER PASS
        BNE     L2              ;   IF THERE WAS INTERCHG
        .EXIT
TABLE:  .BLKB   NREC*RECLEN     ;NREC RECS. OF RECLEN BYTES
FLAG:   .BLKW   1
K:      .BLKW   NREC            ;INDEX ARRAY
        .BLKW   20              ;BUFFER
        .END START
```

Figure 11.6   Index sort of table of records.

array K. The sorting portion uses the bubble sort technique. However, note that it does a comparison on the SCORE field of records in TABLE, but does the interchanges on the contents of the index array K.

The outer loop, beginning at L2, is designed to continue making passes through the K array until it is in the correct order. This condition is indicated by FLAG remaining clear, signifying that no out-of-order sequence was encountered in the most recent pass. Each time through the outer loop, the inner loop LCV is set, the K index, R1, is reset to zero, and FLAG is cleared, prior to entering the inner loop.

The inner loop indexes through the K array, using R1 as an index. For each new value of R1, we extract the corresponding element of K and the next one. These two values from K, when multiplied by the record length, point to two records in TABLE. The contents of the SCORE fields of these two records are compared, and if the first is less than the second, the values from K are interchanged and FLAG is set. Indexing through K one time in this manner places the index of the record with the smallest score in the last element of K. Eventually, there will be a pass in which no interchanges are necessary, so that FLAG remains clear, terminating the process.

Once K has been sorted, it can be used to drive the printing process. For example, if we had a subroutine called PRTREC that printed the record whose address was found in R0, the following code would print the table in the desired order.

```
        CLR     R1
L:      MOV     K(R1),R0
        MUL     #RECLEN,R0
        ADD     #TABLE,R0
        JSR     PC,PRTREC
        ADD     #2,R1
        CMP     R1,#2*NREC
        BLO     L
```

Before leaving this example, note that the techniques used here are general. For example, the program in Fig. 11.6 could be modified easily to sort K alphabetically based on the name field. To do this, the CMP instruction would simply be replaced by a call to a subroutine that compared the two character strings found in the name fields and set the C condition code if they were out of order. All other parts of the program would remain unchanged.

Finally, we should note that the sort technique used in Example 11.3 is not ideal. For one thing, it could be improved easily by decrementing the upper bound on the inner loop LCV each time through the outer loop. (Why is this possible?) However, for large tables the bubble sort algorithm itself is very inefficient relative to other well-known sorting techniques. The other ideas demonstrated here, such as the use of the index array, are applicable to other sort methods.

11.5 Character Strings

A character string is a data item composed of zero or more ASCII character codes. For example, "HELLO", " ", and "1264" are character strings of lengths 5, 0, and 4, respectively. A string of length 0 is said to be empty.

As we have seen in Chapter 7, one 7-bit ASCII character code can be stored in each byte on the PDP-11, or 2 per word. A character string is stored in successive bytes in CM. The address of a string is defined as the address of the first character in it or, if preceded by a count, by the address of the count byte.

When more than one string are stored, there must be some method of discerning where one ends and another begins. The way that this is normally done on the PDP-11 is to store an ASCII "null" character, 000, after the last character. This method, shown in Fig. 11.7(a), works because most strings of practical interest

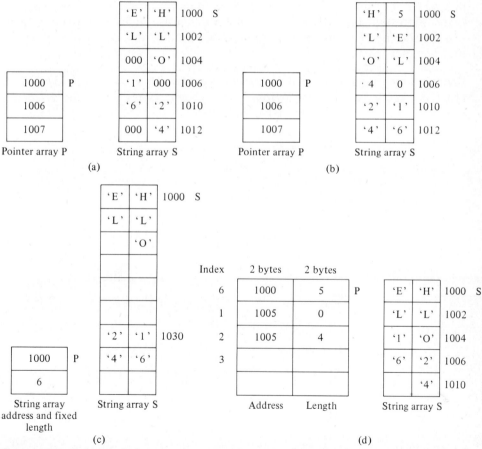

Figure 11.7 Storage of character strings: (a) array of null-terminated strings; (b) array of strings with preceding count byte; (c) array of fixed-length strings; (d) address/length array.

do not contain the null character. An auxiliary array of pointers contains the address of the first byte of each string.

An alternate scheme is as shown in Fig. 11.7(b). Here the number of characters in the string is stored in the first byte, followed by as many ASCII codes. With this method, lengths are limited to 256 characters.

In a third method, the length of strings is constant, as shown in Fig. 11.7(c). This method wastes space, and forces truncation of strings that are longer than anticipated. No pointer array is required because the address of the first string and the fixed length are sufficient to locate all others.

A final method considered is shown in Fig. 11.7(d). Here a separate array of records holds the address and length of each string. The strings themselves are then stored, without intervening nulls or counts, in a separate block of memory.

Manipulation of strings naturally depends on how they are stored. In methods (a) and (b) the address for the nth string is found in location $P + 2n$, where P is the address of the pointer array. Thus we can use index addressing in P to find the address of a particular string in S, then autoincrement to store or extract the characters in S.

Example 11.4 Figure 11.8 demonstrates usage of string storage method (a). This program accepts three strings from the keyboard, using the .TTYIN macro (Section 8.5), then prints them using the .PRINT macro (Section 8.4). Note that

```
        .TITLE STRINGS
        .MCALL .PRINT,.TTYIN,.TTYOUT,.EXIT
;
START:
;
;    FILL STRING ARRAY FROM KEYBOARD
;
        CLR     R1              ;INIT P INDEX
        MOV     #S,R2           ;INIT S INDEX
L1:     MOV     R2,P(R1)        ;STORE STRING ADDR IN P(R1)
L2:     .TTYIN                  ;GET CHAR FROM KEYBOARD
        CMPB    R0,#15          ;IF CR
        BEQ     L2              ;   GET LF
        CMPB    R0,#12          ;IF LF
        BEQ     EOS             ;   IT IS END OF STRING
        MOVB    R0,(R2)+        ;STORE CHAR IN S
        BR      L2              ;NEXT CHARACTER
EOS:    CLRB    (R2)+           ;MARK END OF STRING
        TST     (R1)+           ;INC P INDEX
        CMP     R1,#6           ;REPEAT
        BLO     L1              ;   3 TIMES
;
;    PRINT STRING ARRAY
;
        CLR     R1              ;INIT. LCV/INDEX
L3:     .PRINT  P(R1)           ;PRINT STRING
        TST     (R1)+           ;INC. INDEX
        CMP     R1,#6           ;REPEAT
        BLO     L3              ;   3 TIMES
        .EXIT
P:      .BLKW 100               ;POINTER STORAGE
S:      .BLKB 1000              ;STRING STORAGE
        .BLKW 20
        .END START
```

Figure 11.8 Implementation of string storage using method (a) of Fig. 11.7.

the loop beginning at L2 gets a string of characters, one character at a time, storing these characters in successive bytes of S. When a ⟨CR⟩⟨LF⟩ sequence is found, it marks the end of the string with a null byte, and increments the pointer array index. The address of the first character of each string is stored in P prior to getting the string. For output, the character-by-character processing is handled by .PRINT, so that only one loop is required. Observe that the .PRINT macro uses the given argument as an *address* of the start of the string, and printing is terminated by a null.

Methods of string storage (b), (c), and (d) can be implemented in much the same way as (a) is implemented. For (b) it is necessary only to place the characters beginning at the second byte, saving the first for a count that is developed during the input process. This count is then placed in the first byte using the address stored in P and index deferred addressing. Method (c) does not use a pointer array at all, and increments the S index by a fixed number of bytes after getting each string. Method (d) uses the technique shown in Section 11.3.3. The input process places the string starting address in ADDR(R1), and places the characters into S developing the count at the same time. Then the count is placed in LEN(R1). Here ADDR is equated to 0 and LEN to 2 by direct assignment. R1 is initialized to the address of P and is incremented by 4 each time through the outer loop. The details of these implementations are left as exercises.

11.6 Stacks and Queues

The stack, as introduced in Chapter 9, is a data structure in which data items can be conveniently removed in reverse of the order in which they were added. We have already seen an important application of a stack, namely, subroutine linkage. In that application, the *system stack* was used, meaning that register 6, SP, was used as the pointer to the current top of the stack. It is, however, possible to use any of the registers for a pointer, and other stacks can be established at any convenient location in memory. One might set up such a stack whenever it was necessary to access data on a last-in/first-out basis, and for some reason it was not desired to use the system stack.

When a stack is to be used, space must be allocated for it and the pointer must be initialized to its bottom. For example, a stack of 100_8 words (200_8 bytes) with R5 as its pointer is established and used by the instructions

```
MOV     #S + 200,R5      ;INITIALIZE STACK POINTER
  .
  .
  .
MOV     B, - (R5)         ;PUSH B ONTO STACK
  .
  .
  .
```

```
        MOV     (R5)+,R1            ;POP STACK INTO R1
          .
          .
          .
        HALT
S:      .BLKW 100                  ;ALLOCATE STACK
```

Note that the pointer always contains the address of the item most recently added to the stack. An instruction with autoincrement addressing for the source operand removes this item. This is called "popping" the stack. Conversely, autodecrement addressing in a destination operand causes a push onto the stack. Care must be exercised to ensure that items are not added beyond the allocated space, leading to stack overflow. Stack underflow is said to occur when more items are removed than were placed on the stack. If the program logic is such that either overflow or underflow could possibly occur, the value of the pointer should be compared with the first allocated address before each push, or with the last allocated address before each pop.

The example above used a word stack. It is also possible to have a byte stack. It is necessary only to change the push and pop to the byte forms of the instructions, and to change the .BLKW to .BLKB. Recall that autoincrement and autodecrement addressing change the employed register, other than SP, by 1 in the byte instructions. Byte stacks should not use SP because autoincrement and autodecrement always increment or decrement by 2 with SP.

There are applications that require temporary storage of data items with removal in the same order as entry. A **queue** is a data structure with this property. An example of a need for a queue is an input "buffer," in which keyboard entry is stored prior to its being accessed by the program. Such buffering is needed whenever the rate of accessing the data may be slower than the rate of entry. A stack is inappropriate in this case because it would provide access in the reverse order of entry.

Implementation of queues requires two pointers. One of these pointers points to the next item available for removal, called the FRONT, and another points to the next place where a new item can be placed, called the REAR. This is shown in Fig. 11.9. In Fig. 11.9(a) the characters A, B, C, D, and E have been entered, and none have been removed. In Fig. 11.9(b), A, B, and C, have been removed, and F and G have been inserted. Normally insertions at REAR and removal at FRONT proceed as independent processes, except removal stops when the queue becomes empty. The empty condition is indicated by FRONT becoming equal to REAR.

Obviously, if there is continuing input, the allocated space for the queue will eventually be overrun with the process described above. That is, both FRONT and REAR will go beyond the allocated space. To avoid this, the pointers are simply reset back to the beginning of the allocated storage space when the end of this space is reached. This creates what is called a "circular" queue or buffer. Figures 11.9(c) and (d) show the condition after both pointers have "wrapped around" and started over.

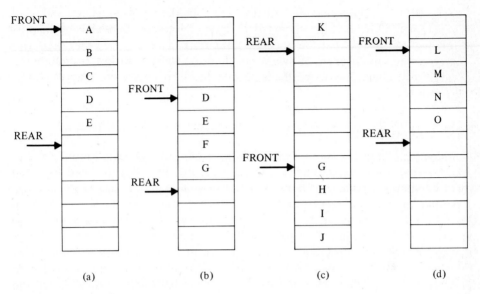

Figure 11.9   Circular input queue.

Implementation of circular queues is done easily in MACRO-11. Sufficient space is allocated to handle the longest anticipated number of items; this will depend on the expected speed of insertions and removals. Two registers are used as pointers, and are initialized to 0. The index addressing mode using these registers then allows insertion or removal. This is shown below.

```
        CLR     R0              ;REAR POINTER
        CLR     R1              ;FRONT POINTER
          .
          .
          .
        MOVB    B,Q(R0)         ;ADD ITEM AT REAR
        INC     R0              ;ADVANCE REAR POINTER
        BIC     #177700 R0      ;WRAP AROUND
          .
          .
          .
        CMP     R0,R1           ;CAN'T REMOVE
        BEQ     L               ;    IF EMPTY
        MOVB    Q(R1),C         ;REMOVE ITEM FROM FRONT
        INC     R1              ;ADVANCE FRONT POINTER
        BIC     #177700,R1      ;WRAP AROUND
L:        .
          .
          .
        HALT
Q:      .BLKB   77              ;64 DECIMAL BUFFER
```

The BIC instruction has the effect of resetting the pointer register to 0 when it is incremented beyond the allocated 77_8 bytes. Note that a check is made prior to removal to be sure that the queue is not empty. This assumes that the queue is large enough to ensure that overflow cannot occur. If overflow is anticipated, an additional check has to be made to distinguish between the empty and the full condition.

11.7 Linked Lists

A linked list is a data structure in which the order is established by one or more pointers that are in separate fields in each record. In a singly linked list, each record contains a pointer to the next record, while a doubly linked list contains a pointer to the next record and one to the previous record. The meaning of "next" and "previous" here refer to the order in which the records are to be accessed. This is called the **logical order,** as opposed to the **physical order** of storage in CM. The program will access a record and, after processing it, get the pointer out of it. This pointer is then used to address the next record to be processed. Linked lists are often used for tables that require efficient insertion or deletion of records.

As an example of a singly linked list, let us reconsider the table of names and scores shown in Fig. 11.3. This is redrawn with an added field for the pointer in Fig. 11.10. The pointer field has been added at the right, but could be anywhere in the record. It is called NEXT because it contains the address of the next record. For convenience, we have shown the records in physically sequential

	NAME	SCORE	NEXT
BASE (600)	/////////	/////	1106
	← 10 bytes →	← 2 bytes →	← 2 bytes →
TABLE (1000)	SMITH	77	1142
1016	JOHNSON	90	1124
1034	WELLINGTON	56	1160
1052	STUMP	65	1034
1070	DAVIDSON	72	1052
1106	GARCIA	95	1016
1124	EDWARDS	82	1000
1142	JONES	77	1070
1160	ROBERTSON	52	600

Figure 11.10 Table as a linked list.

memory locations beginning at 1000_8, although in general the records of a linked list can be scattered throughout the memory.

Accessing a linked list requires the address of the first item to be at some known location. This is most conveniently done by creating a dummy record called BASE with the same format as the actual records. The address of the logically first list record is stored in the NEXT field of BASE. It can reside anywhere in memory.

As noted above, the access order of the records is determined by the addresses stored in the NEXT field of the records. In order to show a concrete example of this, Fig. 11.10 shows addresses in these fields that would allow access in order of the scores, from highest to lowest. As shown, it is said to be "sorted" according to the score field. In a later example we will see how these addresses can be established. Observe that BASE has 1106 in the NEXT field, which is the address of the record with the highest score. If the record at 1106 is examined, we see in its NEXT field the address of 1016, the record which has the next highest score, 90. This continues down to the record with the lowest score, which points back to BASE.

Successive records in a linked list can be accessed using the index addressing mode. For example, to place the second highest score in R0, we would write

```
NEXT  = 12.
SCORE = 10.
        MOV     #BASE,R1      ;GET ADDR OF BASE
        MOV     NEXT(R1),R1   ;GET ADDR OF 1ST REC
        MOV     NEXT(R1),R1   ;GET ADR OF 2ND REC
        MOV     SCORE(R1),R0;GET SCORE OF 2ND REC
```

In the first instruction, we get the address of the BASE dummy record, 600, into R1. The operand NEXT(R1) in the second instruction then refers to the contents of the NEXT field in BASE, namely, 1106, which gets placed into R1. Then the third instruction updates R1 to the contents of the NEXT field in the record at 1106, namely, 1016. Finally, the contents of the SCORE field in the record at 1016, i.e., 90, is moved into R0. This suggests the following scheme for printing all of the scores in highest-to-lowest order.

```
        MOV     #BASE,R1
L:      MOV     NEXT(R1),R1
        MOV     SCORE(R1),R0
        JSR     PC,PUTOCT
        CMP     NEXT(R1),#BASE
        BNE     L
```

Here we use the routine PUTOCT that prints the contents of R0 in octal. (See Section 4.9.) Observe that the loop termination relies on the fact that we use the convention of linking the last record back to BASE. Other conventions are also employed.

When programming with linked list data structures, it is necessary to be able to create the linked list in the desired order, access records in it, delete records

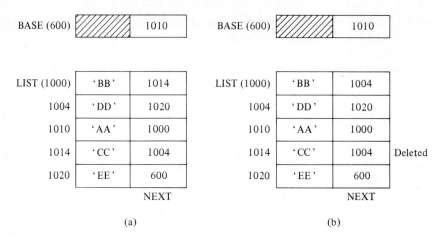

Figure 11.11 Deleting record from a linked list.

from it, and add new records to it. We have already seen how to access it. Deleting a record from it means simply to break it out of the chain and relink the adjacent records. To see the process required, let us consider how to delete the record containing 'CC' in the linked list of five records in Fig. 11.11. Because we access records by using the NEXT field contents, it is necessary only to change this field in the record that logically precedes the one to be deleted. Specifically, it must be changed to the address of the record that logically follows the deleted record. Thus the record containing 'BB' is given the NEXT address of the 'DD'—record 1004 in this example. Note that the "deleted" record is really still there; it is simply ignored during subsequent list accesses because its address is no longer present in the chain.

The instructions for deleting must include a search for the record to be deleted. Usually this is based on the contents of some field. During the search, the address of the *previous* record is always retained in another register to facilitate its change when the target record is found. This is demonstrated by the following code that carries out the operation suggested in Fig. 11.11.

```
        F=0
        NEXT=2
        RECLEN=4

            MOV     #BASE,R1
L:          MOV     R1,R0               ;SAVE PREVIOUS REC PTR
            MOV     NEXT(R1),R1         ;UPDATE POINTER
            CMP     R1,#BASE            ;EXIT IF
            BEQ     OUT                 ;    NOT FOUND
            CMP     F(R1),#"CC          ;IS IT "CC"?
            BEQ     DELETE              ;    IF YES THEN DELETE
            BR      L                   ;    ELSE CONTINUE
DELETE:     MOV     NEXT(R1),NEXT(R0);
OUT:
```

Let us now take up the matter of creating a linked list in a particular order. In the process, we will see how new records are added to such a list, completing our repertoire of linked list operations.

Example 11.5   Let us consider how to create the list as shown in Fig. 11.10, then print out the scores in highest-to-lowest order. The program to do this is shown in Fig. 11.12. In Fig. 11.12(a) we see that the problem is divided into three tasks. First, the table is entered and stored exactly as it was in Example 11.3. Observe that we have added a NEXT field simply by changing RECLEN and adding the displacement definition to the direct assignments. However, we do not read anything into this field. The second task links the records by filling in the NEXT field with the correct addresses. This task begins by placing the *address* of the dummy BASE record into its own NEXT field. This, in effect, creates an empty linked list, i.e., the base is linked to itself. Then a loop is entered that steps through the table in physical order. Each time through the loop the address of the next record is placed in R2 and a jump is made to subroutine LINK. LINK, shown in Fig. 11.12(b), "inserts" the record whose address is in R2 into the linked list. As we shall see below, the record itself is not moved. Rather, the correct linking address is found and placed in its NEXT field. After linking the table, the scores are printed out in the manner discussed previously. Because the linking was done according to the score, these values are accessed and printed in highest-to-lowest order.

The principal new concepts of Example 11.5 are embodied in Fig. 11.12(b) in which the LINK subroutine is shown. This is a "search and insert" process. That is, we first step through the table (in its logical order) looking for the right place to insert the new record. When we find it, we break the chain and insert the new record. We will now consider these two functions one at a time.

The search process uses a loop structure much like the one used in deleting a record. At any given state of the process, there will be some number of records (initially 0) already linked into the list. We step through this list using the NEXT field contents of each record as a "search pointer" R0 to point to the next record to be examined. A copy of the previous search pointer is always placed in R1 so that it can be used in the insertion process at the conclusion of the search. When the search pointer is updated, we compare it to the address of BASE. If R0 ever becomes equal to BASE, we know that the end of the current linked list has been encountered, and we branch to the instructions to insert the new record at the end of the list. Otherwise, we compare the SCORE field contents of the search record with that of the new record. (The latter is pointed at by R2.) If the search record score is less than the new one, we have found the correct position, i.e., it belongs immediately before the first score that it exceeds. At this point a branch is made to the insert instructions.

Observe that the search process can conclude with one of two outcomes— a record with a lower score to place the new record in front of, or no such

```
                .TITLE SORTED LINKED LIST
                .MCALL .TTYIN,.TTYOUT,.PRINT,.EXIT
                .GLOBL GETOCT,GETSTR,PUTOCT
NREC=9.     ;NUMBER OF RECORDS
NAME=0.     ;NAME DISPLACEMENT IN RECORD
SCORE=10.   ;SCORE DISPLACEMENT IN RECORD
NEXT=12.    ;NEXT RECORD POINTER DISPLACEMENT IN RECORD
RECLEN=14.  ;RECORD LENGTH
TABLEN=NREC*RECLEN   ;LENGTH OF TABLE
EOT=TABLE+TABLEN  ;ADDRESS OF END OF TABLE
;
START:
;
;    READ TABLE LEAVING NEXT RECORD POINTER FIELD BLANK
;
        CLR     R3              ;INIT. LCV/INDEX
        MOV     #TABLE,R1       ;INIT RECORD POINTER
        MOV     #TABLE+NAME,R2  ;INIT POINTER TO NAME
L1:     MOV     R2,R0           ;GET
        JSR     PC,GETSTR       ;   NAME
        JSR     PC,GETOCT       ;GET
        MOV     R0,SCORE(R1)    ;   SCORE
        ADD     #RECLEN,R1      ;ADVANCE TO
        ADD     #RECLEN,R2      ;   NEXT RECORD
        ADD     #2,R3           ;INC LCV/INDEX
        CMP     R3,#2*NREC      ;REPEAT
        BLO     L1              ;   NREC TIMES
;
;    DO INSERT SORT TO LINK THE TABLE
;
        MOV     #BASE,BASE+NEXT ;INITIALIZE EMPTY LIST
        MOV     #TABLE,R2       ;INITIALIZE LCV/REC. POINTER
L2:     JSR     PC,LINK         ;LINK NEXT RECORD INTO LIST
        ADD     #RECLEN,R2      ;ADVANCE RECORD POINTER
        CMP     R2,#EOT         ;IF NOT LAST RECORD
        BLO     L2              ;   THEN CONTINUE
;
;    PRINT ORDERED SCORES
;
        MOV     #BASE,R1        ;INIT.REC PTR TO BASE
L3:     MOV     NEXT(R1),R1     ;GET RECORD POINTER
        MOV     SCORE(R1),R0    ;GET SCORE
        JSR     PC,PUTOCT       ;PRINT SCORE
        CMP     NEXT(R1),#BASE  ;IF MORE RECORDS
        BNE     L3              ;   THEN CONTINUE
        .EXIT
```

(a)

```
LINK:
;
;    SUBROUTINE TO INSERT RECORD INTO LINKED LIST
;    SORTED BY SCORE FIELD. RECORD POINTED AT BY
;    R2 IS INSERTED BEFORE THE FIRST SMALLER SCORE
;    OR AT THE END OF THE LINKED LIST.
;
        MOV     #BASE,R0        ;START SEARCH AT BASE
AGAIN:  MOV     R0,R1           ;SAVE PREVIOUS SEARCH PTR.
        MOV     NEXT(R0),R0     ;ADVANCE SEARCH POINTER
        CMP     R0,#BASE        ;IF END OF LINKED LIST
        BEQ     INSERT          ;   THEN ADD AT END
        CMP     SCORE(R0),SCORE(R2);DOES IT BELONG HERE?
        BLO     INSERT          ;   IF SO,INSERT IT
        BR      AGAIN           ;   ELSE LOOK FURTHER
INSERT: MOV     NEXT(R1),NEXT(R2);LINK NEW RECORD
        MOV     R2,NEXT(R1)     ;RELINK PRECEDING RECORD.
        RTS     PC              ;RETURN TO CALLER
TABLE:  .BLKB   NREC*RECLEN     ;NREC RECS. OF RECLEN BYTES
BASE:   .BLKW   RECLEN          ;DUMMY BASE RECORD
        .BLKW   20              ;BUFFER
        .END START
```

(b)

Figure 11.12   Sorting a linked list: (a) read table and sort; (b) inserting a record.

record. In *either* case, the new record is to be placed immediately after the "previous" record. Moreover, the address of this record is always in R1.

The insertion process itself is very simple, requiring only two steps.

1. The NEXT field of the new record has to be set to the address of the record that is to *follow* it in the list. Note that the needed address is available in the NEXT field of what we have called the "previous" record.

2. The NEXT field of the previous record has to be set to the address of the record that is to *precede* it in the list. Note that the address needed here is simply that of the new record.

These steps are shown diagrammatically in Fig. 11.13. The MACRO-11 instructions for the insertion are

```
MOV     NEXT(R1),NEXT(R2)
MOV     R2,NEXT(R1)
```

Note that the order of these instructions is critical. If these steps are done out of order, the address of the succeeding record is overwritten and the chain cannot be relinked.

Before leaving Example 11.5, several observations are in order. First, let us reemphasize that the records need not be located contiguously in memory. They were located contiguously in this example simply because this was the most convenient way to create the table in the first place. In some programs, it may be preferred to establish a large region of memory for miscellaneous data storage, and place records more or less randomly in this region. In this case, a routine can be written that locates the required number of unused locations and returns the starting address. The record data are then written into it, and the NEXT field set to the correct address to link it into the list. Indeed, one of the principal virtues provided by linked lists is the ability to do dynamic storage allocation in this way. The access, insert, delete, and add operations presented here work equally well with this scheme of storage allocation.

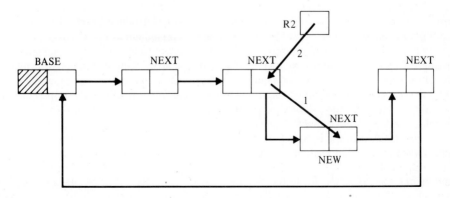

Figure 11.13   Insertion into a linked list.

Finally, it should be observed that any field in the record can be used as the basis for setting the linking order. For example, instead of comparing the score fields, we could have transferred to a subroutine that compared the strings in the NAME field. In this manner the records could be linked alphabetically with only minor changes in the program.

11.8 Summary

This chapter has dealt with two major topics, namely, addressing modes and data structures in MACRO-11.

First, we examined the full set of PDP-11 addressing modes, both from assembly code and machine code viewpoints. Some of this was review because all modes have been introduced by way of examples in earlier chapters. However, by looking at them all together, we were better able to see certain similarities and differences. For one thing, we saw that there are only four basic modes (register, autoincrement, autodecrement, and index), and four other modes that are simply *deferred* or indirect versions of the basic four. Because the basic autoincrement, and index are themselves deferred, however, their so-called deferred versions are actually *second-level* deferred modes. The advantage of thinking of the addressing modes as two groups is that the deferred modes are then seen as simple extensions of the basic modes, rather than as completely different modes.

Attention was called to the fact that with the second-level deferred modes, the word pointed at as a result of the register operations must contain a valid *word* address itself. This is because addresses are 16-bit entities, and therefore cannot reside in bytes. For this reason, even byte forms of instructions cause registers to change by 2 in autoincrement/decrement deferred modes.

Our reexamination of addressing modes also pointed out that the so-called immediate and relative addressing methods are really just special cases of the true PDP-11 addressing modes. The two methods called *absolute* and *relative deferred* addressing, introduced for the first time in this chapter, are similar in this respect. Together, these are referred to as Program Counter Addressing Methods and are among the more widely used methods.

The data structures covered in the chapter included arrays, arrays of records (tables), strings, stacks, queues, and linked lists. Our goal was to introduce briefly the underlying concepts for each of these, and show how they are implemented in MACRO-11.

We saw that arrays can employ one or more indexes to identify their elements. The number of indexes is called the dimensionality of the array. One-dimensional arrays are straightforward because they correspond exactly to the inherently linear organization of the CM. Two-dimensional arrays require some scheme for storing linearly, while allowing location of elements using the two separate (row and column) indexes. Either row-major or column-major storage meets this need.

A powerful concept is found in arrays of records, which can be called tables. The central idea here is that each array element is a group of adjacent bytes in memory called a record. Each record is divided into several *fields* that can be of any length and can contain any type of data. We found that data items in a table are addressed by a *pointer* that selects the record plus a *displacement* of the desired field from the beginning of the record. The index addressing mode, together with direct assignment of mnemonic names to field displacements, facilitates easy access to the data.

The use of tables or arrays brings up the matter of *accessing order*. In this connection, we explored different ways in which arrays and tables can be sorted according to one of the fields. The particular method called *index sort* was demonstrated in an example. Here we sorted a separate array of indexes that is then used to control the order of access to the records in the table.

The concept of *character strings* as data entities was introduced. We saw that there are several ways in which a group of character strings can be stored, including null-terminated sequences, and with a preceding count byte. An auxiliary array of addresses keeps track of where each string begins. It is also possible to store the byte count along with the string addresses in the auxiliary array, so that the strings themselves can be stored without intervening markers or counts.

The final topic discussed in this chapter was *linked lists*. We focused on singly linked lists, although other forms are possible. This data structure requires that the records include a field for a pointer, i.e., address, to the next record. By *next* we refer to the *logical order,* or the order of access. Physically, the records can be located anywhere in memory, not necessarily contiguously. Once any record is accessed, the pointer to the next record can be extracted from the field that we called NEXT using index addressing. We developed techniques for creating such a list from a sequential table, linking it according to descending order in a particular field. This, in effect, creates a "sorted" list, although the records themselves are not moved. We also discussed how to access the linked list, how to add new records, and how to "delete" records. In the latter case, the record is not actually deleted, but rather it is "unlinked" from the chain. The primary advantage of linked lists over sequentially accessed structures is the ease of insertion, deletion, merging, and splitting. Also, linked lists allow for dynamic allocation of storage, a fact that was mentioned without elaboration.

11.9 Exercises

11.1   Assume the following initializations of registers and memory locations prior to *fetching* of each of the sample instructions given. Provide the translation of each, and indicate all changes in registers and memory locations as a result of its execution.

Register	Contents	Label	Location	Contents
R0	000004	A:	000500	000502
R1	000500			
R2	000503	B:	000502	000504
PC	001000		000504	000506

a) MOV A,R0   **b)** MOV #A,R0

c) MOV @#A,R0   **d)** MOV @A,R0

e) MOV 500,R0   **f)** MOV #500,R0

g) MOV @#500,R0   **h)** MOV @500,R0

11.2   Assuming the same initializations as shown in Exercise 1, comment on the instructions below. Say whether or not they are correct, and what changes in registers and memory location occur when executed if they are correct.

a) CLR   @2(R1)   **b)** CLR   @3(R1)

c) CLRB   @2(R1)   **d)** CLRB   @3(R1)

e) CLR   @(R1)+   **f)** CLRB @(R1)+
g) CLRB @(R2)+   **h)** CLRB @−(R2)

11.3 Develop a subroutine that will add two one-dimensional arrays, producing their sum in a third array. Transmit the address of the argument list in R5. (See Sec. 9.10.4.)

11.4 Develop a program that accepts a two-dimensional array from the keyboard in row-major order and stores it in column-major form. Allocate sufficient space for arrays as large as 1000_8 total elements. The number of rows and columns should be read from the keyboard. Use GETOCT or a suitable alternative for keyboard input.

11.5 Write a subroutine that will compute row averages for an array with M rows and N columns. Assume that the array is stored in row-major form. Transmit the address of the argument list in R5. (See Sec. 9.10.4.)

11.6 Write a program that accepts row and column indexes from the keyboard and prints the corresponding element of the T array shown in Fig. 11.1. Assume that it is stored in column-major form. Use GETOCT and PUTOCT or suitable equivalents for I/O.

11.7 Repeat Exercise 11.6, but assume T to be stored in row-major form.

11.8 Assume that there are N students (100 decimal maximum) whose names (10 characters), student numbers (16-bit integers), and test scores (8-bit integers) are to be entered into memory for processing. Write a program that accepts this information from the keyboard and stores it as an array of records, i.e., a table. Assume that you have the subroutines GETOCT and GETSTR mentioned in Sec. 11.3.3.

11.9 Develop a program that will accept a student number from the keyboard and print out the corresponding name and test score from the table referred to in Exercise 11.8.

11.10 Do Exercise 11.8 using an index array. Sort according to student number and print the student numbers and corresponding scores.

11.11 Write a program that functions exactly as that shown in Fig. 11.8, but employs the string storage method shown in Fig. 11.7(b).

11.12 Write a program that functions exactly as that shown in Fig. 11.8, but employs the string storage method shown in Fig. 11.7(c).

11.13 Write a program that functions exactly as that shown in Fig. 11.8, but employs the string storage method shown in Fig. 11.7(d).

11.14 Write a program that accepts octal numbers continuously from the keyboard, placing them in a circular queue of 1000_8 words. When any nonoctal character is entered, the program should print the numbers currently in the queue, removing each number from the queue when printed, then ask for more numbers to be added to the queue. A ^Q should halt the program.

11.15 Do Exercise 11.8 using a linked list.

11.16 Develop a program that provides the user with four commands—ADD (A), DELETE (D), PRINT (P), and HALT (H). If A is entered, it should accept a name (10 characters) and score (8-bit integer), and store them as a linked list of records, ordered according to score. If P is entered, the current list of scores should be printed. If D is entered, a name should be accepted and, if found in the list, the record should be deleted. H should stop the program.

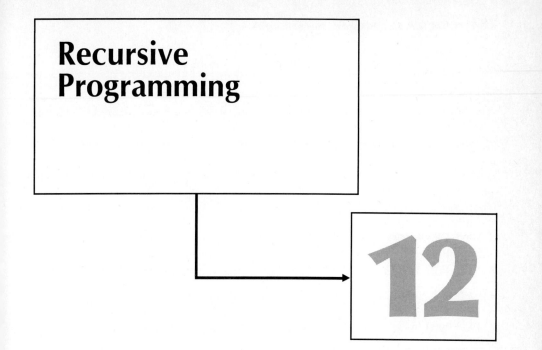

Recursive Programming

12.1 Overview

In Chapter 9 we saw how the system stack is used for subroutine linkage, and how it can be used for argument transmission. We further saw that this method allowed nesting, i.e., subroutines calling other subroutines. In an extension of this same idea, this chapter shows how subroutines can actually call themselves. Mathematically, this concept is known as **recursion,** which is characterized by a function being defined in terms of its own definition. The simplest example is the factorial function. The ease with which such functions are coded in MACRO-11 is impressive. Because of the far-reaching importance of recursive algorithms in computer science, and the fact that this will be the first encounter for many readers, we treat this subject in some detail.

12.2 The Concept of Recursion

In mathematics, a function is said to be **defined recursively** if it is defined in terms of itself. An elementary example of this is the factorial function, $n!$, which we shall call $F(n)$. This is understood to mean the result of the sequence

$$n \times (n - 1) \times (n - 2) \times (n - 3) \times \ldots \times (1)$$

It will be noted here that the sequence

$$(n - 1) \times (n - 2) \times (n - 3) \times \ldots \times (1)$$

is nothing other than $(n - 1)!$. Therefore a valid definition of $F(n)$ is

$$F(n) = n! = n \times F(n - 1)$$

that is recursive. The recursive process begins with a "root formula," in this case $F(0) = 1$.

Many functions can be defined in this way. Other examples include

Power function (X^n):
$F(0) = 1$	(Root formula)
$F(n) = X \times F(n - 1)$	(Recursive formula)

Fibonacci numbers:
$F(0) = 0$	(Root formula)
$F(1) = 1$	(Root formula)
$F(n) = F(n - 1) + F(n - 2)$	(Recursive formula)

Present value of unit annual deposit at interest i:
$F(0) = 0$	(Root formula)
$F(n) = 1 + (1 + i) \times F(n - 1)$.	(Recursive formula)

In each case, there is one or more root formulas that are nonrecursive for particular argument values, as well as the recursive formula. Both are essential elements of recursive calculations.

Recursive definition is also applicable to nonnumeric problems. For example, in the design of language processors such as compilers, it is necessary to examine general expressions such as

$$A + B*(C + C*E + X*(A + 10) + 14)$$

and generate the machine code to carry out the indicated operations. Recursive procedures can be defined to do such translations. Applications such as these make recursion very important in computer science.

The programming of recursively defined functions or procedures requires certain capabilities of the programming language. In particular, a procedure (i.e., a subroutine or function) has to be able to *call itself*. Many widely used high-level languages (e.g., BASIC and FORTRAN) *do not* allow this. However, an assembly language that uses a stack for subroutine linkage and argument transmission, such as MACRO-11, is well suited to the needs of recursive programming.

Before getting into the programming details, let us try to develop a better understanding of the nature of recursion. The factorial function can be used for this purpose. Suppose we wish to compute the factorial of 4 recursively. The steps are as follows.

Step 1:	$F(4) = 4 \times F(3)$.	(Cannot complete, so find $F(3)$.)
Step 2:	$F(3) = 3 \times F(2)$.	(Cannot complete, so find $F(2)$.)
Step 3:	$F(2) = 2 \times F(1)$.	(Cannot complete, so find $F(1)$.)

Step 4:   F(1) = 1 × F(0).   (Cannot complete, so find F(0).)
Step 5:   F(0) = 1.   (By root formula.)
Step 6:   F(1) = 1 × 1 = 1.   (Complete step 4.)
Step 7:   F(2) = 2 × 1 = 2.   (Complete step 3.)
Step 8:   F(3) = 3 × 2 = 6.   (Complete step 2.)
Step 9:   F(4) = 4 × 6 = 24.   (Complete step 1.)

It is seen that evaluation for a high-level argument requires that the function must be evaluated for the entire sequence of lower-level arguments, down to the root formula, in this case, F(0) = 1. This is called the "descent" process. During descent, each attempt to evaluate has to be left "pending" because the result depends on the as yet undetermined lower-level evaluations. Once the descent is complete, which is evident when we finally come to an argument that is the root, the "ascent" process begins. This is a matter of working backwards, completing the steps left pending during the descent.

Also, note that the intermediate results obtained during descent have to be saved for use during the ascent process. That is, in the example above, we had to retain the successive values of n (4, 3, 2, and 1) in order to carry out the multiplications during ascent. This is an important consideration when recursive routines are programmed. It is also important to observe that these values are needed in the *reverse* of the order in which they are calculated. This suggests that a stack will be the ideal data structure for recursion.

It should be said that many functions can be computed either recursively or otherwise. For example, other algorithms for the factorial function are easily devised. In general, a recursive algorithm will require more steps than will the alternatives. The reason recursion is used, then, is not to achieve efficiency, but because the algorithms are often (though not always) less complicated and easier to code. The factorial example used here has been chosen for its familiarity. It is, however, a poor example because it happens to have a recursive algorithm that is both less efficient and more complicated than the alternative. Unfortunately, problems that show the true virtues of recursion are too complex for introductory examples.

12.3 Recursive Programming Examples

Example 12.1   The factorial function is a convenient problem for demonstrating recursive programming. Not only is it a familiar relationship but it also has only one argument N and uses only one previous value of the function. A flowchart showing a recursive algorithm for this function appears in Fig. 12.1. The corresponding MACRO-11 subroutine and a calling program is shown in Fig. 12.2.

The stack plays a major role in this algorithm. The number for which the factorial is to be found, N, is on top of the stack when control is passed to the

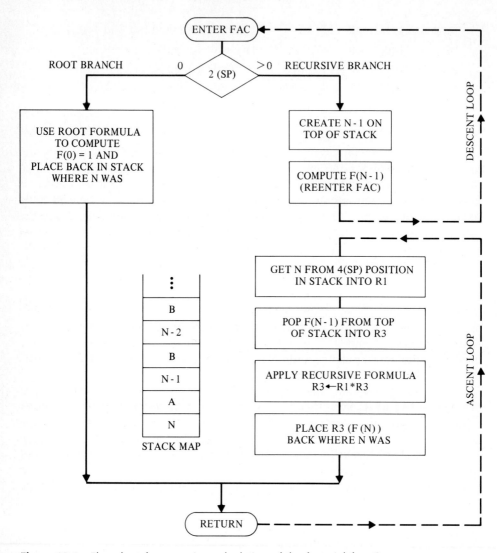

Figure 12.1 Flowchart for recursive calculation of the factorial function.

subroutine. Upon return to the calling point, the result (*N*!) will be on top of the stack, having replaced the argument. Immediately upon entry, the stack contents are

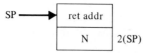

```
                    .TITLE   RECURSIVE FACTORIAL
                    .MCALL   .PRINT,.EXIT
                    .GLOBL   GETDEC,PUTDEC
          START:
                    .PRINT #M1              ;PRINT PROMPT
                    JSR    PC,GETDEC        ;GET N FROM KEYBOARD
                    MOV    R0,-(SP)         ;PUT N INTO STACK
                    JSR    PC,FAC           ;COMPUTE FACTORIAL
          A:        .PRINT #M2              ;PRINT LABEL FOR RESULT
                    MOV    (SP)+,R0         ;POP N! FROM STACK
                    JSR    PC,PUTDEC        ;PRINT N!
                    .EXIT
          M1:       .ASCIZ/ENTER N/
          M2:       .ASCIZ/N! IS:/
                    .EVEN
          ;
          ;         END OF MAIN
          ;
          FAC:
                    TST    2(SP)            ;SEE IF ROOT CASE.
                    BEQ    FAC0             ;IF SO,BR TO FAC0
                    MOV    2(SP),-(SP)      ;IF NOT,SET UP
                    DEC    (SP)             ;  (N-1) AS ARGUMENT.
                    JSR    PC,FAC           ;       AND RECURSE.
          B:        MOV    4(SP),R1         ;GET N
                    MOV    (SP)+,R3         ;POP F(N-1)
                    MUL    R1,R3            ;F(N)=N*F(N-1)
                    MOV    R3,2(SP)         ;PUT F(N) IN STACK.
                    BR     OUT
          FAC0:
                    INC    2(SP)            ;F(0)=1
          OUT:      RTS    PC
          ;
          ;         END OF FAC
          ;
                    .END START
```

Figure 12.2   MACRO-11 implementation of recursive factorial algorithm.

The organization of the stack during recursive calls must be kept in mind so that information can be extracted as needed. All arguments and intermediate results can be addressed from the *current* SP, regardless of the depth of recursion.

There are two cases to be considered with this algorithm, depending on the value of N. We shall first consider the case when $N = 0$, as would arise due to the instruction sequence

```
MOV    #0,-(SP)
JSR    PC,FAC
```

Upon return, we expect the factorial of 0, i.e., 1, to be on top of the stack.

As can be seen in Figs. 12.1 and 12.2, the value of N is examined by testing 2(SP) because N is two bytes (one word) below the current stack pointer. Because the contents of 2(SP) is zero, the branch takes place and it is replaced by its factorial, namely, 1. This is followed immediately by a return to the calling point, leaving the factorial of the argument on top of the stack as promised.

The more interesting case is when N is greater than 0. As an example, suppose the following instruction sequence is executed.

```
     MOV    #2,-(SP)
     JSR    PC,FAC
A:
```

Now, upon reaching the TST 2(SP) instruction in FAC, the test fails and the recursive part of the algorithm is executed.

The recursive part of the algorithm can be explained either intuitively or precisely. The intuitive explanation requires that one simply *believe* that recursion works, without worrying about how it works. That is, when we discover that the argument is greater than zero, we set about to calculate $F(N)$ by the recursive formula,

$$F(N) = N \times F(N - 1).$$

To do this, we need $F(N - 1)$. Because we are confident that our subroutine FAC *will* compute the factorial of a number, we simply use it to compute $F(N - 1)$. That is, we place $N - 1$ on top of the stack and execute JSR PC,FAC. Upon return, $F(N - 1)$ is on top of the stack, and we can proceed with calculation of $F(N)$ by the recursive formula. This line of reasoning requires a certain boldness, but it is very effective in the design of recursive algorithms. The precise explanation, given below, should be understood, but its details tend to obscure rather than enlighten when one is designing a recursive algorithm.

The precise explanation of the recursive part of Figs. 12.1 and 12.2 requires that we examine what happens when the JSR PC,FAC is executed from within FAC. This can best be explained by observing the evolution of the stack as shown in Fig. 12.3 for calculation of 2!. For convenience of discussion, we have labeled the instructions immediately after the JSR PC,FAC in the main program and subroutine as A and B, respectively. Figures 12.3(a), (b), and (c) show the states upon subroutine entry. There are three such states because FAC gets called once from the main program, and twice from itself. Figures 12.3(d), (e), and (f) show the states after the three successive returns.

On the first call, from the main program, the stack has the main program return point on top, and the primary argument in the second position. Because that argument pointed at by 2(SP) is 2 rather than 0, the branch to FAC0 is not executed. Instead, the primary argument is duplicated on top of the stack and decremented, forming $2 - 1 = 1$. The JSR PC,FAC is then executed, creating the stack state shown in Fig. 12.3(b) upon reentry. The value pointed at by 2(SP) is now 1, so it is again placed on top of the stack and decremented. This is followed by JSR PC,FAC, so that the procedure is reentered with the stack state shown in Fig. 12.3(c). Now the value pointed at by 2(SP) is 0, so the branch to FAC0 is executed. This results in the 0 in 2(SP) being incremented to 1 (creating $F(0)$), and RTS PC is executed for the first time. This return, however, is to B, still inside FAC, because that is the address on top of the stack. The state of the stack at this point is shown in Fig. 12.3(d). The instructions at B apply the recursive formula, taking the "current" $N = 1$ (really the original $N - 1$) out of position 4(SP) and $F(N - 1) = 1$ off of the top. The latter is done with a pop so that SP points to the correct return address. After the MUL instruction forms $N \times F(N - 1) = 1$, this value is placed in 2(SP), which is where SP will point after the next return. This second return is also to B, with the stack state

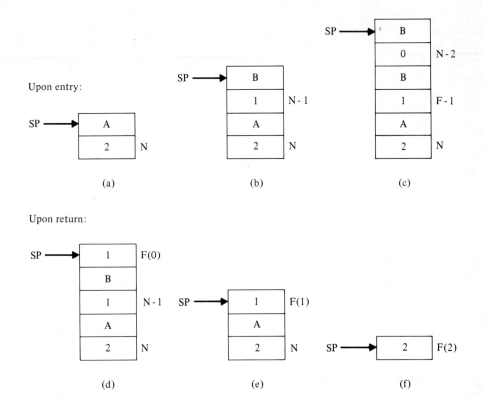

Figure 12.3   States of stack during recursive calculation of 2!.

shown in Fig. 12.3(e). The actions that then take place are exactly the same as before, only this time the operands for the multiply are $N = 2$ and $F(N - 1) = 1$, so that $F(2)$ is formed and placed in 2(SP). The third return is then executed, this time causing return to the main program with $F(2) = 2$ on top of the stack.

It is helpful to think of the process described above as recursive descent, followed by ascent. This is shown by the dashed lines in the flowchart, Fig. 12.1. Note that the descent loop will continue until the value pointed at by 2(SP) is 0. Every time it goes through this loop, it leaves an N and the *internal* return point (B) on the stack. When it finally takes the ROOT branch, the return will therefore be to B. This puts it in the ascent loop where it works its way back down through the stack, computing the successive factorials. It will exit the ascent loop when it works its way down to the A return point placed in the stack by the call from the main program.

The main program in Fig. 12.2 uses subroutines GETDEC and PUTDEC. GETDEC can be seen in Appendix F. Although PUTDEC is not presented in this book, it can be created by minor modifications to the program given in Fig. 8.12.

12.4 Developing Recursive Subroutines

The ideas used in the previous example can be generalized to apply to any recursive definition. The general form for recursion formulas with one previous value is

    SUB:
        Conditional branch to root formula, ROOT.
        Set up arguments for recursive call.
        JSR PC,SUB
        Apply recursive formula.
        Place result in proper place in stack.
        Reset stack pointer to proper return address.
        BR OUT

    ROOT:
        Root formula.
        Place result in proper place in stack.
        Reset stack pointer to proper return address.

    OUT:
        RTS PC

Arguments are always placed in the stack. We saw in the previous example that they are accessed using index addressing into the stack, i.e., n(SP) where n is the number of bytes the needed argument is from the top of the stack in a given state. A simple diagram of the stack will help in determining the proper offset in the stack. Normally, the result is returned on top of the stack. Care must be taken that the stack pointer points at the most recently added return point when the RTS PC instruction is reached.

Some recursion formulas use more than one previous value. The Fibonacci problem, for example, uses $F(N - 1)$ and $F(N - 2)$ to compute $F(N)$. The general structure for two previous values is

    SUB:
        Conditional branch to root formula 1, ROOT1.
        Conditional branch to root formula 2, ROOT2.
        Set up arguments for finding $F(N - 1)$.
        JSR PC,SUB
        Set up arguments for finding $F(N - 2)$.
        JSR PC,SUB
        Apply recursive formula.
        Place result in proper place in stack.
        Reset stack pointer to proper return address.
        BR OUT

    ROOT1:
        Root formula 1.
        Place result in proper place in stack.
        BR OUT

ROOT2:
>   Root formula 2.
>   Place result in proper place in stack.

OUT:
>   RTS PC

Although slightly more complicated than the single root case, the principles for the case of two root formulas are the same. It is seen that two recursive calls must be made before the recursion formula can be applied. Also, there are two conditional branches to root formulas. The stack structure is also more complex because of the need for two previous values of the function.

12.5 Summary

The topic discussed in this chapter was *recursion* and, in particular, recursive subroutines in MACRO-11. We saw that, mathematically, recursion means that a function is defined in terms of itself, with a separately defined "root" formula or formulas to get the process started. In programming, recursion implies that a subroutine has a call to itself from within the body of its definition.

When the subroutine is called from outside (the primary call), it will usually be for some large value of argument. As soon as the subroutine determines that the root formula does not apply, it leaves the evaluation pending, decreases the argument, and calls itself (the recursive call) to evaluate for the smaller argument. This call may result in the need for another recursive call, again leaving the calculation pending. This process, called recursive descent, continues until the root formula applies. Then the ascent process begins, working its way back through the set of pending calculations.

One essential requirement for recursive programming is the retention of the intermediate results of calculations left pending during descent. Another is the retention of the correct return point for each recursive call as well as the primary call. The linkage conventions used by the normal JSR PC,SUB instruction, together with argument transmission through the system stack, make recursive programming straightforward in MACRO-11. We saw this demonstrated with a simple example, as well as with a generalized approach for more complicated problems.

12.6 Exercises

12.1 Enter and assemble the program and recursive subroutine shown in Fig. 12.2. GETOCT and PUTOCT may be used instead of GETDEC and PUTDEC. Link with ODT and execute the program with breakpoints set at FAC, A, and B. At each break, examine the stack and verify the states shown in Fig. 12.3.

12.2 Create a recursive subroutine to calculate x^n, using integer values of x and n. Demonstrate using ODT.

12.3 Create a program and recursive subroutine to calculate Fibonacci numbers. Link with suitable input/output routines. (GETOCT and PUTOCT may be used.) Execute the program to find the largest number for which it can calculate the Fibonacci number.

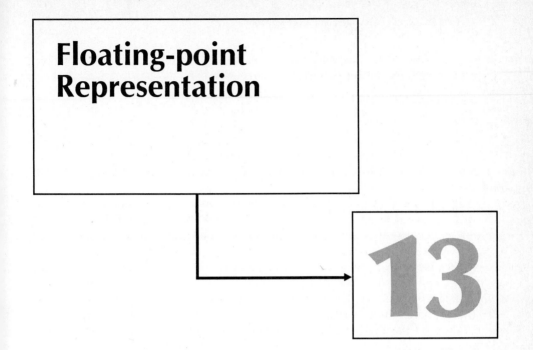

Floating-point Representation

13.1 Overview

You may have noticed that all numerical programming prior to this chapter has been with integers. The PDP-11 does have, however, a convention for storage of noninteger numbers, called **floating point,** and some members of the PDP-11 family have optional instructions to deal with numbers represented in this way. This topic is dealt with in this chapter, and has great importance in many numerical applications. We shall see how these numbers are stored, how operations are carried out with them, and what MACRO-11 directives are available for them. Input and output will also be discussed.

13.2 Concept of Floating-point Representation

Floating point is a way of representing a number in a digital computer that is analogous to **scientific notation.** Recall that in scientific notation the representation of magnitude is separated into two parts, one called the mantissa, and the other, the exponent. For example, 359.628 can be written in scientific notation as 3.59628×10^2, wherein 3.59628 is the mantissa and 2 is the exponent on the base. Note that the same number could be written as 0.359628×10^3. Written in this way, i.e., with the decimal point immediately preceding the most significant digit, the number is said to be **normalized,** and the mantissa can meaningfully be called the **fraction.**

These ideas can be extended to binary numbers. Thus we can represent 110100110 as $0.110100110 \times 2^{1001}$ where the fraction and exponent are both shown in base 2. Now, if we wished to store this number in the computer, we would have to store only the bit patterns

Fraction: 110100110
Exponent: 1001

Note that the base is understood and therefore need not be stored. Also, the "binary point" is understood to be at the extreme left and therefore its location need not be stored. Of course, any usage of this number would have to account for the way it was stored.

The scheme above could be used directly, storing the fraction in one word and the exponent in another. However, this would not be an efficient usage of resources because it is unlikely that an entire 16-bit word would be needed for the exponent, while more than one word may be needed for the fraction. This is so because with normalized floating point representation the *accuracy* with which we can work is controlled by the number of bits available for the fraction, while the allowed size of the number is determined by the number of bits available for the exponent. It is for these reasons that the format for floating-point representation on the PDP-11 has been defined as shown in Fig. 13.1. We see that 23 bits have been reserved for the fraction, eight for the exponent, and 1 for a sign.

We have two other matters to consider before arriving at the way floating-point numbers are actually stored in the PDP-11. The first concerns the sign of the exponent. That is, we need to be able to store very small numbers as well as very large numbers. Therefore positive or negative exponents must be allowed. This is handled by a system known as **excess-200** (octal) representation, in which the exponent plus 200_8 is stored rather than the exponent itself. For example, the exponent in the preceding example, 1001_2, is stored as $11_8 + 200_8 = 211_8$. The full range of exponents possible with this system is then

Actual exponent (Octal)	Excess 200 (Octal)
+ 177	377
+ 1	201
0	200
− 1	177
− 177	001

Note that neither positive nor negative 200_8 is listed as a valid exponent. This is because either would yield 000 in the excess-200 system, and this particular value in the exponent field is used to indicate a floating-point zero as discussed below.

The other matter to be considered is called the **hidden bit,** which is a refinement of the way the fraction is stored. Observe that the normalization process places the binary point to the left of the most significant nonzero bit. This means that

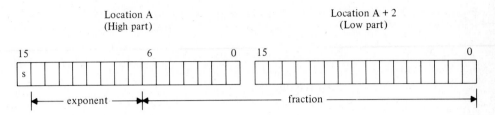

Figure 13.1   Floating-point representation format.

the first bit in what we have called the fraction is *always* a 1! Since this is so, that 1 need not be stored. This "hidden bit" is just *understood* to be there, and is restored by the computer whenever a nonzero floating-point number is processed. This means that although we have only 23 actual bits for the fraction, we in effect have 24, providing greater accuracy.

With this floating-point system, numbers can be represented to approximately seven decimal digits of accuracy, the equivalent of 24 bits. (Showing this is left as an exercise.) Positive or negative numbers as large as approximately 1.7×10^{38} (decimal) can be represented. Also, positive or negative numbers as small as approximately 0.29×10^{-38} (decimal) can be represented. However, as a consequence of the hidden bit assumption, zero cannot be represented internally in the same way as other numbers. This is because the fraction for the number $0.5_{10} = 0.1_2$ is stored as 0 after removing the hidden bit, and therefore a zero fraction cannot be construed as meaning zero. To deal with this, an additional convention is adopted, whereby zero is represented by a zero in the *exponent* field. A so-called *true* or *clean* zero has the fraction *and* sign bits zero. However, whenever the exponent field is zero, a zero value will be used in all operations regardless of the contents of the fraction and sign bits.

Let us now review floating-point representation by considering several examples.

Example 13.1   Convert 384_{10} to floating point as stored on the PDP-11.

384_{10} $= 110000000_2 = 0.11 \times 2^{1001}$
Fraction $= 11$ (Store 1 because of hidden bit)
Exponent $= 1001 = 11_8$ (Store 211_8 as excess-200 value)
Sign bit $= 0$ (Positive number)

Memory (Binary):

Sign	Exponent	Fraction
0	10001001	10000000000000000000000

Memory Word Contents (Octal):

Loc	Loc + 2
042300	000000

Example 13.2   Convert 0.5_{10} to floating point as stored on the PDP-11.

$0.5_{10} = 0.1_2 \times 2^0$
Fraction = 1   (Store 0 because of hidden bit)
Exponent = 0   (Store 200_8 as excess-200 value)
Sign   = 0   (Positive number)

Memory (Binary):

Sign	Exponent	Fraction
0	10000000	00000000000000000000000

Memory Word Contents (Octal):

Loc	Loc + 2
040000	000000

Example 13.3   Convert the following floating-point memory contents (shown in octal) to decimal.

Loc	Loc + 2
042740	000000

Memory (Binary):

Sign	Exponent	Fraction
0	10001011	11000000000000000000000

Fraction = 111 (Hidden bit added)
Exponent = 213_8 (Excess-200)
$\qquad = 213 - 200 = 13_8 = 11_{10}$
Sign   = 0 (Positive)
Value = $0.111 \times 2^{11} = 111_2 \times 2^8 = 1792_{10}$.

Example 13.4   Convert the following floating-point memory contents (shown in octal) to decimal.

Loc	Loc + 2
121432	167000

Memory (Binary):

Sign	Exponent	Fraction
1	01000110	00110101110111000000000

Fraction = 100110101110111 (Hidden bit added)
Exponent = 106_8 (Excess-200 notation)
$\qquad = 106 - 200 = -72_8 = -58_{10}$
Sign   = 1 (Negative)
Value   = $-0.100110101110111 \times 2^{-58}$,
$\qquad = -100110101110111 \times 2^{-73}$,

$$= -19831 \times 1.058791 \times 10^{-22},$$
$$= -2.099689 \times 10^{-18}.$$

13.3 Floating-point Directives

MACRO-11 has special directives useful when working with floating-point numbers. The directive

    A: .FLT2   f

will convert the *decimal* number f and store it in A and A + 2 using the format given in Fig. 13.1. The number f can be written in a variety of ways as suggested by the following examples.

    6
    7.2
    92.6E4
    −4.2E−3

It is also possible to write

    ARY: .FLT2   a,b,c

where a, b, and c are decimal values to be stored in successive, two-word positions in the array ARY.

When using this directive, you must observe the allowable range of magnitude for floating-point numbers. For example,

    .FLT2   1.2E43   (Incorrect)
    .FLT2   1.2E−40   (Incorrect)

will result in assembly error messages because they are outside of the allowed range for floating-point numbers.

A companion directive to .FLT2 is .FLT4. This directive will convert a decimal number to a *four*-word floating point representation, called *double precision*. The format used is similar to that shown in Fig. 13.1, except two additional words are provided for holding more low-order bits. Calculations are sometimes carried out in double-precision floating point because this provides approximately 16 significant decimal digits. We do not consider such problems in this book, however.

We have previously learned that octal is the assumed base for all numerics used in MACRO-11. However, for the .FLT2 and .FLT4 directives, *decimal* is the assumed base, so that

    .FLT2   10

will store decimal 10 rather than octal 10. Sometimes it is desired to use octal in these directives, in which case the numeric must be preceded by ^O. This is called "radix control." For example,

    .FLT2   ^O177

is the same as

     .FLT2   0.127E3

13.4 Floating-point Operations

Because the normal instructions available on the PDP-11 operate on integers, special steps must be taken by the programmer if arithmetic is to be done in floating point. Larger machines and some small machines have additional hardware to handle these and other functions for floating-point numbers. Here we shall consider the two widely used hardware extensions. On many small machines, floating-point capability is not present in the hardware, so it becomes necessary to write subroutines or macros to carry out the needed operations, e.g., move, add, subtract, multiply, and divide. Development of such software is beyond the scope of the present discussion.

13.4.1 Small Machines—FIS Option

The Floating Instruction Set (FIS) option is available for LSI-11 machines as well as older, small PDP-11s such as the PDP-11/03. When installed, this option provides the four instructions shown in Table 13.1.

TABLE 13.1
Floating-point Operations (FIS Option)

Assembler Mnemonics	Translation	Explanation
FADD Rn	07500n	Adds two floating-point numbers found in top four stack locations, leaving sum in top two stack locations.
FSUB Rn	07501n	Subtracts floating-point numbers found in third and fourth stack locations from floating point number found in first and second, leaving difference in top two stack locations.
FMUL Rn	0752n	Multiplies two floating-point numbers found in top four stack locations, leaving result in top two stack locations.
FDIV Rn	07503n	Divides floating-point number found in third and fourth stack locations into floating point number found in first and second, leaving result in top two stack locations.

Notes:

1. Rn = any register, R1 through R6, used as stack pointer.

2. n = integer 0–6 representing register employed.

3. All instructions assume operands are stored in stack positions, with word containing exponent and most significant fraction bits preceding word containing least significant fraction bits.

4. All instructions remove operands from stack and place result back on top of stack.

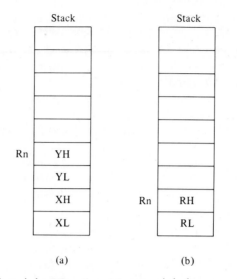

Figure 13.2   Operand stack for FIS option: (a) operands before execution; (b) operands after execution.

All of the FIS option instructions work in the same manner. They assume that the two operands are in a stack, the top of which is pointed at by a selected register. Further, they assume that each operand is stored with the high part preceding (i.e., having a lower address than) the low part. This is shown in Fig. 13.2(a). These operands are removed automatically, and after execution, the result is left on top of the stack as shown in Fig. 13.2(b).

Example 13.5   Because all FIS instructions work similarly, a single example will suffice. Suppose we wish to multiply a floating-point value stored in X and X + 2 by 17_{10}. We could do this using the system stack for the floating-point operands as follows.

```
        MOV     X + 2, − (SP)        ; LOAD
        MOV        X, − (SP)         ;    FLOATING
        MOV     C + 2, − (SP)        ;       POINT
        MOV        C, − (SP)         ;          STACK
        FMUL       SP                ; MULTIPLY
        MOV     (SP) + , X           ; POP PRODUCT
        MOV        (SP) + , X + 2    ;          INTO  X
                    .
                    .
                    .
        HALT
X:      .BLKW   2
C:      .FLT2   17
```

Here we have assumed that a floating-point value was previously placed in X and X + 2. Note that we used .FLT2 to initialize C to 17. It is not permissible to simply place the constant 17 as an immediate-mode operand in the MOV instruction because that would translate to an integer value, whereas FMUL expects a two-word floating-point value.

More complex programming using the floating-point instructions can proceed in the same manner. If desired, macros can be written to move automatically the operands onto and off of the stack, simplifying the programming task.

Note that machines that have the FP11 processor option (see the next section) will *not* have the FIS instructions. The MACRO-11 assembler will recognize the mnemonics and generate the machine code as shown in Table 13.1. However, when the program is executed, an illegal instruction message will result.

13.4.2 Larger Machines—FP11 Floating-point Coprocessor

The PDP-11/34, 11/45, and 11/70 computers can be fitted with a floating-point "coprocessor" called the FP11. This device provides a much larger floating-point instruction set, as well as significantly faster floating-point operations. The same instruction set can also be specified as an option for the smaller 11/23 and 11/24 machines, providing the programming convenience if not the greater speed. Here we shall examine only a few of the FP11 instructions, shown in Table 13.2, that were selected to allow basic floating-point programming.

In order to understand the FP11 instructions, it is necessary to observe that the FP11 has its own registers. These are, in a sense, like the general PDP-11 registers, but they are 32-bits in length. All double-operand FP11 instructions require that at least one of the operands be in an FP11 register. The assembler recognizes the symbols %0, %01, . . ., %5 for the FP11 registers, but it is customary to assign these to the symbols F0, F1, etc. That is, in a program using the FP11 we would include the directives

```
F0 = 0%
F1 = 1%
    .
    .

    .
F5 = 5%
```

In terms of machine code, these registers are designated 0, 1, 2, 3, 4, and 5.

Let us begin our study of FP11 usage by looking at the floating-point equivalent of the ADD instruction. Its MACRO-11 mnemonics are exemplified by

```
ADDF    X,F1
```

This says to take the floating-point value represented in PDP-11 central memory locations X and X + 2 and add it to the floating-point value in the FP11 register

TABLE 13.2
Floating-point Operations (FP11 Floating-point Coprocessor)

Assembler Mnemonics	Translation	Explanation
CLRF DF	1704dd	Stores floating-point zero in memory locations DF. (DF can also be Fn.)
LD SF,Fn	172mss	Moves floating-point number from memory locations SF to FP11 register Fn. (SF can also be Fn.)
LDCIF SI,Fn	177mss	Converts integer in memory location SI to floating-point number in FP11 register Fn. (SI can also be Rn.)
STF Fn,DF	174ndd	Moves floating-point number from FP11 register Fn to memory locations DF. (DF can also be Fn.)
STCFI Fn,DI	175mdd	Converts floating-point contents of Fn to 16-bit two's complement integer and stores it in DI. PDP-11 C condition code is set if number is too large.
ADDF SF,Fn	172nss	Adds floating-point number in memory locations SF to FP11 register Fn. (SF can also be Fn.)
SUBF SF,Fn	173nss	Subtracts floating-point number in memory locations SF from FP11 register Fn. (SF can also be Fn.)
CMPF SF,Fn CFCC	173mss 170000	This instruction sequence will do a comparison of floating-point values and set PDP-11 N and Z condition codes as CMP would for integers. Condition codes C and V are cleared.
MULF SF,Fn	171nss	Multiplies number in FP11 register Fn by floating-point number in SF (SF can also be Fn.)
DIVF SF,Fn	171mss	Divides number in FP11 register Fn by floating-point number in SF. (SF can also be Fn.)

Notes:

1. SF = floating-point source; DF = floating-point destination. These operands can use mode 1 through 7 exactly like normal instructions, in which case the PDP-11 registers are used, and operands are in PDP-11 central memory. If mode 0 is used, e.g., %n, Fn, or even Rn, the floating-point processor registers are used. When the operand is in PDP-11 central memory, the exponent and most significant fraction bits are in location referenced, and least significant fraction bits are in next higher location. Autoincrement and autodecrement modes increment/decrement by 4.

2. SI = integer source (two's complement) in central memory word.

3. Fn = floating-point processor register. Symbols must be defined through assignment, for example, F0 = %0, F1 = %1.

4. n = integer representing floating-point register number.

5. m = integer representing floating-point register number plus 4.

6. dd,ss = destination and source operand address codes. It will be recalled that the assembler also uses %n to refer to the normal PDP-11 registers. No ambiguity results because normal instructions cannot access the FP11 registers, and the FP11 cannot refer directly to a PDP-11 register.

F1. The first argument, X, can use any addressing mode. For example,

```
ADDF    (R1),F1
ADDF    (R2)+,F2
ADDF    F3,F2
```

Thus we see that the first operand can be either a *memory reference operand*, or an *FP11 register operand*, while the second operand *must* be an FP11 register. Because the PDP-11 registers are only 16-bits in length, they cannot be used to hold floating-point operands. Hence any time *register addressing* (mode 0) is used for *either* operand, the register is assumed to be an FP11 register. On the other hand, use of any other mode implies that a PDP-11 register is to be used.

Summarizing, the following differences from addressing in normal instructions must be observed.

1. The nonmemory reference operand, which in the case of ADDF is the second operand, must be an FP11 register selected from F0, F1, F2, or F3.

2. If the addressing *mode* of the memory reference operand (in the case of ADDF, the first operand) is 1, 2, . . ., 7, the register used will be the PDP-11 register, *not* the FP11 register. Also the autoincrement/autodecrement modes will change the register employed by 4.

3. If the addressing mode 0 (i.e., register addressing) is used for the nonmemory reference operand, it must be an FP11 register selected from F0 through F5.

Thus we see that ADDF can be used to add the contents of a memory location to any of the first four FP11 registers, or add the contents of *any* FP11 register to any of the first four FP11 registers. It cannot be used to add into a memory location, or into FP11 registers F4 and F5.

All of the double-operand FP11 instructions are similar to the ADDF in that one of the operands, either the source or the destination depending on the instruction, can be either memory reference or an FP11 register.

Table 13.2 summarizes the addressing rules for each instruction, using the symbols SF (floating-point source) or DF (floating-point destination) to refer to the operand that can reference memory, and Fn for the one that can be only an FP11 register. Similarly, SI and DI refer to source and destination integer operands.

The instructions given in Table 13.2 are sufficient for most floating-point programming. We have included four essential arithmetic operations—ADDF, SUBF, MULF, and DIVF—as well as CLRF. The CLRF instruction creates a true floating-point zero in either central memory or in an FP11 register. Before floating-point arithmetic can be done, it is usually necessary to load a floating value from memory into an FP11 register. This can be done with the LDF (LoaD Floating point) instruction. A companion to this is the LDCIF (LoaD and Convert Integer to Floating) instruction. As the mnemonics suggest, a two's complement integer in a memory location can be converted to floating point and loaded into an FP11 register with this instruction. A floating-point result can be moved from an FP11 register to memory using the STF (Store Floating Point) instruction. The companion STCFI converts to integer (two's complement) before storing.

In order to allow branching, the floating-point compare (CMPF) is included. With this instruction, it is necessary to recognize that the FP11 has its own "status register" with the equivalents of N, Z, V, and C condition codes. The settings of these can be transferred to the PDP-11 PSW with the CFCC (Convert Floating Condition Codes) instruction. Some FP11 instructions, such as STCFI, set the PDP-11 PSW automatically without using CFCC.

There are many FP11 instructions that are not given in Table 13.2. Moreover, all of those that are given have double-precision versions. Full details of all of these are given in *The PDP-11 Processor Handbook* (Digital Equipment Corporation).

The formats of the FP11 instructions are shown in Fig. 13.3. Note that the opcode is viewed to be in two parts, a constant part OC, always 17_8, and a variable part that identifies the specific FP11 instruction. The floating opcodes for the instructions in Table 13.2 are

Mnemonic	FOC (Binary)
CLRF	000100
LDF	0101
LDCIF	1110
STF	1000
STCFI	1011
ADDF	0100
SUBF	0110
CMPF	0111
MULF	0010
DIVF	1001

It will also be noted that there are only two bits allowed for the FP11 register in the format for double-operand instructions. This explains why we are allowed to use only F0 through F3 for this operand. Another consequence of this is that the third *octal* digit in a translated FP11 instruction is composed of the register *and* the least significant bit of the floating opcode.

Thus when we translate an instruction that has an opcode with 0 LSB (e.g., STF) we get the octal value

174ndd

whereas, if it has an opcode with a LSB of 1, it translates to

172mss

where m = 4 + n.

For either single-operand or double-operand FP11 instructions, the six rightmost bits are the address code for an operand that can be either in an FP11 register, or in PDP-11 memory. The FP11 processor is designed to assume it is in the FP11 register designated by the register field (three rightmost bits) if the mode field is zero. In this case the register field must be 0–5 because the FP11 has only six registers. If the mode field is not zero, the register field is assumed to refer to a PDP-11 register, and its contents are used.

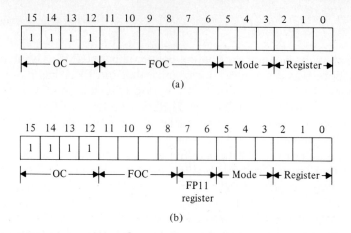

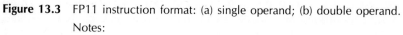

(a)

(b)

Figure 13.3 FP11 instruction format: (a) single operand; (b) double operand.

Notes:

OC = opcode (always 17 octal)
FOC = floating opcode (varies with instruction)
FP11 reg. = floating-point register (0–3 octal)
mode = addressing mode (0–7 octal)
If mode = 0, register taken as FP11 register (0–5)
If mode = 1–7, register taken as PDP-11 register (0–7)

```
                .TITLE FLOATING POINT
                .MCALL .EXIT,.PRINT,.TTYIN
        F0=%0   ;DEFINE FLOATING
        F1=%1   ;   POINT
        F2=%2   ;      REGISTERS
        START:
        ;
        ;       Z=(X+Y)*C/D
        ;
                CLRF    F1      ;CLEAR F1
                ADDF    X,F1    ;ADD X TO F1
                ADDF    Y,F1    ;ADD Y TO F1
                MULF    C,F1    ;MULT BY C
                DIVF    D,F1    ;DIVIDE BY D
                STF     F1,Z    ;MOVE F1 TO Z
        ;
        ;       KF = FLOAT(K)
        ;
                LDCIF   K,F0    ;CONVERT INTEGER TO FLT
                STF     F0,KF   ;MOVE F0 TO KF
        ;
        ;       W = C - D
        ;
                LDF     C,F2    ;MOVE MEM TO FLT REG.
                SUBF    D,F2    ;SUBTRACT D FROM F2
                STF     F2,W    ;MOVE FLT REG TO MEM
                .EXIT
        C:      .FLT2   16.     ;INIT. FLT. NUMBER
        D:      .FLT2   2.
        X:      .FLT2   128.
        Y:      .FLT2   128.
        Z:      .BLKW   2       ;RESERVE FOR FLT NUMBER
        W:      .BLKW   2
        K:      .WORD   200     ;128 DECIMAL
        KF:     .BLKW   2       ;FLOAT K
                .BLKW   20
                .END    START
```

Figure 13.4 Example of use of FP11 instructions for floating-point operations.

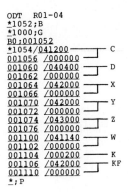

```
ODT   R01-04
*1052;B
*1000;G
B0:001052
*1054/041200 ──────┬─ C
001056 /000000 ──┘
001060 /040400 ──┬─ D
001062 /000000 ──┘
001064 /042000 ──┬─ X
001066 /000000 ──┘
001070 /042000 ──┬─ Y
001072 /000000 ──┘
001074 /043000 ──┬─ Z
001076 /000000 ──┘
001100 /041140 ──┬─ W
001102 /000000 ──┘
001104 /000200 ──── K
001106 /042000 ──┬─ KF
001110 /000000 ──┘
*;P
```

Figure 13.5   Execution of program in Fig. 13.4 under ODT. [OS]

Example 13.6   Figure 13.4 shows the MACRO-11 listing of a simple program that uses many of the FP11 instructions in Table 13.2, as well as the .FLT2 directive. The first five instructions (lines 10–15) implement the equation

$$Z = (X+Y)*C/D$$

where X, Y, C, and D are initialized to the floating-point values 128, 128, 16, and 2, respectively. Lines 19 and 20 demonstrate loading and converting an integer to floating point, then storing it back in memory as floating point. Lines 24, 25, and 26 demonstrate usage of loading a floating-point number C into an FP11 register, forming the result C–D, and storing the result in W. The results of execution of this program (using ODT) are shown in Fig. 13.5. It would be instructive to carry out the steps of this program manually, and verify these results.

13.5 Input and Output of Floating-point Numbers

If floating-point operations are to be used in a program, one must consider how floating-point representation can be accepted as input from a keyboard, and how it can be output to a printer or display unit. These tasks can be done either by using assembly routines or by using existing facilities provided as part of the support software for high-level languages. We shall introduce both approaches without elaboration.

Let us first consider how floating I/O can be handled using existing facilities. Because a frequent use of assembly language is to write critical subroutines for programs written in high-level languages, it is quite natural to handle the input and output in the high-level language. We have already seen in Chapter 9 how to call assembly routines from FORTRAN programs. There, however, we used only integer values. In Fig. 13.6 we see a FORTRAN main program that passes floating-point arguments to and from a MACRO-11 subroutine. All I/O is then done in FORTRAN. Observe that with the FORTRAN convention for argument

```
             PROGRAM FLTIO
       C
       C     FORTRAN MAIN PROGRAM
       C
             READ(5,*)X,Y
             CALL SUB1(X,Y,Z)
             WRITE(7,*)Z
             END
```

(a)

```
                .TITLE FLOATING SUBROUTINE
       F1 = %1
       SUB1::
                CLRF    F1         ;CLEAR FP11 REG. 1
                LDF     @2(R5),F1   ;GET X INTO F1
                MULF    @4(R5),F1   ;MULT BY Y
                STF     F1,@6(R5)   ;STORE IN Z
                RTS     PC
                .END
```

(b)

Figure 13.6 Floating-point operations in MACRO-11 subroutine with I/O in FORTRAN main program: (a) FORTRAN main program; (b) MACRO-11 subroutine.

transmission (see Section 9.10.4), internal access to floating arguments is no different from that for integer arguments. That is, the *addresses* of the real arguments are stored in locations 2, 4, and 6 relative to the argument array address, which is passed in register R5. The compilation, assembly, and linkage steps are exactly as they are shown in Chapter 9.

Another example of using FORTRAN I/O facilities is shown in Fig. 13.7. The short main program, written in FORTRAN, does nothing other than transfer control to the major routine that is written in MACRO-11. The MACRO-11 routine then jumps to FORTRAN subroutines that perform the I/O. This technique is probably not ideal for production programs, but it provides a convenient method for testing. Note that by writing the *main* program in FORTRAN we allow the LINK program be able to resolve references to certain global labels used in FORTRAN input and output routines. If the main program is written in MACRO-11, LINK will not look in the FORTRAN library and certain external references will be unresolved.

Usage of input/output facilities of a higher-level language may not be possible or desirable in certain situations. In this case, routines must be developed for input and output of floating-point numbers. We shall show this approach for output and briefly consider input without going into detail.

For output, the basic goal is to print two decimal integers, D and N, as ASCII character strings, ddddddd and nn. Conventionally, these are printed in the format

$$\pm 0.\text{dddddddF} \pm \text{nn}$$

There are several methods for finding the integers D and N. One way to find N is to compare successive powers of 10, beginning with the most negative

```
            .TITLE FLOATING I/O
            .GLOBL FINP,FOUT
F0=%0
F1=%1
F2=%2
START::
            MOV       #ARG,R5
            JSR       PC,FINP
            CLRF      F1
            ADDF      X,F1              C         MAIN PROGRAM
            ADDF      Y,F1              C
            STF       F1,Z                        CALL START
            MOV       #ARG2,R5                    END
            JSR       PC,FOUT
            RTS       PC                          SUBROUTINE FOUT(C)
ARG:        .WORD     2,X,Y                       WRITE(7,*)C
X:          .BLKW     2                           RETURN
Y:          .BLKW     2                           END
ARG2:       .WORD     1,Z                         SUBROUTINE FINP(A,B)
Z:          .BLKW     2                           READ(5,*)A,B
            .BLKW     20                          RETURN
            .END                                  END
```

(a)   (b)

Figure 13.7   Using FORTRAN I/O for MACRO-11 assembly programs: (a) MACRO-11 portion; (b) FORTRAN portion.

possible N (-38), with the number X. If a power is less than or equal to the number, N is incremented and the next power is tried. When this process is complete, N is the exponent of 10. It can be converted to a string of ASCII digits nn using the procedure such as the one shown in Fig. 8.12, modified for decimal output.

To find D, first observe that we can arbitrarily choose the number of significant digits to be printed. However, this can be no more than seven decimal digits because this corresponds to the maximum accuracy possible with 24 bits. Then note that if X is divided by $10^{(N-K)}$, the whole-number part of the result can be converted to a decimal integer with K digits. These digits will be the decimal digits to the *right* of the decimal point in a normalized decimal floating-point form.

Example 13.7   A procedure implementing these ideas is shown in Figs. 13.8(a) and (b). The macros in Fig. 13.8(a) are used to generate a table of powers of 10 from 1.E-38 to 1.E$+38$. The first part of the executable code, beginning at START, loads the value to be printed into the FP11 register F0, and sets a flag for its sign. The loop beginning at L1 then steps through the POWTEN table, comparing successive table values with the number. When this loop completes, N contains the decimal exponent, and R1 points to one table entry (4 bytes) beyond the actual power of 10. In the next block, beginning at L2, R1 is adjusted to point at $10^{(N-4)}$ in the table. This is divided into F0, leaving there a number that can be represented in decimal with four digits to the left of the decimal point. The sign of the exponent N is used to set a flag ES, and then N is set positive.

The conversion to ASCII and printing is shown in Fig. 13.8(b). The ASCII codes are first developed in the buffer ASC, then printed. The sign of the number,

```
                    .TITLE FLOATING OUTPUT
                    .GLOBL CNVDEC
                    .MCALL  .EXIT,.PRINT
        F0=%0
        F1=%1

                    .MACRO GEN,K
                    .FLT2  1.E^O'K
                    .ENDM  GEN
                    .MACRO DEFPOW
        POWTEN:     .FLT2  1.E-38
                    K1=-37.
                    .REPT 75.
                    GEN   \K1
                    K1=K1+1
                    .ENDR
                    .ENDM DEFPOW
        START:
                    MOV    N0,N         ;INIT. EXPONENT
                    MOV    #POWTEN,R1   ;INIT POWTEN POINTER
                    CLR    ES           ;INIT. EXP SIGN FLAG
                    LDF    X,F0         ;LOAD X INTO F0
                    CLR    IS           ;SET
                    TSTF   F0           ;  INTEGER PART
                    BPL    L1           ;    SIGN
                    INC    IS           ;      FLAG
                    ABSF   F0           ;ABS(X) INTO F0
        L1:
                    CMPF   (R1)+,F0     ;FIND DECIMAL EXPONENT
                    CFCC                ;   BY STEPPING
                    BPL    L2           ;     THRU
                    INC    N            ;       POWTEN
                    BR     L1
        L2:
                    SUB    #4,R1        ;BACK UP 1 FP ENTRY IN POWTEN
                    SUB    K,R1         ;   POINT TO 10**(N-K)
                    DIVF   (R1),F0      ;COMPUTE INTEGER PART
                    TST    N            ;SET SIGN FLAG
                    BGE    L3
                    INC    ES
                    NEG    N
```

(a)

```
        L3:
                    MOV    #ASC,R1      ;SET ASCII BUF POINTER
                    TST    IS
                    BEQ    L4
                    MOVB   #'-,(R1)+    ;PUT "-" INTO BUFFER
        L4:
                    MOVB   #'0,(R1)+    ;PUT "0." INTO BUFFER
                    MOVB   #'.,(R1)+
                    STCFI  F0,ITG       ;PUT INTEGER PART
                    MOV    ITG,R0       ;  INTO R0
                    JSR    PC,CNVDEC    ;PUT INTG PART INTO BUFFER
                    MOVB   #'E,(R1)+    ;PUT "E" INTO BUFFER
                    TST    ES           ;PUT "-" INTO
                    BEQ    L5           ;   BUFFER
                    MOVB   #'-,(R1)+    ;
        L5:
                    MOV    N,R0         ;PUT EXPONENT INTO R0
                    JSR    PC,CNVDEC    ;PUT EXPONENT INTO BUFFER
                    .PRINT #ASC         ;PRINT THE BUFFER
                    .EXIT
        ASC:        .BLKB  12           ;ASCII BUFFER FOR FLOAT PRINT
                    .BYTE  0            ;NUL BYTE TO TURN .PRINT OFF
                    .EVEN
        K:          .WORD  16.          ;4*NUMBER OF DIGITS (MAX 4)
        X:          .FLT2  -1.345E-23.  ;NUMBER TO BE PRINTED
        IS:         .BLKW  1            ;INTEGER PART SIGN FLAG
        ES:         .BLKW  1            ;EXP SIGN FLAG
        N:          .BLKW  1            ;DECIMAL EXPONENT
        N0:         .WORD  -38.         ;INITIAL EXPONENT
        ITG:        .BLKW  1            ;INTEGER PART
                    DEFPOW              ;SET UP POWTEN TABLE USING MACRO
                    .BLKW  20           ;BUFFER
                    .END START
```

(b)

Figure 13.8 Floating-point output: (a) conversion to decimal exponent and fraction; (b) conversion to ASCII and printing.

indicated by the flag IS, determines whether or not to place a "−" symbol as the first character. Next the characters "0" and "−" are stored. Then the previously determined value in F0 is stored as an integer, and placed in R0. The subroutine CNVDEC converts an integer found in R0 to the corresponding string of ASCII decimal characters. It stores these characters beginning at the byte pointed at by R1, advancing R1 accordingly. CNVDEC can be seen in Appendix F. Upon return from CNVDEC, the digits representing the fractional part are in place in the buffer. An "E," and, if indicated by the ES flag, a "−", is then placed in the buffer. Finally, the exponent is loaded into the buffer, again using CNVDEC. The .PRINT macro is then used to print ASC. When executed, the program shown in Fig. 13.8 will print

0.1982E4

If X is changed to −0.04314, it will print

−0.4314E−1

Floating-point input can be accomplished in a manner somewhat parallel to that used in Example 13.7. The objective in this case is to accept a keyboard entry in floating-point notation, e.g.,

−643.961E−13

and store it in the standard internal floating-point representation. A procedure to do this has the following major steps.

1. Read the input line as ASCII characters into a buffer. (The .TTYIN buffer will do.)
2. Set a sign flag if the first character is "−".
3. Store the numeric characters to the left of E in a separate buffer IBUF without the decimal point. Store the number of digits to the right of the decimal point in D.
4. Set an exponent sign flag if "−" follows the E.
5. Store the numeric characters to the right of E in a separate buffer, EBUF.
6. Convert IBUF from ASCII to floating point.
7. Convert EBUF from ASCII to binary and subtract D.
8. Use the converted EBUF as an index into a table of powers of 10, thus obtaining the floating-point representation of 10 to the power of the exponent.
9. Multiply the results of steps 6 and 8, giving the floating-point representation to be stored.

Steps 6 and 7 are very similar to the problem addressed in Fig. 8.11, i.e., the conversion of ASCII character codes to internal representation. However, that procedure must be modified to accept decimal digits. Also, step 6 requires the result to be developed in a floating-point register because many floating-point numbers are too large or too small to be represented in the 16-bit two's complement form. The details of floating-point input are left as an exercise.

Although not included in the algorithms discussed in this section, error checking should be done when converting to and from floating point. The most common errors arise when an operation results in a number too large or too small to be represented in floating point. This is indicated by the exponent going outside of the range -127_{10} to $+127_{10}$. If an operation yields an exponent greater than 127, an *overflow* is said to have occurred, whereas a value less than -127 is called an *underflow*. The FP11 processor provides for the program to monitor these occurrences so that proper action can be taken. Details on this matter may be found in *The PDP-11 Processor Handbook* (Digital Equipment Corporation). Another important matter is rounding or truncation. Because many decimal numbers cannot be represented exactly in binary, conversion sometimes produces unexpected results.

13.6 Summary

We have seen in this chapter that numbers can be stored in the PDP-11 using what is called *floating-point representation*. With this system, two words are used to store a single number. Twenty-three of the 32 bits are used to represent the so-called mantissa or fraction, while eight bits are used to store the exponent on the (understood) binary base, and one bit is used to represent the sign. This system allows positive or negative numbers between 0.29×10^{-38} and 1.7×10^{38} to be represented. This representation allows solution of problems that cannot be handled with integers. Special instructions and directives are available in MACRO-11 for manipulating floating-point numbers. We discussed two sets of floating-point instructions, namely, those for the FIS option, and the FP11 coprocessor. However, you must determine which, if either, of these sets is available on your machine.

The FIS option provides only four instructions—FADD, FSUB, FMUL, and FDIV. These operate on arguments placed in the stack and return the result to the top of the stack. The FP11 coprocessor is available on larger machines, and provides a large set of floating-point instructions. The FP11 has its own registers that it uses in its arithmetic instructions such as ADDF, SUBF, MULF, and DIVF. Special instructions are also provided for moving floating-point data between central memory and the FP11 registers, and for converting between integer and floating-point representation. Several examples were shown, including one in which floating point was converted for output.

13.7 Exercises

13.1 Convert (by hand) the following *decimal* values to PDP-11 floating-point representation. Show in binary as sign, exponent, and fraction bit patterns and as octal contents of two sequential words.

a) 686   b) -12 c) 0.35

d) 6.2×10^{23} e) -9.6×10^{12} f) 512×10^{-4}

g) -3×10^{-8} h) 0.75

13.2 Convert (by hand) the following floating-point word contents to decimal.

a) 043222 000000   b) 143222 000000   c) 031200 000000

d) 042222 162000   e) 000000 000000   f) 111111 111111

g) 100000 000000   h) 011111 111111

13.3 Verify your answers to Exercise 13.1 by assembling a program with these numbers stored using the .FLT2 directive.

13.4 Devise a MACRO-11 program to verify your answers for Exercise 13.2.

13.5 Show that a 24-bit fraction in floating-point representation corresponds to seven decimal-digits of *accuracy*.

13.6 Show that if seven decimal-digit accuracy is to be maintained, the range of positive or negative floating point numbers on the PDP-11 computer is approximately 0.29 $\times$ 10^{-38} to approximately 1.7×10^{38}.

13.7 Create a recursive subroutine to calculate the present value of a unit annual deposit at interest *i,* using floating-point operations. Demonstrate with ODT and compare the result with

$$\frac{(1 + i)^n - 1}{i}.$$

(This exercise requires either the FIS option or the FP11 floating-point processor. It also assumes that Chapter 12 has been covered.)

13.8 Using floating-point operations, write a MACRO-11 subroutine that solves

$$aX^2 + bX + c = 0$$

for both real roots. Create a FORTRAN main program that accepts a, b, and c as floating-point inputs, calls your MACRO-11 subroutine, and upon return prints the results. It should print a message if there are no real roots. Test your program with $a = 2.83$, $b = 8.12$, $c = 2.35$; then with $a = 4.53$, $b = 6.13$, $c = 5.14$. (This exercise requires either the FIS option or the FP11 floating-point processor.)

13.9 Develop a subroutine that will accept keyboard entry in the form $\pm 0.dddddddE \pm nn$ and return it as a floating-point value in F0. (This exercise requires either the FIS option or the FP11 floating-point processor.)

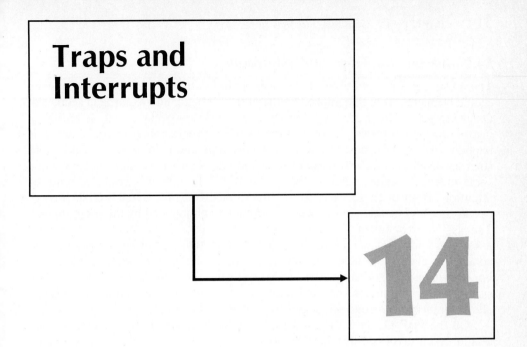

Traps and
Interprets

14

14.1 Overview

This chapter deals with the important concept of **interrupts,** and a special kind of interrupt called a **trap.** The term "interrupt" applies when some event outside of the program itself causes a branch to a special routine. The basic mechanism of interrupts provides a way to take appropriate actions when a *CPU error* occurs, and is called a **trap.** It also provides a more efficient method for performing input/output operations than does the polling method introduced in Chapter 8. We shall see that the PDP-11 uses a method called **vectoring** for traps and interrupts. Vectoring is an important concept in its own right.

Another topic discussed in this chapter is **Direct Memory Access** (DMA). This refers to the ability of some peripheral devices to transfer data to and from memory with minimal intervention by the CPU. DMA is important because it provides much faster data transfer than would otherwise be possible, as well as freeing the CPU for concurrent activity.

The material discussed in this chapter is highly dependent on the hardware and software environment. That is, it may not be possible to carry out the operations shown here on your machine. In general, interrupts and traps cannot be programmed by a nonprivileged user in a multiuser environment. (The examples shown in this chapter were carried out on an LSI-11/03 machine without an operating system. The programs were assembled on a PDP-11/70 and downloaded as machine code to the LSI-11/03 for execution.)

14.2 Reasons for Traps and Interrupts

There are certain conditions under which the instruction execution sequence should be altered from that implied by the normal, programmer-controlled sequence. One example of this happens when an error condition occurs, such as an illegal instruction or addressing error resulting from a programming error. When this happens, it is usually best to interrupt the program and take some special action, such as displaying an error report and halting. Another example occurs when some external device, such as the keyboard of the operator console, requires attention. Both of these cases are characterized by some event whose time of occurrence and location in the program cannot be anticipated by the programmer. That is, an error might occur anywhere in the code, or the need to "service" a keyboard might occur at any moment. Rather than requiring the program to constantly check for these occurrences, modern computers are provided with *interrupt* capability. That is, the hardware itself constantly checks for interrupt signals from various internal and external sources, and on such an occurrence allows branching to routines coded to deal with the event.

On the PDP-11, the CPU can be interrupted because of internal errors, such as addressing errors or illegal instructions, or because of a signal from a peripheral device. Interrupts resulting from CPU errors are called traps, and those caused by peripheral devices are called interrupts. Both are handled in essentially the same way, as described in the following section.

14.3 Trap and Interrupt Vectoring

When the CPU is interrupted, the normal sequence of instruction execution, as provided by the program, has to be altered. That is, control has to be transferred to the place where the so-called servicing or handling routine is located. Because there are many different sources of interrupts, and each needs its own special servicing routine, a way has to be provided to transfer control to the correct routine. On the PDP-11, this problem is solved using a technique called vectoring. With vectoring, each hardware element that can cause an interrupt is designed to send a unique CM address to the CPU along with its interrupt signal. When the CPU receives this address, it fetches the contents of this location and uses it as the address of the service routine. Thus the servicing routine for a device can be stored anywhere in memory, so long as its address is stored in the location set aside for the vector for the device.

This scheme is shown diagrammatically in Fig. 14.1. The vector actually is composed of two words. The first contains the address of the servicing routine, and the second contains a value to be transferred into the PSW when control is passed to the servicing routine. Table 14.1 shows the vector addresses assigned to several devices, and the CPU error traps. Also shown in the table are vector addresses for four instructions—BPT, IOT, EMT, and TRAP. These instructions allow vectoring initiated by the program in much the same way that hardware

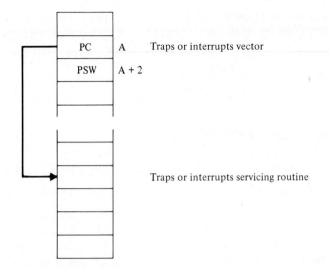

Figure 14.1   Trap and interrupt vectoring.

interrupts and traps are handled. These are called "software interrupts," and are discussed later.

The servicing routine can be simple, such as halting the machine, or complex, such as processing information from an input device. Usually, error trap servicing routines are provided by the operating system, while interrupt servicing routines are provided by the programmer on single-user computers, or by the operating system on multiuser machines. On single-user machines running without an operating system, the programmer is responsible for servicing routines for both traps and interrupts. Whenever a servicing routine is provided, it is the responsibility

Table 14.1
Traps and Interrupts Vector Addresses and Priority Levels

Source	Vector Address(A)	Priority Level
Addressing, time-out, other errors	4	†
Illegal instruction	10	†
BPT instruction	14	†
IOT instruction	20	†
Power failure	24	†
EMT instruction	30	†
TRAP instruction	34	†
Console keyboard	60	4
Console display device	64	4
Line clock	100	6

† Varies with processor.

of the programmer to place its address in the appropriate vector, as well as a suitable value for PSW. This will be clarified in subsequent examples.

14.4 Trap and Interrupt Sequence

Whenever a trap or interrupt occurs, the following sequence of events takes place automatically.

1. The current contents of PSW is pushed onto the stack.
2. The current contents of PC is pushed onto the stack.
3. The contents of the first word of the appropriate vector is placed in PC.
4. The contents of the second word of the appropriate vector is placed in PSW.

Steps 1 and 2 make it possible to return to the place at which the trap or interrupt occurred after execution of the servicing routine. Step 3 transfers control to the servicing routine. By "appropriate" vector, we mean the vector address as given in Table 14.1 for whatever event or device caused the trap or interrupt. For example, if an illegal instruction error occurred, the servicing routine address would be taken from location 10. Step 4 makes it possible for the programmer, by placing an appropriate bit pattern in the second word of the vector, to set the PSW to some condition needed by the servicing routine. This is discussed in connection with interrupts below.

14.5 Error Trap Handling

The term "trap" refers to the capability of the processor to monitor its own operations and to catch (i.e., trap) certain errors or events. We shall demonstrate this process with a very common example, namely, when the word fetched as an instruction does not happen to be a valid opcode. For example, the instruction sequence

```
        MOV     R1,R2
A:      .WORD   075040
```

which is obviously a programming error, results in 075040 being fetched as an instruction. However, this number is not a valid code for any PDP-11 instruction. The CPU always monitors the instruction decoding process and, when an invalid instruction code is discovered, a trap to the servicing routine occurs. Specifically, the previously described sequence of "vectoring" events then causes

1. The current PSW to be placed on the stack.
2. The current PC, i.e., A + 2, to be placed on the stack.
3. The address found in location 10 (see Table 14.1) to be placed in PC.
4. The contents of location 12 to be placed in PSW.

Obviously, someone (you or another programmer) has to be sure that there *is* a proper servicing routine somewhere in memory, and that its address is placed in 10 *prior* to execution of the program under consideration. Also, the proper PSW should be put into location 12 beforehand. If these steps are taken, any illegal instruction error will cause execution of the servicing routine.

Example 14.1 ·Error traps are normally handled by the operating system. That is, a servicing routine is loaded into memory by the operating system, and the trap vector is loaded with the address and PSW for this routine. Therefore if you are using an operating system, you need not (and probably should not) do these things yourself. However, let us assume for the moment that we are using a machine without an operating system, and wish all illegal instructions to ring the console bell and halt the processor. The code to do this is shown below.

```
START:  MOV    #IIERR,@#10    ; SET TRAP
        MOV    #340,@#12      ;  VECTOR
               (PROGRAM)
        HALT
IIERR:  MOV    #7,R0          ; ILLEGAL
L:      TSTB   @#177564       ;   INSTRUCTION
        BPL    L              ;     TRAP
        MOVB   R0,@#177566    ;       SERVICING
        HALT                  ;         ROUTINE
        .END   START
```

The trap vector is first set up by placing the address of the servicing routine, IIERR, into location 10, and the number 340 into location 12. The 340 will cause the bit pattern 11100000 to be placed into PSW upon transfer to IIERR. The significance of this will be explained in Section 14.6.1. The routine beginning at IIERR simply sends an octal 7, the ASCII BELL character, to the console display, ringing the bell, and halts. Obviously, more elaborate servicing routines could be written. Also, trap vectors and servicing routines should be written for other types of errors if these are not provided by an operating system.

A less elaborate but very effective trap-servicing "routine" is provided by the following instructions at the beginning of the program.

```
MOV    #6,@#4
CLR    @#6
MOV    #12,@#10
CLR    @#12
```

Alternately, if the program is to be loaded at absolute location 0, the directive

```
.WORD     0,0,6,0,12,0
```

will accomplish the same result if placed as the first assembled line.

This sets the servicing routine address for addressing errors to location 6, and that for illegal instructions to location 12. Control will then be transferred to one of these locations on the error condition, and the 0 found there will be interpreted as a HALT instruction. Note that this actually uses the second word of the trap vectors to store the (very short!) servicing routine. Also, note that upon halting, the stack will contain the location of the instruction *after* the one that caused the error. This is a helpful debugging aid for very little programming effort in a nonoperating-system environment.

14.6 Interrupts

As noted previously, interrupt in the PDP-11 context refers specifically to those CPU interrupts that originate at peripheral devices, rather than CPU error traps. While they work in much the same way as traps, they have a different purpose and are different in the way that they are used. Their purpose is to allow the CPU to do other tasks while awaiting the need to service a peripheral device such as the console keyboard or display. This way of handling I/O is in contrast to the programmed I/O method considered in Section 8.8.1, in which the CPU constantly tested the device status register while waiting. This can greatly improve the speed in certain applications, and in some cases represents the only viable approach.

Before developing these ideas further, we need to discuss the role of the device status registers and the processor status word (PSW) in interrupt programming. These registers allow interrupts to be enabled or disabled, and to be dealt with in priority order.

14.6.1 Interrupt Enable and Priorities

Interrupt-generating devices have status registers that include a bit called INTR ENBL (interrupt enable). This register is the same as the register discussed in Section 8.8.1, and is shown in Fig. 14.2(a) with the INTR ENBL and READY bits identified. If the INTR ENBL bit is cleared, as it is normally unless set by the program, the associated device *cannot* interrupt the CPU. If it is set, then

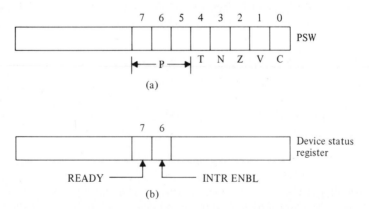

Figure 14.2 CPU priority level and device status: (a) CPU priority level; (b) device status register.

an interrupt signal is sent to the CPU whenever the READY bit in the same register changes from 0 to 1. This means that one of the tasks necessary in programming for interrupts is setting the INTR ENBL in the status register for the device being used. One convenient way to do this is to use the BIS instruction to set bits in the destination operand where ever there is a 1 bit in the source (mask) operand. Let us demonstrate this for the keyboard, which has a status register with address 177560. The instruction

    BIS   #100,@#177560

sets INTR ENBL in this register because 100 octal is 1000000 binary, and is seen to have a 1 in the position corresponding to INTR ENBL. We could also have used the MOV instruction, but BIS has the advantage of leaving the READY bit undisturbed, which may be important. If it is desired to disable the keyboard interrupt capability later in the program, this can be done with the instruction

    CLR   @#177560

It was stated above that interrupt occurs whenever INTR ENBL is set and READY changes from 0 to 1. It is also true that if the READY bit is set and the INTR ENBL changes from 0 to 1, an interrupt will occur. Because of this, an interrupt will occur immediately upon execution of an instruction that sets INTR ENBL for a device that is normally in the ready state such as a display or printer.

Having the INTR ENBL bit set is actually just one of two requirements for a device being allowed to interrupt the processor. The other requirement is that the *CPU priority* must be lower than that of the device. Device priority levels are fixed, as shown in Table 14.1. CPU priority is indicated by bits 5, 6, and 7 in the PSW, and can be set in the program. The programming strategy is to set PSW such that the value represented by bits 5, 6, and 7 is *lower* than that of the device that is to be allowed to interrupt. For example, if the line clock† is to be allowed to interrupt, but not the keyboard or display, the CPU priority level should be set to 4. This can be done by placing 4 into bits in 5, 6, and 7 of the PSW. Most often, however, it is in an interrupt or trap servicing routine that the CPU priority needs to be reset. This is most conveniently done by placing the desired priority into the second word of the interrupt service vector because PSW is reset to the contents of this location upon transfer to the routine. For example, to ensure a CPU priority of 5 during execution of the keyboard interrupt servicing routine, the instruction

    MOV   #240,@#62

should be placed in the initialization portion of the main program.

---

† The line clock is a peripheral device that generates an interrupt 60 times per second. Its status register is at 177546.

Note that the value to be placed in the PSW must be expressed as an octal number that has the desired priority level in bits 5, 6, and 7. The following diagram shows this for priority level 5.

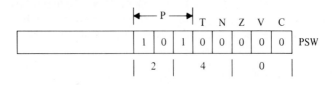

A very common situation is to have several interrupt-servicing routines operating in concert with the main program and its subroutines. The CPU priority is set at 0 for the main program by default. This means that any device can interrupt it. Each servicing routine is assigned a CPU priority, passed through the interrupt vector, that resets the CPU priority at a level that locks out interrupts from less-critical devices. For example, a clock-servicing routine may be assigned a CPU priority of 6, while the keyboard and display are given CPU priorities of 4. This allows any of the three devices to interrupt the main program or subroutines, the clock to interrupt either the keyboard- or display-servicing routines, but no device to interrupt the clock-servicing routine.

14.6.2 Return from Interrupt

Interrupt-servicing routines usually return to the point of interruption. This is made possible by the RTI (Return from Interrupt) instruction. When encountered, the RTI causes the following actions.

1. The top of the stack is popped into PC.
2. The next item in the stack is popped into the PSW.

Because these are the reverse of the actions taken when the interrupt occurred, this will reset PC and PSW to what they would have been had the interrupt not occurred, allowing the program to continue. The RTI instruction has no operands.

Care should be taken to protect any general registers disturbed by the service routine. This is important because an interrupt can occur anywhere in the program, and one must be sure that register values are unchanged during servicing. They are usually pushed onto the stack upon entry and popped back immediately before the RTI.

14.7 An Example of Interrupt Programming

Example 14.2 Consider the need for a program that continuously accepts numerical inputs from the console keyboard and enters them into a sorted list. This program is to be run on a dedicated machine, so that we can access the console keyboard and display device registers directly, rather than by using operating-system routines.

One approach is to use the programmed I/O method described in Section 8.8.1, where we constantly checked the keyboard status register until an entry was received. It could then be converted to binary and sorted into the list. The problem with this approach is that when the list gets long, the time required to sort the new number into the list becomes lengthy. If the keyboard operator entered a number while the sort was being done, part of it could be lost.

An interrupt method for accepting keyboard entry will eliminate this problem. With this method, the main program logic is shown in Fig. 14.3. After setting up the interrupt vector and other needed initializations, the program enters a loop that constantly merges new entries into the list. The variable NSORT represents the number of numbers currently in the list and STP is a stopping flag. Both of these variables have their values updated by the keyboard interrupt-servicing routine. Also, new numbers are placed into the list by this routine. If STP is not set, a check is made to see whether the list has increased since last sorted. If it has, the list is sorted. In either case, the program constantly loops back until the STP flag is set.

Note that the main program algorithm has no "branch point" to an "input routine." Rather, we are depending on the interrupt mechanism to handle this branching, and this cannot be shown in a flowchart because the interrupt could occur *anywhere* in the loop. The loop will be interrupted any time a key is pressed at the keyboard. In a sense, the keyboard process may be thought of as going on in parallel with this loop and sorting process.

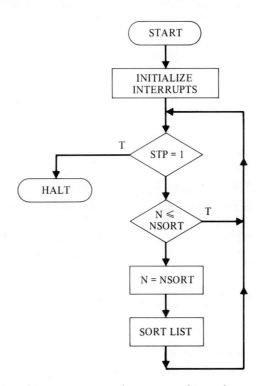

Figure 14.3   Flowchart for main program for interrupt-driven data entry.

```
                      .TITLE INTERRUPTS
           KSR=177560
           KDR=177562
           PSR=177564
           PDR=177566
                      .BLKW 100            ;RESERVE STACK SPACE
           START: MOV    PC,SP             ;SET STACK
                  TST    -(SP)             ;   POINTER.
           ;   INITIALIZATIONS
           ;
                  CLR    @#KSR             ;DISABLE KB INTERRUPTS
                  MOV    #KBIH,@#60        ;SET UP
                  MOV    #300,@#62         ;    INTERRUPT VECTOR.
                  CLR    STP               ;INIT. STOP FLAG
                  CLR    V                 ;INIT. VALUE LOCATION
                  CLR    N                 ;INIT. LEN. OF ENTERED LIST
                  CLR    NSORT             ;INIT. LEN. OF SORTED LIST
                  MOV    #LIST,LLAST       ;INIT. ADDR. OF NEXT LIST ENTRY
                  BIS    #100,@#KSR        ;ENABLE KB INTERRUPT.
           ;   CONTINUOUSLY ACCEPT NEW ENTRIES AND SORT LIST REAL-TIME.
           ;
           L1:
                  TST    STP               ;QUIT IF KBIH
                  BNE    QUIT              ;   SETS STOP FLAG.
                  CMP    N,NSORT           ;IDLE LOOP IF
                  BLOS   L1                ;   N HAS NOT CHANGED.
                  MOV    N,NSORT           ;SORT LEN.=ENTERED LEN.
                  JSR    PC,SORT           ;SORT THE LIST
                  BR     L1                ;KEEP RUNNING TIL STP=0
           QUIT:
                  HALT
           STP:   .BLKW  1                 ;RESERVE
           V:     .BLKW  1                 ;
           N:     .BLKW  1                 ;    STORAGE
           NSORT: .BLKW  1                 ;
           LLAST: .BLKW  1                 ;        SPACE.
           LIST:  .BLKW  1000.             ;1000. DECIMAL LIST SPACE
```

(a)

```
           ;
           ;    SORTING ROUTINE
           ;
           SORT:
                  MOV    NSORT,R2          ;SET SORT PASS
                  DEC    R2                ;   LCV.
                  BLOS   OUTSORT           ;NOTHING TO SORT
                  MOV    #1,MORE           ;SET FLAG FOR INIT.SORT PASS
           WHILE: TST    MORE              ;MAKE MORE PASSES UNTIL
                  BEQ    OUTSORT           ;   NO MORE SWITCHES.
                  CLR    MORE              ;PREPARE SWITCH FLAG
                  MOV    #LIST,R1          ;SET LIST PTR. TO TOP OF LIST
                  MOV    R2,R3             ;INIT. PASS LCV , R3
           PASS:  CMP    (R1),2(R1)        ;SKIP SWITCH
                  BLOS   L2                ;   IF ADJ. ENTRIES IN ORDER.
                  MOV    (R1),TEMP         ;OTHERWISE
                  MOV    2(R1),(R1)        ;   DO THE
                  MOV    TEMP,2(R1)        ;      SWITCH AND
                  INC    MORE              ;         SET THE FLAG.
           L2:    TST    (R1)+             ;INCREMENT LIST PTR.
                  SOB    R3,PASS           ;COMPLETE THE PASS
                  BR     WHILE             ;CONTINUE MAKING PASSES
           OUTSORT:
                  RTS    PC                ;RETURN TO MAIN PROGRAM
           TEMP:  .BLKW  1                 ;TEMP. STORAGE FOR SWITCH
           MORE:  .BLKW  1
```

(b)

Figure 14.4 Interrupt-driven data entry: (a) main program; (b) sorting routine.

```
;
;   KEYBOARD INTERRUPT SERVICING ROUTINE
;
KBIH:
            MOV     R0,-(SP)        ;SAVE R0 ON STACK
            MOVB    @#KDR,R0        ;READ DATA FROM KEYBOARD
            BIC     #177600,R0      ;MASK UNUSED HIGH BITS
            JSR     PC,PRTIT        ;ECHO INPUT
            CMPB    R0,#'S          ;"S" WILL SET STOP FLAG
            BEQ     STPSET
            CMP     R0,#15          ;CR(=15) WILL INDICATE
            BEQ     COMP            ;   ENTRY IS COMPLETE.
            SUB     #60,R0          ;REMOVE ASCII BASE
            BLO     L3              ;IGNOR
            CMP     R0,#10          ;   NONOCTAL
            BHIS    L3              ;      CHARACTERS.
            ASL     V               ;SHIFT PREVIOUS
            ASL     V               ;   VALUE
            ASL     V               ;      1 OCTAL DIGIT LEFT.
            ADD     R0,V            ;ADD ENTERED DIGIT TO VALUE
L3:         BR      OUTKBIH         ;
STPSET:     INC     STP             ;SET STOP FLAG
            BR      OUTKBIH         ;
COMP:       INC     N               ;INC. ENTERED LIST LENGTH
            MOV     V,@LLAST        ;PUT ENTERED VALUE AT BOT. OF LIST
            INC     LLAST           ;ADVANCE "LAST ENTRY" POINTER
            INC     LLAST           ;   TO NEXT WORD.
            CLR     V               ;RESET ENTRY VALUE LOCATION
OUTKBIH:MOV         (SP)+,R0        ;RESTORE R0
            RTI                     ;RETURN FROM KB INTERRUPT
;
;   INPUT ECHO TO SCREEN
;
PRTIT:
            TSTB    @#PSR           ;IDLE LOOP UNTIL PRINTER READY
            BPL     PRTIT           ;   PRINTER IS READY.
            MOVB    R0,@#PDR        ;PRINT THE CHARACTER
            CMP     R0,#15          ;SEND A LF
            BNE     L5              ;   IF IT
L4:         TSTB    @#PSR           ;      WAS
            BPL     L4              ;         A
            MOVB    #12,@#PDR       ;            CR.
L5:         RTS     PC              ;RETURN TO CALLER
;
;   END OF PROGRAM
;
            .EVEN
            .END    START
```

(c)

Figure 14.4 Interrupt-driven data entry: (c) interrupt servicing routine.

The MACRO-11 program for this example is shown in Fig. 14.4. Let us first examine the initializations in the main program, Fig. 14.4(a). By clearing the Keyboard Status Register (KSR), we temporarily disable keyboard interrupts. This prevents keyboard interrupts while initializations are being done. Next, the address of the servicing routine, KBIH (KeyBoard Interrupt Handler), is put into the keyboard vector, location 60. By putting 300 into 62, we establish the bit pattern 11000000 for PSW during execution of KBIH, thus setting a CPU priority level of 6 for this task once it is initiated. The CLRs and MOV instructions simply initialize the various program variables. Finally, the BIS instruction sets the INTR ENBL bit in the KSR, enabling interrupts from the keyboard. After this, the main program loop is begun, with logic as shown in Fig. 14.3.

The sort routine is shown in Fig. 14.4(b). A bubble sort technique is used, in which passes are made through the list until no further interchanges take place. Note that the length of the sorted list is NSORT, rather than N. This is because the length of the list N might get changed while a sort is in progress because of interrupt servicing. One must always be careful when programming with interrupts that the concurrent processes do not interfere with one another.

The interrupt-servicing routine is shown in Fig. 14.4(c). After saving R0 on the stack, we immediately read the Keyboard Data Register. It is not necessary to check its status register because control cannot get to this routine unless READY has changed to 1. After getting this character, we jump to a subroutine to echo it to the display device. Note that a programmed output is done, although we could have also used the interrupt method here. After echoing, we check to see if an "S" was entered, and set the "stop flag" STP to 1 and exit if it was. Otherwise the character is converted to binary and added to the "entry value" that is built up in V. Note that control is returned to the point of interrupt after each entered *digit* is converted. When the entered character is a carriage return, the servicing routine branches to COMP where the completed entry value is placed at the bottom of the list, the list length N is incremented, and the value V reset to 0.

14.8 Software Traps

The concept of vectoring to a servicing routine through an address at a fixed place in memory has applications other than for error traps and interrupts. The PDP-11 has two instructions, TRAP and EMT (Emulate Trap), that allow this vectoring process to be initiated *by the program*. The most common usage of these instructions is to transfer control to an operating-system routine. For example, the .EXIT macro provided by RT-11 expands to EMT 350, which translates to 104350. This instruction acts exactly like a trap through location 30. That is, location 30 will have in it the address of a routine that handles all "system calls," and location 32, the PSW contents needed by this routine. If we were able to examine this RT-11 routine, we would find that it extracted the low byte of the EMT instruction (getting the 350), and used this to branch to the specific code to handle "exit to the operating system."† Similarly, the expansion of .TTYIN yields an EMT 340 (and a branch instruction). This also would cause a trap through 30 to the same routine, but the 340 would cause a branch to a different portion of the servicing routine. In effect, this "software interrupt" gives us a capability to branch to a large number of system routines with a single fixed address, namely, 30. Note that while approximately the same thing could be accomplished with a subroutine transfer (JSR), there are important differences. Perhaps the most significant difference is that the JSR instruction does not preserve the PSW, whereas the EMT instruction does.

---

† The operating system routines are proprietary software owned by Digital Equipment Corporation and are not available for our inspection.

The TRAP instruction is exactly the same as the EMT instruction except that its vector address is at location 34 rather than 30. Having two instructions for software-vectored interrupts makes it possible to have two entirely different servicing routines. Customarily, the EMT instruction is used by DEC operating systems and is therefore not used by application programs. The TRAP instruction is available for application programs that need software-vectored interrupts. However, there are restrictions on both EMT and TRAP programming in some PDP-11 environments as discussed below.

If your program is to run on a single-user, dedicated computer in the absence of an operating system, you may use either EMT or TRAP freely, including setting the trap vectors and programming the servicing routine. However, if there is to be an operating system, you may be restricted or discouraged from setting the trap vectors or programming the servicing routines. For example, if you are programming for a PDP-11/70 in a multiuser environment (e.g., RSTS/E), the trap vector addresses for both EMT and TRAP cannot be altered from a user program. The mechanism whereby this protection is achieved is discussed under "Memory Management" in *The PDP-11 Processor Handbook*. Its purpose is to prevent users from accidentally or deliberately destroying parts of the operating system that are critical to all users. In the RSTS/E environment, one can use the EMT instruction, but vectoring will be to a servicing routine provided by the operating system as discussed earlier in this section. The TRAP instruction is not intended for usage under RSTS/E; its "servicing routine" simply prints an error report. Under the UNIX system, on the other hand, the operating-system service calls are done with the TRAP instruction. For example, TRAP 4 under the UNIX system is a call to the system write function. When operating under a single-user system such as RT-11, it is possible to modify the trap vectors and servicing routines. This means that application programs can do software-vectored interrupts using the TRAP instruction. The EMT vector and servicing routine should not be altered because this may disable parts of the operating system.

14.9 An Example of Software Trap Programming

Example 14.3   Let us illustrate the usage of TRAP programming such as could be done in a single-user environment. As our example, we will use TRAP 0 to read a character into R0, and TRAP 2 to print the character found in R0. This is shown in Fig. 14.5. The program is prepared to use the TRAP by placing the address of the servicing routine into the vector at location 34. In the program, input to R0 just requires a TRAP 0, and output is done by TRAP 2. In the servicing routine, the "argument" (0 or 2) is determined by examining the TRAP instruction itself. The address of the instruction *that follows* the TRAP is on top of the stack upon entry to the routine. This allows us to get the TRAP instruction itself into R1 by the instructions shown. By clearing the opcode in the high byte,

```
                    .TITLE  TRAP DEMO
        START:  MOV     PC,SP           ;INITIALIZE
                TST     -(SP)           ;   STACK POINTER
                MOV     #IO,@#34
                CLR     @#36
                TRAP    0               ;READ INTO R0
                TRAP    2               ;PRINT FROM R0
                TRAP    2
                TRAP    0
                TRAP    2
                HALT
        ;
        ;   TRAP SERVICE ROUTINE
        ;
        IO:
                MOV     R1,-(SP)        ;SAVE R1 ON STACK
                MOV     2(SP),R1        ;GET THE "TRAP N"
                MOV     -(R1),R1        ;   INSTRUCTION INTO R1
                BIC     #177400,R1      ;R1 NOW CONTAINS N
                JMP     @FUN(R1)        ;GO TO FUNCTION N
        ;FUNCTIONS:
        OUT:    TSTB    @#177564        ;PRINT
                BPL     OUT             ;  A
                MOVB    R0,@#177566;    CHARACTER
                BR      IOEND
        IN:     TSTB    @#177560        ;READ
                BPL     IN              ;  A
                MOVB    @#177562,R0;         CHARACTER
                BIC     #177600,R0 ;
                BR      IOEND
        IOEND:  MOV     (SP)+,R1        ;RESTORE R1
                RTI                     ;RETURN FROM TRAP
        FUN:    .WORD   IN,OUT
                .END    START
```

Figure 14.5 Using TRAP for vectoring to servicing routines.

the value of the argument is left in R1. Index deferred addressing then allows transfer to the appropriate address because the .WORD directive causes the assembler to place these addresses in a table labeled FUN. Obviously, up to 256_{10} functions could be added to the routine by extending the FUN table and adding the necessary code.

Once again, note that this example could have been accomplished using subroutines. However, the advantage of doing it with traps is that the servicing routine could be placed *anywhere* in memory, and not necessarily included in the user program. Thus it could be loaded ahead of time and used by any other program without going through a linkage step. Many modern operating systems are implemented in this fashion.

14.10 The Trap Bit and Breakpoint Trap

Suppose we want to display the contents of the registers or certain memory locations after execution of each instruction. This is called "tracing" and is a useful aid in debugging a program. The PDP-11 provides the capability to do this without making major changes to the program being debugged. As shown in Fig. 14.2, bit 4 of the PSW is called the T or *trap bit*. When this bit is set, the CPU will be interrupted and trapped through the vector at locations 14 and 16. To use this feature, the program must place the servicing-routine address in

```
START:      MOV     #TSR,@#14      ;SET TRACE TRAP
            CLR     @#16           ;   SERVICE VECTOR
            MOV     #20,-(SP)      ;SET TRAP BIT
            MOV     #MAIN,-(SP)    ;   AND START TRACING
            RTT                    ;     MAIN PROGRAMS
MAIN:

            {Program to be traced}

            HALT
TSR:        TST     @(SP)          ;IF HALT
            BEQ     FIN            ;   GO TO FINISH

            {Trap service instructions}

            RTT
FIN:        CLR     2(SP)          ;DISABLE TRACE
            RTI
            .END    START
```

Figure 14.6   Using trace traps to debug a program.

14, clear location 16, and set the T bit in the PSW. Once this is done, each subsequent instruction will cause a trap to the servicing routine, which can contain any desired instructions, such as for printing the contents of various registers and locations.

One possible structure for tracing a program is shown in Fig. 14.6. Note that the T bit has to be set rather indirectly because in many PDP-11 configurations the PSW cannot be altered directly. Instead we take advantage of the fact that the RTT (Return from Trace Trap) instruction pops the top two stack items into PSW and PC, respectively. Thus by placing the starting address of the traced program and 20_8 onto the stack, and executing RTT, we start the traced program with the T bit set.

The trap-servicing routine should do the desired printing. If registers are used, they should be first saved on the stack and restored before returning. By using the RTT to return, we ensure that the next instruction in the traced program will generate another trap. When it is found that the *next* instruction is a HALT, we clear the T bit and return with a RTI, terminating tracing and allowing a normal halt in the main program.

The BPT instruction causes a trap through location 14 as if the T bit were set. This provides a mechanism for causing the trace-servicing routine to execute under program control.

14.11 Direct Memory Access (DMA)

We have previously considered two different types of I/O, namely, programmed I/O and interrupts. With programmed I/O, the CPU continually tests the device status register until it is ready, then executes an instruction that transfers the data. This is called polling. As previously mentioned, polling is wasteful in that it ties up the CPU while waiting for a relatively slow I/O process. In other cases, the I/O device may operate faster than the CPU can carry out the polling. With interrupts, we avoid the loss of CPU availability during the waiting period because the device itself will notify the CPU when it is ready. However, the CPU is still required to execute one or more instructions for each item of data transferred, and again may not be able to keep up with rapid I/O processes. There are other I/O methods that reduce the I/O burden on the CPU and greatly speed up the process. One of these is called Direct Memory Access (DMA). This method is possible with certain high-speed devices such as magnetic disk or tape storage units.

The basic idea of DMA is implied by its name, i.e., the I/O device accesses the CM *directly* rather than having the data pass through the CPU. For example, a group of data items can be transferred directly from a magnetic disk storage unit to CM without ever being acted upon by the CPU. This is in contrast to programmed or interrupt I/O in which each data item is brought into the CPU, then transferred to CM. It should be obvious that DMA is potentially much faster than the other methods. In some situations this is merely a welcome improvement in performance. However, in cases such as automatic data acquisition from high-speed events in a laboratory, it may be the only viable method.

With DMA, the CPU is involved only at the beginning of the transfer and at the end. The exact details vary depending on the device, but usually the following steps are involved. First, the program places needed information into the device registers. This will include as a minimum the number of data items to be transferred, type of data (words or bytes), and the CM address that the data are coming from on output or going to on input. Then a program instruction places a code into the device command register that initiates the transfer. From this point on, the device itself carries out the transfer. For example, on input it automatically sends an address to CM, followed by a value to be stored there. It also increments the address for the next item, and decrements the count. All of this takes place in the DMA device. This process continues until the specified number of items has been transferred. While this is going on, the CPU is completely free to do other tasks. When the transfer is complete, a CPU interrupt is generated, causing a transfer of control using the vector stored in location 224. The interrupt servicing routine can then take appropriate action, such as processing the data or beginning another transfer.

The description above of the DMA process is somewhat oversimplified. One thing not mentioned is the possibility of both the I/O device and the CPU needing the data-transfer bus at the same time. (See Section 3.6.) This is solved by the I/O device requesting the bus from the CPU whenever it is ready to transmit a data item. If the CPU is not using the bus, it grants this request. Otherwise, the CPU completes its current operation, then grants the bus request from the I/O device. All of this is done automatically.

The PDP-11 Peripherals Handbook (Digital Equipment Corporation) contains full descriptions of capabilities and programming details for most I/O devices. It should be consulted for DMA programming of specific devices.

14.12 Summary _____

This chapter introduced the general concept of an *interrupt,* which refers to an event external to the program being able to interrupt the program and cause a transfer of control. We saw that the term "trap" is used in the PDP-11 context to refer to interrupts caused by CPU errors, while the term "interrupt" is used specifically for those interrupts caused by peripheral devices. When either a trap or an interrupt occurs, the CPU automatically picks up a new pair of values for PC and PSW, called the *interrupt vector,* from a fixed place in memory called a vector address. Each device or event that can cause a trap or interrupt has a predefined vector address in CM. The programmer can place the address of a *servicing routine* and a suitable PSW into the interrupt vector. This then causes a branch to the servicing routine when the event occurs.

CPU error traps occur without special program instructions, but interrupts must be *enabled.* Also, the programmer can give some interrupt events *priority* over others by placing a so-called CPU priority into the interrupt vector.

The action taken upon trap or interrupt depends on the instructions in the servicing routine. Typically, an error trap-servicing routine will print a message and halt, or exit to the operating system. An interrupt-servicing routine will depend on the peripheral device that generates it. For example, a servicing routine for the keyboard will take the entered character out of the device data register and process it in some way. Servicing routines can be simple or complex.

The RTI or RTT instructions cause return to the point of interruption. The PSW is restored automatically to its value before the interrupt. The RTT is used for return from tracing routines.

The principal advantage of interrupt-driven I/O is that it allows the CPU to do other things while it awaits a signal from the peripheral device, as opposed to testing the status register in a polling loop.

We also saw that a *software trap,* i.e., one controlled by program logic, was possible using the TRAP, EMT (Emulate Trap), or BPT (BreakPoint Trap) instructions. Each of these transfers control using a vector found in a fixed location in memory. The programmer places the servicing-routine address and a new PSW in the interrupt vector. These instructions can be used for programming of system software, such as operating-system functions and debugging aids.

The full capability of trap and interrupt programming cannot always be realized if the program has to be run under an existing operating system. This is because the operating system itself uses these features, and allowing user programs to change the interrupt or trap vectors may disable important system actions.

Finally, we touched briefly on the *Direct Memory Access* (DMA) method of I/O. The key idea here was the CPU initiating a transfer of data to or from memory, then proceeding with other activities while the transfer completes. This greatly enhances overall system performance, especially for programs requiring large amounts of I/O.

14.13 Exercises _____

14.1   The line clock is a peripheral device that generates an interrupt (a "tick") every sixtieth of a second. The status register is at CM location 177546. Write an interrupt servicing routine that updates a location labeled TIME on every tick. Demonstrate how this can be used to determine execution time for a subroutine.

14.2 Write CPU error trap-servicing routines that print out the type of error and the current PC whenever errors occur.

14.3 Write an interrupt-driven servicing routine for printing the contents of a buffer labeled PBUF to the console display. Demonstrate its use in a program. Be sure to include a flag that indicates when printing has been completed, so the main program can test before initiating another print.

14.4 Write a servicing routine that will accept n characters into a buffer whose address is in R0 when TRAP n is executed.

14.5 Write a simple program and include a tracing routine along the lines shown in Fig. 14.6. The contents of all registers should be printed after execution of each instruction.

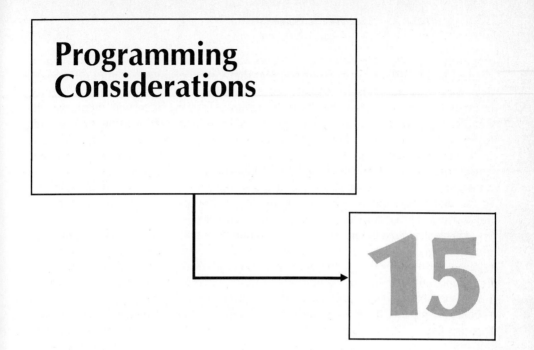

Programming Considerations

15.1 Overview

This chapter deals with a number of programming techniques and special topics that arise in the application of assembly language programming to actual problems in the commercial and industrial world. Included in the discussion are modular programming, programming style and standardization, linking and memory maps, position-independent code, and use of libraries.

The importance of these topics is difficult to see in the context of the small, textbook-type problems we have encountered thus far. However, for larger, more complex problems, the importance of these topics becomes overriding. In fact, it is widely accepted that the ability to deal with large problems through the effective use of techniques discussed here is a far more important skill than merely translating algorithms into assembly language. Here we will describe these techniques, and show their application to a problem that, while still rather small, is larger in scope than examples provided in previous chapters.

15.2 Modular Programming

15.2.1 The Concept of Modular Programming
The problems addressed in examples up to this point in this book have been generally small and uncomplicated, leading to a page or less of assembly language code. In practice, however, programming tasks are often more complex. Taken as a whole, real programs may require hundreds or even thousands of lines of

assembly language code. A problem arises here because the complexity of a single, large program can become so great that the programmer cannot effectively deal with it. This leads to logical errors, compounded by the natural difficulty in error tracing (debugging) in large programs. This problem was mentioned in Chapter 9 as a justification for the need for subroutines, which allow the program to be divided into a number of smaller modules. We will now demonstrate a systematic approach to programming along these lines, called **modular programming.** This topic is sometimes referred to as top-down programming, although that term implies a particular sequence in the design process as well as modularity. In the discussion below, we will attempt to distinguish between these different but closely related and equally important concepts.

The central idea behind modular programming is that even the most complicated programming tasks can be broken down into a series of smaller, more manageable tasks. Each task is then programmed as an independent program module, such as a subroutine or macro. When this is done, several advantages are achieved. First, the smaller tasks are easier to program because they will have a more specific purpose, with more readily defined inputs and outputs and more straight-forward logic. These same characteristics make the tasks of testing, debugging, and maintenance easier to do. Finally, this breakdown allows a large programming task to be handled by a *team* of programmers because each module can be efficiently assigned to a different individual for design, programming, and testing.

Modular design is usually done as a top-down process. That is, the overall problem is first defined in terms of a sequence of logical steps. Each step is described in terms of *function,* i.e., *what* is to be done, rather than *how* it is to be done. This definition can be in the form of a flowchart or "pseudocode." (We will see by example what is meant by pseudocode.) Regardless of how it is presented, this definition is referred to as the *level-one* procedure or algorithm, and is the basis for the main program module. Each step then in the level-one procedure is understood to be an independent module, to be implemented as a macro or subroutine. Next, each of these modules is defined in more detail. This refinement shows *how* the task is to be done, and constitutes a level-two procedure. If the problem is a complicated one, the refinement of a level-two procedure may itself require modularization, requiring separate definition of level-three procedures. This process continues until the problem solution is completely defined in terms of several small, more easily understood modules. These modules have an hierarchical relationship that is often represented by a *System Program Chart* as shown in Fig. 15.1. The purpose of the System Program Chart is to convey information about the program structure, i.e., how the modules are related. It does not indicate program logic, i.e., the sequence in which the modules at a given level are executed.

Once the program is designed using the technique above, and complete specifications have been developed for each module, coding can begin. Normally each module will be coded and assembled separately, and the object-code versions brought together at the linkage step. This creates yet another advantage, namely,

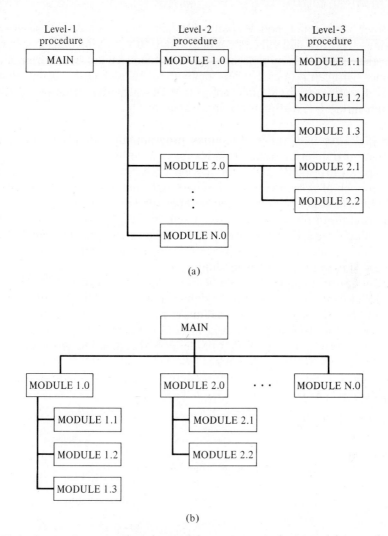

Figure 15.1 System Program Chart for modular program: (a) horizontal format; (b) vertical format.

that changes that may be required in a single module will not necessitate reassembly of the entire program.

Modules can be defined to be either *local* or *global*. The meaning of these terms is that a local (also called internal) module is available *only* to the higher level module to which it is subordinate, while a global (also called external) module is available to *any* other module. Minor modules needed only within a single higher-level module and not subject to frequent change are often made local. In MACRO-11 this is effected by making the module a subroutine internal to the module that needs it, and not defining its entry point as a global label.

On the other hand, major modules that will require significant design, programming, and testing effort are defined to be global. Naturally, any module that is needed by more than one other module must also be made global. Global modules are subroutines with entry point labels defined to be global, by using either the .GLOBL directive or the double colon (: :). As a matter of convenience each global subroutine is usually stored in a separate file.

Example 15.1 As an example of modular programming, let us consider the need for a program to determine the statistics for a set of exam scores. This program is to accept an arbitrary number of scores, each between 0 and 100, and print out the number of scores entered, and the high, low, and average scores. It is also to plot a histogram showing the number of scores in each decile.

The program to do the tasks above would be lengthy and complex if it were done as a single module. However, Fig. 15.2 shows with pseudocode how it can be broken down into seven distinct steps, each of which can be carried out with a relatively simple independent module.

In refining the modules, a specification such as shown in Fig. 15.3 should first be developed. Its purpose is to define more precisely the function of the module and its "interface" to the calling procedure. The interface information includes input data requirements, output data expected, argument transmission methods, and how it is called. A well-defined specification gives sufficient information for a competent programmer to develop an algorithm and program the module, and to use it. The refined procedure for the READ subroutine is shown as pseudocode in Fig. 15.4.

BEGIN:

1. Read scores from keyboard, storing values in array X and count of scores in N. (Subroutine READ)

2. Add all scores and leave sum in R0. (Subroutine SUMX)

3. Calculate average score, rounded to nearest integer, storing result in AVG. (Subroutine AVGX)

4. Find highest and lowest scores in X and store results in HIGH and LOW. (Subroutine HILO)

5. Count number of scores in each decile, storing counts in array F. (Subroutine FREQ)

6. Print N, HIGH, LOW, and AVG. (Subroutine PRINT)

7. Plot histogram of F. (Subroutine PLOT)

END;

Figure 15.2 Level-one procedure for Test Score program.

Function: Prompts user for successive integer scores.
Accepts only those between 0 and 100. Counts
valid entries.

Inputs:
R1:   Address of first location where scores are to
be stored

Outputs:
R1:   As input
R2:   Count of valid entries
$(R1), (R1+1) \ldots (R1+R2-1)$: scores

External Calls:
GETDEC: Gets decimal value from keyboard.
GETCHR: Gets character from keyboard.

Calling Sequence: MOV   #S,R1
JSR   PC,READ

Figure 15.3   Specification for READ subroutine.

BEGIN READ:

1. Save registers R0, R1 on the stack.
2. Clear count register R2.
3. Prompt "ENTER SCORE." (Macro .PRINT)
4. Accept decimal number from keyboard into R0.
(Subroutine GETDEC)
5. Check score for 0–100 range. (Subroutine CHKSCR)
6. If not OK
THEN
print "INVALID ENTRY, REENTER LAST VALUE"
GOTO 3
7. Store score in location pointed at by R1 and
advance R1 to next word. (R1 points to location
for entry.)
8. Increment count register R2.
9. Prompt "MORE SCORES? (Y or N)?"
10. Accept character from keyboard. (Subroutine GETCHR)
11. If "Y"
THEN GOTO 3
12. Restore registers R0, R1.

END;

Figure 15.4   Typical level-two procedure (READ) for Test Score program.

Observe that several of the tasks in Fig. 15.3 are described in function only, to be defined in detail as separate modules. These include the score validation procedure, CHKSCR, the decimal input procedure GETDEC, and the character input GETCHR. If the detailed description of these were incorporated in the READ definition, clarity would be lost. Note also that the system-supplied macro .PRINT is used to print user prompt messages. The procedure includes register protection to prevent side effects.

In a complete program design, specifications and refinements for each module would be developed as exemplified above. We omit these here in the interest of brevity.

The System Program Chart for the test score program is shown in Fig. 15.5. It shows each module in the entire program in relation to the others. Thus we see that the main program, SCORE, uses READ, SUMX, AVGY, HILO, FREQ, PRNT, and PLOT. Further, it may be seen that READ uses GETCHR, which

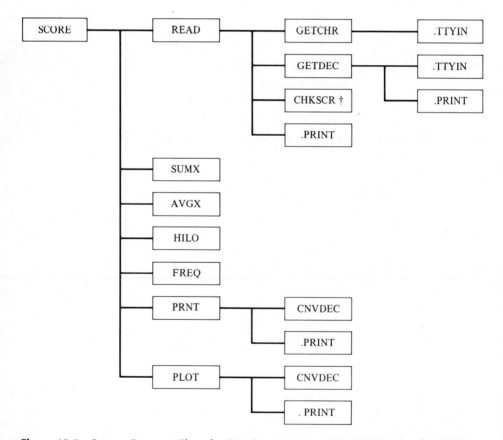

Figure 15.5 System Program Chart for Test Score program. †CHKSCR is local to READ.

in turn uses the system-supplied macro .TTYIN. This diagram, therefore, conveys a concise picture of the overall program structure. Note that the CHKSCR module is local to READ because it is a single module needed only by READ. All others are defined to be global modules.

Once all modules have been designed and expressed in the form of pseudocode or flowcharts, supported by detailed specification of input, output, and linkage information, coding is straightforward. It is necessary only to convert the steps in the algorithm to the instructions and syntax provided by MACRO-11. This has been done for the example above, and the code resulting is presented in Appendix F. The reader is encouraged to study this code, comparing it to the design. This code also exhibits the style and standards recommended in the following section.

15.3 Programming Style and Standardization

When one is first learning how to program, the challenge of "making it work" tends to be all-consuming, and little attention is paid to clarity of the logic, or the general appearance of the code. While it may seem that function is more important than form, in practice it has been found that large programming projects proceed more efficiently if efforts are made to make the code easy to understand. This can be done through the use of certain programming conventions and abundant internal documentation, i.e., comments in the code. Clarity is also improved by following *uniform conventions* or *standards* as to the way the internal documentation is done, the placement of the instructions in a line, and other matters of appearance. Large organizations often have established "programming standards" that set forth these rules that all programmers are expected to follow. Here we shall examine some of the more important issues commonly found in such standards. These issues pertain to coding, symbols, and internal documentation.

Example 15.1, discussed in Section 15.2 and presented in Appendix F, has been coded adhering to these standards. Examination of that code will clarify the general statements of the standards presented below.

15.3.1 Coding Standards

MACRO-11 is a very powerful language that allows many programming techniques. However, clarity is enhanced if certain capabilities of the language are not used, or if absolutely necessary, used only with careful explanation in adjacent comments. The following rules should be followed whenever possible.

1. **Line Format**
   Begin labels in column 1, instruction mnemonics in column 9, operands in column 17, and comments in column 33. If operands extend beyond column 32, leave one space and begin comment.

2. **Program Modularity**

   Design program such that it is composed of a number of small, single-function modules. (See Section 15.2.)

3. **Subroutine Linkage and Argument Transmission**

   Use only standard argument transmission and linkage methods. (See Section 9.11.)

4. **Subroutine Success/Failure Indication**

   Set the condition codes in the PSW to indicate abnormal return from subroutines, following the normal meanings of these codes.

5. **Side Effects**

   Subroutines must not have any effects other than setting the registers and locations designated for output in the specification. Save and restore all registers except result registers.

6. **Structure**

   Program or module control should flow down the listing except for loops. Use only standard control structures, and implement consistently. (See Section 5.4.)

7. **Instructions vs. Data**

   Do not modify instructions. Do not use instructions as data nor data as instructions.

8. **Choice of Instructions**

   Use instructions for their intended purposes only, e.g., to add 4 to R1 code ADD #4,R1 rather than CLR (R1)+,(R1)+. Note, however, that TST (Rn)+ or TST −(Rn) is a common and efficient method of incrementing or decrementing a register by 2. Always explain in comment field.

9. **Location Counter Addressing**

   Use location counter addressing (Section 11.2.3) only when necessary, e.g., for position-independent code. Avoid use for branch destination.

10. **Module Format**

    Each program module should be organized as follows.

    ```
    .TITLE     name
    .MCALL     M1,M2 . . . (if required)
    .GLOBL     A1,A2  . . . (if required)
    (prologue—see Section 15.3.3)
    .PAGE
    .PSECT DATA
    (Allocations for local data)
    (Assignment of local symbols)
    (Definition of local macros)
    .PAGE
    .PSECT PROG
    (Code section, beginning with local SUBROUTINES)
    .END     ; (name) or
    .END     name (if main module)
    ```

    The example in Appendix F shows this technique.

15.3.2 Symbols

Careful choice of symbols will improve clarity in a program. The following rules will help in this regard.

1. Choose meaningful mnemonic labels and symbols.
2. Use R0, R1, R2, R3, R4, R5, SP, and PC for the registers.
3. In a large module, use local labels, e.g., 4$, 5$, unless a mnemonic label would improve clarity or is needed for external reference.
4. Assign ASCII codes to standard mnemonic symbols, e.g.,

   CR = 15
   BEL = 7

5. When addressing device registers, assign to symbols used in the applicable hardware manual.
6. Never define a symbol to be global without justification.

15.3.3 Documentation

As discussed above, all program modules must have abundant internal documentation. Some of the commonly followed documentation rules are given below, although these will vary from one organization to another.

1. **Use of the Line Comment Field**
   Through the use of the comment field, indicate the purpose of each instruction or group of instructions. For example,

   ```
   MOV    R1,R0    ; INTERCHANGE
   MOV    R2,R1    ;    REG 1 AND
   MOV    R0,R2    ;       REG 2.
   ```

   Note that successive lines of multiline comments are slant-indented to indicate that they go together. Comments must indicate the *significance* of the instruction and not just reiterate the instruction mnemonic. For example, write

   ```
   CLR    R1    ; INITIALIZE SUM TO ZERO
   ```

   rather than,

   ```
   CLR    R1    ; CLEAR R1
   ```

2. **Comments in Code Body**
   Any comment too lengthy for the comment field should be placed "in-line" preceding the code which it describes. Such comments are preceded and followed by a line containing a single semicolon in column 1. The comment itself should begin in column 3, with any desired indentation appearing in column 9. For example,

   ```
   ;
   ; THE FOLLOWING CODE MOVES A BLOCK
   ; OF DATA FROM ONE LOCATION TO
   ; ANOTHER. DEFINITIONS ARE:
   ;        R1:   POINTS TO ORIGINAL LOCATION OF FIRST
   ;              ELEMENT TO BE MOVED
   ;        R2:   POINTS TO DESTINATION FOR FIRST ELEMENT
   ;        R3:   NUMBER OF BYTES TO BE MOVED
   ;
   ```

3. Module Prologue

Every program module must have a *prologue* section giving the following information.

a) Version number and date of last revision.

b) Narrative description of module function.

c) Author.

d) List of input arguments indicating their meaning and transmission conventions.

e) List of output arguments indicating their meanings and transmission conventions.

f) List of internal variables indicating their meanings.

g) Indication of any side effects caused by executing the module. Normally, there should be none.

h) List of external module calls, including brief narrative of what they do.

The prologue should begin with a line of the form

```
; + +   ***************************************************************************
```

and end with

```
; — —   ***************************************************************************
```

This allows special programs to automatically extract the prologues from a group of modules for use in external documentation of the program.

15.4 Linkage and the Memory Map

It is often necessary to know exactly where a particular instruction or data item is stored in memory at execution time. We already have seen this need when we learned to use ODT to examine memory contents during execution. There are other times when the programmer needs this information, such as when trying to determine the exact location of a program error, and when trying to make maximum use of limited memory. In order to develop these abilities, we have to examine the processes by which run-time addresses are determined. We shall begin by reviewing the address assignment process during assembly, and then examine the linkage process and the memory map.

15.4.1 Assembly-time Addresses

Address assignment begins with the assembly process. As we have seen beginning in early chapters of this book, the assembler translates the MACRO-11 mnemonics and assigns successive addresses to each machine code instruction or data item. This address assignment begins at 000000 for each separate module processed by the assembler. (Also see the discussion on .PSECT below.)

Thus the addresses assigned by the assembler are actually *relative* to the beginning of the module. These are the addresses shown in the leftmost column of the assembly listing, and are also reflected in the symbol table shown at the bottom of the listing. They are called *relocatable addresses*.

If a module was loaded into memory beginning at location 000000, the relocatable addresses assigned by the assembler would also be the run-time addresses. To determine the location of a particular instruction or data item, we would then need only examine the assembler listing. However, this is seldom the case for a number of reasons. First, space must be reserved for the system stack, which is customarily placed immediately before the program. Second, if there are two or more modules, obviously they cannot all be loaded beginning at zero. Instead, each module must be stored in successive blocks of memory after leaving room for the stack. Because of this, each module has a unique *loading point address* or *offset* from location 000000 at run time. One of the functions of the linker is to assign these offsets as it builds an executable program. Run-time addresses are then the relocatable addresses determined by the assembler plus the offset. The linker does this addition automatically in order to determine the addresses actually referred to in the instructions, such as those introduced through operands of the form ''#label.''

Example 15.2 Let us clarify the above with a simple example. Figure 15.6(a) shows the assembler listing for a main program that calls the subroutine defined in Fig. 15.6(b). Observe that the three arrays—A, B, and C—are defined globally, as are the entry points START and SUB1. The last instruction of SUB1 is also given a global label ESUB1 for reasons soon to be seen. Also note that the address of A introduced by the immediate operand in line 7 of the main program is marked with an apostrophe. This means that this address must be *modified,* i.e., increased by the offset during linkage because at run time the absolute address of A must be used and only the relocatable address relative to the module beginning is known at assembly time. Additionally, the address of SUB1 as used in line 10 is listed as 000000 and marked G. This means that SUB1 is global, and its address will be determined by the linker and the machine code modified accordingly. The need for similar modifications in the code for SUB1 can be seen by the apostrophes and Gs in Fig. 15.6(b).

The assembler listing also contains a *symbol table* as can be seen in Fig. 15.6. All symbols used in the module are listed here along with their values that are marked with R, G, or RG. Symbols such as L1 in the main program that will be modified by addition of the offset upon linkage are marked R, meaning ''relocatable.'' Those such as SUB1 that are listed in the .GLOBL directive but not defined within the module are indicated by ''****** G''. This means that they are global, and the linker will have to provide the run-time address by using the relocatable address and offset of *some other module* where it is defined.

Symbols that are *defined globally within the module,* such as by being to the left of : :, or to the left of : and appearing in the .GLOBL list, are marked RG. This means that the linker can determine the run-time address using the relocatable address and offset of the current module, but the address so determined may be used in another module. Although not used in this example, symbols defined by direct assignment will also be listed in the symbol table with an equal sign between the symbol and the assigned value.

```
LINKAGE EXAMPLE MACRO V03.01 17-JAN-83 14:40:32 PAGE 1


      1                                          .TITLE LINKAGE EXAMPLE
      2                                          .MCALL .EXIT
      3                                          .GLOBL SUB1
      4 000000                         A::       .BLKW  300
      5 000600                         START::
      6 000600  012701  000300                   MOV    #300,R1
      7 000604  012702  000000'                  MOV    #A,R2
      8 000610  012722  177777         L1:       MOV    #-1,(R2)+
      9 000614  077103                           SOB    R1,L1
     10 000616  004767  000000G                  JSR    PC,SUB1
     11 000622  000000                           HALT
     12 000624                         B::       .BLKW  200
     13         000600'                          .END START




   SYMBOL TABLE

   A 000000RG     B 000624RG    L1 000610R    START 000600RG
   SUB1 = ****** G

   . ABS.  000000      000
           001224      001
   ERRORS DETECTED:  0
```

(a)

```
SUB1 FOR LINKAGE EXAMPLE        MACRO V03.01 17-JAN-83 14:43:53 PAGE 1


      1                                          .TITLE SUB1 FOR LINKAGE EXAMPLE
      2                                          .GLOBL A,B
      3 000000                         C::       .BLKW     100
      4 000200                         SUB1::
      5 000200  012701  000100                   MOV     #100,R1
      6 000204  012702  000000'                  MOV     #C,R2
      7 000210  012703  000000G                  MOV     #A,R3
      8 000214  012704  000000G                  MOV     #B,R4
      9 000220  011312                 L1:       MOV     (R3),(R2)
     10 000222  011314                           MOV     (R3),(R4)
     11 000224  005722                           TST     (R2)+
     12 000226  005723                           TST     (R3)+
     13 000230  005724                           TST     (R4)+
     14 000232  077106                           SOB     R1,L1
     15 000234  000207                 ESUB1::   RTS     PC
     16         000001                           .END    ;(SUB1)




   SYMBOL TABLE

   A = ****** G    C 000000RG    ESUB1 000234RG    L1 000220R
   SUB1 000200RG
   B = ****** G

   . ABS.  000000      000
           000236      001
   ERRORS DETECTED:  0
```

(b)

Figure 15.6 MACRO-11 list file for linkage example: (a) main program; (b) subroutine SUB1.

15.4.2 Linkage and the Load Maps

When the object modules for the program in Fig. 15.6 are linked, the result is an executable program, sometimes called a "load module" or "memory image" module. The organization of the load module is shown in Fig. 15.7. Figure 15.7(a) shows the file called "name.MAP" produced by the LINK program. Figure 15.7(b) shows a pictorial representation. Either of these representations can be called the "load map" for the program. The essential information contained in the load map consists of the run-time, absolute addresses of the global symbols defined in each module. Thus we see that A is stored beginning at 001000, and C, at 002224. Because these are the first addresses in the main program and SUB1, respectively, these addresses indicate the load points or offsets for the two modules. The fact that A is stored at 001000 indicates that 1000_8 bytes were reserved immediately before the main program; this space will be used for the system stack. The global label ESUB1 placed at the end of SUB1 is also listed in the load map. This allows us, for purposes of this example, to see the address

```
RT-11 LINK  V06.00      Load Map        Mon 17-Jan-83 14:51:18
E12P2 .SAV       Title:  LINKAG  Ident:

-----------------------------
| Section  Addr   Size | Global  Value    Global  Value    Global  Value
|                      |
|                      -----------------------
| . ABS.  000000 001000    (RW,I,GBL,ABS,OVR) |
|         001000 001462    (RW,I,LCL,REL,CON) |
-----------------------------------------------
                          A       001000  START   001600  B       001624
                          C       002224  SUB1    002424  ESUB1   002460

Transfer address = 001600, High limit = 002462 = 665.   words
```

(a)

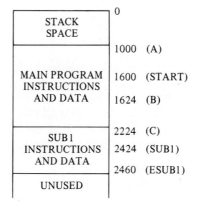

(b)

Figure 15.7 Memory map for linkage example: (a) map file from LINK; (b) diagram of memory. [OS]

of the last word used by the program. This label is unnecessary and is usually omitted.

In addition to the load points of each module, we are sometimes interested in other absolute run-time addresses available from the load map. For example, the *entry* point of each module is sometimes needed. Because these are always global labels, they are listed in the *map* symbol table. Thus we see that the main module entry point START is located at 001600, and that for SUB1 is located at 002424.

The last line of the MAP file gives the *transfer address and the high limit* for the load module. The transfer address is where the PC must be set to begin execution. This is established by placing the entry label for the main program module in the .END directive. As can be confirmed by comparison with the label ESUB1, the high limit is the address of the first location of unused memory. This is numerically equal to the length of the entire load module in bytes. This value is divided by 2 and converted to decimal to give the program length in decimal words as the last item in the MAP listing.

Figure 15.7 also gives information labeled *Section, Addr,* and *Size.* The meaning of this information will be discussed below when .PSECT is introduced.

15.4.3 Finding Run-time Addresses

Run-time addresses can be calculated as the sum of the relocatable addresses found in the assembler listing and the load point addresses found in the MAP listing from the linker. For example, the run-time address of L1 in the SUB1 module is

```
    000220   (From Fig. 15.6b)
+   002224   (From Fig. 15.7)
    002444   (Absolute address of L1)
```

Care must be taken to be sure that the correct load point address is used. A common error is to assume that the entry point is the same as the load point. This is true only if there is no code or data before the module entry point.

15.4.4 Program Sections

The load map in Fig. 15.7(b) shows that all of one module including instructions and data is loaded first, followed by all of the next module. This creates a load module that has instructions and data intermixed, i.e.,

data   — module 1
instructions — module 1
data   — module 2
instructions — module 2

While there is nothing really wrong with this, there are situations in which it would be more desirable to have all instructions grouped together, and all data grouped together and thus separate from instructions, i.e.,

data   − module 1
data   − module 2
instructions − module 1
instructions − module 2

One advantage of this organization is that it is easier to distinguish between instructions and data when examining memory contents. Other advantages have to do with efficiency of memory allocation by the operating system.

MACRO-11 allows the programmer to specify the organization above through a concept called *program sections,* implemented with the .PSECT directive. When the assembler encounters the directive

.PSECT   name1

in the source code, it will begin placing all subsequent translated instructions or data into a "program section" identified by "name1". When the next directive

.PSECT   name2

is encountered, the assembler stops placing code in "name1" and starts placing it in the section called "name2". The programmer can choose any name, and there can be any number of .PSECT directives. This therefore allows the source assembly language instructions and data allocation directives to occur in a sequence convenient and logical from a programming point of view, while at the same time providing enough information so that the linker can create an efficient load module organization.

Example 15.3   To show the usage of .PSECT to force separate data and program sections, let us modify the example in Fig. 15.6. As shown in Fig. 15.8, we simply place the directive

.PSECT DATA

before all data-generating directives, and

.PSECT PROG

before all groups of instructions. Note that in Fig. 15.6(a) there are two .PSECT DATA directives because there are data before and after the instructions.

The effects of these .PSECT directives can be seen first in the assembly listing, Fig. 15.8, which should be compared with Fig. 15.6. Note that in Fig. 15.8(a), A is assigned the relocatable address 000000, and B immediately follows the end of the 300-word A array, in spite of the intervening instructions. Also observe that START is assigned the relocatable address 000000, and the instructions are assigned the successive word addresses up to 000022. In order to accomplish this separate address assignment into the two sections, the assembler uses a separate location counter for each section. The counter for a particular section

```
LINKAGE EXAMPLE MACRO V03.01 17-JAN-83 15:01:52 PAGE 1


     1                                         .TITLE LINKAGE EXAMPLE
     2                                  ;            WITH .PSECT USAGE
     3                                         .MCALL   .EXIT
     4                                         .GLOBL   SUB1
     5  000000                                 .PSECT   DATA
     6  000000                         A::     .BLKW    300
     7  000000                                 .PSECT   PROG
     8  000000                         START:: 
     9  000000  012701  000300                 MOV      #300,R1
    10  000004  012702  000000'                MOV      #A,R2
    11  000010  012722  177777         L1:     MOV      #-1,(R2)+
    12  000014  077103                         SOB      R1,L1
    13  000016  004767  000000G                JSR      PC,SUB1
    14  000022  000000                         HALT
    15  000600                                 .PSECT   DATA
    16  000600                         B::     .BLKW    200
    17          000000'                        .END     START


     SYMBOL TABLE

     A 000000RG  002      B 000600RG  002      L1 000010R  003
     START 000000RG  003      SUB1 = ****** G

     . ABS.   000000      000
              000000      001
     DATA     001200      002
     PROG     000024      003
     ERRORS DETECTED:  0
```

(a)

```
SUB1 FOR LINKAGE EXAMPLE      MACRO V03.01 17-JAN-83 15:02:43 PAGE 1


     1                                         .TITLE SUB1 FOR LINKAGE EXAMPLE
     2                                  ;            WITH .PSECT USAGE
     3                                         .GLOBL   A,B
     4  000000                                 .PSECT   DATA
     5  000000                         C::     .BLKW    100
     6  000000                                 .PSECT   PROG
     7  000000                         SUB1:: 
     8  000000  012701  000100                 MOV      #100,R1
     9  000004  012702  000000'                MOV      #C,R2
    10  000010  012703  000000G                MOV      #A,R3
    11  000014  012704  000000G                MOV      #B,R4
    12  000020  011312                 L1:     MOV      (R3),(R2)
    13  000022  011314                         MOV      (R3),(R4)
    14  000024  005722                         TST      (R2)+
    15  000026  005723                         TST      (R3)+
    16  000030  005724                         TST      (R4)+
    17  000032  077106                         SOB      R1,L1
    18  000034  000207                 ESUB1:: RTS      PC
    19          000001                         .END     ;(SUB1)


     SYMBOL TABLE

     A = ****** G      C 000000RG  002      ESUB1 000034RG  003
     L1 000020R  003      SUB1 000000RG  003
     B = ****** G

     . ABS.   000000      000
              000000      001
     DATA     000200      002
     PROG     000036      003
     ERRORS DETECTED:  0
```

(b)

Figure 15.8 MACRO-11 list file for .PSECT example: (a) main program; (b) subroutine SUB1.

```
RT-11 LINK  V06.00      Load Map        Mon 17-Jan-83 15:54:11
E12P3 .SAV      Title:  LINKAG  Ident:

-----------------------
|Section  Addr   Size |  Global  Value   Global  Value   Global  Value
|                     ---------------------
| .ABS.   000000 001000   (RW,I,GBL,ABS,OVR)|
| DATA    001000 001400   (RW,I,LCL,REL,CON)|
-----------------------------------------------
                         A      001000  B       001600  C       002200
   PROG   002400 000062   (RW,I,LCL,REL,CON)
                         START  002400  SUB1    002424  ESUB1   002460

   Transfer address = 002400, High limit = 002462 = 665.   words
```

(a)

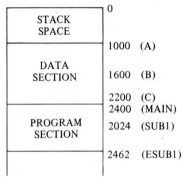

(b)

Figure 15.9   Memory map for .PSECT example: (a) map file from LINK; (b) diagram of memory. [OS]

begins at 0 at the first occurrence of the .PSECT directive with its name and is incremented in the normal manner until a section of a different name is indicated by another .PSECT directive.

The assembler writes the name of each program section and the code placed in that section into the object module. The linker then puts together a load module in which sections of like names are grouped together, even though they may have come from different modules. This creates a load map such as shown in Fig. 15.9, which should be compared with Fig. 15.7. Note that in the load map in Fig. 15.9 three sections are shown—.ABS, DATA, and PROG. The .ABS section is created automatically by the linker and, in fact, is the space for the system stack and certain absolute locations used by the operating system. The other two come from the .PSECT directives in the source code.

15.5 Position-independent Code

In certain situations we want the machine language version of a program or subroutine to be able to execute properly regardless of where it is placed in memory. An example is a library routine furnished by the operating system and needed by many different users in a multiuser environment such as RSTS/E or RSX-11M. In such a case, the operating system must be able to load the machine code into any available portion of the central memory without having to modify it in any way. That is, it must be "Position-Independent Code," or PIC.

Early in our study of machine and assembly language programming we learned that programs can reside anywhere in the central memory. It might therefore be thought that *all* machine code is "position-independent." Unfortunately, this is not necessarily the case as we will see in the following examples.

Example 15.4   Suppose we need a routine to print a character in an environment that allows access to the device registers. In Chapter 8 we saw that this could be done with the assembly code

```
LOOP:    TSTB     177564
         BPL      LOOP
         MOVB     R0,177566
```

Here we have used relative addressing, although 177564 is the *absolute* address of the printer status register (PSR), and 177566 is the *absolute* address of the printer data register (PDR). If this was assembled and then linked using the standard 1000_8 offset provided by LINK, we would have the translated absolute instructions

Location	Instructions	
001000	105767	
001002	176560	(PC rel addr of PSR)
001004	100376	
001006	110067	
001010	176554	(PC rel addr of PDR)

Recall that in relative addressing (code 67), the operand address is found by adding the current PC to the PC relative address as stored in the second word of the instruction. Hence

$$1004 + 176560 = 177564$$

is found for the operand address for the TSTB instruction. Now suppose that we ignored the fact that this code was linked for loading at 001000, and arbitrarily entered the *same* machine code at 000500. (This could be done, for example, by using ODT.) We would then have

000500	105767
000502	176560
000504	100376
000506	110067
000510	176554

When the TSTB operand address is computed now we get

$504 + 176560 = 177264$

which is *not* the address of the printer status register. Similarly, the address of the printer data register is incorrect, and this code will not work at this location in memory.

The principle we see in Example 15.4 is that when *relative addressing* is used to refer to *absolute addresses* outside of the set of instructions in question, the resulting machine code is not position independent. The code will work well as long as the machine code is *loaded* beginning at the location where the linker *assumed* it would be loaded, but if it is relocated without modification elsewhere in memory, it will fail. The cure for this difficulty is to use absolute addressing to refer to any absolute addresses outside of the routine to be relocated.

Example 15.5 Modify the previous example to make the code position independent.

```
LOOP:    TSTB    @#177564
         BPL     LOOP
         MOVB    R0,@#177566
```

This (regardless of load point) translates to

```
105737
177564   (Absolute address of PSR)
100376
110037
177566   (Absolute address of PDR)
```

Because no addresses were assumed in the translation, this code can be located anywhere without modification.

Another problem of position dependence arises when a translated instruction incorporates an *absolute* (e.g., rather than PC-relative) address that lies *within* the body of code to be relocated. Shown below is perhaps the most common example of this.

Example 15.6 Determine if the following program segment is position-independent.

```
A:        .WORD    0,2
START:    MOV      #A,R1
          MOV      (R1),R2
            .
            .
            .
```

Assuming the standard 1000_8 offset provided by LINK, this translates to

```
001000    000000  ← A
001002    000002
001004    012701
001006    001000  (Absolute address of A)
001010    011102
             .
             .
             .
```

If this code was relocated, without modification, to 002000, we would have

```
002000    000000  ← A
002002    000002
002004    012701
002006    001000  (Wrong absolute address of A)
002010    011102
```

Now the address of A is 002000, although the code still assumes it to be 001000. Once again, relocation has resulted in incorrect results. Therefore the code is position dependent.

Example 15.7 Modify the code in Example 15.6 to be position-independent. One way to accomplish the operation above with position-independent code is to use the assembler location counter

```
A:        .WORD    0,2
START:    MOV      PC,R1
          ADD      #A−.,R1
          MOV      (R1),R2
```

To see how this works, keep in mind that the intent is to place the correct address of A into R1, regardless of where the code exists in memory. During execution, the MOV PC,R1 instruction will capture the address of the ADD instruction and place it into R1. The ADD instruction, due to the immediate addressing, adds the value found in the following word to R1. Now, if the value stored there is the distance from the ADD to A, the resulting sum will be the true address of A. The *assembler* can be caused to compute this distance by using the syntax #A−. because "." represents the *current location counter* as ADD is being translated. This code (regardless of location) translates to

```
000000
000002
010701
066701
177772
011102
```

which is position-independent.

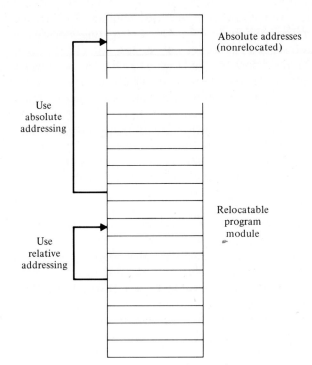

Absolute addresses
(nonrelocated)

Use
absolute
addressing

Relocatable
program
module

Use
relative
addressing

Figure 15.10   Requirements for position-independent code.

Summarizing, we can say that position-independency has been achieved for the block of code to be relocated if

1. It contains no *relative* addresses of locations *outside* of itself.
2. It contains no *absolute* addresses to locations *within* itself.

These rules are shown pictorially in Fig. 15.10.

15.6 Libraries [OS]

When developing a new program, it often happens that several of the needed modules already exist. These could come from earlier stages of a large program development effort, from an unrelated earlier project, or from the large body of programs that have been developed over many years. In any event, it is most convenient to have access to the needed modules without having to include them directly in the new program. That is, we would like simply to refer to the existing modules and have them immediately available to our program. We have already seen that this can be achieved through the linking process by listing each individual object module along with the new program object module. For example,

```
LINK
*PROG,PROG=MAIN,SUBA,SUBB,SUBC
*^Z
```

This becomes awkward, however, when the number of object modules is large. It would be more convenient to gather all the existing modules into a single file that could be referenced whenever any of the contained object modules was required. This is indeed possible, and the composite file is called an *object library*. A related concept is a *macro library*, in which there is a collection of macro definitions in MACRO-11 assembly language. Libraries of either kind can be "private," i.e., created by the user, or "public," i.e., provided to all users by the system. Below we shall see how libraries are created, and how they are used. Note that while the command syntax is dependent on the operating system, the concepts are generally applicable to almost any operating system. We shall show our examples assuming the RSTS/E environment.

15.6.1 Creating an Object Library
Suppose you had developed a set of subroutines in MACRO-11 and wanted to make them available for use in other programs. To accomplish this, you must first assemble the subroutines (with global entry point labels) as separate modules, then merge them into a library file. The merging operation requires a special system program that not only concatenates the separate files but also creates a "directory" so that the individual modules can be found later by the linker. In RSTS/E, this program is called LIBR, and its use is shown in the following example.

Example 15.8   As an example, let us create an object library containing the subroutines in Fig. 15.11. These are stored in the three separate files—SUBA.MAC, SUBB.MAC, and SUBC.MAC. First, assemble each file to create the object files.

```
MACRO
*SUBA,SUBA = SUBA
*SUBB,SUBB = SUBB
*SUBC,SUBC, = SUBC
*^Z
```

The object files now exist as SUBA.OBJ, SUBB.OBJ, and SUBC.OBJ. To create the library called MYLIB.OBJ (or any other convenient name), enter the following sequence.

```
RUN   $LIBR
*MYLIB.OBJ,MYLIB.LST = SUBA,SUBB,SUBC/N
*^Z
```

This creates the two files—MYLIB.OBJ and MYLIB.LST. The OBJ file is to be used in a LINK operation, and the LST file can be printed to see the contents of the library. The listing file for the example above is shown in Fig. 15.12. Note that the module name comes from the .TITLE directive in the module, while the GLOBALS are all labels in each module that were defined in a .GLOBL directive or by the : : operator.

```
                        .TITLE  SUBA
                        .MCALL    .PRINT
            SUBA::
                        .PRINT    #MSG
                        RTS       PC
            ENTRY2::
                        .PRINT    #MSG2
                        RTS       PC
            MSG:        .ASCIZ/SUBROUTINE SUBA/
            MSG2:       .ASCIZ/SUBROUTINE SUBA,ENTRY2/
                        .END             ;(SUBA)

                            (a)


                        .TITLE    SUBB
                        .MCALL    .PRINT
                        .LIST     ME
            SUBB::
                        .PRINT    #MSG
                        RTS       PC
            MSG:        .ASCIZ/SUBROUTINE SUBB/
                        .END             ;(SUBB)

                            (b)


                        .TITLE  SUBC
                        .MCALL    .PRINT
            SUBC::
                        .PRINT    #MSG
                        RTS       PC
            MSG:        .ASCIZ/SUBROUTINE SUBC/
                        .END             ;(SUBC)

                            (c)
```

Figure 15.11 Subroutines for library example: (a) SUBA.MAC; (b) SUBB.MAC; (c) SUBC.MAC.

```
        RT-11 LIBRARIAN V03.07   MON 17-JAN-83 15:19:57
        MYLIB                    MON 17-JAN-83 15:19:57

        MODULE          GLOBALS          GLOBALS          GLOBALS

        SUBA            ENTRY2           SUBA
        SUBB            SUBB
        SUBC            SUBC
```

Figure 15.12 MYLIB.LST showing directory of object library. [OS]

The LIBR command has several variations that are necessary or convenient when maintaining an object library. Some of these are shown below.

To add a module,

```
RUN  $LIBR
*MYLIB,MYLIB = MYLIB/NEW.OBJ
*^Z
```

To delete a module,

```
RUN  $LIBR
*MYLIB,MYLIB = MYLIB/D
module to be deleted? name to be deleted
module to be deleted? ⟨CR⟩
*^Z
```

To replace a module with the current OBJ file,

```
RUN  $LIBR
*MYLIB,MYLIB=MYLIB,name/R
*^Z
```

15.6.2 Using an Object Library
Object libraries are used at the linkage step. The library name is simply listed on the right-hand side of the LINK command. For example, suppose we wish to use one or more of the three subroutines in MYLIB.OBJ in a main program, as shown in Fig. 15.13.

After assembling this program, we execute the command

```
LINK
*MAIN,MAIN=MAIN,MYLIB
*^Z
```

The LINK program will recognize MYLIB as a user library and will search it for external labels referred to in MAIN or in already-loaded library modules. When it finds a label, it extracts the module to which it belongs and links it into the load module. Modules in the library but that do not contain any global labels referred to in MAIN or other modules are not included in the load module. The program can now be run in the normal manner.

```
RUN    MAIN
```

It is possible to use more than one library. LINK will search all libraries listed in the LINK command in a left-to-right order until all external labels are identified. These may all be libraries you have created, or they can be those supplied by the system. For example, the FORTRAN library may be available on your system, in which case you can link with it to gain access to its many subroutines. See your computer center staff for the name and location of such libraries.

15.6.3 Macro Library
The LIBR command can also be used to create a library of macro definitions. A macro library is quite different from an object library in that it is composed of MACRO-11 source code as opposed to object code. This is because macros are introduced at the *assembly* step rather than at the linkage step.

```
              .TITLE  MAIN
              .MCALL  .EXIT
              .GLOBL  SUBA,SUBB,SUBC,ENTRY2
      START:
              JSR     PC,SUBA
              JSR     PC,SUBC
              JSR     PC,ENTRY2
              .EXIT
              .END    START
```

Figure 15.13 Main program using library subroutines.

Example 15.9 As an example of defining a macro library, suppose that a file named MACRO.MAC has been created containing definitions of the macros PUSH and SAVREG. (See Section 10.3.4.) To create the library enter

```
RUN   $LIBR
*SYSMAC.SML = MACRO.MAC/M
*^Z
```

This creates the special file SYSMAC.SML that will contain the macro definitions and a directory of the contained macro names.

To use this macro library, the MACRO-11 module that requires SAVREG and/or PUSH must contain

```
.MCALL     SAVREG,PUSH
```

Then when this module is to be assembled, we issue the command

```
MACRO
*MAIN,MAIN = MAIN,SYSMAC.SML
*^Z
```

When .MCALL is encountered during assembly, the file SYSMAC.SML will be searched for the macros listed. However, only those listed in the .MCALL *and* referenced in the program will be taken from the library and included in the program.

Because MACRO-11 normally searches only *one* macro library, namely, SYSMAC.SML, a problem arises if macros from two different libraries are needed. The most common example of this occurs when an individual user has a macro library, and also needs macros available in the system library, which is also called SYSMAC.SML but is stored under a public account. One solution to this problem is to extract the macros needed from the system library and include them in your macro library. Alternatively, the system manager may be willing to add your macros to the system library. The latter approach has an advantage in that the system macro library is automatically searched for macro listed in .MCALL without having to list SYSMAC.SML in the MACRO command.

15.7 Summary

In the preceding sections we have dealt with several ideas that are important in the development of large assembly language programs. One of these topics was *modular programming*. It can be argued that a "complicated problem" is simply one that has not been broken down into small enough steps, and this is the idea behind modular programming. The "top-down" approach to modular programming suggests that the original problem be broken into a number of major functional steps, each of which becomes a program module. However, if any module so defined is itself overly complicated, we describe it in terms of functional steps, and so on until the entire problem is described in terms of simple, single-purpose modules. The formal design procedure, applicable to large programming efforts, then suggests that each module be described by a specification and a procedure or algorithm, expressed as a flowchart or in pseudocode. The latter terms refer to step-by-step description using precise but informal language that can be unambiguously interpreted by another programmer.

The modular programming idea is augmented by standards of style and program logic. These standards include cosmetic things, such as formatting the line of assembly code in a uniform way and the format of internal documentation. However, they also include restrictions on usage of nonstandard control structures, and on some features of MACRO-11.

Both modularity and standardization address the problem of making programming easier for *people* to read and follow. The importance of this is that most often large programming projects are handled as team efforts, and it is necessary for one programmer to be able to understand another's work. Also, these practices make program maintenance a more manageable task.

Modular programming is enhanced by making each major module a separate file so that all can be assembled and stored as separate object-code modules. This has several advantages, including minimizing the amount of machine time for reassembly when localized changes have to be made. When this is done, the linkage program (LINK) is used to build a "load-module" that is a combined machine-code module ready for loading and executing. In this building process, the linker assigns a "load point address" to each module. Whenever necessary, it adds this so-called offset to the address assigned by the assembler to arrive at the correct run-time code for the load point of the module. Also, any global labels are given absolute addresses by the linker. Thus the linkage step is one of conversion of the "relocatable" code produced by the assembler to "absolute" code ready for execution. An important output of the linker is the "load map" of the program. This is a list of global symbols (labels) and their absolute addresses as assigned by the linker. The programmer can use this information along with the assembler listings for each module to arrive at the run-time addresses of all data and instructions, should this be necessary.

Finally, it was shown that the directive .PSECT can be used to control where each portion of a module is to be loaded. Often this feature is used to cause the load module to have all data from many modules located in one section of memory, and all instructions in another. There are certain advantages to this organization.

In Section 15.6.1 we saw that a system program called $LIBR on RSTS/E can be used to create object or macro libraries. This makes code that has been thoroughly debugged available in other programs with minimal effort.

15.8 Exercises

15.1 Based on the problem description, and the level-one procedure shown in Fig. 15.2, develop specifications and level-two procedures for steps 2 through 5 for Example 15.1 in Sec. 15.2. Use Figs. 15.3 and 15.4 as guides.

15.2 Develop MACRO-11 implementations of the procedures defined in Exercise 15.1. Follow the standards set forth in Sec. 15.3. Compare your work with Appendix F.

15.3 A program is required to analyze a paragraph of text entered at a keyboard. It must count the number of words, the average word length, and the average number of words per sentence, and print out these values. Words are separated by spaces, commas, or periods. Develop the level-one procedure as pseudocode or flowchart.

Then write specifications and level-two procedures for each module. If necessary, modularize the level-two procedures so that each program module has a single, simple purpose. Your work must have sufficient clarity so that it can be programmed by a classmate without further communication. (Your instructor should assign Exercise 15.4 or 15.5 with this exercise.)

15.4 Using the standards set forth in Sec. 15.3, implement the modular program defined in Exercise 15.3. Test it using the text of Exercise 15.3 as the entered paragraph.

15.5 Using the standards set forth in Sec. 15.3, implement the program defined by a classmate for Exercise 15.3. Test it with the text of Exercise 15.3 as the entered paragraph.

15.6 Enter and assemble the program and subroutine shown in Fig. 15.6. Link it with the SUB1 object module *before* the main program, i.e.,

```
LINK
*E12P2.SAV,E12P2.MAP=SUB1.OBJ,MAIN.OBJ
*^Z
```

Examine the listing and map files and determine the absolute run-time addresses of L1 in both modules.

15.7 Revise the program in Fig. 15.8 such that there are three sections defined as follows.

DATA: contains all data
MAIN: contains only instructions for main program
SUB1: contains only instructions for SUB1

Assemble and link and examine the load map and listing. State why this might be more convenient than having a single instruction section.

15.8 Examine each of the following code segments and state whether or not it is position-independent. If necessary, revise to make it position-independent.

```
a)   ADD     R1,R2              b)  A: WORD    4
     MOV     R2,R3                  S: MOV     #2,R1
                                       ADD     A,R1

c)   MOV     #177564,R1         d)  A: WORD    4
 L:  TSTB    (R1)                      MOV     #A,R1
     BPL     L                         ADD     (R1),R3
     MOV     #177566,R1
     MOVB    R0,(R1)

e)   CLR     200
```

Appendixes

$\boxed{\text{A}}$ Programming References

The following notes apply to Table A.1.

1. Normal settings of N, Z, V, and C condition codes are

   N = 1 if MSB of result is 1 (implies negative result if operands are viewed as two's complement numbers).

   Z = 1 if result is 0

   V = 1 if operation caused a two's complement overflow

   C = 1 if addition caused a carry out of the MSB, or if a subtraction required a borrow into MSB.

2. Set means set to 1; cleared means cleared to 0.

3. Instructions shown with (B) have byte form, e.g., MOVB.

4. ■ is 0 for word form of instruction or 1 for byte form.

5. For discussion of byte form of instructions, see Section 7.7.

6. S and D mean source and destination operand, respectively. Any addressing mode is allowed.

7. Rn means register operand, i.e., R0, R1, . . ., R5, SP, and PC. Other addressing modes not allowed.

8. L means label operand.

9. See Tables 13.1 and 13.2 for floating-point instructions.

10. Several PDP-11 instructions are omitted from this table because their explanations would be beyond the scope of this text. See *The PDP-11 Processor Handbook*.

TABLE A.1
MACRO-11 Instructions

Assembly Mnemonics and Translation— Notes 3–8	Explanation	Effects on Condition Codes
General		
MOV(B) S,D ■ 1SSDD	Copy of S is placed into D. Sec. 4.2.1	N, Z: Note 1 V: Cleared. C: Unaffected.
ADD S,D 06SSDD	S is added to D. Sec. 4.2.2	N, Z, V, C: Note 1
SUB S,D 16SSDD	S is subtracted from D. Sec. 5.2	N, Z, V, C: Note 1
INC(B) D ■ 052DD	D is incremented by 1. Sec. 4.2.4	N, Z, V: Note 1 C: Unaffected.
DEC(B) D ■ 053DD	D is decremented by 1. Sec. 5.4	N, Z, V: Note 1 C: Unaffected.
NEG(B) D	D is replaced by its two's complement, i.e., D is negated. Sec. 6.3	N, Z, V: Note 1 C: Cleared if result is 0, set otherwise.
CLR(B) D ■ 050DD	D is set to 0. Sec. 4.2.3	N, V, C: Cleared. Z: Set.
MUL S,Rn 070nSS	If n = 1, 3, 5 then 16-bit S × Rn is formed in Rn. If Rn = 0, 2, 4 then 32-bit S × Rn is formed with high word in Rn and low word in Rn + 1. Sec. 6.14.1	N, Z: Note 1 V: Cleared. C: Set if product exceeds 16-bit two's complement number.
DIV S,Rn 071nSS	n must be 0, 2, or 4. The 32-bit value in Rn (high word) and Rn + 1 (low word) is divided by S. Quotient is placed in Rn and remainder in Rn + 1. Sec. 6.14.2	N, Z: Note 1, except unspecified if V = 1. V: Set if S = 0 or if quotient exceeds 16-bit two's complement number.
ADC(B) D ■ 055DD	C condition code (carry bit) is added to D. Sec. 6.13	N, Z, V, C: Note 1
SBC(B) D ■ 056DD	C condition code (carry bit) is subtracted from D. Sec. 6.13	N, Z, V, C: Note 1
NOP 000240	No operation. Used as a "filler" or place holder.	N, Z, V, C: Unaffected.
Logical		
BIC(B) S,D ■ 4SSDD	Clears each bit in D that is 1 in S. Used to clear unwanted portions of S. Sec. 7.9	N, Z: Note 1 V: Cleared. C: Unaffected.
BIS(B) S,D ■ 5SSDD	Sets each bit in D that is 1 in S. Used to set particular bits in S. Sec. 7.9	N, Z: Note 1 V: Cleared. C: Unaffected.
COM(B) D ■ 051DD	Flips bits in D (1's become 0's and 0's become 1's). A one's complement operation. Sec. 7.9	N, Z: Note 1 V: Cleared. C: Set.

TABLE A.1 (cont.)

Assembly Mnemonics and Translation— Notes 3–8	Explanation	Effects on Condition Codes
BIT(B) S,D ■ 3SSDD	See Test and Compare. Sec. 7.9	See Test and Compare.
XOR Rn,D 074nDD	Exclusive OR. A particular bit in D is set only if it had been set in either D or Rn originally, but not if it had been set in both. Sec. 7.9	N, Z: Note 1 V: Cleared. C: Unaffected.

Test and Compare

CMP(B) S,D ■ 2SSDD	D is subtracted from S with result formed in ALU. S and D unchanged; affects only condition codes. Sec. 5.2	N, Z, V, C: Note 1
TST(B) D ■ 057DD	Tests D against 0. Affects only N and Z condition codes. Sec. 5.2	N, Z: Note 1 V, C: Unaffected.
BIT(B) S,D ■ 3SSDD	S is ANDed with D bit by bit in the ALU. S and D unchanged. Affects only condition codes. Yields nonzero only if every 1 bit in S is matched with a 1 bit in D. Sec. 7.9	N, Z: Note 1 V: Cleared. C: Unaffected.

Rotate/Shift

ROR(B) D ■ 060DD	All bits in D are rotated one position to right. C bit rotates into MSB, and LSB rotates into C. Sec. 6.12	N,Z: Note 1 C: Set to previous value of LSB. V: Set to N$\vee$C (based on new values).
ROL(B) D ■ 061DD	All bits in D are rotated one position to left. C bit rotates into LSB, and MSB rotates into C. Sec. 6.12	N, Z: Note 1 C: Set to previous value of MSB. V: Set to N$\vee$C (based on new values).
ASR(B) D ■ 062DD	Arithmetic shift right. Does a divide by 2, preserving the sign of D by replicating the old MSB. Sec. 6.12	N, Z: Note 1 C: Set to previous value of LSB. V: Set to N$\vee$C (based on new values).
ASL(B) D ■ 063DD	Arithmetic shift left. Does a signed multiply by 2. LSB set to 0. Sec. 6.12	N, Z: Note 1 C: Set to previous value of MSB V: Set to N$\vee$C (based on new values).
SWAB D 0003DD	Swaps low and high bytes. D must be word address or register.	N: Set if MSB of low byte of result (bit 7) is set. Z: Set if low byte of result is 0. V, C: Cleared

Control

HALT 000000	Stops the instruction execution cycle. Sec. 4.2.5	N, Z, V, C: Unaffected.
JMP D 0001DD	Jumps to D. Addressing mode 0 not allowed. Unlimited range.	N, Z, V, C: Unaffected.
JSR Rn,D	Jumps to subroutine D, saving previous contents of register n on stack and returns address in Rn. Secs. 9.3, 9.5	N, Z, V, C: Unaffected.

TABLE A.1 (cont.)

Assembly Mnemonics and Translation— Notes 3–8	Explanation	Effects on Condition Codes
RTS Rn 00020n	Returns from subroutine to address in Rn; restores Rn from top of stack. Secs. 9.3, 9.5	N, Z, V, C: Unaffected.
SOB Rn,L 077n00 + 6-bit offset	Subtracts 1 from Rn and branches backwards to label L if Rn is not 0 after subtraction. Sec. 5.5	N, Z, V, C: Unaffected.
Branches (See Table A.2.)	Conditional and unconditional transfer of control. Range limited to $+177_8$ or -200_8 words. Secs. 5.2, 6.8, 6.9, 6.10	N, Z, V, C: Unaffected.

Condition Code Set/Clear

CLN, CLZ, CLV, 250, 244, 242, CLC 241	Clears the condition code indicated by last letter of mnemonic. Sec. 6.11	N, Z, V, C: All but the one cleared are unaffected.
CCC 000257	Clears all condition codes.	N, Z, V, C: Cleared.
SEN, SEZ, SEV 270, 264, 262, SEC 261	Sets the condition code indicated by the last letter of mnemonic. Sec. 6.11	N, Z, V, C: All but the one set are unaffected.
SCC 000277	Sets all condition codes. Sec. 6.11	N, Z, V, C: Set.

Software Traps

EMT 104000 + arbitrary 8-bit number	Emulates trap. Saves PSW and PC on stack and transfers control to address found in location 30 with new PSW taken from 32. Not for general use because it is used by DEC system programs. Low byte of opcode used to pass information to servicing routine. Sec. 14.8	N, Z, V, C: Set to values found in bits 3, 2, 1, and 0 of location 32.
TRAP 104400 + arbitrary 8-bit number	Exactly like EMT except PC and PSW are taken from locations 34 and 36. Used for non-DEC system software, e.g., the UNIX system. Sec. 14.8	N, Z, V, C: Set to values found in bits 3, 2, 1, and 0 of location 36.
BPT 000003	Breakpoint trap. Used to force execution of trace trap routine. Works much like EMT with PC and PSW taken from locations 14 and 16. Sec. 14.10	N, Z, V, C: Set to values found in bits 3, 2, 1, and 0 of location 16.
IOT 000004	I/O trap. Used to force execution of service routine whose address is in location 20, with PSW taken from 22. Works much like EMT.	N, Z, V, C: Set to values found in bits 3, 2, 1, and 0 of location 22.

TABLE A.1 (cont.)

Assembly Mnemonics and Translation— Notes 3–8	Explanation	Effects on Condition Codes
Software Traps		
RTI 000002	Return from interrupt. Used to return from interrupt or trap service routine. PC and PSW are popped from stack. Sec. 14.6.2	N, Z, V, C: Loaded from bits 3, 2, 1, and 0 in stack.
RTT 000006	Return from trap. Used to return from trace trap. Allows the return-point instruction to be executed before the next trace trap. PC and PSW are popped from the stack. Sec. 14.10	N, Z, V, C: Loaded from bits 3, 2, 1, and 0 in stack.

TABLE A.2
Branch Instructions

Instruction and Usage	Assembly Mnemonic		Base Code	Branch Condition
General Usage				
Unconditional **BR**anch	BR	L	000400	Unconditional
Branch if **EQ**ual	BEQ	L	001400	$Z = 1$
Branch **N**ot **E**qual	BNE	L	001000	$Z = 0$
Unsigned Branch Instructions				
Branch if **HI**gher	BHI	L	101000	$C \vee Z = 0$
Branch if **LO**wer	BLO	L	103400	$C = 1$
Branch if **HI**gher or **S**ame	BHIS	L	103000	$C = 0$
Branch if **LO**wer or **S**ame	BLOS	L	101400	$C \vee Z = 1$
Unsigned Overflow Checking				
Branch on **C**arry **S**et	BCS	L	103400	$C = 1$
Branch on **C**arry **C**lear	BCC	L	103000	$C = 0$
Signed Branch Instructions				
Branch if **G**reater **T**han	BGT	L	003000	$Z \vee (N \not\equiv V) = 0$
Branch if **L**ess **T**han	BLT	L	002400	$N \not\equiv V = 1$
Branch if **G**reater than or **E**qual to	BGE	L	002000	$N \not\equiv V = 0$
Branch if **L**ess than or **E**qual to	BLE	L	003400	$Z \vee (N \not\equiv V) = 1$
Signed Overflow Checking				
Branch if **OV**erflow **S**et	BVS	L	102400	$V = 1$
Branch if **OV**erflow **C**lear	BVC	L	102000	$V = 0$
Sign Checking				
Branch if **PL**us	BPL	L	100000	$N = 0$
Branch if **MI**nus	BMI	L	100400	$N = 1$

TABLE A.3
PDP-11 Addressing Mode Explanations

Mode	Name	Assembly Mnemonics	Explanation
0	Register	Rn	Rn contains operand. Sec. 4.3
1	Register Deferred	(Rn)	Rn contains address of operand. Sec. 5.7
2	Autoincrement	(Rn)+	Rn contains address of operand. After the operand is fetched or stored, Rn is incremented (by 2 if the operation is a word operation, or by 1 if it is a byte operation, but always by 2 if R6 is used). Sec. 5.7
3	Autoincrement Deferred	@(Rn)+	Rn contains address of address of operand. After the operand is fetched or stored, Rn is incremented by 2. Sec. 9.10.3
4	Autodecrement	−(Rn)	Decrement contents of Rn by 2 if the operation is a word operation, or by 1 if it is a byte operation, but always by 2 if R6 is used. After that, Rn contains address of operand. Sec. 5.7
5	Autodecrement Deferred	@−(Rn)	Decrement contents of Rn by 2. After that, Rn contains address of address of operand. Sec. 9.10.3
6	Index	X(Rn)	Address of operand is X + contents of Rn. The value of X is stored in the word following the instruction. The PC is incremented by 2. Sec. 9.10.4
7	Index Deferred	@X(Rn)	Address of address of operand is X + contents of Rn. The value of X is stored in the word following the instruction. The PC is incremented by 2. Sec. 9.10.4

Note:

Examples of usage are shown in the indicated sections for each mode.

TABLE A.4
Program Counter Addressing

Address Code	Name	Assembly Mnemonics	Explanation
27	Immediate	#symbol	Operand is the value of symbol. This value is automatically stored following the instruction.
37	Absolute	@#symbol	Operand is in location whose address is the value of symbol. Symbol value is automatically stored following the instruction.
67	Relative	symbol	Operand is in location whose address is the value of symbol. The PC relative address of symbol (see *Notes*) is automatically stored following the instruction.
77	Relative deferred	@Symbol	Address of operand is in location whose address is indicated by value of symbol. The PC-relative address of symbol (see *Notes*) is automatically stored following the instruction.

Notes:

1. Symbol can be a numeric constant, a label, a symbol given a value by assignment, or even an expression. In all cases, a value is first determined, then used as indicated.

2. PC-relative address is the symbol value minus the *current* PC. See Sec. 5.6.2.

TABLE A.5
MACRO-11 Directives

Assembly Mnemonics	Explanation
General	
.TITLE string	Assigns *string* as title of the module. Sec. 4.5
.END label	Marks end of module and sets the starting address for execution to *label*. Sec. 4.5
.END	Marks end of module. Use this form for subroutines. Sec. 9.12
.MCALL list	Causes the system macro library (SYSMAC.SML) to be searched for macros in *list*. Sec. 8.2
.GLOBL list	Places symbols in *list* in the global symbol table. This is necessary when symbols are referenced in separately assembled modules. Secs. 4.9, 9.12
Symbol = Expression	Assigns the value determined by *expression* to *symbol*. Sec. 10.2
Symbol = = Expression	Like =, but also makes *symbol* global. Sec. 10.5
Storage	
.BLKW n	Advances the location counter by *n* words. Used to reserve *n* words without initialization. The *n* can be a previously defined symbol. Sec. 5.6.2
.BLKB n	Advances the location counter by *n* bytes. Used to reserve *n* bytes without initialization. Sec. 7.6
.WORD n1, n2 . . .	Reserves space and initializes one word for each listed value. Symbols or expressions can be included in list, in which case their values are stored. Sec. 5.6.2
.BYTE n1, n2 . . .	Reserves space and initializes one byte for each listed value. Expressions or symbols with values representable with 8 bits can be included in list. Sec. 7.6
.ASCII/string/ or .ASCII ⟨n⟩	Reserves space and initializes bytes to the ASCII codes corresponding to characters in string or to octal value *n*. Sec. 7.6
.ASCIZ/string/ or .ASCIZ ⟨n⟩	Exactly like .ASCII except last character code is followed by a null (000). Sec. 7.6
.EVEN	Advances location counter to next even location. Sec. 7.6
.ODD	Advances location counter to next odd location.
.FLT2 n1, n1, . . .	Reserves two words for each listed item and converts value to floating point representation. The *n* is assumed to be *decimal*. Sec. 13.3
Macro and Conditional Assembly	
.MACRO name, a1, a2, . . .	Defines macro called *name* with arguments a1, a2, ... Sec. 10.3
.ENDM name	Ends definition of macro called name (name is optional). Also used to end .IRP and .IRPC blocks. Secs. 10.3, 10.4
.REPT expression	Repeats instructions up to .ENDR a number of times determined by expression. Sec. 10.4

TABLE A.5 (cont.)

Assembly Mnemonics	Explanation
.ENDR	Ends .REPT blocks. Sec. 10.4
.IF cond arg	Instructions up to next .ENDC or .IFF will be assembled if argument meets condition. Sec. 10.5
.ENDC	Ends conditional assembly block. Sec. 10.5
.IFF	Can be used only between .IF and .ENDC. Instructions up to next .IFT or .ENDC will be assembled only if argument does *not* meet condition in .IF. Sec. 10.5
.IFT	Can be used only between .IF and .ENDC. Instructions up to next .IFF, or .ENDC will be assembled only if argument meets condition in .IF. Sec. 10.5
.IFTF	Can be used only between .IF and .ENDC. Instructions up to next .IFF, .IFT, or .ENDC will be assembled regardless of argument in .IF. Sec. 10.5
.IIF .IF cond arg, statement	Statement can be any instruction or directive and is assembled only if argument meets condition. Sec. 10.5
.MEXIT	Can be used only between .MACRO and .ENDM. Causes all subsequent instructions and directives in the macro to be skipped. Sec. 10.5
.NARG symbol	Can be used only between .MACRO and .ENDM. Causes the count of actual arguments to be assigned to symbol. Sec. 10.5
.NTYPE symbol, arg	Can be used only between .MACRO and ENDM. Causes the addressing code of argument to be assigned to symbol. Sec. 10.5
.NCHAR symbol, ⟨string⟩	Causes the count of characters in string to be assigned to symbol.
.ERROR symbol; message	Causes message and symbol to be printed in .LST file. Used to generate macro error reports.

Miscellaneous

.LIST ME	Causes all subsequent macro expansions to be listed. Useful for seeing how macro expansion works. Sec. 10.3.1
.NLIST	Listing suppressed up to the next .LIST directive.
.LIST	Causes listing to resume after a prior .NLIST.
.PSECT name	Causes subsequent code to be assembled into section called *name*. Sec. 15.4.4
.PAGE	Causes a form-feed character to be placed in the .LST file. Will cause a page eject on a line printer.

B Text Editors

B.1 Overview

A text editor is a system-supplied program that allows you to create or modify text files. These files can be viewed as a collection of lines of text of any kind, e.g., MACRO-11 programs, FORTRAN programs, and data. On a typical PDP-11 installation there will be several different text editors to choose among. While each of these has the same essential capabilities, they differ slightly in the details of their usage. This appendix discusses several text editors, including the DEC Editor called EDT (V2.0) that should be available under RSTS/E and RSX-11M. Also discussed are EDIT and TECO as supplied with RT-11, and *ed* that is part of the UNIX operating system.

Presented here is only a minimum set of commands necessary for convenient creation and alteration of MACRO-11 programs with these editors. In particular, only the line and character editing features are considered. Readers wishing to use the more extensive capabilities of these editors should consult the appropriate manuals.

B.2 EDT [RSTS/E, RSX-11M]

EDT is the newest of the editors available under the RSTS/S and RSX-11M operating systems, and therefore has more modern features. However, some of these features, such as full-screen editing, require special terminals, and are therefore not discussed here. EDT is presented here as a *line editor*, meaning that the file is treated as a collection of lines that can be modified, added, or deleted on a one-at-a-time basis. Those who have access to DEC's VT100 or comparable terminals may wish to use instead EDT's full-screen capability that allows editing of an entire screen full of lines at one time. Other EDT features are discussed in *The EDT Editor Manual* (DEC order no. AA–J726A–TC).

When EDT is entered, the name of the file to be edited is given. If this file does not exist, it is created so that new text can be inserted. If it does exist, it is read into a portion of memory called the EDT "buffer." It is only the contents of this buffer that is changed by EDT commands, until EDT is left with the EX command. EX causes the buffer to replace the file, thus making your changes permanent. However, a temporary copy of the original file is saved under a file named fn.BAK that is automatically deleted after a short period. Thus if you wish to go back to the original version, you should delete the edited version and rename the .BAK version immediately. A short summary of EDT commands is presented in Table B.1. These commands are shown in examples below.

B.2.1 Entering EDT

The command line necessary for entering EDT is

```
EDT      filename.extension ⟨CR⟩
*
_
```

TABLE B.1
Summary of Editor Commands

Action	EDT [RSTS/E, RSX-11M] Type: line Key: ⟨CR⟩ = carriage return	TECO [RT-11] Type: character Key: ⟨CR⟩ = carriage return $ = ESC
Enter editor		
New file	EDT fn1 ⟨CR⟩	R TECO ⟨CR⟩ *EW fn1$$
Existing file	EDT fn1 ⟨CR⟩	R TECO ⟨CR⟩ *EB fn1$Y$$
Insert text		
	*I ⟨CR⟩ text *^Z (Inserts before line pointer)	*I text text $$ (Inserts before char. pointer)
Leave editor		
Saving changes	*EX ⟨CR⟩	*EX$$
Discarding changes	*QUIT ⟨CR⟩	*EK$$ *^C *^C
Pointer movement		
Beginning of buffer	*%BE ⟨CR⟩	*J$$
End of buffer	*%E ⟨CR⟩	*ZJ$$
Down n lines	*+n ⟨CR⟩	*nL$$
Up n lines	*−n ⟨CR⟩	*−nL$$
Forward n char.	Not available	*nC$$
Backward n char.	Not available	*−nC$$
Position at entry	At first line	Before first char.
Display		
Buffer	*%WH ⟨CR⟩	*HT$$
n lines	*T.#n ⟨CR⟩	*nT$$
Delete		
Forward n lines	*D.#n ⟨CR⟩	*nK$$
Forward n char.	Not available	*nD$$
Backward n char.	Not available	*−nD$$
Find string		
	*"string" ⟨CR⟩ or 'string' ⟨CR⟩	*string$$
Substitute string		
	*S/old/new/ ⟨CR⟩	*FSold$new$$
Read/write second file		
Read into buffer	*INC fn2 ⟨CR⟩	*ER fn2$A$$
Write buffer to file	*WR fn2 ⟨CR⟩	*EF$EW fn2$HPW$$

TABLE B.1 (cont.)

Action	EDIT [RT-11] Type: character Key: $ = ESC	ed [the UNIX system] Type: line Key: ⟨CR⟩ = carriage return
Enter editor		
New file	EDIT/CREATE fn1 ⟨CR⟩	ed ⟨CR⟩
Existing file	EDIT fn1 ⟨CR⟩ *R$$	ed fn1 ⟨CR⟩
Insert text		

	*I text
	  text$$
	(Insert before char. pointer.)
		⟩ a ⟨CR⟩
		  text
		. ⟨CR⟩
		(Insert after line pointer.)

Leave editor		
Saving changes	*EX$$	⟩ w fn ⟨CR⟩ ⟩ q ⟨CR⟩
Discarding changes	*^C	⟩ q ⟨CR⟩ ? ⟩ q ⟨CR⟩
Pointer movement		
Beginning of buffer	*B$$	⟩ 1 ⟨CR⟩
End of buffer	*/$$	⟩ $ ⟨CR⟩
Down n lines	*nA$$	⟩ +n ⟨CR⟩
Up n lines	*−nA$$	⟩ −n ⟨CR⟩
Forward n char.	*nJ$$	Not available
Backward n char.	*−nJ$$	Not available
Position at entry	Before first char.	At last line
Display		
Buffer	*B/L$$	⟩ 1,$p ⟨CR⟩
n lines	*nL$$	⟩ .,.+n−1p ⟨CR⟩
Delete		
Forward n lines	*nK$$	⟩ .,.+n−1d ⟨CR⟩
Forward n char.	*nD$$	Not available
Backward n char.	*−nD$$	Not available
Find string		
	*string$$	⟩ /string/ ⟨CR⟩
Substitute string		
	*old$=cnew$$	⟩ s/old/new/ ⟨CR⟩
Read/write second file		
Read into buffer	*ER fn2$R$$	⟩ r fn2 ⟨CR⟩
Write buffer to file	*EW fn2B/W$$	⟩ w fn2 ⟨CR⟩

Here filename.extension is the file that you wish to create or modify. If it does not exist on your account, it will be created and you will be informed that it is a new file. The symbol ⟨CR⟩ means to press the RETURN key. The asterisk * is the EDT "command prompt," signifying that EDT is waiting for your command. Available commands are discussed below. The computer response is indicated by underlining.

B.2.2 Leaving EDT

After the file has been created or modified and you wish to leave EDT, one of two commands can be entered—EXIT or QUIT. If you use EXIT (EX is an acceptable abbreviation), the edited file will be saved, and control will be returned to the operating system. Using QUIT (which cannot be abbreviated) results in a return to the operating system *without saving the edited file*. This is used when for some reason you wish to abandon the changes you have made in the file.

Normally, then, an EDT session looks like this.

```
EDT     MYFILE.MAC
*
```

(Various editing operations)

```
* EX
READY
```

B.2.3 Creating a New File with EDT

To create a new file, enter the EDT command line with a new file name, including its extension. Then, to the first command prompt (*) enter the INSERT command (abbreviated I). This sequence is shown below, along with the computer response (underlined).

```
EDT     MYPROG.MAC     ⟨CR⟩
input file does not exist
[EOB]
* I ⟨CR⟩
```

Here, ⟨CR⟩ means carriage return, i.e., the RETURN key. The response tells us that MYPROG.MAC does not exist on the logged-on account, which is to be expected when you are creating a new file. The [EOB], meaning end-of-buffer, is further indication that the file is empty.

After the I⟨CR⟩, EDT awaits entry of the file. It is said to be in insert mode. You can then enter each line, followed by a ⟨CR⟩. After the last line is entered, enter a control-Z (^Z) to leave the insert mode and return to command mode.

Upon reaching the command mode, you can either edit the lines just entered (see Section B.2.4), or leave EDT with an EXIT command, saving the file (see Section B.2.2).

The entire file creation sequence is shown below. A ⟨CR⟩ is required after each user input.

```
EDT      MYPROG.MAC
input file does not exist
[EOB]
*I
            .TITLE MYPROG
START:
            CLR   R0
            INC   R0
            HALT
            .END START
^Z
*EX
READY
```

It must be observed that while in the insert mode, *everything* that is typed is accepted as text without regard to its meaning. This means that EDT will not respond to commands. A very common and frustrating error when working with an editor is to be in insert mode without realizing it, and expect EDT to respond to its normal commands. In addition to the frustration of "nothing working right," when you finally do realize what has happened and leave the insert mode, you find that all of your attempts have been entered as text into your file! To avoid such difficulties, be sure to issue ^Z when you have finished inserting new lines.

B.2.4 Modifying a File with EDT

EDT provides several commands that can be used to modify a file. However, before we discuss these, we need to discuss some general aspects of EDT. First, note that the file is viewed as a collection of lines of text. When EDT is entered, each of these lines is given a number, beginning with 1 for the first line. These line numbers are temporary and are removed upon completion of the editing session. While editing, however, they provide a convenient means for referring to particular lines in the file. EDT also uses what is called the "current line pointer." At any instant this pointer has the value of the "current" line number. It is represented by the period (.) in some commands. The line numbers and current line pointer play an important role in the use of many of the EDT commands discussed below.

Most EDT commands have the form

Command range

where "command" is the name or abbreviation for the command, and "range" indicates the lines that the command is to be applied to. In general, range is of the form

start:finish

or

start#number

If the : and # are missing, only the line numbered start is affected. As a simple example of this, consider the DELETE command, abbreviated D. To delete line 3 of the file being edited, enter

```
*D 3
1    line deleted
        4              (Next line is displayed here.)
*
```

As the response indicates, line 1 was deleted and the current line pointer is advanced to line 4. The following examples show forms of the range specification.

```
* D   3:10           deletes lines 3 through 10.
* D   .              deletes current (. is optional).
* D   3#4            deletes four lines beginning with line 3.
* D   .#4            deletes four lines beginning with current line.
* D   BEFORE         deletes all lines in file before current line.
* D   REST           deletes current line and all following lines in the file.
* D   WHOLE          deletes entire file.
```

Although these examples of the various range specifications are shown using the DELETE command, they work equally well for all other commands that require a range specification. Note in particular that the period (.) range specification means the current line. Thus to display the current line and the next 24, enter the TYPE command as follows.

```
*T  .#24              types 24 lines beginning with the current line.
```

With the understanding above, we can now look at the EDT commands. These are grouped below into major categories according to their general purpose. Abbreviations are used instead of the full command word. Also, several common range specifications are shown for each command.

B.2.4.1 Commands to move current-line pointer

```
*%BE                 moves to beginning of file (first line).†
*%E                  moves to end of file (EOB mark).†
*F"KZW"              finds the next line containing KZW searching down.
                        Does not print the line.
*"KZW"               finds next line containing KZW searching down. Prints
                        the line.†
*+5                  moves five lines down.†
*-5                  moves five lines up.†
*10                  moves to line 10.†
```

---

† Note that these are actually forms of the TYPE command with the null abbreviation.

B.2.4.2 Commands to display the file

*T .#3	displays three lines beginning with the current line.
(.#3)	
*T WHOLE	displays entire file.
(%WH)	
*T "KZW"	displays next line containing "KZW".
("KZW")	

Note that the TYPE command can be abbreviated with T, or with nothing at all, i.e., just a carriage return, called the "null" abbreviation. This leads to the shorter form of the instructions above as shown in parentheses. When this is done, however, words like WHOLE and BEGIN or their abbreviations must be preceded by %.

B.2.4.3 Commands to alter lines in the file

*D	deletes current line.
*D .#5	deletes five lines beginning with current line.
*S/CAT/DOG/.:"CAT"	substitutes DOG for next occurrence of CAT. This is a combined search and replace.
*S/MOV/ADD/	substitutes ADD for MOV only in current line.†
*S/MOV/MOVB/.#4	substitutes MOVB for all occurrences of MOV in four lines beginning with the current line.†
*S/HALT/.EXIT/WH	substitutes .EXIT for all occurrences of HALT in the whole file.†
*I	switches to insert mode. All subsequent text is entered into the file *before* the current line. Return to command mode with ^Z.
*R	deletes current line *and* enters insert mode. All subsequent text entry replaces current line. Return to command mode with ^Z.

B.2.4.4 Commands to read or write files

*INC file.ext	reads contents of file.ext into file being edited; lines read will be inserted before current line. (INC is an abbreviation for INCLUDE.)
*WR file.ext 2:4	writes lines 2 through 4 of file being edited into file.ext. Edited file is not changed.

B.2.4.5 Commands to reorder lines

*M 7:20 TO 5	moves lines 7 through 20 to immediately before line 5; deletes them from original position.
*M 7#5	moves five lines beginning with line 7 to immediately before current line; deletes them from original position.

---

† Note that other characters, e.g.. " or $, can be used instead of / in the SUBSTITUTE command. This is necessary when one of the strings contains a /. For example, S "A/B"B/A".

<u>*</u>CO 7:20 TO 5   copies lines 7 through 20 to immediately before line 5
                                              without deleting them from their current position.

B.2.4.6 Commands to leave EDT

*EX   SAVES or REPLACES the permanent file with the edited
                                              file and leaves EDT.

*QUIT   leaves EDT *without* saving modified file. (All changes
                                              are lost.)

Note that whenever EDT is entered with an existing file, a backup file of the
same name, but with extension .BAK, is automatically created. This is important
if it is necessary to recover the previous version after leaving EDT with the EX
command.

B.2.4.7 Version 1.0 of EDT

Some PDP-11 installations may use Version 1.0 of EDT. The subset of commands
discussed in this appendix are only slightly different in this earlier version. The
differences are

1. The # character used in range specifications is a semicolon in Version 1. For example
   D 3;4 instead of D 3#4.
2. The keywords (or abbreviations) BEGIN, END, REST, TO, and WHILE must be
   preceded by % in Version 1.
3. The read and write commands for Version 1 are

   INC/FI:file.ext
   WR 2:4/FI:file.ext

4. In Version 1.0, the command

   S/CAT/DOG/

   will do a combined search and replace, whereas in Version 2.0 it does the change
   in the current line only.
5. Version 1.0 numbers lines in increments of 10, and does not number inserted lines
   until EDT is reentered. Version 2.0 numbers in increments of 1, and numbers inserted
   lines with digits to right of a decimal point, e.g., 5.1, 5.2.

B.3 EDIT and TECO [RT-11]

EDIT and TECO are editors commonly available on RT-11 systems. Generally
speaking, TECO is a more powerful editor than EDIT. However, at the level
of detail considered here they are substantially the same. Both are *character*-
oriented editors, meaning that the file is viewed as a collection of characters,
and most commands operate on characters. The pointer, sometimes called dot(.),
always points to a position *between* two characters. Upon entry, dot is before
the first character in the file, and various commands cause it to move forward

or backward in the file. Most commands operate on particular characters or strings of characters, and dot usually identifies the beginning of the range over which the command applies.

EDIT and TECO also recognize groups of characters in the file called *lines* and *pages*. A line is defined as a string of characters ending in the carriage return and linefeed characters. (Linefeed is inserted automatically when ⟨CR⟩ is pressed.) Some commands operate on lines. A page is a group of characters (possibly divided into lines) ending with a form-feed character (octal 14). Small files usually comprise a single page. If the file is larger, the editor works on a page at a time. File read commands cause a page to be loaded from the input file into a region of memory called the "buffer." Changes or additions made by the editor actually affect only the contents of this buffer, until a command is given to write the buffer, as a page of characters, into the output file. For the small programs usually encountered by beginning programmers, the entire file fits on one page, so that the terms "file" and "page" are synonymous, and EDIT or TECO can load the entire file into the buffer.

Note that an editor called EDIT is also available on many RSTS/E and RSX-11M systems. This editor is similar to, but not identical with, the EDIT discussed here. TECO is available on RSTS/E and RSX-11M, but has slightly different commands for entry. EDT is the recommended editor for RSTS/E and RSX-11M.

A short summary of EDIT and TECO commands is presented in Table B.1. While these should be sufficient for elementary usage, one should consult the users' manuals for a more complete list. For EDIT, consult Section 5 of the *RT-11 System User's Guide* (DEC order no. AA–5279B–TC), or for TECO the *TECO PDP-11 User's Guide* (DEC order no. AA–5530–TC).

As can be seen from Table B.1, the formats of EDIT and TECO commands are almost identical, differing primarily in the command characters. For example, J refers to the beginning of the TECO buffer, while B has this meaning in EDIT. Because of this similarity, many of the examples below are shown for EDIT only. With the aid of Table B.1, little difficulty will be had in carrying out similar operations using TECO.

B.3.1 Entering EDIT or TECO

The command line for entering EDIT to create a new file on RT-11 is

```
.EDIT/CREATE fn.ext ⟨CR⟩                          [EDIT—create new file]
*
_
```

This brings up the EDIT command prompt, *, as shown above. Here fn.ext is the file to be created. If the file already exists and you wish to modify it, use

```
.EDIT fn.ext ⟨CR⟩                                 [EDIT—edit existing file]
*R$$
*
_
```

where $ stands for the ESCape key. The R is a command that causes the contents (actually only the first page) of the named file to be read into the buffer for editing.

The corresponding commands for TECO are

 .R TECO ⟨CR⟩   [TECO—create new file]
 *EW fn.ext $$
 *

or to edit an existing file

 .R TECO ⟨CR⟩   [TECO—existing file]
 *EB fn.ext $Y$$

The EW command tells TECO to open the named file so that the TEXT added to the buffer can be written into it as discussed below. For the case of an existing file, the EB command is used to open the named file for input and output. The Y command (given in the same line) causes the contents of fn.ext to be read into the buffer.

B.3.2 Leaving EDIT or TECO

After having added or modified the text in the buffer, you usually want to write it to the output file and return to the operating system. To do this with either EDIT or TECO, enter

 *EX$$ [EDIT, TECO]

If you wish to discard your changes, i.e., to leave the original input file unchanged, enter

 *^C   [EDIT]

or

 *^C   [TECO]
 *^C

B.3.3 Creating a New File with EDIT or TECO

EDIT and TECO have the same commands for entering the "insert text" mode, namely,

 *I text ⟨CR⟩   [EDIT, TECO—enter insert mode]
 text ⟨CR⟩

 .

 .

 text ⟨CR⟩
 $$ [EDIT, TECO—return to command mode]
 *

Thus to create a MACRO-11 source file using EDIT, enter the following sequence, with ⟨CR⟩ at the end of each line.

```
.EDIT/CREATE MYPROG.MAC                        [Enter EDIT]
*I            .TITLE MYPROG                     [Enter insert mode]
START:
        CLR     R0
        INC     R0
        HALT
        .END        START
$$                                              [Leave insert mode]
*EX$$
                                                [RT-11 prompt]
.
```

For TECO, this would look the same except for the entry sequence, which is discussed above.

Note that once in insert mode, everything you enter is accepted as text until $$ is entered. This can create some confusion if you do not remember that you are in insert mode and expect the editor commands to be obeyed. If commands are not being executed, enter $$ to be sure you leave insert mode.

B.3.4   EDIT and TECO Command Structure and Conventions

Both EDIT and TECO provide a number of commands that can be used to manipulate the contents of a text file. These commands have the general form

n command string $

Here command is a one- or two-character command word recognized by the editor. A summary of these commands is shown in Table B.1. Note that the command word for a particular action is not always the same for EDIT and TECO. Some commands require an argument called string after the command word. The preceding n indicates the range of characters or lines over which the command is to be executed. The $ represents the ESC (escape) key, *not* the $ key. This symbol is displayed whenever ESC is pressed, however.

As an example, suppose you wish to delete the third and fourth lines of a file being edited by EDIT. To do this, we use the "advance line" command A and "delete line" command K.

```
*2A$$                          [EDIT—advance pointer two lines]
*2K$$                          [EDIT—delete two lines beginning at pointer]
*
.
```

The example above assumed that the pointer was at the beginning of the buffer, as it is upon entry.

Several EDIT and TECO commands can be typed in one line, then all can be executed. To do this, each command is terminated by $, and the last entered command is followed by $$. For example,

```
*2A$2K$$                                               [EDIT]
*
.
```

accomplishes the same objective as above. In general, a single $ merely marks the end of a command; the second $ causes all pending commands to execute, and the command prompt to be displayed.

The n in a command can also refer to a number of *characters*, depending on the command. For example, to delete the 16th and 17th characters in the fourth line, we could, using EDIT, issue the commands

*B$$	[EDIT—place pointer before first char. in buffer]
*3A$$	[EDIT—advance pointer three lines]
*15J$$	[EDIT—advance pointer fifteen characters]
*2D$$	[EDIT—delete two characters]

More compactly, this could be entered

*B$3A$15J$2D$$ [EDIT]

Here we demonstrate the EDIT commands B that places the pointer *before* the first character in the file, nA that advances n *lines*, nJ that advances n *characters*, and nD that deletes n *characters*. There are corresponding commands in TECO as shown in Table B.1.

The n preceding a command can be replaced by special symbols for some commands. For example, because B means beginning of buffer and / means end of buffer in EDIT, one can display the entire buffer by

*B/L$$ [EDIT—display entire buffer]

The symbol H means the same as B/ if TECO is used. Also, the symbol 0 (zero) refers to characters between the beginning of the current line and the pointer, and blank refers to those between the pointer and the end of the current line. Thus

*0L$$ [EDIT]

prints the current line up to the pointer, and

*L$$ [EDIT]

prints the rest of the line. This feature helps to see where the pointer is at any time.

B.3.5 Search (Find String) and Substitute String Commands
Search commands are among the most important commands in an editor because they allow rapid location to the text to be changed. In EDIT, the command

*GRABBIT$$ [EDIT]

will find the next occurrence of the character string "RABBIT", beginning the search at the current pointer location. The pointer will be left immediately after the T. Naturally, any string can be the target of the search.

Another useful command is the substitute string command. For example, suppose you wished to change the first occurrence of MOV in your file to MOVB. The following commands will do this in EDIT.

```
*B$$                                   [EDIT—pointer to beginning of buffer]
*GMOV$ = CMOVB$$                       [EDIT—replace MOV with MOVB]
```

This says, "Get MOV and Change it to MOVB." The preceding B$$ ensured that the search began at the beginning of the file.

B.3.6 File Reads and Writes

As noted earlier, EDIT and TECO operate on the text buffer, rather than on your file. Text can be read from any file into the buffer, and written from the buffer into any file. It is necessary, however, to first open the files. The EDIT commands for open and reading are

```
*ER fn$$                                     [EDIT—open fn for read]
*R$$                                   [EDIT—read from fn into buffer]
*
-
```

The R$ command reads a page from the file opened by the ER command, and places it in the buffer. Note that when EDIT is entered with the command EDIT fn, the file fn is automatically opened for read and writing. A subsequent ER command will close the currently open read file and open another, allowing the text buffer to receive text from more than one file.

The text buffer, or portions of it, can also be written out to files. The EW command opens a file for writing, and the W command writes into it. For example, the EDIT commands

```
*EW fn$$                                                        [EDIT]
*20W$$
*
-
```

cause 20 lines, beginning with the current line, to be written to fn. If issued again, the EW command will close the current write file and open another, so that many different files can be written to. Note that the EX command automatically writes the entire buffer to the current write file before leaving EDIT. Also, entering EDIT with EDIT/CREATE fn or with EDIT fn opens fn for write, so that the EW command does not normally have to be used; its principal use is to write portions of the buffer to separate files.

Reading and writing files from TECO is like EDIT except that it is necessary to close the current write file before another can be opened. The command for doing this is EF. An example will clarify this. Suppose you wish to load the buffer from file M1, append the file M2, and write the entire buffer to both M3 and M4. The following commands do this.

```
.R TECO
*ER M1 $Y$$                                      [TECO—open and read M1]
*ER M2 $A$$                                    [TECO—open and append M2]
```

```
*EW M3 $HPW$$          [TECO—open and write to M3]
*EF $$                 [TECO—close M3]
*EW M4 $HPW$$          [TECO—open and write to M4]
*EF$$                  [TECO—close M4]
*EK$$                  [TECO—kill the buffer]
*^C                    [Leave TECO]
*^C
```

In this sequence, observe that PW is the file write command and H stands for the entire buffer. To write only selected characters, use

   *.,. + nPW

that writes n characters beginning with the one following the pointer into the currently open output file.

B.3.7 Moving Lines

Groups of lines can be moved from one place in the buffer to another by using the SAVE (S) and UNSAVE (U) commands. The block of lines to be moved is first saved by setting the pointer to the beginning of the first line to be moved and issuing the S command. For example,

   *4S$$ [EDIT—put four lines in SAVE buffer]

saves four lines beginning with the current line in the "SAVE buffer." Now suppose you wish to place these four lines immediately *before* the tenth line in the buffer. The following commands will do this.

   *B$9A$$ [EDIT—position pointer to line 10]
   *U$$ [EDIT—copy saved lines at pointer]

Note that the U command places the saved lines *at* the pointer. Because the pointer was positioned before the first character in the tenth line, this places it *before* line 10. The saved lines remain in the SAVE buffer until the command

   *0U$$ [EDIT—kill SAVE buffer]

is given. If the lines are not wanted in their *original* location, they can be deleted using the K command.

B.4 *ed* (The UNIX System)

The UNIX system text editor is called **ed.** It is a relatively powerful editor that is line-oriented; i.e., operations are done on lines rather than on individual characters. Lines have automatically assigned numbers that are referred to by the commands. Also, there is a line pointer, called dot (.), that always points to the "current" line. Most commands operate on the current line if no other specification is given.

Like most editors, *ed* actually operates on text in its "buffer," rather than directly on a file. Thus to edit an existing file, it is necessary to read it into the buffer, and upon completion, the modified buffer must be written out to a file.

A short summary of *ed* commands is shown in Table B.1. While these should be sufficient for elementary usage, the document, *A Tutorial Introduction to the UNIX Text Editor*, in the *UNIX User's Manual* can be consulted for more information and examples. The following discussion shows the basic principles of usage. Underlining indicates computer response.

B.4.1 Entering *ed*
To invoke *ed*, issue the command

   ed ⟨CR⟩   [*ed*—enter/create]
   ⟩

or

   ed fn ⟨CR⟩   [*ed*—enter/edit]
   ⟩

The latter command reads an existing file into the buffer upon entry to *ed*. This is the normal way to begin editing of an existing file. Use the first command if you are creating a file. Upon entry, *ed* displays its command prompt, ⟩.

Before leaving *ed*, you must decide whether or not to keep the results of your editing session. If you do want to keep them, you must first write the buffer to a file. To do this, use the write command, **w.**

   ⟩ w fn ⟨CR⟩

This says, "Write the buffer contents to file fn." If you entered *ed* with *ed* fn, then you can simply enter

   ⟩ w ⟨CR⟩

and *ed* will assume that you wish to save the modified file under the same name as the original.

After having written the buffer to a file, leave *ed* by the quit command

   ⟩ q ⟨CR⟩

This returns you to the UNIX system command level.

If you do not wish to save the results of your editing, just issue **q** without doing a write. This will cause *ed* to respond with a question mark (?), saying, in effect, "Are you sure?" A second *q* will then get you out of *ed*.

   ⟩ q   [*ed*—quit]
   ?   ["Are you sure?" prompt]
   ⟩ q   [*ed*—leave for sure]

B.4.2 Creating a New File with *ed*

The complete sequence for creating a file with *ed* is shown below.

```
ed 〈CR〉
〉 a 〈CR〉
              .title myprog 〈CR〉
start: 〈CR〉
              clr      r0 〈CR〉
              inc      r0 〈CR〉
              halt 〈CR〉
              end      start 〈CR〉
. 〈CR〉
〉 w myprog.mll 〈CR〉
〉 q 〈CR〉
```

The commands *a* and *w* are discussed further below.

B.4.3 *ed* Command Structure

Ed provides a number of commands that allow files to be created or modified. The general form of these commands is

start,end command parameter 〈CR〉

For example, the command-letter *p* means to print. Therefore to print lines 3 through 10 in the buffer, we issue

〉 3,10p 〈CR〉

Here 3 is the starting line number, 10 is the ending line number, and *p* is the command letter.

The print command does not take a parameter. On the other hand, the write command uses a parameter to specify the file to be written to. Other *ed* commands also use parameters.

B.4.4 Special Characters for start and end

When specifying the start and end line numbers in *ed* commands, certain special characters may be used. These are

Special Characters	Meaning
.	Current line number
$	End of buffer
1	First line in buffer

Thus to print the entire file, you can enter

〉 1,$p 〈CR〉

or to print the text from the current line to the end of the buffer

⟩ .,$p ⟨CR⟩

These characters can also be used with other *ed* commands.

B.4.5 Moving Dot
The line pointer in the *ed* buffer is called dot. Whenever a file is read into the buffer, dot is placed at the last line in the file. Because most commands use dot as the line at which the command is to be done if no other line number is given, it is sometimes necessary to move the dot. This can be done with the commands

⟩ +n ⟨CR⟩	advances dot n lines, i.e., down.
⟩ −n ⟨CR⟩	moves dot backwards n lines, i.e., up.
⟩ 1 ⟨CR⟩	places dot at first line.
⟩ $ ⟨CR⟩	places dot after last line.

Dot is also moved by many other commands. For example, the search command (see below) sets dot at the line where the target string was found. The current value of dot, i.e., the number of the current line, can be found by

⟩ .= ⟨CR⟩

B.4.6 Displaying the Buffer
All or part of the buffer can be displayed at the terminal with the print command. For example, to print the entire buffer, use

⟩ 1,$p ⟨CR⟩

or to print the current and next n lines enter

⟩ .,.+np ⟨CR⟩

Actually, print is the "implied" command if just ⟨CR⟩ is entered. Thus

⟩ ⟨CR⟩

advances the pointer and displays the then-current line. Because it advances dot, continued ⟨CR⟩s will display line after line.

B.4.7 Deleting Lines
The *ed* command to delete one or more lines is **d.** For example, to delete lines 4 through 16, enter

⟩ 4,16d ⟨CR⟩

or to delete the current line and the next n lines, enter

⟩ .,.+nd ⟨CR⟩

To delete every line between the current line and the end, enter

⟩ .,$d ⟨CR⟩

Everything *above* the current line can be deleted by

⟩ 1,.−1d ⟨CR⟩

Note that *ed* renumbers lines after deleting.

B.4.8 Adding Lines to the Buffer

There are two commands for adding lines to the buffer, append, **a,** and insert, **i.** The only difference is where the new lines are placed. The append command places new lines *after* the current line, i.e., after dot, whereas the insert command places them before dot. For example, suppose you wished to add more lines after line 6. Enter

⟩ 6 ⟨CR⟩		puts dot at line 6.
	mov r1,x	prints line 6.
⟩ a ⟨CR⟩		enters append mode.
	add r2,r1 ⟨CR⟩	enter new line.
	clr r3 ⟨CR⟩	enter new line.
. ⟨CR⟩		leaves append mode.
⟩ 6,8p ⟨CR⟩		prints line 6 and new lines.
	mov r1,x	
	add r2,r1	
	clr r3	
⟩		

Note that *ed* renumbered the file accounting for the new lines.

The *a* command works well except when you wish to add lines *before* the first line. This can be done using the *i* command. For example,

⟩ 1 ⟨CR⟩		sets dot to first line.
⟩ i ⟨CR⟩		enters insert mode.
	clr r3 ⟨CR⟩	new line.
	mov r1,−(sp) ⟨CR⟩	new line.
. ⟨CR⟩		leaves insert mode.
⟩		

This results in the two new lines being placed as the first two lines in the buffer.

Once the append or insert mode is entered, all subsequent keyboard entry is placed into the buffer until that mode is exited. Return to the *ed* command mode is done with the sequence

. ⟨CR⟩

Often users who forget to leave append or insert mode after entering their text wonder why *ed* is not responding to commands. Note that commands are treated as text to be added to the buffer until the append or insert mode is exited. If *ed* does not respond to your commands, do a .⟨CR⟩ to be sure you are not adding text to the buffer. If you are already in the *ed* command mode, the dot just prints the current line.

B.4.9 Search and Substitute String Commands

The search command allows an arbitrary string to be found in the file, and the substitute command causes one string to be replaced by another. These are among the more important commands in any editor.

In order to search for a string, enter

⟩ /string/⟨CR⟩

This will cause dot to be moved to the line with the next occurrence of "string" in it. If you wish to search for the *next* line containing string, just enter

⟩ //⟨CR⟩

This works because *ed* remembers what you searched for last. Also, note that *ed* searches forward from dot and starts over at the top if necessary. A ? is reported if the string is not found. Another useful extension in search is printing all lines that contain string. This is executed as follows.

⟩ g/string/p ⟨CR⟩

There are some characters that have special significance when searching for a string. These are

Special Characters	Meaning
.	Any character
∧	Beginning of a line
$	End of a line
[]	Used to denote classes of characters
*	Repetition
\	Treat next char. as "nonspecial"

Because of the special significance of ., if you enter

⟩ /6.29/ ⟨CR⟩

you will find things like 6A29 and 6229 in addition to 6.29 because . means *any* character. Going on, the command

⟩ /∧string/ ⟨CR⟩

finds only an occurrence of string that starts a line, and

⟩ /string$/ ⟨CR⟩

finds the next occurrence of string that ends a line. The command

⟩ /[0123456789]/ ⟨CR⟩

finds the next occurrence of any decimal digit.

Often you may want to change one string to another. This is done with the substitute command. For example, to change the first occurrence of r0 to r1 in the current line, enter

⟩ s/r0/r1/⟨CR⟩

The first string, R0 in this case, is changed to the second. To do this replacement in *every occurrence* in the current line, enter

⟩ s/r0/r1/g ⟨CR⟩

where **g** stands for "global" change. If you want to change *every* occurrence of string 1 in the next ten lines to string 2, enter

⟩ .,10s/string1/string2/g ⟨CR⟩

If you wish to see each line changed (not a bad idea), enter instead

⟩ .,10g/string1/s/string1/string2/gp ⟨CR⟩

This makes use of the global command, *g*, which is in general

⟩ m,ng/string/command ⟨CR⟩

and means to do *command* in every line from m to n containing string.

The search and substitute commands can be combined. Thus to find the first occurrence of end and change it to end1, enter

⟩ /end/s/end/end1/ ⟨CR⟩

In effect, the result of the search becomes the line number for the substitute command. This works in a more general sense also. That is, any place a line number is needed, a "context search expression" can be used. For example, to delete three lines *following* the next occurrence of mov, enter

⟩ /mov/+1,3d ⟨CR⟩

where /mov/+1 is a context search expression meaning one line beyond the next one containing mov.

B.4.10 Reading and Writing Files from *ed*

As discussed above, *ed* operates on text in a buffer. This text can be created in *ed* using the append or insert commands, or can be read from one or more files. When *ed* is entered using the UNIX system command line

ed junk ⟨CR⟩
46
⟩

the contents of junk are automatically read into the buffer. The 46 is a report that this file has 46 characters in it.

There is also a file read command in *ed*. Therefore if you wished to read a second file, say junk2, into the buffer, you could enter

⟩ r junk2 ⟨CR⟩
15
⟩

This causes the entire contents of junk2 to be added to the buffer. The entry junk2 is added at the end of the buffer if no line number is given. However, if we enter

⟩ 3r junk2 ⟨CR⟩

junk2 is added after line 3. To add it before the current contents of the buffer, enter

⟩ 0r junk2 ⟨CR⟩

Files can also be written from *ed*. To do this, use the command

⟩ n,mw fn ⟨CR⟩

This writes buffer lines n through m into the file named fn. If n,m is omitted, the entire buffer is written.

Note that n and m can be context expressions. so that you could enter

⟩ /.macro/,/.endm/w mac2.mll ⟨CR⟩

that would write all lines from and including the one with .macro to and including the one containing .endm into mac2.mll.

B.4.11 Moving Lines with *ed*

The move command, **m,** can be used to move lines from one point to another in the *ed* buffer. Its general form is

⟩ start,end m to ⟨CR⟩

where *start* and *end* are the line numbers of the first and last lines in the group to be moved, and *to* is the line number where it is to be placed. The entire group is inserted *after* the line numbered *to*, and is deleted from its original location. Note that the line numbers can be replaced with context expressions. (See Section B.4.9.)

C Debugging Tools (ODT and Adb)

C.1 The Purpose of Debugging Tools

MACRO-11 programs that are not working properly are difficult to debug because errors are often caused by misunderstanding of the action of instructions, directives, or addressing modes. A powerful method of debugging such a program is a system-supplied program that allows you to execute your program up to some preselected "breakpoint," and then to stop to allow examination of the contents of each register and memory location. **ODT** is such a system program available under RSTS/E, RT-11, and RSX-11M. A similar program for the UNIX system environment is **adb.**

Many commands are provided by debugging tools, including those for setting breakpoints, running the program, examining locations, modifying locations and registers, and single-step execution. Because these programs allow memory locations and registers to be examined and set, they also can be used as a primitive input/output means while learning MACRO-11.

C.2 Using ODT [RSTS/E, RSX-11M, RT-11]

To use ODT, you link it to your MACRO-11 program with LINK. Then when you issue a RUN command for your program, ODT "takes over." From that point on, you issue ODT commands, such as to set breakpoints, run the program, and examine contents. To use ODT effectively, you will need to look at the MACRO listing of your program in order to determine addresses.

ODT is available under the RT-11, RSX-11M, and RSTS/E operating systems. There are only minor differences among these operating systems with respect to ODT, and these are discussed at the appropriate points below.

C.2.1 Linking with ODT

Before ODT can be used, it first has to be linked to your MACRO-11 object file. In the following it is therefore assumed that you have a MACRO output file such as PROG1.OBJ. To link with ODT, enter the sequence below. Computer response is indicated by underlining.

```
RUN    $LINK    ⟨CR⟩                                        [RSTS/E, RT-11]
*PROG1.SAV,PROG1.MAP = PROG1.OBJ,ODT/T    ⟨CR⟩
```

The system then responds

```
Transfer Symbol?
```

to which you respond

```
O.ODT    ⟨CR⟩
*^Z
```

394

<u>MCR</u>)RUN $TKB   ⟨CR⟩   [RSX-11M]
<u>TKB</u>)PROG1/DA,PROG1 = SUBLIB,PROG1 ⟨CR⟩
<u>TKB</u>) ^Z
<u>MCR</u>)

At this point you have an executable file named PROG1.SAV [RSTS/E, RT-11] or PROG1.TSK [RSX-11M] that consists of your program linked with ODT. Naturally, PROG1 could be replaced by any MACRO-11 file name.

C.2.2 Running ODT
To execute under control of ODT, enter

RUN   PROG1   ⟨CR⟩

where PROG1 is the run file produced by linking with ODT. The file extension is assumed and need not be given. The response will be

<u>ODT   RO1.04</u>
*

It now awaits your ODT command. Normally, you next want to set breakpoints, or examine memory locations. The computer response will be slightly different for RSX-11M. For example, the ODT prompt is an underscore (_) rather than an asterisk (*).

C.2.3 Leaving ODT
Returning to the operating system can be accomplished in two ways. The first way is to allow your program to execute to a HALT instruction. (See Section C.2.8.) The second way is to enter ^C. For RSTS/E, this will always work even if your program gets into an infinite loop while executing under ODT. For RSX-11M, the ^C gets you the ODT prompt; entering X will then cause exit to the operating system.

C.2.4 Addressing When Using ODT
When using ODT, in this book, we have always worked in terms of the absolute addresses of various instructions and data in the program. These absolute addresses are found by adding the *load point* addresses of the module under consideration to the addresses shown in the MACRO-11 listing (the .LST file). This address calculation is discussed in Section 15.4.3. For many cases, the load point address is 1000_8, because under RSTS/E and RT-11 this is the size of the space automatically reserved by LINK (for stack and other uses) and placed in memory before your program. This makes the addition process simple mental arithmetic, and MACRO-11 listing addresses are easily related to the absolute addresses needed by ODT. When the load-point address is a less convenient number for addition, it is easier to make use of the *relocation calculation* features of ODT described in Section C.2.11.

C.2.5 Examining and Changing Memory Location Contents
A frequent use of ODT is to examine the contents of locations in central memory. To do this, after the command prompt (* under RSTS/E or _ under RSX-11M) enter the address of the location to be examined, followed by /. For example,

```
*1000/012705    ⟨CR⟩
*
```

The computer responds with the contents, in this case 012705, shown in octal. In order to look at several sequential locations, enter linefeed ⟨LF⟩ instead of ⟨CR⟩ after the displayed contents.

```
*1000/012705     ⟨LF⟩
001002/ 010504   ⟨LF⟩
001004/ 060503   ⟨LF⟩
       .
       .
       .
```

This is a good way to see exactly how your program is stored in memory. Just continue pressing ⟨LF⟩ until the HALT instruction is displayed. If you wish to see the contents of a location displayed as a *byte* rather than as a word, use \ instead of /. For example,

```
*1056\ 124 = T    ⟨LF⟩
001057\110 = H    ⟨LF⟩
001060\111 = I    ⟨LF⟩
       .
       .
       .
```

Note that the contents are shown in 8-bit octal representation, and as the equivalent ASCII character, if it is printable. Also, the automatic incrementation caused by ⟨LF⟩ is by 1 instead of 2, so each successive byte is displayed.

Sometimes you will want to change the contents of a location. To do this, enter the location address and / or \ as if you were going to examine its contents. Then instead of ⟨CR⟩ or ⟨LF⟩, type the new value. For example,

```
*1000/012705 012703    ⟨CR⟩
*
```

This will change the original contents, 012705, to 012703. This provides a convenient means of making program or data changes directly to the machine code without going through source file editing and reassembling. Of course permanent changes *must* eventually be done in the source program because changes made with ODT are only temporary and in no way alter the MACRO-11 source file.

C.2.6 Examining and Changing the General Registers
The general registers, R0 through R5, SP, and PC, can also be examined and changed with ODT. The procedure is much the same as for memory locations,

except instead of the address we use $n, where n is the register number. For example, to examine the contents of R0, R1 and SP, enter the following sequence.

```
*$0/ 002607    ⟨CR⟩
*$1/ 001310    ⟨CR⟩
*$6/ 001000    ⟨CR⟩
*
-
```

If you want to examine several sequential registers, e.g., R0, R1, R2, and R3, just enter ⟨LF⟩ rather than ⟨CR⟩. For example,

```
*$0/ 002607         ⟨LF⟩    (R0)
001146 /001310      ⟨LF⟩    (R1)
001150 /001000      ⟨LF⟩    (R2)
001152 /176314      ⟨CR⟩    (R3)
*
-
```

Note that a register displayed as a result of a ⟨LF⟩ is shown with a six-digit octal number preceding the /. This is an address internal to ODT where the register contents are placed when ODT interrupts execution of your program. (The registers themselves are released for other uses.) These addresses are of no concern to the user of ODT. Under RSX-11M, ODT displays $1, $2, $3, etc., instead of these internal addresses.

To change the contents of a register, just enter the new value following the displayed value, then a ⟨LF⟩ or ⟨CR⟩. For example, to change the contents of R0, R1, R2, and R3 to 0, 10, 22, and 35, enter

```
*$0/ 002607   0       ⟨LF⟩
001146 /001310 10     ⟨LF⟩
001150 /001000 22     ⟨LF⟩
001152 /176314 35     ⟨CR⟩
*
-
```

Naturally, the new values must be entered in octal.

C.2.7 Examining the Processor Status Word (PSW)

As discussed in Section 6.4, the condition codes N, Z, V, and C are the rightmost four bits in the PSW. Sometimes it is helpful to examine these codes during debugging. To do this, enter $S followed by /. For example,

```
*$S/174012    ⟨CR⟩
```

Because only the right four bits are of interest, it is necessary only to translate the right two octal digits to binary, i.e.,

$$12_8 = 001010_2$$

This tells us that, for this example,

$$N = 1 \qquad V = 1$$
$$Z = 0 \qquad C = 0$$

C.2.8 Execution

ODT can also be used to execute your program. To do this, you need to issue the command n;G. This means "GO" starting at address n. For example, if the starting address is 1000 (as it often is under RSTS/E or RT-11), the GO command is

    * 1000;G

This will initiate the instruction execution sequence, causing instructions in your program to be executed one after the other until a 000000 (HALT instruction) is found in some word, or a "breakpoint" is encountered. (See Section C.2.9.)

Under RSTS/E and RT-11 you will not want to issue the GO command unless breakpoints have been set because if HALT is encountered, control will be returned to the *operating system,* aborting the ODT session. If this happens, you must reenter ODT if you wish to continue debugging. RSX-11M returns the ODT prompt when HALT is encountered.

C.2.9 Setting Breakpoints

Breakpoints are addresses where you wish execution to stop when your program is being executed under control of ODT. A common situation in which this is needed occurs when you wish to examine memory locations, registers, etc., after your program has executed. To do this, you need execution to stop and return to ODT command mode immediately *before* the HALT instruction in your program is reached. Otherwise, if HALT is executed under RSTS/E or RT-11, you are returned to the operating system, preventing further ODT commands. This is accomplished by setting a breakpoint at the address of the HALT instruction.

Breakpoints are set by giving the command n;B where n is the address of the breakpoint. For example, if you wish execution to stop before execution of the instruction at location 1020, issue the command

    *1020;B
    *

A subsequent n;G command will now be terminated before the instruction at 1020 is fetched.

Sometimes you may want to have the program stop at several different points to allow examination of intermediate results. Multiple breakpoints and the proceed command (;P) are provided for this purpose. Up to eight breakpoints (0–7) can be set by repeated use of the n;B command. For example, suppose you wish to set breakpoints at 1020, 1030, and 1050

    *1020;B   sets breakpoint 0.
    *1030;B   sets breakpoint 1.
    *1050;B   sets breakpoint 2.
    *

Execution is then initiated by the n;G command. It will stop before executing the instruction at 1020. Execution is resumed by issuing the ;P command. Thus with the breakpoints above, we would have

```
*1000;G                   initiates execution at 1000.
B0;001020                 stops before execution at 1020.
*;P                       proceeds to next breakpoint.
B1;001030                 stops before execution at 1030.
*;P                       proceeds to next breakpoint.
B2;001050                 stops before execution at 1050.
*
```

Normally, one would use other ODT commands to examine locations and/or registers before proceeding to the next breakpoint. If you issue a ;P command after stopping at the last set breakpoint, the program will execute to the HALT instruction, returning control to the operating system, or to the ODT command level if using RSX-11M.

Breakpoints can be reset by the command r;nB where r is the new address and n is the breakpoint number. For example, to reset breakpoint 2 to 1044 in the example above

```
*1044;2B
*
```

To remove a breakpoint, use ;nB. For example,

```
*;1B
*
```

will remove breakpoint 1. To remove all breakpoints, use ;B. For example,

```
*;B
*
```

will remove all breakpoints set in the example above.

In order to see the breakpoints settings, the $B/ command can be used. For example, after the breakpoints were set at 1020, 1030, and 1050, we would see

```
*$B/001020       ⟨LF⟩     shows setting of breakpoint 0.
001224/001030    ⟨LF⟩     shows setting of breakpoint 1.
001226/001050    ⟨LF⟩     shows setting of breakpoint 2.
001230/006412    ⟨LF⟩     shows that breakpoint 3 is not set.
001232/006412    ⟨CR⟩     shows that breakpoint 4 is not set.
*
```

The numbers 001224, 001226, etc., printed by RSTS/E and RT-11, are internal to ODT and have no meaning in the context of your program. The number 006412 is also an address internal to ODT that is assigned to all unset breakpoints. It will vary depending on the length of your program. It will, however, always be beyond the end of your program and therefore cannot be encountered in execution. Note that RSX-11M displays $1B, $2B, etc., instead of internal addresses.

C.2.10 Single-instruction Mode

Occasionally you may want to examine the progress of the computations after execution of each instruction. This could be done by setting breakpoints at each instruction. A more convenient way, however, is to use the single-instruction execution feature of ODT. Actually, we will see that this is somewhat of a misnomer because any number of instructions can be executed before interruption when using this feature.

For RSTS/E and RT-11 single-instruction mode uses three commands, ;kS, n;P, and ;S. The ;kS command causes entry into the single-instruction mode, and ;S returns you to normal ODT command mode. Here k has no meaning whatever, and can be any nonzero value. It just distinguishes this from the ;S command. The n;P command causes execution of the next n instructions. Breakpoints have no effect while in single-instruction mode. This usage is demonstrated below.

*;1S	enters single-instruction mode. [RSTS/E, RT-11]
*1000;G	initiates execution at 1000
B8;001002	stops before executing at 1002
*;P	executes one instruction
B8;001004	stops before executing at 1004
*3;P	executes three instructions
B8;001012	stops before executing at 1012
*;S	returns to normal ODT command mode
*	

For RSX-11M there is only one single-instruction command, namely, nS. When nS is entered, n instructions are executed. If n is omitted, 1 is assumed. Thus S ⟨CR⟩ "single-steps" through the program.

C.2.11 Relative Addresses

When the module load point (also called the offset) is a conveniently added number such as 1000_8, it is a simple matter to relate absolute addresses required by ODT to the address given in the MACRO-11 listing, which are relative to the module load point. However, when the offset is an inconvenient number such as 1254_8, the mental addition is awkward. Therefore, a different approach is suggested. This is provided by a feature of ODT that allows addresses to be stated relative to the module load point, rather than as absolute addresses.

This use of relative addresses is facilitated by eight ODT *relocation registers,* numbered 0 through 7. You must set these to the load-point addresses of the modules in the program being debugged. For single-module programs, the single load point is usually 1000_8 for RSTS/E, or 1254_8 for RSX-11M systems. If in doubt, see the load map in the .MAP file. This number should be put into relocation register 0, which is accomplished as follows.

*1254;R	sets relocation register 0 to 1254
*	

```
EXP C1   MACRO V04.00   19-FEB-83 16:09:22 PAGE 1

     1                                        .TITLE EXP C1
     2 000000   005003            START:  CLR     R3
     3 000002   012701   000034'          MOV     #A,R1
     4 000006   012711   177777           MOV     #177777,(R1)
     5 000012   012702   000020           MOV     #16.,R2
     6 000016   005703                    TST     R3
     7 000020                     LOOP:
     8 000020   006111                    ROL     (R1)
     9 000022   103001                    BCC     SKIP
    10 000024   005203                    INC     R3
    11 000026                     SKIP:
    12 000026   077204                    SOB     R2,LOOP
    13 000030   006111                    ROL     (R1)
    14 000032   000000                    HALT
    15 000034                     A:      .BLKW   1
    16 000036                             .BLKW   20
    17            000000'                 .END    START


SYMBOL TABLE

A 000034R      LOOP 000020R     SKIP 000026R      START000000R


. ABS.   000000      000
         000076      001
ERRORS DETECTED:   0
```

Figure C.1   Bit counting program used in relative addressing example.

For programs with more than one module, the load points for each of the modules receiving the most attention during the ODT session can be read from the load map (see Sec. 15.4) and placed in other relocation registers, e.g.,

<u>*2556;1R</u>   sets relocation register 1 to 2556
<u>*4224;2R</u>   sets relocation register 2 to 4224
<u>*</u>

Once the relocation registers are set, you can refer to the locations within a module using the notation n,k where n is the number of the relocation register containing the module load point, and k is the relative address read from the MACRO-11 listing.

An example will clarify this procedure. The MACRO-11 listing of a simple program is shown in Fig. C.1. When linked, it will be loaded at 1000. We wish to examine its representation in memory using ODT with relative addressing. The following sequence shows how this is done.

RUN BIT   ⟨CR⟩   BIT is the name of the program file for
                                        Fig. C.1.

<u>ODT</u> <u>R01-04</u>
<u>*1000;R</u>   sets relocation register 0.
<u>*0,0/005003</u>   ⟨LF⟩   examines rel addr 0.
<u>0,000002 /012701</u>   ⟨LF⟩   examines rel addr 2.
<u>0,000004 /001034</u> 0R=<u>0,000034</u>   ⟨LF⟩   examines *contents* of rel addr 4 as rela-
                                        tive to load point.

<u>0,000006 /012711</u>   ⟨LF⟩
<u>0,000010 /177777</u>   ⟨LF⟩

```
0,000012 /012702    ⟨LF⟩
0,000014 /000020    ⟨LF⟩
0,000016 /005703    ⟨LF⟩
0,000020 /006111    ⟨LF⟩
0,000022 /103001    ⟨LF⟩
0,000024 /005203    ⟨LF⟩
0,000026 /077204    ⟨LF⟩
0,000030 /006111    ⟨LF⟩
0,000032 /000000    ⟨LF⟩
0,000034 /000000    ⟨CR⟩
0,32;B                              sets breakpoint at rel addr 32.
*0,0;G                              executes from rel addr 0.
B0;0,000032
*0,34/177777       ⟨CR⟩            examines rel addr 34
*$3/000020
*;P
?M-HALT AT USER PC 001034
READY              [RSTS/E]        [returns the ODT prompt under RSX-11M]
```

In the first ODT command we set relocation register 0 to the load-point address, 1000. In the second command, we ask for the contents of relative location 0 using the notation 0,1. After it prints the contents, we press ⟨LF⟩ to get automatic display of the next location. Note that the next address is automatically displayed in the relative notation. These addresses and contents should be compared with those shown in the listing in Fig. C.1.

Observe that absolute addresses in the machine code, such as the 001034 in location 000004, can also be shown as relative addresses. This is done by entering nR after the displayed contents, where n is the number of the relocation register where the load-point address is stored. This is demonstrated in the fourth line of the ODT sequence in the example above.

The ODT commands discussed in this section and preceding sections are summarized in Table C.1.

TABLE C.1
Summary of ODT Commands

Examine/Change Commands			
*n/ contents ⟨CR⟩ examines word contents.		*$r/ contents new ⟨CR⟩	replaces register r contents with new.
*n \ byte = C ⟨CR⟩ examines byte contents.		*$S/ contents ⟨CR⟩	examines PSW. (N, Z, V, and C are found by converting two rightmost octal digits to binary.)
*n/ contents new ⟨CR⟩ replaces contents with new.			
*n/ contents ⟨LF⟩ examines next word contents.			
*$r/ contents ⟨CR⟩ examines register r contents.			

TABLE C.1 (cont.)

Execute/Breakpoint Commands

_*_n;B	sets breakpoint to n.
_*_;bB	removes breakpoint number b.
_*_;B	removes all breakpoints.
_*_n;bB	resets breakpoint number b to n.
_*_$B/ <u>contents</u> ⟨LF⟩	examines breakpoint settings.
_*_n;G	executes beginning at n.
_*_;P	proceeds after halting at breakpoint. (Single-instruction mode disabled.)
_*_m;P	proceeds past breakpoint m times before stopping (Single-instruction mode disabled.)

Single-instruction Mode [RSTS/E, RT-11]

_*_;1S	enables single-instruction mode. (Must also issue n;G to begin.)
_*_;P	proceeds to next instruction. (Single-instruction mode enabled.)

_*_m;P	executes m instructions before stopping. (Single-instruction mode enabled.)
_*_;S	disables single-instruction mode.

Single Instruction [RSX-11M]

_ns	executes n instructions.
_s	executes one instruction.

Addresses

_*_a;kR	sets relocation register k to load-point address a.
*k, _rel_;command	In all places where an address n is used, this notation can also be used. Contents of relocation register k is added to _rel_ to get absolute address.
_*_n/_contents_ kR = <u>k,rel</u>	Converts contents to an address relative to relocation register k

Notes:

underscore	Machine response
n	Address. Can be either absolute or in the k,rel notation.
contents	Word contents in octal
byte	Byte contents in octal
C	Byte contents as ASCII
r	General register number (0–7)
b	Breakpoint number (0–7)
m	Breakpoint or single instruction proceed count
a	Load-point address
k	Relocation register number (0–7)
rel	Address relative to load point

C.3 Using Adb [in the UNIX System]

C.3.1 Invoking and Leaving Adb

To use **adb** you must first assemble and link your program as explained in Section D.4.2. For purposes of discussion, let us assume that the program in Fig. C.1 is stored in file bit.m11. It is assembled and linked as follows.

```
$ macro -ls maclib.mll bit.mll    ⟨CR⟩
$ link bit.mll    ⟨CR⟩
$
```

Now *adb* can be executed as follows.

```
$ adb bit.out    ⟨CR⟩
```

Adb does not give any prompts or other indication of successful entry. You can confirm that it is executing by issuing any *adb* command. For example, you can have it search for ''start'' and display the contents of the corresponding instruction (in octal) by

```
start ?o    ⟨CR⟩
```

This gives the response

```
start:                          05003
```

In order to leave *adb*, issue the quit command

```
$q    ⟨CR⟩
$
```

Note that *adb* does not give a command prompt. The $ in $q is part of the quit command.

C.3.2 Adb Number Conventions and Display Formats

Adb allows numbers to be input or displayed in octal, decimal, or hex. Octal numbers are input or displayed with leading 0's. Decimal numbers do not have leading 0's. Thus

```
0143    013    07
```

are octal, whereas

```
143    13    7
```

are decimal. Hex numbers, used infrequently in MACRO-11, have a preceding #. For example,

```
#143    #13    #7    #af
```

are hex. You can request the format for output using the codes in Table C.2 (Formats for Display). For example, lowercase o asks for octal display, while c asks for character, and i asks for the mnemonics obtained by ''disassembling'' the machine code.

TABLE C.2
Summary of adb Commands

Enter adb (after linking)		
$ adb fn.out ⟨CR⟩		

Leave adb
$q

Examine/Change Location Commands

n,k?o	⟨CR⟩	displays octal contents of k words at n.
n,k?b	⟨CR⟩	displays octal contents of k bytes at n.
n,k?d	⟨CR⟩	displays decimal contents of k words at n.
n,k?c	⟨CR⟩	displays character contents of k bytes at n.
n?s	⟨CR⟩	displays string of char. from n to null.
n?w value	⟨CR⟩	changes contents of word at n to value.

(Note: See Formats for Display.)

Examine/Change Register Commands

$r	⟨CR⟩	displays PSW, PC, SP, R5, R4, R3, R2, R1 and R0. Instruction at PC is also displayed.
value>n	⟨CR⟩	changes contents of register n to value.

(Note: Applies to active process only. See Sec. C.3.5.)

Execute/Breakpoint Commands

n:b	⟨CR⟩	sets a breakpoint to address n.
n:d	⟨CR⟩	removes breakpoint at address n.
$b	⟨CR⟩	displays all breakpoints.
:r	⟨CR⟩	executes from normal entry point.
n:r	⟨CR⟩	executes from address n.
:c	⟨CR⟩	continues after halting at breakpoint.
n:c	⟨CR⟩	continues from n after halting at breakpoint.

:k	⟨CR⟩	terminates subprocess started by :r.

(Note: The :r command starts a subprocess.)

Single-instruction Command

n:s	⟨CR⟩	executes a single instruction at n.
:s	⟨CR⟩	executes a single instruction at normal entry point.
n,k:s	⟨CR⟩	executes k instructions starting at n.

(Note: The :s command will initiate a subprocess if one is not active.)

Formats for Display

o	displays word as octal number.
d	displays word as decimal number.
x	displays word as hex number.
b	displays byte as octal number.
c	displays byte as character.
i	displays one or more words as assembler mnemonics (not exactly MACRO-11, however).
s	displays bytes as characters up to null.

Addresses

0n	Octal address
n	Decimal address
#n	Hex address
symbol	Any label in fn.mll file
symbol + 0n	Octal number 0n beyond symbol in fn.m11 file
symbol + n	Decimal number n beyond symbol in fn.mll file

Numbers

0n	Octal number
n	Decimal number
#n	Hex number

C.3.3 Adb Commands

The general *adb* command has the form

> address,count command modifier ⟨CR⟩

This means that the command is to be performed "count" times beginning at "address." If omitted, address defaults to the current pointer into the file being worked on. (See Section C.3.4.) Count defaults to 1 if omitted.

In this appendix we consider only the commands summarized in Table C.2. The UNIX sysyem manual should be consulted for a more complete list.

One of the commands most frequently used is to display the contents of a memory location. This is the ? command. Its modifier is a format that specifies the way the contents are to be displayed. The more commonly used formats are given in Table C.2. As an example,

> 022?d ⟨CR⟩

will display the contents of location 022 octal as a decimal value. That is, we specified the address in octal, but requested the contents to be displayed in decimal.

C.3.4 Adb Addresses

Most *adb* commands are applied at a particular address. For example,

> address ?o

displays the word at address. In general, address can be any expression, even those which involve symbols from the source file. For example,

> start +014 ?o

displays the octal contents of the word that is 014 (octal) bytes beyond the label "start". Note that numeric constants such as the 014 are treated according to the conventions given above. Values of symbols are taken from the symbol table produced by the assembler; *adb* finds these symbols and values in fn.out.

If an address is given as a numeric constant, it must be the run-time address, i.e., load-point address plus the offset from the beginning of the module.

Adb uses an address pointer called dot (.). It initially has a value equal to the fn.out file load point, i.e., the first location in your program. It is advanced to the given address by *adb* commands that require the address (except breakpoint and execute commands). Whenever address is omitted, *adb* uses dot. For example,

> ?c ⟨CR⟩

will display the byte currently pointed at by dot as a character.

A ⟨CR⟩ or ⟨LF⟩ will repeat the previous command after incrementing dot. Thus four successive bytes beginning at label m can be printed as follows.

> m?c ⟨CR⟩
> 01020:   t
> ⟨CR⟩

01021:	h
⟨CR⟩	
01022:	i
⟨CR⟩	
01023:	s

Note that the advancement of dot is affected by the requested format. Above it is incremented by 1 because of the c format request. If we had instead used m?o, repeated ⟨CR⟩s would have advanced dot by 2 each time. When the i format is requested, dot is advanced by the number of bytes implied by the instructions, i.e., as many as six bytes for a three-word instruction.

C.3.5 An Adb Example

As an example of *adb* usage, let us assume that Fig. C.1 has been assembled and exists as expcl.out in the working directory. Enter *adb* with

    $ adb expcl.out   ⟨CR⟩

The program is displayed in octal by

start,15?o	⟨CR⟩				
start:	05003	012701	034	012711	0177777
	012702	020	05703		
loop:	06111	013001	05203		
skip:	077204	06111	0104401		
a:	0				

Note that labels are printed for convenient reference to the source code. The machine code is the same as shown in Fig. C.1 except for the 0104401 at skip +04; this is the TRAP 1 instruction that is the standard UNIX system exit call.

Let us now set breakpoints at start and skip +04 so that we can use *adb* to execute the program. To do this, we enter

    start:b   ⟨CR⟩
    skip+04:b   ⟨CR⟩

To see what we have done, display the breakpoints

    $b ⟨CR⟩
    breakpoints
    count bkpt   command
      1   skip+o4
      1   start

The "count" and "command" headings refer to advanced features of *adb* not discussed here.

Now to execute the program we enter a :r command. This will initiate the program execution as a "subprocess," but will then stop so we can examine the registers before execution of the first instruction. (The register contents before the subprocess begins have no meaning.) Computer responses are underlined.

```
:r     ⟨CR⟩                        executes to first breakpoint.
expcl.out: running
breakpoint        start:    clr   r3
   $r     ⟨CR⟩                     displays registers.
   ps     0170010
   pc     0         start:
   sp     0177704
   r5     0
   r4     0
   r3     0
   r2     0
   r1     06                       This value is "left over" from adb.
   r0     012                      This value is "left over" from adb.
   start:      clr     r3          is about to be executed.
```

At this point we can change values in registers and locations, and such changes will be in effect during the run. For example, let us set r4 to 22 and location start +010 to 077. The value in r4 has no effect, but the value in start +010 represents the bit pattern for which the 1-bits are to be counted. The steps to make these changes are

```
022>r4 ⟨CR⟩                        sets r4 to 22 octal.
start +010?w 077 ⟨CR⟩              sets location start +010 to 077.
start +010:     0177777 = 077
```

To continue the execution to the breakpoint we enter

```
:c ⟨CR⟩                            continues execution.
expc1.out:running
breakpoint      skip +04     sys     exit
```

We can now examine registers and memory locations as shown below.

```
   $r     ⟨CR⟩                     displays registers.
   ps     0170000                  N = 0, Z = 0, V = 0, C = 0.
   pc     032       skip +04
   sp     0177704
   r5     0
   r4     022                      as we set it.
   r3     06                       is the number of 1-bits in 077.
   r2     0
   r1     034
   r0     012                      is unchanged.
   start, 15?o     ⟨CR⟩            displays program in octal.
       start:     05003    012701    034       012711    077
                  012702    020      05703
       loop:      06111    0103001   05203
       skip:      077204   06111     0104401
       a:         077
```

Note that the changes to r4 and start +010 are reflected here. Also, the contents of **a** has been changed as a result of execution of the program.

At this point the subprocess started by :r is still pending. To complete it, enter the :c command

```
:c    ⟨CR⟩
expc1.out; running
process terminated
```

The "process terminated" message is normal. If it had not appeared, it would be a good idea to "kill" the process with the :k command because pending processes can cause *adb* to respond to later commands in unexpected ways.

When the subprocess has finished, the changes made while it was active or pending are lost. That is, if we did another start 15?o command, we would see start +010 and **a** back at their original values. Register contents are also lost.

C.3.6 Other Usages of Adb

The preceding example demonstrated the usage of *adb* that parallels ODT usage in early chapters of this book, i.e., as a rudimentary I/O tool and to see the contents of memory and registers as a program executes. It has other uses, including examination of memory dumps (core files) created by aborted programs, and making permanent changes to object files.

To examine core files, enter *adb* with

```
$ adb fn.out    core    ⟨CR⟩
```

where fn.out is the program file that aborted, and core is the core image when it aborted (it will be in your working directory as a result of the abort). Once in *adb,* you can examine core in much the same way as you examine fn.out. The only difference is that / is used instead of ?. For example, to display in octal the 22 (octal) words beginning at the label data, enter

```
data,022/o    ⟨CR⟩
```

Registers are examined exactly as shown earlier.

To use *adb* to modify an object file, enter it with

```
$ adb −w fn.out    ⟨CR⟩
```

Let us say that you wish to change the number at start +0100 from 012701 (MOV) to 112701 (MOVB). Just enter

```
start+0100?w    112701    ⟨CR⟩
start+0100    012701 = 0112701    reports change.
```

Because *adb* was entered with the −w parameter, this change is permanent in fn.out, even after leaving *adb.* (Obviously, this does *not* change the source fn.mll file that fn.out came from.)

$\boxed{\text{D}}$ Operating System Dependencies

D.1 Overview

In order to show specific examples of machine interaction in the body of this text it was necessary to assume a particular operating system. The widely used Digital Equipment Corporation (DEC) operating system called RSTS/E was used for this purpose. This appendix shows the commands required for machine interaction with other operating systems, namely, RT-11, RSX-11M, and the UNIX system. It also summarizes the more important RSTS/E commands for reference purposes.

> *Note:* Also presented here are macros and subroutines for use of .TTYIN, .TTYOUT, and .PRINT as employed in the examples in this text. These are normally available on RT-11 systems, but must be installed if RSTS/E, RSX-11M, or the UNIX system is employed. Instructions for this installation are also given here. (See Section D.5). Examples given in the text and certain commands given in this appendix will not work if this installation is not carried out.

D.2 Operating Systems—General Concepts

The operating system provides a framework of programs that allows the programmer to use the computer more effectively. Among the essential services provided by the operating system are

1. Interpretation of keyboard commands, e.g., RUN and DIR. This is done by the "keyboard monitor" program of the operating system.
2. Systematic storage and retrieval of files.
3. A collection of supporting "utility" programs that allows manipulation of files, e.g., create, modify, merge, and delete.
4. Libraries of macros and object programs to support application programs.
5. A collection of language processors such as assemblers, compilers, and interpreters.
6. The allocation of resources such as central memory, CPU time, and use of peripheral devices to multiple, simultaneous users.

The PDP-11 computer has a variety of available operating systems that differ in capability and features. Some of the more widely used include RSTS/E, RSX-11M, RT-11, and the UNIX system.

Although MACRO-11 itself is the same regardless of the operating system, there are certain steps in the overall MACRO-11 programming task that vary depending on which system is in use. Some of these differences are minor, especially among the various DEC-supplied systems. There are more significant differences when the DEC systems are compared to the UNIX system, which was developed by Bell Laboratories.

In the following sections, the essential features of RSTS/E, RT-11, RSX-11M, and the UNIX system are presented. These features are summarized in Table D.1. While the information given here should be adequate for using MACRO-

TABLE D.1
Operating System Command Summary

	RSTS/E	RT-11
System Prompt	READY	
Terminate execution of a task	^C	^C or DEL (rubout)
File naming conventions		
MACRO source	fn.MAC	fn.MAC
Listing	fn.LST	fn.LST
Object	fn.OBJ	fn.OBJ
Map	fn.MAP	fn.MAP
Load module	fn.SAV	fn.SAV
Assemble	RUN $MACRO *fn,fn, = fn *^Z or MACRO fn,fn = fn	RUN MACRO *fn,fn = fn *^Z or MACRO fn/LIST
Link	RUN $LINK *fn,fn = fn *^Z or LINK fn,fn = fn	RUN LINK *fn,fn = fn *^Z or LINK fn/MAP
Execute a program	RUN fn	RUN fn
Using the debugging program	RUN $LINK *fn,fn = fn,ODT/T TRANSFER SYMBOL? O.DOT *^Z RUN fn	RUN LINK *fn,fn = fn,ODT/T TRANSFER SYMBOL? O.ODT *^Z RUN fn
List file at terminal	TYPE fn.ext or PIP fn.ext	TYPE fn.ext or PIP fn.ext
Interrupt/restart terminal listing	^S stops ^Q restarts	^S stops ^Q restarts
Copy a file	PIP new.ext = old.ext	PIP new.ext = old.ext
Rename a file	PIP new.ext = old.ext/RE	PIP new.ext = old.ext/R
Delete files	PIP fn.ext/DE	PIP fn.ext/DE
Directory of files stored on your account	DIR	DIR

411

	RSTS/E	RT-11
Delete previous character on current line	DEL or RUBOUT	DEL or RUBOUT
Delete current line	^U	^U
Logoff system	BYE or GOODBYE	BYE or Turn computer off

	RSX-11M	The UNIX System
System Prompt	MCR⟩ or ⟩	$ or @ (varies locally)
Terminate execution of a task	ABORT fn.TSK (^C returns a system prompt, allows task to continue)	^C (varies locally)
File naming conventions: MACRO source Listing Object Map Load module	 fn.MAC;v fn.LST;v fn.OBJ;v fn.MAP;v fn.TSK;v (v is version number. Most usage assumes latest version if omitted.)	 fn.m11 fn.lst fn.obj fn.map fn.out
Assemble	RUN $MAC MAC⟩fn,fn = MACLIB,fn MAC⟩^Z or MAC fn,fn = MACLIB,fn (MACLIB is Fig. D.2)	macro − ls maclib.m11 fn.m11 (maclib is Fig. D.4)
Link	RUN $TKB TKB⟩fn,fn = SUBLIB,fn TKB⟩^Z or TKB fn,fn = SUBLIB,fn (SUBLIB is Fig. D.3)	link fn

TABLE D.1 (cont.)

	RSX-11M	The UNIX System
Execute a program	RUN fn.TSK or RUN fn.	fn.out or fn
Using the debugging program	RUN$TKB TKB)fn/DA,fn = SUBLIB,fn TKB)^Z RUN fn	adb fn.out
List file at terminal	TYPE fn.ext or PIP TI: = fn.ext	cat fn.ext or pr fn.ext
Interrupt/restart terminal listing	^S Stops ^Q Restarts	^S Stops ^Q Restarts (varies locally)
Copy a file	PIP new.ext = old.ext	cp old.ext new.ext
Rename a file	PIP new.ext = old.ext/RE	mv old.ext new.ext
Merge files	PIP new.ext = old1.ext, old2.ext (entered as one line)	cat old1.ext old2. ext)new.ext
Delete files	PIP fn.ext/DE or ERASE fn.ext	rm fn.ext
Directory of files stored on your account	DIR	ls
Delete previous character on current line	DEL or RUBOUT	# (varies locally)
Delete current line	^U	@ (varies locally)
Log off system	BYE or GOODBYE	login or Break communication (varies locally)

11, the descriptions of these operating systems are by no means complete. A reference manual giving a complete description is therefore cited for each system.

Because of the similarity among the DEC-supplied systems—RSTS/E, RT-11, and RSX-11M—their treatment here is integrated. That is, after a brief description of each system, covering its unique features, all common features are covered in a single section.

D.3 DEC-supplied Operating System

D.3.1 Programming in MACRO-11 under RSTS/E

RSTS/E is a timesharing operating system supplied by DEC. Typical RSTS/E installations serve 16 to 63 users, or other independent jobs, running simultaneously.

As implied by the term "timesharing," the principal criterion for servicing each user under RSTS/E is equal time allocation. That is, RSTS/E cycles through all tasks currently loaded in memory, giving each an equal fraction of the CPU time. This tends to provide a more uniform response for each user than other resource-sharing methods. RSTS/E is also characterized by fixed upper limits on user regions in memory, normally 32KB (16,384 words).

Sign-on to the RSTS/E system begins by establishing a physical connection between the terminal and computer. This will depend on local factors, and may require using a telephone and modem (e.g., acoustical coupler). You must obtain directions for this from local support people.

After establishing the connection, RSTS/E responds as shown by underlining. User response is also shown

RSTS V7.0 Timesharing Job 15 KB4 19-NOV-82 08:15 AM

#88,15 ⟨CR⟩   (You must use your assigned account number.)
Password: JKGIQU ⟨CR⟩   (You must use your assigned password. It will *not* be
                                echoed to screen.)
READY

The number 88,15 above is an account number. You must obtain your own account number from the system manager or your instructor. Similarly, the password is specially assigned.

The READY is the system prompt provided by RSTS/E. It signifies that RSTS/E is waiting for your command, e.g., to use the editor (EDT), or to assemble a program (MACRO). RSTS/E always returns with this prompt whenever it completes an operation. (Some RSTS/E systems may use a slightly different prompt. This will be apparent the first time you sign on.)

In order to sign off of RSTS/E, issue the command

BYE ⟨CR⟩

The exact response to the BYE command varies depending on the installation.

For example, it may report the amount of disk space being used. At some installations, you may be asked to confirm that you really wish to sign off.

Occasionally you may lose the connection to the computer during a session. If this happens, immediately reestablish the connection and go through the sign-on process again. Usually this results in the prompt

JOB m IS ATTACHED UNDER THIS ACCOUNT
JOB NUMBER TO ATTACH TO?

This indicates that RSTS/E is still running under your earlier sign-on, known to the system as JOB m, and all you have to do is enter the job number to reconrect to it. That is

JOB NUMBER TO ATTACH TO ? n⟨CR⟩
ATTACHING TO JOB n

Your session can then be resumed where you left off.

MACRO-11 programming requires creation of the program in a source file, assembling the source file to produce the object file, linking the object file to produce the load module, and finally executing the program. These steps are shown below for the RSTS/E environment. Machine prompts are underlined.

Creation of source file using EDT:

```
EDT MYPROG.MAC ⟨CR⟩
*I⟨CR⟩
                .TITLE FIRST TRY ⟨CR⟩
                .MCALL .PRINT, .EXIT ⟨CR⟩
START:          .PRINT #MSG1 ⟨CR⟩
                .EXIT ⟨CR⟩
MSG1:           .ASCIZ/HI THERE!/ ⟨CR⟩
                .END START ⟨CR⟩
^Z
*EX ⟨CR⟩

READY
```

Further details in the use of EDT are given in Section B.2.

Assembling:

```
RUN $MACRO ⟨CR⟩
*MYPROG.OBJ, MYPROG.LST = MYPROG.MAC⟨CR⟩
ERRORS DETECTED = 0
*^Z
READY
```

If this step produces a message saying that .PRINT was not found, see Section D.5.1.

Linking:

```
RUN $LINK ⟨CR⟩
*MYPROG.SAV,MYPROG.MAP = MYPROG.OBJ ⟨CR⟩
*^Z
```

READY

Execution:

```
RUN MYPROG.SAV ⟨CR⟩
HI THERE!
```

Section D.3.4 covers other useful commands and information on RSTS/E. A complete description of the operating system features is given in *RSTS/E System User's Guide* (DEC order no. AA–5133B–TC, AD–5133B–T1).

D.3.2 Programming in MACRO-11 under RSX-11M

RSX-11 designates a family of DEC operating systems that allows "multiprogramming" on the PDP-11. The term "multiprogramming" means that there are several jobs in memory at once and executing concurrently. There is a similarity here to timesharing (see Section D.3.1), in that both have several jobs in memory at the same time, and both "timeshare" the CPU. The difference is that under multiprogramming the job currently executing will continue until interrupted by some event, e.g., the need to perform I/O, whereas in timesharing the executing job will be interrupted when its allowed time interval is consumed. Also, in multiprogramming the job with the highest *priority* will be executed next, whereas timesharing cycles from one job to the next in a fixed order, with each job getting one execution interval per cycle. (However, RSTS/E can also be installed with a priority system.) Another distinguishing feature of RSX-11 is that tasks can use any required amount of memory (up to the system memory size less the operating system size), whereas RSTS/E limits each task to some prescribed maximum.

Another feature of RSX-11 is that it allows "multitasking." This means that a single user can initiate several tasks for concurrent execution.

The member of the RSX-11 family emphasized here is RSX-11M. Its unique characteristics include the ability to allow many different users to be logged-on at the same time. Each can have one or more tasks executing concurrently. It is usually installed on smaller PDP-11 computers, although it will also run on the larger PDP-11 machines.

RSX-11S is a small, single-user version of RSX-11 that does not support files. It is not suitable for program development work, and will not accept many of the commands discussed here.

RSX-11M-PLUS is an extended version of RSX-11M. It is designed for running on the PDP-11/44 and PDP-11/70 machines, and supports more simultaneous users and tasks than RSX-11M. In general, all of the RSX-11M commands discussed here will work on RSX-11M-PLUS.

Sign-on to the RSX-11M system begins by establishing a physical connection to the computer from the terminal. The exact steps to do this will differ at each installation, so local assistance will be required. See your local support people or your instructor.

After establishing the connection, RSX-11M responds as shown by underlining below. User response is also shown.

```
MCR)HELLO
ACCOUNT OR NAME:     88,15 (CR)      (You must use assigned account number.)
PASSWORD: JKGIQU (CR)                (You must use assigned password. It will
                                       not be echoed to screen.)

RSX-11M BL26 MULTIUSER SYSTEM
```

(Message varies locally.)

```
MCR)
```

The number 88,15 above is an account number. It and the password must be assigned to you by the system manager or your instructor.

The MCR) symbol, meaning Monitor Console Routine, is the RSX-11M system prompt. It signifies that it is waiting for your command, e.g., to use the editor (EDT), or assemble a program (MAC). RSX-11M always returns with this prompt whenever it completes an operation. (Some RSX-11M systems may provide a slightly different prompt, for example just).)

As mentioned above, RSX-11M allows a single user to initiate several programs simultaneously. Complete program units are referred to as *tasks*. After one task has been initiated, a ^C will cause the system prompt MCR) to appear, allowing another task to be initiated. Stopping a task before it completes requires use of the ABORT command. (See Section D.3.4.)

In order to sign-off of RSX-11M, issue the command

```
MCR)BYE (CR)
```

This will terminate your session. Certain messages may be displayed, depending on the local RSX-11M installation.

MACRO-11 programming under RSX-11M requires creation of the program in a source file, assembling the source file to produce an object file, linking the object file to produce a load module, and finally executing the program. These steps are shown below. Machine prompts are underlined.

Creation of source file using EDT:

```
MCR)EDT MYPROG.MAC (CR)
*I (CR)
            .TITLE FIRST TRY (CR)
            .MCALL .PRINT, .EXIT (CR)
```

```
START:      .PRINT #MSG1 ⟨CR⟩
            .EXIT ⟨CR⟩
MSG1:       .ASCIZ/HI THERE!/ ⟨CR⟩
            .END START ⟨CR⟩
^Z
*EX ⟨CR⟩

MCR⟩
```

Further details in the use of EDT are given in Section B.2.

Assembling:

```
MCR⟩RUN $MAC ⟨CR⟩
MAC⟩MYPROG.OBJ,MYPROG.LST = MACLIB.MAC,MYPROG.MAC ⟨CR⟩
MAC⟩^Z

MCR⟩
```

Note that this assumes the presence of MACLIB.MAC in your account. See Section D.5.2 for instructions on how to place it there if it is not already available. MACLIB.MAC provides for .PRINT, .EXIT, .TTYIN, and .TTYOUT macros as used in this book.

Linking (called task building in RSX-11M):

```
MCR⟩RUN $TKB ⟨CR⟩
TKB⟩MYPROG.TSK,MYPROG.MAP = SUBLIB.OBJ,MYPROG.OBJ ⟨CR⟩
TKB⟩^Z

MCR⟩
```

Note that this assumes the presence of SUBLIB.OBJ in your account. See Section D.5.2 for instructions on how to place it there if it is not already present. SUBLIB.OBJ supports the .PRINT, .TTYIN, and .TTYOUT macros used in this book.

Execution:

```
MCR⟩RUN MYPROG.TSK ⟨CR⟩
HI THERE!
MCR⟩
```

Section D.3.4 covers essential commands available under RSX-11M. A complete description of the features of this operating system is given in the *RSX-11M MCR Operations Manual* (DEC order no. AA–H263A–TC).

D.3.3 Programming in MACRO-11 under RT-11

RT-11 is a single-user operating system provided by DEC. Although most often used on smaller machines, it can be run on all PDP-11s except the PDP-11/70. It closely resembles RSTS/E in most of the commands provided.

RT-11 can be configured with any one of three different control programs, called monitors. Use of the Single-Job monitor, called SJ, will be assumed in this discussion. Under this monitor, up to 28K words of memory and a wide range of peripheral devices can be used.

Because RT-11 is a single-user system, elaborate sign-on procedures with account numbers and passwords are not used. After the computer is turned on, you simply load the monitor program and begin. The steps required to load the monitor program will vary depending on the hardware configuration and must be determined locally.

Upon loading the SJ monitor (called bootstrapping), the console terminal will print

RT-11SJ(S) V04.01B   (Version number may vary.)

<u>.</u>

The . is the RT-11 system prompt. It signifies the RT-11 is waiting for your command, and will reappear at the completion of each task.

Note that upon loading, the monitor normally executes a "start-up" command file called STARTS.COM before displaying the prompt. This feature can be used to automatically execute commands needed to properly initialize the RT-11 system to your hardware configuration, or to perform other start-up chores. See the *RT-11 System User's Guide* for details on how to use this feature. If you do not have a STARTS.COM file on the system storage device, an error report will be issued. It can be safely ignored.

MACRO-11 programming requires creation of the program in a source file, assembling the source file to produce an object file, linking the object file to produce a load module, and finally executing the program. These steps are shown below for the RT-11 environment. Machine prompts are underlined.

Creation of source file using EDIT:

EDIT/CREATE MYPROG.MAC ⟨CR⟩

<u>*</u>I	.TITLE FIRST TRY ⟨CR⟩
	.MCALL .PRINT, .EXIT ⟨CR⟩
START:	.PRINT #MSG1 ⟨CR⟩
	.EXIT ⟨CR⟩
MSG1:	.ASCIZ/HI THERE!/ ⟨CR⟩
	.END START ⟨CR⟩
$$	(Note: $ represents ESC key)
<u>*</u>EX$$	

<u>.</u>

Assembling:

```
.RUN MACRO (CR)
*MYPROG.OBJ,MYPROG.LST=MYPROG.MAC (CR)
ERRORS DETECTED: 0
*^C
```

:

Linking:

```
.RUN LINK (CR)
*MYPROG.SAV,MYPROG.MAP=MYPROG.OBJ (CR)
*^C
```

:

Execution:

```
RUN MYPROG.SAV (CR)

HI THERE!
```

:

Section D.3.4 covers the essential commands available under RT-11. A complete description of the operating system features is given in the *RT-11 System User's Guide* (DEC order no. AA–5279B–TC).

D.3.4   More Information on RSTS/E, RSX-11M, and RT-11

The preceding sections gave the minimum commands necessary to create, assemble, link, and run MACRO-11 programs under these three DEC operating systems. This section presents more details on these and other commands. To save space, all three systems are treated together here. Wherever there is a difference in a command or feature among these operating systems, the forms are given for each, with the system identified in square brackets at the right, e.g., [RSTS/E], [RSX-11M], or [RT-11].

D.3.4.1   File name conventions

File names are composed of two parts, a name and an extension, separated by ".", i.e.,

fn.ext

The name is arbitrary except that it must begin with an alphabetical character and be no more than six characters in length. The extension is three or fewer characters and are usually chosen to indicate the type of file. For example, a

MACRO-11 source file should be named

    name.MAC

Similarly, object files have the extension .OBJ, listing files .LST, map files .MAP, and load module files .SAV [RT-11, RSTS/E], or .TSK [RSX-11M]. The importance of these standard extensions is that certain system programs, such as MACRO and LINK or TKB, will *assume* the correct extension if none is given. Also, it is of great convenience to be able to tell the type of file by merely looking at its name.

Certain system commands can refer to several files at once. With these commands, the * can be used in place of either the file name or extension, and refers to all files that match the given part. For example, *.MAC refers to all files in your account with the extension .MAC, while PROG.* refers to all files named PROG regardless of the extension. The ''?'' character can also be used in a file name reference, meaning, ''Accept any character'' in that position. For example,

    PROG??.MAC   [RSTS/E, RSX-11M]

refers to PROG.MAC, PROG01.MAC, PROGAB.MAC, and all others in your account beginning with PROG and having the extension .MAC. (RT-11 uses * instead of ? for this purpose.) Certain commands such as PIP and DIR are greatly enhanced by these conventions. The * and ? used in this way are sometimes called ''wild cards,'' in analogy to the usage of this term in certain card games.

Under RSX-11M, several different versions of a file may exist at the same time. The version number is appended to the file name with a semicolon. For example,

    MYPROG.MAC;1   [RSX-11M]
    MYPROG.MAC;2
    MYPROG.MAC;3

are three versions of the same program, retained in three separate files. A new version is created each time a file is edited, or when a file is written into a name that already exists on the storage device. The version number can be included in the file specification, or omitted for some commands. If omitted, the latest, i.e., highest version number, is assumed.

D.3.4.2 Assembly
The following sequence will assemble a MACRO-11 source file named fn.MAC. Computer response is underlined.

```
RUN$MACRO ⟨CR⟩                                    [RSTS/E]
*fn.OBJ,fn.LST = fn.MAC⟨CR⟩
ERRORS DETECTED = 0
*^Z

READY      (READY is prompt.)
```

MCR⟩RUN $MAC⟨CR⟩   (MCR⟩ is prompt.)   [RSX-11M]
MAC⟩fn.OBJ,fn.LST = MACLIB.MAC,fn.MAC⟨CR⟩
MAC⟩^Z
MCR⟩
(*Note:*   MACLIB is for .PRINT, .TTYIN and .TTYOUT. See Section D.5.2.)

.RUN MACRO ⟨CR⟩   (. is prompt.)   [RT-11]
*fn.OBJ,fn.LST = fn.MAC ⟨CR⟩
ERRORS DETECTED: 0
*^C
:

This creates a listing file as well as an object file. If a listing is not wanted, just enter

---

*fn.OBJ = fn.MAC⟨CR⟩   [RSTS/E, RT-11]

MAC⟩fn.OBJ = MACLIB.MAC,fn.MAC⟨CR⟩   [RSX-11M]

Furthermore, the extensions OBJ, MAP, and MAC can be inferred from the positions of these files in the command line and can therefore be omitted. This allows simpler forms of the command line

*fn,fn = fn⟨CR⟩

with a listing, or

*fn = fn⟨CR⟩

without a listing. This works for RSTS/E, RT-11, or RSX-11M.

As noted in Section D.3.4.4, some installations may recognize an even simpler form for assembly, namely,

MACRO   fn,fn = fn⟨CR⟩   [RSTS/E]
MAC   fn,fn = MACLIB,fn⟨CR⟩   [RSX-11M]
MACRO   fn/LIST⟨CR⟩   [RT-11]

D.3.4.3 Linking or task building

An object program must be linked before it can be executed. As explained in Section 15.4, this process resolves external address references and relocates all code to the run-time addresses. In an RSX-11M environment this is called "task building" instead of linking, and the linking program is called TKB standing for Task Builder. The command lines for linking are

---

RUN $LINK⟨CR⟩   [RSTS/E]
*fn.SAV,fn.MAP = fn.OBJ⟨CR⟩
*^C

READY

MCR⟩RUN $TKB⟨CR⟩   [RSX-11M]
TKB⟩fn.TSK,fn.MAP = SUBLIB.OBJ,fn.OBJ⟨CR⟩
TKB⟩^Z
MCR⟩
(*Note:* SUBLIB is required for .PRINT, .TTYIN, .TTYOUT. See Section
D.5.2.)

.RUN   LINK⟨CR⟩   /   [RT-11]
*fn.SAV,fn.MAP = fn.OBJ⟨CR⟩
*^C

.

or

. LINK ⟨CR⟩
FILES? fn/MAP⟨CR⟩

.

This produces a load module called fn.SAV [RSTS/E, RT-11] or fn.TSK [RSX-11M], and a load map fn.MAP. If the map is not needed, simply omit fn.MAP from the RSTS/E or RSX-11M command line, or omit the /MAP from the RT-11 command line. As with assembly, file extensions will be inferred if they are omitted, allowing the simpler command line

*fn,fn = fn⟨CR⟩

If supported locally (see Section D.3.4.4), linking can also be done by

LINK fn,fn = fn⟨CR⟩

To link with ODT, the command line is

RUN $LINK⟨CR⟩   [RSTS/E]
*fn,fn = fn,ODT/T⟨CR⟩
TRANSFER SYMBOL ? O.ODT   ⟨CR⟩
*^Z

READY

MCR⟩RUN $TKB⟨CR⟩   [RSX-11M]
TKB⟩fn/DA,fn = SUBLIB,fn⟨CR⟩
TKB⟩^Z
MCR⟩
(*Note:* SUBLIB is required for .PRINT, .TTYIN, and TTYOUT macros.
See Section D.5.2)

.RUN LINK⟨CR⟩   [RT-11]
*fn,fn = fn,ODT/T⟨CR⟩
TRANSFER SYMBOL ? O.ODT⟨CR⟩
*^C

.

Because of /T required for linking with ODT, the single-line form of LINK cannot be used.

If several object programs are to be linked together, they are simply listed, separated by commas, to the right of the "=" symbol, e.g.,

```
*fn,fn = fn1,fn2,fn3⟨CR⟩
*^Z
```

This will work for linking up to six object files. For more than six object files, enter /C after the sixth object file, then a ⟨CR⟩. This will give another * on a new line. You can then enter more object files, and if needed another /C in order to link any number of object files.

D.3.4.4 Execute commands
Programs, either those supplied by the system or your own, are caused to execute by the RUN command

```
RUN    name ⟨CR⟩
```

This assumes that *name* is an executable file, called a load module. Such files have the extension .SAV [RSTS/E, RT-11], or TSK [RSX-11M] and are the result of the linking process.

So-called system programs, such as MACRO and EDT, are also executed using the run command. The only difference between running your program and running a system program is that the load module for the system program is available without your having to assemble or link it. On RSTS/E and RSX-11M, system programs are often given names beginning with $ (e.g., $MACRO and $LINK). This alerts the operating system that it is a system program, so that it looks for the file in a system account instead of your account. RT-11 does not adhere to this convention.

RSTS/E allows definition of "command files" using what DEC calls the Concise Command Language, CCL. Similar files are possible with RSX-11M and RT-11, but are called "indirect files." Using this facility, or by installation procedures, the system manager often defines "single-line commands" that replace the normal RUN command. If this has been done at your installation, many system programs can be run using the single line command, e.g., MACRO fn,fn = fn, instead of RUN $MACRO. (Try it and see if it is accepted on your system.)

D.3.4.5 Utilities
Utilities are system-supplied programs that perform file operations frequently needed by many users. This includes listing, copying, merging, deleting, and listing of a directory of all files on your account.

Many of these operations can be done using the Peripheral Interchange Program (PIP), available under RSTS/E, RT-11, and RSX-11M. The general form of the PIP command line is

```
PIP output = input⟨CR⟩
```

On some systems, it may be necessary to use

RUN $PIP ⟨CR⟩   [RSTS/E, RX-11M]
* [command string]
*^C

Here command string is the list shown after PIP in this section, and *input* stands
for the input file and *output* the output file. For RT-11, PIP must be used instead
of $PIP in the command above.

In the following sections, the first form of the PIP command is used in the
examples. If these do not work, use the second form.

Copying a file: When the command is given exactly as above, a copy of
the input is created. For example,

PIP   PROGB.MAC = PROGA.MAC⟨CR⟩

creates a copy of PROGA.MAC and puts it into PROGB.MAC.

Merging files: If there are several input files, they are merged into the output.
That is

PIP D.MAC = A.MAC,B.MAC,C.MAC⟨CR⟩	[RSTS/E, RSX-11M]
RUN PIP⟨CR⟩ *D.MAC/U = A.MAC,B.MAC,C.MAC⟨CR⟩ *^C	[RT-11]

creates D.MAC as a combination of the three input files A, B, and C. The input
files are not affected by merging or copying. One should not attempt to merge
files of differing extension, because they may not be of the same format.

Renaming a file: To simply rename a file, as opposed to creating a copy,
enter

PIP new.ext = old.ext/RE⟨CR⟩	[RSTS/E, RSX-11M]
RUN PIP⟨CR⟩ * new.ext = old.ext/R⟨CR⟩ *^C	[RT-11]

Accessing other users' files: Files under RSTS/E or RSX-11M can be copied
from other users' accounts if the "protection code" is set to 40 or less. To do
this, the file owner must sign on with his or her account number and enter

PIP   fn.ext⟨40⟩/RE⟨CR⟩

The recipient can then copy the file by signing on to his or her account and
entering

PIP   fn.ext = [n,m]fn.ext⟨CR⟩

where n,m is the account number of the file owner.

Deleting files: To delete a file, issue the command

    PIP   fn.ext/DE⟨CR⟩   [RSTS/E, RSX-11M]

Several can be deleted at once also.

    PIP   A.MAC,A.LST,A.SAV,A.OBJ/DE⟨CR⟩   [RSTS/E, RSX-11M]

Actually, all of the above (and more!) could be accomplished more easily with

    PIP   A.*/DE⟨CR⟩   [RSTS/E, RSX-11M]

because this means delete all files named A regardless of extension. Obviously, the delete command should be used with care. The commands above for RT-11 use D instead of DE, e.g.,

```
RUN PIP⟨CR⟩                                                        [RT-11]
*fn.ext/D⟨CR⟩
*^C
```

Listing files: A listing of any printable file can be displayed on the terminal by

PIP	fn.ext	⟨CR⟩	[RSTS/E]
PIP	TI:=fn.ext	⟨CR⟩	[RSX-11M]

Alternately, the command

    TYPE   fn.ext   ⟨CR⟩   [RT-11, RSTS/E]

will do the same. Note that .OBJ, .SAV, and .TSK files are not printable.
    If it is desired to generate a listing at the system line printer, use the command

    QU   fn.ext⟨CR⟩   [RSTS/E]

Before using QU on a centralized system, however, check to see that your computer center allows this, and has a method for returning your listing to you.

Directory listing: File space is often limited. Therefore, you may have to periodically "clean up" your account, deleting unneeded files. To see what files you have saved, use the DIR command

    DIR⟨CR⟩   [RT-11, RSTS/E, RSX-11M]

This lists the names, extensions, sizes, protection codes, and creation dates for all files on your account. If you wish to see only those with a particular extension, e.g., .MAC, use the following.

    DIR   *.MAC⟨CR⟩   [RT-11, RSTS/E, RSX-11M]

See Section D.3.4.1 for more ways to specify a group of files of similar name.

Interrupting a task: Sometimes it is necessary to interrupt a task that is running too long or producing unwanted results. To do this, enter

^C	[RSTS/E, RT-11, RSX-11M]
^C	[RSX-11M]
MCR)ABORT fn.TSK	

Note that ^C simply returns the system prompt under RSX-11M, allowing other commands to be entered. The ABORT command must then be used to interrupt a task.

The ^C can also be used to exit a system program, e.g., LINK, or MACRO. Often a ^Z will work equally well in this function, however.

When working at a cathode ray tube (CRT) terminal, it is often desired to temporarily suspend a long listing on the screen. This can be done with a ^S. The listing can be resumed with ^Q. These controls work on RSTS/E, RSX-11M, and RT-11.

D.4 The UNIX™ Operating System†

D.4.1 Background

The UNIX system is a multiuser timesharing operating system developed by Bell Laboratories. Originally, it was developed for PDP-11 computers, but has now been adapted to many other machines. It has many unique features that make it quite different from other contemporary operating systems, and is viewed by many as representative of future trends. Here we will examine it in sufficient depth only to allow development of MACRO-11 programs.

> *Note:* It should be noted that the UNIX system is delivered with an assembler called **as** that is very similar to MACRO-11, but not identical to it. For one thing, it does not support macro definitions and usage. It is therefore not recommended for use with this book. There is a true MACRO-11 assembler available for the UNIX systems, and it is the one that should be used. Information on obtaining and installing it and the associated linker is given in Section D.5.

EDT and ODT are not available under the UNIX system. However, there are comparable programs called **ed** and **adb,** respectively, that serve the same purposes. The usage of *ed* is shown in Section B.4; and *adb*, in Section C.3.

D.4.1.1 Lowercase usage

Unlike most other systems, the UNIX system is oriented entirely around usage of the lowercase alphabet. Thus all commands and programs are normally entered in lowercase. If you have a terminal that does not provide lowercase, e.g., older

---

† UNIX™ is a trademark of Bell Laboratories.

printing terminals, you will experience strange behavior at times, but no insurmountable difficulties. For one thing, any uppercase characters that come from the system will be preceded by a ''\'' character.

In this section, all user input is shown in lowercase. The UNIX system output is shown in uppercase or lowercase. The UNIX system commands are shown in **boldface** at the first usage and *italics* thereafter in order to distinguish them from normal words.

D.4.1.2 The UNIX system shell

The component of the UNIX system that interprets user commands is called the **shell.** An interesting feature of the shell is that it can be changed locally. This means that things such as the prompt symbol and other special symbols may differ depending on the installations. You will therefore have to check locally to confirm some of the information given here. Commands likely to vary are shown as they are most often implemented, and attention is called to possible variations.

D.4.1.3 Sign-on/sign-off

Sign-on to the UNIX system begins by establishing a physical connection between the terminal and the computer. This procedure will be dependent on your particular installation. Therefore, you will have to get local instructions for this step. After establishing the connection, the UNIX system responds as shown by underlining. Required user input is also shown.

UNIX V7
Login: Uname ⟨CR⟩   (Uname is your assigned user name.)
Password: password ⟨CR⟩   (You must use your assigned password. It will *not* be
                               printed.)

           WELCOME TO UNIX
$ ($ is default prompt; varies locally.)

Note that you must obtain your user name and password from the system manager. The $ is the system prompt, signifying that the UNIX system awaits your command. As noted previously, the prompt may be a different symbol, e.g., @, at your installation. The system prompt will always return whenever the UNIX system completes an operation.

In order to sign off of the UNIX system, you can either break the connection, or issue the command

   $ **login** ⟨CR⟩

This in effect signs you off and prepares the terminal for the next user to sign on. Some installations accept the command

   $ **bye** ⟨CR⟩

that signs you off and breaks the connection.

D.4.1.4 Special control characters

There are several special control characters that will be useful when you are using the UNIX system. These characters will vary depending on the shell at your installation. Those shown below are the defaults for the indicated functions if they were not changed locally. You should check locally and write in the local characters in the space provided.

	Default	Local
Terminate a program:	DEL(RUBOUT), BREAK	_____
Delete current line of input:	@	_____
Delete the previous character:	#	_____
End-of-file:	^d	_____
Interrupt printing:	none	_____
Resume printing:	none	_____

The end-of-file character ^d is important because interactive programs "read" the terminal as if it were a file. An end-of-file character issued at the keyboard will interrupt such a program. In particular, the *shell* itself is such a program, so that an end-of-file issued in response to a *system prompt* will sign you off of the UNIX system! This can be disconcerting if you do it accidentally.

The print interrupt and resume control characters are helpful when listing a long file at the terminal. However, these may not be available at your site.

D.4.2 MACRO-11 Programming under the UNIX System

Macro-11 programming requires creation of the program in a source file, assembling the source file to produce the object file, linking the object file to produce the load module, and finally executing the program. These steps are shown below for the UNIX system environment. Machine prompts are underlined.

D.4.2.1 Creation of source file using ed

The UNIX system editor **ed** is described in Section B.4. Its use for file creation is demonstrated below.

```
$ ed ⟨CR⟩
⟩ a                                              enters append mode.
                    .title first try ⟨CR⟩
                    .mcall .print,.exit ⟨CR⟩
start:              .print #msg⟨CR⟩
                    .exit ⟨CR⟩
msg:                .asciz/hi there!/ ⟨CR⟩
                    .end start ⟨CR⟩

.⟨CR⟩                                            leaves append mode.
⟩ w myprog.mll ⟨CR⟩                              writes to file myprog.mll.
⟩ q ⟨CR⟩                                         leaves ed.

$
```

D.4.2.2 Assembling

To assemble a program, issue the command

$ **macro** −ls maclib.m11 myprog.m11 ⟨CR⟩

This concatenates the MACRO-11 source files maclib.m11 and myprog.m11 and assembles them, placing the object program into myprog.obj. The −ls option causes the listing file to be created and placed in myprog.lst. If the listing file is not wanted, simply omit −ls.

The file maclib.m11, described in Section D.5.3, is assumed to be in your current directory; it contains macros that simulate the RT-11 macros .TTYIN, .TTYOUT, .PRINT, and .EXIT that are used in the examples in this text. The procedure for getting maclib into your directory is shown in Section D.5.3. If these macros are in your *system* library (your system manager will know), you do not need maclib. Instead, use the command

$ macro −ls myprog.m11 ⟨CR⟩

Note that the last four characters in the source files, i.e., .m11, can be omitted because if omitted *macro* will search your directory for a file ending in these characters before it looks for a file without them.

D.4.2.3 Linking

To link a program, issue the command

$ **link** myprog.obj ⟨CR⟩

This produces a load module called myprog.out. It also creates a load map in myprog.map.

D.4.2.4 Execution

To execute the load module, simply enter the name of the .out file. For example,

$ myprog.out ⟨CR⟩
hi there!
$

The .out part of the name is optional because the UNIX system assumes that it is an executable module.

D.4.3 More Information on the UNIX System

Section D.4.2 gave the minimum information necessary to create, assemble, link, and execute a MACRO-11 program under the UNIX system. This section presents more details that will be useful as you gain more experience with the UNIX system.

Space does not allow a full coverage of all the UNIX system features, so you may also wish to consult the *UNIX Reference Manual,* in several volumes, which should be available locally. In particular, you should consult the portions of these manuals entitled *UNIX for Beginners* (Volume I), *A Tutorial Introduction to the UNIX Text Editor* (Volume I), and *A Tutorial Introduction to ADB* (Volume II). the UNIX system also provides extensive "on-line" documentation. In fact, any portion of the manuals can be printed at your terminal with the command "**man** subject." For example,

$ man files ⟨CR⟩

prints a discussion of the UNIX file system, which is summarized below. Another useful feature of the UNIX system is a tutorial program called **learn.** Provided that this program is installed at your site, simply typing *learn* will lead you through a series of lessons on the various aspects of the UNIX system.

D.4.3.1 File name conventions

Files can have names up to 14 characters in length. Although any combination of characters can be used, it is most convenient to use consistent naming conventions. The conventions suggested for MACRO-11 are

Macro source file:	fn.m11
Listing file:	fn.lst
Object file:	fn.obj
Map file:	fn.map
Load module file:	fn.out

In the above, fn can be any ten or fewer characters. The last four characters are recognized by various programs such as the assembler, *macro,* and linker, *link;* also, they allow easy recognition when you examine your directory.

Sometimes it is convenient to be able to refer to a group of files having some common characters in their names. For example, you may wish to refer to all object files. The file reference

*.obj

refers to all files ending in .obj. Similarly,

a*b

refers to all file names beginning with "a" and ending in "b", such as a103b and aab. A question mark, ?, plays a similar role, but refers to a single character. For example,

mac?.m11

refers to maca.m11, macl.m11, and all other file names beginning with mac, ending with .m11, and having any single character in between.

The discussion above presents a simplified view of the UNIX file system. A more in-depth treatment is presented in the *UNIX Reference Manual,* where it is shown that files are cataloged in an hierarchical structure of directories. A directory is simply a file containing file names. As a consequence of this, the complete identification of a file includes, in addition to its name, the chain or "path" of directories used to locate it in the UNIX system of files. For example,

/usr/tom/myprog.m11

is the complete identifier of a file named myprog.m11. Here "tom" is the name of the directory containing the file myprog.m11, "usr" is the name of the directory containing the name tom, and "/" is the so-called root directory containing usr. Each directory probably contains other entries also. For example, usr may contain other directories such as bill and joe. Thus another "path name" might be

/usr/bill/myprog.m11

and another

/usr/joe/myprog.m11

Each of these identifies a unique file in the UNIX system. In particular, note that myprog.m11 in the directory joe is a completely different file from the one of the same name in the directory tom.

As might be surmised from the above, the UNIX system provides every user with a personal directory identified by

/usr/uname

where

uname	= The assigned user name used in logging on
usr	= Directory of all unames on the system
leftmost "/"	= the UNIX system root directory

When you log on, the UNIX system "puts you into your personal directory," which is then the current working directory. The significance of this is that any file *in* the working directory may be referred to by its name only; i.e., the path name is assumed to be that of the working directory if omitted. This feature makes it possible to ignore the presence of this hierarchical file directory system for most usages. You simply use ordinary file names and they get placed in your personal directory. As long as you do not take special steps to change the working directory, you do not need to use path names to refer to your files. On the other hand, you will need to be aware of these matters in order to access other users' files. This is discussed later in Section D.4.3.2.

The path name to your personal directory may have to be modified slightly to allow for local implementation details. To see the exact path name for your UNIX system, enter

$ **pwd** ⟨CR⟩   (This means "print working directory.")

It will respond something like this

/usr/uname

where uname is your assigned user name.

There may be more directory names in the path. That is, the *pwd* command may produce

/u/f/uname

Whatever precedes uname is the "system path" that must also precede the uname of the owner of any desired file.

D.4.3.2 Utility commands

Utility commands are available for various file operations. These include listing, copying, merging (concatenation), deleting, and listing of the directory of all of your files. These are presented below.

Copy of a file: A file can be copied by the **cp** command. For example,

$ cp old new ⟨CR⟩

copies the file "old" into the file "new."

Merging (concatenation):   When two or more files are to be merged into one, the **cat** command is used.

$ cat old1 old2 old3 ⟩ new ⟨CR⟩

Here the file called "new" will be the combination of old1, old2, and old3. A curious use of *cat* is to list a file, discussed below.

Rename: Sometimes you may want to change the name of a file. To do this, use the move command, **mv.**

$ mv old new ⟨CR⟩

This differs from *cp* in that old no longer exists after the *mv*.

Accessing other users' files: Files belonging to other users can be accessed by using the correct "path name" instead of just the file name. This is related to the UNIX system hierarchical directory scheme mentioned in Section D.4.3.1. Suppose, for example, you wish to copy a file named mac.m11 from the user named jeff. Issue the command

$ cp /usr/jeff/mac.m11 mac.m11 ⟨CR⟩

The file mac.m11 will now be in your directory. Of course, you do not actually have to copy it; you could just refer to it in jeff's directory in any UNIX system command, using the path name. This is because a path name can be used *anywhere* in lieu of a file name.

The above assumes that /usr/uname is the path name from the system root to a user personal directory. Because the root can be different at each installation, you should use the *pwd* command to check this. (See D.4.3.1.)

Deleting files: A file can be deleted by using the remove, **rm,** command. For example,

$ rm a.m11 a.lst a.obj a.map a.out ⟨CR⟩

will delete the four files listed. This (and more!) could also be accomplished using the wild card character. For example,

$ rm a.* ⟨CR⟩

Note that this deletes *all* files beginning with "a.". Obviously, one should use *rm* with caution. For example, *rm* * will delete *all* of your files, no questions asked! A better way is to use the "interactive" option

$ rm −i a.* ⟨CR⟩

This will *ask* before deleting each referenced file.

Listing files: A listing of any printable file can be obtained using either the **pr** or **cat** commands. The *pr* command will generate a print out in page format, with the file name and date printed at the top. It is not especially useful at a CRT terminal because the automatic "form feed" at the end of each page rolls the listing off the screen.

For listing at your terminal, *cat* is a more useful command. For example,

$ cat macprog.m11 ⟨CR⟩

will list the MACRO-11 source file called macprog.m11. The reason this works is that the UNIX system looks at the terminal as a *file*. In effect, you are telling the UNIX system to add macprog.m11 to the "terminal display file," i.e., the screen or printer.

Directory listing: In order to see the names of the files in your current working directory, use the list directory command, **ls.** For example,

$ ls ⟨CR⟩

This will show the names of all files in the current working directory, listed alphabetically. If you wish to see files in a different directory, give the path name to the directory. For example, to see the file in the user tom's directory, enter

$ ls /usr/tom ⟨CR⟩

An interesting use of the *ls* command is to see the complete structure of all UNIX system files. For example, if you issue

$ pwd ⟨CR⟩

and get

/usr/bill

this indicates that usr is the name of the directory containing the user log-on names (yours is bill). To see the names of all users, simply enter

$ ls /usr ⟨CR⟩

Suppose that one of the entries in this file was tom. To see his files, enter

$ ls /usr/tom ⟨CR⟩

Finally to see all files in the root directory, enter

```
$ ls / ⟨CR⟩
```

This will show the directory name usr, plus many other directories used by the UNIX system.

D.4.3.3 Concurrent processes

The UNIX system allows you to have several tasks (called *processes* in UNIX system terms) running at the same time. To use this feature, the command line of the first process must be ended with an ampersand, **&.** This will cause the system prompt to return *before* the first process completes, allowing a second process to be initiated.

As an example, suppose you wish to execute program a.out that runs a long time. While it is running, you might want to edit another file, say macprg.m11. To do this, enter

```
$ a.out & ⟨CR⟩          (Starts process a.out.)
29885                   (This is the process "number.")
$ ed macpgr.m11 ⟨CR⟩    (Starts ed process.)
⟩
```

(Editing commands)

```
⟩ w
⟩ q
$
```

The only problem with this sequence of commands is that any terminal output generated by a.out will be interspersed with your editing activity. To avoid this, the output of a.out can be diverted to a file, say a.output, as follows.

```
$ a.out ⟩a.output & ⟨CR⟩
29885               (This is the process number.)
$ ed macro.m11 ⟨CR⟩
⟩
```

(Editing commands)

```
⟨ w
⟩ q
$
```

The file a.output can then be printed using the *cat* command when a.out completes. This technique works with any number of concurrent processes.

When using concurrent processes, it is important to be able to see what processes are currently active. To do this, issue the **ps** command. For example,

```
$ ps ⟨CR⟩
29885   07   1:00   a.out
29613   07   0:09   −sh
$
```

This tells you that two processes are active under your log-on, namely a.out and sh (the shell). The process number, your keyboard number (which is how the UNIX system distinguishes you from the other current users) and the process name are given for each.

A process initiated by a command line ending in & cannot be terminated with the usual DEL or BREAK key. Instead, use the **kill** command, e.g.,

    $ kill 29885 ⟨CR⟩

This will terminate process 29885.

D.5 Installing .TTYIN, .TTYOUT, .PRINT, and .EXIT Macros

If you are using RT-11, this section is of no concern to you. However, if you are not working on RT-11, it will probably be necessary to install the input, output, and exit macros in order to run many of the examples and problems in this book. Listings of these macros and installation procedures are given in this section.

D.5.1 RSTS/E Installation

The macro definitions for .TTYIN, .TTYOUT, .PRINT, and .EXIT suitable for RSTS/E are shown in Fig. D.1. In order to make these available for your MACRO-11 programs, you must type them into a file, then transform it into a library file called SYSMAC.SML. The exact steps to do this are

```
EDT MACLIB.MAC ⟨CR⟩
* I ⟨CR⟩
```

                   (Type in Fig. D.1.)

```
^Z
*EX ⟨CR⟩
```

READY

```
RUN $LIBR ⟨CR⟩
* SYSMAC.SML = MACLIB.MAC/M ⟨CR⟩
*^Z
```

READY

The macro library file SYSMAC.SML created above is automatically searched for all macros listed in a .MCALL directive whenever the RUN $MACRO command is issued.

The procedure above creates SYSMAC.SML on your personal account. If there are many people using these macros, disk storage space can be saved by placing SYSMAC.SML on the system account [1,2]. The system manager can do this if he or she sees the need. If there is already a SYSMAC.SML file on [1,2], these can be added to it. Note that if there is *not* a SYSMAC.SML file

```
;
;    MACRO DEFINITIONS FOR .TTYIN,.TTYOUT,.PRINT & .EXIT
;    FOR RSTS/E ENVIRONMENT.
;
         .NLIST
         .MACRO  .PRINT,A
         .IF NB  <A>
         MOV     A,%0
         .ENDC
         EMT     ^O351
         .ENDM   .PRINT
;
         .MACRO  .TTYIN,A,?E
E:       EMT     ^O340
         BCS     E
         .IF NB  <A>
         MOVB    %0,A
         .ENDC
         .ENDM   .TTYIN
;
         .MACRO  .TTYOUT,A,?E
         .IF NB  <A>
         MOVB    A,%0
         .ENDC
E:       EMT     ^O341
         BCS     E
         .ENDM   .TTYOUT
;
         .MACRO  .EXIT
         EMT     ^O350
         .ENDM   .EXIT
;
         .LIST
;
```

Figure D.1   Macro listing for RSTS/E environment.

on an individual user's account, RSTS/E will automatically look for it in [1, 2].
Therefore it does not make any difference where it resides.

Alternately, SYSMAC.SML can be placed in the account of a particular
user, e.g., the instructor, and referenced by all users in the MACRO-11 assembler
command line. That is, enter

```
RUN    $MACRO
*fn,fn = (n,m)SYSMAC.SML,fn
*^Z
```

where n,m is the number of the account containing SYSMAC.SML. Its protection
code must be set to 40 as noted in Section D.3.4.5.

D.5.2 RSX-11M Installation

The macro definitions for .TTYIN, .TTYOUT, .PRINT, and .EXIT suitable for
RSX-11M are shown in Fig. D.2. Note that these call three subroutines, TTYIN,
TTYOUT, and PRINT, shown in Fig. D.3. In order to make these available for
your MACRO-11 programs, you must have Fig. D.2 in a file called MACLIB.MAC,
and the assembled form of Fig. D.3 in a file called SUBLIB.OBJ in your account.
The exact steps to do this are shown below.

```
MCR)EDT MACLIB.MAC(CR)
EDT) I (CR)
```

(Type in Fig. D.2)

```
;
;    MACRO DEFINITIONS  FOR .TTYIN,.TTYOUT,.PRINT & .EXIT
;    FOR RSX-11M ENVIRONMENT.  USES SUBROUTINES DEFINED IN
;    SUBLIB.MAC.
;
        .NLIST
        .MACRO   .PRINT,A
        .IF NB   <A>
MOV     A,%0
        .ENDC
        JSR      PC,PRINT
        .ENDM    .PRINT
;
        .MACRO   .TTYIN,A
        JSR      PC,TTYIN
        .IF NB   <A>
        MOVB     %0,A
        .ENDC
        .ENDM    .TTYIN
;
        .MACRO   .TTYOUT,A
        .IF NB   <A>
        MOVB     A,%0
        .ENDC
        JSR      PC,TTYOUT
        .ENDM    .TTYOUT
;
        .MACRO   .EXIT
        .MCALL   EXIT$S
        EXIT$S
        .ENDM    .EXIT
;
        .LIST
;
```

Figure D.2 Macro listing for RSX-11M environment.

^Z

EDT⟩ EX ⟨CR⟩

MCR⟩ EDT SUBLIB.MAC ⟨CR⟩

EDT⟩ I⟨CR⟩

(Type in all three parts of Fig. D.3)

^Z

EDT⟩ EX ⟨CR⟩

MCR⟩RUN $MAC
MAC⟩SUBLIB.OBJ = SUBLIB.MAC ⟨CR⟩
MAC⟩ ^Z
MCR⟩

Note that if many people need these macros, considerable effort could be saved by having only one person prepare the files above. Others could then copy MACLIB.MAC and SUBLIB.OBJ into their accounts using the commands shown in Section D.3.4.5, or simply refer to them in the LINK command line as is shown for SYSMAC.SML in Section D.5.1.

```
                  .TITLE SIMRT - SIMULATE RT11 MACROS
                  .MCALL QIO$S,WTSE$S,WSIG$S
         ;
         ;     THIS SUBROUTINE WILL SIMULATE THE FUNCTION OF THE RT11
         ;     .TTYIN MACRO WITH RSX-11M MACROS.  EACH CALL TO THIS
         ;     SUBROUTINE WILL RETURN ONE CHARACTER FROM A LINE ENTERED
         ;     FROM THE TERMINAL KEYBOARD.  THE CHARACTER WILL BE RETURNED
         ;     IN REGISTER ZERO, RIGHT JUSTIFIED AND ZERO-PADDED.
         ;     THIS ROUTINE ASSUMES THAT LOGICAL UNIT 5 IS ASSIGNED TO
         ;     THE TERMINAL (TI:).  THIS IS THE TASK BUILDER DEFAULT.
         ;
         ;
         ;
         TTYIN::
                  CMP     NCHAR1,IOSB1+2    ;INPUT BUFF1 EMPTY?
                  BLO     20$               ;NO, SKIP TERMINAL READ
         10$:     QIO$S   #IO.RLB,#5,#1,,#IOSB1,,<#BUFF1,#80.>
                  BCC     40$               ;QIO OK, SKIP RECOVERY
                  CMPB    $DSW,#IE.UPN      ;ALLOCATION FAILURE?
                  BNE     30$               ;NO, SKIP RETRY
                  WSIG$S
                  BR      10$               ;REQUEUE READ REQUEST
         ;
         30$:     MOV     #177777,R0        ;SET ALLOCATION ERROR CODE
                  IOT                       ;ABORT TASK
         ;
         40$:     WTSE$S  #1                ;WAIT FOR READ COMPLETION
                  CMPB    IOSB1,#IS.SUC     ;SUCCESSFUL READ?
                  BEQ     50$               ;YES, CONTINUE
                  MOV     #177776,R0        ;SET READ ERROR CODE
                  IOT                       ;ABORT TASK
         ;
         50$:     CLR     NCHAR1            ;RESET CHARACTER COUNTER
                  MOV     IOSB1+2,R0        ;GET INPUT LINE LENGTH
                  MOVB    #15,BUFF1(R0)     ;ADD ON A CARRIAGE RETURN
                  MOVB    #12,BUFF1+1(R0)   ;ADD ON A LINE FEED
                  ADD     #2,IOSB1+2        ;ADJUST INPUT LINE LENGTH

         20$:     MOV     NCHAR1,R0         ;GET NEXT CHAR OF INPUT LINE
                  MOVB    BUFF1(R0),R0
                  INC     NCHAR1            ;INCREMENT CHARACTER COUNTER
                  CMP     R0,#12            ;RETURNING A LINEFEED?
                  BNE     60$               ;NO, RETURN TO CALLER
                  MOV     IOSB1+2,NCHAR1    ;EMPTY THE INPUT BUFF1
         60$:     RTS     PC                ;RETURN TO CALLING ROUTINE
         ;
         ;    LOCAL DATA
         ;
         IOSB1:   .WORD   0                 ;I/O STATUS BLOCK
                  .WORD   0
         NCHAR1:  .WORD   0                 ;NO. OF CHARACTERS TRANSFERRED
         BUFF1:   .BLKB   82.               ;TERMINAL-INPUT BUFF1
                  .PAGE
```

Figure D.3   Subroutines for RSX-11M macros.

```
;
;       THIS SUBROUTINE WILL SIMULATE THE FUNCTION OF THE RT11
;       .TTYOUT MACRO.  EACH CALL TO THIS SUBROUTINE OUTPUTS
;       THE LOW-ORDER BYTE OF REGISTER ZERO TO LOGICAL UNIT 5,
;       WHICH IS ASSUMED TO BE ASSIGNED TO THE USER'S TERMINAL
;       (TI:).  THIS IS THE TASK BUILDER DEFAULT.
;
;
;
TTYOUT::
        MOVB    R0,BUFF2
        QIO$S   #IO.WLB,#5,#1,,#IOSB2,,<BUFF2,#1,#0>
        BCC     20$             ;QIO OK, SKIP RECOVERY
        CMPB    $DSW,#IE.UPN    ;ALLOCATION FAILURE?
        BNE     10$             ;NO, SKIP RETRY
        WSIG$S
        BR      TTYOUT          ;REQUEUE WRITE REQUEST
;
10$:    MOV     #177775,R0      ;SET ALLOCATION ERROR CODE
        IOT                     ;ABORT TASK
;
20$:    WTSE$S  #1              ;WAIT FOR WRITE COMPLETION
        CMPB    IOSB2,#IS.SUC   ;SUCCESSFUL WRITE?
        BEQ     30$             ;YES, CONTINUE
        MOV     #177774,R0      ;SET WRITE ERROR CODE
        IOT                     ;ABORT TASK
;
30$:    RTS     PC              ;RETURN TO CALLING ROUTINE
;
;   LOCAL DATA
;
IOSB2:  .WORD   0               ;I/O STSTUS BLOCK
        .WORD   0
BUFF2:  .BLKB   1               ;OUTPUT BUFF2
        .EVEN
        .PAGE
```

Figure D.3   (cont.)

```
;
;     THIS SUBROUTINE WILL SIMULATE THE FUNCTION OF THE RT11
;     .PRINT MACRO.   THIS SUBROUTINE WILL HANDLE UP TO AN
;     80-CHARACTER STRING.   THE STRING TO BE PRINTED SHOULD
;     BE DELIMITED BY A BYTE OF ZEROS.   THE STRING WILL BE
;     OUTPUT TO LOGICAL UNIT 5 (ASSUMED TO BE ASSIGNED TO THE
;     USER'S TERMINAL (TI:).   THIS IS THE TASK BUILDER DEFAULT.
;     STRING WILL BE PRECEDED BY A LINEFEED AND FOLLOWED BY
;     A CARRIAGE RETURN.
;
;
;
PRINT::
        MOV     R1,-(SP)        ;SAVE REGISTER 1
        MOV     R2,-(SP)        ;SAVE REGISTER 2
        MOV     R0,R1           ;POINT TO BEGINNING OF STRING
        CLR     R2              ;CLEAR CHARACTER COUNTER
;
10$:    TSTB    (R1)+           ;NULL BYTE FOUND?
        BEQ     20$             ;YES, GO TO OUTPUT
        INC     R2              ;NO, INCREMENT CHARACTER COUNTER
        CMP     R2,#80.         ;LESS THAN 80. CHARACTERS?
        BLO     10$             ;YES, LOOK AT NEXT CHARACTER
;
20$:    TST     R2              ;NULL STRING?
        BEQ     50$             ;YES, BYPASS OUTPUT
;
25$:    QIO$S   #IO.WLB,#5,#1,,#IOSB3,,<R0,R2,#40>
        BCC     40$             ;QIO OK, SKIP RECOVERY
        CMPB    $DSW,#IE.UPN    ;ALLOCATION FAILURE?
        BNE     30$             ;NO, SKIP RETRY
        WSIG$S
        BR      25$             ;REQUEUE WRITE REQUEST
;
30$:    MOV     #177775,R0      ;SET ALLOCATION ERROR CODE
        IOT
;
40$:    WTSE$S  #1              ;WAIT FOR WRITE COMPLETION
        CMPB    IOSB3,#IS.SUC   ;SUCCESSFUL WRITE?
        BEQ     50$             ;YES, CONTINUE
        MOV     #177774,R0      ;SET WRITE ERROR CODE
        IOT
;
50$:    MOV     (SP)+,R2        ;RESTORE REGISTER 2
        MOV     (SP)+,R1        ;RESTORE REGISTER 1
        RTS     PC              ;RETURN TO CALLING ROUTINE
;
;
;   LOCAL DATA
;
IOSB3:  .WORD   0               ;I/O STATUS BLOCK
        .WORD   0
        .END
```

Figure D.3 (cont.)

D.5.3 Installation for the UNIX System

The macro definitions for .TTYIN, .TTYOUT, .PRINT, and .EXIT suitable for PDP-11 UNIX system installations are shown in Fig. D.4. In order to make these available for your MACRO-11 programs, you must have the code in Fig. D.4 in a file called maclib.m11 in your UNIX system personal directory. The exact steps to accomplish this are shown below.

```
$ ed ⟨CR⟩
⟩ a⟨CR⟩
```

(Type in Fig. D.4.)

```
.⟨CR⟩
⟩ w maclib.m11 ⟨CR⟩
⟩ q
$
```

```
;       These macros allow the RT11 macros .ttyin,.ttyout,
;       .print and .exit to be used in a UNIX system environment.
;
        .nlist
        .macro      .ttyout   src,?a,?b
        mov         src,b
        mov         #1,%0                   ;file descriptor to r0
        trap        4                       ;sys write
        .word       b                       ;address of a write buffer
        .word       1                       ;byte count
        br          a
b:      .byte       0,0
a:
        .endm       .ttyout
;
        .macro      .ttyin    a,?a,?b
        clr         %0                      ;standard input file descriptor
        trap        3                       ;unix read sys call
        .word       b                       ;address of read buffer
        .word       1                       ;byte count
        mov         b,%0                    ;pick up char just read
        .iif nb     <a> movb  %0,a
        br          a
b:      .byte       0,0
a:
        .endm       .ttyin
;
        .macro      .print    src,?b,?m,?k,?c
        mov         src,%0
m:      tstb        (%0)+
        bne         m
        sub         src,%0                  ;length
        mov         %0,k                    ;set length
        mov         src,b                   ;set buff address
        mov         #1,%0                   ;fd = std out
        trap        4                       ;sys write
b:      .word       0
k:      .word       0                       ;kount
        .ttyout     #12
        .ttyout     #15
c:
        .endm       .print
;
        .macro      .exit
        trap        1
        .endm       .exit
;
        .list
;
```

Figure D.4 Macro listing for a UNIX system environment.

Now whenever you assemble a MACRO-11 program that uses any of these macros, enter

    $ macro − ls maclib.m11 fn.m11 ⟨CR⟩

where fn.m11 is your program.

If many people will be using these macros, your UNIX system manager may wish to place them in a file where they can be accessed by all users.

MACRO-11 itself and the associated linker will also have to be installed on your UNIX system if not already present. These programs were developed at Harvard University and are available from the USENIX Association, P.O. Box 7, El Cerrito, California 94530. The necessary programs are on the 1981 USENIX distribution tape. The local UNIX system manager will know how to do the installation.

$\boxed{\text{E}}$ Subroutines for Simplified I/O

E.1 Installation

In order to make the simplified I/O routines GETOCT and PUTOCT described in Section 4.9 available to all students, the instructor or computer center staff should carry out the installation procedure for the appropriate operating system. These procedures are shown below.

E.1.1 RSTS/E

1. Sign on with account number (n,m) (instructor's account).
2. Create source file.

```
EDT GPOCT.MAC ⟨CR⟩
*I ⟨CR⟩
                    (Type in all three parts of Fig. E.1.)
^Z
*EX ⟨CR⟩
READY
```

```
GETOCT:
            .GLOBL   GETOCT
            .MCALL   .PRINT,.TTYIN,.EXIT,.TTYOUT
    ;
    ;       GETOCT CONVERTS KEYBOARD OCTAL (0-177777) TO
    ;       BINARY NUMBER IN R0.  SEE DEMO BELOW FOR EXAMPLE
    ;       USAGE.
    ;
            MOV      R1,-(SP)       ;SAVE R1 IN STACK
    1$:     CLR      R1             ;CLEAR RESULT REGISTER
            .TTYOUT  #'*            ;PROMT USER FOR INPUT
    2$:     .TTYIN                  ;GET CHARACTER
            CMPB     R0,#15         ;IF CR
            BEQ      2$             ;   LOOK FOR LF.
            CMPB     R0,#12         ;IF LF
            BEQ      4$             ;   NUMBER IS COMPLETE.
            SUB      #60,R0         ;CONVERT ASCII TO BIN.
            BCS      3$             ;INVALID OCTAL DIGIT
            CMPB     R0,#8.         ;
            BCC      3$             ;INVALID OCTAL DIGIT
            ASL      R1             ;MULTIPLY CURRENT
            ASL      R1             ;     RESULT BY
            ASL      R1             ;         EIGHT.
            ADD      R0,R1          ;ADD NEW DIGIT
            BR       2$             ;GET NEXT DIGIT
    3$:     .TTYIN                  ;BAD CHAR. HANDLING
            CMPB     R0,#12         ;CLEAR .TTYIN BUFFER
            BNE      3$
            .PRINT   #6$            ;PRINT ERROR MSG.
            BR       1$             ;   AND START OVER.
    4$:     MOV      R1,R0          ;PUT RESULT INTO R0
            MOV      (SP)+,R1       ;RESTORE R1
            RTS      PC             ;RETURN TO CALLING POINT.
    5$:     .ASCIZ/*/
    6$:     .ASCIZ/SOME CHARACTER WAS NOT OCTAL. START OVER./
    ;
    ;       END      OF      GETOCT
    ;
                            (a)
```

Figure E.1 I/O subroutines (a) GETOCT; (b) PUTOCT; (c) GETSTR and DEMO.

444

```
;
PUTOCT:
        .GLOBL PUTOCT
;
;       PUTOCT DISPLAYS CONTENTS OF R0 AS OCTAL
;       NUMBER AT USERS TERMINAL.
;
        MOV     R0,-(SP)        ;SAVE REGISTERS IN STACK
        MOV     R1,-(SP)
        MOV     R2,-(SP)
        MOV     R3,-(SP)
        MOV     R4,-(SP)
        MOV     #3$,R1          ;INITIALIZE PLACE VALUE POINTER
        MOV     #6,R2           ;INITIALIZE LCV (6 DIGITS)
        MOV     #4$,R3          ;INITIALIZE RESULT DIGIT POINTER
1$:     MOV     #-1,R4          ;INITIALIZE DIGIT VALUE
2$:     INC     R4              ;UPDATE DIGIT VALUE
        SUB     (R1),R0         ;SUBTRACT PLACE VALUE
        BCC     2$              ;    UNTIL OVER SUBTRACTED.
        ADD     (R1)+,R0        ;CORRECT FOR OVER SUBTRACT
        ADD     #60,R4          ;CONVERT DIGIT TO ASCII CHAR.
        MOVB    R4,(R3)+        ;STORE CHAR. IN PRINT ARRAY
        SOB     R2,1$           ;REPEAT FOR NEXT DIGIT
        .PRINT  #4$             ;PRINT RESULT
        MOV     (SP)+,R4        ;RESTORE REGISTERS
        MOV     (SP)+,R3
        MOV     (SP)+,R2
        MOV     (SP)+,R1
        MOV     (SP)+,R0
        RTS     PC              ;RETURN TO CALLING POINT
3$:     .WORD   100000,10000,1000,100,10,1 ;PLACE VALUES
4$:     .BLKB   6               ;RESULT ARRAY
        .BYTE   0               ;NULL CHAR TO TURN OFF .PRINT
        .EVEN
;
;       END     OF      PUTOCT
;
```

(b)

```
;
GETSTR::
;
;       ACCEPTS A STRING AND STORES IT WITH A TERMINATING
;       NULL BEGINNING AT ADDRESS IN R0.
;
        MOV     R0,-(SP)        ;SAVE REGISTERS
        MOV     R2,-(SP)        ;SAVE REGISTERS
        MOV     R0,R2
        .TTYOUT #'*             ;PROMPT USER FOR INPUT
1$:     .TTYIN                  ;GET CHAR FROM KEYBOARD
        CMPB    R0,#15          ;IF CR
        BEQ     1$              ;    GET LF
        CMPB    R0,#12          ;IF LF
        BEQ     2$              ;    ITS END OF STRING
        MOVB    R0,(R2)+        ;STORE CHARACTER
        BR      1$              ;NEXT CHARACTER
2$:     CLRB    (R2)+           ;MARK END OF STRING
        MOV     (SP)+,R2        ;RESTORE REGISTERS
        MOV     (SP)+,R0
        RTS     PC
DEMO:
;       DEMO CALLING PROGRAM FOR GETOCT AND PUTOCT
;
        .GLOBL  GETOCT,PUTOCT
        .PRINT  #1$
        JSR     PC,GETOCT       ;GET A NUMBER INTO R0
        MOV     R0,R1           ;PROTECT R0 FROM .PRINT
        .PRINT  #2$
        MOV     R1,R0           ;PUT NUMBER BACK INTO R0
        JSR     PC,PUTOCT       ;PRINT R0
        .EXIT
1$:     .ASCIZ/PLEASE ENTER OCTAL NUMBER:/
2$:     .ASCIZ/IT WAS:/
        .END    DEMO
```

(c)

3. Assemble.

```
RUN $MACRO (CR)
*GPOCT = GPOCT (CR)
ERRORS DETECTED = 0
*^Z
READY
```

4. Lower protection code to 40.

```
PIP GPOCT.OBJ(40)/RE (CR)
READY
```

E.1.2 RSX-11M

The following procedure assumes that the .TTYIN, .TTYOUT, and .PRINT macros are on the account (n,m). (See Section D.5.2.)

1. Sign on with account number (n,m) (instructor's account).

2. Create source file.

```
MCR)EDT GPOCT.MAC (CR)
*I (CR)
                            (Type in all three parts of Fig. E.1.)
^Z
*EX (CR)
MCR)
```

3. Assemble.

```
MCR)RUN $MAC (CR)
MAC)GPOCT = MACLIB,GPOCT (CR)
MAC)^Z
MCR)
```

4. Lower protection code to 40.

```
MCR)PIP GPOCT.OBJ (40)/RE (CR)
MCR)
```

E.1.3 RT-11

1. Power up and load the RT-11 operating system.

2. Create source file.

```
.EDIT/CREATE GPOCT.MAC (CR)
*I
(Type in all three parts of Fig. E.1.)
$$
*EX$$
.
```

3. Assemble.

```
.RUN MACRO ⟨CR⟩
*GPOCT = GPOCT ⟨CR⟩
*^C
.
```

E.1.4 The UNIX System

The following procedure assumes that the .TTYIN, .TTYOUT, and .PRINT macros are in the log-on directory. See Section D.5.3.

1. Log-on.

2. Create source file.

```
$ ed ⟨CR⟩
⟩ a ⟨CR⟩
(Type in Fig. E.1.)
. ⟨CR⟩
⟩ w gpoct.m11 ⟨CR⟩
⟩ q ⟨CR⟩
$
```

3. Assemble.

```
$ macro maclib.m11 gpoct.m11 ⟨CR⟩
$
```

4. Make public.

```
$ chmod 755 gpoct.m11 ⟨CR⟩
```

E.2 Usage

After the preceding installation, any user can access GETOCT, PUTOCT, or GETSTR by linking to GPOCT.OBJ [RSTS/E, RSX-11M, RT-11], or gpoct.m11 [the UNIX system]. The linkage process is shown below. Calling these routines is demonstrated in the small program DEMO that is included in GPOCT. (See Fig. E.1.)

E.2.1 RSTS/E

```
RUN $LINK ⟨CR⟩
*MYPROG,MYPROG = MYPROG(n,m),GPOCT.OBJ ⟨CR⟩
*^Z
```

        (The (n,m) must be the same as the one used during installation.)
READY

E.2.2 RSX-11M

This assumes that SUBLIB.OBJ is on the user's account. See Section D.5.2.

```
MCR⟩RUN $TKB ⟨CR⟩
TKB⟩MYPROG,MYPROG = SUBLIB,MYPROG,GPOCT ⟨CR⟩
TKB⟩^Z
MCR⟩
```

E.2.3 RT-11

```
.RUN LINK ⟨CR⟩
*MYPROG,MYPROG = MYPROG,GPOCT ⟨CR⟩
*^Z
.
```

E.2.4 The UNIX System

This assumes that the path for gpoct.obj is p, and is a public file.

```
$ link myprog p/gpoct ⟨CR⟩
$
```

F An Example of Modular Programming

This program is the implementation of the design developed in Section 15.2.2.

```
        .TITLE TEST SCORE ANALYSIS
        .MCALL .EXIT
        .GLOBL READ, SUMX, AVGX, HILO, FREQ, PRNT, PLOT
;++ ***********************************************************************
;
;    VERSION:  1.0                        LAST REVISED:   03 JULY 1982
;
;
;   FUNCTION: COMPUTES HIGH, LOW, AVERAGE SCORES AND
;             PLOTS FREQUENCY IN EACH DECILE FOR
;             TEST SCORES IN RANGE 0-100.
;
;   AUTHOR: E. F. SOWELL
;
;---------------------------------------------------------------------------
;
;   COPYRIGHT:  1982 GOOD-CODE INC.
;               NO PART OF THIS PROGRAM MAY BE
;               REPRODUCED IN ANY FORM WITHOUT PRIOR
;               WRITTEN PERMISSION OF GOOD-CODE.
;               GOOD-CODE MAKES NO WARRANTIES
;               WITH RESPECT TO THE VALIDITY OF
;               THIS SOFTWARE, AND DISCLAIMS ANY
;               IMPLIED WARRANTIES.  IN NO CASE SHALL
;               THE LIABILITY OF GOOD-CODE EXCEED PURCHASE
;               PRICE OF THE SOFTWARE.
;
;---------------------------------------------------------------------------
;
;   INPUTS:
;             AN ARRAY OF SCORES FROM THE KEYBOARD FOR
;             SUBROUTINE READ.
;
;   OUTPUT:
;           N: NUMBER OF SCORES
;        HIGH: HIGHEST SCORE
;         LOW: LOWEST SCORE
;         AVG: AVERAGE SCORE (ROUNDED)
;           F: ARRAY OF COUNTS IN EACH DECILE
;
;   INTERNALS:
;             R0, R1, R2, R3: USED VARIOUSLY AND RESTORED.
;
;   EXTERNAL CALLS:
;             READ: READS SCORES INTO (R1) AND COUNT INTO R2.
;             SUMX: SUMS SCORES INTO R0.
;             AVGX: COMPUTES AVERAGE INTO R0.
;             HILO: FINDS ADDRESS OF LOW (R2) AND HIGH (R3).
;             FREQ: COUNTS SCORES INTO EACH DECILE (R2).
;             PRNT: PRINTS N, HIGH, AVG, AND LOW.
;             PLOT: PLOTS FREQUENCY HISTOGRAM.
;
;-- ***********************************************************************
        .PAGE
```

```
;-------------------------------------------------------------------------------
;
;                       L O C A L     D A T A
;
;-------------------------------------------------------------------------------
        .PSECT  DATA
X:      .BLKW   1000.                   ;SCORES
N:      .BLKW   1                       ;COUNT
AVG:    .BLKW   1                       ;AVERAGE SCORE
HIGH:   .BLKW   1                       ;HIGH SCORE
LOW:    .BLKW   1                       ;LOW SCORE
F:      .BLKW   100.                    ;FREQ. ARRAY
ARG:    .WORD   N,HIGH,AVG,LOW          ;ARG LIST FOR PRNT
;
;-------------------------------------------------------------------------------
;
        .PAGE
;
;-------------------------------------------------------------------------------
;
;                       C O D E     S E C T I O N
;
;-------------------------------------------------------------------------------
        .PSECT  PROG
START::
        MOV     #X,R1                   ;READ DATA FROM KEYBOARD
        JSR     PC,READ                 ;   INTO X ARRAY, AND
        MOV     R2,N                    ;       READ COUNT INTO R2.
        JSR     PC,SUMX                 ;SUM ALL SCORES INTO R0
        JSR     PC,AVGX                 ;AVERAGE SCORE INTO R0
        MOV     R0,AVG                  ;   AND SAVE.
        MOV     R2,R0                   ;FIND HIGH
        JSR     PC,HILO                 ;   AND
        MOV     (R2),LOW                ;     LOW
        MOV     (R3),HIGH               ;       SCORES.
        MOV     #F,R2                   ;COUNT SCORE FREQUENCIES
        JSR     PC,FREQ                 ;   IN DECILES, STORED IN F.
        MOV     #ARG,R1                 ;PRINT N, HIGH,
        JSR     PC,PRNT                 ;   AVG, AND LOW.
        JSR     PC,PLOT                 ;PLOT HISTOGRAPH OF F
        .EXIT
        .END    START
;
;-------------------------------------------------------------------------------
;
```

```
        .TITLE READ
        .MCALL .PRINT
        .GLOBL  GETDEC, GETCHR
;++ ************************************************************************
;
;   VERSION: 1.0                         LAST REVISED: 03 JULY 1982
;
;   FUNCTION:  PROMPTS USER FOR SUCCESSIVE INTEGER SCORES
;              BETWEEN 0 AND 100, SAVING THEM IN AN ARRAY.
;              ALSO COUNTS ENTRIES.
;
;   AUTHOR: E. F. SOWELL
;
;----------------------------------------------------------------------
;
;   INPUTS:
;           R1: ADDRESS OF THE FIRST LOC. WHERE DATA IS TO BE STORED
;
;   OUTPUTS:
;           R1: AS INPUT
;   (R1)-(R1+R2): ARRAY OF SCORES
;
;   INTERNALS:
;           R0: USED BY GETDEC, GETCHR, .PRINT, BUT IS RESTORED
;               TO INPUT VALUE
;
;   SIDE EFFECTS:
;           NONE
;
;   EXTERNAL CALLS:
;       GETDEC: GETS DECIMAL VALUE FROM KEYBOARD
;       GETCHR: GETS CHARACTER FROM KEYBOARD
;
;-- ************************************************************************
        .PAGE
;----------------------------------------------------------------------
;
;               L O C A L   D A T A
;
;----------------------------------------------------------------------
;
        .PSECT   DATA
PRMT1: .ASCIZ /ENTER SCORE (0 TO 100):/
PRMT2: .ASCIZ /MORE SCORES (Y OR N)?/
ERRMSG: .ASCIZ /INVALID.  REENTER LAST VALUE./
;
;----------------------------------------------------------------------
;
;               L O C A L    S Y M B O L S
;
;----------------------------------------------------------------------
;
YES   = 'Y
MINSCR = 0.
MAXSCR = 100.
        .PAGE
```

```
;
;-------------------------------------------------------------------------------
;
;                    C O D E    S E C T I O N
;
;-------------------------------------------------------------------------------
;
;                    L O C A L     S U B R O U T I N E
;
;-------------------------------------------------------------------------------
;
        .PSECT  PROG
CHKSCR:         ;(CHECKS SCORES)
        CMP     R0,#MINSCR      ;SET CARRY BIT
        BLO     OUT             ;IF SCORE
        CMP     #MAXSCR,R0      ;  OUT OF RANGE.
OUT:    RTS     PC              ;RETURN TO READ
;
;-------------------------------------------------------------------------------
;
;       ENTRY POINT
;
READ::
        MOV     R0,-(SP)        ;SAVE
        MOV     R1,-(SP)        ;REGISTERS
        CLR     R2              ;INIT COUNTER
REPEAT: .PRINT  #PRMT1          ;ASK FOR INPUT
        JSR     PC,GETDEC       ;GET SCORE (RETURN IN R0)
        JSR     PC,CHKSCR       ;CHECK
        BCC     OK              ;   SCORE.
        .PRINT  #ERRMSG         ;PROMPT
        BR      REPEAT          ;   IF BAD SCORE.
OK:     MOV     R0,(R1)+        ;STORE SCORE
        INC     R2              ;INCREMENT COUNT
        .PRINT  #PRMT2          ;PROMPT
        JSR     PC,GETCHR       ;   FOR MORE.
        CMPB    R0,#YES         ;GET NEXT
        BEQ     REPEAT          ;   SCORE.
        MOV     (SP)+,R1        ;RESTORE
        MOV     (SP)+,R0        ;   REGISTERS.
        RTS     PC              ;RETURN TO CALLER
        .END    ;(READ)
;
;-------------------------------------------------------------------------------
;
```

```
        .TITLE     GET CHARACTER
        .MCALL     .TTYIN
;++ ***************************************************************************
;
;   VERSION: 1.0                        LAST REVISED: 04 JULY 1982
;
;   FUNCTION:  INPUTS A SINGLE CHARACTER INTO R0
;              BUT CONTINUES TO READ JUST TO EMPTY
;              THE BUFFER.
;
;   AUTHOR:  E. F. SOWELL
;
;-------------------------------------------------------------------------------
;
;   INPUTS:
;       NONE
;
;   OUTPUT:
;
;       R0: INPUT CHARACTER IS IN LOW BYTE.
;
;   INTERNALS:
;       R5: TEMP STORAGE (RESTORED)
;
;-- ***************************************************************************
;
;                    L O C A L     S Y M B O L S
;
;-------------------------------------------------------------------------------
LF = 12
;
;-------------------------------------------------------------------------------
;
;                    C O D E      S E C T I O N
;
;-------------------------------------------------------------------------------
;
        .PSECT PROG
GETCHR::
        MOV     R5,-(SP)        ;SAVE REGISTER 5 ON STACK
        .TTYIN                  ;GET LINE FROM KEYBOARD
        MOV     R0,R5           ;SAVE FIRST CHAR
REST:   .TTYIN                  ;GET RID OF REST OF LINE
        CMPB    R0,#LF
        BNE     REST
        MOV     R5,R0           ;PUT FIRST CHAR BACK INTO R0
        MOV     (SP)+,R5        ;RESTORE R5
        RTS     PC              ;RETURN TO CALLER
        .END    ;(GETCHR)
;
;-------------------------------------------------------------------------------
;
```

```
        .TITLE  GETDEC
        .MCALL  .TTYIN,.PRINT
;++ *************************************************************************
;
;   VERSION: 1.0                         LAST REVISED: 04 JULY 1982
;
;   FUNCTION:   GETS DECIMAL ASCII CHARACTERS FROM THE KEYBOARD
;               AND CONVERTS THEM TO BINARY.
;
;   AUTHOR:   E. F. SOWELL
;
;-------------------------------------------------------------------------
;   INPUTS:
;       NONE
;
;   OUTPUT:
;       R0: VALUE ENTERED FROM KEYBOARD
;
;   INTERNALS:
;       R3: TEMP STORAGE (RESTORED)
;
;
;-- *************************************************************************
;
;                  L O C A L    D A T A
;
;-------------------------------------------------------------------------
        .PSECT  DATA
BAD:    .ASCIZ  /BAD INPUT.....TRY AGAIN/
;
;-------------------------------------------------------------------------
;
;               L O C A L    S Y M B O L S
;
;-------------------------------------------------------------------------
CR = 15
LF = 12
;
        .PAGE




;-------------------------------------------------------------------------
;
;                  C O D E    S E C T I O N
;
;-------------------------------------------------------------------------
;
        .PSECT  PROG
GETDEC::
        MOV     R3,-(SP)        ;SAVE R3 ON STACK
G0:     CLR     R3              ;CLEAR RESULT REGISTER
G1:     .TTYIN                  ;GET LINE FROM KEYBOARD
        CMPB    R0,#CR          ;IF CR
        BEQ     G1              ;  GET LF.
        CMPB    R0,#LF          ;IF LF
        BEQ     GEND            ;   NUMBER IS FINISHED
        SUB     #'0,R0          ;REMOVE ASCII BASE
        BCS     G2              ;BAD CHARACTER
        CMP     R0,#10.
        BCC     G2              ;BAD CHARACTER
        MUL     #10.,R3         ;DECIMAL SHIFT OF PREVIOUS RESULT
        ADD     R0,R3           ;COMBINE NEW DIGIT
        BR      G1              ;GET NEXT CHARACTER
G2:     .TTYIN                  ;GET RID OF
        CMPB    R0,#LF          ;   REST
        BNE     G2              ;    OF LINE
        .PRINT  #BAD            ;     PRINT MESSAGE
        BR      G0              ;THROW AWAY BAD NO. & GET ANOTHER
GEND:
        MOV     R3,R0           ;PUT NUMBER INTO OUTPUT REGISTER
        MOV     (SP)+,R3        ;RESTORE R3
        RTS     PC              ;RETURN TO CALLER
        .END    ;(GETDEC)
```

```
          .TITLE  SUMX
;++ ***********************************************************************
;
;    VERSION 1.0                            LAST REVISED:   03 JULY 1982
;
;    FUNCTION: ADDS INTEGERS FROM ARRAY.
;
;    AUTHOR: E. F. SOWELL
;
;-----------------------------------------------------------------------
;
;    INPUTS:
;              R1: ADDRESS OF FIRST LOC. WHERE DATA IS STORED
;              R2: NUMBER OF VALUES TO BE ADDED
;
;    OUTPUTS:
;              R0: SUM
;              R1: AS INPUT
;              R2: AS INPUT
;
;    INTERNALS:
;              NONE
;
;    SIDE EFFECTS:
;              NONE
;
;    EXTERNAL CALLS:
;              NONE
;
;-- ***********************************************************************
          .PAGE
;-----------------------------------------------------------------------
;
;                    C O D E    S E C T I O N
;
;-----------------------------------------------------------------------
;
          .PSECT   PROG
SUMX::

          MOV     R1,-(SP)        ;SAVE
          MOV     R2,-(SP)        ;  REGISTERS.
          CLR     R0              ;INIT. SUM
LOOP:     ADD     (R1)+,R0        ;ADD R2 VALUES
          SOB     R2,LOOP         ;  INTO R0.
          MOV     (SP)+,R2        ;RESTORE
          MOV     (SP)+,R1        ;  REGISTERS.
          RTS     PC              ;RETURN TO CALLER
          .END    ;(SUMX)
;
;-----------------------------------------------------------------------
;
```

```
        .TITLE  AVGX
;++ **********************************************************************
;
;   VERSION: 1.0                        LAST REVISED: 03 JULY 1982
;
;   FUNCTION:  FINDS AVERAGE BY DIVIDING SUM BY COUNT.
;
;   AUTHOR: E. F. SOWELL
;
;-----------------------------------------------------------------------
;
;   INPUTS:
;               R0: SUM OF SCORES
;               R2: NUMBER OF SCORES
;
;   OUTPUT:
;               R0: AVERAGE (ROUNDED TO THE NEAREST INTEGER)
;               R2: AS INPUT
;
;   INTERNALS:
;               R1: USED IN DIVIDE OPERATION, BUT RESTORED
;
;   SIDE EFFECTS:
;               NONE
;
;   EXTERNAL CALLS:
;               NONE
;
;-- **********************************************************************
        .PAGE
;-----------------------------------------------------------------------
;
;                    C O D E    S E C T I O N
;
;-----------------------------------------------------------------------
;
        .PSECT  PROG
AVGX::
        MOV     R1,-(SP)        ;SAVE REGISTERS
        MOV     R0,R1           ;SET UP
        CLR     R0              ;  DIVIDE.
        DIV     R2,R0           ;QUOTIENT TO R0, REMAINDER TO R1
        ASL     R1              ;ROUND RESULT
        CMP     R1,R2           ;  RATHER
        BLO     OUT             ;     THAN
        INC     R0              ;        TRUNCATE.
OUT:    MOV     (SP)+,R1        ;RESTORE REGISTERS
        RTS     PC              ;RETURN TO CALLER
        .END    ;(AVGX)
;
;-----------------------------------------------------------------------
;
```

```
        .TITLE HILO
;++ **********************************************************************
;
;   VERSION: 1.0                          LAST REVISED:  03 JULY 1982
;
;   FUNCTION:  FINDS ADDRESS OF THE LOWEST
;              AND THE HIGHEST VALUES IN THE ARRAY OF SCORES.
;
;   AUTHOR:  E. F. SOWELL
;
;----------------------------------------------------------------------
;
;   INPUTS:
;           R0: COUNT OF SCORES
;           R1: ADDRESS OF FIRST LOCATION WHERE DATA IS STORED
;
;   OUTPUTS:
;           R0: AS INPUT
;           R1: AS INPUT
;           R2: ADDRESS OF LOWEST VALUE
;           R3: ADDRESS OF HIGHEST VALUE
;
;   INTERNALS:
;           NONE
;
;   SIDE EFFECTS:
;           NONE
;
;   EXTERNAL CALLS:
;           NONE
;
;----------------------------------------------------------------------
        .PAGE




;----------------------------------------------------------------------
;
;                       C O D E    S E C T I O N
;
;----------------------------------------------------------------------
;
        .PSECT  PROG
HILO::
        MOV     R0,-(SP)        ;SAVE
        MOV     R1,-(SP)        ;  REGISTERS.
        MOV     R1,R2           ;INITALIZE RESULT
        MOV     R1,R3           ;  POINTERS.
LOOP:
        CMP     (R1),(R2)       ;CHECK VALUE AGAINST
        BHIS    1$              ;  CURRENT LOW VALUE.
        MOV     R1,R2           ;ESTABLISH NEW LOW POINTER
1$:     CMP     (R1),(R3)       ;CHECK VALUE AGAINST
        BLOS    2$              ;  CURRENT HIGH VALUE.
        MOV     R1,R3           ;ESTABLISH NEW HIGH POINTER
2$:     TST     (R1)+           ;INC. R1 BY TWO
        SOB     R0,LOOP         ;NEXT VALUE
        MOV     (SP)+,R1        ;RESTORE
        MOV     (SP)+,R0        ;  REGISTERS.
        RTS     PC              ;RETURN TO CALLER
        .END    ;(HILO)
;
;----------------------------------------------------------------------
;
```

```
        .TITLE  FREQUENCY COUNTER
;++ ******************************************************************
;
;   VERSION: 1.0                        LAST REVISED: 03 JULY 1982
;
;   FUNCTION:     CREATES AN ARRAY OF COUNTS OF
;                 SCORES IN N INTERVALS BETWEEN
;                 MINSCR AND MAXSCR.
;
;   AUTHOR: E. F. SOWELL
;
;------------------------------------------------------------------
;
;   INPUTS:
;             R0:  COUNTS
;             R1:  ADDRESS OF FIRST LOCATION OF SCORES ARRAY
;             R2:  ADDRESS OF FIRST LOCATION OF RESULTS
;
;   OUTPUTS:
;             R0:  AS INPUT
;             R1:  AS INPUT
;             R2:  AS INPUT
;             (R2) TO (R2+2 N):  ARRAY OF FREQUENCIES
;
;   INTERNALS:
;             R4, R5:  USED AS LCV AND DIVISION REGISTERS
;                      BUT RESTORED.
;
;   SIDE EFFECTS:
;             NONE
;
;   EXTERNAL CALLS:
;             NONE
;
;-- ******************************************************************
        .PAGE
;
;
;                 A S S I G N E D    V A L U E S
;
;------------------------------------------------------------------
;
MAXSCR = 100.                    ;MAX SCORE
MINSCR = 0.                      ;MIN SCORE
N      = 10.                     ;NUMBER OF INTERVALS
W      = <MAXSCR-MINSCR>/N       ; INTERVAL WIDTH
;
;------------------------------------------------------------------
        .PAGE
```

```
;-----------------------------------------------------------------------------
;
;                    C O D E      S E C T I O N
;
;-----------------------------------------------------------------------------
;
        .PSECT  PROG
FREQ::
        MOV     R0,-(SP)        ;SAVE
        MOV     R1,-(SP)        ;  REGISTERS
        MOV     R2,-(SP)        ;    ON
        MOV     R4,-(SP)        ;      THE
        MOV     R5,-(SP)        ;        STACK.
        MOV     #N+1,R4         ;CLEAR
LOOP1:  CLR     (R2)+           ;  RESULTS
        SOB     R4,LOOP1        ;    ARRAY.
        MOV     4(SP),R2        ;RESTORE FREQUENCY POINTER
LOOP2:  CLR     R4              ;OFFSET IN FREQ ARRAY
        MOV     (R1)+,R5        ;  IS
        DIV     #W,R4           ;    (SCORE/W)*2.
        ASL     R4
        ADD     R2,R4           ;COMPUTE ADDRESS IN FREQ ARRAY
        INC     (R4)            ;COUNT AT SCORE
        SOB     R0,LOOP2        ;NEXT SCORE
        MOV     (SP)+,R5        ;RESTORE
        MOV     (SP)+,R4        ;  REGISTERS
        MOV     (SP)+,R2        ;    FROM
        MOV     (SP)+,R1        ;      THE
        MOV     (SP)+,R0        ;        STACK.
        RTS     PC              ;RETURN TO CALLER
        .END    ;(FREQ.)
;
;-----------------------------------------------------------------------------
;
```

```
        .TITLE   PRINT
        .MCALL .PRINT
        .GLOBL CNVDEC
;++ ******************************************************************
;
;   VERSION: 1.0                          LAST REVISED:  04 JULY 1982
;
;   FUNCTION    PRINTS TESTS STATISTICS.
;
;   AUTHOR:     E. F. SOWELL
;
;---------------------------------------------------------------------
;
;   INPUTS:
;         R1: ADDRESS OF ARRAY OF RESULT ADDRESS
;            (R1): ADDRESS OF NO. OF SCORES
;           2(R1): ADDRESS OF HIGHEST SCORE
;           4(R1): ADDRESS OF AVBERAGE SCORE
;           6(R1): ADDRESS OF LOWEST SCORE
;
;   OTUPUTS:
;         R1: AS INPUT
;
;   INTERNALS:
;         R0: ARGUMENT TRANSMISSION (RESTORED)
;         R2: TEMP. FOR R1 (RESTORED)
;
;   SIDE EFFECTS:
;         NONE
;
;   EXTERNAL CALLS:
;         CNVDEC: CONVERTS R0 TO A STRING OF ASCII DECIMAL CHARACTERS
;
;-- ******************************************************************
        .PAGE
;---------------------------------------------------------------------
;
;                     L O C A L    D A T A
;
;---------------------------------------------------------------------
;
        .PSECT DATA
MSG1:   .ASCII <15><15>/                                      /
        .ASCII /TEST STASTICS/
        .ASCIZ <15><15>/RESULTS:/
NUM:    .ASCIZ <15>/    NUMBER TAKING TEST=   /
HIGH:   .ASCIZ <15>/    HIGHEST SCORE      =  /
AVG:    .ASCIZ <15>/    AVERAGE SCORE      =  /
LOW:    .ASCIZ <15>/    LOWEST SCORE       =  /
;
;---------------------------------------------------------------------
        .PAGE
```

```
;-------------------------------------------------------------------------------
;
;           C O D E     S E C T I O N
;
;-------------------------------------------------------------------------------
;
        .PSECT  PROG
PRNT::
        MOV     R0,-(SP)            ;SAVE
        MOV     R1,-(SP)            ;   REGISTERS
        MOV     R2,-(SP)            ;     ON STACK.
        MOV     R1,R2               ;R1 WILL BE USED BY CNVDEC
        .PRINT  #MSG1               ;PRINT HEADER
        MOV     @(R2)+,R0           ;CONVERT
        MOV     #NUM+23.,R1         ;   AND
        JSR     PC,CNVDEC           ;     PRINT
        CLRB    (R1)                ;       NUMBER
        .PRINT  #NUM                ;         OF TESTS.
        MOV     @(R2)+,R0           ;CONVERT
        MOV     #HIGH+23.,R1        ;   AND
        JSR     PC,CNVDEC           ;     PRINT
        CLRB    (R1)                ;       HIGHEST
        .PRINT  #HIGH               ;         SCORE.
        MOV     @(R2)+,R0           ;CONVERT
        MOV     #AVG+23.,R1         ;   AND
        JSR     PC,CNVDEC           ;     PRINT
        CLRB    (R1)                ;       AVERAGE
        .PRINT  #AVG                ;         SCORE.
        MOV     @(R2)+,R0           ;CONVERT
        MOV     #LOW+23.,R1         ;   AND
        JSR     PC,CNVDEC           ;     PRINT
        CLRB    (R1)                ;       LOWEST
        .PRINT  #LOW                ;         SCORE.
        MOV     (SP)+,R2            ;RESTORE
        MOV     (SP)+,R1            ;   REGISTERS
        MOV     (SP)+,R0            ;     FROM STACK.
        RTS     PC                  ;RETURN TO CALLER
        .END    ;(PRINT)
;
;-------------------------------------------------------------------------------
;
```

```
            .TITLE CNVDEC
;++ *************************************************************************
;
;   VERSION: 1.0                          LAST REVISED: 03 JULY 1982
;
;   FUNCTION:   CONVERTS R0 INTO 3-DIGIT DECIMAL ASCII IN
;               BUFFER POINTED TO BY R1.
;
;   AUTHOR:  E. F. SOWELL
;
;-------------------------------------------------------------------------
;
;   INPUTS:
;       R0: CONTAINS CHARACTER TO BE CONVERTED
;       R1: POINTER TO THE BUFFER
;
;   OUTPUT:
;       R0: AS INPUT
;       R1: POINTS TO NEXT AVAILABLE BUFFER BYTE.
;
;   INTERNALS:
;       R2: USED AS LOOP CONTROL VARIBLE (RESTORED)
;       R3: PLACE VALUE ARRAY POINTER (RESTORED)
;       R4: DIGIT VALUE (RESTORED)
;
;   SIDE EFFECTS:
;       NONE
;
;   EXTERNAL CALLS:
;       NONE
;
;-- *************************************************************************
;
;                     L O C A L      D A T A
;
;-------------------------------------------------------------------------
            .EVEN
            .PSECT  DATA
PV:         .WORD   100.,10.,1,     ;PLACE VALUES
;




;-------------------------------------------------------------------------
;
;                     C O D E    S E C T I O N
;
;-------------------------------------------------------------------------
;
            .PSECT  PROG
CNVDEC::
            MOV     R0,-(SP)        ;SAVE
            MOV     R2,-(SP)        ;  REGISTERS
            MOV     R3,-(SP)        ;    IN
            MOV     R4,-(SP)        ;      STACK.
            MOV     #PV,R3          ;INITIALIZE PLACE VALUE POINTER
            MOV     #3,R2           ;INITIALIZE LCV (3 DIGITS)
1$:         MOV     #-1,R4          ;INITIALIZE DIGIT VALUE
2$:         INC     R4              ;UPDATE DIGIT VALUE
            SUB     (R3),R0         ;SUBTRACT PLACE VALUE
            BCC     2$              ;  UNTIL OVERSUBTRACTED.
            ADD     (R3)+,R0        ;CORRECT FOR OVERSUBTRACT
            ADD     #60,R4          ;  CONVERT DIGIT TO ASCII CHAR.
            MOVB    R4,(R1)+        ;STORE CHAR IN PRINT ARRAY
21$:        SOB     R2,1$           ;REPEAT FOR NEXT DIGIT
            CLRB    (R1)            ;STORE NULL BYTE
            MOV     (SP)+,R4        ;RESTORE
            MOV     (SP)+,R3        ;  REGISTERS
            MOV     (SP)+,R2        ;    FROM
            MOV     (SP)+,R0        ;      THE STACK.
            RTS     PC              ;RETURN TO CALLER
            .BLKW   20.             ;ODT BUFFER
            .END    ; (CNVDEC)
;
;-------------------------------------------------------------------------
;
```

```
        .TITLE    PLOT
        .MCALL    .PRINT
        .GLOBL    CNVDEC
;++ **********************************************************************
;
;  VERSION: 1.0                            LAST REVISED:  04 JULY 1982
;
;  FUNCTION  PLOTS HISTOGRAM OF SCORE FREQUENCIES.
;
;  AUTHOR:  E. F. SOWELL
;
;----------------------------------------------------------------------
;
;  INPUTS:
;          R2: ADDRESS OF FREQUENCY ARRAY
;
;  OUTPUT:
;          R2: AS INPUT
;
;  INTERNALS:
;          R0: USED AS LOOP CONTROL  (RESTORED)
;          R1: USED AS POINTER (RESTORED)
;
;  SIDE EFFECTS:
;          NONE
;
;  EXTERNAL CALLS:
;          CNVDEC:  CONVERTS  R0  TO A STRING OF  ASCII  DECIMAL
;                   CHARACTERS.
;
;-- **********************************************************************
        .PAGE




;----------------------------------------------------------------------
;
;                 L O C A L      D A T A
;
;----------------------------------------------------------------------
;
        .PSECT    DATA
BUF:    .BLKB     80.             ;PLOT LINE BUFFER
MSG1:   .ASCII    <15><15>/                        /
        .ASCIZ    /FREQUENCY PLOT/
;
;----------------------------------------------------------------------
;
;                 L O C A L     S Y M B O L S
;
;----------------------------------------------------------------------
;
DASH   = '-
SPA    = 40
BAR    = 174
STAR   = '*
MAXSCR = 100.                     ;MAX SCORE
MINSCR = 0.                       ;MIN SCORE
N      = 10.                      ;NUMBER OF INTERVALS
W      = <MAXSCR-MINSCR>/N        ;INTERVAL WIDTH
;
        .PAGE
```

```
;-------------------------------------------------------------------------------
;
;                      C O D E        S E C T I O N
;
;-------------------------------------------------------------------------------
        .EVEN
        .PSECT  PROG
PLOT::
        MOV     R0,-(SP)        ;SAVE
        MOV     R1,-(SP)        ;  REGISTERS.
        .PRINT  #MSG1           ;PRINT HEADER
        CLR     R0              ;INIT LCV
L0:     MOV     #BUF,R1         ;SET
        JSR     PC,CNVDEC       ;
        CMP     #MAXSCR,R0      ;  UP
        BEQ     L1              ;
        MOVB    #DASH,(R1)+     ;    LABEL
        ADD     #W-1,R0         ;
        JSR     PC,CNVDEC       ;       FOR
L1:     CMP     R1,#BUF+9.      ;
        BHIS    L2              ;         EACH
        MOVB    #SPA,(R1)+      ;
        BR      L1              ;           LINE
L2:     MOVB    #BAR,(R1)+      ;              OF PLOT.
        MOV     (R2)+,R3        ;SET UP
L3:     BEQ     L4              ;  CORRECT NUMBER
        MOVB    #STAR,(R1)+     ;   OF *'S
        DEC     R3              ;      IN EACH LINE
        BR      L3              ;         OF PLOT.
L4:     CLRB    (R1)+           ;STORE NULL CHAR.
        MOV     R0,-(SP)        ;PROTECT R0 FROM .PRINT
        .PRINT  #BUF            ;PRINT LINE
        MOV     (SP)+,R0        ;RESTORE R0
        CMP     #MAXSCR,R0      ;TRUE EXIT
        BEQ     OUT             ;  GET OUT HERE
        INC     R0              ;DO NEXT
        BR.     L0              ;  LINE OF PLOT.
OUT:
        MOV     (SP)+,R1        ;RESTORE
        MOV     (SP)+,R0        ;  REGISTERS.
        RTS     PC              ;RETURN TO CALLER
        .END    ;(PLOT)
;
;-------------------------------------------------------------------------------
```

$\boxed{G}$ Assembly and Execution Errors

G.1 The Purpose of This Appendix

One of the frustrations encountered in learning to program is the cryptic error message. This is particularly acute in assembly language because messages are extremely brief, and errors are all too common. This appendix is intended to help you understand these error messages, and to give you some suggestions for correcting the problem. Unfortunately, we are not always able to give a definite cause of the error because often a single error code can be caused by several different programming errors. Once the problem is localized, however, it is usually not too difficult to identify the fault from among the listed possible causes of the error code. Presented here are the errors most frequently encountered during assembly, linkage, and execution of the program.

G.2 Assembly Errors

Certain programming errors are detected during the assembly process. The count of these errors is printed at the terminal after the MACRO command line. For example,

```
MACRO JUNK,JUNK=JUNK ⟨CR⟩
?MACRO-W-ERRORS DETECTED: 2
READY
```

When this occurs the .LST file should be examined to determine the nature of the errors. The LST file for this example is shown in Fig. G.1. The errors are marked by one or more letters printed at the left of the offending lines.

In Fig. G.1, the error code is "M", standing for "multiple definition of a label." Each line that attempts to define A is so marked, so that two errors are

```
      1                                          .TITLE ERROR REPORTS
M     2              000010              A = 10
      3  000000                         START:
      4  000000     000402                       BR     B
M     5  000002     000074   000054      A:       .WORD  74,54
      6  000006     010203               B:       MOV    R2,R3
      7  000010     000000                        HALT
      8  000012                                   .BLKW  20
      9              000000'                       .END   START


      SYMBOL TABLE

      A = 000010      B 000006R      START 000000R

      . ABS.  000000        000
              000052        001
      ERRORS DETECTED:   2
```

Figure G.1 Example of assembler error report (one error per line).

```
         1                                              .TITLE  ERROR REPORTS
         2 000000                             START:
         3 000000   000402                            BR      B
         4 000002   000074    000054          A:      .WORD   74,54
         5 000006   010203                    B:      MOV     R2,R3
    AQ   6 000010   016167    000002' 000000          MOV     A(R1)+,R3
         7 000016   000000                            HALT
         8 000020                                     .BLKW   20
         9           000000'                          .END    START


         SYMBOL TABLE

         A 000002R      B 000006R      START 000000R

         . ABS.   000000        000
                  000060        001
         ERRORS DETECTED:   1
```

Figure G.2 Example of assembler error report (multiple errors per line).

created by the single programming error of using A both as an assigned symbol and a label.

When two errors are found on a single line of the program, both error codes are printed together. This is shown in Fig. G.2, where "AQ" is printed at line 6. The code "A" means "addressing error" and "Q" means "questionable syntax." Note that this is counted as a single error.

Table G.1 gives a list of all error codes that can be produced by the assembler. In some cases there are many things that could cause the error. Here we give only the most common meanings of these codes, omitting the causes less likely to occur in elementary programming.

Errors made in the assembly command line are printed at the terminal preceded by a question mark. For example, an attempt to assemble a nonexistent file will have the following effect.

```
MACRO MYPROG,MYPROG = MYPROG ⟨CR⟩
?MACRO-F-FILE NOT FOUND
READY
```

Usually this is a result of mistyping the source file name. Otherwise, check your directory to be sure it has not been deleted.

G.3 Linkage Errors

Certain programming errors cannot be detected by the assembler, but result in error reports when linkage is attempted. These are printed immediately after the LINK command line, preceded by a question mark. The errors most commonly encountered in elementary programming are shown in Table G.2, along with corrective actions.

TABLE G.1
Assembler Error Codes

Code	Probable Meaning	Probable Cause and Correction
A	1. Addressing error Operand address cannot be determined. 2. Relocation error	1. Invalid addressing mode. See Table 11.1 for valid modes. 2. Expressions that add labels, or other operations that would make it impossible to relocate the program during linkage. Avoid such operations.
B	Bounding error	A .BYTE, .ASCII, or .ASCIZ directive, or changing the location counter by assignment, places later instruction or word data at odd address. Use .EVEN after these directives.
D	Doubly defined symbol usage	Marks a line in which a symbol that is multiply-defined is referred to. This will go away when M-code errors are fixed.
E	End directive missing	The .END was omitted. Place .END at end of source file.
I	Illegal character	A character not recognized by the assembler occurs in the line. Do not use control characters [,], {,}, |, and ~.
L	Line buffer overflow	The line is longer than 132 characters. Error during editing may have removed ⟨CR⟩ ⟨LF⟩ at end of line. Delete and retype line.
M	Multiply-defined symbol	Symbol appears to left of : or = more than once in program. Be sure all symbols are different in the first six characters.
N	Number error	The digit 8 or 9 has been used without a decimal point, and assembler tried to treat it as octal. Either use octal equivalent, or include decimal point.
O	Directive out of context	Often an .ENDM, .ENDC, or .ENDR without matching beginning. Review macros, conditional assembly, and repeat structures.
P	1. Phase error	1. Some operation on a label would cause its value to change in second assembly pass. Often caused by storage directive, e.g., .BLKW X where X is defined afterwards. Define symbols before they are used if they will affect storage allocation.
	2. The .ERROR directive has been encountered.	2. A macro containing .ERROR has an error in usage. Check macro definition and usage for consistency.
Q	Questionable syntax	Something in the line is not recognized by the assembler. Check operand addressing and spelling of mnemonics.

TABLE G.1 (cont.)

Code	Probable Meaning	Probable Cause and Correction
R	Misuse of register symbol	A symbol R0, R1, ..., R5, PC, or SP has been used illegally. Do not use these symbols for labels or any purpose other than register reference.
T	Truncation error	Some operations lead to a value too large to fit in a word or byte. For example, .BYTE 777 or .WORD 771000. If large values are needed, store as double precision or floating point.
U	Undefined symbol	An undefined symbol was used in an operand or directive. All symbols must appear to the left of = or :, or must be in .GLOBL directive.

Most linkage errors deal with misuse of global symbols. Recall that a symbol is defined by appearing to the left of = or :, and is made global by placing it in .GLOBL. Alternatively, appearing to the left of :: or == both defines a symbol and makes it global. Global symbols must be defined once and only once in the group of modules being linked together.

Table G.2 gives the wording for the error messages as they appear under RSTS/E. Other operating systems will have somewhat different wording, but have enough similarity to allow identification of the error.

TABLE G.2
Linkage Errors [RSTS/E]

Message	Probable Cause and Correction
?LINK-W-FILE NOT FOUND dev:fn.ext	The file fn.ext could not be found on the device dev. File name was probably mistyped, or perhaps you forgot to assemble the program. Check your directory.
?LINK-W-UNDEFINED GLOBALS: X SUB1 SUB2	The symbols X, SUB1, and SUB2 were listed in .GLOBL in at least one linked module, yet did not appear as *defined* globals in any module. All .GLOBL symbols must appear to left of :: or ==, or must appear to left of : or = *and* be in .GLOBL, in one module.
?LINK-W-MULTIPLE DEFINITION OF X	The symbol X is global and *defined* in more than one module. A global symbol can appear only to the left of :: or == *and* be in .GLOBL, in one module.

G.4 Execution Errors

There are many kinds of programming errors that cannot be detected until an attempt is made to actually execute the program. These are called "execution-time" or "run-time" errors. An example is the instruction sequence

```
MOV     A,R2
MOV     @3(R2),R1
```

This is not an error if the contents of A has an odd value, but it is an error if it is even. (See Section 11.2.2.) Because the contents of A is not known until execution, the assembler has no way of detecting this as an error. Yet it could easily result in an error at run-time.

Regardless of the type of run-time error, a message of the form:

?M-message AT USER PC n   [RSTS/E]

is printed at the terminal. Messages are as shown in Table G.3 for RSTS/E; similar messages are printed for other operating systems. Note that the PC location n is the address of the instruction that *follows* the offending instruction. This is because PC is advanced *before* the instruction is executed. Also, this is the address after relocation by the LINK process, so the load point has to be subtracted from this number to find the offending instruction in the .LST file.

For some types of errors, the reported message and n are meaningless. For example, a bad branch instruction may transfer control to a data area or unused portion of memory where a completely unrelated error message is generated. These errors are very hard to locate, but are best approached by studying the listing file.

TABLE G.3
Execution Errors [RSTS/E]

Message	Probable Cause and Correction
?M-HALT AT USER PC n	This means that 000000 (i.e., HALT) was encountered as an instruction. Examine the .LST file to see if n is one word beyond your HALT. If so, it is not really an error.
?M-TRAP TO 4 AT USER PC n	This means that an instruction attempted to fetch a *word* from an *odd* address. Usually caused by (Rn), −(Rn) or (Rn)+ in a *word* instruction when Rn can become odd. Be sure Rn is set to an address at all times. Also caused by @X(Rn) when the sum of X and contents of Rn is odd for word or byte instruction. See Section 11.2.2.

TABLE G.3 (cont.)

Message	Probable Cause and Correction
?M-TRAP TO 10 AT USER PC n	This means that a number was fetched as an instruction that is not a valid opcode. Usually caused by control getting into data area, such as a .BLKW or .WORD, appearing after a nonbranch instruction, or a bad branch destination or no HALT instruction. Put all data before START: or after HALT, and check branches. Note that the reported n is a word after the illegal instruction and does *not* show how control got there.
?M-MEMORY MANAGEMENT VIOLATION AT USER PC n	This occurs whenever an instruction refers to a memory location that a normal user is not allowed to access or change. Usually caused by using (Rn), −(Rn), or (Rn)+ without first putting a valid address into Rn. Also, loops without proper limits and using (Rn)+ or −(Rn) can cause this. Check addressing modes and loop limits.
?M-BPT TRAP AT USER PC n ?M-IOT TRAP AT USER PC n ?M-TRAP TRAP AT USER PC n	These are caused by attempting to execute BPT, IOT or TRAP instructions, which are not allowed under RSTS/E. May be result of getting data instead of an instruction. See TRAP TO 10 message above.

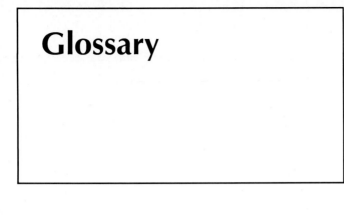

Glossary

Absolute Address A value in the machine code program that represents an actual CM address, rather than the distance between two CM addresses.

Address *See* Byte Address, Word Address.

Addressing The way in which an operand is identified.

ALU *See* Arithmetic Logic Unit.

Arguments The quantities that are provided to or returned from a subroutine or macro.

Arguments, Actual/Dummy Actual arguments are those used when a macro is invoked. Dummy arguments are those used in its definition. Actual arguments replace the dummy arguments during expansion.

Arithmetic Logic Unit (ALU) The electronic assembly that actually carries out instructions.

Array A data structure in which all elements are of identical type, and each can be identified by one or more indexes.

ASCII A system of binary codes for printable and control characters. American Standard Code for Information Interchange. See Table 7.1.

ASCII Base Octal 60 is called the ASCII base because when it is added to an integer value between 0 and 9 (decimal), the corresponding ASCII code is produced.

Assembler The program that translates an assembly language program to machine code.

Assignment *See* Direct Assignment.

Autoincrement/Autodecrement Addressing modes indicated by $(Rn)+$ or $-(Rn)$, respectively. See Section 5.7.2.

Base The number that, when raised to successive powers, produces the position values in a positional notation number system. With index addressing, base means base address, such as the first address of any array or table. *See also* Offset.

Base Code The number that represents a branch instruction. The Base Code plus the offset yields the machine code translation of a branch instruction.

Binary A system in which numbers are represented by a sequence of 1's and 0's called bits. In the positional binary system, each bit represents the coefficient of a power of 2.

Bit Short for binary digit. A bit can be a 0 or a 1.

Bit Pattern (Bit String) A group of 0's and 1's, e.g., 10111010. This term is a way of referring to the contents of a byte, word, or register without imparting a particular meaning to it.

Borrow In subtraction, the process of adding the base value from the next higher digit to a digit of the minuend in order to allow subtraction of a larger digit in the subtrahend. The higher digit is decremented by 1.

Breakpoint An address where program execution is to be stopped during the use of ODT or adb. See Section C.2.9.

Buffer A block of storage locations in which data is placed temporarily. Used when rates of entry and removal are different. Usually organized as a queue.

Byte A unit of information composed of 8 bits. Sometimes viewed as a unit of memory, because the PDP-11 assigns unique addresses to each byte.

Byte Address The unique number assigned to each byte by CM.

Carry An addition to the left adjacent digit necessitated by a sum larger than the maximum allowed digit value. If this occurs while adding the MSBs, a carry error condition occurs setting the C condition code.

Central Memory Unit (CM) Also called main memory. The collection of cells where data and program instructions are stored.

Central Processor Unit (CPU) The unit within the computer consisting of the arithmetic logic unit, general registers, program status register, and control unit.

Character String A group of characters in a specified sequence, e.g., "ABC", "123", "A + B*C".

Circular Buffer/Queue A queue in which the pointers are reset to the beginning when they reach the end.

CM *See* Central Memory Unit

Code Often used to refer to a program or program segment, either in machine language, assembly, or any computer language.

Column-major An arrangement of a two-dimensional array in which all elements of the first column are followed by those of the second column, and so on.

Compiler A program that translates an entire program module from its source language, e.g., FORTRAN, into a machine-language program. *Contrast with* Interpreter.

Complement *See* One's Complement, and Two's Complement.

Concatenation Joining together. Thus "ABC" concatenated with "123" is "ABC123".

Condition Codes (N, Z, V, C) The four rightmost bits in the Processor Status Word

(PSW). These bits are set or cleared depending on whether the previous result yielded a negative (N), zero (Z), overflow (V), or carry out of the MSB (C). *See* Table A.1.

Conditional Assembly   A group of assembly program lines that are assembled or skipped depending on a condition check of some symbol or expression at assembly time.

Console   The terminal, composed of a keyboard and display device, that the operator uses to control the computer.

Contents   Refers to the bit pattern currently held in a register or CM location.

Contiguous   A group of locations in sequential locations in CM or mass storage are said to be contiguous.

Control (transfer of)   Resetting PC. An imaginary pointer to the program instruction to be executed next.

CPU   *See* Central Processor Unit

CPU Priority   The value represented by bits 5, 6 and 7 in the PSW. Any interrupt-enabled device with a higher priority (*see* Table 14.1) can interrupt the CPU.

DEC   Digital Equipment Corporation. Also, the decrement instruction in MACRO-11. See Table A.1.

Decimal   A system in which numbers are represented by a sequence of digits selected from 0, 1, 2,..., 9. Each digit acts as a coefficient on successive powers of 10.

Deferred Addressing   An addressing mode whereby the referenced register or location contains the address of the operand rather than the operand itself. Also called indirect addressing.

Delimiter   Any character that marks the beginning and/or end of a string of characters. Thus in /ABCD/ the "/" is the delimiter. In normal text, spaces and punctuation marks "delimit" words.

Destination   The CM location or register where the result of an operation is to be placed.

Device Register   A register that is associated with a peripheral device such as a printer, keyboard, or line clock. Such devices usually have a status register, a data register, and others if required. They have assigned addresses like CM locations, but are not physically part of CM.

Direct Assignment   The use of the direct assignment directive to give a symbol a value, e.g., A = 4. The equal sign (=) signifies direct assignment.

Direct Memory Access (DMA)   The capability to transfer data directly between a peripheral device and the CM with minimal CPU intervention.

Directive   An instruction recognized by the assembler that does not generate a machine code instruction. Rather, it causes the assembler to take some action, e.g., reserve a block of words.

DMA   *See* Direct Memory Access.

Double Precision   The representation of numbers using twice the normal word length. Thus a double-precision two's complement number on the PDP-11 occupies two words or 32 bits, while double-precision floating point occupies four words.

EBCDIC   Extended Binary Coded Decimal Interchange Code. A character code system like ASCII but employing eight bits rather than seven.

EDT A text editor program often used to create and modify MACRO-11 programs and other text files. See Section B.2.

Expansion The process whereby the assembler replaces the macro reference by its defining instructions.

Expression An algebraic expression such as A + 2 or <X+2>/4. Such expressions are evaluated by the MACRO-11 assembler and reduced to a value.

Extended Instruction Set (EIS) A group of extra instructions available as an option on most PDP-11 computers. SOB, XOR, MUL, and DIV are among these.

Fetch Fetch refers to the ALU getting an instruction, operand, address, or any other data item out of the CM. The ALU must send the address of the desired item to the CM.

Field A subunit of a record. For example, a record holding name, identification number, and score has three fields, one for each of these items.

File A collection of data stored on a mass storage device. Often this data is a program in source, object, or load module form.

Flag Any symbol, location, or register whose value or contents control some program action.

Floating Point A system in which a number is represented as a fraction (mantissa) and an exponent, each stored separately.

Forward Reference The use of a symbol in a program before the place where it is defined.

General Register (GR) *See* Register.

Global A symbol that can be referred to outside of the module in which it is defined is said to be global or external. *Contrast with* Local.

Hexadecimal (Hex) A positional system for number representation in which the base is 16. Used as a shorthand for binary, because hex to binary (and reverse) conversion is very easy. Bit strings of length 4 convert directly to hex digits.

High-level Language A computer programming language that allows a problem to be *conveniently* defined by the programmer, rather than in the machine language or assembly. FORTRAN, Pascal, and BASIC are examples of high-level languages.

I/O *See* Input/Output.

Immediate Addressing The addressing method indicated by #A. The assembler places the value of A immediately after the instruction code.

In-line Instructions or data that are placed directly into a program, as opposed to being placed remotely and transferred to by branching instructions, JSR or JMP.

Index Addressing The addressing mode indicated by X(Rn) where X is any symbol, expression, or value. The contents of Rn is added to the value of X to determine the operand address.

Indirect Addressing *See* Deferred Addressing.

Input/Output (I/O) The processes whereby data is transferred to (input) and from (output) the computer. This transfer can be to/from external storage devices, or keyboards, card readers, display devices, and so on.

Instruction A bit pattern that has a particular meaning to the computer. Can also refer to the assembly mnemonics for a machine code instruction.

Instruction Execution Cycle   The process whereby an instruction is fetched, decoded, its operands fetched, and executed. The design of the machine is such that this process continues automatically once started and until HALT is encountered.

Instruction Set   A collective term meaning all of the machine code instructions that a particular computer recognizes.

Interpreter   A program that translates a programming language, e.g., BASIC, into machine code one statement at a time for immediate execution. *Contrast with* Compiler.

Interrupt   In general, an event that triggers an automatic transfer of control to a special "servicing" routine. On the PDP-11, interrupts due to CPU errors are called traps and the word interrupt is reserved for those from peripheral devices.

Interrupt Vector   The two words of memory set aside for each interrupt-capable device to contain the servicing routine address and the new PSW.

Invoke   To use a previously defined macro or subroutine. *Synonymous with* Reference.

Label   An identifier for a memory location. In MACRO-11, a symbol appearing to the left of : or ::.

LC   *See* Location Counter.

LCV   *See* Loop Control Variable.

Least Significant Bit (LSB)   The rightmost bit in a word or byte.

Library   A collection of existing programs, subroutines, or macros that can be used by reference to their names.

Link (LINK)   Linking refers to the process of converting one or more object programs into a load module. LINK is the system-supplied program that does this. See Section 15.4.

Linked list   A data structure in which a pointer to the logically next item is stored along with each item is called a singly linked list. Doubly linked lists also store pointers to previous items.

Listing   The contents of the .LST file created by the assembler. Contains the machine code and source code side by side, along with the address where each instruction and data item is stored.

Load   Place a machine language program into the computer memory in preparation for its execution.

Load Module   The machine code program properly linked for execution. Also called memory image module. The output of the LINK program with file name extension .SAV.

Local   A symbol that cannot be referred to outside of a limited area, e.g., a module, is said to be local. Sometimes called internal. *Contrast with* Global.

Location   Refers to a particular word or byte in CM. Each location has a 16-bit address.

Location Counter (LC)   A pointer to the next available location for storage of translated code during the assembly process.

Logical Order   The order of items in a list that reflects some logical scheme, e.g., alphabetical or numerical order. May be different from physical order in memory.

Loop Control Variable (LCV)   A register or memory location that is used to determine exit conditions from a loop.

Machine Language (Code) Instructions or a program expressed as binary (or equivalent octal or hex) codes recognized directly by the computer hardware. Also called native code.

Macro Instruction (Macro) A group of instructions that can be introduced into the machine code by giving a single instruction in the assembly source program. Some macros, e.g., .EXIT, are supplied by the system. Others are written by the programmer to meet special needs. See Chapter 10.

Mask A bit pattern that is used as the source operand in BIT, BIS, BIC, and XOR instructions. The pattern is selected to have a 0 or a 1 in each position that produces the desired effect, e.g., test, set, or clear, in the corresponding bit of the destination.

Mass Storage Device A device for permanent storage of data or programs accessible by the computer. Magnetic tape or disk units are the most common.

Memory *See* Central Memory Unit (CM).

Minuend The number from which another number (the subtrahend) is to be subtracted in a subtraction problem, e.g., in $A - B$, A is the minuend and B is the subtrahend.

Mnemonic As used in assembly programming, a short string of alphabetical characters that represent an opcode e.g., MOV, and ADD.

Module An independent group of instructions such as a subroutine.

Most Significant Bit (MSB) The leftmost bit in a word or byte.

MSB *See* Most Significant Bit.

Negation The mathematical operation of changing the sign of a number, e.g., negating 2 yields -2, and negating -3 yields 3. In the two's complement number system, negation is accomplished by finding the two's complement.

Normalize A process that adjusts the exponent in a floating-point number such that the binary point is immediately to the left of the most significant 1-bit.

Null-terminated String A character string stored in sequential bytes of memory and followed by a 000, which is the ASCII null character.

Object Program (Module) A program expressed as machine code but not linked for execution. The output of the assembler with file name extension .OBJ.

Octal A positional system for number representation in which the base is 8. Used as a shorthand for binary, because octal to binary (and reverse) conversion is very easy. Bit strings of length 3 convert directly to octal digits.

ODT (On-line Debugging Technique) A program used to control execution and examine results of a machine language program being debugged. See Section C.2.

Offset In index addressing, offset is the distance in bytes between the base address and the desired address. Thus in 2(R1), R1 contains the base address and 2 is the offset, whereas in A(R1), A is the base address and R1 contains the offset. Offset is also used to mean an address given relative to a load point of a module. Also, offset refers to the distance from the word following a branch instruction to the target address.

One's Complement The bit pattern formed by changing all 1's to 0's and all 0's to 1's in a binary number. Also the number system that uses the one's complement of positives to represent the negatives.

Opcode (Operation Code)   The numerical code, often expressed in octal, that represents a particular machine language instruction.

Operand   The data item referred to in an instruction.

Operating System   The program that provides overall control of the computer. It processes user commands such as RUN, MACRO, and DIR. It also keeps track of user files, and many other tasks necessary for convenient use of the computer. See Section D.1.

Overflow (Signed Overflow)   An error condition caused by an arithmetic operation that invalidates the sign bit. Causes the V condition code to be set. *See also* Unsigned Overflow.

Parity   The setting or clearing of the MSB in a byte containing a character code so that the number of 1-bits is even (even parity) or odd (odd parity). This allows error checking after transmission.

PC   *See* Program Counter.

Peripheral Device   Components of a computer system other than the CPU and CM. Printers, mass storage devices, line clocks, and keyboards are peripheral devices.

PIP (Peripheral Interchange Processor)   A system supplied program that performs various operations on files, e.g., copy, merge, list, and delete. See Section D.3.4.5.

Pointer   The register or location containing the address of the operand in deferred addressing.

Polling   Repeated checking of a peripheral device such as a printer or keyboard to see if it is ready to receive or send data to the CPU.

Pop   Remove an item from the top of a stack.

Positional Notation   A means for representing a number in which each digit position implies a definite position or place value. Decimal, binary, octal, and hexadecimal are examples.

Processor Status Word (PSW)   The special register within the ALU that contains the status of the CPU. This includes the condition codes, trap bit, processor priority bits, and certain other information.

Program Counter (PC)   Register 7, used to hold the address of the next instruction to be executed.

Program Counter Addressing   Addressing modes 2, 3, 6 and 7 used with R7(PC) as the register. See Table 11.3.

Pseudocode   A method of expressing an algorithm that uses normal language with IF, THEN, ELSE, and WHILE clauses. Indentation is used to "set off" the clauses. An alternative to flowcharting.

Pseudo-ops   Another term for an assembler directive. *See* Directive.

PSW   *See* Processor Status Word

Push   Place an item on top of a stack.

Queue   A data structure in which the last item entered is the last to be removed. There are two pointers, with one pointing to the next item for removal, and the other, at the next available place for entry.

Real Line   A line extending from minus to plus infinity on which every real number can be placed.

Reference   The use of a symbol, macro, or subroutine.

Register   Most often this refers to one of the eight general registers in the CPU—R0, R1,..., R5, SP, and PC. Also used in a general sense to mean electronic elements within the computer or peripheral devices that can hold a bit pattern. These are often used for special purposes and are distinct from the CM.

Relative Addressing   The addressing method indicated by a symbol, e.g., A. The assembler places the PC-relative address of the operand immediately after the instruction code.

Relocation   The process whereby the addresses in the object program are adjusted to reflect the locations in CM where it is to be placed for execution. Performed by LINK.

Row-major   An arrangement of a two-dimensional array in which all elements of the first row are followed by those of the second row, and so on.

RSTS/E   Resource-sharing Timesharing System/Extended. A widely used DEC operating system on PDP-11 computers. Used in moderate to large systems serving many users through interactive terminals.

RSX-11M   Real-time System Executive Operating System. A small to moderately sized real-time multiprogramming operating system for PDP-11 computers. RSX-11M-PLUS supports larger systems.

RT-11   Real-time Operating System for PDP-11 computers. Small, single-user DEC operating system for PDP-11 computers.

Run-time Address   The address of an instruction or data item when the program is loaded into CM for execution. The .SAV file has run-time addresses. See Section 15.4.3.

Servicing Routine   A group of instructions that carries out certain actions when an interrupt or trap occurs.

Sign Bit   The MSB. Note that while the MSB is always referred to as the sign bit, it is not always restricted to that role. When the word is viewed as a 16-bit positive integer, it has no special significance.

Sign Extension   The process of replicating the MSB of a byte when it is moved into a register. This ensures an arithmetically correct conversion from 8-bit to 16-bit representation.

Signed Branches   Those branch instructions intended for usage with two's complement, i.e., signed numbers—BGT, BLT, BGE, and BLE.

Signed Number   The representation of a number in a system that allows both positive and negative values, such as the two's complement system.

Signed Overflow   *See* Overflow.

Source Program   A program in the form originally expressed by the programmer, e.g., a MACRO-11 program. Usually saved with file name extension .MAC.

SP   *See* Stack Pointer

Stack   A data structure in which the last item entered is the next available for removal. A register usually acts as a pointer to the most recently entered item, which is said to be on "top" of the stack.

Stack Pointer (SP)   Register 6, used as a pointer into a stack storage area in the CM.

Store   This term refers to the ALU sending a data item to the CM. The ALU also has to send the address where it is to be stored.

String Usually just a shorter way of saying character string. However, other kinds of strings are possible, e.g., bit strings.

Subroutine A separate program module to which control is transferred for performance of a particular task. After completion, control is returned to the calling point.

Subtrahend The number to be subtracted in a subtraction problem, i.e., in $A - B$, B is the subtrahend and A is the minuend.

Symbol Table The list of all symbols used or defined in an assembly program, along with the values assigned to each. Included in the .LST file.

System Program A program that is provided to all users of a computer as part of the operating system, e.g., the MACRO-11 assembler and EDT.

System Stack A stack that uses R6 (SP) as its pointer. Various instructions, e.g., JSR, EMT, use this stack. Storage is in the user's program area (immediately before program in RSTS/E, RT-11, and RSX-11M).

Table In programming, this refers to a one-dimensional array in which each element is a record composed of several fields. Similar to a two-dimensional array except that items in a record can be of different types whereas elements in an array are all of the same type.

Trap *See* Interrupt.

Two's Complement The number system used on the PDP-11 to represent both positive and negative integers. Also used as a synonym for the verb "negate" in the two's complement system.

UNIX System An operating system for PDP-11 (and other) computers developed by Bell Laboratories. See Section D.4.

Unsigned Branch Those branch instructions intended for usage with positive integers only—BHI, BLO, BHIS, and BLOS. The instructions BEQ and BNE can be used either for signed or unsigned numbers.

Unsigned Number The representation of a number in a system that does not allow for a sign. The positional binary system for positive integers is an example.

Unsigned Overflow Error condition caused by a carry out of the MSB, setting the C condition code.

Utilities Programs that perform frequently needed operations such as copying files. Usually provided by the operating system.

Vectoring Transferring to a servicing routine through the use of special memory locations containing the routine address and the PSW.

Word A unit of memory. On the PDP-11 the CM is composed of a large number of words, each of which holds 16 bits. It can be viewed as a combination of two bytes.

Word Address The unique number assigned to each word in CM. Always an even number, and usually expressed in octal. Corresponds to the address of the low (rightmost) byte in the word.

Word Length The number of bits in the fundamental unit of a computer's memory, 16 on the PDP-11.

Answers to Selected Exercises

Chapter 1

3. d) PIP NEW.MAC=OLD1.MAC,OLD2.MAC ⟨CR⟩

or

EDT NEW.MAC ⟨CR⟩
*INC OLD1.MAC ⟨CR⟩
*INC OLD2.MAC ⟨CR⟩
*EX ⟨CR⟩
READY

Chapter 2

1. a) See powers of 2 table inside back cover.
$1 \times 128 + 1 \times 64 + 1 \times 32 + 1 \times 16 + 0 \times 8 + 1 \times 4 + 1 \times 2 + 1 \times 1 = 247_{10}$

e) Double dabble

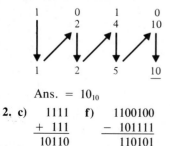

Ans. = 10_{10}

2. c)
```
   1111
 +  111
  10110
```
f)
```
 1100100
 - 101111
  110101
```

3. d) $001\ 111\ 101\ 000\ =\ 1750_8\ =\ 1\times 8^3\ +\ 7\times 8^2\ +\ 5\times 8^1\ +\ 0\times 8^0\ =\ 1000_{10}$

4. b) $384/8\ =\ 48$ R 0 ; $\quad D_0\ =\ 0$
   $48/8\ =\ 6$ R 0 ; $\quad D_1\ =\ 0$
   $6/8\ =\ 0$ R 6 ; $\quad D_2\ =\ 6$
   Ans. $=\ 600_8\ =\ 110000000_2$

6. a)
```
    432     d)      375
   +371            −177
   ────            ────
   1023             176
```

7. a)
```
   E12A     d)     AC79
  +0E5B           −79AC
  ─────           ─────
   EF85            32CD
```

Chapter 3

1. a) $29652_{10}\ =\ 71724_8\ =\ 0\ 111\ 001\ 111\ 010\ 100_2$

	Word	High Byte	Low Byte
Binary	0111001111010100	01110011	11010100
Octal	71724	163	324
Hex	73D4	73	D4

5. b) 001072

8. Any *even* number between 0 and 177776.

Chapter 4

1. a) 010503   **g)** 060604

2. See numerical opcode list inside back cover.
   f) CLR   R3

3. b) Because the opcode field is 4 bits, $2^4\ =\ 16$ possible codes.

   c) Assume a word length of 16, and an addressing mode field of 3. If all 16 registers are to be allowed in addressing operations, 4 bits are required for the register field, and $3\ +\ 4\ =\ 7$ bits are required for each address code. This leaves $16\ -\ 14\ =\ 2$ bits for opcodes. There can be no more than four double-operand instructions. Other schemes are possible.

4. R0:3   R1:1

Chapter 5

1. c) BHI   BLO   BLOS   BHIS   BEQ   BNE   BR
        X   X   X   X

2. e) $001400\ +\ 375\ =\ 001775$

9. h) $101375\ -\ 101000\ =\ 375$
       opcode $=\ 101000$ (BHI)
       offset $=\ 375\ =$ two words backwards *from the instruction.*

10. i) R3:000120 ; 000120:701

Chapter 6

1. a) 000016_8 b) 177762_8
2. b) -4682_{10} d) 65_{10}
3. a) 153173 is a negative number, no overflow.
   e) 000105 is a positive number, overflow.
4. e) BPL BEQ BHIS BMI BLT BLO BGT BHI BLE BLOS
        X   X   X   X
5. e) NZVC = 0000
   j) NZVC = 1011

10. Observe that a carry can result from adding the low order words, adding the carry bit to the middle word, and adding the middle words. Thus six instructions are required, including three ADCs.

Chapter 7

1. f) BEL or $^\wedge$G (control key and G)
2. h) $002_8 = 0000010_2$ j) $074_8 = 00111100_2$
3. e) The word contains the character string "mg".

High   Low
byte   byte

"g"	"m"

9. e)   BIT   BIC   BIS   XOR
   NZVC = 000? 173777   177777   173777
   The C bit is unaffected by BIT, so it is left at the previous value.

Chapter 8

1. d) An input line is accepted into the .TTYIN buffer, and the first character is placed in R0, then into B. The .PRINT will initiate printing of CM contents beginning at *address* B, stopping at the first byte containing a null character (000). The input character is therefore printed, along with others found in memory.

10. See Sections 8.9.2 and 8.9.4.

Chapter 9

3. See GETDEC in Appendix F.
7. f) 000504:000000 (registers unaffected)
   i) R1:000506; 000500:000500

Chapter 10

1. B   = 8.   ; CHANGE TO 10. FOR DECIMAL
   D   = 6-<<B-8.>/2> ; D IS NUMBER OF DIGITS—6 OR 5
   S   = 6*<B-8.>   ; THIS SETS PV TO PV8 IF B=8.
   PV = PV8+S   ;   OR TO PV10 IF B=10.

PV8: .WORD 100000,10000,1000,100,10,1; FOR OCTAL
PV10: .WORD 10000.,1000.,100.,10.,1.   ; FOR DECIMAL

Chapter 11

1. b)

	Address	Contents
Translation	001000	012700
	001002	000500
After execution:		
	PC:001004	
	R0:000500	
c) *Translation:*	001000	013700
	001002	000500
After execution:		
	PC:001004	
	R0:000502	

2. a) Correct usage of index deferred addressing. Clears location 000504.

b) Error because $3 + 000004$ yields an odd address that cannot possibly contain a 16-bit address.

Chapter 12

3. Provided that sufficient stack space is available, F(24) can be computed while F(25) is too large for the 16-bit word.

Chapter 13

1. g) $-3 \times 10^8 = -0.1000000011011001010101 \times 2^{-11000}$
(found by subtraction method using 2^{-n})

Sign $= 1$
Exponent $= 200 - 30 = 150_8 = 01101000$
Fraction $= 00000001101100101011001$

	LOC	LOC $+ 2$
Words:	132000	154531

2. d) 042222   162000

Sign	Exponent	Fraction
0	10001001	0010010111001000000000000

Fraction $= 10010010111001$ (hidden bit added)
Exponent $= 211 - 200 = 11_8 = 9_{10}$
Sign $= 0$ (positive)
Value $= .10010010111001 \times 2^9 = 0.29378125 \times 10^3$

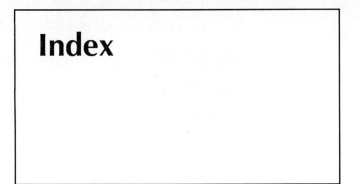

Index

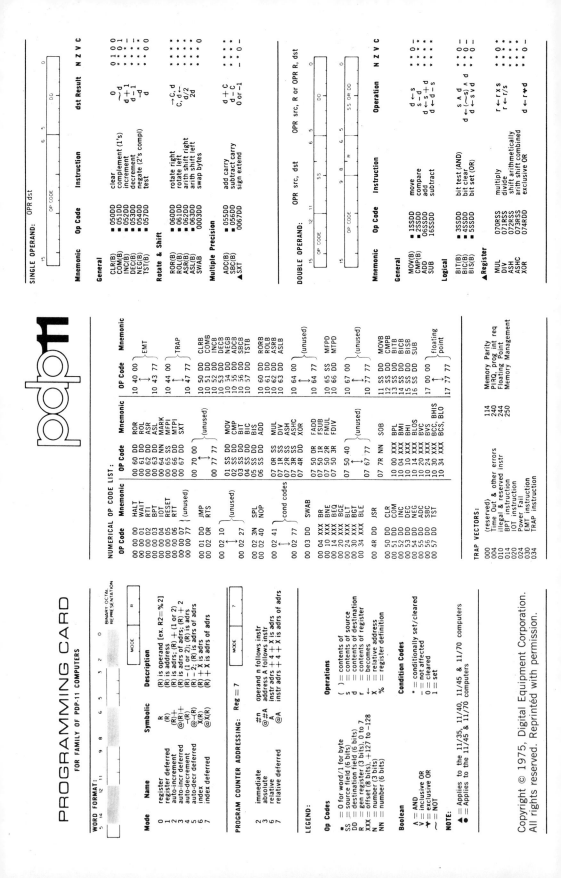

PROGRAMMING CARD
FOR FAMILY OF PDP-11 COMPUTERS

WORD FORMAT:

bits: 15 14 | 12 11 | 9 8 | 6 5 | 3 2 | 0 — MODE | R — BINARY OCTAL REPRESENTATION

Mode	Name	Symbolic	Description
0	register	R	(R) is operand [ex. R2= %2]
1	register deferred	(R)	(R) is address
2	auto-increment	(R)+	(R) is adrs; (R) + (1 or 2)
3	auto-incr deferred	@(R)+	(R) is adrs of adrs; (R) + 2
4	auto-decrement	-(R)	(R) - (1 or 2); (R) is adrs
5	auto-decr deferred	@-(R)	(R) - 2; (R) is adrs of adrs
6	index	X(R)	(R)+X is adrs
7	index deferred	@X(R)	(R)+X is adrs of adrs

PROGRAM COUNTER ADDRESSING: Reg = 7

2	immediate	#n	operand n follows instr
3	absolute	@#A	address A follows instr
6	relative	A	instr adrs + 4 + X is adrs
7	relative deferred	@A	instr adrs + 4 + X is adrs of adrs

LEGEND:

Op Codes
■ = 0 for word/1 for byte
SS = source field (6 bits)
DD = destination field (6 bits)
R = gen register (3 bits), 0 to 7
XXX = offset (8 bits), +127 to -128
NN = number (3 bits)
NN = number (6 bits)

Boolean
$\wedge$ = AND
$\vee$ = inclusive OR
$\forall$ = exclusive OR
$\sim$ = NOT

Operations
( ) = contents of
s = contents of source
d = contents of destination
r = contents of register
$\leftarrow$ = becomes
X = relative address
% = register definition

Condition Codes
* = conditionally set/cleared
- = not affected
0 = cleared
1 = set

NOTE:
▲ = Applies to the 11/35, 11/40, 11/45 & 11/70 computers
▲● = Applies to the 11/45 & 11/70 computers

NUMERICAL OP CODE LIST:

OP Code	Mnemonic
00 00 00	HALT
00 00 01	WAIT
00 00 02	RTI
00 00 03	BPT
00 00 04	IOT
00 00 05	RESET
00 00 06	RTT
00 00 07 — 00 00 77	(unused)
00 01 DD	JMP
00 02 0R	RTS
00 02 10 — 00 02 27	(unused)
00 02 3N	SPL
00 02 40	NOP
00 02 41 — 00 02 77	cond codes
00 03 DD	SWAB
00 04 XXX	BR
00 10 XXX	BNE
00 14 XXX	BEQ
00 20 XXX	BGE
00 24 XXX	BLT
00 30 XXX	BGT
00 34 XXX	BLE
00 4R DD	JSR
00 50 DD	CLR
00 51 DD	COM
00 52 DD	INC
00 53 DD	DEC
00 54 DD	NEG
00 55 DD	ADC
00 56 DD	SBC
00 57 DD	TST
00 60 DD	ROR
00 61 DD	ROL
00 62 DD	ASR
00 63 DD	ASL
00 64 NN	MARK
00 65 SS	MFPI
00 66 SS	MTPI
00 67 DD	SXT
00 70 00 — 00 77 77	(unused)
01 SS DD	MOV
02 SS DD	CMP
03 SS DD	BIT
04 SS DD	BIC
05 SS DD	BIS
06 SS DD	ADD
07 0R SS	MUL
07 1R SS	DIV
07 2R SS	ASH
07 3R SS	ASHC
07 4R DD	XOR
07 50 0R	FADD
07 50 1R	FSUB
07 50 2R	FMUL
07 50 3R	FDIV
07 50 40 — 07 67 77	(unused)
07 7R NN	SOB
10 00 XXX	BPL
10 04 XXX	BMI
10 10 XXX	BHI
10 14 XXX	BLOS
10 20 XXX	BVC
10 24 XXX	BVS
10 30 XXX	BCC, BHIS
10 34 XXX	BCS, BLO
10 40 00 — 10 43 77	EMT
10 44 00 — 10 47 77	TRAP
10 50 DD	CLRB
10 51 DD	COMB
10 52 DD	INCB
10 53 DD	DECB
10 54 DD	NEGB
10 55 DD	ADCB
10 56 DD	SBCB
10 57 DD	TSTB
10 60 DD	RORB
10 61 DD	ROLB
10 62 DD	ASRB
10 63 DD	ASLB
10 64 00 — 10 64 77	(unused)
10 65 SS	MFPD
10 66 DD	MTPD
10 67 00 — 10 77 77	(unused)
11 SS DD	MOVB
12 SS DD	CMPB
13 SS DD	BITB
14 SS DD	BICB
15 SS DD	BISB
16 SS DD	SUB
17 00 00 — 17 77 77	floating point

TRAP VECTORS:

000	(reserved)
004	Time Out & other errors
010	illegal & reserved instr
014	BPT instruction
020	IOT instruction
024	Power Fail
030	EMT instruction
034	TRAP instruction
114	Memory Parity
240	PIRQ, prog int req
250	Memory Management

SINGLE OPERAND: OPR dst

General

Mnemonic	Op Code	Instruction	dst Result	N Z V C
CLR(B)	■050DD	clear	0	0 1 0 0
COM(B)	■051DD	complement (1's)	~d	* * 0 1
INC(B)	■052DD	increment	d+1	* * * -
DEC(B)	■053DD	decrement	d-1	* * * -
NEG(B)	■054DD	negate (2's compl)	-d	* * * *
TST(B)	■057DD	test	d	* * 0 0

Rotate & Shift

Mnemonic	Op Code	Instruction	dst Result	N Z V C
ROR(B)	■060DD	rotate right	→C, d	* * * *
ROL(B)	■061DD	rotate left	C, ←d	* * * *
ASR(B)	■062DD	arith shift right	d/2	* * * *
ASL(B)	■063DD	arith shift left	2d	* * * *
SWAB	0003DD	swap bytes		* * 0 0

Multiple Precision

Mnemonic	Op Code	Instruction	dst Result	N Z V C
ADC(B)	■055DD	add carry	d+C	* * * *
SBC(B)	■056DD	subtract carry	d-C	* * * *
▲SXT	0067DD	sign extend	0 or -1	- * * -

DOUBLE OPERAND: OPR src, dst   OPR src, R or OPR R, dst

General

Mnemonic	Op Code	Instruction	Operation	N Z V C
MOV(B)	■1SSDD	move	d←s	* * 0 -
CMP(B)	■2SSDD	compare	s-d	* * * *
ADD	06SSDD	add	d←s+d	* * * *
SUB	16SSDD	subtract	d←d-s	* * * *

Logical

Mnemonic	Op Code	Instruction	Operation	N Z V C
BIT(B)	■3SSDD	bit test (AND)	s ∧ d	* * 0 -
BIC(B)	■4SSDD	bit clear	(~s)∧d	* * 0 -
BIS(B)	■5SSDD	bit set (OR)	d←s∨d	* * 0 -

▲Register

Mnemonic	Op Code	Instruction	Operation	N Z V C
MUL	070RSS	multiply	r←r×s	* * 0 *
DIV	071RSS	divide	r←r/s	* * * *
ASH	072RSS	shift arithmetically		* * * *
ASHC	073RSS	arith shift combined		* * * *
XOR	074RDD	exclusive OR	d←r⊕d	* * 0 -